Charles Henry Stanley Davis

**History of Wallingford, Conn.**

from its settlement in 1670 to the present time, including Meriden, which was one

of its parishes until 1806, and Cheshire, which was incorporated in 1780 (Volume 2)

Charles Henry Stanley Davis

**History of Wallingford, Conn.**
*from its settlement in 1670 to the present time, including Meriden, which was one of its parishes until 1806, and Cheshire, which was incorporated in 1780 (Volume 2)*

ISBN/EAN: 9783337017507

Printed in Europe, USA, Canada, Australia, Japan

Cover: Foto ©ninafisch / pixelio.de

More available books at **www.hansebooks.com**

# HISTORx OF WALLINGFORD, CONN.

from its settlement in 1670 to the present
time, including MERID̄IN, which was one of
its parishes until 1806 and CHESHIRE which
was incorporated in 1780

by

Charles Henry Stanley Davis, M.D.

Part 2

Meriden, Conn.
Published by the author
1870

cous, forbearing one another and forgiving one another, if any man have a ground against any. Forget not your relations to Christ, to one another, and to your Minister. In all these, cherish the spirit of Him whose you are and whom you serve."

This was followed with a "declaration of general principles" and signed by "Leveritt Griggs, Scribe of the Consociation, Meriden March 14, 1838."

Mr. Granger published

"A sermon preached to the Congregational Church and Society in Meriden, at the request of several respectable Anti Abolitionists."

In the introduction Mr. Granger states that

"The preaching and publication of the following sermon, have been occasioned by a humiliating scene — a scene that will be incorporated into the future history of our hitherto quiet and peaceable town, and go down the line of posterity to the latest period of recorded time."

"April 15, 1846. The Church met this day by special appointment, and after deliberation adopted the following vote. Resolved, that the system of Slavery, as it exists in the United States, is essentially sinful and admits of no justification from the word of God."

# CHAPTER XXXIII.

## BIOGRAPHIES.

"To wryte of a Mannes Lyfe mote bee enowe to saie of somme he was ybore and deceased ; odher somme lacketh recytalle, as manie notable matters bee contained in yee storie."

*Life of W. Canynge, bie Rowley.*

### DR. AARON ANDREWS

Was a Son of Denizen Andrews of Meriden, and was born in that part of Wallingford. He settled as a Physician in the first, or Old Society. He owned and occupied the house now owned by Samuel B. Parmelee Esq. Doct. Andrews when living, was regarded by his friends and neighbors as a very skillful and able physician, and as such won a highly enviable position with them and the profession, and it is to be regretted that a more extended notice of him could not be made.

### DR. JOHN ANDREWS

Was a Son of Dr. Aaron Andrews, and was for many years an influential and very successful physician in Wallingford, and enjoyed an extensive practice with the confidence of the community. He was often called by the choice of his fellow citizens to fill important offices. He was a member of the Convention in 1818, which gave the State of Connecticut her present constitution. He married Abigail Atwater, a daughter of Capt. Caleb Atwater, for his first wife, and Anna Noyes, daughter of Rev. James and Anna Noyes, for his second wife. After her decease he left Wallingford and went to Penfield, Ohio, to spend his old age with his son, and died at the house of his son William, aged 86 years. His remains were, at his request, brought to Wallingford for interment.

### HON. SHERLOCK J. ANDREWS

Is the son of Dr. John Andrews, and was born in Wallingford, Nov. 17, 1801. He was graduated at Yale College in 1821, and studied law in the Yale Law School. He removed to Cleveland, Ohio, in 1825, and was a member of Congress from Ohio from 1841 to 1843. He was for several years Judge of the Superior Court of Cleveland, and in 1851 was a member of the convention that formed the present constitution of Ohio. He married in 1828 Ursula McCurdy Allen, daughter of the Hon. John Allen, late of Litchfield, Conn., and has five children; a son and four daughters.

### HON. WILLIAM ANDREWS

Son of the late Dr. John Andrews, was born in Wallingford, and is now a successful farmer at Penfield, Ohio. He has been honored by frequent elections to the Legislature of Ohio, and is a highly respected citizen of his adopted state.

### HON. JOHN WHITING ANDREWS

Son of the late Dr. John Andrews, was graduated at Yale College in 1830. After finishing his law studies, he went to Columbus, Ohio, where he soon took high rank as a lawyer, and as such commands the respect of the people of the whole Community in which he lives.

## JONATHAN ATWATER

Was a merchant of New Haven. In 1702, Feb. 12, he bought of Henry Cook of Wallingford, one hundred and eighteen acres of land, near the Honey Pat Brook in the western part of Wallingford, now Cheshire. The same farm has been in the family name ever since, and has come down as follows : first to Jonathan Atwater Jr. ; second to his son Abraham Atwater ; third to Samuel Atwater, and fourth to Flamen Atwater ; and then recently to the heirs of Flamen, who had lived to the age of 70 or more years, and was born on the place. This branch of the Atwater family emanates from a different branch than others of the same name in Cheshire and Wallingford, although of the same original stock.

## CAPT. CALEB ATWATER,

Son of Joshua and Sarah (Yale) Atwater, and grandson of John Atwater, the first of the name who permanently settled in the village of Wallingford, was born Sept. 5, 1741. At suitable age after the decease of his father, he articled himself as an apprentice to learn the art, trade and mystery of shoe and harness making and tanning leather. At the termination of his apprenticeship, he commenced business for himself, adopting as his motto, Be diligent, be honest, and owe no man. In the different branches of his business he was successful, and as soon as his means would permit he opened a store of goods. At this time his business rapidly increased, and for many years he was extensively and successfully engaged as a merchant. He was endowed with extraordinary good judgment and business talent. He seldom if ever failed of success in any of his numerous enterprises.

He was one of the Connecticut Land Company which purchased of the state of Connecticut the Western Reserve or New Connecticut in Ohio; and though one of the largest purchasers, he found it convenient to pay cash in full for all of his purchases on receiving his deeds. Among other lands in the different counties of the Reserve, was the entire township of Atwater in Portage Co., which, with the exception of 200 acres set apart for religious purposes by him, he gave to his son Joshua; and he afterwards caused a tract of land in Auburn, Granger County, to be surveyed into 65 lots of 100 acres each, giving one lot to each of his grandchildren, numbering over fifty, and the balance of his western land to be divided among his children. He was at this time a man of great wealth.

For many years he was a worthy member of the Congregational church, and was highly esteemed and honored by all who knew him. At the advanced age of 91, in the full enjoyment of his mental faculties, he died deeply lamented.

### DEACON JOSHUA ATWATER

Was an only son of Caleb and Abigail (Jones) Atwater, and was born February 8, 1773. He was bred a merchant, and for several years occupied the old stand of his father, where he prosecuted quite an extensive business. He was a highly respected gentleman, honorable and honest in all his business transactions. He was a deacon of the Congregational church for many years, and occupied a highly respectable position among all classes of his fellow citizens in his native town and wherever known. He died at the age of 89 years, beloved and respected by all who knew him.

### CALEB ATWATER

Son of Joshua, and grandson of Capt. Caleb Atwater, was born July 11, 1804; removed to Atwater, Ohio, in 1823, to take charge and dispose of Western Reserve Lands, and to engage in merchandize. That country at that date was quite new. For over forty years he resided in the town of Atwater and city of Cleveland, an interested observer of the growth and advance of the Western Reserve and entire state of Ohio to its present greatness. In 1865 he removed from Cleveland to his native town, Wallingford, the oldest remaining member of his father's family.

### DEACON JOHN ATWATER

Son of Joshua Atwater, born July 19, 1815, now resides at his father's old homestead, which was the home of his grandfather and great grandfather, it being the same farm originally owned and occupied by his great great grandfather John Atwater, who was son of David Atwater of New Haven, and who was one of the original Planters of New Haven, A. D. 1637.

### HON. EDGAR ATWATER

Son of Joshua and Elizabeth Atwater, and grandson of Caleb Atwater, was a young man of more than ordinary promise and ability. As a public speaker he was endowed with an uncommon gift. In 1841 he was elected a Senator from the sixth Senatorial district to the Connecticut Legislature, and was a popular and a very influential member of that body. He died in 1850, at the age of 38 years, lamented by all who knew him.

### JOHN BAULCOT

Of Farmington, Eng., came into Wallingford about the beginning of the last century, and settled in the eastern section of the town on an old road that formerly ran south from the site of the late Col. Russel Hall's barn. This old road on which lived a number of families has long since been closed, and the dwellings they once occupied are now gone to decay. His will was dated Feb. 19, 1745-6, and is recorded in the books of the Probate Court at New Haven. The inventory of his property amounted to £1839, 10s. 2d. After giving to the Congregational Church at Wallingford the sum of £3 for a Silver Cup, he gave "all the remainder of his property to the Lord Jesus Christ, the interest of which to be expended towards keeping up two lectures in said first church, to be called Baulcot's Lectures, forever; but if any of his brothers' or sisters' children claim the property within forty years, then the estate shall go to them." He married Naomi Thorp, Dec. 20, 1710.

### THOMAS BEACH

Was a son of John, of Stratford. He married Ruth Peck, May 12, 1680. He located on the farm late the property of Cephas Johnson, and built the old house that was taken down to make way for the present one built by Mr. Johnson on the old site. He died in Meriden May 13, 1741, aged 82 years, and was interred in the old burying-ground on burying-yard hill, about a mile to the south-west of Meriden center.

### JOHN BEACH

Came from New Haven to Wallingford with the first company of Planters in 1670, and located himself in the southerly portion of the town, and I suppose him to be a brother of Thomas Beach above. He was a man of some consequence in the settlement, and was frequently elected to some of the offices in the gilt of the people.

## STEPHEN BEACH

Was born in Wallingford, March 15, 1790. Without the advantages of a collegiate education, but with a remarkable love of learning, and strong intellectual powers, he became a good scholar and an excellent preacher. He was admitted to Deacon's Orders in St. Michael's Church, R. I., by Bishop Griswold, on the twentieth of October, 1815. Immediately after his ordination he removed to the northern part of Vermont, where, for several years, he officiated in the three parishes of St. Albans, Fairfield and Sheldon. He was the only clergyman of the Episcopal church of that day, north of Vergennes. He was admitted to Priest's orders by Bishop Griswold, in Holderness, N. H., August 20, 1817. In 1822 he removed from Vermont to take charge of the parish at Salisbury in the state of Connecticut. Here also he was known, as he had been in Vermont, as a successful founder of churches, and his name is gratefully remembered throughout that part of the State. In 1833 he removed from Salisbury to Essex in the same State, taking charge of that parish in connection with St. Stephen's Church, East Haddam. Under his zealous ministry, each of these parishes soon grew to require and be able to support the entire service of a minister; and in 1836 Mr. Beach resigned the parish at Essex and became pastor at East Haddam. His ministry in this place, abundantly blessed, was continued for two years only, when he died at the age of forty-seven, on the fourteenth day of January, 1838.

In 1814 he was married to a daughter of Amos Billings of Guilford, Vermont. Two of his sons are highly respectable clergymen of the Episcopal church; one, Amos Billings, rector of Christ church, Binghampton, N. Y., the other, Alfred Billings (now D. D.), rector of St. Peter's church, New York city.

Although called in the Providence of God to occupy positions in the church to which he belonged remote and comparatively but little known, yet it may be said with truth, that few of its ministers have been more useful, or have in the same period of time done more in this country for the extension of that church, and its permanent establishment in destitute places, than did Mr. Beach.

As a preacher, he was remarkably clear, earnest, plain and instructive. He excelled in extemporaneous preaching. Taking a strong hold of what he regarded as truth or duty, his conduct was always consistent with his professions and convictions. At the same time, he was singularly humble and charitable, and was therefore greatly respected and beloved by all who knew him, and not less by those who were not, than by those who were, of his own church and persuasion.

### MOSES YALE BEACH.

The life of Moses Y. Beach, well known as the late proprietor of the *New York Sun*, the pioneer of the penny press, while it presents no remarkable variety of changes or incidents, is attractive in tracing the steps of a determined man.

His great grandfather and grandfather, both bearing the name of Moses Beach, each lived in succession on the same farm, to good old age, ranking among the more respectable men of the settlement ; and when each in turn had answered the call of nature, their possessions passed to Moses Sperry Beach, who married Lucretia Yale, a daughter of Captain Elihu and Lucretia (Stanley) Yale, a descendant of Thomas Yale, who

settled in Wallingford in 1670. Of this couple, Moses
Yale Beach was an only son. When at the age of four
months Mr. Beach was deprived of his mother by the
hand of death ; and as his father's business called him
much from home, he was confided to the care of his
step-mother. As soon as his age would permit he was
taught to do "chores," and at the age of ten years he
took charge of considerable of the out-door work on the
farm, besides going a long distance to school. From
four o'clock in the morning until eleven o'clock at night
he was generally up and doing, and yet found leisure to
exercise his mechanical ingenuity in the manufacture of
playthings for himself and others.

At a suitable age he was, at his own solicitation, bound
an apprentice to Mr. Daniel Dewey, a cabinet maker at
Hartford. His industry soon excited the attention of
his master, who was a close man, but who finally made
a contract by which young Beach was allowed two cents
an hour for extra work. Mr. Beach afterwards said,
that he never felt happier at any time during his life, at
success in any thing, than he did on the occasion of
closing that contract. Early and late he worked, and
the pennies began to accumulate. Finally he made a
bargain for his time after he should arrive at the age
of eighteen years, for which he was to pay the sum of
$400. This arrangement gave him new life, and when
the time had come round he had saved between one
and two hundred dollars more than enough to pay for
his freedom, with which he commenced life.

He went to Northampton and worked a short time as
a journeyman. After a while he formed a copartnership
with a young man by the name of Loveland. Their
work was much celebrated ; in testimony of which they

received the first premium of the Franklin Institute. While thus employed under a fair sky, he married Nancy Day of West Springfield, Mass.

In 1835 he removed to New York, where he shortly after bought the interest of Mr. Wisner in the *New York Sun*, on a credit of $5,200. In the course of the following year, he bargained with Benjamin H. Day, his partner, for the remaining half, for the sum of $19,500. The first six months after he became the entire owner of the paper it did not prove as profitable as he had expected, and he was ready to sell it out, and offered it and all the property he then possessed, if any one would take it off his hands and pay his obligations to Mr. Day; but not succeeding in effecting a sale, he went to work with renewed ardor, and before two years had passed, the last dollar was paid off and he was once more in the ascendant.

From 1838 his course was steadily upward. His ability and enterprise in the management of his business excited the envy of some; but notwithstanding this, there are very few, if any, who knew him personally, who did not value him as a friend. Notwithstanding his many and severe labors, together with his failing health in middle life, he lived to the age of sixty-nine years, and died possessed of the largest estate of any native of Wallingford who had died in the town.

CHILDREN.

Drusilla Brewster, b. Nov. 30, 1820; m. Alexander Kursted of Tannersville, N. Y., Jan. 1, 1848. In 1849 they removed to Delaware County, N. Y. Moses Sperry, b. Oct. 5, 1822; m. Chloe Buckingham of Waterbury, in 1842. Resides in Brooklyn, N. Y. Henry Day, b. Aug. 8, 1824; m. Annie Fordham. Re-

K K

sides at May's Landing, N. J. Alfred Ely, b. Sept. 1,
1826; m. Harriet E. Holcomb of Boston, Mass., June 30,
1847. Resides in Stratford, Conn. Joseph Perkins, b.

RESIDENCE OF MOSES Y. BEACH, WALLINGFORD.

July 16, 1828; m. Eliza M. Betts of New York city,
March 20, 1850. Resides in Cheshire, Conn. Eveline

Shepherd, b. July 27, 1830; d. Aug. 18, 1836. Mary Ely, b. Aug., 1834; d. 1834 William Yale, b. Jan. 7, 1836; m. Emma A. Munson of Wallingford, where he now resides

### REV. JOSEPH BELLAMY, D. D.

Was born in Wallingford, parish of Cheshire, 1719. He was a son of Matthew, and grandson of Matthew of Fairfield and Killingworth, Conn. He was graduated at Yale College—studied for the ministry, and settled at Bethlem in 1740. He married Frances Sherman of New Haven, April 27, 1744. She died August 30, 1785. He died March 6, 1760.

He was a large, well-built man of commanding appearance, ha! a smooth, strong voice, and could fill the largest house, without any unnatural elevation. He was possessed of a truly great mind, and generally preached without notes. He usually had some great doctrinal point to establish, and would keep close to his subject until he had sufficiently illustrated it ; then, in an ingenious, close and pungent manner, he would make the application.

When he felt well, and was animated by a large audience he would preach incomparably. Though he paid little attention to language, yet when he became warm, and filled with his subject, he would, from the native vigor of his soul, produce the most commanding strokes of eloquence, making his audience alive. There is nothing in his writings, though a learned and great divine, equal to what was to be seen and heard in his preaching ; and it is difficult for any one who never heard him to form a just idea of the force and beauty of his preaching. He died at Bethlem in Litchfield county, Conn.

### STEPHEN ROWE BRADLEY, LL.D.

Was born in Wallingford, Cheshire Parish, Oct. 20, 1754, and graduated at Yale in 1775. He was the aid of Gen. Wooster when that officer was slain. He settled in Vermont, and became one of the most popular men in that State. In 1791 he was elected to the Senate of the United States, and continued a member of that body for sixteen years. He died at Walpole, New Hampshire, Dec. 16, 1830, aged 75 years.

### JOHN BROCKETT

Was one of the earliest settlers in Wallingford ; was there with his friend John Moss in 1668, and possibly before, making preparations for the settlement of a village there, and was selected by the New Haven committee to act as one of the sub-committee to manage the affairs of the new settlement until such time as it should become strong enough to manage its own affairs. The lot which was assigned him and on which he located himself, was at the south end of the village, a short distance below the present residence of Constant Webb, and extending over to Wharton's brook, embracing a portion of the land of Giles Hall and the house of the late Edward L. Hall. He died March 12, 1689, aged 80 years. His eldest son John was born in England, and settled near Muddy River in North Haven, as a Physician. He died Nov., 1720, and was the progenitor of most of the Brockett families in that locality.

### JAMES CARRINGTON, ESQ.

Was born in Wallingford and was during his whole life one of the most prominent of her citizens. He was the first post-master ever appointed for Wallingford, having the appointment in 1798, and continued in the discharge of its duties until the close of his life. In person he was a large, well-built man, of commanding appearance and address. For many years he conducted the singing in the old Congregational meeting-house, until it was taken down in 1824, giving great satisfaction as a leader. He was superintendent of the gun factory for the late Eli Whitney, Esq., at Whitneyville, and such was the confidence of Mr. Whitney in his ability, that he gave him the entire charge of the business for many years. His death was lamented by a large circle of friends and neighbors.

### LIVERIUS CARRINGTON, ESQ.

Studied medicine with Dr. Billious Kirtland of Walling-ford, but never practised his profession. He entered into the mercantile business in early life as a partner with the late George B. Kirtland, and continued with him through life. He was remarkable for his fund of liveliness. He had a peculiar way of pleasing his patrons and friends, especially the young; and his many noble qualities will long live in their memories. The firm of Carrington and Kirtland, at the decease of Mr. C., was one of the oldest, if not the oldest, in New Haven county.

### DANIEL CLARK

Married Elizabeth, daughter of James Miles of Walling-ford. She died April 19, 1755. He was a sea captain, and engaged largely in the shipping business. Being successful, he built at the foot of town hill, a house which was then the largest in the township, being 40 feet square on the front, and three stories high. It was after-ward occupied by Nathaniel Hitchcock, and finally sold to Joel Rice, who caused it to be taken down. He died Aug. 17, 1774, aged 63.

## COL. THADDEUS COOK

Son of Samuel, the son of Samuel, was born in that part of the town now embraced in the township of Cheshire. On the breaking out of the war of the Revolution he entered into the service of his country ; was made Colonel of his regiment, and was under the command of Gen. Gates during the memorable battle at Saratoga in 1777, and greatly distinguished himself as a brave and skillful officer. He died in Wallingford, Feb. 28, 1800, aged 72 years.

### SAMUEL COOK

Son of Col. Thaddeus, was born in Wallingford, and was eminently qualified for a public man. Although possessed of a large real estate, he was ever ready to serve the public in almost any position to which he might be called. He was often a member of the General Assembly, and a selectman of the town. He was noted for his natural gift in controlling those brought under his special authority. One look from him at one naturally indolent, was sufficient to arouse in him spirited action. A person once said to me, that he always loved and feared the presence of old Esq. Cook. He was active in the establishment of the Union Academy, which flourished for some years after its charter was granted, and was an honor to the town. As a farmer he had few if any superiors in his town or State. He died Sept. 27, 1824, aged 66 years.

### CAPT. JOEL COOK

Born in Wallingford in 1760. At the age of 16 he entered the army of the Revolution with his father, Col. Isaac Cook of Wallingford, and served to the end. In 1811 he was at the battle of Tippecanoe. In 1813 he resided in New Haven, and in 1849 he removed from Yonkers to Deer Park, Long Island, where he died on the 18th day of Dec., 1851, aged 92 years. It was this man who built the small stucco house standing on the east side of East street in the city of New Haven.

### REV. BENJAMIN DOOLITTLE.

In the year 1718, Rev. Benjamin Doolittle, of Wallingford, preached in Northfield, Mass. ; the people desired him to settle, and promised him £65 as annual salary, and quite a liberal amount of money and land as "settlement." Mr. Doolittle continued there until January 9, 1748, when he died, in the fifty-fifth year of his age, and the thirtieth of his ministry. On the Northfield records, one of their highways is laid out, "from Pochaug meadow to a little brook where Mr. Doolittle's horse died." The following is the epitaph on his tombstone :

" Blessed with good intellectual parts,
Well skilled in two important arts,
Nobly he filled the double station
Both of a preacher and physician.
To cure man's sicknesses and sins,
He took unwearied care and pains ;
And strove to make his patient whole
Throughout, in body and in soul.
He loved his God, loved to do good,
To all his friends vast kindness showed,
Nor could his enemies exclaim
And say, he was not kind to them.
His labors met a sudden close :
Now he enjoys a sweet repose,
And when the just to life shall rise,
Among the first he'll mount the skies."

### LIEUT. ABRAHAM DOOLITTLE

Was an inn-keeper during the French war. His house
was the most noted tavern on the main road between
Boston and New York. Lord Loudon, while on his way
to Canada, put up at Doolittle's house with his coach
and four splendid horses. The landlord was much in
the habit of using large words out of their appropriate
place and meaning. On this occasion he felt a special
call for them. In the morning he carefully looked at
the fine blooded team in presence of his titled guest
and on each of the horses employed every superlative of
a considerable character until he came to the fourth ani-
mal. "What do you think of that one?" asked his
lordship. "It is a *precarious* good horse," replied the
landlord. The word *precarious* stuck to Mr. Doolittle
as long as he lived. The house was removed from its
old site, and is now the building on the south corner,
opposite the Congregational church. It was placed
where it now stands by Eben Smith, who occupied it
as a hotel for several years.

### DEA. THOMAS FENN

The son of Thomas Fenn of Wallingford, was born in
Wallingford in the year 1735, and removed to Westbury in early life with his father, April 19, 1760. He
represented the towns of Watertown and Waterbury,
in thirty-five Sessions, beginning in 1778. He was a
Justice of the Peace and a Deacon of the Congregational Church of Watertown for many years. Through
a long life he was an influential and much respected citizen. He married Abiah, daughter of Richard Welton
of Waterbury, by whom he had six sons and two
daughters. He was a captain in the Revolutionary
army. He died August 1, 1818.

## HON. SAMUEL A. FOOT, LL.D.

Was a son of Rev. John Foot of Cheshire, and was born Nov. 8, 1780. He graduated at Yale College in 1797, studied law, and commenced practice in his native village. He married Miss Eudocia Hull, daughter of Gen. Andrew Hull, of Cheshire, and became a partner with Mr. Hull in commercial business at New Haven. In 1819 he was elected a member of Congress, and reëlected in 1823 and 1834. He was elected Speaker of the House of Representatives of Conn. in 1825-6, and was chosen a Senator in Congress from 1827 to 1833. In 1834 he was elected Governor of Connecticut, and during that year received from Yale College the degree of LL.D. He died Sept. 16, 1846, aged 66 years. He left three sons, viz.: the Hon. John A. Foot, of Cleveland, Ohio; Rear Admiral Andrew H. Foot, U. S. N., who died at New Haven; Augustus E. Foot, Esq., of Cleveland, Ohio.

## HON. LYMAN HALL.

Was born in Wallingford. He graduated at Yale College in 1747, studied medicine, and located himself at Midway, Georgia. Having earnestly and zealously espoused the cause of his country in her struggle with the mother country during the Revolution, his efforts contributed much to induce the people of Georgia to join the confederacy. He was in May, 1775, elected to Congress, as a member of which he signed the Declaration of Independence, and continued in that body till the close of 1780. In 1783 he was elected Governor of Georgia. He died Feb. 1791, aged 66 years. He was a son of the Hon. John and Mary (Lyman) Hall, of Wallingford.

### DANIEL HART

Was born in Wallingford, and removed to Goshen in early life. He owned and occupied when living in Wallingford the house now occupied by the heirs of Lyman Hall, and known as the Aaron Yale place. He was a man of worth, and much respected.

### REV. LUTHER HART

Was his son, and was born at Goshen, July 27, 1783. His mother was a woman of superior mind. She came from a family on Long Island. In childhood he was distinguished for his great fondness for books and love of music. In his sixteenth year he became converted and united with the church at Torrington, where the family then resided. He felt a desire then to enter the ministry. The expense however was an effectual barrier to his desires, and he learned the trade of a house carpenter of his father. In the meantime he became acquainted with the rudiments of an English education, and acquired an intimate acquaintance of men and things, of human nature as seen in the affairs of common life, of which clergymen as a class are lamentably deficient. His trade he never forgot through life, and during his preparatory studies continued to exercise his skill as a worker on wood for profit, and at a later period for exercise and recreation. In the latter part of the year 1802, or early in 1803, he commenced his preparatory course of studies under the direction of his pastor, the Rev. Alexander Gillette. In September, 1803, he entered Yale college. He at once took high rank, and at his graduation in 1807, received one of the highest honors of the institution. After a year devoted to teaching, he commenced his theological studies under the Rev Dr. Porter of Washington, Conn., and finished them at Andover. Mass. In a short time he was called to Plymouth, Conn., where he was ordained and installed over the Congregational church and society in Sept., 1810. He married a daughter of Gen. Daniel and Martha (Humiston) Potter. He was an interesting and able preacher, and few men in the State were more generally acceptable He was lively and pleasant in conversation, easy and agreeable in his manners. He died April 25, 1834; left no children.

### NATHANIEL HART

Of Wallingford, owned the farm on which afterwards lived Jeremiah Hall, who married his daughter. The old Hart house stood a little south of the one in which Mr. Hall lived. Mr. Hart was a carpenter and joiner, and when in advanced life, used to boast of having built eleven meeting-houses, one of which is now (1870) standing in Farmington. In his old age he went to Goshen to reside with his sons. He built the steeple on the old three story Congregational meeting house in Wallingford, about 1745 He died some sixty years ago, aged ninety years.

### GIDEON HOSFORD

Was an inn-keeper in Wallingford, and is said to have built the house now known as the residence of the late Abijah Ives, on the plains, in which for many years he kept an inn. This house is still standing on its original foundation, on the corner of the old colony road and the road leading to Hosford's bridge, in a rather dilapidated condition.

### DR. ZEPHANIAH HULL.

Was a son of John and Sarah Hull, of Wallingford, and was born in what is now Cheshire, in 1728. Studied the profession of medicine at an early age; married

Hannah, daughter of ———— Cook, March 28, 1749, and
soon after removed to Bethlem in Woodbury, probably
through the influence of Dr. Bellamy, who was a native
of the same town and a few years his senior. He died
Nov. 10, 1760, the same day with his wife, in the "Great
Sickness." They were buried in one grave, and two of
his children and a young man living in his house died a
few days later. Soon after these deaths, and while others
were sick in the house, a Deacon Strong, near by, raised
a flock of eleven quails, which flew over the house and
dropped in the garden. Immediately after, three of them
rose and flew into the bushes, but the other eight were
found dead, and in an hour afterwards putrified, became
offensive and were buried. As a physician and as a
man Dr. Hull ever sustained a high character, in the
place of his adoption.

### JAMES HUMISTON, ESQ.

Was a prominent citizen of Wallingford. He frequently
represented his town in the Legislature of the State.
Was often one of the select men of the town, and as
proprietor of the old mill which to this day bears his
name, conducted a large business. Subsequently he
added to his milling business that of wool carding, dye-
ing, dressing cloth, &c., continuing the same to the
close of his life.

### TURHAND KIRTLAND

Was born in Wallingford, November 16, 1755. He
was a descendant of John Kirtland, who was one of the
thirty-six heads of families who settled at Saybrook in
1635. In the year 1776 he was in the provisional
service at New York, at the time of the defeat of the
American army on Long Island, and was engaged on

board the boats which conveyed our retreating forces
over to the mainland. He, with most of the company,
was attacked with the malignant camp distemper,
typhoid dysentery, and was discharged at Saw-pits.
After his recovery and return home, he pursued for a
number of years the occupation of carriage-making and
farming, in his native town. He was one of the original
members of the Connecticut Land company, which
purchased the title to the Western Reserve, or New
Connecticut. As agent for the company, he conducted
a boat loaded with surveyors, emigrants and provisions
up the Mohawk river through Wood creek, Oneida and
Ontario lakes, into Niagara river; from thence hauled
it around the falls on the Canada side, and navigated up
the river and through Lake Erie into Grand river, a little
above the present city of Painesville, in the year 1798.
In the same capacity he annually visited the West until
1803, when he removed his family to Ohio, and located
at Poland, where he resided until his death, August 16
1844. As agent or proprietor, he disposed of extensive
tracts of new lands ; and he took an active and influential part in promoting settlements and introducing
schools and various improvements. For a time he was
a Senator in the State Legislature, and Associate Judge
in the court of Common Pleas of Ohio. He was
distinguished for his integrity and active business habits.
As one of the earlier settlers, he saw the Connecticut
Reserve in its primitive condition a perfect wilderness,
and lived to see it thickly peopled by the best regulated
and most intelligent population to be found in the
Union out of New England. When in Wallingford he
owned and occupied the house and farm of the late
Amos Dutton.

### GEORGE B. KIRTLAND, ESQ.

During his whole life was an example worthy of imitation. He was universally regarded as an honest, upright and intelligent merchant and business man. He made it a principle never to recommend an article beyond what it would bear. He died in 1869, having lived out the full number of years allotted to man, greatly lamented by the whole community, and especially by the Episcopal church, of which he was a consistent and worthy member. He was the last male member of the once highly respectable Kirtland family in Wallingford.

### JARED POTTER KIRTLAND, M.D., LL.D.

A son of Turhand and Mary Kirtland, and grandson of Dr. Jared Potter, a distinguished physician of Wallingford. He was born Nov. 10, 1793, in the town of Wallingford. He received his classical education chiefly in Cheshire and Wallingford academies, and was for a time a pupil of Rev. Dr. Tillotson Bronson, the then Principal of the Cheshire Episcopal Academy.

In 1810 he commenced the study of medicine, and became a private pupil of Drs. Eli Ives and Nathan Smith, of New Haven, until 1812, when he entered the first class in the Medical Department of Yale College, and was the first who signed the matriculation book in the charge of Prof. Jonathan Knight. At the close of the medical term, he with others formed a class for the study of botany and mineralogy, which, together with their medical studies, was pursued under Prof. Eli Ives and Benjamin Silliman. In 1814 he entered the Medical Department of the University of Pennsylvania, and soon after passed an examination for a medical degree before the medical faculty of Yale College. The subject of his Thesis was, "Our Indigenous Vegetable Materia Medica," a private subject of one of his teachers, Dr. Benjamin Smith Barton, and in consonance more with his own taste than other points of his profession.

In May, 1814, he married Caroline, daughter of Joshua and Elizabeth (Cook) Atwater of Wallingford, and soon after commenced the practice of medicine in that place, which he continued until 1817, when at a town meeting held at Durham he was invited to locate in that town as a physician, which invitation he accepted His practice here soon became large; but with it he found time to interest himself in the culture of fruits and flowers, of which he was very fond. In 1823 he removed to Poland, Trumbull Co., Ohio, where, although continuing to practice his profession of medicine whenever called upon, he gave his time and thoughts mainly to the culture of his farm, garden and orchard.

In 1837 he removed to Cleveland, Ohio, an l at first established himself in the town or city ; but soon tiring of the confined limits of a city residence, he purchased one hundred and seventy-five acres of land about five miles west of the city of Cleveland, situated immediately on the Lake shore. Here, while at times continuing his professional labors, he has found time to examine and describe all the fishes of Ohio's lakes and rivers ; to collect and compare innumerable fresh water shells, connected with which he made a discovery in the science, new and distinct, viz.: the sexual or male and female character of the muscle, which is indicated by the form of the shell. He found time to examine the native wild plants botanically, to examine and to study the geological formation of the State, to study and gather specimens of birds by hundreds. He has investigated the habits of the honey-bee, has found time to superintend and direct a large farm on which all the best grains and grapes, and the best breeds of cattle, sheep, hogs, &c., have been tried and compared, comparative values of manures tested, and their components analyzed.

In 1827 he was elected a representative to the Legislature of Ohio, and re-elected several times ; was chairman of the committee on the Penitentiary in the House. In 1835 he was elected Professor of the Theory and Practice of Medicine in the Medical College of Ohio. In 1841, having resigned his position in the Medical College of Ohio, he became Professor of the Theory and Practice of Medicine in the Willoughby Medical School ; and afterwards, when the medical department of the Western Reserve College was established at Cleveland, he accepted a similar position in that college, which his health compelled him to resign in 1864. He was at one time President of the Ohio State Medical Society; and when in attendance at public gatherings has universally been called upon to assume the duties of the chair. In 1861 he received the degree of LL.D. from Williams College. Genial in spirit, full of intelligent conversational power, possessing the retiring manner and dignity of a well-bred gentleman of the old school, he wins the hearts of the old and young ; while the intelligent and all who seek knowledge, rejoice in obtaining an hour in his society. He is now over 76 years old.

### JARED LEWIS, ESQ.

Was born in Wallingford, and was for several years a justly celebrated hotel keeper and merchant in the village. He owned and occupied the lot on which now stands the house and store of Lorenzo Lewis, his grandson. He was a prominent politician. One of the parties at one time assumed the name of Lewis, and the opposition that of Cooke. Politics never ran higher in Wallingford than at this time. He was the father of Isaac Lewis, who was keeper of a hotel and merchant at Meriden, and who was the father of the late Patrick Lewis, and of Isaac Lewis, who is and has been a very successful business man in Meriden for several years.

### CHARLES BARNY MC CARTY

A native of Ireland, came to America in the latter part of the last century, and found his way to Wallingford, a peddler of small articles of dry-goods. In making his trips about Wallingford, he formed the acquaintance of Miss Dacia Hall, a daughter of Charles and Sarah (Atwater) Hall, and married her. In a few years he was enabled by his industry and success in business, to build and stock a store with dry-goods and groceries. His ambition led him to invest in real-estate quite too largely for his means, by which, with other matters, he became involved, from the effects of which he never fully recovered. He lived to an advanced age. His children were Dr. Charles B., who was a physician in Yalesville; Mary, died in Yalesville; Sarah, died unmarried in 1869; Ann, died unmarried; Henry Hobart, died April 23, 1870, from an injury received two days before.

### JOHN MOSS

Was in New Haven as early as 1645, perhaps earlier, and was a member of the General Court during several sessions. In 1670 at the May session he was active in procuring the act of incorporation of Wallingford, and succeeded on the 12th day of May, 1670, at Hartford. He was evidently the leading man of the new settlement,

L. L.

and was the pioneer of the settlers, being on the ground certainly as early as 1667. His house lot was situated at the extreme south end of the village, adjoining that of his friend (John Brockett) who was associated with him in promoting the interest and advancement of the settlement. He died A. D. 1707, aged 103.

### ELISHA M. POMEROY, ESQ.

Came into Wallingford a tinner by trade, and married Lydia Mattoon. About the year 1820 he invented his justly celebrated Razor Strop, which soon became noted in every part of the United States. In this enterprise he was prosperous beyond his most sanguine expectations. He was a man of enterprise and good business talents, and of easy address and gentlemanly deportment. After his retirement from business he was chosen Judge of the Probate Court, and a Justice of the Peace. In the discharge of the duties of these offices, he was eminently well qualified, and his decisions compare favorably with those of any of his predecessors. He reared a large and highly respectable family of children, and died at the advanced age of 78 years, in Wallingford, the place of his adoption. His eldest son, George V. Pomeroy, is a merchant in New York city. The late Jerome B. Pomeroy M. D. is also a son of the Judge.

### JARED POTTER, M. D.

Was born in East Haven, Conn., Sept. 25, 1742. His classical studies were commenced under the Rev. Philemon Robbins of Branford. He entered Yale college in 1756, and was graduated in 1760. His medical studies were begun under Dr. Harpins of Milford, and afterward pursued under the Rev. Jared Elliot of Killingworth. He commenced practice in East Haven in 1763, but soon removed to New Haven, where he established a favorable reputation and secured a good share of patron-age. The premonitory tumults of the approaching conflict with the mother country induced him to remove his family to a place of less exposure to impending dangers. Hence in the year 1773 he changed his location to Wallingford, where he went into professional practice and continued with the exception of the time spent in the service of his country, until his death, July 30, 1810.

He was a descendant of John Potter, who signed the plantation covenant of New Haven, June 4, 1639. At the commencement of the Revolution, when the first six regiments were raised by the Province of Connecticut, he was appointed surgeon of the fourteenth regiment under Colonel (afterwards General) Wooster, and went with them to Canada, and was present when the British port of St. John's was captured in September, 1775, by General Montgomery. From there he removed with the army to Montreal, where he was placed in charge of a hospital, and remained until our forces returned in the next summer. The term of enlistment having expired, he was immediately re-appointed surgeon, and was attached to Colonel Douglas's regiment, destined to re-enforce the continental army in New York city. He was in the battles of Long Island and White Plains, and at the close of the campaign, when the regiment was disbanded, he returned to Wallingford

Too many physicians throw aside their books, or pay little attention to them after they are engaged in extensive practice. This was not the case with Dr. Potter. He was an uncommonly diligent student, not merely while acquiring the rudiments of his profession, but to the end of his life. For many years he kept a medical school, in which several of the most eminent physicians

of Connecticut were educated; and it is worthy of
remark that the late Dr. Samuel Hopkins of Hartford,
who was considered the most able practitioner of his
county if not in the State, was his pupil. Dr. Potter
imbibed much of the spirit of Elliot for philosophical
investigations, and took pains to become well acquainted
with the practice and opinion of all the most celebrated
writers, ancient and modern, upon nearly every disease.
His reading was consequently very extensive. He
was in the habit of purchasing annually all of the new
medical works which appeared ; and was also well read in
the reviews and other periodical literature of the day.
As a physician he was a superior judge of symptoms,
and was a very energetic and successful practitioner in
acute diseases; but it is said that he was very skeptical
of the power of medicine in most chronic complaints,
and for that reason, his practice in such cases was rather
inefficient and sometimes almost inert. Dr. Potter was
well known as having had a peculiar fondness for discuss-
ing questions of speculative theology and the politics
of the day ; and when conversing on these subjects his
strict command of his temper and an uncommon urban-
ity of manner, joined to a large share of wit and humor,
usually gave him a decided advantage over most of his
opponents. Like his preceptor Elliot, his practice and
consultations were very extensive, and like him too for
many years he was probably the most distinguished and
influential physician in the State. He was one of the
founders, and a Vice President of the State Medical
Society. It is said that he was always able to recollect
the name and face of any person who had once been
introduced to him, and the circumstances of their meeting. His great colloquial powers, and the frankness and

candor with which he uniformly treated his medical
brethren, made his presence and advice as a counsellor
always acceptable. He died in Wallingford, deeply lamented by the whole community.

### THOMAS RICHARDSON

Of Farmington in 1672, and of Waterbury in 1674,
received and accepted a grant of land called the bachelors' property in 1699. He was one of the eighty four
first proprietors of the town in 1692. He died Nov. 14,
1712. Mary, his wife, died one week afterwards, Nov.
21. Both were victims of the " great sickness" that then
prevailed in the place.

Thomas, their second son and fourth child, received a
grant of land in March, 1695, which he accepted as a
bachelors' proprietor March 26, 1699. He remained in
Waterbury long enough to secure his right, and then
removed to Wallingford, and was there in July, 1705.
After his father's decease he returned to Waterbury and
was appointed a fence-viewer in 1713, grave-digger in
1714-15-16, hayward in 1714-17-18-19. March 30
he sold his house and six acres of land on the north side
of West Main-st., to Thomas Richards, and returned to
Wallingford, where he was living in 1722, a farmer. He
had brothers and sisters, viz., Mary, Sarah, John, Israel,
Rebecca, Ruth, Johannah, Nathaniel and Ebenezer.
He married for his second wife, Rachel, daughter of
John and Hannah Parker, of Wallingford.

### THOMAS RUGGLES

Came to Wallingford about 1812, and purchased the old
homestead of Mr. Joel Hall. He was a gentleman of
means, and a graduate of Yale College. He soon after
purchased the house of Salmon Carter in the village,
and became the principal of the Union Academy. He

continued in charge of the Academy until the death of
his father-in-law, Mr. Charles Hall, which occurred in
1817, at which time he by his will became the possessor
of one-half of Mr. Hall's estate. Having repaired the
buildings, he occupied them during the rest of his life.
He had by his first wife a child, Hannah, who died young.

### SAMUEL GEORGE SIMPSON

Son of Robert, alias Samuel George, and Mary Simpson,
was born in New Haven in 17—. Samuel G. sen., came
to America a lieutenant in the British army, about the
year 1767, on a mission from the King of England to
persuade the people of the colonies to receive the Stamp
Act and other measures of the English government,
which were then looked upon as odious and burdensome
by the people. Mr. Simpson was a relation of the King
by his marriage into a German family, Mr. Simpson
himself being a German, and of a highly respectable
and wealthy family. After taking up his residence in
New Haven under the assumed name of *Robert*, he
married Mary Johnson, daughter of a reputable family.
Of this marriage Samuel George was an only child.
After the decease of Mr. Simpson in 1776, his widow
married Josiah Merriam of Wallingford, in the parish of
Meriden, and removed to that place, taking her little son
along with her, who, when about twenty years of age,
married Mary, daughter of John and Eunice Yale of
Meriden. She died April 2, 1799. After a suitable
lapse of time he married Malinda, daughter of John and
Lois Hall of Wallingford. He purchased and settled on
the Dr. Russel or Henry place, situated on the old
Tank-hood road, a short distance east of the residence of
Mr. Hall. He disposed of this place and removed to
Ohio, but after a residence of a few years he returned

to Wallingford, where he died, highly respected for his honesty and integrity.

Children: Alfred, Henry, George, Harmon, Samuel The latter married Martha Benham and is a successful manufacturer in his native town; has had one son, Samuel G., and two daughters.

## EBEN SMITH

Was a man of some note in Wallingford sixty years ago. He bought the old Doolittle hotel that formerly stood a little to the west of the Dr. Potter house, lately Rice Hall's, and placed it upon the corner of Main street and the street running east and west past the Congregational meeting-house, and in front of the same, and occupied it as a hotel. At that time there were three hotels in the village, viz.: Jared Lewis's house, Chauncey Cook's, now Dwight Hall's, and Eben Smith's house. He was the father of Mrs. Lyman Carmon.

## TITUS STREET, ESQ.

Son of Samuel, was born in Wallingford. In early life he went to Cheshire, where he commenced business in a small store, with his friend Samuel Hughs (afterwards his partner) as clerk. Here he was married to Miss Amaryllis, daughter of Reuben and Mary Atwater, by whom he had two children, Augustus Russell and Mary, the wife of Gov. Hoppen of Rhode Island. He afterward located in New Haven with Mr. Hughs as partner, and after a few years' successful business in the city he retired with a large fortune, and continued in retirement until his decease. He was a descendant of the Rev. Samuel Street, the first settled Congregational minister in Wallingford Augustus Russell Street, son of Titus, was the founder of the Yale Art Building on the grounds of Yale College in New Haven.

### CAPT. WILLIAM TODD

Was born in North Haven and came to Wallingford a young man. He became acquainted with Miss Harriet Johnson, and in due time married her. He was a house joiner and carpenter, and as a builder was deservedly popular. Being possessed naturally of a good constitution, he was enabled to continue the business of his trade until near the close of his life, which occurred in 1869, at the advanced age of 83 years. After the death of his first wife, he was married twice; first, to the widow of Capt. Joel Rice, and secondly, to the widow Merrit Tuttle. He had a large family of children, most of whom are living.

### JOHN TYLER

Was a native of Wallingford, and was graduated at Yale College in 1765. He was educated a Congregationalist, but having embraced the doctrines of the Church of England, prepared for Holy Orders under the care of Dr. Johnson of Stratford. In 1768 he went to England to receive ordination, with a view to becoming Rector of Christ Church, in Chelsea, Norwich, Conn.; and having accomplished this object he returned the next year and entered on the duties of his office. For three years during the Revolution, owing to the popular excitement which prevailed against Episcopacy in New England, (it being regarded almost synonymous with Toryism), Mr. Tyler's church was closed; and from April 1776 to April 1779 not an entry was made in its records. He however, during this time held divine service in his own house, and was never molested in the performance of it. At one time he was afraid to drink the water of his own well; and yet he was regarded as a man of great benevolence and liberality. As an evidence of the kindly feeling which both he and his church maintained toward their Congregational neighbors, it may be mentioned that when the Congregationalists in 1794 lost their place of worship by fire, the Episcopalians at once proffered them the use of theirs on the following condition : "The Rev. John Tyler, our present pastor, to perform Divine service one half the day on each Sabbath, and the Rev. Walter King, pastor of said Presbyterian Congregation, to perform Divine service on the other half of said Sabbath, each alternately performing on the first half of the day." The offer was gratefully accepted and this amicable arrangement continued for three months. Mr. Tyler died Jan. 20, 1823, aged 81 years. He published a sermon preached at the opening of Trinity church in Pomfret, 1771 ; and a sermon preached at Norwich on the Continental Thanksgiving, 1795. Mrs. Sigourney writes thus concerning him : "He was an interesting preacher ; his voice sweet and solemn, and his eloquence persuasive. The benevolence of his heart was manifest in daily acts of courtesy and charity to those around him. He studied medicine in order to benefit the poor, and to find out remedies for some of those peculiar diseases to which no common specifics seemed to apply. During the latter years of his life he was so infirm as to need assistance in his clerical duties."

## ADOLPH WILHELM AUGUST FRIEDRICH, BARON VON STEINWEHR

Was born at Blankenburg in the duchy of Brunswick, Sept. 25, 1822. His father was a major in the ducal service, and his grandfather a lieutenant-general in the Prussian army. He was educated at the military academy of the city of Brunswick, and entered the army of the duchy as a lieutenant in 1841. In 1847 he resigned and came to the United States for the purpose of offer-

ing his services to the government in the Mexican war ;
but failing to obtain a commission in the regular army,
he returned to Germany after marrying a lady of Mobile.
In 1854 he again came to America and purchased a farm
in Wallingford. At the commencement of the civil
war he raised a regiment, the 29th New York Volunteers, which he commanded at the first battle of Bull
Run, forming part of the reserve under Col. Miles. On
Oct. 12, 1861, he was commissioned brigadier-general of
volunteers, and appointed to the command of the 2d
brigade of Blenker's division. This division was attached
in May, 1862, to the Mountain department under Gen.
Fremont. When Sigel assumed command of the corps
after the organization of the army of Virginia, General
Steinwehr was promoted to the command of the 2d
division, and participated in the campaign on the Rapi-
dan and Rappahannock in August.

### ANDREW WARD

Was admitted a Freeman in 1638 at Boston. In 1638
he was at Wethersfield, and with twenty others purchased the town of Stamford. He also with others
purchased Hempsted on Long Island, but in consequence
of difficulties with the Dutch government, removed to
Fairfield, and died Oct., 1650, leaving a widow Esther,
and children. He was a man of great worth and consequence in the colony, and was frequently called upon
by the Governors and members of the Legislature to
act with them on important committees. He was the
ancestor of those of the name in Hartford, and the
father of Andrew, who was the father of William, who
married Lettice, daughter of John Beach of Wallingford,
and had Zenas, who settled in Woodbury, and Mocock,
who was a lawyer in Wallingford.

### ELISHA WHITTELSEY

Was a merchant in Wallingford, and for many years was Town Clerk, in which office he gained the esteem and confidence of all who had business with him. He was a highly respected and honored gentleman, and a man of strict integrity and usefulness. At his death he was greatly lamented by all. He was born July 1, 1753, and died Sept. 16, 1822, aged 67 years.

### JARED POTTER WHITTELSEY

Was the third son of Elisha and Sarah (Jones) Whittelsey, and was born in Wallingford, March 8, 1787. In 1808, being then in his twenty-first year, he commenced business in Catskill, N. Y., where he remained four years. In 1812 he removed to New York city, where he carried on the wholesale flour business, retaining his flour-mills and his store in Catskill, Cairo, and Schoharie, until the year 1832, when he removed his family to Wallingford and erected the present buildings on the ground where he was born ; and during the remainder of his life he devoted his time to improving and beautifying the streets of his native town, by setting out shade trees, opening walks and highly improving his own grounds. He was a man of sterling worth, very methodical in habit, of thorough business qualities and a finely balanced mind. During his residence in Wallingford, he gave largely to the Episcopal church, and gave more to erect the present Congregational church than any of its members. In his religious belief he was a Unitarian. His donations were made during his lifetime, and yearly he gave to the following societies, viz.: Children's Aid Society, Five Points House of Industry, Association to improve the condition of the Poor, and other societies. During the war he gave largely to the sanitary commission. He never

spoke of his donations, and they were not known until
after his death. Mr. Whittelsey was frequently offered
positions of trust in private and public, but he refused
them, for he wished to be quiet after a busy life. Mr.
Whittelsey was the father of ten children, only two remaining at the time of his death; six died between the
ages of nineteen and twenty-seven. He married Oct.
22, 1814, Lydia G. Archer of New York city, who lived
with him fifty-five years, and died only a month before
him. Mr. Whittelsey died January 25, 1869, in the ·
eighty-second year of his age.

### CAPT. THOMAS YALE

Son of Thomas the emigrant, was one of the original
settlers or planters of Wallingford, and was one of the
most active and efficient among them. As selectman or
townsman, he was ever ready to work for the interest
of the village. He was frequently elected to represent
the people in the General Court, and was greatly distinguished for his devotion to the interests of his constituents, whom he ably represented for a number of
successive years. He married Rebecca Gibbons,
daughter of William, of New Haven. She died Dec.
11, 1667. After her decease, he married Sarah, daughter of John Nash, of New Haven. She died May 24,
1716; and he then married Mary Beach, of Wallingford,
July 31, 1716. He had by the two last no children. He
was chosen one of the number to assist in the formation
or gathering of a church in the place, after the Congregational order; and was a signer to the call of the first
and second ministers, viz.: Rev. Samuel Street and
Rev. Samuel Whittelsey. In 1710 he was, with the
exception of Mr. Street, the only surviving signer of the
Plantation covenant of Wallingford. He was a Justice

of the peace, and a Captain of the train-band, &c. He died at the age of 89 years, July 26, 1736.

### CHARLES YALE, ESQ.

Was born in Wallingford, parish of Meriden, April 20, 1769. He married Huldah Robinson of Meriden, and commenced the manufacture of japanned and tin ware, for this and the southern market ; and for several years kept a depot for the sale of his goods at Richmond, Virginia, in connection with his brother Selden. In, this enterprise they were very successful, and in a few years they each had accumulated a very handsome property. The failing health of Selden compelled him to retire from the firm. Upon this, Mr. Yale formed a business connection with his son-in-law, under the name of Yale and Dunby, and soon after purchased in his own name the old Mills at the first falls on the Quinnipiac River, which had borne the name of Tyler's Mills for more than one hundred years. He repaired and remodeled the whole concern, and changed the name to Yalesville. Here he entered largely into the manufacture of britannia wares and tea-pots, which found a ready sale in New York and elsewhere. In this business he continued until the close of his life. He died Nov. 2, 1835, aged 47 years.

### HON. ELIHU YALE

Of New Haven, son of the late Ira and Harriet (Cook) Yale of Wallingford, was born July 25, 1807, in the house built by his grandfather Elisha Yale in Yalesville district, and resided at home with his parents until Jan. 6, 1824, when he left his home to learn a trade in the city of New Haven. After the term of his apprenticeship was concluded, he returned to his native town, where he was soon after made a freeman and elected a consta-

bie.   The year following he went to Cheshire, where he
married Julia Ann, daughter of the late Capt. Thaddeus
Rich, formerly of Bristol, Conn., May 25, 1830.   He was
appointed post master at Cheshire in 1832, and continued
in the office with the exception of a few months until
1851, when he removed to New Haven.   He was a Justice of the Peace for about 18 years, and a selectman in
Cheshire five consecutive years, clerk of the school society for about fourteen  years, and  judge of the  Probate
court in  1850–7, and was in  1853 elected a member of
the common council of New  Haven, and was  re-elected
for five consecutive years.   In 1859 he was elected chief
of the Police of the city of New Haven, and  was re-
elected to the same office in 1864.   After serving nearly
two years he resigned the office, believing that he had
contributed his share to the public service.

In 1750 he prepared and published a genealogy of the
Yale family, from the  first of the name who appeared in
this country down to 1850.   He has in  manuscript a
genealogy of the  Cook family, which he has carefully
prepared and hopes soon to publish.   Besides he has
collected a large amount of genealogical matter for this
work, and many  of the Biographical  notices which
appear in this work, have been prepared by him. He was
elected a member of the New  England  Historical and
Genealogical Society, on the 7th of May, 1856, and is a
member of the New Haven Colony Historical Society.

—..—

## MERIDEN BIOGRAPHIES.

### HON. WALTER BOOTH

Was born in Woodbridge, Conn., Dec. 8th, 1791. When
about sixteen years of age, he came to Meriden and
spent his first night in this town at the old white house
on the Hanover road, which stands first northwest of
the old residence of the late J. C. Breckenridge. The
greater part of his life since then has been spent here,
a few years excepted which he spent in business in
Baltimore. But it is not only as a citizen of Meriden,
that Deacon Booth was known ; he was widely known
throughout the state. At one time he was appointed to
fill the office of General of our State Militia, both as a
Brigadier and a Major General. In 1850 he was sent
to Washington to represent the State of Connecticut in
the House of Representatives, which position he held
for two years; besides having previously held sundry
minor offices in both town and state. At twenty-two
years of age he was elected deacon in the Center
Congregational Church in this city, which office he had
held at the time of his death 56 years. He had also
been a director in the Meriden National Bank for
twenty years, and at one time its President.

But above all he was eminently a good man, a man of
strict integrity and a Christian man. Up to his last
illness he was active in all his church duties, and seldom
was he absent from his place in the sanctuary and the
Sabbath school where he was a teacher, and of which
he was the first superintendent, and also in the social
prayer-meetings. Many will recall the fervor of his
prayers and the unction of his exhortations in the social

meeting; and the testimony of all who knew him, is uniform as to the steadfastness of his Christian principle, and the purity of his Christian character.

He was a man of great simplicity and plainness of manners, and was averse to all pageantry and parade, and strictly economical in his expenditures. He showed himself ever ready to aid any enterprise, either in business, or civil and religious affairs, which promised to promote the secular or religious interests of his native town.

His illness, which lasted little less than two weeks, was a malignant form of erysipelas; first indicating itself in his face, and from there creeping to his brain, rendering him delirious for a greater part of the time. His friends, however, and physician, Dr. Catlin, did not deem him dangerous until Wednesday of the week in which he died. Dr. Townsend of New Haven was called in as counsel on Tuesday, and did not then think his chances for recovery were doubtful. But notwith-standing the tender nursing of his wife and friends who were continually by his bedside, and in spite of the skill and faithfulness of his physician, the destroying disease made headway, and on Saturday morning, April 30, 1870, lapsing into unconsciousness, he gently and with-out a struggle or a groan breathed his life away.

### FENNER BUSH

Son of John and Bathsheba (Dodge) Bush, was born in East Lyme, Conn., in the year 1791. His father died when Fenner was quite young, and as the family were in very poor circumstances, he was put out to live when but six years of age. He was employed in assisting on the farm and at house-work. When eleven years old he was put in the family of a ship-builder, and was to be taught the trade when old enough; but soon after, his master ran off with his wife's sister, and the boy was returned to his former master. In his twelfth year he went to live with a joiner, with a view to learn the trade. When eighteen years old, his master furnished him with a new suit of clothes, and for the first time he attended church. The last four years of his apprenticeship (he served nine years), his master treated him with less rigor, but his situation was far from being respectable.

FENNER BUSH.

When he was twenty-one, he had no home or property, except a right in a small piece of land that his father left, worth perhaps two hundred dollars. He worked for his master three months, at fourteen dollars per month, and at the close of this term, he took his forty-two dollars and started off on foot to a neighboring town, to make purchases of some tools. On his way he lost his money, all he had in the world; but by good luck found it again, purchased his tools, and returned and set up business in opposition to his former master, who politely told him that he was "a — — fool, for he would not earn enough to pay his board." But he was

M M

ambitious, and moreover a good workman, and soon had so much to do, that his former master offered to sell out to him.  Fenner accepted the offer, and hired help to meet his engagements.

He now found the necessity of something which had been entirely neglected ; for he could neither read nor keep accounts.  He therefore gave up business, hired a room, and for two winters devoted himself to study, three months of which were given to learning to read. He again commenced business, and pursued his trade with considerable success.  In 1816 he married Eunice Kirtland of Saybrook, and commenced keeping house, taking two apprentices to board.  About this time he was taken sick with typhus fever, and for a long time was very sick ; and for nearly two years was unable to work.  During his sickness he spent all he had earned from the beginning, and got into debt several hundred dollars.  But by diligent attention to business he paid up his debts and bought the house that he lived in.

In April, 1824, he removed from Saybrook to Meriden and became interested in the comb business in connection with Mr. Julius Pratt.  He worked here with untiring industry twelve hours a day, at $1 25 per day ; after a few years the time was reduced to eleven hours, and the wages increased to $1 75 a day.  For twenty years he labored here, when the shop was destroyed by fire, and he lost the earnings of twenty years.  It was through his management that the shop was re-built and the machinery introduced early in the July following the fire.  Mr. Bush has been interested in the comb business up to this time ; is now one of the largest stockholders, and until within a few years, was one of the directors.  By steady and persevering industry and economy he has accumulated considerable property.

Mr. Bush is a whole-souled, liberal man, loved and respected by every one who has met him. He has contributed largely to benevolent objects, assisted liberally to build three churches and five school-houses, and paid liberally for the support of the Anti-Slavery cause and of Christianity.

Mr. Bush served in the war of 1812, and in 1848 was elected senator from the 6th district to the Connecticut Legislature.

His two daughters, Temperance Janet and Eunice Kirtland, married respectively Randolph Lindsley and P. J. Clark.

### LIEUT. COMFORT BUTLER

Son of John and Sarah (Foster) Butler, was born in Middletown, Nov. 16, 1743. He was the sixth generation from Richard Butler, one of the original proprietors in Hartford in 1639, and who was admitted freeman in Cambridge, Mass., in 1634. Comfort Butler was apprenticed to the shoemaking business in Middletown at an early age, and being much troubled by a fellow apprentice of a quarrelsome disposition, he told his master that if he must fight, he preferred to fight the enemies of his country rather than one of his mates ; and that if he would allow him to enlist in the army he would serve out the balance of his time after his return. His master consented, and young Butler enlisted, although only about sixteen. To his great surprise he found his fellow apprentice was a member of the same company. But it seems that their fighting propensities found ample scope without troubling each other, and they became fast friends and remained such until the close of the war, when Comfort returned home, fulfilled his agreement

with his master, finished his trade, married Mary,
daughter of Divan Berry, in 1765, and removed to Wallingford in the Meriden parish.   He had nine children,
viz.: Samuel, John, Hannah, Lemuel, Esther, Asa, Divan,
Mary and Phebe.   He died February 19, 1826.

### JOHN BUTLER

Son of Comfort and Mary (Berry) Butler, was born in
Meriden, Sept. 5, 1770.   He was early in life apprenticed
to a shoemaker, and subsequently engaged in the tanning
and shoe-making business on his own account, and was
the principal shoemaker and tanner in Meriden for
nearly sixty years.   He was considered by all who knew
him an honest, upright man in all his intercourse with

JOHN BUTLER.

the world.   He was " Uncle John" to everybody.   He
was remarkable from a boy for his industrious and frugal
habits.   After he had arrived at an age when he was
subject to military duty, his residence was in the center
of the town ; and on training days he would manage to
have his work where he could see the military move-

ments, and when the time of roll-call arrived, he would leave his work and go and answer to his name, drill a while with the company, and return to his work again, thereby making the most of his time. He was very regular in his habits, rising before the sun and retiring before nine in the evening. He was very exact in his accounts, and when he gave his apprentices money he always wanted to know what use it was put to, and usually made a note of it. For instance, I find in his account-book among others, the following entry : " Gave Stephen Seymour twenty-five cents to see a striped jackass." He raised a numerous family of children, most of whom are residents of Meriden at this date, and are universally esteemed by the community. Mr. Butler married 1st, August 17, 1796, Ruth Parker, who died Sept. 30, 1799 ; m. 2d, March 15, 1800, Philomela Cowles, who died March 25, 1807 ; m. 3d, April 17, 1810, widow Susannah Hall. His children were Albert, Ruth A. (m. Morris Stevens), Henry C., Philomela, Lyman, John, Levi, Susan (m. Sydney P. Hall), and Isaac. John Butler died Oct. 6, 1852, æ. 82 years and 21 days, in the full hope of a blissful immortality.

### LEMUEL BUTLER

Son of Comfort and Mary (Berry) Butler, was born in Meriden, Feb. 3, 1775. He was a farmer, a plain, unassuming man, perfectly reliable at all times. He was a soldier in the war of 1812, and raised a numerous family, most of whom now reside here, and are very estimable citizens, some of whom are occupying responsible positions both in religious and secular affairs. Dec. 4, 1810, he married Salina, daughter of Jesse Merriman, who was born March 20, 1786, and died Sept. 25, 1842. Their children were: Joel I., Eli, Hiram, Harriet, (m.

Andrew A. Bradley), and George. Lemuel Butler
died Dec. 11, 1852.

LEMUEL BUTLER.

HENRY C. BUTLER

Son of John and Philomela (Cowles) Butler, was born
in Meriden, March 6, 1807. By honest and persevering
industry, Mr. Butler has accumulated a large property,

HENRY C. BUTLER.

and for his moral worth he is highly respected by his
fellow citizens. Though often solicited to accept offices

of trust in the town, he has always refused, with the exception of acting as moderator at every annual town meeting since the town hall was built. He married 1st, July 1, 1832, Sophronia Hotchkiss, who died April 17, 1841. He married 2d, Nov. 25, 1841, Elizabeth Foster, who died June, 1847. He married 3d, May 31, 1848, Mrs. Mary L. Woodruff, widow of Dr. Isaac Woodruff. His children by his 1st wife were: Lucy C. (m. Wm. L. Squires), Mary P. and John H.; by 2nd wife: Henry W. and Aaron C.

### JOEL I. BUTLER

Son of Lemuel and Selina (Merriman) Butler, was born in Meriden, Nov. 12, 1811. He has occupied numerous positions of trust and responsibility in matters pertain-

JOEL I. BUTLER.

ing to the government and the town. He is President of the Meriden Bank, and U. S. Internal Revenue Assessor, and a man in whom the people have the most implicit confidence in every respect. Mr. Butler married 1st, Aug. 27, 1835, Mary A. Morton, who died Aug. 21, 1837. He married 2nd, July 27, 1840, Sarah A. Hotch-

kiss, who died Sept. 11, 1853.   He married 3d, Jan. 17,
1855, Ursula M. Hart.   By his 2nd wife he had two children, Mary Ann and Emma S.

## BENJAMIN HOPKINS CATLIN

The eldest son of Benjamin and Rhoda Catlin, was born
in Harwinton, Litchfield county, Conn., Aug. 10, 1801.
His advantages for education were limited to the district
school near his father's residence, till his sixteenth year,
when an academy was built in his native town, in which
he had the opportunity of pursuing the higher branches
of study not then taught in our common schools.   At
this academy and under the tuition of the Rev. Luther
Hart of Plymouth, he pursued his preparatory studies.
He studied medicine and surgery nearly four years
under the instruction of different physicians and at the
Medical Institution of Yale College, where he received
his diploma, March 4, 1825.   July 13th of the same
year, he opened an office in Haddam, Middlesex County,
there being a vacancy occasioned by the death of Dr.
Andrew Warner.   The first week he had patients to
attend, and in two or three months was in full practice.
He remained here more than sixteen years, his practice
extending into all the adjoining towns.   The last day of
March, 1842, Dr. Wyllis Woodruff of Meriden died.
The same evening a messenger was sent to Dr. Catlin
by some of the leading citizens of Meriden, requesting
him to come to Meriden to fill the vacancy.   He came
up the next day, April 1, made arrangements for his
removal, and commenced practice in Meriden April 5.
He was elected a Fellow of the Connecticut Medical
Society, and in 1840 received the honorary degree of
M. D. from Yale College.   In 1854 he was elected Vice-
President of the Connecticut Medical Society, re-elected

in 1855, appointed President in 1856, and re-elected in
1857. He has been a permanent member of the American Medical Association since May, 1853, and has since
that time attended most of the annual meetings as
delegate from the New Haven County Medical Society,
or from the State society. In 1860 he was elected an
Honorary Member of the New York State Medical
Society, and in 1869 a Corresponding Member of the
Gynæcological Society of Boston. When the first Congregational society removed to West Meriden, Dr.
Catlin was elected deacon, which office he has held until
the present time.

### TIMOTHY FISHER DAVIS, M. D.

Was the son of Eliphaz and Hannah (Sawyer) Davis,
and was born in Marlboro, Mass., March 13, 1810. After
receiving his early education at the common schools
of his native town, he was apprenticed to a trade in
Springfield, Mass. In 1837, having then a wife and two
children, he entered the office of Dr. Riley of Goshen,
Conn., to pursue the study of medicine, still working at
his trade during his spare hours, for the support of his
family. After leaving the office of Dr. Riley he practiced his profession for a time in Goshen, and then
concluded to remove to Litchfield as offering a wider
field for his business. In Litchfield he remained several
years, engaged in a constantly increasing and lucrative
practice; but hearing that there was a better opening in
Plymouth, and being urged by a number of influential
persons in that town, he removed his family there and
commenced practice about the year 1846. Here he
opened a drug store, built a house, and obtained an extensive practice in the town and beyond it, being
frequently called to the neighboring towns of Wolcott,

Bristol, Bethlem, and Watertown. These long rides in a hilly country soon wore upon his health, and he began looking for some easier field of practice. At this time his old friend and fellow student, Dr. William H. Allen of Meriden, died, and his widow wrote to Dr. Davis a letter urging him to remove to Meriden and take her late husband's practice. This was just the field that he was looking for, and accordingly in 1850 he removed to Meriden, and the year following removed his family.

DR. TIMOTHY FISHER DAVIS.

For nearly eighteen years Dr. Davis practiced his profession in Meriden with success. He was a skillful and prudent operator, a careful and discriminating prescriber, ever improving the lessons of experience. In 1843 he received a diploma from the Botanic Medical Society of Connecticut, and in 1850 an honorary diploma, he being at that time Vice President of the Society. He afterwards held the office of President. He was one of the founders of the State Eclectic Medical Society, and held the offices at different times, of Secretary, Treasurer,

Vice President and President, and was for several years one of the Board of Censors.

Dr. Davis was most genial, kind and companionable in his social relations. Fond of society, with a genial humor which led him to enjoy the present and not be too careful of the future, quick in his perceptions, liberal in pecuniary matters, and despising money-hoarding, he lived in as much enjoyment as falls to the lot of most men, and was personally esteemed as a friend and physician throughout the community. He was not a man of fluent speech, and of consequence not what we call a great talker. But he was a capital listener, and would attend with great eagerness and delight to hear men of sense talk. He was fond of horticulture, and evinced much taste and skill in the cultivation of his land. He had the true idea of success in this business, viz.: that "a little land should be well tilled."

In 1866 a small pimple on his lower lip began troubling him, and soon proved to be a cancer. At that time he was very busy, and thinking that he could not neglect his patients, he was careless of himself and suffered the disease to make great progress before he could be prevailed upon to do anything for it. He had at different times two operations, one by Dr. Ellsworth of Hartford, and the other by Dr. Gurdon Buck of New York; but the operations were undertaken too late. He lingered until the 24th of February, 1870, when he passed away in his sixtieth year. At the funeral services, the attendance of the most prominent citizens in the city testified to the high esteem in which he was held. The funeral services were performed by Rev. M. I. Steere. The rector of the Episcopal Church and the pastor of the Methodist Church were also present. His pastor said

of him, " During his long and distressing sickness I do
not think so much as a shadow of distrust or fear passed
over his soul. He steadfastly contemplated death as
though it were life. He saw light in its darkness, and
the Father's love shining within its shadows. He felt
that his life was with Christ in God, and that death
could not disturb it. His language ever was, ' I am
ready ; I am sinking into the arms of Jesus.' And the
pressure of his hand as I rose from his bedside, often
told me how, deeper than I, he felt the sentiments of
hope and goodness." Dr. Davis was a member of the
order of Free and Accepted Masons, and was buried
with Masonic honors. He married Miss Mary Parsons,
November 1, 1832. She died April, 1834, in Pleasant
Valley, Conn., leaving one child, Mary Markham
Morehouse, who married Edwin Miner in 1853, and
is now living in New Haven, a widow. Dr. Davis married for his second wife, Miss Moriva Hatch of Springfield, Mass., in 1836, and had : Julia, born April, 1838 ;
died December, 1839 ; Charles Henry Stanley,[1] born
March 2, 1840 ; Julia Moriva, born July, 1844 ; Wilbur
Fisk, born Sept., 1846, died July 15, 1847 ; Wilbur Fisk,
born July, 1848 ; a graduate of the Cambridge Law
School in 1870.

---

1 Charles Henry Stanley Davis was born March 2, 1840. He was prepared for college in the public schools of Meriden, and pursued the studies
of the Freshman and Sophomore classes under Rev. Messrs. Wilder and
Foster. His plans for entering college were broken up by the war, and in
1862 after a short residence in Springfield, Mass., he removed to New
York and entered the medical department of the New York University,
where he was graduated in the spring of 1865, attending the last course of
lectures ever delivered by Dr. Valentine Mott. After attending a course
of lectures at the Bellevue Hospital Medical school and following hospital
practice, he removed to Boston, attending the summer course at the Harvard University Medical school. During his residence in Boston he edited

## JACOB EATON

Was a graduate of Harford University, Pennsylvania, and of the New Haven theological seminary. His first and only pastorate was over the Hanover Congregational Church, where he was ordained May 28, 1857. This church, then in its infancy, enjoyed a revival of religion at the beginning of his ministry, which continued after his ordination, and was the means of increasing the membership and the strength of the church by an addition of about twenty-five new members. This relation was sustained harmoniously till the outbreak of the rebellion. The following pastoral note, under date of September 30, 1861, copied from the records of the church in Hanover, speaks for itself:

"The Congregational church in Hanover has been subjected to many changes since my settlement as pastor. God has blessed it by adding to its numbers from year to year. These additions have averaged ten each year during my ministry here. But our church and society have been greatly weakened by numerous removals. The darkest hour has arrived. The terrible rebellion in our Southern states

the first volume of the Boston *Medical Register*. In the fall of 1866, he removed to Baltimore, where he remained through the winter attending the lectures in the medical department of the University of Maryland and following hospital practice. In 1867 he returned to Meriden, succeeding his father in the practice of his profession. In 1863 Rev. Dr. Brown, Rev. Messrs. Duer, Jones, Post, Owen and others organized the America Philological Society, and Dr. Davis was elected the first corresponding Secretary and afterwards one of the Vice Presidents. In September, 1868, he was elected member of the N. E. Historical and Genealogical society of Boston, and during 1868 and the following year was elected corresponding member of the Wisconsin, Minnesota and Chicago Historical societies. In 1870 he was made a member of the New Haven Colony Historical society. He is also a member of several medical and scientific societies, and has contributed largely to the medical and periodical press. He married September 23, 1869, Carrie E. daughter of George W. Harris, Esq.

has seriously affected our manufacturing and pecuniary interests. We feel it most deeply. My mind and heart have been deeply interested in our national conflict. After mature reflection, I have asked of my people a leave of absence for one year, that I may enlist in the Grand Army of Freedom. May God be with those I shall leave behind. May He save me through His grace, and may He save our beloved country and our government, from anarchy and dissolution.

"Signed,    JACOB EATON."

In accordance with the purpose here expressed, he enlisted in the 8th Connecticut Regiment, sharing its fortunes under Burnside on the Atlantic coast as a private. He was promoted at length to a Lieutenancy, and served as an officer till wounded on the bloody field of Antietam, a musket ball entering his hip and disabling him for many months. Incapacitated thus for service in the ranks, he received an honorable discharge and returned to his people again to break unto them the bread of life and fight the good fight. His heart more than ever was with the country in its trial, and with the brave men who were fighting our battles. After preaching about a year, again he enlisted in the 7th Connecticut Regiment, and was promoted to a chaplaincy. Here he did valiant service for Christ and his country. He died at Wilmington, N. C., March 20, 1865, of typhoid fever, induced by fatigue and over exertion in ministering to the wants of the recently rescued federal prisoners in the hospital at that place. Mr. Eaton was a man of strong affection and love of home, of most deep and tender sympathies, and of ardent devotion to the cause of Christ and the country. He was a warm friend, when once friendship was established, and self-sacrificing for others weal. His character was impulsive. He was strong in his detestation of whatever he thought wrong, and bold in his defense of what he deemed right.[1] Humble as was the life and death of this man, it may be doubted whether any of all the martyrs of the Great Rebellion offered a truer sacrifice to their country than his. Twice he left his peaceful profession for the camp and the battlefield ; but he finally died, not in the work of death, but as a minister of mercy.

## JOEL H GUY

Son of Orchard and Lois (Hall) Guy, was born in Meriden June 4, 1804. He attended the district school winters, until he was sixteen years old. At the age of twenty he commenced teaching, and taught for ten winters at an average salary of eight dollars per month and board. He then acted as salesman for Meriden manufactures for four or five years. After this Mr. Guy, in connection with his brother, bought a store in Middletown where he carried on business until 1840, though residing in Meriden most of the time. In 1840 he built the store now standing east of his present residence, and under the title of J. H. Guy & Co., he carried on the grocery business, the Company being the firm of Julius Pratt & Co. In 1846 Mr. Guy bought out his partner and carried on the business until about 1850. Mr. Guy has been a very energetic business man, honest and straightforward in all of his dealings. Since 1844 he has held the office of postmaster at different times for twelve years. He was President of the Meriden Bank thirteen years, and has been President of the 1st National Bank seven years. He has also held the office of constable, deputy-sheriff, assessor and collector, justice of the peace and alderman. He has also acted more than

1 Funeral Discourse by Rev. H. C. Hayden.

any other man in Meriden as administrator and trustee of estates.   Mr. Guy married Nov. 9, 1830, Semira Wetmore of Middlefield, and has one daughter born in 1833.   He has been extensively engaged in the insurance business about twenty years.

### JULIUS HALL.

The oldest house in Meriden is now standing about three miles east of the center.   It was built by Daniel Hall in the earlier part of the last century.   He was the grandson of John Hall, the first emigrant, and was born January 27, 1689.   His son John was born Jan. 29, 1724, and died May 13, 1795, leaving twelve children.   Joseph, the fifth son, born Oct. 8, 1770, succeeded to the old homestead.   He died March 13, 1831, leaving six children, of whom two, Sherman, born April 26, 1806, and

JULIUS HALL.

Julius, the subject of this sketch, born June 7, 1813, still survive.   They are the fourth generation born in this old house.   Julius Hall married Laura L. Parker, May 1, 1852, and has six children.   Some years ago he built the house in which he now lives, just north of the old house.

The immense timbers and old stone chimney, in the fire-place of which a load of wood might easily be placed, bid fair to stand for several generations to come. Mr. Hall is a plain, unassuming man, whose whole attention is given to his farm. Respected by his friends and neigh-bors for his moral worth, he never sought after office, or mingled in town affairs, but lives as did his ancestors for four generations in this town, a tiller of the soil, happy and content in the bosom of his family.

### EDWARD WALKER HATCH, M. D.

Was born in Blandford, Hampden Co., Mass., Aug. 31, 1818. His parents were Timothy Linus and Sarah Walker (Shepard) Hatch. He was graduated at the Berkshire Medical College, Pittsfield, Mass., in the class of 1842. He was married Oct. 15, 1846, to Miss Nancy C. Boies, daughter of David Boies Esq., of Blandford. He was then in the practice of his profession in New Jersey. He removed from New Jersey to Meriden in December, 1849.[1] In 1853 he built and occupied the house on the corner of Main and Butler streets, now occupied by Henry C. Butler, Esq. He was appointed trustee of the State Reform School by the Legislature of 1858, and in July, 1859 was appointed by the trustees superintendent. He still occupies that position. He made a public profession of his faith in Christ in 1853, and in 1853 he connected himself with the First Congregational church of Meriden, at West Meriden, and still retains his connection there. His success as

---

[1] His children are Edward Walker Hatch Jr., born at Little Falls, N. J., Jan. 12, 1848, died July 28, 1849; Sarah Elizabeth, born at Blandford, Mass., Nov. 2, 1849; Caroline Bigelow, born Sept. 30, 1852; Mary Boies, born March 6, 1859; Frances Catharine, born Sept. 6, 1863, died April 9, 1864.

N N

superintendent of the Reform School is well known not only to the people of this town, but to the people of the State and to all in the country at large who are interested in the success of such institutions.   Dr. Hatch was a warm and earnest advocate of the Union all through the war of the rebellion.   He has always been interested in the cause of education, and is well known as an able, zealous advocate of total abstinence.

EDWARD WALKER HATCH, M. D.

He is active as one of the executive committee of the Connecticut Temperance Union, is earnestly interested in sabbath schools, and is one of the Board of Directors of the Connecticut Industrial school for girls, just established at Middletown.

### DR. ISAAC I. HOUGH

Was born in Wallingford, in the parish of Meriden, in 1781.   His father, Dr. Ensign Hough, commenced practice in this town in 1769, and died in 1813.   The parents of Dr. Isaac Hough were small in stature and weight.   His mother especially was a feeble, delicate woman.   Their son Isaac was large from his birth, and in childhood was so heavy that his mother could not lift him ; and when no one was near to raise him into her lap, she would stretch out her limbs and roll him up. When ten weeks old he weighed twenty pounds, and previous to his death had attained the weight of about three hundred and fifty pounds. He studied medicine under his father, and under the instruction of Dr. Hall of Middletown. His father requested him not to marry

ISAAC I. HOUGH, M. D.

early, as several members of the family would be dependent upon him. The result was, he did not marry at all.

At the time he commenced practice, Meriden contained about twelve hundred inhabitants; but his practice extended to all adjoining towns, and was for several years quite extensive. He was a very efficient practitioner and believed fully in the power of medicine and administered it freely. He had a good library of medical and miscellaneous works, and in his earlier years his reading was extensive. He took and read for many years the *North American Review* and most of the medical journals published while he was in practice. For a person so large and fleshy he was remarkably active in body and mind. He always kept some of the best horses in the country and drove them rapidly. He was an early riser, up and off to see his patients earlier than they ·were ready to receive him. He spent but little time investigating cases, but would see at once the prominent points of acute cases, and prescribe with skill and good jugdment. His prognosis of a cure was generally very correct. He had no taste for the management of chronic cases, and no patience to listen to the multitudinous complaints of chronic patients. He much preferred to laugh at what appeared to him their absurd notions, and consequently would often lose their confidence. He had great faith in the medical properties of opium, and prescribed it freely in fevers and in acute and chronic cases. His presciptions unfortunately led some of his friends and patients to its habitual use. His charges for professional services were very moderate, and he accumulated no property from that source.

For many years he kept a public house in the building now standing on the corner of Broad and Main streets; and during a portion of the time he found it very profitable, especially during the war of 1812. From this source he accumulated considerable property, and retired from active business at the early age of fifty-three. It is believed that this was an unfortunate movement for him. When Dr. Catlin moved to Meriden in 1842, Dr. Hough took a deep interest in his welfare, and rode in consultation with him more than he had done for several years previous. For several of the latter years of his life he read but little, as it affected his head unpleasantly, and he thought it imprudent to indulge in this pleasure. He always took a deep interest in the welfare of his friends and neighbors, and was sometimes so minute in his inquiries as to cause offense, though he never did it from bad motives; it was only that he might rejoice in their prosperity, or sympathize with them in their adversity.

Dr. Hough's knowledge of men was very extensive, and his judgment of character very accurate. Keeping a public house on one of the great thoroughfares of the State, half way between Hartford and New Haven, all of the prominent men of the State and many of the nation were more or less frequently his guests. Being very social and inquisitive he formed a very extensive acquaintance. He knew something about, not only every Doctor in the State, but the ministers, lawyers, judges and politicians. Six or eight four horse stages stopped daily at the Doctor's inn. He was so remarkable in personal appearance that he was always noticed and remembered by those who saw him. According to the custom of those days his house was well stocked with the best of liquors (none of the mixed poisonous liquors so much used now), but he never tasted them himself, and at the commencement of the temperance reform in 1828–30, he sold out his tavern for $6,000 and removed across the street to the house now occupied by Wm. Merriman. A student of Yale College, while passing through Meriden, called at the Doctor's bar and said, " Doctor, I have a bad cold, what is best for me to take?" The Doctor handed him a glass of water. Dr. Hough never united with any church, but he was a constant attendant upon the service of the Congregational church and a liberal supporter of its institutions, and a friend of good morals.

I have said that it was unfortunate for him that he

gave up business so early in life. It affected his health and
mind unfavorably. Being naturally so active, he suffered
from ennui. At the best he was a poor sleeper, and his
wakefulness was increased by his lack of employment of
body and mind during the day. He has been known to
take his horse and wagon and ride twenty or thirty miles
till he was thoroughly fatigued, when he would sleep
well. He almost uniformly called himself well, except
to his most intimate friends. He never could bear to have
people talk to him of their bodily complaints ; so he
seldom troubled other people with a recital of his own.
Says Dr. Catlin (to whom I am indebted for most of the
facts in this sketch of Dr. Hough) : "I knew that he
suffered much pain in his limbs, and for several years he
had an organic affection of the heart. He expected to
die suddenly, and was not disappointed. He had been
unwell more than usual for a few days. I was called in
to see him several times ; he was sometimes in his chair,
at others on the lounge. I was in one afternoon, when
he appeared more comfortable and quite cheerful. Early
the next Monday (I think), word was sent me that he
was dead. I found him on 'the floor. He had appar-
ently got up, put on his dressing-gown, slid down by the
side of his bed, and died alone, evidently from dropsy
of the heart. He was fearful he should give his friends
trouble, either by being confined by sickness, when his
great weight would be burdensome, or after he was dead.
To provide against the latter event, he went to Hartford
some years before his death, and was measured for his
coffin, which he had made, boxed up and sent home. He
told me he did not suppose the maker expected he would
examine it, but he had a desire to see how the work was
done. He appeared satisfied with its appearance. It

was kept in the loft of a carriage house." Dr. Hough
died in the building now occupied (1870) by the 1st
National Bank.

He was very sensitive in regard to his weight. He
once drove on to the hay-scales, and while engaged
in conversation a bystander endeavored to weigh
the doctor with his horse and gig, hoping afterwards
to weigh the horse and gig, thus getting his exact
weight; but the doctor happened to look around, and
discovered what was going on, and he instantly whipped
up his horse and left the scales before the operation was
completed. Dr. Hough died Feb. 26, 1852, æ. 71 years.
I remember hearing the following verses when I was a
boy :

> " Dr. Hough, he keeps good stuff,
> And lives just under the steeple ;
> By hook or by crook, he keeps his good looks
> And takes the cash from the people."

These lines so pleased the doctor that he was often in
the habit of repeating them.

### LEVI SILLIMAN IVES

Was born in Meriden parish on the 16th of September,
1797. At an early age he removed with his parents to
Lewis county, N. Y., where he lived until he was sent to
the academy at Lowville. During the last months of
the war with Great Britain he served in the army, but
upon the return of peace went back to school, entering
Hamilton college in 1816. At first he studied for the
ministry of the Presbyterian church, but before he was
ordained, illness compelled him to leave the college, and
upon his recovery to health his religious views became
changed and he allied himself with the Protestant Episcopal denomination. In 1820 he removed to New York

where he studied theology under Bishop Hobart, who ordained him in August, 1822. Three years later he married Rebecca, a daughter of the Bishop. After his ordination his first mission was to Batavia, Genesee Co. ; subsequently he took charge of Trinity church, Philadelphia, where he was ordained to the priesthood by Bishop White, and in 1827 removed to Lancaster, Pa., and officiated at Christ church. During the next year he returned to New York and served as assistant minister at Christ church for about six months, when he became rector of St. Luke's church. Here he remained until he was consecrated Bishop of North Carolina in 1831. While in North Carolina he became quite popular for his efforts in behalf of education and his success in providing for the spiritual welfare of the slaves. He also became widely known as a theological author from his works on the "Apostles' Doctrine and Fellowship," and the "Obedience of Faith," published in New York in 1849.

When the Oxford tract excitement broke out in the Episcopal church, he strongly sided with the tractarian movement, and this position caused his alienation from his diocese. The fact was that he doubted the truth of the Protestant faith for a long time, and in 1852, while on a visit to Rome, openly renounced his faith and was admitted to the Catholic church. This conversion on his part was severely denounced by the Protestant religious papers in the United States, and upon his return he defended the act in a work entitled "The Trials of a Mind in its Progress to Catholicism." (London and Boston, 1864). After his return to America, he became Professor of Rhetoric in St. Joseph's theological seminary, and lectured in the convents of the Sacred Heart and the Sisters of Charity. He also occasionally lectured in public, and served as an active president of a conference of St. Vincent de Paul. In 1857 he conceived the idea of founding a home in New York for vagrant and orphan children of Catholic parentage, and, having obtained the approval of Archbishop Hughes, set energetically to work to carry out his design. The result of his philanthropic labors was the establishment of the Catholic Male Protectory, and the house of the Holy Angels, two of the most deserving charitable institutions in New York. Dr. Ives died at Fordham, N. Y., Oct. 13, 1867.

## ISAAC C. LEWIS

Son of Isaac and Esther (Beaumont) Lewis of Wallingford, was born Oct. 19, 1812. When he was about eleven years old his father died, and five years after his mother died. He attended school until the death of his father. About a year afterwards he was sent to live with Mr. Levi Yale, and the following summer with Moses Andrews in the west part of Meriden. At the end of the summer he went to live with his grandfather, Jared Lewis of Wallingford, who soon after died, when Isaac returned to Meriden to live with his brother Patrick Lewis. When in his fifteenth year he returned to Wallingford and was apprenticed to Hiram Yale to learn the britannia ware trade. His employer died when he was nineteen years old. He remained with the family a short time, then returned to Meriden and worked about two years for Lewis and Holt. In 1834, being then in his twenty second year, Mr. Lewis formed a copartnership with George Cowles under the title of Lewis and Cowles, and hired rooms in a factory in East Meriden for the manufacture of britannia metal goods. They remained here about two years, when they closed up business, Mr. Cowles going north, and Mr. Evans west

This was in the summer of 1836. Mr. Lewis returned in the fall and commenced business again with Mr. Lemuel Curtis as partner, under the name of Lewis and Curtis, in a factory belonging to Mr. Samuel Cook in East Meriden. After about two years the partnership was dissolved, Mr. Curtis coming to Meriden center. Mr. Lewis soon after purchased a house and small farm about one mile east of Meriden center, and built a shop and put in a horse-power. Business increased to such an extent that a small engine was put in; but that proving to be insufficient, he bought the factory where he first commenced business with Mr. Cowles. He soon after associated with Daniel B. Wells, a former apprentice, under the name of I. C. Lewis & Co. Mr. Wells died soon after, and Mr. Lewis bought his interest. In 1852 the Britannia Company was formed, with Mr. Lewis as President. He remained President of the company about twelve years, when he declined holding the office any longer. He is still a member of the company, and takes an active interest in the business. Mr. Lewis married in 1836, Harriet, daughter of Noah Pomeroy, and has had six children, viz.: Melissa N., Martha E., Henry J., Isaac, Frank, and Katie A. Three are now living. Mr. Lewis represented the town in the Legislature in 1848, 1859, 1862, and 1866. He has given largely toward the support of the Universalist society in Meriden, and for fifteen years has been super-intendent of the Sunday-school. Mr. Lewis commenced life without a dollar, and by his own exertions and strict attention to business has accumulated a large fortune. He never had a note protested, never was sued, nor has he ever entered a suit against any man. Uni-versally loved and respected, he affords another example in this town, of what honest industry and enterprise can accomplish.

## WILLIAM W. LYMAN

Son of Andrew and Anna (Hall) Lyman, was born in Woodford, Vt., March 29, 1821. When seven years of age his father died, and he removed to Northford, Conn. where he lived six years. In 1836 he came to Meriden and learned the trade of making britannia ware, of Griswold & Couch, serving five years. In 1844 he went into business on his own account, manufacturing britannia spoons in connection with Ira Couch, but after a short time bought him out. The shop stood a few rods north of his present residence. He remained there two years, and then removed his works to the Twiss factory in Prattsville. He was in business here for a short time with Lemuel J. Curtiss, but finally dissolved partnership and removed to the Frary shop, near the present works of the Malleable Iron Co. He was there about five years. He has been a member and director of the Meriden Britannia Co. since its organization. In Dec. 1858 he patented a fruit can which is known throughout the country as " Lyman's Fruit Jar." One house in Delaware has bought over 60,000 of these jars. He has also patented an ice pitcher, copper bottom tea-pot, butter dish and numerous other articles. Mr. Lyman represented Meriden in the Legislature in 1849, and is President of the Meriden Cutlery Co. In 1844 he married Roxanna G. Frary, and has one daughter, who married Henry Warren, of Watertown, Conn.

## JOHN PARKER

Son of Stephen and Rebecca Parker was born in Cheshire, Conn., in 1805. Receiving his early education in the common schools of his native town, he at an early period of life took a decided stand on the side of Christ, and even then it was his earnest desire to prepare for the ministry and devote his life to preaching the gospel. To this end he entered upon the study of theology at the Wesleyan University in Middletown, Conn., where he was graduated in 1831. He then removed to Massachusetts and was stationed at Webster two years. He afterwards supplied the pulpit at Newtown in 1833–4; Holliston, 1835; Lowell, 1836–7; Lynn, 1838–9; Holliston, 1840. In 1840 he came to Meriden and entered into business with his brother Charles.

In 1843 the Second Adventists were making a great excitement, and had quite a large number of followers in Meriden. Mr. Parker collected a number of these together and formed a society of Primitive Methodists. They assembled for worship in the building now used by the Messrs. Parkers as a spectacle-shop. It then stood where the office is now situated. It was through the exertions of Mr. Parker that the Methodist church grew and prospered in the town; and he, with his brother Charles, jointly contributed between thirty and forty thousand dollars toward the erection of the present church edifice. During his residence in Meriden, Mr. Parker has enjoyed the confidence and respect of the people, and has always been looked to as a friend and counselor. He has filled acceptably the offices of Selectman, Justice of the Peace, and Judge of Probate; and in 1870 was elected a Representative to the State Legislature. Mr. Parker was married in March, 1832, to Miss Emily Ward of Ashfield, Mass. She died June 1, 1867. He married for his second wife, Grace A. Belden, January 22, 1868. The following children were by his first wife Emily, born November 2, 1842, died December 17, 1843 ; George White, born September 1, 1846 ; Mary, born July 28, 1848, died Aug. 4, 1848 ; Frank Milton, born July 7, 1850, died October 7, 1850

### NOAH POMEROY

Was born March 1, 1786, in Saybrook, Conn., and was the youngest of five children, three sons and two daughters. His father, Charles Pomeroy, was a merchant of that place, and died a short time previous to the birth of his youngest child. If a long and honorable line of ancestry is capable of conferring distinction, the subject of this sketch could scarcely have desired a more auspicious birth ; for his family trace their ancestry into the eleventh century, to a distinguished Norman Knight, who fought at the battle of Hastings, under William. One of the descendants of the knight, Eltwood Pomeroy, emigrated to Massachusetts in 1630, from England, and was well known in the early Indian wars of New England ; and the history of the Indian, French and Revolutionary wars, bears honorable record of the bravery and patriotism of many of his descendants.

Noah Pomeroy was descended from Eltwood, and his only inheritance was the good name and strong physical and mental capacities of his ancestors. After the death of his father, his brothers and sisters were kindly cared for and educated by his paternal grandfather, a man of considerable property and good standing in Colchester, Conn. ; while he from necessity remained with his mother who removed with him to Meriden. When he was about five years old his mother contracted a second marriage, which to him proved of little advantage. He continued to live with his mother and step-father until he was ten

years old, when penniless and scarcely possessing a
knowledge of the English alphabet, he commenced the
world for himself.

His first great object was to secure an education which
would enable him to transact the common business in-
cident to a life of action and enterprise, such as his
youthful preception had already foreshadowed as his
destiny. In attempting to accomplish this, he was
obliged to struggle with difficulties which those alone
can rightly estimate who have had the same to contend
with. The meagre earnings of the summer, with the
most rigid economy, afforded a bare surplus to apply to
the purpose of his education during the winter; and
often this was lawfully claimed and obtained by his step-
father.

At fifteen he commenced peddling tin ware, but this
gave offence to some of his nearest relatives. After
repeated solicitations by other members of the family,
he was induced about three years afterwards to commence
an apprenticeship with a carpenter and joiner; a trade
in those days being esteemed next to a profession. He
continued, however, but a short time in this employment.
He had already selected the business most congenial to
his feelings for his future occupation, and returning to
his peddling wagon, he made use of it as the most direct
and honorable means within his power, by which he
could eventually make himself master of that business,
and establish himself in the manufacture of tin ware.
Accordingly at twenty, he apprenticed himself to a tin-
smith for six months, for which he paid a stipulated sum,
and in that almost incredibly short period, gained such
an insight into the business as to enable him to become
a complete master of the trade, which usually required

four or five years to learn. In the succeeding year he engaged in the manufacture of plain tin ware. During the same year he married Miss Mary Merriman, a lineal descendant of Lieut. Nathaniel Merriman, who was one of the first settlers of Wallingford, and who commanded in the early Indian wars. During the eleven years succeeding, he prosecuted a small yet successful business at various localities. In the Autumn of 1807, he removed to Plymouth, Conn., where he continued his business until 1815, with the exception of one winter spent at Baltimore. It was during his residence at Plymouth that the second war with Great Britain commenced, of which he was an enthusiastic supporter. He was tendered a lieutenant's commission in the regular army, which however he did not accept. In 1815 he returned to Wallingford, from whence he removed to Meriden in 1818, where he permanently established his business and purchased a farm on which he ever afterward lived. From this time he continued gradually to increase the yearly amount of his manufactures, yet not so fast as to endanger his credit. He was among the first to engage extensively in the manufacture of japanned and ornamented tin ware in this country. In 1839 he retired nominally from his business, which he left to his sons, and applied his energies, which were not in the least abated, to the improvement of his farm.

During his residence in Meriden he exercised a controlling influence in its affairs. He held all the offices within its gift, and that of selectman repeatedly until he declined an election. He filled the office of justice of the peace by appointment of the State Legislature, as long as it possessed the power to appoint. During his whole residence in Meriden he was scarcely ever removed by a change in party politics. His knowledge of common law, and his impartial judgment may be estimated by the fact, that of all the cases which were ever brought before him, an appeal from his decision was never carried to the county court. An ardent advocate of progression and reform, and contending for the broadest religious and political liberty,. he earnestly urged the necessity of calling the convention which remodeled the constitution of the state, and expunged many of those statutes which have been known as "blue laws." In 1832 he was elected a member of the House of Representatives, and in 1837 he was chosen senator from the sixth district, and in that capacity exerted his influence for the abolition of the law which imprisoned for debt. In 1833 when the Meriden Bank was established he was appointed one of the directors, and in 1849 was chosen president, which office he shortly after resigned. Mr. Pomeroy died Nov. 23, 1868, in the eighty-second year of his age.

JULIUS PRATT

Was born Nov. 24, 1791, at Saybrook, Conn., and was the son of Deacon Phineas (and Hepsibah) Pratt, who was the son of Azariah, (born Aug., 1710), who was the son of John Jr. (born Sept. 5, 1671), who was the son of John (born Feb. 20, 1644), who was the eldest son of William, who came to this country with Rev. Thomas Hooker in 1633. Julius Pratt married Lydia, daughter of John De Wolfe of Westbrook, January 9, 1817. She was born March 18, 1795. His father's residence, where he himself lived in early life, was about one mile west of Pautapaug Point. At the age of fifteen he commenced work with his brothers Abel and Phineas, in ivory-comb making, and at the age of twenty-two engaged with his brother Philo in the silversmith business in Pautapaug. In February 1858 he removed to Meriden, and in connection with Messrs. Bush, Williams, Howard, Reed, Starkey, Rogers and Spencer, soon commenced the manufacture of ivory combs on Harbor brook, a little south of the Middletown and Waterbury turnpike bridge. Finding his water-power too small for his increasing business he removed to what is now called Prattsville. Joined with Mr. Webb he continued to be a leading member of the ivory comb business, and his energy and enterprise contributed in a large degree to the development of this branch of manufactures, which in a few years distanced foreign competition, and at the present time is a large and important business, the goods being exported to nearly all parts of the world. While Mr. Pratt was heavily engaged in business at Prattsville, he was also interested in another company at Crow Hollow, afterward at Hanover, where much of his time was occupied. He was one of the pioneers in the manufacture of cutlery, and had the pleasure while living, of seeing that business well established on a firm and profitable basis. He was a stockholder and director in the Home National Bank of Meriden from its commencement. In this connection, as in all other business relations, his counsel was sought and relied upon at all times.

As a citizen he always enjoyed the respect and confidence of the community where he lived. Uncompromising in principle, unflinching in the discharge of duty, sagacious as an adviser, modest in demeanor, active and liberal in private and public charities, and affectionate towards his family and friends, it may well be said that the best blood of the Puritans flowed in his

O o

veins. He never sought for preferment, but was called to represent his town in the State Legislature of 1852, and was elected Senator of the Sixth District of Connecticut in 1854. In his business intercourse he may have left the impression at times that he was austere ; but his apparent sternness arose from the promptness and decision with which he always transacted his business. His language was direct, final and rigidly business like. He was seldom misunderstood, and but few ever attempted to swerve or cajole him. Beneath his apparent harshness was an inner life as gentle as a dove. He loved with a woman's heart, but he spoke with the promptness of a business man, and in all his movements there was a kind of military precision which, to the unobserving, might easily be misapprehended. He died August 31, 1869. His children are, Harriet Melinda, born April 24, 1818 ; Julius H., born August 1, 1821 ; William McLain, born December 12, 1837.[1]

#### BENJAMIN TWISS

Was born in Meriden Oct. 31, 1798. He early commenced the manufacture of wooden clocks in Prattsville, and did a large business. Later in life he manufactured coffee-mills at the same place. He was one of the most active men of the day in town affairs, holding at different times the offices of constable, justice of the peace, selectman and assessor. He was appointed postmaster in

---

1 William McLain Pratt graduated at the Rensselaer Polytechnic Institute, at Troy, N. Y., with the degree of civil engineer, in the class of 1857. He visited South America in 1860 and 1861, crossing the continent from Buenos Ayres to Valparaiso, via Mendoza and the Andes. He enlisted as a private in the 8th Regiment of Connecticut Volunteer Infantry, in May, 1862, and was wounded in the battle of Antietam, September 17, 1862. He was promoted to the office of second lieutenant in November, 1862, and that of first lieutenant and adjutant in June, 1863.

1853, but resigned. He took an active interest in the establishment of the Reform school; also in the Air-line railroad. He married March 7, 1832, Miss Lucy G .'rancis of Wethersfield, Conn. Mr. Twiss died January 23, 1854.

### HON. DEXTER R. WRIGHT

Was born in Windsor, Vermont, on the 27th of June, 1821. His ancestors were among the first settlers of Vermont, and one of them was killed in the frontier wars with the Canadians and Indians. Alpheus Wright, his father, held a commission in the war of 1812, and was severely wounded in the battle at Plattsburg.

During the boyhood of Dexter, his father removed to the northern part of New York, where he carried on the milling and lumber business, together with a woolen factory. All of his sons were employed in these various branches of business, and each learned some useful trade. Dexter, however, being of a studious turn of mind, prepared himself for college and entered the University at Middletown, from which he graduated in 1845. In the same year, he became principal of the Meriden Academy, and continued as such for nearly a year and a half; having given instruction to many youths who are now among the energetic and successful business men of Meriden. He was noted for his firm discipline and thorough teaching; and the Academy flourished under his administration.

In the year 1846, he entered the Yale law school at New Haven, from which he graduated in 1848. During his studies at Yale, as well as throughout his collegiate course, he gave great promise of future eminence in his profession; and particularly in that branch of it pertaining to advocacy. In 1848 he commenced the practice of law in Meriden, and soon after married Miss Maria H. Phelps, daughter of Col. E. L. Phelps, of East Windsor, Conn.

In 1849 he was elected senator for the 6th senatorial district, and was the youngest man that had ever been elected to the state senate from that district. He served with credit to himself and satisfaction to his constituents. After the adjournment of the Legislature, he sailed for California, where he remained for two years practising in the territorial courts and taking part in the early political history of that state.

In 1851 he returned to Meriden and continued the practice of his profession until 1862, when he entered the Union army as colonel of the fifteenth regiment, Connecticut volunteers. His practice in Meriden during this period was large and successful, and he had the confidence and esteem of all men as a thorough lawyer, an honest man, and a good citizen. The people of Meriden are largely indebted to his cultivation and taste as a pioneer in beautifying the village, and in urging forward general public improvements, and his spirit in those matters has become, largely from his example, the prevailing spirit of the people of the present city.

He was commissioned Lieut. Col. of the 14th Regiment of Connecticut Volunteers, early in 1862; and he assisted in raising a company for that Regiment. He had also aided in raising companies for every preceding regiment, for that purpose speaking in different parts of the State. Owing to his zeal in the cause of the Union, Gov. Buckingham, without consulting Col. Wright's wishes, commissioned him Colonel of the 15th Regiment of Connecticut Volunteers; thus promoting him before he entered the field. The latter Regiment

he recruited to its full number and six hundred in excess
in an unprecedentedly short time, by his personal exertions and great influence and popularity.

His regiment went to Virginia in August, 1862, where
for several months he commanded a brigade. He participated in the battle of Fredericksburg, Dec. 13, 1862,
under Burnside. After about a year's service in the
field, he was discharged upon surgeon's certificate of
disability, and subsequently, upon special request of
Gov. Buckingham, he was appointed commissioner on
the Board of Enrollment for the 2nd Congressional
District, the duties of which he discharged with marked
ability and zeal in the cause of the nation. In 1863 he
was elected to the General Assembly of Conn. as a
representative from the town of Meriden.

Having served in the field and as commissioner for
three years with great pecuniary sacrifice, Col. Wright
removed, at the close of the war, to New Haven, Conn.;
where he resumed the practice of the law, and has continued therein to the present time. He has served as
United States assistant District Attorney for a term of
years, and discharged the duties of that office with
ability and satisfaction to the public.

His present law partner is H. Lynde Harrison, Esq.,
who is himself somewhat identified with the history of
Wallingford. Mr. Harrison taught school in Wallingford in 1858–9, and represented the 6th senatorial district, of which Meriden is a part, in 1865 and 1866; and
he is a young man of ability and promise.

Mr. Wright is a thoroughly educated man. His
studies are not confined to the legal profession alone;
but he is well read in every department of general literature and national science. He has even pursued his

studies into medicine ;. and several years ago, the honorary degree of M. D. was conferred upon him by a
medical college in the city of New York. His maxim
is that of Lord Bacon, " All knowledge is my province ;"
and he is not satisfied with the mastery of one^profession
only. His personal integrity has never been questioned,
and his professional honor is fully up to the high standard always maintained by the Connecticut bar. His
mind works quickly and logically, and has been well
trained for the successful practice of the most drastic
profession pursued by men. His diction is at all times
polished and elegant ; his command of language and
power of characterization is almost wonderful ; and his
manners are dignified and well calculated to please all
with whom he comes in contact. As a lawyer he is remarkably strong ; as an examiner of witnesses he is
powerful; in the presentation of facts in argument to
court or jury, he is clear and forcible ; in the preparation
of his cases for trial, thorough and exhaustive ; and, in
his drafting of pleadings, neat, clear and logical.

Since his removal to New Haven in 1864, he has, by
strict attention to his business, built up a large and
lucrative practice. He is a laborious worker, and is
devoted to his calling, and has attained a position in
his profession, which his many friends are glad to see
him occupy.

Col. Wright, though a republican in sentiment, par-
ticipates but little in politics; yet the republicans have
few men in Connecticut who could shed more honor
upon their party than he, were he to actually enter upon
political life. Though not a native of Meriden, he has
been for so many years identified with her interests and
progress, that this notice of him is due more to the town

than to him ; and the people of Meriden can never feel less than a strong interest in his future success and welfare.

## WILLIAM YALE

Son of Samuel and Eunice (Payne) Yale, was born March 13, 1784. He attended the schools of the town until he was old enough to work, when he was apprenticed to learn the tin business, and finally went into the business on his own account. It was his custom to go to Boston and purchase a box of tin ; then with the assistance of a sail-maker, he would make two bags in which he would put the tin ; then swinging it across his horse's back, he would bring it to Meriden, and make it into long tin combs, pint-cups and other articles.

In 1817 he bought the farm of Benjamin Merriam, which comprised nearly the whole of what is now West Meriden. The land was purchased for $2500, he giving a note for $1800 for one year, and paying the remainder in cash. Previous to the note coming due, he learned that it was the intention of Mr. Merriam to demand the payment of it in specie, and he prepared himself accordingly, by gradually accumulating the whole amount in sixpence and one shilling pieces. As he brought the coin home, Lyman Collins and Joel Hall counted it and put it in bags, upon which they put their private seal. This was continued until the whole amount was deposited in the bags. The day that the note became due, Mr. Yale stationed his son at the hotel, to watch for any stranger that might come. In the afternoon a gentleman drove up to the hotel, and enquired where Esq. Yale lived. The boy at once informed Messrs. Collins and Hall, and they repaired to Mr. Yale's to meet the stranger, who soon made his appearance.

After a few remarks, the decanter with sugar, lemons, etc., was brought out, according to the custom of the times, and all took a drink. The stranger then remarked, that he was the sheriff of Hartford county, and had come to demand payment of the note which was due that day, and that he was ordered to demand specie payment. " Very well," replied Mr. Yale, " I have anticipated your demand, and am prepared to meet it." He then told Messrs. Collins and Hall to bring out the bags and examine the seals, and they were found all right. Mr. Yale then untied the bags and emptied the contents on the table, first sixpences and then shillings ; then turning to the sheriff said, " There is $1800. which I tender to you in payment of my note, due this day." The sheriff was completely nonplussed. "It will take me a week to count it," said he. "Very well," replied Mr. Yale, "I don't doubt it, for it has taken me six months to get it." The sheriff took another drink, then filling the bags, he took his departure, after asking Mr. Yale if he did his own coining.

Mr. Yale took an active interest in the affairs of the town, and was much respected by his townsmen. He married Mary Johnson, Nov. 20, 1803, and died Jan. 23, 1833, in the forty-ninth year of his age. Mary, his wife, died April 1, 1854, æ. sixty-nine years. His son, Edwin Rodolphus Yale, was born Aug. 8, 1804, and was extensively engaged in business in Meriden for many years. He is now the proprietor of the Mansion House, Brooklyn, N. Y.

### SAMUEL YALE

Was the son of Samuel and Eunice (Payne) Yale, and was born April 4, 1786. He was the third of a family of nine children, six sons and three daughters. At an early age he was engaged with his father in the manufacture of cut nails, in a little shop which stood nearly in front of the present center Congregational church. He and his father worked the nail machine with their own hands, and each nail was headed separately. The elder Mr. Yale soon after commenced the manufacture of pewter buttons, which met with a ready sale, his son working with him. The father died Sept. 18, 1804, in his forty-seventh year, and after his death the son continued the business in connection with his brother Hiram, employing two or three men. Samuel and Hiram afterwards removed to Richmond, Va., where they remained several years engaged in the tin business. They finally returned to Meriden, where, in connection with two other brothers, William and Charles, they commenced the manufacture of tin and britannia ware. Their goods were sold chiefly by peddlers. The Yales were very enterprising men and imported from England more skilled artizans, and soon took the lead in the manufacture of britannia goods, such as tea-sets, church services,[1] etc. Charles and Hiram removed to Wallingford and commenced business, and had for an apprentice Mr. Samuel Simpson. Samuel Yale remained in Meriden and continued the tin and britannia business, occupying a shop on Liberty-st., and afterwards on the corner of Broad and East Main-st. He continued here until 1858, when he retired from business. The shop is still standing a few rods east from Broad-st.

Mr. Yale in his younger days was deputy sheriff for several years. When the Meriden Bank was organized

[1] The author has in his possession a flagon which was manufactured by the Yale Brothers. It was a part of the communion service of the First Baptist church in Meriden.

he was chosen one of the directors, and held the office until his death. He was President and trustee of the Meriden Academical Association while it was in existence. In 1850 he erected the building known as the Odd Fellows Building ; and in 1856 erected the brick building on the northeast corner of Broad and Main-sts. Mr. Yale died March 12, 1854, æ. 79 years. His wife died in 1865 in her 79th year.

### WM. HUBBARD YALE

Son of Jonathan and Alma (Hubbard) Yale, was born in Meriden Nov. 22, 1817, in the house in which he now

WILLIAM HUBBARD YALE.

lives. The house was known to the old residents of the town as the "Penfield place," and was built by Mr. Wm. Yale's grandfather. Mr. Yale gives most of his time to the cultivation of his farm, but finds time to take an active interest in town affairs. To his memory the author is indebted for many facts contained in this volume. Mr. Yale married June 27, 1841, Miss Maria M. Hubbard.

JAMES S. BROOKS

Was born in Haddam, Conn., March 1, 1796. He came
to Meriden when he was sixteen years old, a poor boy,
and was apprenticed to David Plant, to learn the business of carpenter and joiner. He served his apprenticeship, and worked at the business a few years. Major
Elisha A. Cowles was engaged in business in Meriden at
that time, and having become acquainted with young
Brooks, he employed him to travel and sell dry-goods
and Yankee notions for him. Mr. Brooks with a single
horse and wagon, in which he carried his goods, drove to
South Carolina, and there carried on business in connection with Mr. Cowles, under the name of J. S. Brooks
& Co., for nearly twenty years; his family residing, in
the meantime, in Meriden. When he returned to Meriden to live, he was engaged in numerous enterprises, at
one time manufacturing augers, and at another as one of
the firm of Parker, Snow, Brooks & Co., occupying the
buildings now used by Parker Brothers. Mr Brooks
was one of the pioneers in building the Hartford, New
Haven and Springfield railroad, was a Director for several years, Vice President, and for a number of years
acting President. He was largely identified with the
affairs of the town, serving as Selectman, Judge of Probate, Justice of the Peace and as Representative of the
town to the State Legislature in 1839, 1844, 1855 and
1857. He was very active in church affairs, and gave
the land on which the West Meriden Congregational
church was built, and the sum of one thousand dollars
towards the building. He had a good knowledge of
human nature, and a quick perception of the character
and intent of men. He was ardent in his temperament,
strong in his attachments, and kind as a friend and

neighbor. Possessing strong common sense and good
mother-wit, and an indomitable will and perseverance,
he made his influence felt in the community.    Mr.
Brooks married, Aug. 31, 1823, Millicent A., daughter
of Patrick Clark of this town.    He died Oct. 29, 1862,
leaving ten children : six daughters and four sons.    One
of the latter, John C., died in 1864, after nearly three
years' service in the Union Army.    He occupied the
house just north of the depot in West Meriden.

### LEMUEL J. CURTIS

Son of Elisha and Abigail (Hall) Curtis, was born Jan.
15, 1814.    He attended school until he was sixteen years
old, when he was apprenticed to Ira Yale of Wallingford
to learn the britannia ware business.    After serving
about twelve months, he, together with Mr. Wm. Elton,
bought out Mr. Yale and formed a partnership in which
they continued about one year.    In the summer of 1836
Mr. Curtis and Mr. Isaac C. Lewis went to Illinois, in-
tending to settle there and carry on business together ;
but Mr. Lewis was taken sick, and they soon returned
to Meriden, and formed a partnership and commenced
manufacturing britannia ware about two miles east of
the town.    The partnership was soon dissolved, and Mr.
Curtis, together with his brother Edwin E. Curtis, manufactured britannia ware in Meriden for a few years.    Mr.
Lemuel Curtis then formed a partnership with Mr. William Lyman, and when the Meriden Britannia Company
was formed in 1852, they both became members of the
company.    Mr. Curtis has been one of the directors of
the company since its organization, and an active member until 1868.    He has long been an active member of
the Episcopal Church ; was vestryman for several years,

and is now one of the wardens. He married Dec. 24,
1835, Bedotha P. Button, and has had two children.

### ASHABEL GRISWOLD

Was born in Rocky Hill, Conn., April 4, 1784. He
removed to Meriden in 1808, eating his first meal in

ASHABEL GRISWOLD.

Meriden at the residence of Mr. James Frary, in the
north part of the town. On this occasion he first met
Mr. Frary's daughter Lucy, whom he afterward married.
Previous to his coming to Meriden he had learned the
block-tin business of Captain Danforth of Rocky Hill,
and soon after coming here he commenced business in a
small shop near the residence of Mr. Samuel Clark, in
Clarksville, now Fraryville, manufacturing tea-pots and
other articles from block-tin. In 1810 he built the house
just north of the residence of Mr. Wm. Lyman, and near
this he built a shop which he occupied until 1842, when
he retired from business. Mr Griswold was a very energetic business man and highly respected in the community. He was President of the Meriden Bank for
some years, one of the wardens of the Episcopal church,

Justice of the Peace, and represented the town in the Legislature in 1831 and 1847. He married 1st, Lucy Frary ; 2nd, the widow of Andrew Lyman, and died May 30, 1853, æ. 69 years.

### ELI IVES

Son of Othniel and Sarah (Yale) Ives was born in the house now occupied by his brother Othniel Ives Jr. in the eastern part of the town, January, 1809. He remained on the farm until his twenty-second year, when with Mr. Noah Pomeroy he commenced the manufacture of tin ware. In 1837 he went to Wetumpka, Alabama, and commenced business in which he retained an interest, although living most of the time in Meriden. In 1843 he bought the Tyler mills in Yalesville, and carried on the milling business and manufacture of britannia spoons. In 1849, in company with Mr. Bennett Jeralds he commenced manufacturing britannia spoons and other articles in Prospect, Conn. The business was

ELI IVES.

carried on until 1854. In 1852 Mr. Ives was admitted as a partner in the firm of Goodrich and Rutty, and

the firm was changed to Goodrich, Ives and Rutty.
Mr. Goodrich retired in 1864, and Edwin R. Crocker
and Nelson Payne were admitted, making the firm Ives,
Rutty and Co. He has been a member of the common
council, and also one of the aldermen. His services
have been often called for in the settlement of estates,
and he has taken an active interest in city improvements.

### LAUREN MERRIMAN

Son of Asaph and Damaris Merriman, was born in
Meriden in 1787. He early commenced the manufacture of block tin buttons in his own house, and afterwards

LAUREN MERRIMAN.

in a small shop which is now occupied as a dwelling-
house, and stands opposite the north end of Foster and
Merriman's shop. He afterwards commenced the manufacture of ivory combs in Crow Hollow, where he
continued until 1830, when he sold out the business.
He was a very active and enterprising man, devoted
entirely to his business, and accumulated a large property. He married Temperance Todd of Bristol, Conn.,
and had six children. His three sons have been actively

engaged in business in this town ; viz., Asaph, Nelson,
and Lauren T.  Mr. Merriman died in April, 1867, æ.
80 years.

### ORVILLE H. PLATT

Son of  Daniel G. and  Almira Platt, was born in
Washington, Litchfield county, Conn., July 19, 1827.
He received his early education in his native town, and
studied law with G. H. Hollister Esq., of Litchfield.
He was admitted to the bar, and in the spring of 1851
he removed to Meriden and commenced the practice of
law.  He was appointed Judge of Probate in 1853–4–5
and 6: was Clerk of the Senate in 1855–6; Secretary
of State in 1857; State Senator in 1861–2; and Representative in 1864–9.  He was speaker of the House of
Representatives in 1869.  Mr. Platt has always ranked
high in the legal profession.  His success as a lawyer
has been dependent on an unshaken conviction of his
probity, untiring diligence and devotion to the interests
of his clients, and his comprehensive knowledge of the
law, and his admirable judgment.  The impulse he has
communicated while living, to all schemes of public
enterprise and improvement, will doubtless continue ;
but his aid and influence would be missed in many
channels which no other could successfully fill.  Mr.
Platt married May 15, 1850, Miss Annie Bull of To-
wanda, Penn., and has had two children, Daniel G. who
died young, and James P. who is now in Yale College.

### SAMUEL PADDOCK

Was born in Middletown, Conn., Feb. 22, 1784, and removed to Meriden in 1806.  For over fifty years he was
one of the active and influential men of the town,
holding several offices in the gift of the town.  He was

by occupation a farmer. August 20, 1803, he married Miss Polly Sears. January 22, 1823, he married for his second wife Charlotte Yale. He died August 7, 1800.

SAMUEL PADDOCK.

One of his sons, Charles Paddock, is an extensive farmer in the eastern part of the town. Another son, Samuel C. Paddock, is well known as a business man in Meriden.

### CHARLES PARKER

Son of Stephen and Rebecca Parker, was born in Cheshire, Conn., January 2, 1809. When nine years of age he was placed with a farmer by the name of Porter Cook, where he remained until he was fourteen. He continued on a farm until he was eighteen, when he went to work in Southington casting buttons for Anson Matthews. He remained there one year and then removed to Naugatuck, then a part of Waterbury, where he worked for Horace and Harry Smith about six months. In August, 1828, Mr. Parker came to Meriden and hired out to Patrick Lewis, making coffee-mills. In December, 1829, he went into business for himself with a capital of

P P

seventy dollars, taking a contract from Lewis and Holt.
for thirteen months to manufacture coffee-mills. His
shop stood nearly opposite his present residence. During the thirteen months Mr. Parker cleared thirteen
hundred dollars. He then took in as partner, Mr. Jared
Lewis, and took another contract from Lewis and Holt,
to manufacture coffee-mills, ladles and skimmers. In
January, 1831, he sold out to Mr. Jared Lewis and
bought an acre of ground lying west of his present
residence. On this ground was an old brown house, and
Mr. Parker paid for the house and ground, six hundred
and fifty dollars. On the back of this lot he built a shop
which was finished in the spring of 1832, in which he
manufactured coffee-mills and waffle irons. Mr. Parker
then went to market with his own goods. In Nov.
1833 Lewis and Holt failed, thus leaving the whole
market in Mr. Parker's hands. In 1833 he associated
with his brother Edmund and Heman White, under
the firm name of Parker and White, and carried on
business until 1835, when Edmund Parker was sent to
Montgomery, Alabama, with clocks and dry goods. In
1836 he returned, and Mr. White went to Montgomery
with dry goods, which sold readily. In October, 1837, he
made a second trip to Alabama with a large stock of
dry goods; but the hard times came on and he lost
heavily, much embarassing the firm of Parker and White,
who did not fully recover from their embarassment for
over six years. They were often advised by their friends
to fail, but did not, and paid all debts in full with interest.
During this time Edmund Parker sold out his interest to
Mr. White, and in 1843 the partnership was dissolved,
Mr. White going south, where he soon failed. He came
back to Meriden and hired out to Mr. Parker for one

hundred dollars a month. He built the house now owned and occupied by Mr. John W. Miles, corner of Broad and Elm streets. He died there of consumption. Mr. Parker's business steadily increased, and in 1844 he added largely to his buildings, putting in steam power, having previously used horse power. He was the first to manufacture plated spoons and forks, and the first to plate hollow ware in Meriden. Mr. Parker owns besides his shop in Meriden center, a factory in East Meriden, one about two miles west of Meriden, one in Yalesville, one in West Meriden, and occupies the Twiss shop in Prattsville. His business now amounts to about one million dollars a year.

His success in life has been owing to strict economy and close application to business; he often working fifteen hours a day, attending to his large correspondence evenings. He has been distinguished for good sense, great industry, method in business, and punctuality in all his engagements. At the age of thirty-one, Mr. Parker experienced religion, and after two years united with the Methodist church. He gave the Methodists the lot on Broad street on which their church was built, and also gave three-quarters of what the building cost; and he with his brother John jointly contributed between thirty and forty thousand dollars towards the erection of the present Methodist church. His liberality has been great but unostentatious; and whenever he has conferred a favor he has endeavored to conceal it from the world. Mr. Parker has always refused to accept office, though often urged to do so, until Meriden was incorporated a city; when he was elected Mayor, which office he held two years.

Mr. Parker married October 6, 1831, Miss Abi Lewis

Eddy, of Berlin, and has had ten children ; four are
now living. The youngest son, Dexter Wright Parker,
was graduated at West Point in the spring of 1870, he
Leing then in his twenty-first year.

## EDMUND PARKER

The youngest son of Stephen and Rebecca Parker, was
born in Cheshire, Conn., Feb. 9, 1811. He removed
to Meriden at an early age, and shortly after became
connected with his brother Charles and Mr. Heman
White, in the manufacture of hardware, under the name
of Parker and  White, which firm were  really the
pioneers of the business enterprise of Meriden.    To
their energy, perseverance and success, is due in a
great measure the growth and present prosperity of
the town.    Upon the dissolution of Parker and White
he associated himself with his brother John in the brass
and iron-foundry business, and in the manufacture of
coffee-mills and other hardware, under the firm name of
J. & E. Parker, which partnership continued until his
health failed in 1865, when he sold out his interest to
his brother Charles. He was Selectman and also
County Commissoner for several years. He embraced
Christianity at an early age, and for many years was a
member of the Methodist Episcopal Church in Meriden.
He joined the Episcopal Church in 1858, in which
communion he remained until his death, which occurred
April 19, 1866, at the age of fifty-five years. Mr.
Parker was distinguished for the clearness and strength
of his judgment, the ease and accuracy with which he
transacted business, and the kindness and affability
which he uniformly manifested in all the relations of
life ; and while always attentive to business, he was

EDMUND PARKER.

never neglectful of the duties of friendship nor of social life generally. Mr. Parker married Miss Jennette Bradley of Branford, and had seven children, four of whom are now living.

### JOSEPH J. WOOLLEY

son of Joseph and Fannie (Burroughs) Woolley, was born at Bridgeport, Conn., September 17, 1832. He

REV. JOSEPH J. WOOLLEY.

studied for the ministry in the M. E. Church, and joined the New York East Conference in 1856, and was stationed at South Norwalk, Conn. When the war broke out in 1861, he was commissioned as chaplain in the 8th Regiment, Conn. Volunteers, and was connected with the Burnside expedition into North Carolina, being actively engaged in the battles of Roanoke Island and Newbern. Constant exposure for weeks brought on an attack of typhoid fever, and he came home in the spring of 1862. Immediately after his recovery he presented the cause of the Chaplain's aid Commission in this State ; and it was while engaged in this work, that he was invited to become the Pastor of the Center Congregational Church in Meriden, Conn., where he was installed October 22, 1862 ; having been previously ordained by Bishop Simpson in the Methodist Church. Mr. Woolley was brought up in the Congregational Church under the pastorate of Dr. N. Hewitt, but was converted in the Methodist Church, which will account for his connection with that church, for which he still cherishes the warmest affection. Mr. Woolley has been twice married. His first wife was the daughter of Charles Briscoe of Bridgeport, Conn., with whom he lived five years ; during four years of which she was an invalid, being confined to her room the greater part of the time. She died May 6th, 1860, leaving no children. In Dec. 1861 he married the daughter of Dea. Stephen G. and Mary A. Ferris of South Norwalk, Conn., by whom he has two children, a son and daughter.

In his present pastorate, Mr. W. succeeded the Rev. O. H. White of New Haven. The church membership at that time was 154 ; it is now 224. His church is the original church of Meriden, having been organized in October, 1729.

### HORACE C. WILCOX

Son of Elisha B. and Hepsibah (Cornwall) Wilcox, was born in Middletown, Ct., Jan. 26, 1824. He lived on his father's farm until he was twenty years old, attending school until he was eighteen. In his twentieth year he

commenced peddling, and followed this business for nearly two years. In 1850 he came to Meriden and began
selling britannia ware for Mr. James Frary, and finally
furnished Mr. Frary with stock, and took all of the goods
that he manufactured. He followed this business for
several years, taking also the goods manufactured by
Messrs. Wm. Lyman and John Munson of Wallingford,
and I. C. Lewis & Co. Mr. Wilcox took in partnership his brother Dennis C. Wilcox, and under the firm
name of H. C. Wilcox and Co., remained until Dec.,
1852, when the Meriden Britannia Company was formed.
The Company comprised Mr. Horace Wilcox, his brother
Dennis, and the men for whom he had been selling
goods. Mr. Lewis was elected President, and Mr.
Wilcox Secretary and Treasurer. Mr. George R. Curtis,
then the Cashier of the Meriden Bank, was admitted
into the Company and filled the office of Treasurer, Mr.
Wilcox continuing Secretary until 1865, when he was
appointed President of the Company. The principal
trait in Mr. Wilcox's character is an indomitable energy
and perseverance. From a borrowed capital of three
dollars, with which he commenced business, he has accumulated a large property. The success of the Meriden
Britannia Company demonstrate his enterprise and
sagacity. Success as the result of the skillful use of
means and the powers of nature, persistent success,
always proves ability. Judged by this standard, Mr.
Wilcox is no ordinary man. He married first, August 9,
1849, Charlotte A., daughter of Jabez Smith of Middletown, by whom he had five children. He married second, May 31, 1865, Miss Ellen M., daughter of Edmund
Parker, by whom he has two children.

ALMER HALL.

Son of David and Thankful Hall, was born in Wallingford, Sept. 10, 1793. His early boyhood was spent with
his parents on the farm. His opportunities for intellectual improvement were limited. After leaving the farm,
he commenced for himself by peddling tin ware and
"Yankee notions" over the Alleghany mountains, through
Virginia, Tennessee and other States, for Charles Yale
of Wallingford. After following this business a few
years, he opened a small store in Wallingford for the
sale of dry goods and groceries. He continued in that
business several years. In 1827 he commenced the
manufacture of britannia spoons, but did not succeed
well in the business. In 1834 he went into company
with Walter Martin for the purpose of manufacturing
wooden screws. They soon failed, and Mr. Hall lost
$9,000, all that he was worth. He became very de-
spondent, and had no ambition to commence business
again ; but visiting New York, a friend gave him seven
pounds of German silver and told him to begin life
again. In 1837 Mr. Hall formed a copartnership with
William Elton under the .firm name of Hall, Elton &
Co., for the purpose of manufacturing German silver
ware. They were the first successful manufacturers of
this ware in this country. He continued in this business
until his death, Jan. 15, 1865, at the age of seventy-two
years. He was the last one of the constituent members
of the Baptist Church, which was organized in May,
1817. Four weeks afterwards he was chosen deacon,
and ever after used the office well, "purchasing to himself a good degree." He had a more than ordinary gift
for prayer and exhortation, and used it well to the last.
He was thoroughly versed in the great doctrines of

grace. It was his delight to hear them preached, and to converse about them in private. Mr. Hall was a quiet, unassuming man, and was possessed of that charity which "thinketh no evil." He was inclined to put the best construction on the acts of others, and to impute to them the best motives possible. He was confiding and unsuspecting, so much so as to suffer loss from some with whom he transacted business. For many years he was the chief support of the church, when it could not have been sustained without him. Mr. Hall married, 1st, Miss Lois Twiss of Meriden ; 2nd, Miss Fanny Silliman Ives of Meriden ; 3rd, March, 1840, Mrs. Clarissa Cooke of Wallingford. He had seven children, two of whom are living, viz.: Almer I. and Jane A., wife of Mr. D. W. Fields of Wallingford.

### ELIHU YALE.

Son of Theophilus and Azubah (De Wolf) Yale, was born in Wallingford in 1747. He married Lucretia, daughter of Abraham and Prudence Stanley of the same town, Nov. 24, 1774. He was a blacksmith, and was one of the first in Connecticut who commenced the manufacture of scythes and bayonets. Being successful in business, from a small beginning he accumulated a large estate. He was in the service of his country during the Revolution, and was an active and efficient man in all his undertakings. He died suddenly, having attended Church during the day, Sunday evening May 12, 1806, in his fifty-ninth year, leaving seven children.

# CHAPTER XXXIV.

## MISCELLANEOUS LAWS. LETTERS. CATHOLIC CHURCH. LAWYERS. MERIDEN GRAYS.

At a special town meeting holden at Wallingford Jan. 27, 1794, "Voted unanimously that this town do disapprove of the measures taken by the General Assembly in October last relative to the sale of the western territory belonging to this State, and the appropriation of the avails thereof; and that we deem it our duty to use every prudent method to prevent the aforesaid measures being carried into effect, and that the above Vote be inserted in the *Connecticut Journal.*"

At the October session of the General Assembly, 1726, a grant of three hundred acres of land in the town of Goshen was made to John Hull of Wallingford, James Wadsworth of Durham and Hezekiah Brainerd of Haddam (father of the missionary David Brainerd), for public services. It was called the Esquires' Farm, from its being given to these persons, each of whom had the title of Esquire.

[ *From the* CONNECTICUT JOURNAL, *April* 29, 1768.]

As I have never burthened the public to read or you to publish any of my productions, I flatter myself the subsequent succint suggestions will be forgiven. As economy is the watchword of this reign, as candor was of the former, in the courtly and ministerial style, it has crossed the Atlantic, and is in high vogue in America as well as in Westminster he city of the great king. The story is this: A few days since a strolling man in soldier's regimental garb, calling himself James McCannon, with a blazing woman, came into my house in early morn, begged for cider, then three mugs deep, as I was informed; after some admonitions given him, my affairs pressing my immediate departure, I left him in the house, on which he soon became very boisterous, attempted to pilfer some things which my domestic discovered; finally carried off a brass save-all, of a stand of candlesticks ( then undiscovered ), what else is at present unknown. This, though trifling in its value intrinsically, but as an ancient patrimonial legacy of high estimation, not only is a standing evidence of their prudent economy, but *ex vi termini* a memento of economy and save-all. And hereby I beg leave to give warning to all families to beware of such strolling pilferers, if they would save all. I beg leave also to ask the public, whether it would not be of public utility, to have task-masters in every town to compel them to labor, as they are passing every day in our streets, and will be probably more and more, or some other similar salutary measure. I ask pardon for one more hint which pops into my head, while my pen is moving, as a supplemental suggestion to economy and save-all. A respectable physician of the city of London, of high renown in the faculty, told the subscriber that he required his servants to save all the rags, not that it was of the least avail to him, but only a specimen of economy—save-all, and withal added, " The rags in this city are worth sixty thousand pounds sterling a year." I hope the paper mill manufacturers will not esteem the foregoing hint burthensome, though the public may what precedes. Gentlemen, if it appear more eligible to save your pains and paper than print this, remember and save all.

I am your most humble servant,

E. HALL.

*Wallingford,* 5 *o'clock, April* 27*th.*

[*From the* CONNECTICUT GAZETTE.]

At a meeting of the true sons of Liberty in Wallingford, in New Haven county, on the evening of the 13th day of January, 1766, after duly formed by choosing a moderator and a clerk, the following resolves were come into, viz.:

*Resolved*, 1 That the late act of Parliament, called the Stamp Act, is unconstitutional, and intended to enslave the true subjects of America.

*Resolved*, 2. That we will oppose the same to the last extremity, even to take the field.

*Resolved*, 3. That we will meet at the Court House in New Haven, on the third Tuesday of February next ; and we desire all the sons of liberty in each town in the county would meet there by themselves or representatives ; there to consult what is best to be done in order to defend our liberties and properties, and break up the stop to public affairs.

*Resolved*, 4. That this meeting be adjourned to the first Tuesday of February next, then to choose our representatives to attend the aforesaid meeting.

A true copy, examined.

P. P. CLARK.

## CATHOLIC CHURCH.

The first Roman Catholic service in Meriden was held at a private residence in the north-east part of the town. The building now occupied as a residence near the corner of Liberty and Broad streets, and which then stood on the corner of Olive and South Broad streets, was soon after purchased and used by the Catholics for many years. Rev. Thomas Quinn was the first settled pastor, although Rev. Messrs. Stevens and Hugh Riley had previously had pastoral care of the society. During Rev. Mr. Quinn's pastorate, the present church of St. Rose of Lima was built at a cost of about $25,000. Soon after the completion of the Church, Father Quinn was removed to another field of labor, and was succeeded by Rev. Thomas Walsh, the present pastor. Rev. Mr. Sheridan was curate for a while under Father Walsh, and was succeeded by the Rev. Mr. Plunkett, who in 1870 was removed. The church has recently been enlarged.

The Holy Sacrifice of the Mass was offered up for the first time in Wallingford on the 22nd of December, 1847, by a missionary Priest, in a private house on Main street, occupied by James Hanlon. Fifteen persons composed the congregation. From 1847 to 1857 the Catholics of Wallingford had divine service in private houses and in the hall of the tavern when it could be obtained, and it was attended by the Priest from Meriden. On the 23d of November, 1857, the corner stone of the present Catholic church was laid by the Rev. Thomas Quinn, then pastor of the Meriden church. Wallingford has ceased to be an out-mission to Meriden since 1868 ; Rev. Hugh Mallon being then appointed pastor. The Catholic population of Wallingford is now about one thousand.

## LUTHERAN CHURCH.

The corner-stone of the St. John's German Evangelical church was laid Friday, Oct. 19, 1866, Rev. Dr. Bohrman of Albany preaching the sermon. In the stone were deposited a Bible, Catechism, Records of the Church, a copy of the *Recorder*, and several evangelical newspapers. Rev. Gustavus A. Schmidt was the first pastor, and was succeeded by Rev. Charles Groeber.

## LAWYERS.

Benajah Andrews was for many years the leading lawyer of Meriden. He was Judge of Probate in this district from 1844 to 1846, and from 1847 to 1850. Dexter R. Wright, a graduate of the Wesleyan University, of the class of 1845,[1] and Tilton E. Doolittle, a graduate of Yale College of the class of 1846, practised law in this town for many years. Orville H. Platt came here in 1851[2] and has held many important offices in the gift of the town. Savilian R. Hall practiced here for a short time, and removed to New Haven, as did Messrs. Wright and Doolittle. The lawyers at present in Meriden are as follows: George W. Smith, Cooke Lounsbury, George A. Fay, E. A. Merriman, Leverett L. Phelps and Ratcliffe Hicks.

### MERIDEN GRAYS.

2d Brigade, Conn., State Militia. In 1830 the roll was as follows: *Captain,* Almeron Miles; *Lieutenant,* John S. Blake; *Ensign,* Osamas Crocker; *Sergeants,* Alfred P. Curtiss, Alanson Curtiss, Edmund Parker, Harrison W. Curtiss; *Bugler,* Elam L. Johnson; *Fifer,* Henry P. Judd; *Drummer,* John Miles Jr.; *Bass Drummer,* Loyal Smith; Almon Ives, Benj. H. Royce, Charles Parker, Charles Ranney, Daniel Hart, Edwin Birdsey, Ezra Rutty, Edward N. Hall, Geo. Thrall, Harrison Curtiss, Henry Penfield, Henry W. Saltonstall, Horace Redfield, Isaac W. Curtiss, James S. Lathrop, Lyman Ives, Norman W. Pomeroy, Nelson Payne, Sydney P. Hall, Wm. H. Yale, Wm. D. Cutler, Wm. Green, John Houseman, Alanson Carter, Wm. Seymour, Wm. White, Elias M. Barnes, Hiram H. Royce.

---

1 See Biographical notices.
2 See Biographical notices.

COL. WILLIAM M. PRATT

MAJ. THEODORE BYXBEE

COL. CHARLES L. UPHAM

CAPT. ROGER M. FORD

CAPT. JARED R. COOK

# GENEALOGIES.

"To trace lineage -- to love and record the names and actions of those without whom we could never have been, who moulded and made us what we are, and whom the very greatest of us all must know to have propagated influences into his being, which must subtly but certainly act upon his whole conduct in this world—all this is implied in ancestry and the love of it, and is natural and good."   *Westminster Review, July, 1853.*

## INTRODUCTION.

FEW know the amount of time, patience and labor, that is required in compiling genealogies, and no one can estimate the difficulty of collecting these materials, who has not had experience in similar undertakings. It has been said, that it was useless to tell antiquaries anything about the cost of such works, for they understood it ; and it was equally useless to tell others, for they could not comprehend you. It is probable that this work would not have been printed for several years had not the services of Mr. ELIHU YALE been called into requisition. He has spent many years in examining town church and family records, and in an extensive correspondence with the descendants of the families noticed in this work. Every one who has had any experience in labors of this kind, knows that errors are unavoidable. The neglect of parents in having the births, deaths, and marriages in their respective families recorded, renders it imposssible in many cases, to collect from the town records a correct list of a family. I have carefully compared these records with those of the neighboring towns, the published genealogies of some of the families, and also the records of the Probate office, and the office of the Register of deeds for the county. Thus in some instances I have supplied the record of whole families, not found upon the town records at all. It was my intention to bring the record of each family down to the present generation, but the work has grown to such a size that it will be impossible except in a few instances. Of the Parker, Street, and Brown families I have the record of several thousand names of collateral branches, and also the records of numerous Meriden families, since the incorporation of the town. These Meriden pedigrees I had hoped to have incorporated in this work, but perhaps sufficient inducement may be offered to print them separately ; they would occupy about two hundred pages. Any corrections or additions to the families mentioned in these genealogies will be thankfully received by the author.

# ABERNATHY.

## WILLIAM.

WILLIAM ABERNATHY came to Wallingford from Branford. He was a native of Scotland, and was an active man among the settlers. The name of his 1st wife was Sarah.[1] His 2nd wife was Elizabeth.

Children: 1 *Elizabeth*, b Oct. 15, 1673; 2 *William*, b J n. 23 1675; 3 *Sarah*, b Oct. 10, 1677; 4 *Mary*, b Mar. 27, 1679; 5 *Samuel*, b Jan. 10, 1683, d Mar. 14, 1723; 6 *Daniel*, b Sept. 3. 1686; 7 *Susannah*, b July 18, 1689.

## 2. WILLIAM

WILLIAM AND MARY ABERNATHY. He died Feb., 1728. She died Jan. 1, 1757.

Children: 8 *Mary*, b April 30, 1700; 9 *Jemima*, b Aug. 20, 1702; 10 *Sarah*, b Dec. 15, 1705; 11 *Ann*, b June 7, 1706; 12 *John*, b Feb. 27, 1708, killed by lightning May 12, 1727, æ 19; 13 *Caleb*, b Feb. 11, 1710, m. to Lois Gaylord by Capt. Yale, Sept. 26, 1733; 14 *Susannah*, b April 28, 1712, m. Samuel Yale.

## 5. SAMUEL.

SAMUEL ABERNATHY married Elizabeth Peck Nov. 21, 1711.

Children: 15 *Abraham*, b March 1, 1712; 16 *Samuel*, b Dec. 28, 1718, d July 28, 1724; 17 *Jasper*, b Feb. 24, 1721, d Dec. 2. 1741.

## 13. CALEB.

CALEB and LOIS ABERNATHY, of Wallingford, married. 1733.

Children: 18 William, b July 1, 1734; 19 *Mary*, b Nov. 23. 1736; 20 *John*, b July 2, 1738; 21 *Mary*, b Dec. 9, 1797; 22 Jared, b Oct. 31, 1741.

1 Hinman's Letters of Com , 17, 18.

## ALLING AND ALLEN.

### JAMES.

JAMES ALLING is the first of this name that I find in Wallingford, with his wife Abigail, before 1700. The name has not been numerous.

Children: 1 *Abigail*, b. June 23, 1701 ; 2 *James*, b. Nov. 15, 1702 ; 3 *Stephen*, b. Oct. 13, 1704 ; 4 *Mary*, b. March 3, 1708 ; 5 *Samuel*, b. Jan. 15, 1710, m. Mary Blakeslee, June 23, 1726 ; 6, *Ebenezer*, b. April 8, 1713.

### 2. JAMES.

JAMES and MARY (Beadles) ALLING were married Sept. 23, 1731.

Children: 7 *Marshal*, b. Aug. 1, 1732 ; 8 *Rebecca*, b. Feb. 7, 1734 ; 9 *Abigail*, b. Dec. 1, 1735 ; 10 *Josiah*, b. Feb. 19, 1738.

### 6. EBENEZER.

EBENEZER ALLING married Sarah Atwater, Dec. 19, 1742. He died Nov. 3, 1760.

Children: 11 *Sarah*, b Feb. 8, 1745 ; 12 *Daniel*, b. Oct. 22, 1747, d. July 11, 1746 ; 13 *Abel*, b. Jan. 30, 1749 ; 14 *Enos*, b. Jan. 17, 1752 ; 15 *Damaris*, b. March 15, 1755 ; 16 *Abigail*, b. July. 6, 1757 ; 17 *Eunice*, b. Dec. 19, 1760.

### EPHRAIM.

EPHRAIM ALLING married Hannah ——— .

Children: 18 *Daniel*, b. Nov. 18, 1743 ; 19 *Esther*, b. Jan. 24, 1744.

———————

## ANDREWS.[1]

### WILLIAM.

WILLIAM ANDREWS, of Hampsworth, England (carpenter), was one of the fifty-three persons besides women and children who shipped at Hampton, 15 miles west-south-west of London,

———————

[1] Andrews' Hist. New Britain ; Bubson's Hist. of Gloucester, 57, 58;

about the 6th of April, 1635, on board of the *Jame* of London, of 300 tons, Wm. Cooper, Master. Several of the 53 passengers had their wives and children with them, but no record of their names was kept. They landed at Boston, where Wm. Andrews was made a freeman in 1635. He was early at New Haven with Eaton and Rev. John Davenport. He built the first meeting-house there in 1644. He is known to have had three sons and one daughter, and is supposed to have had two other daughters whose names are now unknown. The name of his first wife who was the mother of all his children, is also now unknown. He married his 2nd wife, Anna Gibbands, Dec. 7, 1665 ; she was a daughter of William Gibbands, who was Colonial Secretary in 1657. Mr. William Andrews died at East Haven, March 4, 1676. Mrs. Anna, his wife, died A. D. 1701.

Children : 1 *William*, born in England, died Jan. 3, 1663, left no sons ; 2 *Samuel*, born in England, 1632, died Oct. 6, 1704 ; 3 *Nathan*, born in England, 1638. Ancestor of the East Haven branch. Daughters, supposed three.

Samuel and Nathan were of the original proprietors of Wallingford in 1670. Nathan was one of the twelve selected to lay the foundation for the formation of the Church in Wallingford, and was an active member of the plantation, after giving directions for its government, until they became sufficiently strong to support a minister.

## 2. SAMUEL.

SAMUEL ANDREWS, son of William the emigrant, married Elizabeth, daughter of Deacon Wm. Peck, of New Haven. He took the oath of fidelity May 2, 1654 ; settled in Wallingford in 1670. Made his will April 17, 1703, amount of estate

Dodd's Hist. of E. Haven, 101, 102 ; Eaton's Annal of Warren 376, 377 ; Eaton's Hist. of Thomaston, 135, Hale's Lawrence Family, 10-12, Hinman's Conn. Settlers, 51-55 ; Michas, M. Centennial Celebration, 152, 153 ; Savage's Gen. Dict., 1. 51, 57 ; Walker's Memorials of Walker Family, 215, Ward's Hist. Shrewsbury, 221-5.

616 HISTORY OF WALLINGFORD.

£331 2s. 6d. He died in Wallingford, Oct. 6, 1704, æ. 73 years. She died in Wallingford.

Children: 4 *William*, b. 1658 ; 5 *Samuel*, b. Feb. 1, 1661, d. 1662, æ. about 1 year ; 6 *Samuel*, b. April 30, 1663, m. Anna Hall, Aug. 27, 1686 ; 7 *William*, b. Feb. 9, 1664, m. to Hannah Parker, by Mr. Moss, Jan. 12, 1692 ; 8 *John*, b. July 4, 1667 ; 9 *Nathaniel*, b. Aug 2, 1670, m. Susannah Tyler; she d. June 5, 1721 ; 10 *Twins*. b. May 30, 1673, d. 1 day after birth ; 11 *Elizabeth*, b. July 16, 1674, m. Benjamin Hull ; 12 *Mary*, b. March 27, 1677 ; 13 *Joseph*, b. June 1, 1679, m. Abigail Paine ; 14 *Margery*, b. Jan. 15, 1681 ; 15 *Dinah*, b. July 25, 1684. ~~~ . *Theua Hall*

3 NATHAN.

NATHAN ANDREWS, son of William the emigrant, married 1st, Elizabeth Miles, July 26, 1686 ; 2nd, Hannah Gibbons, of New Haven. He went to Wallingford in 1670. - Lot 8 on the west side of Main street was assigned him for his house lot. He died in 1712.

Children by 1st marriage : 16 *Elizabeth*, b. April 8, 1688 ; 17 *Daniel*, b Aug. 15, 1690. d. Aug. 15, 1690 ; 18 *Tamer*, b. Aug. 15, 1690, d. Jan. 11, 1727 ; 19 *Samuel*, b. Aug. 15, 1691, d. Jan. 31, 1727 ; 20 *Daniel*: 21 *Mary*: 22 *Jonathan*, m. Jemima —————; 23 *Abigail*; by 2nd marriage, 24 *William*, b. Sept. 4, 1729.

6. SAMUEL.

SAMUEL ANDREWS, son of Samuel and Elizabeth, married Hannah, or Anna Hall, August 27, 1686.

Children : 25 *Thomas*, b. March 11, 1687, m. Felix —— ; 26 *John*, b. April 18, 1692, d May 6, 1693 ; 27 *John*, b. May 5, 1693. m. Hannah Merriman. July 19, 1714 : 28 *Elizabeth*, b Nov. 27, 1695, d July 19, 1697 ; 29 *Samuel*, b 1697, m Abigail ———; 30 *Elisha*, b. Apr. 28, 1701 ; 31 *William*, b July 6, 1702, m. Mary Foster ; 32 *Anna*, m. Joseph Roys of Wallingford.

### 7. WILLIAM.

WILLIAM ANDREWS, son of Samuel and Elizabeth, married to Hannah Parker, by Mr. Moss. Jan. 12, 1692. He died July 8, 1726. (Estate £291)

Children: 33 *Thankful* A., m. Matthias Hitchcock.

### 8. JOHN.

JOHN ANDREWS, son of Samuel and Elizabeth, married Sarah ————.

Children: 34 *Ruth*, b. Oct. 1, 1723.

### 9 NATHANIEL.

NATHANIEL ANDREWS, son of Samuel and Elizabeth, married Susannah Tyler, Dec. 13, 1705. She died June 25, 1721; and he married Elizabeth Clark, Oct. 16, 1721. He died March 5, 1735. Elizabeth Clark died Sept. 10, 1751

### 13. JOSEPH.

JOSEPH ANDREWS, son of Samuel and Elizabeth Andrews, married Abigail Payne Nov. 10, 1704. He made his will Oct. 12, 1741 and died Nov. 20, 1741, æ. 62 yrs., 6 mos., 11 days. She died June 25, 1721.

Children: 35 *Caleb*, b. June 23, 1701; 36 *Caleb*, b. March 12, 1706, d Nov. 20, 1741; 37 *Joseph*, b March 3, 1708, d 1741; 38 *Giles*, b March 19, 1710, m Abigail Curtiss, April 7. 1731; 39 *Mary*, (twin) b June 15, 1714; 40 *Mary*, (twin), b June 15, 1714, m John Hulls of Wallingford; 41 *Nathaniel*, b March 16, 1717, d 1741; 42 *Andrew*, b Aug. 16, 1719, d. 1792, m Hester ——, she d Sept. 6. 1750; 43 *Stephen*, b May 24, 1722, d 1775, æ. 73

### 20. DANIEL.

DANIEL ANDREWS son of Nathan and Elizabeth, married 1s, Mehitable ——, she died. He married 2d, Sarah ——, she died of small pox, 1712.

Children by first wife: 44 *Nathaniel*, b. July 12, 1714, 45 *Elnathan*, Sept. 12, 1717. By 2nd wife: 46 *Zebel*, b. June, 1720, m. Sarah Cook, Jan. 16, 1746; 47 *Hanna* A.

May 12, 1723 ; 48 *Mehitable*, b. April 30, 1726 ; 49 *Ephraim*, b. May 13, 1731. By 3d wife, Deliverance: 50 *Margery*, b. Nov. 6, 1733 ; 51 *Abigail*, b. May 1, 1736 : 52 *Lydia*, b. June 16, 1740.

## 22. JONATHAN.

JONATHAN ANDREWS, son of Nathan and Elizabeth ; married Jemima Hotchkiss April 11, 1727.

Children : 53 *Abel*, b. Jan. 28, 1728. m. Lettis Williams Feb. 10, 1757, and settled in Cheshire ; 54 *Esther*, b. May 9, 1730; 55 *Mary*, b. Jan. 14, 1734; 56 *Daniel*, b. June 4, 1737 ; 57 *Jemima*, b. Nov. 24, 1740.

## 25. THOMAS.

THOMAS ANDREWS, son of Samuel and Elizabeth, married 1st Felix ————. He died in 1756, leaving widow Elizabeth.

Children : 58 *Elizabeth*, born April 23, 1717, m. R. Strong of Waterbury, Conn. ; 59 *Benjamin*, b. Nov. 26, 1718; 60 *Enos*, b April 13. 1719, m. Content ———; 61 *Sarah*, b. July 15, 1720 ; 62 *Lois*, b. July 15, 1722, m. Leverius Carrington ; 63 *Martha*, b. Sept. 25, 1730 ; 64 *Thankful*, m. Jason Hitchcock.

## 26. JOHN.

JOHN ANDREWS, son of Samuel and Elizabeth, married Hannah Merriman, July 23, 1714. She died Sept. 28, 1738.

Children : 65 *Ephraim*, b. Oct. 14, 1714 ; 66 *Phebe*, b. Sept. 11, 1716 ; 67 *Denizen*, b. May 14. 1718, d. April 13, 1725 ; 68 *Eben*, b. Jan. 15, 1720 : 69 *Anna*, b. Nov. 17, 1721 ; 70 *Hannah*, b. Jan. 13, 1722 : 71 *Peter*, b. Dec. 6, 1723 ; 72 *John*, b. Nov. 23, 1727 : 73 *Hannah*, b. Oct. 24, 1729 ; 74 *Mary*, b. Sept. 15, 1732, m. Joseph Parker in 1758 ; 75 *Elizabeth*, b. Aug. 20, 1736.

## 29. SAMUEL.

SAMUEL ANDREWS, son of Samuel and Anna, married Abigail Tyler, daughter of John and Abigail. He died Oct. 5, 1784, aged 87 years. She died Feb. 13, 1786, aged 89 years. Interred in Meriden.

Children : 76 *Elon*, b Nov. 26, 1721, m. Sarah ————. He died

Sept. 22. 1784. 77 *Jacob*, b. Nov. 18, 1723; 78 *Nicholas*, b. Dec. 27. 1725, died Dec. 21, 1784, æ. 26 years; 79 *Laban*, b. Apr. 25, 1728, m. Prudence Stanley, Apr. 5, 1758; 80 *Dawson*, b. Aug. 27, m. Abigail Whiting, May 11, 1757; 81-2 *Moses* and *Aaron*, twins, b. Aug. 29. 1734; the former was a physician in Meriden; 83 *Samuel*, b. April 27. 1737.

## 30. ELISHA.

ELISHA ANDREWS, son of Samuel and Annah, married Mabel Andrews.

Children: 84 *Zuba*, b. April 1, 1721, m. John Couch of Meriden, Conn.; 85 *Elisha*, b. Dec. 25, 1727, d. young; 86 *Titus Elisha*, b. Jan. 5, 1728; 87 *Dinah*, b. Mar 23, 1729, m. Silas Merriman; 89 *Mabel*, b. May 24. 1731. m. Benjamin Tyler of Farmington; 90 *Bartholomew*, b. Jan. 30, 1735, m. Sarah Andrews; 91 *Noah*, b. Feb. 4, 1737. d. in the old French war; 92 *Anna*, b. Dec. 15, 1738, d. in childhood; 93 *Lucy*; 94 *Anna*.

## 31. WILLIAM.

WILLIAM ANDREWS, son of Samuel and Anna, married Mary Foster, Nov. 1, 1727. He died July 8, 1756. Will dated Oct. 6, 1736.

Children: 95 *Samuel*, b. Aug. 21, 1727, m. Lydia ———— , 96 *Anna*, b. Feb. 15, 1729; 97 *Eunice*, b. Feb. 18, 1750: 98 *Titus*, b. June 3, 1732; 99 *William*, b. Feb. 13, 1724; 100 *Thankful*; 101 *Mary*; 102 *Rhoda*; 103 *Titus*, b. March 7, 1751.

## 35. CALEB.

CALEB ANDREWS, son of Joseph and Abigail (Payne), married, 1st, Esther Beecher, May 22, 1727. She died Oct. 25, 1729. He married 2nd, Mary Culver, July 5. 1733. He died Nov. 20, 1741. Estate £1314.

Children by first marriage: 104 *Sarah*, b. Aug. 22, 17*9*; by 2nd marriage: 105 *Lament*, b. July 28, 1730, d. December 6, 1736.

## 38. GILES.

GILES ANDREWS, son of Joseph and Abigail, married Abigail Andrews. They settled in Sheffield, Mass.

Children: 106 *Amos*, b. Jan. 19, 1732 ; 107 *Joseph*, b May 2, 1743, d. Nov. 8, 1744.

#### 41. NATHANIEL.

NATHANIEL ANDREWS, son of Joseph and Abigail, married 1st, Esther ———; 2nd, Ruth ———; He died July 2, 1756. .

Children by Esther: 108 *Amos*, b. April 15, 1733. Children by Ruth: 109 *Rhoda*, b. Feb. 1, 1743 ; 110 *Nathan*, b. Feb. 2, 1750 ; 111 *Daniel*, b. May 29, 1751 ; 112 *Moses*, b. April 8, 1752.

#### 42. ANDREW.

ANDREW ANDREWS, son of Joseph and Abigail, married 1st, Esther ———. She died. He married 2nd, Elizabeth Dunbar. He died Feb. 22, 1772, æ. 72 years, 6 months, and 6 days.

Children: 113, 114, *Johanna* and *Sarah*, b. July 31, 1740, twins ; the latter married Bartholemew Andrews ; 115 *Margery*, b. March 23, 1742, d. in 1751 ; 116 *Esther*, b. Feb. 24, 1743 ; by 2nd wife : 117 *Eunice*, b. Dec. 6, 1746 ;- 118 *Caleb*, b. Dec. 9, 1748 ; 119 *Margery*, b Nov. 23, 1751 ; 120 *Margery*, b. June 14, 1752 ; 121 *Andrew*, b. Aug. 9, 1756 ; 122 *Joseph*, b. Nov. 26, 1758, died on board of the old prison ship, Jersey ; 123 *Nathaniel*, b. May 20, 1761 ; 124 *Elizabeth*, b. June 20, 1763 ; 125 *Mary*, b. May 20, 1766, m. Joseph Blakeslee ; 126 *Abigail*, b. April 26, 1770, m. Charles T. Jackson, of Litchfield, Conn.

#### 43. STEPHEN.

STEPHEN ANDREWS, son of Joseph and Abigail, married twice ; 1st, Mabel ———, she died. 2nd, Hannah ———. He died in Meriden.

Children: 127 *Mary*, b. April 5, 1747, m. a Mr. Bailey ; 128 *Abigail*, b Oct. 29, 1749 ; 129 *Benjamin*, b. Oct. 16, 1751 ; *Abigail*, b. Oct. 16, 1753 ; 130 *Mabel*, b. Sept. 23, 1761 ; 131 *Sarah ; Content.*

#### 46. ELNATHAN.

ELNATHAN ANDREWS, son of Daniel and Mehitable, married Hannah ———.

Children : 132 *Beta*, b March 16, 1740, d. in Cheshire : 133 *Inacta*, b. Sept. 22. 1742-3 ; 134 *Damaris*, b. March 23. 1745 : 135 *Hannah*, b. Jan. 10, 1746 : 136 *Elizabeth*, b. June 21, 1758 : 137 *Mary*, b Aug. 29, 1761.

### 47. JEHIEL.

JEHIEL ANDREWS, son of Daniel and Sarah ; married Sarah Cook

Children : 138 *Mabel*, b. July 19, 1746 ; 139 *Thankful*, b Dec. 9, 1748 : 140 *Lois*, b. Aug. 8, 1750 ; 141 *John*, b. Nov. 12, 1752 ; 142 *Ebenezer*, b. May 4, 1754 ; 143 *Sarah*, b. Dec. 29, 1756 : 144 *Eunice*, b. March 14, 1759 : 145 *Chloe*, b Dec. 16, 1760.

### 53. ABEL.

ABEL ANDREWS, son of Jonathan and Jemima, married 1st, Sarah ———— ; she died, and he married, 2nd, Lettis Williams, Feb. 10, 1757, and settled in Cheshire, where they both died.

Children by 1st marriage ; 146 *Sarah*, b. Feb. 1, 1744. By 2nd marriage ; 147 *Samuel;* 148 *Mamre;* 149 *Abel*, m. twice ; 150 *Chauncey*, d. in Cheshire ; 151 *Esther*, d. in Cheshire.

### 59. BENJAMIN.

Benjamin Andrews, son of Thomas and Felix, married Susannah ————.

Children : 153 *Samuel*, b. Sept. 21, 1741.

### 60. ENOS.

Enos Andrews, son of Thomas and Felix ————, married Content—*Curtis 15 July 1743*

Children : 154 *Thomas*, b. Aug. 8, 1744 ; 155 *Bede*, b. April 2, 1746 ; 156 *Asahel*, b Nov. 13, 1747 ; 157 *Hullah*, b. Nov. 3, 1751 ; 158 *Thankful*, b. Mar. 1, 1754 ; 159 *Enos*, b. Oct. 12, 1760.

### 65. EPHRAIM

EPHRAIM ANDREWS, son of John and Hannah, married Hannah ————.

Children : 160 *Asahel*, b Nov. 5, 1736.

## 68. EBEN.

EBEN ANDREWS, son of John and Hannah, married Elizabeth Andrews, Dec. 13, 1739.

Children: 161 *Joel*, b Aug. 11, 1740.

## 72. JOHN.

JOHN ANDREWS, son of John and Hannah, married Abigail ———.

Children: 162 *Abigail*, b Sept. 21, 1740; 163 *Lydia*, b Nov. 13, 1741.

## 76. ELON.

ELON ANDREWS, son of Samuel and Abigail, married Sarah ———. He died Sept. 22, 1784, aged 63 years. She died April 30, 1797, aged 60.

Children: 164 *Isaac*, d Oct. 24, 1754; 165 *Eunice*, b July 23, 1758; 166 *Isaac*, b March 8, 1762.

## 77. JACOB.

JACOB ANDREWS, son of Samuel and Abigail, married Ruth ———.

Children: 167 *Abigail*, b Oct. 29, 1749; 168 *Benjamin*, b Oct. 16, 1751; 169 *Abigail*, b Oct. 16, 1753.

## 78. NICHOLAS.

NICHOLAS ANDREWS, son of Samuel and Abigail, married Lydia ———, March 31, 1761. He died Dec. 21, 1784, æ. 50 years. He when living owned land now owned by Charles E. Yale.

Children: 170 *Amos*, b July 24, 1762.

## 79 LABAN.

LABAN ANDREWS, son of Samuel and Abigail, married Prudence Stanley.

Children: 171 *Abigail*, b Sept. 21, 1740; 172 *Lydia*, b Nov. 13, 1741.

## 80. DENIZEN.

DENIZEN ANDREWS, son of Samuel and Abigail, married Abigail Whiting, May 11, 1787. He died at Meriden, June. 1807, æ. 77 years. She died Oct. 1, 1796, æ. 60 years.

Children: 173 *Sarah*, b March 16, 1758; 174 *Abner*, b
August 25, 1759. He was paralyzed, died in Meriden, during
the Revolutionary war: 175 *Abigail*, b March 23, 1671, 176
*Whiting*; 177 *Samuel*; 178 *Jaram*; 179 *Denizen*; 180 *Oliver*,
was a farmer in Meriden, and died there; 181 *Loyal*; 182
*Harvey*; 183 *Sarah*; 184 *Philomelia*.

### 81. MOSES.

Dr. MOSES ANDREWS, son of Samuel and Abigail, married
Lucy ———. He died in Meriden, Oct. 2, 1811, æ. 77. She
died June 13, 1832, æ. 86 years.

### 82. AARON.

DR. AARON ANDREWS, son of Samuel and Abigail, married Sarah Whiting of Stamford, Dec. 18, 1771, and settled in
the old village of Wallingford. He owned and occupied the
house now owned and occupied by Samuel B. Parmelee Esq.,
during his life-time. She died Aug. 28, 1836, æ. 92 years,
5 months and 19 days.

Children: 185 *Sherlock*, b. Oct. 19, 1772, d. at Geneva, N. Y..
Aug. 28, 1795, m Selina, dau. of Samuel Tyler, of Wallingford; 186 *Betsey*, b. Dec. 11, 1774, m. Oliver Clark, and d.
Sept. 10, 1828, at Oswego, N.Y; 187 *John*, (M. D.) b. June
13, 1777, m. Abigail Atwater; 188 *William*, b. Dec. 26, 1779,
d. in St. Bartholomew, Nov. 9, 1809; 189 *Drake*, b. Dec.
27, 1781, m. Lucy Whittelsey, and d. in Illinois, May 21,
1841; 190 *Aaron*, b. Dec. 20, 1784, d. in the West Indies,
July, 30, 1837.

### 89. BARTHOLOMEW.

BARTHOLOMEW ANDREWS, son of Elisha and Mabel, married
Sarah Andrews, of Wallingford. They both died at Wallingford.

Children: 191 *Elisha*, b Jan 5, 1761; went to Ballston
Spa, N. Y.; 192 *Thomas*, b. May 17, 1762; d. in Walling-
ford, left Betsey and Orrin; 193 *Esther*, m Ezra Reid; 194
*Sally*, b. April 17, 1771, d. in Wallingford; 195 *Noah*, b.
April 17, 1744, d. in Wallingford; 196 Eunice, b. Sept. 8,

1776, m. Asaph Merriman, of Wallingford; 197 *Lyman*, settled at Ballston Spa, N. Y.; 198 *Caleb*, b. Nov. 11, 1782, went to Nova Scotia, N. B.; 199 *Margery*, m. Constant Abbot.

## 94. SAMUEL.

SAMUEL ANDREWS, son of William and Mary, married Lydia ———.

Children: 200 *Christopher*, b. Oct. 29, 1752; 201 *Lydia*, b. Dec. 29, 1757.

### 123. NATHANIEL.

NATHANIEL ANDREWS, son of Andrew and Esther, married Lois Blakeslee, May 7, 1781. He died Nov. 21. 1836, aged 75 years, 8 months and 1 day. Mrs. Lois his wife died, March 8, 1823, aged 61 years, 1 month and 29 days.

Children: 202 *Ira*, b Aug. 30, 1781, m. Julia, dau. of Jeremiah Hull; 203 *Andrew*, b Sept. 6, 1783; 204 *Salmon*, b April 3, 1788; 204 *Joseph*, b. Feb. 9, 1791; 205 *Polly*, b May 18, 1793, m Nathan Hull; 206 *Viney*, b Sept. 7, 1795; 207 *Orrin*, b. Dec. 4, 1797, m. —— Cook, dau. of Chester Cook; 208 *Nathaniel*, b 1800; 209 *Aaron*, b April 18, 1803; 210 *Ives*, b March 28, 1805.

### GIDEON.

GIDEON ANDREWS, married Hannah ———, and had at his decease the following

Children: 212 *Caleb*, m 1st, Esther Benham, May 22, 1727. She d. Oct. 25, 1727. Married 2d, Mary Culver, July 5, 1735; 213 *Jedediah;* 214 *Lydia;* 215 *Sarah:* 216 *Phebe;* 217 *Esther;* 218 *Samuel.*

### 170. AMOS.

AMOS ANDREWS, son of Nicholas and Lydia ———, married Content ———.

Children: 219 *Abigail*, b Feb. 17, 1752; 220 *Sybil*, b July 6, 1754; 221 *Lois*, b April 13, 1756; 222 *Mary*, b Mar. 18, 1758; 223 *Amos*, b Jan. 16, 1760.

TIMOTHY.

TIMOTHY ANDREWS married Temperance Griswold, Aug. 23, 1741. She died Nov. 25, 1743, a. 23. He married a second wife, Rachel. She died Jan. 11, 1756, aged 33. He settled at Newark Valley, near Oswego, N. Y.

Children by 1st wife: 224 *Lydia*, b Oct. 27, 1743; by 2d wife, 225 *Elisha*, b Dec. 12, 1746; 226 *Timothy*, b. April 27, 1749; 227 *Phineas*, b Nov. 25, 1752; 228 *Benjamin*, b Dec. 18, 1755.

### 185. SHERLOCK.

SHERLOCK ANDREWS, son of Doctor Aaron and ——, married Salina, daughter of Samuel Tyler, of Tyler's Mills, now Yalesville, Wallingford. He died at Geneva, N. Y., in 1795. She died at Columbus, Ohio, aged 94 or 95.

Children: 229 *Samuel*, was a lawyer at Columbus, Ohio, 230 *Sarah*, m. —— Wilcox, a lawyer at Columbus, Ohio.

### 187. JOHN.

Dr. JOHN ANDREWS, son of Dr. Aaron and ——, married Abigail, daughter of Caleb Atwater, by whom he had all his children. His 2d wife was Anna, daughter of Rev James and Anna Noyes.

Children: 231 Hon. *Sherlock J.*, b Nov. 1801, graduated at Yale, and a lawyer at Cleveland, Ohio ; 232 *Jane*, b Dec., 1803, m John M. Wolsey, Esq., of New Haven; 233 *William*, b 1806, a farmer at Elyria, Loraine Co., Ohio ; 234 *John Whiting*, b 1809, graduated at Yale. A lawyer at Columbus, Ohio.

### 189. DRAKE.

DRAKE ANDREWS, son of Dr. Aaron and ——, married Lucy Whittelsey, Oct 12, 1812. He died in Illisia, May 21, 1841. Of his family I have no further information.

### 229 IRA.

Col. IRA ANDREWS, son of Nathaniel and ——, married Julia Hall, daughter of the late Jeremiah Hall of Wallingford. He died Jan. 14, 1861, aged 79 years, 4 months, 15 days. She

was born the 5th of March, A. D. 1788, and is living Jan., 1870.
Children: 235 *Janet*, b June 9, 1806, m Miller ; 236 *Ali*, b
Mar. 6, 1800, resides in Bridgeport, Conn ; 237 *Gad*, b Nov.
19, 1803 ; 238–9 *Burr* and *Sarah* ( twins), b Oct, 14, 1806 ;
240 *Lee*, b April 2, 1809 ; 241 *Joseph D.*, b March 9, 1824 ;
242 *Jane*, b June 24, 1830.

## ATWATER.[1]

### JOHN.

JOHN, son of Daniel Atwater of New Haven, settled in
Wallingford in 1682 on a lot in the village designated as No.—
on the east side of the Main street, being forty rods long and
twenty rods wide, and was first settled by Daniel Atwater
for his son Joshua, who died before taking possession of it in
1680.    He was married to Abigail Mansfield, Sept. 13, 1682,
and was a weaver by trade.    She died Sept. 24, 1717.
Children: 1 *John*, b. Aug. 17, 1683, m. Elizabeth Mix,
Aug. 4, 1713 ; 2 *Abigail*, b Oct. 17, 1685 ; 3 *Mercy*, b Feb. 6,
1687 ; 4 *Hannah*, b Dec. 17, 1690 ; 5 *Joshua*, b Sept. 18,
1693, m. Mary Peck and Sarah Yale ; 6 *Moses*, b July 17,
1696. m. Sarah Merriman and Mary Hotchkiss ; 7 *Phineas*,
b Sept. 23, 1699, m. Mary Ward ; 8 *Ebenezer*, b Feb. 6,1703,
m. Jane Andrews ; 9 *Caleb*, b Oct. 9, 1705, m. Mehitable
Mix ; 10 *Benjamin*, b Dec. 8, 1708, m. Elizabeth Porter.

### I. JOHN.

JOHN, son of John and Abigail Atwater of Wallingford,
married Elizabeth, daughter of ——— Mix, August 4, 1713.
Children: 11 *Elizabeth*, b Nov. 17, 1721, m ———Ives ;
12 *Enos*, b Dec 3, 1717 ; 13 *Stephen*, b Sept. 8, 1714 ; 14
*John*, b Jan. 27, 1718 ; 15 *Sarah:* 16 *Hannah*, b Dec. 28,
1722, m Bela Hitchcock of Cheshire ; 17 *Ebenezer*, b 1723,
d. Oct. 21, 1755 ; 18 *Stephen*, b Feb. 2, 1720, m Elizabeth Yale.

1 Atwater's Gen. Reg. of Atwaters, 30 ; Hinman's Com. Settlers, 76 ;
Savage's Gen. Dict., I. 75, 76.

June 6, 1739 ; 19 *Titus*, b 1724, d. Dec. 26, 1758 ; 20 *Amos*, died without issue.

## 5. JOSHUA.

JOSHUA, son of John, m Mary, dau. of John Peck, 17 Jan. 1723 ; m 2nd, Sarah, dau. of Theophilus Yale, Sept. 4, 1740 He died Nov. 29, 1757.

Children: by 1st marriage ; 21 *Joshua*, b Mar. 8, 1724, d 1747 ; 22 *Mary*, b Feb. 12, 1727. By 2nd marriage : 23 *Caleb*, b Sept. 5, 1741 ; 24 *Sarah*, m —— Hall.*

## 6. MOSES.

MOSES, son of John Peck, m Sarah Merriman, Dec. 28, 1722. She died Feb. 1733, and he married 2nd, Mary Hotchkiss, Apr. 22, 1734.

Children : by 1st marriage ; 28 *Abigail*, b Sept. 13, 1725 ; 26 *Sarah*, b Oct. 29, 1727 ; 27 *Moses*, b Nov. 22, 1729 ; 28, *Mercy*, b Aug. 15, 1731. By 2nd marriage ; 29 *Elihu*, b Jan. 18, 1735 ; 30 *David*, b Feb. 23, 1736 ; 31 *Mary*, b Aug. 1. 1734 ; 32 *Hannah*, b May 1. 1739.

## 7. PHINEAS.

PHINEAS, son of John Atwater, m Mary Ward Nov. 9, 1727, and died Oct., 1781. He resided in Cheshire.

Children : 33 *Reuben*, b Oct. 13, 1728 ; 34 *William*, b 1730; 35 *Thomas*, b Aug 14, 1733 ; 36 *Phineas*, b Dec. 12, 1735 , 37 *Damaris*, b 1738, m Samuel Tyler of Wallingford ; 38 *Menab*, b July 8, 1741, d Sept. 13, 1754 ; *Ambrose*, b Dec. 19, 1743, m Sarah Tryon.

## 8 EBENEZER.

EBENEZER, son of John Atwater m, Jane Andrews, Dec. 30, 1737.

Children : 40 *Caleb*, b Sept. 8, 1738, m Phebe Talmage ; 41 *Samuel*, b January 30, 1740, m Hannah Bristol ; 42 *Ebenezer*, b July 13, 1742 ; 43 *Ephraim*, b Nov. 27, 1743, m Abigail Rowe ; 44 *Esther*, b Feb. 4, 1716 ; 45 *Elizabeth*, b April 13, 1748 ; 46 *Abigail*, b Sept. 19, 1754 ; 47 *Comfort*, b March 16, 1757.

#### 9. CALEB.

CALEB, son of John Atwater, married Mehitable Mix, Nov. 10, 1726.

Children: 48 *Sarah*, b Nov, 28, 1727 ; 49 *Eunice*, b Sept. 10, 1786, m Phineas Cook.

#### 10. BENJAMIN.

BENJAMIN, son of John Atwater, married Elizabeth Porter, Nov. 28, 1739. She died January 13, 1774, æ. 66 years.

Children: 50 *Elizabeth*, b April 25, 1780; 51 *Mary*, b Dec. 20, 1735 ; 52 *Comfort*, b Sept. 19, 1749, d January 22, 1789 ; 53 *Benjamin*, b January 9, 1750, d January 19, 1781.

#### 12. ENOS.

ENOS, son of John 2nd, married Hannah Moss, July 9, 1740. Children: 54 *Heman*, b March 4, 1743, d Sept. 27, 1752 ; 55 *Asaph*, b Aug. 1, 1745 ; 56 *Mehitable*, b July 23, 1747, m Eli Bronson of Waterbury ; 50 *Enos*, b Oct. 25, 1748, m Hannah Moss, July 3, 1741 ; 58 *Eunice*, b Sept., 1750 ; 59 *Heman*, b Aug. 29, 1752, went to Southington ; 60 *Kezia*, b Oct. 10, 1754 ; 62 *Anna*, b Nov. 17, 1756 ; 63 *Titus*, b Jan. 6, 1761.

#### 14. JOHN.

JOHN, son of John 2d, m Hannah Thompson, Feb. 22, 1744. Children : 63 *Jeremiah*, b Nov. 10, 1744 ; 64 *Phebe*, b Aug. 11, 1747, m —— Dutton ; 65 *Hannah*, b Feb. 17, 1749, m Samuel Hull of Cheshire ; 66 *John;* 67 *Jesse;* 68 *Mary*, m —— Peck of Waterbury.

#### 18. STEPHEN.

STEPHEN, son of John 2d, m Hannah Hotchkiss, Feb. 23, 1744.

Children: 69 *Elizabeth*, b Sept. 12. 1746 ; 70 *Lois*, m John Upson ; 71 *Stephen*, b Sept. 4, 1749, d Aug. 25, 1750; 72 *Sarah*, b Nov. 25, 1751, m Enos Johnson ; 73 *Hannah*, b Nov. 27, 1754, m John Hall ; 74 *Naomi*, b Aug. 17. 1756, m Enos Bushnell ; 75 *Ruth*, b Aug. 17, 1756, m Jonathan Hall ; 76 *Stephen*, b May 13, 1758.

#### 19. TITUS.

TITUS, son of John 2nd, m Margaret Scott, Dec, 14, 1758,

Children: 77 *Chloe*, b Sept. 29, 1750. m Samuel Cook ; 78 *Amos*, b June 12, 1752, m Mary- , his wife d Oct. 2, 1799, a 38 ; 79 *Miriam*, b 1754. m Calvin Cowles ; 80 *Rhoda*, b May 15, 1756.

### 23. CALEB.

CALEB, son of Joshua and Sarah, m Abigail Jones for his 1st wife, and Ruth Wadsworth, Jan. 22, 1776, for his 2nd wife.

Children : 81 *Sarah*, b July 19, 1767 ; 82 *Mary*, b April 23, 1769 ; 83 *Lucy*, b Dec. 8, 1770 : 84 *Joshua*, b Feb. 8, 1773, m Elizabeth Cook, dau. of Aaron : 85 *James W.*, b June 30, 1777 ; d Oct. 30, 1777 ; 86 *Abigail*, b Dec. 13, 1778, m Doct. John Andrews ; 87 *Catharine*; 88 *Ruth*.

### 27. MOSES.

MOSES, of Wallingford, son of Moses, m Emma Newton, Dec. 18, 1755.

Children : 89 *Sarah*, b Nov. 16, 1755 ; 90 *Lyman*, lived in Broad Swamp, Cheshire.

### 29. ELIHU.

ELIHU, of Wallingford, son of Moses, married Abigail Tryon.

Children : 91 *Freeman*, b Feb. 16, 1766. went to Canandaigua, N. Y. ; 92 *Mary*, b March 2, 1767 ; 93 *Abiah*, b Nov. 3, 1769 ; 94 *Sally*, b Jan. 23, 1773 ; 95 *Elihu*, b June 9. 1776, went South ; 96 *Jesse*, was Postmaster at New Haven, m Widow Hudson, left no children.

### 30. DANIEL.

DANIEL, son of Moses of Wallingford, was an apothecary at New Haven, m Eunice Thompson of Stratford, Nov. 15, 1770, and was killed in a skirmish with the British troops at Compo Hill, April 28. 1777.

Children : 97 *Chester*, b Dec. 21. 1772. d Mar. 30, 1773 ; 98 *Chester*, b April 14, 1774, no issue ; 99 *Sylvester*, b Feb. 17, 1776, d Sept. 9. 1776 ; 100 *David*, b 1777, graduated at Yale 1797, d 1805.

### 33. REUBEN.

REUBEN, son of Phineas of Wallingford, m Sarah Hull N

April 29, 1752, and Mary Russel January 28, 1755.   He died Aug. 19, 1801.

Children: 101 *Sarah*, b June 14, 1753 ; 102 *Merab*, b June 19, 1757 ; 103 *Phineas*, b Nov. 25, 1758 ; 104 *Elizabeth M. A.*, b Sept., 1760, m Andrew Hull of Cheshire ; 105 *Russel*, b June 20, 1762, went to Blandford, Mass. ; 106 *Nabby*, b April 2, 1764, m Dr. Elnathan Beach of Cheshire ; 107 *Amaryllis*, b April 2, 1764, m Titus Street of Wallingford, Cheshire, and of New Haven ; 108 *Reuben*, b May 18, 1767.

### 34. WILLIAM.

WILLIAM, son of Phineas, of Wallingford, married Esther Tuttle.

Children : 109 *Rufus*, b Nov. 29, 1754, m 1st, Mary Tuttle of Wallingford, Dec. 18, 1777.   He removed to Nova Scotia ; 110 *Lyman*, b Feb. 8, 1757 ; 111 *William*, b Feb. 16, 1759, went to Nova Scotia ; 112 *Chloe*, b Sept. 21, 1763 ; 113 *Ira*, b June 21, 1765, d April 4, 1738, in Wallingford ; 114 *Asenath*, b Oct. 30, 1768 ; 115 *Esther*, b Oct. 4, 1771 ; 116 *Ward*, went to Nova Scotia.

### 36. PHINEAS.

PHINEAS married Mary ———, and 2nd, widow Hannah Ives, of Goshen, Conn., June 15, 1760.

Child : 117 *Ward*, b 1760.

### 39. AMBROSE.

AMBROSE, son of Phineas, married Sarah Tryon.

Children : 118 *Amelia*, b July 3, 1767, m Thaddeus Tuttle; 119 *Linus*, b July 23, 1769 ; 120 *Jonathan*, b Oct. 18, 1770 ; 121 *Ambrose*, b April 5, 1773, d June 23, 1778 : 122 *Thomas*, b April 19, 1774 ; 123 *Sarah*, b April 19, 1775 ; 124 *Mary*, b Oct, 17, 1778 ; 125 *Phineas*, b July 12, 1782 ; 126 *Menab*, b April 17, 1782, m John P. Wetmore ; 127 *Clara C.*, b May 6, 1786, m Joshua Tuttle ; 128 *William*, b May 9, 1789.

### 40. CALEB.

CALEB, son of Ebenezer, of Wallingford, m Phebe Tallmage.

Children: 129 *June*, b Nov. 17, 1765; 130 *Ebenezer*, b Feb. 16, 1768.

### 41. SAMUEL.

SAMUEL, son of Ebenezer, m Hannah Bristol, May 5, 1768. Children: 131 *Silvia*, b Feb. 21, 1769, m ―――― Winchell, 132 *Merab*, b May 11, 1771, m ―――― Ives, d 1857; 133 *Samuel*, b Oct. 7, 1773, d in Orange, Conn.; 134 *Joshua*, b Feb. 20, 1779; 135 *Ebenezer*, d in Cheshire.

### 43. EPHRAIM.

EPHRAIM, son of Ebenezer, m Abigail Rowe, d Oct. 22, 1776, at Danbury, Conn.

Children: 136 *Lovely*, b Oct. 26, 1772, m Noah Andrews, of Wallingford; 137 *Eunice*, b Sept. 18, 1744, m ―――― Matthews; 138 *Ephraim*, b March 5, 1777.

### STEPHEN.

STEPHEN, son of David, settled in Meriden, then in Wallingford, m Elizabeth Yale. He came from New Haven.

Children: 139 *Ruth*, b June 6, 1740; 140 *Stephen*, b Sept. 16, 1742, settled in Cheshire; 141 *Eunice*, b Sept. 28, 1744; 142 *Daniel*, b Aug. 30, 1747, d unmarried; 143 *Mary*, b June 25, 1750, m ―――― Merriam; 144 *Elizabeth*, b July 27, 1752; 145 *Christopher*, b Jan. 6, 1757, d Sept. 10, 1776; 146 *Isaac*, b Dec., 1758.

### ABRAHAM.

ABRAHAM, son of Jonathan, the son of Jonathan, the son of Daniel, the son of David, m Mary Bull in May, 1738, and settled in Cheshire, then belonging to Wallingford. He died Jan. 4, 1786, æ 70 yrs. She died May 15, 1811, æ 83 yrs.

Children: 146 *Esther*, b Dec. 19, 1738; 147 *Mary*, b April 28, 1740; 148 *Chloe*, b Oct. 27, 1742; 149 *Isaac*, b June 15, 1746; 150 *Lois*, b June 12, 1749; 151 *Timothy*, b Oct. 30, 1751; 152 *Abigail*; 153 *Samuel*, b 1757 died Jan. 12, 1748; 154 *Esther*, b Dec. 10, 1763

### BENJAMIN.

BENJAMIN, son of Joseph Atwater, the son of Jonathan, m

Phebe ————. She died March 1, 1799, æ 64. He died Feb. 6, 1799, æ 72.

Children: 155 *Joseph;* 156 *Sarah,* b April 26, 1756, m Charles Hull, 2nd, Aaron Hall, of Wallingford ; 157 *Benjamin,* b Sept. 26, 1757 ; 158 *Titus,* b Aug. 29, 1759. d unm. at Cheshire ; 159 *Moses,* b May 12, 1765, d at Canandaigua, N. Y. ; 160 *Aaron,* b Nov. 10, 1776 ; 161 *Joel,* b April 22, 1769 ; 162 *Anna,* b Aug. 23, 1777, d Aug. 29, 1776 ; 163 *Jeremiah,* d in Canandaigua ; 164 *Anna,* m Stephen Jarvis, of Cheshire.·

### JOSEPH.

JOSEPH, son of Joseph, son of Jonathan, son of Daniel of Wallingford, m Phebe Hall, Aug. 18, 1756. He d Aug. 22, 1769. She d March 23, 1767, æ. 23 yrs..

Child : 165 *Phebe,* b Oct. 15, 1757, d Jan. 19, 1766, æ. 9 yrs.

### 54. HEMAN.

HEMAN, son of Enos Atwater, settled at Southington, and was the owner of Atwater mills.

### 84. JOSHUA.

JOSHUA, son of Caleb, of Wallingford, m Elizabeth Cook, dau. of Aaron Cook, Oct. 22, 1793.

Children : 166 *Elizabeth,* b Aug. 4, 1794, m John Barker ; 167 *Caroline,* b June 17, 1796, m Dr. Jared P. Kirtland ; 168 *Emily,* b Feb. 7, 1798, m Dr. Friend Cook ; 169 *Abigail,* b Dec. 28, 1800, d at Durham, Sept. 23, 1823 ; 170 *Mary,* b Oct. 18, 1802, d July 24, 1804 ; 171 *Caleb,* b July 11, 1804, m Julia A. Royce, and 2nd, Elizabeth S. Clark ; 172 *Joshua,* b Aug. 26, 1806, m Mary H. Day ; 173 *Thomas Cook,* b Aug. 20, 1808, m Harriet E. Cook ; 174 *Lucretia,* b June 26, 1800, d June 29, 1822 ; 155 *Edgar,* b Oct 12, 1812, m Sarah S. Yale, d 1860 ; 176 *John,* b Jan. 19, 1815, m Caroline, and 2nd, Eliza Hall, dau. of Russel Hall ; 177 *William,* b Aug. 5, 1817, m Elizabeth Helfenstein ; 178 *Mary Ann,* b May 29, 1819, m Lieut. Garrit Barry.

### 105. RUSSEL.

RUSSEL, son of Reuben Atwater, of Cheshire (then Wallingford), m Clarissa Chapman, Oct. 24, 1790, and died Oct. 3 1798. She was born Nov. 22, 1762

Children: 179 *Phineas*, b Nov. 10, 1791; 180 *Merab*, b April 28, 1793, d March 19, 1794; 181 *Russell*, b Jan. 8, 1795, d Dec. 22, 1823. 182 *Fredrick*, b Nov. 6, 1796; 183 *Henry*, b Sept. 21, 1798; 184 *Thomas*, b Sept. 21, 1798, d April 15, 1803.

## 108. REUBEN.

REUBEN, son of Reuben Atwater, m Eliza Willard, and 2d, Sarah Lamb. He died February, 1831.

Children: 183 *Catharine*; 184 *Clinton Edward*.

## 113. IRA.

IRA, son of William Atwater, m Lois ——. He was a shoemaker, and lived and died at what is now Yalesville.

Children: 185 *Mary*, m and went to Bethany; 186 *Martha*, m Henry Hough; 187 *William*, d March, 1828; 188 *John*, d South; 189 *Luman*, of Fair Haven, Conn.; 190 *Esther;* 191 *Lois;* 192 *Chloe.*

## 116. WARD.

WARD, son of Phineas, m Abigail Atwater. She died in New Haven in 1822.

Children: 193 *Rebecca*, b Sept. 23, 1787, d Sept 22, 1788; 194 *Harriet*, b Feb. 23, 1789, d May, 1795; 195 *James*, b May 1, 1790, d Oct. 21, 1791; 196 *James Ward*, b Feb. 11, 1794, d Dec. 8, 1820; 197 *William*, b June 20, 1795, d Jan. 1810; 198 *Harriet*, b March 14, 1797, d Sept., 1798; 199, *Abigail*, b Sept. 4, 1798, d Nov. 11, 1799; 200 *Richard*, b March 25, 1802, d Oct. 3, 1848; 210 *Edward*, b June 29, 1803; 202 *Charlotte*, b Sept., 1804.

## 120. AMBROSE.

AMBROSE, son of Phineas Atwater, m Sarah Tryon

Children: 203 *Amelia*, b July 3, 1767, m Thaddeus Tuttle; 204 *Linus*, b Feb. 22, 1769; 205 *Jonathan*, b Oct. 18, 1770; 206 *Ambrose*, b April 5, 1773, d June 23, 1778; 207 *Thomas*, b April 19, 1775; 280 *Sarah*, b Feb. 11, 1777, m Asa Lyon;

209 *Mary*, b Oct 17, 1778, m Peter B. Smith; 210 *Phineas*, b July 12, 1770; 211 *Merab*, b April 17, 1782, m John P. Wetmore; 212 *Clara*, b May 6, 1786, m Joshua Fuller; 213 *William*, b May 9, 1789.

### 137. STEPHEN.

STEPHEN, son of Stephen and Elizabeth Yale Atwater, m Anna Moss, March 23, 1780. Settled in Cheshire.

Children: 214 *Hannah H.*, b Feb. 8, 1781; 215 *Richard*. b Feb. 10, 1783; 216 *Tempa*, b Sept. 11, 1787; 217 *Anna Maria*, b Aug. 28, 1789; 218 *Betsey*, b Dec. 9, 1794; 219 *Merab*, b June 22, 1797; 220 *Matilda*, b June 5, 1805.

### 147. ISAAC.

ISAAC, son of Abraham Atwater, son of Jonathan of Cheshire, settled in Columbia, now Prospect, m Eunice —♦—, May 16, 1771. He died Sept. 13, 1776, at New York.

Children: 221 *Pamelia*. b March 28, 1772; 222 *Abraham*, b March, 6, 1774; 223 *Hannah*, b Oct. 15, 1775.

### 149. TIMOTHY.

TIMOTHY. son of Abraham Atwater, son of Jonathan of Cheshire, m Lucy ——.

Children: 224 *Deborah*, b May 28, 1773; 225 *Lucy*, b Aug. 8. 1775; 226 *Cato*, b Oct. 18, 1777; 227 *Isaac*, b Oct. 5, 1779; 228 *Lucinda*, m March 4, 1782; 229 *Timothy Glover*, b July 20, 1784, d in Cheshire; 230 *Charlotte*, b July 22, 1786; 231 *Phineas*, b Jan. 20, 1789; 232 *Esther*, b July 1, 1791; 233 *Aaron*, b March 11. 1793, m Betsey Atsom.

### 151. SAMUEL.

SAMUEL, son of Abraham Atwater, son of Jonathan, settled in Cheshire, m Patience ——.

Children: 204 *Flamen*, b March 30, 1783; 235 *Roxanna*, b Jan. 15, 1785; 236 *Nancy*, b May 15, 1789; 237 *Nancy*, 2d, b Sept. 13, 1789; 238 *Mary Ann*, b Jan. 4, 1792; 239 *Patience*, b March 13, 1794; 240 *Nabby Ann*, b Dec. 13, 1797, 241 *Abigail Ann*, b Oct. 19, 1800; 242 *Lois*, b July 15, 1803; 243 *Lois Maria*, b Feb. 13, 1806, m Joseph Hitchcock of Cheshire.

### 153. JOSEPH.

JOSEPH, son of Benjamin of Cheshire, m Hannah Hitchcock, Sept. 17, 1783.

Children: 244 *Joseph Hall*, b Feb. 29, 1784, m, had *Joseph H.*; 245 *Phebe*, b Nov. 25, 1786; 246 *Almon*, b March 5. 1788; 247 *Hannah*, b April 20, 1790, m Belina Clark of Cheshire; 248 *Freeman*, b April 17, 1796, m —— Beach.

## BEAUMONT.

### DEODATE.

DEODATE BEAUMONT was born in Wallingford as early as the commencement of the present century, and perhaps earlier. He was a mechanic and farmer, and owned and occupied the house and lot now owned by his son Elijah Beaumont in Wallingford.

Children: *John; Elijah; Elizabeth*

## BARKER.[1]

### JOHN.

JOHN and SARAH BARKER were in Wallingford previous to 1739, from Branford, where he was born. He built the large brick house now owned by Samuel C. Ford, Esq. His farm was a large one, and one of the best in the county of New Haven. Of his history very little can now be learned.

Children: 1 *Sarah*, b July 22, 1739; 2 *John*, b May 2, 1741; 3 *Mary*, b March 10. 1742, m Solomon Johnson; 4 *Edward*, m Rachel, dau. of Constant Kirtland; 5 *Eunice*, m John Beadles, Jan. 18. 1764.

1 For collateral branches, see Abbott's Hist. Andover, Mass., 20-1; Barry's Hist. Hanover, Mass., 206-7; Blood's Hist. Temple, N. H., 203; Bolton's Hist. Westchester Co., N. Y., 501; Deane' Hist. Scituate, Mass., 216; Eaton's Hist. Thomaston, Me., 130; Goodman's Fowl family Gen., 189; Hanson's Hist. Gardner, Me., 156; Savage's Gen. Dict., I. 115, 116.

## 4. EDWARD.

EDWARD BARKER, son of John and Sarah Barker, m Rachel, dau. of Constant and Rachel Kirtland of Wallingford, and remained on the old homestead until his death.

Children: 6 *John*, m Elizabeth Atwater, of Wallingford ; 7 *Sarah*, m Wm. H. Jones, New Haven.

## BEACH.[1]

Genealogists have been somewhat divided and in doubt regarding the earliest families of this name. Hinman assigns John of Stratford, to Thomas of Milford ; but John of Stratford had two children born to him before John the son of the Milford Thomas was born. Savage thinks John of Stratford was probably son of Richard of New Haven, if not his brother. Savage also thinks Benjamin of Stratford was son of Richard of New Haven. But if so, he would have been only fifteen years old when first announced in Stratford, which is out of the question. The probabilities seem to indicate that John, Benjamin and Richard, who all appear in Stratford, and Thomas of Milford, were brothers. The latter had a home lot in Milford in 1648. The Beaches of Litchfield, and George Beach Esq. of Hartford, are said to be of this stock. Richard Beach of New Haven I take to be the man who was in Stratford in 1663, and as keeper of the ordinary or tavern, desired a grant of land from the town, and also exemption from military duty. He bought of Thomas Wheeler, who bought from Robert Rice, the lot where Mr. Meacham now lives. Wheeler moved to Pagusset ( Derby), and sold to R. Beach, who sold to Mr. Fenn of Milford, and he sold in 1667 to Rev. Israel Chauncey, the second pastor of the Congregational church in Stratford, part of this land, with part of the land owned by John Brinsmade, one of the first settlers ( on the river side), and

---

1 For collateral branches, see Hinman's Conn. settlers, 163, 164 ; Littell's Passaic Valley Gen., 35–7 ; Savage's Gen. Dict.. I. 144.

the land owned by William Beardsley, with a piece of Nicholas Knell's lot on the back street and now (1868) owned by Alfred E. Beach, son of the late Moses Yale Beach of Wallingford, a lineal descendant of John, brother of Richard.

Benjamin Beach, a brother also of John, as I suppose, was in Stratford in 1659. From him descended Benjamin Beach, the merchant and owner of vessels, who was a man of property and built the old house that was taken down by Mr. Patterson some years ago, and which stood where Mr. Dutcher, in 1863, lived. Benjamin Beach senior's descendants settled in part in Trumbull. The year of John Beach's birth is now unknown: he died suddenly, intestate, in 1667, and the names of his ten children are given on the probate records, but not that of his wife. He became one of the original proprietors of Wallingford, and is represented in the inventory of his estate as having property in Wallingford to the amount of £92 19s.; and in Stratford to the amount of £312 13s. He seems to have bought in Wallingford with a view to the settlement of his sons there. John Jr., Isaac and Thomas removed to Wallingford, but the first two died in Stratford. Indeed, Isaac in 1694 united with Stratford church, and is entered as of Wallingford. His grave-stone with that of his brother Nathaniel's and also of Nathaniel's wife, yet remain in the old cemetery at Stratford. As John Beach senior's estate was administered in Fairfield county probate court, he evidently had not transferred his residence to Wallingford.

References in the Stratford Records establish the identity of the Wallingford Beaches with the family of John Beach of Stratford, through his son Thomas principally, as will be seen.

Children of John Beach of Stratford: 1 *Elizabeth*, b March 8, 1652, m Eliasaph Preston, went to Wallingford; *John*, b April, 1654, m Hannah, dau. of Thomas Staples of Fairfield, 1679; 3 *Mary*, b Sept., 1656; 4 *Thomas*, b May, 1659, m Ruth Peck of Wallingford, and 2nd, Phebe, dau. of Timothy Willcoxen; 5 *Nathaniel*, b March, 1662, m Sarah Porter, April 29,

1693, went to Wallingford ; 6 *Hannah,* b Dec., 1665, m Zachariah Fairchild, Nov. 3, 1681, after his decease she m John Barrit ; 7 *Sarah,* b Nov., 1667 ; 8 *Isaac,* b June 27, 1659, m Hannah Birdsey, was a tailor in Stratford ; 9 *Joseph,* b Feb. 5, 1671, m Abiah, dau. of Ebenezer Booth ; 10 *Benjamin,* b March, 1674, m Mary —————.

John Beach's house lot extended from Main-st, to Back-st, originally called Front street, and covered the present lots now occupied by the Masonic Lodge, Alfred Barnet and Mrs. Hubbell, with a part of Mrs. Linsley's and Miss Poor's grounds.

I will now attempt to trace, so far as I can by existing records, the settlement and increase of the above named ten children of John Beach of Stratford:

### 1. ELIZABETH.

ELIZABETH m Eliasaph Preston. He was born with his twin brother Hackaliah, April 9, 1643 : was a son of William Preston, one of the first settlers of New Haven. Their mother was probably William Preston's 2d wife, and a daughter of Robert Seabrook, another of whose daughters was the wife of Thos. Fairchild, and an original proprietor in Stratford. Eliasaph Preston removed to Wallingford soon after its settlement in 1674, and was the first Deacon of the Congregational church in that place. He died in 1705, æ. 62 years. Elizabeth was his second wife. His first wife Mary Kimberly died in 1674, April 28. She was the widow of Thos. Kimberly, and died in 1672.

The children of Eliasaph and Elizabeth Preston were: 11 *Elizabeth,* b Jan. 29, 1676 ; 12 *Hannah,* b July 12, 1678 ; 13 *Eliasaph,* b Jan. 26, 1679–80 ; 14 *Joseph,* b March 10, 1681–2 ; 15 *Esther,* b Feb. 28, 1683–4 ; 16 *Lydia,* b May 25, 1686 ; 17 *Jehiel,* b Aug. 25, 1688, d Nov., 1689.

### 2. JOHN.

JOHN BEACH m Hannah, dau. of Thomas Staples of Fairfield, 1679.

Their children recorded at Stratford were: 18 *Mary,*

b July 14, 1683, m Archibald Dunlap, June, 1704, and 2nd,
———— Smith ; 10 *Ruth*, b about 1685, m Samuel Fairchild,
1704 , 2 : *Mehitable*, b Sept. 30, 1690 ; 21 *Ebenezer*, b Sept.
14, 1692 ; 22 *Hester*, b May 3, 1694. John Beach 2nd d in
Stratford, 1712.

### 4. THOMAS.

THOMAS BEACH, married 1st, Ruth Peck, a sister of John
Peck, and settled in Wallingford May 12, 1680 ; 2nd, Phebe,
dau of Timothy Willcoxen of Stratford. She was born in 1669.
Her father was son of William, an original proprietor of
Stratford, whose house-lot was situated about where Mrs.
Turk's home-lot now lies ( 1863 ), and probably covered Mr.
Wm. Benjamin's lot besides. Phebe's mother was Johannah,
dau. of Deacon John Birdsey, an original proprietor of Strat
ford.

Children : 23 *Hannah*, b Feb. 26, 1680, d Sept. 18, 1683 :
24 *Ruth*, b Oct. 24, 1684, died young ; 25 *Thomas*, b Dec. 9,
1685, d Dec. 13, 1685 : 26 *Benoni*, b Oct. 20, 1686, d Dec. 5,
1686. Mrs. Ruth Beach died Dec. 5, 1686. Children by
2nd marriage : 27 *Timothy*, b Jan. 11, 1689, m Hannah
Cook, Nov. 25, 1713 ; 28 *Nathan*, b Aug. 18, 1692, m
Jemima Curtiss, Sept. 29, 1713 ; 29 *Moses*, b Feb. 19, 1695, m
Esther Tyler, Sept. 21, 1722, 2nd Susannah ———— ; 30 *Gershom*,
b May 23, 1697, m Deliverance How of Wallingford ; 31 *Caleb*,
m Eunice ———— : 32 *Thankful*, b Sept. 20, 1702 ; 33 *Phebe*, b
May 23, 1710 ; 34 *Joanna*, b Oct. 9, 1705, m Mr. Royce. Mr.
Thomas Beach died in Meriden, where he was buried in the
old cemetery, May 13, 1741, æ 82 years.

### 5. NATHANIEL.

NATHANIEL BEACH m Sarah Porter, daughter of Nathaniel
Porter. She was born 1667. Her mother was a daughter of
Philip Groves, the first and only ruling elder in Stratford
church. She died in 1738, and her grave-stone yet stands
with that of her husband who died in 1747.

Children : 35 *Ephraim*, b May 25, 1687, m 1712, Sarah,
dau. of Andrew Patterson, d Oct. 30, 1717 ; 36 *Elizabeth*, b

Nov 11, 1689 ; 37 *David*, b May 15, 1692, m 1717, Hannah
Sherman, dau. of Matthew, son of Samuel Sen. : 38 *Josiah*, b
Aug. 18. 1694, m 1722, Patience Nichols : 39 *Nathaniel*, b
Dec. 22, 1696, m 1720. Sarah, dau. of Solomon Burton, d 1734 ;
40 *Sarah*, b Nov. 12, 1699 ; 41 *Daniel*, b Jan 15, 1700, m
1724, Hester, dau. of Benj. Curtiss, son of John, son of William Curtiss ; 42 *Anna*, b March, 1704, m Elnathan Beers, Jan.
25, 1728 ; 43 *Israel*, b May, 1705, m 1731, Hannah Barrett,
dau. of Joseph, son of John, son of William.; 44 *James*, b
Aug. 13, 1709, m Sarah Curtiss 1710, dau. of John, son of
Benjamin, son of John.

### 8. ISAAC.

ISAAC BEACH, married Hannah Birdsey, daughter of John,
in 1693. Mr. Birdsey was a son of John, an original settler
in Stratford. Her mother was Phebe, daughter of William
Willcoxen, also among the first settlers of Stratford. Hannah was born February, 1671. Isaac Beach settled in Wallingford on land given him by his father John Beach, but in
1694 was received into the church at Stratford as from Wallingford. He died in Stratford in 1741, and his grave-stone
still remains. Hannah his wife died Oct. 15, 1750, in her 79th
year, and was buried in the Episcopal burying-ground, Stratford. He sold land in Wallingford to Joseph Rice in 1699.

Children: 45 *William*, b July 7, 1794, m Sarah Hull of
Derby, dau. of Joseph Hull ; 46 *Elnathan*, b July 7, 1698, m
Abigail Uffont, 2d, Hannah, dau. of Samuel Cook ; 47 *John*,
b Oct. 6, 1700, Episcopal clergyman at Newtown, Ct., d Mar.
19, 1782 ; 48 *Mary*, b Dec. 16, 1703 ; 49 *Hannah*, b May 26,
1709 ; 50 *Dinah*, b Oct. 14, 1713.

### 9. JOSEPH.

JOSEPH BEACH, son of John No. 1, married Abiah, dau. of
Ebenezer Booth, son of Richard, an original settler in Stratford. He died in 1737, æ. 66. His grave-stone yet remains.

Children : 51 *Sarah*, b July 13, 1697 ; 52 *Agar*, b April 8.
1699 ; 53 *Abraham*, b April 29, 1701 ; 54 *Hannah*, b Feb. 12,
1702, m Zachariah Tomlinson, grandson of Henry and great

grandfather of Gov. Gideon Tomlinson, d in 1812 55 *Jo-seph*: 56 *Huah*. b Jan. 12, 1712 13, m Samuel Judson in 1737. His first wife in 1734 was Bethiah Beach.

### 10. BENJAMIN.

BENJAMIN BEACH of Stratford, m Mary ——.
Children: 57 *Bethia*, b April 23, 1674; 58 *Peter*, b Sept. 14, 1696; 59 *Eunice*, b Aug. 3, 1690; 60, 61, *Benjamin* and *Mary*, b May 19, 1702, the former went to Durham, Conn.

### 46. ELNATHAN.

ELNATHAN BEACH, son of Isaac and Hannah Beach, was a merchant settled in Wallingford, in the southerly part of what is now Cheshire, and for several years was engaged with Captain Samuel Cooke, in foreign trade, in which they were very successful. Mr. Beach soon became a man of great wealth and high standing in the community. He presented the Congregational society of Cheshire with a bell for their meeting-house, and by his last will left a bequest of several pounds as a fund for the relief of the poor of the parish of Cheshire. He married first Miss Abigail Ufford of Stratford, May 9, 1720. She died Dec. 2, 1738. He married second, Hannah, daughter of Capt. Samuel Cooke, Feb. 8, 1742. She died May 18, 1754, æ. 21 years. He died Aug. 16, 1742, æ 45 years.

Children by first marriage; 79 *Isaac*, b April 7, 1721, d Jan. 27, 1724; 80 *Elnathan*, b July 21, 1723, at Cheshire, d May 18, 1754, æ 31, 81 *Isaac*, b March 3, 1725, d Oct. 13, 1471, æ 16 years; 82 *John*, b 1733, a farmer at Cheshire; 83 *Hannah*, b Nov. 12, 1728; 84 *Abigail*, b Dec. 17, 1730; 85 *Samuel*, b Dec 26, 1737, Dea. of the church, grad. a ord. at Y. 1757; 86 *Sarah*, b March 25, 1727, m Jonathan Atwater of New Haven; 87 *Lois*, b Aug 18, 1732, m Col. Thaddeus Cook of Wallingford, d April 4, 1753; 88 *Esther*.

Child by second marriage: 89 *Abraham*, b Aug. 29, 1743, graduated at Yale, 1757, and was a distinguished clergyman of the Protestant Episcopal Church in the city of New York. He died 1828, æ. 85 years.

## 45. WILLIAM.

WILLIAM BEACH, eldest son of Isaac and Hannah Beach of Stratford, married Sarah Hull, daughter of Joseph Hull of Derby (ancestor of Com. Isaac Hull), in 1725. Her mother was Mary Nichols, dau. of Isaac 2d of Stratford and Derby. Children: 62 *Isaac*, b and bap. Oct., 1726, bap. in the Cong. church, Stratford ; 63 *Ann*, b April, bap. May, 1729, m Wm. Sam'l Johnson, bap. in Cong. church ; 64 *Abel*, b and bap. Nov. 31, 1731, m Mary Lewis 1757, d 1768 ; 65, 66 *Henry* and *Abijah*, b May, 1734, bap. in the Episcopal church.

## 63. ANN.

ANN BEACH, daughter of William and Sarah Hull Beach, married in Nov., 1749, at the age of 20 years, Wm. Sam'l Johnson, aged 22 years, son of Rev. Samuel D. D. by his wife Charity, wid. of Benj. Nichols, oldest son of Hon. Matthias Nichols of Islip, L. I. Wm. Samuel Johnson had by wife Ann,

Children : 67 *Charity*, b July, 1750; 68 *Sarah*, b April, 1754; 69 *Gloriance Ann*, b March, 1757 ; 70 *Mary*, b April, 1759; 71 *Samuel William*, b Oct., 1761 ; 72 *Elizabeth*, b Dec., 1763 ; 73 *Robert Charles*, b May, 1766.

## 71. SAMUEL.

SAMUEL WM. JOHNSON, son of Anna and Wm. Samuel Johnson, married Nov., 1791, Susan, dau. of Pierrepont Edwards Esq., and grand-daughter of Rev. President J. Edwards. Children : 74 *Anna Frances :* 75 *William Samuel ;* 76 *Sarah Elizabeth ;* 77 *Edwards ;* 78 *Robert Charles.*

## 85. SAMUEL.

DEA. SAMUEL BEACH graduated at Yale College in 1757. He was an Attorney at Law in his native town, Cheshire, and was a highly respected citizen. and filled with honor many offices of public trust, and was a delegate to the convention which formed the constitution of the United States. He married Mary ——.

Children ; 90 *Mary Ann*, b July 31, 1760; 91 *Samuel IV.*,

b Feb. 11, 1762, was a farmer in Cheshire, where he died
Sons, Samuel W., Albert and Rufus. By second marriage, 12
*Burrag*, m      Bowden, was a graduate of Yale College in
1793 and became an Attorney at Law in his native town,
where he died æ. 70. He had daughters, Elizabeth, wife of
Rev. Dr. Fuller, Augusta, Amelia.

## 29. MOSES.

MOSES BEACH, son of Thomas and Phebe, of Wallingford,
married Esther Tyler, Sept. 26, 1722. She died Sept. 16,
1750, æ 55. He married Susannah ———. She died
April 9, 1770, æ 62 yrs. Mr. Beach died in Wallingford.
He was a farmer and resided on, and owned the farm called
(at the present time) the Wooden Farm, in the southern
part of Yalesville.

Children: 93 *Ephraim*, b Aug. 2, 1723, m Lydia - —, d
August 29, 1751; 94 *Titus*, b April 4, 1725; 95 *Moses*, b
Nov. 8, 1726, m Dinah Sperry, March 19, 1756; 96 *Lois*, b
April 29, 1729, d Jan. 4, 1731; 97 *Esther*, b May 16, 1731;
98 *Asahel*, b Jan. 11, 1736, m Keziah Roys, Feb. 11, 1757, and
settled in Westbury in Waterbury, previous to 1764.

## 28. NATHAN.

NATHAN BEACH, son of Thomas and Phebe of Wallingford, married Jemima Curtiss, Sept. 29, 1713. He lived in
the house late the property of Jason Beach.

Children: 99 *Joseph*, b June 10, 1764; 100 *William*, b
Nov. 18, 1716, m Susannah Holt, Oct. 15, 1739; 101 *Lydia*,
b Feb. 26, 1719; 102 *Nathan*, b May 28, 1721; 103 *Stephen*,
b April 6, 1729; 104 *Elihu*, b Dec. 14, 1734.

## 95. MOSES

MOSES BEACH, son of Moses and Esther, married Dinah
Sperry of New Haven, March 19, 1756. She died April 8,
1768, leaving one child, a daughter; 105 *Mary*, b Feb. 14, 1758.
She became the wife of Turhand Kirtland of Wallingford.
She died Nov. 24, 1792. The 2nd wife of Mr. Beach was
Parthenia Tallman of Branford. By this marriage they had

one child, a son. She d July 5, 1797, æ 60. 106 *Moses Sperry*, b March 7, 1776, d at Norwalk, Ohio, in 1826, æ 50 yrs., m Lucretia Yale of Wallingford.

### 104. MOSES.

MOSES SPERRY BEACH, only son of Moses and Parthenia, married Lucretia Yale, daughter of Elihu and Lucretia (Stanley) Yale. She died 1800, and had by this marriage two children: 107 *Sally*, m Horatio Green of Springfield, Mass.; 108 *Moses Yale*, b Jan., 1800, d July 1, 1868, æ 68. He married 2nd, Lois Ives, daughter of Abijah Ives, of Wallingford. She died at New Haven, Huron Co., Ohio.

Children: 109 *Tallman*, b in Wallingford, d at New Haven, Ohio; 110 *Abraham Stanley*, b in Wallingford, d supposed in Canada; 111 *Abijah*, M. D., b in Wallingford, resides in Ohio; 101 *Asahel*, b in Wallingford, d in Kansas.

### 30. GERSHOM.

GERSHOM BEACH, son of Thomas and Deliverance Howe Beach.

Children: 112 *Ruth*, b Aug. 21, 1722; 113 *Aaron*, b Jan. 14. 1727; 114 *Joanna*, b Aug. 17, 1724, m —— Chittenden; 115 *Gershom*, b Sept. 24, 1729.

## CHESHIRE BRANCH.

### 82. JOHN.

JOHN BEACH, son of Capt. Elnathan and Abigail. married Eunice Eaton in 1744, and settled on a farm left him by his father. His house stood almost opposite the present residence of Edward Andrews, south part of Cheshire, Conn. It was a large two story red house, and was in its day considered a first class house.

Children: 186 *Hannah*, b Jan. 29, 1756, m Samuel Rice, 1776, Feb. 15; 187 *Isaac*, b Aug. 25, 1758, d Dec., 1776; 188 *Elnathan*, b Aug. 30, 1760, m Abigail Atwater; 189 *James Eaton*, b Sept., 1762, m Huldah Sherman of Bridgeport; 190 *John*, b May, 1764, m 1st. Lucy Cornwall, 2d. Lois

Doolittle ; 191 *Eunice*, b Jan. 4, 1766, m Dan Bradley ; 192 *Abijah*, b 1768, m Jemima Cornwall ; 193 *Bildad*, b Sept., 1770, m 1st, Huldah Hotchkiss, 2d, Hannah Cossit ; 194 *Abraham*, b 1772, d in 1772 : 195 *Lois*, b Dec., 1774, m Calvin Lawrence.

### 188 ELNATHAN.

ELNATHAN BEACH, M. D., was a physician in his native village, where he married Abigail Atwater. He built and occupied the house now known as the Bronson house, opposite the south west corner of the public Green in the village. He died in Western N. Y.

Children: 196 *Hannah :* 197 *Narcissa :* 198 *Julia :* 199 *Eliza*.

### 189. JAMES.

JAMES EATON BEACH married Huldah Sherman of Bridgeport, where he died quite advanced in life, and highly respected by the community generally. A fine marble monument has been erected to the memory of both him and his wife.

Children : 200 *Polly :* 201 *Laura :* 202 *Isaac*, now resides in Bridgeport.

### 191. EUNICE.

EUNICE BEACH married Dan Bradley, and settled at Marcellus, N. Y.

Children : 203 *Nancy :* 204 *Harriet :* 205 *Augustus* , 206 *William :* 207 *Dan*.

### 190. JOHN.

JOHN BEACH married Lucy Cornwall, daughter of Abijah Cornwall of Cheshire, and sister of Thomas T. Cornwall, Sept. 20, 1786. She died, and he married Lois Doolittle of Cheshire He died in western New York, Dec. 23, 1844, æ. 80 years. His wife Lucy died Feb. 14, 1814.

Children : 208 *Abraham*, b Nov. 9, 1787, d March 1, 1788, in his 2d year ; 209 *Horace*, b April 11, 1789, m Ann Atwater of New Haven, no issue. His widow m Laban Smith, is living in 1869. He died in 1826 : 210 *Isaac*, b June 5, 1792, m

S s

Nancy Cooper of Meadville, Pa., May 15, 1823, she died
March 2, 1857; 211 *William*, b Feb. 6, 1797, d Sept., 1820;
212 *John*, b July 16, 1794. m Polly Prescott of New Haven,
Feb. 14, 1819, d Oct. 17, 1849; 213 *Matilda*, b Feb. 13, 1799,
was the wife of John H. Cooley of New Haven; 214 *Lorraine*, b March 24, 1802, m Minerva Porter of Marcellus,
N. Y., Nov. 20, 1823. She dying, he m Sarah Elizabeth
Plant of Stratford, Ct., no issue; 215 *Lucy Ann*, b Dec. 15,
1810, d Aug. 17, 1845. She m Samuel Porter Rhodes of
Marcellus, April 26, 1829. Her children were: 216 *Edward*,
b June 26, 1830, d June 3, 1831; 217 *Edward P.*, b Jan. 14,
1832, d March 31, 1836; 218 *Augusta Comstock*, b Sept. 30,
1833, d Oct. 31, 1859; 219 *William Porter*, b May 2, 1826;
220 *Samuel Porter*, b May 2, 1838; 221 *Ann Elizabeth*, b Nov.
15, 1840; 222 *John Beach*, b Aug. 8, 1843; 223 *Mary Matilda*, b Aug. 12, 1845, d Aug. 22, 1845.

### 192. ABIJAH.

ABIJAH BEACH married Jemima Cornwall, daughter of
Abijah Cornwall of Cheshire, Nov. 6, 1796. He was a
merchant, inn-keeper and farmer in his native town Cheshire
until his death, which occured Dec. 2, 1821. She died at
the house of her son-in-law, Edward A. Cornwall Esq., Dec.
17, 1853. Mr. Beach while living built the house now owned
by Burrit Bradley Esq., and also that of Martin Branin in the
village of Cheshire, long occupied for a store and hotel by
Mr. Beach and others.

Children: 224 *Richard*, b July 14, 1799, m Lucinda
Hitchcock, of Cheshire; 225 *Palmina*, b April 19, 1802, m
Truman Atwater; 226 *Elnathan*, b Sept. 1, 1804, m Mary
Bullard, of Cheshire; 227 *Eunice*, b Feb. 11, 1809, m Edward
A. Cornwall Esq., of Cheshire; 228 *Abijah*, b Dec., 1812,
d Jan. 9, 1813.

### 193. BILDAD.

BILDAD BEACH, married for his 1st wife Huldah Hotchkiss,
and his 2nd, Hannah Cossit, and removed to Marcellus, N.
Y., where the family still reside.

Children: 229 *Emily*, 230 *Laura*; 231 *Hannah*; 232 *Merab*; 233 *Merab*.

### 224. RICHARD.

RICHARD and Lucinda Beach were married Nov 21, 1824; he resided in his native town, Cheshire, until 1830, as a merchant. He built a store on the canal, at what is now West Cheshire, and gave it the name of Beachport. In 1830 he removed to Burton, Grange Co., Ohio, where he prosecuted the mercantile business with good success, until near the close of his life.

Child: 234 *Ann Palmina*, b July 14, 1826, d Dec. 17, 1848. She married Wm. Tolles, of Burton, Ohio, June 9, 1846, had two children, both deceased.

### 226. ELNATHAN.

ELNATHAN and Mary Ann Bullard Beach were married Jan 18, 1824. He resided at Cheshire and Hartford, and finally removed to Michigan.

Children: 235 *Lucretia H.*, b Aug., 1824, died 1827; 236 *Elizabeth Eunice*, b Jan. 26, 1826, m Chester S. Steele of Hartford, Conn., Nov. 22, 1852, 3 children; 237 *William A.*, b 1828; 238 *Henry Bullard*, b Oct., 1830; 239 *Mary Ann Beach*, b Sept. 9, 1832, m William Carey, of Pittsfield, Mass. in 1863, and has had three children; 240 *Edward F.*, b Sept. 6, 1834; 241 *Cornelia*, b Sept. 9, 1836; 242 *George*, b July 3, 1840, died Sept. 15, 1842.

## WALLINGFORD BRANCH.

### 27 TIMOTHY.

TIMOTHY, son of Thomas and Phebe Beach, born in Wallingford, married Hannah Cook, Nov. 25, 1713.

Children: 115 *Thomas*, b Aug. 6, 1714, d Sept. 27, 1714; 116 *Thomas*, b Dec. 16, 1751; 117 *Keziah*, b Oct. 18, 1717; 118 *Prudence*, b Oct. 6, 1719; 119 *Hannah*, b April 21, 1722; 120 *Ebenezer*, b Feb. 9, 1724; 121 *Thankful*, b Dec. 19, 1725; 122 *Keziah*, b May 18, 1733.

### 28. NATHAN.

NATHAN, son of Thomas and Phebe Beach, born in Wallingford, married Jemima Curtis, Sept. 29, 1712. Children: 123 *Joseph*, b Jan. 10, 1714; 124 *William*, b Nov. 18, 1716, m Susannah ———, she d Sept. 24, 1742; 125 *Lydia*, b Feb. 26, 1719; 126 *Nathan*, b May 23, 1721; 127 *Sarah*, b Oct. 22, 1723; 128 *Enos*, b Jan. 30, 1726; 129 *Stephen*, b Oct. 16, 1729; 130 *Elihu*, b Dec. 17, 1734; 132 *Eunice*, b March 3, 1737.

### 31. CALEB.

CALEB, son of Thomas Beach, of Wallingford, m Eunice —. Children: 133 *Sarah*, b Oct. 20, 1728; 134 *Margaret*, b Aug. 28, 1735.

### 116. THOMAS.

THOMAS, son of Timothy Beach, m Hannah ——. Children: 135 *Damaris*, b April 5, 1714; 136 *Amzi*, b July 14, 1716; 137 *Abigail*, b Oct. 15, 1718; 138 *Londrey*, b March 5, 1727; 139 *Asa*, b Oct. 3, 1752.

### 123. JOSEPH.

JOSEPH, son of Nathan and Jemima Beach, of Wallingford, m Experience ———. Children: 140 *Lydia*, b Sept. 13, 1735; 141 *Mehitable*, b Nov. 2, 1732; 142 *Mary*, b Dec. 22, 1740; 143 *Elizabeth*, b Feb. 24, 1743; 144 *John*, b Jan. 25, 1745; 145 *Joel*, b Sept. 23, 1747; 146 *Sarah*, b Sept. 21, 1749.

### 128. ENOS.

ENOS, son of Nathan and Jemima Beach, m Anna ——. Child: 147 *Joanna*, b April 1, 1751, in Wallingford.

### 124. WILLIAM.

WILLIAM, son of Nathan and Jemima Beach, m Susannah ——— for his first wife. His 2nd wife was Martha Clark. He built the house in which lived the family of the late Mr. Charles Parker, on Parker's Farms, in Wallingford. He went west with his family. Susanna d Sept. 24, 1742. Children: by first m, 148 *Benjamin*, b May 21, 1740; by

2nd m, 149 *Solomon*, b March 31, 1744 ; 150 *Isaac*, b April 16, 1746 ; 151 *Thankful*, b Sept. 25, 1747.

## 98. ASAHEL.

ASAHEL, son of Moses and Esther Beach of Wallingford, m Keziah Royce, Feb. 11, 1757. He removed to Waterbury, and from thence to Kingsbury, N. Y., in 1799

Children: 152 *Esther* ; 153 *Keziah*.

## JOHN JR.

JOHN Jr., son of John Beach of Stratford, was among the first planters of Wallingford. He died in 1709.

Children: 154 *Nathaniel* ; 155 *Lettice*, b Dec. 24, 1679, m Wm Ward ; 156 *Mary*, b Jan. 11, 1681, d Sept. 1, 1688 ; 157 *Hannah*, b March 17, 1684, m Eliphalet Parker, Aug. 5, 1708 ; 158 *Thomas*, b Feb. 14, 1686, m Hannah Atwater, May 9, 1711 ; 159 *John*, b Oct. 15, 1690, m Mary Royce, Feb. 22, 1717 ; 160 *Samuel*, b Nov. 29, 1696, m Phebe Tyler, April 29, 1718.

## 160. SAMUEL.

SAMUEL BEACH, son of John Jr., m Phebe Tyler. Family mostly settled at North Haven.

Children: 161 *Beulah*, b March 1, 1719 ; 162 *Rhoda*, b Nov. 26, 1720 ; 163 *Zopher*, b Feb. 10, 1723 ; 164 *Phebe*, b Jan. 2, 1725 ; 165 *Benoni*, d June 5, 1738 ; 166 *Esther*, b Jan. 6, 1733 ; 167 *Eunice*, b Jan. 27, 1735 ; 168 *Lamineas*, b Jan. 15, 1737 ; 169 *Hannah*, b Nov. 8, 1739 ; 170 *Daniel*, b. March 24, 1740.

## 159. JOHN.

JOHN BEACH, son of John, married Mary Royce, Feb. 22, 1718-9.

Children: 171 *Adna*, b Jan. 11, 1718, m Hannah Miles ; 172 *Edmund*, b Feb. 18, 1720 ; 173 *Linus*, b Dec. 5, 1721 ; 174 *Amos*, b Jan. 3, 1724 ; 175 *Mary*, b April 28, 1726 ; 176 *Jacob*, b Dec. 5, 1728 ; 177 *Roya*, b Oct. 13, 1733 ; 178 *Samuel*, b Dec. 22, 1729 ; 179 *Baldwin*, b July 26, 1736.

### 158. THOMAS.

THOMAS BEACH, son of John, m Sarah Sanford, Feb. 19,
1712. She died, and he married Lois ——.

Children: by 1st marriage, 180 *Barnabas*, b July 1, 1716;
181 *Abel*, b May 12, 1728, d May 7, 1729. By 2d marriage,
182 *Amos*, b Oct. 14, 1747; 183 *John*, b Oct. 15, 1744; 184
*Lois*, b July 1, 1749; 185 *Adna*, b May 17, 1759.

## BARTHOLOMEW.[1]

### DANIEL.

DANIEL AND SARAH BARTHOLOMEW are the first of the
name in Wallingford. Of their origin and subsequent history, nothing has come to my knowledge. The records in relation to this family as well as many others, have been so kept
as to render it almost impossible to trace them.

Children: 1 *Samuel*, b April 11, 1735; 2 *Reuben*, b Sept.
19, 1736; 3 *William*, b Feb. 1, 1738; 4 *Jacob*, b June 11,
1740; 5 *Susannah*, b April 11, 1745.

### JOSEPH.

JOSEPH BARTHOLOMEW m Mary ———, Jan. 13, 1741;
probably a brother of Daniel.

Children: 6 *Hannah*, b Jan. 29, 1742; 7 *Andrew*, b Nov.
24, 1744; 8 *Joseph*, b Sept. 6, 1746; 9 *Jonathan*, b May 6,
1751; 10 *Joseph*, b Aug. 25, 1752.

### TIMOTHY.

TIMOTHY BARTHOLOMEW m Mary Hull, July 12, 1737; m
2nd, Abigail Phelps, Jan. 11, 1742.

Child: 11 *Timothy*, b Aug. 11, 1745.

### JOHN.

JOHN AND JERUSHA BARTHOLOMEW of Wallingford, had
12 *John Porter*, b Nov. 10, 1740.

---

1 For collateral branches, see Savage's Gen. Dict., I. 120–130.

## BEADLES.[1]

### NATHANIEL.

NATHANIEL BEADLES came to Wallingford, probably soon after the commencement of the last century, and located himself on a farm on the west side of the river, and near the line which divides Cheshire from Wallingford. The house is still standing, and is the first house north of the residence of the late John Cook. He died about 1764 Elizabeth, his wife, died in Wallingford.

Children : 1 *Nathaniel*, b Dec. 15, 1703, m Elizabeth Hitchcock, Nov. 10, 1726 ; 2 *Mary*, b Sept. 18, 1708 ; 3 *Josiah*, b Aug. 3, 1711 ; 4 *Samuel Sharp*, graduated at Yale College in 1757, estate settled in 1763, died Jan. 5, 1762.

### 1. CAPT. NATHANIEL.

CAPT. NATHANIEL BEADLES, son of Nathaniel and Elizabeth Beadles, married Elizabeth Hitchcock, Nov. 10, 1726. He died Feb. 10, 1762.

Children : 5–6 *Elizabeth* and *Susannah* (twins), b Sept. 17. 1727 ; 7 *John*, was a captain of the militia ; 8 *Hannah ;* 9 *Sarah ;* 10 *Lois*, b 1743, m John Hull, she died Sept. 6, 1802, æ. 59 ; 11 *Mehitable ;* 12 *Nathaniel*, died March 4, 1763.

### 7. CAPT. JOHN.

CAPT. JOHN BEADLES, son of Nathaniel and Elizabeth Beadles of Wallingford, m daughter of John Barker. They had a large family, some of whom settled in the State of New York.

Children : 13 *John ;* 14 *Henry*, m —— Blakeslee, dau. of Joseph ; 15 *Alfred*, m —— Byington, and settled in Cheshire, a wagon maker.

— -

1 For collateral branches see Hinman's Conn. Settlers, 104, 105 ; Savage's Gen. Dict., t. 144, 145.

## BELLAMY.[1]

### MATTHEW.

MATTHEW BELLAMY ( a weaver ), the ancestor of those of the name in Wallingford, appears first at Fairfield, Conn., then at Killingworth, where he married Sarah Wood, Sept. 26, 1705. She died March 8, 1721. He married for his second wife, Mary Johnson, May 31, 1722. He died June 7, 1752, æ. 77 years. Mary died May 10, 1730, æ. 66 years. By 1st marriage ;

Children : 1 *Mary*, b Sept. 5, 1706, m Benjamin Gray, May 10, 1731 ; 2 *Matthew*, b June 1, 1708, m Rachel Clark, Sept. 14, 1754, æ. 46 ; 3 *John*, b Jan. 26, 1713, m Màrtha ——; 4 *James*, b Sept. 29, 1716 ; 5 *Joseph*, *D. D.*, b Feb. 20, 1719, grad. at Yale ; 6 *Samuel*, b Jan. 18, 1721. By 2d marriage, 7, 8, *Sarah* and *Anna*, b Jan. 25, 1722 ; 9 *Moses*, b June 29, 1725, m Elizabeth Martin, Dec. 8, 1762 ; 10 *Aaron*, b July 23, 1728, m Desire Parker, Dec. 20, 1753 ; 11 *Hannah*, b May 17, 1731.

### 2. MATTHEW.

MATTHEW BELLAMY, m' Rachel Clark, Jan. 26, 1734, by Rev. Samuel Hall of Cheshire.

Children : 12 *Thankful*, b Nov. 23, 1734 ; 13 *Lois*, b Jan. 15, 1737 ; 14 *Ann*, b Feb. 11, 1738 ; 15 *Reuben*, b Dec. 31, 1742 ; 16 *Matthew*, b Feb. 9, 1745 ; 17 *Asa*, b Dec. 19, 1753 ; 18 *Silas*, b Jan. 14, 1755.

### 5. JOSEPH.

JOSEPH BELLAMY, D. D., settled as · Pastor over the Congregational church at Bethlem, in 1740 ; married Frances Sherman of New Haven, April, 27, 1744. She died Aug. 30, 1785. He married 2d, the widow of Rev. Andrew Storrs of Watertown, Conn. He died March 6, 1760.

Children : 19 *Lucy*, b Aug. 1, 1745, m Abijah Gurnsey,

---

1 For collateral branches, see Cothren's Hist. Woodbury, 507 ; Hinman's Conn. Settlers, 182–5 ; Savage's Gen. Dict., I. 160–1.

Aug., 1772; 20 *Rebeca*, b Oct. 15, 1747, m Rev. Mr. Hunn, of Preston, Conn.; 21 *Daniel*, b Nov. 10, 1750, d May, 1826; 22 *Jonathan*, b Nov. 18, 1752, d at Oxford, N. J., in 1777; 23 *Samuel*, b March 13, 1756, d Nov. 11, 1802; 24 *Elizabeth*, b Dec. 23, 1759. m Charles Sheldon, of Springfield, Mass.; 25 *William*, b June 28, 1770; 26 *Joseph Sherman*, b 1713.

### 10. AARON.

AARON BELLAMY, m Desire Parker, Dec. 20, 1753. He resided in the southwest part of Cheshire on the farm late the property of Elias Gaylord Jr., and at this time (1869), the property of Amos Rice.

Children: 27 *Rhoda*, b Oct. 30, 1754; 28 *Desire*, b July 3, 1758; 29 *Mary*, b April 18, 1761.

## BENHAM.[1]

### 1. JOSEPH.

JOSEPH BENHAM came from New Haven to Wallingford in 1670, with the first settlers in the village, and some of his children were born after his removal there. The name of his wife who died in Wallingford was Winifred. He died in 1702.

Children: 1 *Mary*; 2 *Joseph*, b May 25, 1659, m Hannah Ives, Aug. 17, 1682; 3 *Sarah*, b 1660, d 1668; 4 *Johanneh*, b July 25, 1662; 5 *Elizabeth*, b Sept. 13, 1664; 6 *John*, b Dec. 28, 1666, d 1670; 7 *John*, b Nov. 3, 1671, in Wallingford; 8 *Mary*, b May 18, 1673; 9 *Samuel*, b May 12, 1673; 10 *Sarah*, b Sept. 6, 1676; 11 *James*, b about 1679, d 1745; 12 *Winifred*, b Aug. 21, 1684.

### 2. JOSEPH.

JOSEPH BENHAM, Jr. m Hannah Ives, Aug. 17, 1682, and settled in Wallingford.

Children: 13 *Mary*, b May 18, 1683; 14 *Joseph*, b Dec.

---

1 For collateral branches, see Hinman' Conn. Settlers, 195, 196; Savage's Gen. Dict., i. 155.

15, 1685, m Hope, dau. of Samuel Cook ; 15 *Abigail*, b April 14, 1688, d 1741.

### 11. JAMES.

JAMES BENHAM, m Esther Preston, Dec. 9, 1702, in Wallingford. She died a widow July 3, 1764.

Children: 14 *Jehiel*, b Feb. 23, 1703-4, d July 9, 1780, æ. 76 ; 15 *Sarah*, b April 12, 1706, m Henry Hotchkiss, Nov. 23, 1736 ; 16 *Esther*, b March 18, 1709 ; 17 *Samuel*, b Nov. 9, 1711, m Phebe ——— ; 18 *John*, b Dec. 17, 1714, m Mary ——— ; 19 *Lydia*, b Jan. 9, 1717 ; 20 *Mary*, b July 27, 1719 ; 21 *Eunice*, b Aug. 5, 1723.

### 14. JOSEPH.

JOSEPH BENHAM, 3d, married Hope, dau. of Samuel and Hope Cook. She died Jan. 31, 1731.

Children: 22 *Hannah*, b Dec. 2, 1708, m Samuel Beach, March 23, 1732 ; 23 *Esther*, b March 18, 1709 ; 24 *Joseph*, b April 5, 1711, m Mary ——— ; 25 *Enos*, b Sept. 8, 1713, m Anna ——— ; 26 *Thankful*, b Feb. 14, 1716 ; 27 *Phebe*, b May 20, 1718, m Robert Austin ; 28 *John*, b Oct. 4, 1723 ; 29 *Lois*, b April 30, 1727 ; 30 *Esther*, b March 22, 1730.

### 17. SAMUEL.

SAMUEL BENHAM m Phebe ———, she died, and he married Dorothy Hotchkiss, Dec. 27, 1742.

Children: 31 *Esther*, b March 4, 1737 ; 32 *Oliver*, b July 30, 1743, m Dorothy ———.

### 18. JOHN.

JOHN BENHAM m Mary Curtis, Sept. 23, 1747.

Children: 34 *John*, b July 15, 1750 ; 35 *Mary*, b Nov. 6, 1752 ; 36 *Hope*, b Dec. 21, 1754.

### SERG'T JOSEPH.

SERG'T JOSEPH BENHAM, m Mary Curtis, April 5, 1732, and 2d, Mary Bunnell. Aug. 3, 1735. He died April 18, 1754.

Children: 37 *Benjamin*, b May 23, 1733 ; 38 *Reuben*, b Sept. 30, 1734, m Abigail Clark Sept. 10, 1758 ; 39 *Asa*, b June 10, 1736 ; 40 *Shradrack*, b Jan. 14, 1736 ; 41 *Martha*, b

Aug. 11, 1737, m Benjamin Cook, Aug. 2, 1759 ; 42 *Nathaniel*, b Jan. 18, 1739 ; 43 *Abigail*, b Jan. 14, 1740, d Nov. 1, 1743 ; 44 *James*, b Feb. 1, 1745 ; 45 *Daniel*, b July 31, 1758, d May 16, 1761.

## 26. ENOS.

ENOS BENHAM m Anna Hull Aug. 3, 1741.

Children : 46 *Asaph*, b Dec. 23, 1741 ; 47 *Enos*, b April 6, 1744, d May 2, 1751 ; 48 *Molly*, b Nov. 16, 1746, d Sept. 8, 1753 ; 49 *Samuel*, b Oct. 1, 1749, d Jan. 5, 1751 ; 50 *Polly*, b March 1, 1752 ; 51 *Theophilus*, d Feb. 1, 1759 ; 52 *Samuel*, b March 8, 1758 ; 53 *Molly*, d June 29, 1748 ; 54 *Anna*, b Aug. 29, 1755, d Sept. 29, 1760 ; 55 *Enos*, b Nov. 5, 1761, d May 2, 1760.

## 39. REUBEN.

REUBEN BENHAM m Abigail Clark, Sept. 10, 1758.

Child : 56 *Reuben*, b June 9, 1761.

## NATHAN.

NATHAN BENHAM married Mary ——.

Children : 57 *Hannah*, b Jan. 9, 1722 ; 58 *Patience*, b Dec. 23, 1723 ; 59 *Ebenezer*, b Oct. 31, 1726, m Elizabeth Hotchkiss Nov. 23, 1750 ; 60 *Joel*, b March 2, 1730, m Esther Andrews.

## JOSEPH.

JOSEPH BENHAM m Em. Curtis Jan. 7, 1735.

Children : 61 *Sarah*, b Oct. 26, 1735, d Dec. 29, 1736 ; 62 *Isaac*, b Aug 29, 1736 ; 63 *Samuel*, b June 8, 1755, d April 22, 1759 ; 64, *Uri*, b Dec. 15, 1751. He settled on a farm near the Honey-pot brook in Cheshire ; 65 *Sarah*, b Dec. 25, 1741 ; 66 *Elizabeth*, b March 23, 1745, d Aug. 10, 1758 ; 67 *Em.*, b June 5, 1745, d May 20, 1751 ; 68 *Lois*, b July 13, 1750; 69 *Elisha*, b Nov. 17, 1753.

## 60. JOEL.

JOEL BENHAM, married Esther Andrews, Dec. 7, 1752, m 2d, Elizabeth——.

Children : 70 *James*, b Oct. 26, 1753 ; 71 *Elizabeth*, b Mar.

7, 1755 ; 72 *Ebenezer*, b July 21, 1756 ; 73 *Lyman*, by 2nd wife, b Oct. 1, 1760.

### 59. EBENEZER.

EBENEZER BENHAM married Elizabeth Hotchkiss Nov. 23, 1780.

Child : 74 *Sarah*, b Sept. 18, 1763.

### 62. ISAAC.

ISAAC BENHAM married Lucy Cook, May 11, 1758.

Child : 75 *Elizabeth*, b Oct. 19, 1758.

---

### BLAKESLEE.[1]

The name of Blakeslee, on the early records, is written in twenty-five or more different ways. It is now generally spelled as above.

There is a tradition among the descendants that two brothers of the name of Blakeslee came from the west of England, designing to settle in the Plymouth Colony, and that one of them died on the passage. The other came to Plymouth, where he died in the early days of the Colony, leaving one son. who was placed with a blacksmith in New Haven, Conn., to learn the trade. It is also asserted that the brothers brought an anvil with them, and that it was seen but a few years since in Roxbury, Conn.

#### SAMUEL.

SAMUEL and Elizabeth Blakeslee appear to be the first of the name in Wallingford ; they were in the place about the year 1712 ; of their history very little now appears.

Children : 1 *Obedience*, b June 13, 1713, m Joshua How ; 2 *Jemima*, b Oct. 13, 1717 ; 3 *Susannah*, b March 15, 1719, m Andrew Parker, April 27, 1736 ; 4 *Elizabeth*, b July 8, 1721, m Gamaliel Parker ; 5 *Abigail*, b Sept. 8, 1723, m Elijah Oakley ; 6 *Zeruah*, b Jan 16, 1726, m Nathaniel Ives, Nov. 8,

---

1 For collateral branches, see Bronson's Hist. Waterbury, 469–77 ; Savage's Gen. Dict., I. 189–190.

1741: 7 *Phe'*, b Nov. 1, 1728; 8 *Thankful*, b Nov. 26, 1729, m Justus Hoalt, April 26, 1849; 9 *Hannah*; to *Joseph*, b Apr. 1, 1732; 11 *Miriam*, b Oct. 4, 1735, m Joshua How Oct. 14, 1756; 12 *Phebe*, b July 1, 1744.

### 10. JOSEPH.

JOSEPH BLAKESLEE married Lois Ives, April 1, 1757.

Children: 13 *Elizabeth*, b July 14, 1758; 14-15 *Lois* and *Joseph* (twins), b Jan. 9, 1762; 16 *Joseph*, b 1766, d Dec 19, 1831, æ. 65; 17 *John W.*

---

## BRISTOL.[1]

### HENRY.

HENRY BRISTOL was in Wallingford in the early part of the last century, and settled in the parish of New Cheshire, where he died, 1750; m Desire Bristol.

Children: 1 *Jonathan*, b Dec. 27, 1725; 2 *Lydia*, b March 16, 1728; 3 *Desire*, m Thomas Brooks, Feb. 12, 1728; 4 *Austin*, d before his father, 1750; 5 *Henry*, d before his father, 1748; 6 *Amos*, m Joanna Parker of Wallingford; 7 *Simeon*, graduated at Yale College; 8 *Gideon*, b 1722, d July 15, 1747, æ. 25; 9 *Augustus*, b 1720, d Feb. 4, 1742, æ. 22.

### 1 JONATHAN.

JONATHAN BRISTOL m Elizabeth ———, m 2nd, Susannah Peck, Oct. 16, 1761.

Children: 10 *Gideon*, b June 11, 1755; 11 *Lowly*, b Feb. 20. 1753; 12 *Jonathan*, b August 1, 1760, m Thankful ———.

### 5 HENRY.

HENRY and Lois Bristol, of Cheshire in Wallingford; he died 1748-9.

Children: 13 *Mary*, b March 12, 1742; 14 *Sarah*, b June 10, 1744; 15 *Damaris*; 16 *Henry*.

---

1 For collateral branches, see Redfield's Gen. of the Redfield family. 36.

6. AMOS.

AMOS and Joanna ( Parker) Bristol.

Children : 17 *Thomas*, b March 28, 1741 :  18 *Augustus*, b July 19, 1743 ; 19 *Hannah*, b March 20, 1745 ; 20 *Amos*, b May 6, 1751 ; 21 *Ezra*, b January 9, 1753 ; 22 *Reuben*, b Oct. 1, 1755 ; 23 *Lydia*, b Sept. 15, 1757 ; 24 *Lucy*, b Sept. 10, 1759.

## BROCKETT.[1]

### JOHN.

JOHN BROCKETT came to Wallingford with John Moss from New Haven, in 1667 or 1668, and was chosen by the people of New Haven as one of the committee to manage the affairs of the settlement.   He was frequently called to fill many of the public offices of the village, and after its incorporation, to represent the town in the General Court.   His house lot was No. 1, at the extreme south end of the village, extending from the Old Colony road east toward Wharton's Brook, twenty rods wide and forty rods long ; subsequently it was extended to the Brook.   The land on which now stands the house of the heirs of the late Edward Hall, is a part of this grant. He died March 12, 1689, æ. 80 years.

Children : 1 *John*, b in England, was a physician, and settled near Muddy river in North Haven : 2 *Benjamin*, b 1648, m Lydia Elcock, he died May 22, 1679 ; 3 *Abigail*, b March 10, 1649 ; 4 *Samuel*, b Jan. 14, 1650, m Sarah Bradley, May 21, 1682 ; 5 *Jabez*, b Oct. 24, 1654, m Dorothy Lyman, Nov. 20, 1691 ; 6 *Silence*, m Joseph Bradley ; 7 *Mary*, m William Pennington of New Jersey.

### 1. JOHN.

DR. JOHN BROCKETT m Elizabeth ————, and settled at Muddy River as a farmer and physician, and remained there

---

1 For collateral branches, see Savage's Gen. Dict., i. 257, 258.

during his life-time. He died 1720. He settled the estate of his father in 1689-90. At his death he gave all his property to his widow Elizabeth, by will. He had a son Moses, b April 23, 1679.

## 2. BENJAMIN.

BENJAMIN BROCKETT m Lydia Elcock, Dec. 16, 1720.
Children: 8 *Martha*, b Oct. 2, 1721 ; 9 *Zilla*, b June 17, 1723, d March 20, 1737 ; 10 *Alice*, b Feb. 12, 1725 ; 11 *Hezekiah*, b Dec. 31, 1727 ; 12 *Lydia*, b March 14, 1729, d Nov. 17, 1729 ; 13 *Lydia*, d March 7, 1731 ; 14 *Benjamin*, b May 2, 1733 ; 15 *Zenich*, d March 21, 1737 ; 16 *Lydia*, b March 20, 1737 ; 17 *Sarah*.

## 4. SAMUEL.

SAMUEL BROCKETT m Sarah Bradley, Nov. 21, 1682.
Children: 18 *Samuel*, b Feb. 15, 1682, m Rachel Brown, April 15, 1699 ; 19 *Daniel*, b Sept. 30, 1684 ; 20 *John*, b Nov. 8, 1685, m Huldah Ells ; 21 *Joseph*, b Oct. 25, 1688 ; 22 *Josiah*, b July 25, 1691 ; 23 *Alice*, b April 23, 1693 ; 24 *Josiah*, b July 25, 1698, m Deborah Abbott.

## 5. JABEZ.

JABEZ BROCKET, m Dorothy Lyman, Nov. 20, 1691.
Children : 25 *Joseph*, b Sept. 17, 1692 ; 26-27 *James* and *Dorothy* (twins), b March 16, 1695 ; 28 *Mary*, b March 16, 1699 ; 29 *an infant dau*, b May 14, 1696, d June 10, 1696 ; 30 *Caleb*, b July 5, 1697 ; 33 *Gideon*, b April 15, 1699, d May 8, 1705 ; 32 *Andrew*, b July 6, 1701.

## 18. SAMUEL.

SAMUEL BROCKETT m Rachel Brown, April 15, 1699 ; she died Jan. 24, 1718. He married Elizabeth How, Aug. 5, 1718.
Children : 33 *Titus*, b June 28, 1700, m Mary Turhand ; 34 *Sarah*, b Aug. 26, 1702 ; 35 *Isaac*, b Sept. 3, 1705, m Mary Sedgwick, June 16, 1733 ; 36 *Rachel*, b March 20, 1708 ; 37 *Abigail*, b Feb. 11, 1711 ; 38 *Samuel*, b June 21, 1714.

## 20. JOHN.

JOHN BROCKETT married Huldah Ells, March 1, 1711.

Children: 39 *Daniel*, b April 3, 1712, m Rachel ——; 40 *David*, b Nov. 28, 1714; 41 *Anna*, b Feb. 2, 1715, m Gideon Hotchkiss, Jan. 18, 1737; 42 *Christopher*, b April 3, 1718; 43 *Mehitable*, b April 3, 1719; 44 *Elisha*, b May 31, 1726; 45 *John*, b Feb. 14, 1728.

## 24. JOSIAH.

JOSIAH BROCKETT m Deborah Abbot, Nov. 16, 1725. He m 2nd, Mary ——, who survived him and m Captain Isaac Bronson of Waterbury, Feb. 13, 1755, she d Aug. 1, 1816.

Children by 1st wife: 46 *Hannah*, b Sept. 22, 1725; by 2nd, 47 *Job*, b Sept. 20, 1727, m Martha Ebenathe; 48 *Sarah*, b Dec. 7, 1728, m James Bronson, Aug. 22, 1750; 49 *Abigail*, b July 23, 1732; 50 *Mary*, b Feb. 22, 1735; 51 *Elizabeth*, b April 15, 1736.

## 33. TITUS.

TITUS BROCKETT m Mary, daughter of Henry Turhand, of Wallingford, Feb. 12, 1728. He was one of the most active Episcopalians in the place, and was one of the four largest contributors toward the erection of the second church edifice, in 1762, which, until within a few years, occupied the lot on the corner opposite the Isaac Peck house, on which a schoolhouse is about being erected, the lot having been given to the town for [that purpose by the late Moses Yale Beach Esq. Mr. Brockett died July 29, 1773, æ. 74 years. His wife died May 1, 1777, æ. 64 years.

Child: 52 *Turhand*, b March 7, 1733, d May 23, 1738; The disease of which Mr. Titus Brockett died was smallpox. He was a member of Parson Andrews' Episcopal church, and a strong Tory. Parties had been formed for and against the British Government. In Wallingford they ran extremely high, and just two years before, Rev. Mr Andrews delivered his celebrated Fast-day sermon, that compelled him to leave for Nova Scotia. At the funeral of Mr. Brockett the Whigs would not have him buried with other members of the family, but compelled Turhand Kirtland and two others, to have the grave dug on a wet, springy place, directly under the east fence of the burying ground, so that the water immediately filled the grave, though in mid-summer. It was therefore necessary to sink the coffin with two rails till the earth could be returned. For a long time these rails remained standing up out of the grave, and did not decay. Some of the family supposed that the timber was supernaturally preserved, as a testimony against the wicked whigs.

### 35. ISAAC.

ISAAC BROCKETT married Mary Sedgwick, a daughter of Samuel and Ruth Sedgwick of Hartford, June 16, 1731. She died Jan. 19, 1734. He married Elizabeth Culver, Feb. 25, 1737, who after his death married Daniel Frisbie, May 4, 1748. He died Oct. 18, 1746. He was an ardent churchman.

Child by 1st marriage: 53 *Rachel*, b May 23, 1732, m Constant Kirtland. Children by 2d marriage: 54 *Ruth*, b Feb. 3, 1738; 55 *Esther*, b Oct. 6, 1739; 56 *Hannah*, b Oct. 6 1741; 57 *Ruth*, b Oct. 26. 1744.

### 38. SAMUEL.

SAMUEL BROCKETT married Ruth ——. He was a son of Samuel and Rachel Brockett.

Children: 58 *Eunice*, b Jan. 15, 1744; 59 *Zuer*, b Mar. 24, 1746; 60 *Joel*, b June 14, 1749; 61 *Joel*, b July 28, 1750; 62 *Zenas*, b July 12, 1752; 63 *Benjamin*, b Oct. 1, 1760.

### 39. DANIEL.

DANIEL BROCKETT, son of John and Huldah, m Rachel ——.

Children: 64 *Daniel*, b July 3, 1737; 65 *Daniel*, b April 13, 1740.

### 45. JOHN.

JOHN BROCKETT, son of John and Huldah Brockett, married Jemima ——.

Children: 66 *Christopher*, b June 2, 1749; 67 *Susannah*, b Nov. 17, 1750.

### 47. JOB.

JOB BROCKETT, son of Josiah and Deborah Brockett, m Martha Ebernathe.

Child: 68 *Lucretia*, b July 27, 1756.

T T

## BROWN.[1]

### FRANCIS.

FRANCIS BROWN married Mary Edwards, in England, and came over to America, and to New Haven, in advance of the colony; was one of the company that spent the winter of 1637–8 in a hut which they had erected on the east corner of what is now College and George-sts. He was one of the subscribers to the colony compact, or constitution, in 1639.

Children: 1 *Lydia;* 2 *John;* 3 *Eleazer;* 4 *Samuel;* 5 *Ebenezer.*

### 4. SAMUEL.

SAMUEL married Mercy Tuttle, May 2, 1667, and was one of the original subscribers for the settlement of the village of Wallingford. Lot No. 7, west side of the Main street, was assigned to him for his encouragement, as a house lot. But it does not appear that he ever built upon it;. why he did not is unknown. This lot was subsequently assigned to John Moss, who built a house upon it; and it remained in the family until the death of the late Ebenezer Morse, a few years since. In 1850 Moses Y. Beach purchased this lot, and erected that elegant mansion, now known as the Beach House, upon it. ' Samuel Brown died in Wallingford, Nov. 4, 1691, æ. 46 yrs.

Children: 6 *Abigail,* b March 11, 1669, d young; 7 *Sarah,* b Aug 8, 1672; 8 *Rachel,* b April 14, 1677; 9 *Francis,* b Oct. 7, 1679; 10 *Gideon,* b July 12, 1685; 11 *Samuel,* b Oct. 29, 1699.[2]

------------

## BUNNEL.[3]

### PETER.

PETER BUNNEL came from England in the May-flower, with the Pilgrims, and landed at Plymouth, Mass.. in 1620.

1 Durrie refers to 45 works for collateral branches.

2 Bronson in Hist. of Waterbury gives descendants of above.

3 For collateral branches, see Hinman's Conn. settlers, 405, 406.

### RICHARD.

RICHARD BUNNEL came from England in 1630, and settled at Watertown, Mass.

### BENJAMIN.

BENJAMIN BUNNEL was an early settler in Wallingford ; was made a freeman in 1670. He was at New Haven in 1668, and possibly previous to that date. He married Mary Brooks, and had a daughter, 1 *Lydia*, b Aug. 27, 1713.

### 2. ABNER.

ABNER BUNNEL, born in 1676.

Children : 3 *Abner ;* 4 *David ;* 5 *Enos*, m Truelove ——, she d May 7, 1717, æ. 22 ; 6 *Ebenezer*, b 1716.

### NATHANIEL.

ENSIGN NATHANIEL BUNNEL was an early settler in that part of Wallingford now Cheshire, where he married Desire, daughter of Benjamin Peck, May 10, 1709. She was born Aug. 26, 1687, and died in 1721. He married Mary Brooks, Feb. 17, 1726, and died of small pox, May 4, 1732, æ. 46 yrs. He appears to have been the ancestor of all who have gone from Cheshire that bear the name of Bunnel.

Children : 7 *Desire*, b March 26, 1711 ; 8 *Ebenezer*, b May 21, 1713, m Lydia Clark ; 9 *Benjamin*, b April 16, 1715 ; 10 *Parmineas*, b March 1, 1717 ; 11, 12, *Jared* and *Desire* (twins), b June 25, 1719 ; 13 *Abner*, b March 24, 1721, m Elizabeth Preston, Feb. 19, 1746 ; 14 *Joseph*, b Jan. 17, 1723. By 2nd marriage : 15 *Patience*, b Nov. 28, 1726 ; 16 *Hezekiah*, b Nov. 21, 1727, m Esther —— ; 17 *Rachel*, b Nov. 15, 1728, m Samuel Thompson, June 27, 1747 ; 18 *Rebecca*, b Jan. 6, 1730 ; 19 *Stephen*, b July 6, 1731.

### 8. EBENEZER.

EBENEZER BUNNEL m Lydia Clark of Cheshire, 1738.

Children : 20 *Nathaniel*, b June 4, 1739 ; 21 *Jared*, b Oct. 6, 1741 ; 22 *Lydia*, b May 4, 1744 ; 23 *Israel*, b March 17, 1747 ; 24 *Ebenezer*, b Feb. 15, 1750, d March 1, 1756 ; 25

*Lydia*, b Jan. 26, 1753; 26 *Hannah*, b April 11, 1756; 27 *Desire*, b Jan. 7, 1759; 28 *Miriam*. b March 20, 1762.

### 9. BENJAMIN.

BENJAMIN BUNNEL married Lydia Fox, Dec. 22, 1743.

Children: 29 *Benjamin*, b July 15, 1747; 30 *Samuel*, b Jan. 7, 1750.

### 10. PARMINEAS.

PARMINIAS BUNNEL m Rachel Curtis, Sept. 20, 1739. After his death she married Samuel Thompson, June 7, 1741.

Children: 31 *Desire*, b May 19, 1740; 32 *Parmineas*, b Jan., 1742; 33 *Mary*, b Jan. 6, 1745; 34 *John*, b April 18, 1746; 35 *Rachel*, b July 2, 1748; 36 *Desire*, b Nov. 7; 1750; 36 *Damaris*, b June 30, 1752; 38 *John*, b July 25, 1754.

### 13 ABNER.

ABNER BUNNEL m Elizabeth Preston, Feb. 19, 1756.

Children: 39 *David*, b Dec. 2, 1747; 40 *Abner*, b Nov. 18, 1749; 41 *Elizabeth*, b Nov. 20. 1751; 42 *Enos*, b May 15, 1753, m Naomi, dau. of Stephen and Hannah Atwater; 43 *Reuben*, b Feb. 22, 1755; 44 *Samuel*, b May 12, 1757; 45 *Esther*, b March 26, 1759; 46 *Jehiel*, b Oct. 6, 1763

### 14. JOSEPH.

JOSEPH BUNNEL m Hannah Hotchkiss, Feb. 28, 1745.

Children: 47 *Eunice*, b May 23, 1745; 48 *Miriam*, b May 31, 1747.

### 16. HEZEKIAH.

HEZEKIAH BUNNEL m Esther ——.

Children: 49 *Nathaniel*, b Jan. 23. 1734, m Lois Rice, June 17, 1759; 50 *Titus*, b Nov. 9, 1735; 51 *Esther*, b Nov. 31, 1737.

### 19. STEPHEN.

STEPHEN BUNNEL married Mary Hendrick, Sept. 26, 1752.

Children: 52 *Lois*, b July 1, 1754; 53 *Mary*, b March 27, 1756: 54 *Levi*, b July 19, 1759: 55 *Eunice*, b June 10, 1761.

### 23. ISRAEL.

ISRAEL BUNNEL married Jerusha Dowd, daughter of Benjamin Dowd of Middletown. He was a large landholder in Cheshire, and one of the most prominent and active men in the town, and for many consecutive years served as selectman, and in various other offices in the gift of his fellow-townsmen. His death was greatly lamented by all who knew him, and especially by his neighbors and friends.

Children: 56 *Nathaniel*, d in Cheshire ; 57 *Rufus* ; 58 *Virgil* ; 59 *Israel* ; 60 *Jairus*, d in New Haven ; 61 *Ebenezer* ; 62 *Dennis* ; 63 *Hannah* ; 64 *Jerusha*, m Doct. Pierre E. Brandon.

## CANNON.

### LYMAN.

LYMAN CANNON, married ——— . a daughter of the late Elisha Smith, of Wallingford. He carried on the tin business with considerable success during his whole life in Wallingford. He was a Deacon in the Congregational church.

Children : *Burdett*, d in Wallingford ; *William*, resided in New Haven ; *James*, d in New Haven in 1808 ; 1 *daughter*.

## CARTER.

This name appears in Wallingford before 1738, in the persons of William and Anna Carter. They had a daughter born Nov. 20, 1738, and a son, William, born Nov. 14, 1748, and perhaps others. Dea. Salmon Carter was one of the old inhabitants sixty years ago, in Wallingford. He carried on cabinet making and a small store. He by close application to business and rigid economy in all his affairs, accumulated a very handsome estate. He married ——— Hough, daughter of Joseph and ——— Hough, of Wallingford. In appearance he was a sedate, and remarkably dignified man in his manners and address, but little seen in the public streets, except on business

Children: 1 *Salome*, d unm.; 2 *Betsey*, m Lyman Collins. of Meriden; 3 *William*, m wid. Hiram Yale, of Wallingford, left no children.

## CARRINGTON.[1]

This family is one of great antiquity. Sir Michael Carrington, who was a standard bearer to Richard I., 1189, is the first of whom I find any record. His grandson Sir William Carrington was an officer under Edward I., 1272–1307. Sir Edmund Carrington, Kt., was an officer under Edward II., 1307–27. Sir William Carrington, Kt., temp. of Edward III. 1327–77. Sir Thomas Carrington, Kt., Steward (of the household) to Edward III., was the father of John Carrington, who in the beginning of the reign of Henry IV. for his adherence to Richard II. (who was deposed) was compelled to flee from his country, and on returning assumed for disguise the name of Smith. He died 1446, and was father of Hugh (Carrington) Smith, who appears to have been the father of (1445–1500) Sir John Carrington Smith, Baron of the Exchequer, temp. Henry VIII., whose fourth son (1509–47) Francis (Carrington) Smith, of Ashley Tolville, Leicester, was great grandfather of Charles (Carrington) Smith, who was created Oct. 31, 1643, Lord C——, Baron of "Wotton Warren" in Warwickshire, 4th of Nov., following Viscount Carrington in the Peerage of Ireland, was murdered by his valet at Pontoise in France, Feb. 21, 1664, and was succeeded by Francis Carrington Smith, 2d Baron and Viscount. He died in 1705. Charles, his son, died young, in May, 1706. The title and honor thus became extinct.

John Carrington was an early settler in Farmington, and

---

1 For collateral branches, see Andrews' Hist. New Britain, 338 ; Campbell's Hist. Virginia, 624–625 ; Foot's Hist. Virginia, 2nd series, 575; Hinman's Conn. Settlers, 491–492 ; Mead's Hist. of Old Churches and Families of Virginia, II. 29.

one of the "eighty-four proprietors" in 1672. He signed the articles for the settlement of Mattatuck, Waterbury, in 1674, and appears to have joined the new plantation early; for he is named in all the divisions of fences. It appears that for some cause he did not fully comply with the conditions of the new plantation covenant, and was consequently declared to have forfeited his rights. Feb. 6, 1682. But little is known of him. He died in the early part of 1690, leaving a widow who died before the inventory of his effects was rendered, June 30. 1690. His son John was the administrator, and the estate amounted to £120 11s. John had £23, and each of the other children had £12 ; their guardians were instructed o put out the three youngest, and not to be governed or over-ruled by John the administrator. John's brothers were Ebe-nezer, Samuel and Ezekiel. John Carrington's house-lot of two acres was on West Main-st., the south side, about where Leavenworth street now runs. It was bounded north and south on the highway, east on Timothy Stanley, west on George Scott. It was sold in 1710, by the heirs to Timothy Stanley and George Scott, for £12.

Children: 1 *John*, b 1667, d 1692 in Farmington, he was a cooper; 2 *Mary*, b 1672, m William Parsons of Farming-ton, Ct.; 3 *Hannah*, b 1675. m Joshua Holcombe of Sims-bury, Ct.: 4 *Clark*, b 1678, m Sarah Higason, and lived in Farmington ; 5 *Elizabeth*, b 1682, m John Hoskins of Wind-sor ; 6 *Ebenezer*, b 1687, removed to Hartford, d in Waterbury, had no issue.

### 1. JOHN.

JOHN CARRINGTON, first of Waterbury, married Miss ——— Hunn, from Mass. He married for his second wife Miss ———. He lived on a farm at Red Stone Hill in Farmington, where he died.

Children by 1st marriage : 7 *Nathaniel*, m, had no issue, d on the old homestead ; 8 *John*, m Mabel Beach in New York, was a merchant in Goshen, d a young man ; 9 *Jeremiah*, b 1746, m Mindwell Cook and settled in Wallingford, where he kept a tavern a great number of years; 10 *Deborah*, m ——— Rice, she died at Onondaga, N. Y., a woman of great worth; 11 *Keziah*, m 1st,——— Munson, 2d, Esq. Oliver Stanley of Wallingford; 12 *Martha,* m Fisk Beach of Goshen, brother of Mabel, had 8 children. By 2d marriage: 13 *Jonathan*, b 1748, m Azubah Burns of Bristol, d 1733 ; 14 *Solomon*, d in the old prison ship New York; 15 *Phineas*, d supposed in the service of the U. States; 16 *David*.

## 8. JOHN.

JOHN CARRINGTON, son of John and ——— Hunn Carrington, married Mabel Beach, of Goshen, Conn. He was a merchant in Goshen. He died of a fever in New York while a young man.

Children: 17 *Harvey*, m ——— Catlin, children, John and Lucia; 18 *Elisha*, m Judy Thompson, she died leaving 7 daughters and 1 son; 19 *Miles*, resides in Augusta N. Y., is accounted a good man; 20 *Anna*, m a lawyer named Dawes, had 2 children, she died young; 21 *Mabel*, m., and lived in humble circumstances.

### JEREMIAH.

JEREMIAH CARRINGTON, son of John and ——— Hunn Carrington, married Mindwell Cook, daughter of Isaac and Jerusha, of Wallingford, and was the keeper of the hotel now kept by Dwight Hall in the village of Wallingford, for a number of years. He died Dec. 17, 1812, æ. 66 years. She died Jan. 7, 1813, æ. 64 years.

Children: 22 *James*, b 1770, d July 6, 1836, æ. 66, m Patty McLean, she died March 12, 1836, æ. 64; 23 *Liverius*, b 1778, d Dec. 22, 1848, æ. 70.

### 22. JAMES.

JAMES CARRINGTON, son of Capt. Jeremiah and Mindwell Carrington, m Patty McLean of Wallingford. He was an energetic and thorough business man, and for many years was in the employ of Eli Whitney Esq., as superintendent of the Gun Factory at Whitneyville. He was Postmaster at

Wallingford many years, and leader of the singing in the old three-story meeting house, being a fine musician, and possessed of a remarkably full, well-toned bass voice.

Children: 24 *Miles*, now of Mobile, Ala.; 25 *James Whitney*, Astoria, N. Y.; and several daughters.

### 23. LIVERIUS.

LIVERIUS CARRINGTON, son of Capt. Jeremiah and Mindwell Carrington, m 1st, Thankful Hall, 2nd, Eliza Kirtland, 3d, Sarah Kirtland Yale, wid. of Selden Yale, and sister to Eliza, his 2nd wife. He studied medicine with Dr. Kirtland of Wallingford. Not liking the professsion he formed a partnership with the late George B. Kirtland, and entered the mercantile business, in which he continued until his decease in 1840.

Children by 1st marriage: 27 *William*, b about 1807, successor to the old firm, C. & K.; 28 *Anna*, and an infant, both of whom died, Anna at the age of 17. Children by 2nd marriage: 29 *Sarah K.*; 30 *Anna*, m Joel Peck, late deceased. Children by 3d marriage: 31 *Kirtland*, business clerk; 32 *Ellen*.

## CLARK.[1]

### 1. EBENEZER.

EBENEZER CLARK, son of James, of New Haven, born Nov. 29, 1651, m Sarah, daughter of James Peck, of New Haven, May 6, 1678; she died May 20, 1696, æ. 37 years. He died April 30, 1721, æ. 70 years. He married Elizabeth Royce for his 2nd wife, Dec. 22, 1696. He was the first of this name in Wallingford.

Children: by 1st m, 1 *Caleb*, b March 6, 1678; 2 *Sarah*, b Aug. 20, 1681, m Isaac Cook, Oct. 11, 1706; 3 *Josiah*, b Feb. 6, 1683, m Mary Burr; 4 *Stephen*, b Dec. 18, 1686; 5

---

[1] Durrie refers to fifty-two works containing notices of the Clark family.

*Hannah*, b Aug. 18, 1689, d before her father ; 6 *Sylvanus*, b Feb. 1, 1691-2. m Damaris Hitchcock in 1717 ; 7 *Obadiah*, b Oct. 17, 1694, d before his father ; 8 *Stephen*, b Dec. 7, 1696, d Mar. 25, 1750. By 2nd marriage : 9 *Eliphalet*, b Dec. 28, 1697 ; 10 *Elizabeth*, b Sept. 24, 1698, d before her father ; 11 *Susannah*, b April 29, 1700, d before her father ; 12 *Caleb*, b Sept. 26, 1701, m Lois How, Jan. 19, 1722 ; 13 *Phebe*, b May 20, 1703 ; 14 *Daniel*, b Feb. 7, 1712, m Elizabeth ——, she d April 17, 1755 ; 15 *Abigail*, b June 8, 1705 ; 16 *James*, b Sept. 29, 1713, d before his father ; 17 *Susannah*, b Sept. 30, 1717 ; 18 *Sarah*, b Sept. 24, 1721, d June 18, 1722.

### 3. JOSIAH.

JOSIAH CLARK, son of Ebenezer and Sarah Clark of Wallingford, m Mary Burr, April 21, 1710.

Children : 19 *Solomon*, b March 6, 1711 ; 20 *Mary*, b Mar. 22, 1723.

### 6. SYLVANUS.

SYLVANUS CLARK, son of Ebenezer and Sarah Clark, married Damaris Hitchcock, April 22, 1717.

Children : 21 *Jonah*, b Jan. 31, 1718 ; 22 *Thankful*, b Dec. 21, 1719, m James Curtis, Nov. 11, 1738.

### 8. STEPHEN.

STEPHEN CLARK, son of Ebenezer and Sarah Clark, m Lydia Hotchkiss of Cheshire. She died Nov. 1, 1737, æ. 41. He died Nov. 25, 1750, æ. 64 years, at Cheshire. His second wife was Ruth ——.

Children by 1st marriage : 23 *Lydia*, b Nov. 25, 1718 ; 24 *Sarah*, b Sept. 24, 1721 ; 25 *Andrew*, b Oct. 24, 1727, m Mehitable Tuttle, Feb. 7, 1748. Children by 2nd marriage : 26 *Desmania*, b Sept. 26, 1751 ; 27 *Amasa*, b Nov. 25, 1753 ; 28 *Mary*, b Oct. 4, 1756 ; 29 *Stephen*, b Dec. 16, 1785, m Mehitable —— ; 30 *Levi*, b Jan. 11, 1761.

### 12. CALEB.

CALEB, son of Ebenezer and Elizabeth Clark, married Lois How, Jan. 19, 1722.

Children: 31 *Margery*, b April 14, 1723 : 32 *Eunice*, b Mar. 23, 1725 : 33 *Phebe*, b Mar. 1, 1728 ; 34 *Lois*, b Aug. 31, 1730.

### 14. DANIEL.

DANIEL, son of Ebenezer and Elizabeth Clark, married Elizabeth Miles, Sept. 17, 1741; she died April 17, 1755. He m again in 1741 ; he died Aug. 17, 1774, æ. 63 yrs.

Children : 35 *Lois*, b Nov. 12, 1743 ; 36 *Archibald*, b Sept. 1, 1745–6, m Polly Ives, of North Haven : 37 *Ebenezer* : 38 *Daniel*, was a town pauper for years ; 39 *Abigail;* 40 *James*.

### 25. ANDREW.

ANDREW, son of Stephen and Lydia Clark, m Mehitable Tuttle, Feb. 7, 1748–9.

Children : 41, *Stephen*, b Jan. 16, 1749 ; 42 *Lydia*, b March 23, 1752 ; 43 *Mehitable*, b Aug. 21, 1758.

### WILLIAM.

WILLIAM CLARK married Mindwell Rowe, Aug. 29, 1749. Children : 44 *Sylvanus*, b Oct. 4, 1750 ; 45 *Josiah*, b Aug. 8, 1752.

### ABRAHAM.

ABRAHAM CLARK married Martha Tyler, Oct. 5, 1721

Children : 46 *Mary*, b March 1, 1724 : 47 *Lydia*, b March 1, 1726 ; 48 *Hannah*, b Sept. 12, 1727 ; 49 *Rufus*, b March 1, 1728 ; 50 *Keziah*, b Oct. 31, 1731.

— — ·

# COOK.[1]

The ancestors from whom most of the Cooks in New England trace their descent, came from Herefordshire and Kent, in England The ancestral branch from whom those of the name trace their origin, now resident in various parts of the state, came from Kent, and were of the Puritan stock.

---

1 For collateral branches see Andrews' Hist. New Britain, Conn., 207 ; Babson's Hist. Glouce ter, Mass., 74 ; Bronson's Hist. Waterbury, 485–7 ; Cope s Record of Cope family of Penn., 44, 78, 79–82, 157, 175, 176 ; Fox s Hist. Dunstable, Mass., 242 ; Freeman's Hist. Cape Cod, Mass , 11. 360, 389, 634, 642, 643 ; Hinmans's Conn. Settlers, 698 703 ; Hobart's

Henry Cook was at Plymouth, Mass., before 1640. He had sons, Isaac, John, Henry and Samuel. Isaac is supposed to have remained at Plymouth, and John to have settled at Middletown. Henry and Samuel settled at Wallingford, and are the ancestors of most of the name of Cook in Connecticut, and of many in various parts of the country.

### SAMUEL.

SAMUEL COOK came to New Haven in 1663, m Hope, daughter of Edward Parker of New Haven, May 2, 1667. They went to Wallingford in April, 1670, with the first planters. He was, perhaps, the first and only shoemaker and tanner of leather in the place. After the decease of his wife Hope, he married Mary Roberts, July 14, 1690. He was regarded as a very good man by his friends and neighbors, and was frequently called to fill offices of responsibility and trust in the village, and in the church of which he was a member. He died March, 1702. He left an estate of £340. His widow m Jeremiah How, sen., April 9, 1705.

Children by 1st marriage: 1 *Samuel*, b March 3, 1667–8, in New Haven; 2 *John*, b Dec. 3, 1669, in New Haven; 3 *Hannah*, b March 3, 1671–2, in Wallingford; 4 *Isaac*, b March 10, 1673, d April 7, 1673; 5 *Mary*, b April 23, 1675, m Nathaniel Ives, April 5, 1699; 6 *Elizabeth*, b August 22, 1677, d young; 7 *Judith*, b Feb. 29, 1679, m Jeremiah How jr., April 20, 1704, she d March 20, 1708; 8 *Isaac*, b Jan. 10, 1681; 9 *Joseph*, b Feb. 25, 1683; 10 *Hope*, b Sept. 27, 1686, m Joseph Benham, Dec. 18, 1706, she d Jan. 30, 1731. . By 2nd marriage: 11 *Israel*, b May 8, 1692; 12 *Mabel*, b June 30, 1694; 13 *Benjamin*, b April 8, 1697, d 1717, unmarried, was

Hist. Abingdon, Mass., 363–4; Hollister's Pawlet, Vt., 179, 180; Howell's Hist. Southampton, L. I., 210–12; Judd and Boltwood's Hist. Hadley, Mass., 465–471; Kellogg's Memorials of John White, 77; Kidder's Hist. New Ipswich, N. H., 352; Mitchell's Hist. Bridgewater, Mass., 141; Nash's Gen. of Nash Fam., 33, 34; Stiles's Hist. Windsor, Conn., 572–4; Savage's Gen. Dict., 1. 445–51; Bond's Hist. and Gen. Watertown, Mass., 163, 164; Jackson's Hist. Newton, Mass., 247–50.

a tanner and currier; 14 *Ephraim*, b April 19, 1699; 15 *Elizabeth*, b Sept 10, 1701, m Adam Mott, Aug 28, 1717.

## 1. SAMUEL.

SAMUEL COOK, son of Samuel and Hope Cook, married Hannah Ives, daughter of William of New Haven, March 3, 1692, John Moss Esq. officiating. She died May 29, 1714. He then married Elizabeth Bedel, of Stratford. He died Sept. 18, 1725, æ. 58 years, at Wallingford. His widow married Capt. Daniel Harris, of Middletown, Conn. He was a farmer in the western part of the township, near the line which now divides Cheshire from Wallingford. Some of his descendants are still occupying the same land. Estate, £300.

Children: 16 *Hannah*, b May 28, 1693, m Jeremiah Hull, she died Nov. 22, 1735, æ. 43 years; 17 *Samuel*, b March 5, 1695; 18 *Aaron*, b Dec. 28, 1696; 19 *Lydia*, b Jan. 13, 1699, m Daniel Dutton, d Oct. 12, 1738, 20 *Moses*, b Jan. 4, 1700, d Dec. 25, 1711; 21 *Miriam*, b Nov. 4, 1703, m Benjamin Curtis, Dec. 12, 1727; 22 *Thankful*, b Dec. 24, 1705, d Aug. 19, 1714; 23 *Esther*, b March 8, 1707, m Abel Yale, July 22, 1730; 24 *Eunice*, b Feb. 25, 1709; 25 *Susannah*, b Sept. 5, 1711, m Joseph Cole, Dec. 1, 1735; 26 *Hope*, d Sept. 18, 1728. By 2nd marriage: 27 *Moses*, b Nov. 6, 1716; 28 *Thankful*, b Nov. 14, 1718, m Stephen Hotchkiss, Dec. 31, 1742; 29 *Asaph*, b June 23, 1720; 30 *Hannah*, b Nov. 4, 1721, m Zephaniah Hull, of Cheshire, and settled at Bethlem.

## 2. JOHN.

JOHN COOK, son of Samuel and Hope Cook, married Hannah Hall, and settled in the western part of the township near Scott's Rock in Cheshire. He died April 30, 1739, æ. 70 years.

Children: 31 *Ezekiel*, b April 20, 1700, d Nov. 7, 1722; 32 *Naomi*, b Jan. 27, 1704, d Nov. 20, 1707; 33 *John*, b Aug. 23, 1707, d Nov. 1, 1722; 34 *Mary*, m John McKay, she d 1763, in Cheshire, Conn.

## 8. ISAAC.

ISAAC COOK, son of Samuel and Hope Cook, married Sarah Curtis, Oct. 11, 1705. He d Feb. 1, 1712, in Wallingford. His widow married Caleb Lewis, in 1714. Estate, £103.

Children: 35 *Sarah*, b July 20, 1707 ; 36 *Amos*, d in childhood ; 37 *Mindwell*, b May, 1709, m Caleb Evarts of Guilford, Conn. ; 38 *Isaac*, b July 22, 1710.

## 9. JOSEPH.

JOSEPH COOK, son of Samuel and Hope Cook, married Abigail ——. After her death, he married Eleanor Johnson, Oct. 14, 1714, and remained in Wallingford until 1743, when in the autumn of that year, he went to Goshen in Litchfield county, and was among the earliest and most prominent men in the place. He died Nov. 7, 1764, æ. 82 years.

Children by 1st marriage : 39 *Lois*, b April 25, 1700, d in infancy ; 40 *Samuel*, b Feb. 18, 1702 ; 41 *Abigail*, b Jan. 18, 1703. By 2d marriage : 42 *Phebe*, b Oct. 7, 1715, m Eli Pettibone, Feb. 21, 1751, she d about 1767 ; 43 *Benjamin*, b Jan. 5, 1718 ; 44 *Daniel*, b Aug. 19, 1720 ; 45 *Walter*, b Dec. 21, 1722 ; 46 *Joseph*, b Jan. 18, 1726 ; 47 *Lois*, b May 23, 1729 ; 48 *Lambert*, d at Goshen ; 49 *Hannah*, b Nov. 15, 1735, m Roger Pettibone, Jan. 25, 1752, she d April 29, 1763.

## 11. ISRAEL.

ISRAEL COOK, son of Samuel and Mary Cook, married Elizabeth, daughter of Ebenezer Clark of Wallingford, Feb. 22, 1717. He settled in what is now Cheshire, and afterward moved to Vermont with some of his children, where it is supposed he died.

Children : 50 *Catharine*, b July 3, 1718, m Isaiah Smith, of New Haven, May 20, 1750; 51 *Ebenezer*, b Dec. 13, 1719 ; 52 *Sarah*, b May 5, 1722, m 1st, Jonathan Hall, Dec. 25, 1739, 2d, Jehiel Andrus, Jan. 16, 1745 ; 53 *Deborah*, b Oct. 1, 1725, m Elisha Perkins, June 20, 1748 ; 54 *Anna*, b July 4, 1727; 55 *John*, b 1731, bap. in Cheshire, June, 1751 ; 56

*Amos*, b Dec. 5, 1734 ; 57 *Benjamin*, b about 1736 ; 58 *Abel*, b May 6, 1738 ; 59 *Charles*, doubtless settled in Vermont ; 60 *Ezekiel*, b and bap. at Cheshire, June, 1751, supposed settled in Vermont.

## 14. EPHRAIM.

EPHRAIM COOK, son of Samuel and Mary Cook, married Lydia Doolittle. She died Dec. 25, 1785, æ. 84 years. He died March 22, 1774, æ. 75 years. He was licensed by the county court, April 24, 1727, to prosecute the business of tanning and dressing leather in Cheshire.

Children : 61 *Mary*, b Feb. 13, 1723, d same year ; 62 *Mamre*, b Dec. 21, 1725, m Daniel Hotchkiss, of Cheshire ; 63 *Lydia*, b March 2, 1726, m Jason Hitchcock, Sept. 20, 1741 ; 64 *Mary*, b April 7, 1728, m John Smith of Cheshire ; 65 *Ephraim*, b April 7, 1730 ; 66 *Tirzah*, b Oct. 3, 1733, m Samuel Smith of Cheshire ; 67 *Elam*, b Nov. 10, 1735 ; 68 *Elizabeth*, b Feb. 10, 1738, m Ebenezer Brown of Cheshire ; 69 *John*, b Dec. 27, 1739 ; 70 *Merriman*, b 1741, d unmarried in Cheshire ; 71 *Thankful*, no account of this person recorded ; 72 *Phebe*, m Timothy Gaylord, May 4, 1748.

## 17. CAPT. SAMUEL.

CAPT. SAMUEL COOK, son of Samuel and Hannah Ives Cook, married Hannah Lewis, daughter of Ebenezer and Elizabeth Lewis, of Wallingford, Feb. 8, 1721. He was a wealthy shipping merchant, from the port of New Haven, where he died Nov. 7, 1745 (Thanksgiving Day), leaving an estate of £20103. He was buried at Cheshire, where a fine altar tomb marks his resting place. His benefactions to the church and poor of Cheshire are lasting monuments to his memory and worth.

Children : 73 *Hannah*, b Dec. 22, 1722, m Elnathan Beach. She died May 18, 1754 ; 74 *Rhoda*, b Oct. 22, 1724, m Benjamin Hitchcock, of Cheshire, Feb. 27, 1745 ; 75 *Damaris*, b Nov., 1726, m Rev. Ebenezer Boone, of Farmington, Dec. 19, 1750, then removed to Vermont ; 76 *Thaddeus*, b Sept. 10, 1728 ; 77 *Lowly*, b May 10, 1730, m Andrew

Hull of Cheshire, Oct. 17, 1750; 78 *Samuel*, b Nov. 16, 1733; 79 *Eunice*, b June 29, 1735, m Samuel Hull, of Cheshire, b Feb., 1755; 80 *Levi*, b Nov. 10, 1737, m Isaac Benham of Cheshire; 81 *Aaron*, b Nov. 30, 1739.

Elnathan Beach was a partner with Capt. Cook, whose dau. he married. Andrew Hull was the Hon. father of the late Gen. Andrew Hull of Cheshire, and great grandfather of Rear Admiral Andrew Hull Foote, U. S. N. Samuel Hull was brother to Andrew Hull, and grandfather to the late Mrs. Jonathan Law, of Cheshire and Hartford.

### 18. AARON.

AARON COOK, son of Samuel and Hannah (Ives) Cook, married 1st, Sarah, daughter of James Benham, Nov. 14, 1723. He married 2d, Sarah Hitchcock. She died Aug. 11, 1735, and for his 3d wife he married Ruth Burrage, of Stratford, Feb. 7, 1736. He was a very large landholder in the south-eastern part of Wallingford, Northford survey. He died Oct. 14, 1756, æ..60 years. Mrs. Ruth Cook died July 2, 1786, æ. 79 years.

Children, by 1st m.: 82 *Samuel*, b Sept. 25, 1725, d before his father; 83 *Stephen*, b Dec. 28, 1727; 84 *Titus*, b Feb. 25, 130; 85 *Abel*, b Feb. 23, 1732. By 2d marriage: 86 *Sarah*, b June 2, 1735. By 3d marriage: 87 *Lydia*, b 1736, m Uriah Collins, she d Jan. 9, 1793; 88 *Ruth*, b Sept. 7, 1738, m William Collins, she d June 9, 1790; 89 *Esther*, b May 14, 1740; 90 *Elizabeth*, b March 16, 1741-2, d Jan. 27, 1751; 91 *Aaron*, b June 5, 1744; 92 *Miriam*, b June 30, 17 46, d Dec. 1. 1750; 93 *Lucy*, b Sept. 20, 1748, d April 29, 1760; 94 *Elizabeth*, b June 7, 1751, d Oct. 19, 1762.

### 27. MOSES.

MOSES COOK, son of Samuel and Elizabeth Cook, m Sarah Culver, June 18, 1740, and went to Branford. Subsequently he went to Waterbury, where his wife died, Jan. 4, 1760, and he afterwards m Dinah Harrison, widow of Benj., June 7, 1762. He was killed by Moses Paul, an Indian, in the town

of Woodbridge, Dec. 12, 1771. (Paul was executed at New
Haven in June, 1772). Mr. Cook was æ. 54 years. Mrs
Dinah Cook d Oct. 4, 1792.

Children by 1st m. : 95 *Charles*, b June 3, 1742 ; 96 *Moses*,
b May 30, 1744, in Branford, d 1832 ; 97 *Sarah*, b June 13,
1747, d April 5, 1823 ; 98 *Esther*, b June 27, 1750, m Joseph
Beebe, she d in Ohio, 1810 ; 99 *Elizabeth*, b May 15, 1752,
m Benj. Baldwin, she d 1797 ; 100 *Hannah*, b ' m. 11, 1755,
m Titus Bronson, she d 1841 ; 101 *Lydia*, b March 27, 1760,
'm —— Hickox.

### 29. ASAPH.

ASAPH COOK, son of Samuel and Elizabeth Cook, m Sarah
Parker, of Wallingford, and went to Granville, Mass., where
he remained until about the close of the Revolution, when
he removed to Granville, N. Y., where he d in 1792 ; she d in
1818, æ. 96 years.

Children : 102 *Samuel*, b Aug. 18, 1744 ; 103 *Amasa*, b
1746, m Miriam Loomis, of Granville. N. Y., subsequently of
Essex Co., N. Y. ; 104 *Asaph*, b March 6, 1748 ; 105 *Joseph*,
b April 13, 1750 ; 106 *Susannah*, b April 13, 1750, m Ichabod
Parker, she d 1770 ; 107 *Sarah*, b 1752, m Wm Meacham,
2nd, Zeruah Everest, she d 1777 ; 108 *Thankful*, b 1754, m
Gideon Beebe, of Adams, Mass. ; 109 *Hannah*, b June 5,
1758 ; 110 *Charles*, b May 9, 1764 ; 111 *Lois*, b 1766, m John
Merrick, of Granville, N. Y.

### 38. ISAAC.

ISAAC COOK, son of Isaac and Sarah Cook, m Jerusha
Sexton, of Wallingford, Oct. 13, 1733. He died March 16,
1780, æ 80 years. She died Oct. 13, 1795. He was a tanner
and currier of leather.

Children : 112 *Amos*, b Dec. 5, 1734 ; 113 *Jerusha*, b Nov.
19, 1736, m Gideon Hosford, Feb. 23, 1757 ; 114 *Isaac*, b
July 28, 1739 ; 115 *Caleb*, b Nov. 14, 1741 ; 116 *Minikcell*, b
Dec. 9, 1743, d Jan. 26, 1744 ; 117 *Ambrose*, b March 19,
1744, d in infancy ; 118 *Ambrose*, b June 30, 1746 ; 119 *Elihu*,

U u

b Aug. 16, 1747, d Aug. 31, 1747; 120 *Mindwell*, b April 20, 1750, m Capt. Jeremiah Carrington, of Wallingford.

### 43. BENJAMIN.

BENJAMIN COOK. son of Joseph and Eleanor Cook, married Hannah Munson, Jan. 20, 1741. She was celebrated in her day as a skillful midwife in Wallingford, where they lived at the time of his decease, which occurred about 1790. He was a weaver and farmer.

Children: 121 *Benjamin*, b Oct. 8, 1743; 122 *Martha*, m Col. Isaac Cook of Wallingford; 123 *Joel*, b Aug. 31, 1745, d young; 124 *Merriman*, b Oct. 1, 1748; 125 *Lois*, b 1752, m Oliver Doolittle, Jan. 16, 1776; 126 *Phebe*, b May 3, 1756, m Isaac Doolittle of Wallingford.

### 44. DANIEL.

DANIEL COOK, son of Joseph and Eleanor Cook, m Elizabeth Pond, Feb. 6, 1746. He moved from Wallingford to Goshen, where she died, Sept., 1791.

Children: 127 *Samuel*, b Aug. 2, 1747, in Wallingford, went to Goshen, Conn.; 128 *Amasa*, b Oct. 26, 1749; 129 *Philip*, b Feb. 2, 1752; 130 *Lois*, b Feb. 27, 1754, m Joel Gaylord, of Goshen, Conn.; 131 *Lydia*, b Oct. 29, 1756, m Moses Bartholomew, of Goshen, Conn.; 132 *Daniel*, b Aug. 18, 1761; 133 *Moses*, b April 25. 1764; 134 *John*, b Sept. 8, 1767, no report from him.

### 45. WALTER.

WALTER COOK, son of Joseph and Eleanor Cook, m Reuema Calling, and went to Goshen, Conn. Subsequently he went to Richmond, Mass. He was a farmer and shoemaker.

Children: 135 *Eunice*, b Nov. 10, 1754, in Wallingford; 136 *Pitman*, b June 28, 1757, in Wallingford; 137 *Walter*, b Sept. 10, 1764, in Goshen; 138 *John*, b Oct. 2, 1767, in Goshen; 139 *Sinai*, b Oct. 12, 1769, in Goshen; 140 *Susannah*, b Feb. 26. 1790. in Goshen; 141 *Lucy*, m Abijah Newton, of Goshen, Conn.

### 48. LAMBERT.

LAMBERT COOK, son of Joseph and Eleanor Cook, married 1st, Abigail ——, and settled in Goshen, Conn. She died Oct. 8, 1758. He married Mindwell Loomis, for his 2nd wife. Dec. 13, 1759. He died at Goshen, Conn.

Child by 1st marriage: 142 *Mary*, b July 17, 1757. By 2nd marriage: 143 *Abigail*, b Jan. 25, 1760; 144 *Joseph*, b Feb. 25, 1762; 145 *Hannah*, b Dec. 25, 1763; 146 infant, b June 11, 1765, d æ. 1 day.

### 51. EBENEZER.

EBENEZER COOK, son of Israel and Elizabeth Cook. He married Eunice ——. This family left Wallingford soon after the war of the Revolution.

Children: 147 *Ebenezer*, b May 19, 1760; 148 *Munson*, b March 1, 1762; 149 *Eunice*, b Feb. 28, 1766; 150 *William*, b July 3, 1772.

### 55. JOHN.

JOHN COOK, son of Israel and Elizabeth Cook, married Naomi Abernathy, and removed to Guildhall, Vermont. She died in 1809, aged about 75 years. He died at Guildhall in 1812, aged 81 years.

Children: 151 *Benjamin*, b Jan. 24, 1764; 152 *Naomi*, b March 12, 1766, m Laban Beach; 153 *John*, b March 16, 1768. d at Guildhall, Vt.; 154 *Ruth*, b Feb. 7, 1769; 155 *Lemuel*, b Feb. 7, 1770; 156 *Enos A.*, b Jan 7, 1773; 157 *Raphael*, b May 8, 1775; 158 *Abigail*, b May 2, 1777. d at Guildhall, Vt.; 159 *Anna*, b July 4, 1779, m —— Stoddard; 160 *Beulah*, m Eli How, she died in 1810; 161 *Zaccheus*, b Sept. 13, 1781.

### 57. BENJAMIN.

BENJAMIN COOK, son of Israel and Elizabeth Cook, married Martha Benham, Aug. 2, 1759, and doubtless left Wallingford soon afterwards.

Children: 162 *Martha*, b March 11, 1760, in Wallingford; 163 *Benjamin*, b May 6, 1675.

## 58. ASHBEL.

ASHBEL COOK, son of Israel and Elizabeth Cook, married
Rachel ———. He left Wallingford about 1768, when it is
supposed he went to Vermont.

Children: 164 *John;* 165 *Simeon,* d young; 166 *Israel;* 167
*Ashbel;* 168 *Simeon;* 169 *Rice,* b Aug. 12, 1780, in Rutland,
Vt.; 170 *Orel.*

## 65. EPHRAIM.

EPHRAIM COOK, son of Ephraim and Lydia Cook, married
Elizabeth Hull, Jan. 1, 1752. He was a farmer, shoemaker,
tanner and currier of leather; he died in Cheshire, Conn.,
Jan. 18, 1789, æ. 59 yrs.

Children: 171 *Lois,* b Jan., 1753, d Nov. 4, 1753, æ. 10
mos.; 172 *Ephraim,* b 1754, d Dec. 2, 1764, æ 10 yrs.; 173
*Lydia,* b Dec. 20, 1756; 174 *Anna,* b Feb. 5, 1764; 175
*Urina,* b 1765, d Dec. 11, 1771, æ. 6 yrs.; 176 *Clarinda,* b
1770, d Dec. 5, 1772, æ. 2 yrs.

## 67. ELAM.

ELAM COOK, son of Ephraim and Lydia Cook, married
Abigail Hall, Jan. 8, 1761. He died in Cheshire, Feb. 3,
1808, aged 73 years. She died in Ohio, Sept. 26, 1816, aged
81 years.

Children: 177 *Merriman,* b Nov. 12, 1761, went to Barton,
Ohio; 178 *Samuel,* b 1764, settled in Cheshire, Conn.; 179
*Esther,* b March, 1769, m John Ford of Prospect, and went
to Ohio, she was the mother of Gov. Ford of Ohio; 180
*Ephraim,* b Dec. 21, 1775; 181 *Elam,* b 1780, settled in
Cheshire; 182 *Joseph II..* b Feb. 1, 1782; 183 *Abigail,* b
July 10, 1784, married Hon. Peter Hitchcock of Ohio, for-
merly of Cheshire.

## 69. JOHN.

·JOHN COOK, son of Ephraim and Lydia Cook, married
Obedience ———; he died in Cheshire, Oct. 2, 1764, æ. 25
yrs. His widow married Daniel Ives, Dec. 7, 1769.

Child: 184 *Ephraim,* b 1763, d Oct. 2, 1765, æ. 2 yrs.

## 76. THADDEUS.

Col. THADDEUS COOK, son of Capt. Samuel and Hannah Cook, m 1st, Lois, daughter of Capt. Elnathan Beach, of Cheshire, Nov. 28, 1750. She died April 4, 1753, a. 21 yrs. He m 2nd, Sarah, daughter of Hon. Benjamin Hall, of Che shire She died Sept. 5, 1774, at 44 years. His 3d wife was Abigail ———, she survived him. After having served his country during the Revolution, under the brave Gen. Gates, and his townsmen in almost every office of trust or honor within their gift, he died Feb. 27, 1800.

Child by 1st marriage: 185 *Lois*, b April 1, 1753. By 2d marriage: 186 *Sarah*, b July 23, 1755, m Dr. Gould Gift Norton, of Cheshire, she d Sept., 1838; 187 *Samuel*, b April 19, 1758; 189 *Eunice*, b Jan. 15, 1761, d Feb. 26, 1776, æ. 15 yrs.; 190 *Lucy*, b 1762, m Amos Harrison Ives. She d Feb. 30, 1836, in Cheshire; 191 *Thaddeus*, b May 3, 1764, gradua ted at Yale, 1783, d Oct. 3, 1789; 192 *Sally*, m Nathan Har rison, of New Branford; 193 *Clarissa*, m ——— Hall, and had a dau., Sukey Hall.

## 78. SAMUEL.

SAMUEL COOK, son of Capt. Samuel and Hannah Cook, m Jerusha Hollingworth, March 4, 1756. It was the intention of his father that he should receive a liberal education at col lege, but for some cause now unknown, he gave it up, and settled on a farm in the north part of Cheshire, where he d Jan. 5, 1800, æ. 67 years.

Children: 194 *Hannah*, b April 20, 1758, m a Mr. Wright : 195 *Temperance*, b Aug. 6, 1760; 196 *Perez*, b Dec. 1, 1762 ; 197 *Jerusha*, b Jan. 7, 1767, d July 29, 1803 ; 198 *Eunice*, b March 23, 1769; 199 *Damaris*, b Feb. 23, 1772 ; 200 *Abigail*, b June 27, 1775, m Elkanah Doolittle, of Cheshire. She d Dec. 16, 1800.

## 81. AARON.

AARON COOK, son of Capt. Samuel and Hannah Cook, m Mary, dau. of Capt. Cornelius Brooks, of Cheshire. He d Sept. 29, 1776, æ. 37 yrs. She d Sept. 30, 1776, æ. 38 yrs.

He was a farmer, about three and one-half miles south-east of Cheshire meeting-house, where his father formerly lived.

Children: 201 *Jerusha*, b 1757, m Robert Hotchkiss. She d May 19, 1824 : 202 *Cornelius*, b Oct. 9, 1763 ; 203 *Sue*, m ‹ Samuel Cook, she d Dec. 24, 1824 ; 204 *Aaron*, b 1768, d in Cheshire ; 205 *Stephen*, b 1771, m Eunice Beadles, of Wallingford : 206 *Mary*, m Shelden Spencer, Esq.

### 83.  STEPHEN.

STEPHEN COOK, son of Capt. Aaron and Sarah Cook, m 1st, Anna Culver, Dec 25, 1751.  After her decease he m Thankful Preston, March 2, 1771, and for his 3d wife he married Anna Tyler.  Anna his ·1st wife died Dec. 10, 1769. Mrs. Thankful his 2d wife died Sept. 20. 1776, and Anna his 3d wife died Sept. 23, 1817, æ. 80 years.

Children by 1st wife: 207 *Samuel*, b Oct. 22, 1752 ; 208 *Stephen*, b March 25, 1755, went to Vermont ; 209 *Anna*, b Oct. 5, 1757 ; 210 *Elihu*, b July 2, 1760, went to Vermont ; 211 *Ruth*, b June 30, 1763, d æ. 90 yrs.  By 2d marriage : 212 *Lyman*, b June 30, 1772. went to Ohio ; 213 *Jared*, b Aug. 9, 1775.  By 3d marriage : 214 *Lemuel*, b Sept. 2, 1779 ; 215 *Malachi*, b Aug. 28, 1781.

### 84.  TITUS.

TITUS COOK, son of Capt. Aaron and Jerusha Cook, married Sarah Merriman, Jan. 18, 1753.  She died Feb. 16, 1795.  He died April 4, 1809, æ. 80 years, and was buried in Northford, Conn.

Children : 216 *Sarah*, b Nov. 14, 1753 ; 217 *Jerusha*, b May 27, 1757 ; 218, 219 *Lucy* and *Titus*, b April 23, 1761, d in childhood ; 220 *Abigail*, b July 19. 1763 ; 221 *Esther*, b July 21, 1765 ; 222 *Caleb*, was accidentally killed : 223 *Sally :* 224 *Titus*, b Nov. 7, 1775 ; 225 *Lydia*, b April 1, 1778.

### 85.  ABEL.

ABEL COOK, son of Capt. Aaron and Sarah Cook, married Mary, daughter of Dea. Benjamin and Elizabeth P. Atwater of Wallingford. Nov. 16, 1757. She was born Dec. 30, 1735. and died Jan. 13. 1774. æ. 30. He died Aug. 10, 1776, æ. 44 years.

Children: 226 *Atwater*, b Nov. 3, 1758; 227 *Porter*, b July 27, 1760; 228 *Elizabeth*, b March 13, 1763; 229 *Abel*, b March 27, 1765; 230 *Chester*, b Aug. 13, 1767, d young; 231 *Daniel M*, b Feb 16, 1770; 232 *Mary*, b April 2, 1773, m Col. Eliakim Hall, d Dec. 1, 1839; 233 *Chester*, b Oct. 6, 1775.

### 91. AARON.

AARON COOK, son of Capt. Aaron and Ruth B. Cook, married 1st, Lucretia Dudley. She died April 16, 1771, æ. 27 years. He married 2d, Elizabeth Taintor. She died April 24, 1816, æ. 65 years. He died Sept. 14, 1825, æ. 80 years. and was interred in Northford grave-yard.

Children ; 234 *Oliver Dudley*, b 1766, grad. at Yale College, 1735 ; 253 *Aaron*, b 1768 ; 236 *Kilborn*, b 1771, settled in North Guilford, Conn. By 2nd marriage : 237 *Increase*, b 1773, grad. at Yale College, 1793 ; 238 *Nathaniel*, b 1775, m Susan Baldwin ; 239 *Lucretia*, b 1780, d Nov. 14, 1844 ; 240 *Apollos*, b 1786, settled at Cattskill, N. Y. ; 241 *Thomas Burrage*. 242 *Elizabeth*, b 1776, m Joshua Atwater, she d Apr. 4, 1842. æ. 66 years ; 243 *Lydia*, m Doct. Amos G. Hull ; 244 *Henrietta*.

### 95. CHARLES.

CHARLES COOK, son of Moses and Sarah Cook, married Sybil Munson, Aug. 1, 1764. He resided severally in New Haven, Waterbury and Watertown, Conn. He died in 1797. æ. 55 years.

Children : 245 *James Munson*, b June 11, 1765. in New Haven ; 246 *Sarah*, b Dec. 22, 1766.

### 96. MOSES.

MOSES COOK, son of Moses and Sarah Cook, married Jemima Upson of Waterbury. March 4, 1766. He was a musician during the Revolutionary war. He died Dec. 25, 1831. She died March 6 1821.

Children : 247 *Joseph*, b March 4. 1767 ; 248 *Lucy*, b Sept. 29, 1769, d unmarried, Dec. 8, 1835 ; 249 *Daniel*, b Sept. 5. 1773 ; 250 *Hannah*, b March 5, 1775, m Horatio Upson, Waterbury ; 251 *Anna*, b March 8, 1778, m Mark Leavenworth ; 252 *Elias*, b Dec. 26, 1783, m 2nd, Mrs. Charry Bartholomew.

### 102. SAMUEL.

SAMUEL COOK, son of Asaph and Sarah Parker Cook, m Chloe Atwater, daughter of Titus and Margarette, of Cheshire. He went with his father to Granville, Mass., and subsequently to Granville, Washington Co., N. Y. He died in 1823, æ. 79 years.

Child : 253 *Moses*, settled at Hartford, Washington Co., N. Y.

### 104. ASAPH.

ASAPH COOK, son of Asaph and Sarah Parker Cook, married Thankful Parker, June 17, 1776 ; she was born in Wallingford, April, 1776. They removed to Granville, N. Y. In 1818 they went to Ridgefield, Four Corners, Ohio, where he died in 1826, æ. 78. He was at the battle of Lexington, Mass., as were several of his brothers. His widow died in 1819.

Children : 254 *Eluthcras*, b March 21, 1777, d Nov., 1780 ; 255 *Hannah*, b Feb. 25, 1779, m Lewis Stone, Aug. 3, 1839 ; 256 *Asaph*, b March 23, 1781, d August 2, 1842 ; 257 *Rhoda*, b January 7, 1784, d Sept. 30, 1805 ; 258 *Chloe*, b July 21, 1786, d Oct., 1845 ; 259 *Eluthcras*, b Dec. 25, 1787, d Dec. 27, 1864 ; 260 *Sarah*, b Jan. 2, 1790, d March, 1829 ; 261 *Thankful P.*, b April 26, 1792, d unmarried, Aug. 3. 1858 ; 262 *Erastus*, b Feb. 6, 1795, d July 30, 1849 ; 263 *Edwin*, b Aug. 25, 1797, d Nov. 3, 1807 : 264 *Israel*, b Dec. 4, 1801, d unmarried, Jan. 6, 1854 ; 265 *Elmira*, b Oct. 15, 1803, d unmarried, Jan. 10, 1852.

### 105. JOSEPH.

JOSEPH COOK, son of Asaph and Sarah Parker Cook, went early in life with his father and family to Granville, N. Y. ;

thence to Hartford, Washington Co., N. Y.; and in 1803 to
Adams, Jefferson Co., N. Y.; from there in 1805 to live with
his sons in Ohio. He died at Oxford, Erie Co., Ohio, æ
nearly 86 yrs. The name of his wife was Rachel Langdon.
I have ascertained the names of only two of their children,
to wit:

266 *Chauncey*, b 1775, resided in Erie Co., Ohio; 267
*Charles L.*, b 1778.

### 110. CHARLES.

CHARLES COOK, son of Asaph and Sarah Parker Cook,
married Elizabeth Curtis of Granville, N. Y., daughter of
David Curtis; he died at Sackett's Harbor, N. Y., May 13,
1855, æ. 91 yrs.

Children: 268 *Betsey*, b Feb. 4, 1791, m Rev. E. Rossiter,
she died Nov., 1833: 269 *Daniel C.*, b May 20, 1793, d 1813,
was a physician; 270 *Horace*, b Nov. 5, 1775; 271 *Charles*, b
May 12, 1778; 272 *Elisha*, b April 12, 1801; 273 *Theda
Louisa*, b Nov. 10, 1802, m B. F. Darrow, 1831, d 1832; 274
*Laura E.*, b Sept. 10, 1804, m Ephraim Read, settled in Ohio;
275 *Hiram E.*, b Jan. 15, 1807, d Aug., 1822, was a physician.

### 112. AMOS.

AMOS COOK, son of Isaac and Jerusha Cook, married
Rhoda, daughter of Gideon Hosford, Feb. 23, 1757; she died
May 10, 1810. He died at Wallingford.

Children: 276 *Elihu*, b April 25, 1757; 277 *Rhoda*, b
April 16, 1761, m John Davis; 278 *Roswell*, b Dec. 6, 1764;
279 *Uri H.*, b Jan. 19, 1767, supposed to have settled in Nor-
way, Herkimer Co., N. Y., 1789; 280 *Amos*, b Nov. 29, 1768;
281 *Lucinda*, b Oct. 31, 1771, m Stephen Hart in 1790; 282
*Sybil*, b Oct. 10, 1778, m Thomas Welton, Jan. 3, 1797; 283
*Lyman*, b Sept. 21, 1780; 284 *Desire*, b March 5, 1783.

### 114. ISAAC.

Col. ISAAC COOK, son of Isaac and Jerusha Cook, married
Martha, daughter of Benjamin Cook, March 6, 1760; he was

in the service of his country during the Revolution. as Colonel. He died June, 1810, æ. 71 yrs.

Children: 285 *Joel*, b Oct. 12, 1760, a distinguished officer in the war of 1812 ; 286 *Lemuel*, b March 17, 1762 ; 287 *James*, b Jan 29, 1764, m Chloe Royce, May 4, 1786 ; 288 *Lucy*, b Jan. 29, 1766 ; 289 *Isaac*, b July 16, 1768. settled at Chillicothe, Ohio; 260 *Martha*, b June 30, 1770 ; 291 *Mindwell*, b July 17, 1772, m Asahel Barham, Jan. 6, 1791 ; 292 *Phebe*, b Feb. 9, 1777, m David Stocking, 1805.

### 115. CALEB.

CALEB COOK Esq., son of Isaac and Jerusha Cook, married Abigail Finch, Jan. 12, 1764. She died Dec. 22, 1794. He then married Mrs. Lydia Foot. She died May 31, æ. 89. He was a magistrate for many years, and died in his native town, Nov 17, 1821, æ. 80 years.

Children : 293 *Viney*, b Nov. 26, 1764, m Abel Cook, Dec. 19, 1790 ; 294 *Augustus*, b Jan. 25, 1767 ; 295 *Caleb*, b July 27, 1768, d young ; 296 *Abigail*, b Nov. 8. 1769 ; 297 *Nabby*, b April 10, 1777, m Ira Hall, she d 1859 ; 298 *Betsey*, b Feb. 18, 1779, d unmarried, Jan., 1859 ; 299 *Mary Ann*, b Aug. 23, 1783 : 300, 301, *Caleb* and *Amelia*, b June 4, 1786, the former m Sarah Eaton, the latter d Aug. 31, 1786.

### 118. AMBROSE.

AMBROSE COOK, son of Isaac and Jerusha Cook, married Esther Peck. He died at the age of 78, March 5, 1824. She died Sept. 13, 1822, æ. 78.

Children: 302 *Chauncey*, b Feb. 1, 1767, m Eunice Dutton ; 303 *Samuel*, b July 8, 1769, m Martha Cook; 304 *Jerusha*, b April 25, 1771, m Hunn Munson, Esq. ; 305 *Abigail*, b Apr. 9, 1773, supposed died young ; 306 *Charles*, b April 26, 1775, m Sylvia, dau. of Elihu Yale ; 307 *Esther*, b Oct. 9, 1777, m Benajah. son of Stephen Yale ; 308 *Lydia*, b Oct. 13, 1779, m Andrew Hall, M. D. : 309 *Nancy*, b Nov. 13, 1782, m Richard Hall ; 310 *Orrin*, b Feb. 14, 1784, m Miss —— Stone, of Guilford, Conn.; 311 *Diana*, b Nov. 28. 1786, m Andrew Bartholomew.

### 121. BENJAMIN.

BENJAMIN COOK, son of Benjamin and Hannah Cook, married April 19, 1770, Esther Rice, dau. of Reuben Rice of Wallingford. He died 1821, ae. 78 years. He was a large, corpulent man.

Children: 312 *Hannah*, m Linus Hall; 313 *Rice*, went west, m a Miss Twiss; 314 *Keziah*, b Jan. 27. 1774: 315 *Munson*, b Aug. 27, 1776; 316 *Daniel*, d about 1860, in western New York; 317 *Betsey*, d unmarried; 318 *Charlotte*, b Oct. 26, 1787, m John Malone.

### 124. MERRIMAN.

MERRIMAN COOK, son of Benjamin and Hannah Cook, m Mary Osborn, May 2, 1768. He went to Malta, Saratoga Co., N. Y. He died Sept 27, 1827. ae. 80, and she died May 20, 1832, ae. 83 years.

Children: 319 *Joseph*, b Sept. 1, 1768, m Mary Ann Tolman; 320 *Eunice*, b Dec., 1770, m John Scarrit; 321 *Lydia*, b 1773, m Benj. Hall, d Nov. 8, 1856; 322 *Polly*, b March, 1775, m Samuel Hall; 323 *Elihu*, b May 1, 1777, m Sarah Cooley; 324 *Susannah*, b May 9, 1779, m Isaac Darrow; 325 *Lois*, b May 27, 1782, m Amy Hulin; 325 1-2 *Samuel*, m 1st, Mary Culver, 2d, Sally Galpin; 326 *Lyman*, b Sept. 16, 1783; 327 *Catharine*, b 1786, d 1796; 328 *Marcus*, b 1789; 329 *Sherlock*, b 1781, m Milly Thurston.

### 128. AMASA.

AMASA COOK, son of Daniel and Elizabeth Cook, married (after his removal to Goshen ) Rachel Norton, March 5, 1772. She died Dec. 17, 1819. He died Dec. 4, 1821, ae. 72 years.

Children: 330 *Sally*, b Dec. 28, 1772, m Samuel Chamberlain, she d Aug. 1, 1828; 331 infant, b Oct. 28, 1774, d same day.

### 129. PHILIP.

PHILIP COOK, son of Daniel and Elizabeth Cook, married Thankful Tuttle, of Goshen, Conn. He removed to Nassau.

N. Y., where she died Jan. 9, 1816, ae. 64. He died March 26, 1825, ae. 73 years.

Children: 332 *Samuel*, b March 4, 1776; 333 *Augustus*, b Jan. 25, 1778, deaf and dumb, d 1843; 334 *Erastus*, b Dec 18, 1779; 335 *Silas*, b Nov. 22, 1781, d Aug. 24, 1811; 336 *Gratia T.*, b Oct. 27, 1784, d unm. Oct. 4, 1840; 337 *Laura H.*, b Jan. 4, 1787, m Samuel McLellan, M. D.

### 132. DANIEL.

DANIEL COOK, son of Daniel and Elizabeth Cook, married Eliza Porter, of Goshen. He died near the south-west corner of the town.

Children: 338 *Amasa*, he was killed by a cart, 1817; 339 *Phineas*, m Irene Churchill.

### 133. MOSES.

MOSES COOK, son of Daniel and Elizabeth Cook, married Lydia Thompson. She died Jan. 21, 1821, æ. 72 years. He died Feb. 23, 1841, ae. 77 years.

Children: 340 *George*, b July 24, 1791; 341 *Harriet*, b May 25, 1794, m Samuel Cook; 342 *Betsey*, b March 6, 1797; 343 *Frederick*, b Nov. 9, 1801; 344 *Moses*, b March 2, 1808.

### 151. BENJAMIN.

BENJAMIN, son of John and Naomi Cook, married Charity Elliott, of Guildhall, Vt. He died May, 1843.

Children: 345 *Elias*, b Sept. 29, 1798; 346 *Naomi*, b May 25, 1800, d unm. June 15, 1818; 347 *Benjamin*, b April 17, 1802; 348 *Charity*, b April 8, 1804, d unm. April, 1820; 349 *Ira*, b Feb. 23, 1806; 350 *Abigail*, b Sept. 16, 1808; 351 *Esther*, b Feb. 12, 1811, m Isaac Brooks; 352 *Anderson*, b March 30, 1813, m Catherine M. Cramer; 353 *Selina*, b April 7, 1816, m Frederick Rich, of Petersham; 354 *Lorenzo*, b April 15, 1819, d unm. June 6, 1855; 355 *Semantha*, b June 18, 1822, m Marshall Twitchell, d Dec. 1, 1854.

### 155. LEMUEL.

LEMUEL COOK, son of John and Naomi Cook, married Hannah Gustin, and settled at Guildhall, Vt. She died June 1, 1828.

Children: 356 *Thomas*, b May 7, 1802, d at the west, 357 *Mary*, b Aug 6, 1805, m ——— Cheney, May 1, 1831; 358 *Beulah*, b Dec 22, 1808, m 1831, d June 8, 1846; 359 *Dr. Raphael*, b May 5, 1810, d Aug., 1834, ae. 24 yrs; 360 *Rebecca*, b March 31, 1813, d Feb 5, 1831, at Guildhall, Vt.; 361 *Lemuel*, b Nov. 20, 1817, d Feb. 12, 1855, ae. 38 yrs; 362 *Adelphia*, b Jan. 13. 1824, m Dec., 1855.

## 156. ENOS.

ENOS A. COOK, son of John and Naomi Cook, m Susan Palmer, at Granby, Vt. After his decease she went to New Portage, Ohio, with her children, of which the following are a part, viz. :

363 *Raphael*, d in Vermont ; 364 *Enos A.*, residence unknown ; 365 *Orrin*, m Harriet Cook ; 366 *Ambrose*, residence in 1862, Spencer, Medina Co., Ohio.

## 157. RAPHAEL.

RAPHAEL COOK, son of John and Naomi Cook, m Sally Fox, of Canada. He died at Guildhall, Vt. His widow m Eli Howe, of Guildhall.

Children : 367 *Moses M.*, is a printer by profession ; 368 *Naomi*, went to Stanstead, Canada East.

## 161. ZACCHEUS.

ZACCHEUS COOK, son of John and Naomi Cook, of Wallingford and Guildhall, married Phebe Elliot, and settled at Dryden, N. Y., and probably died there.

Children : 366 *John*, resided at Guildhall, Vt. ; 370 *Harriet*, m Orrin Cook, son of Enos.

## 169. RICE.

RICE COOK, son of Ashbel and Rachel Cook, was born at Rutland, Vt., removed to Stillwater, N. Y. Married Ann ———. He lived in Troy, N. Y., in 1837.

Children : 371 *Mary Ann* ; 372 *Sarah Ann* ; 373 *Rachel* ; 374 *Rebecca* ; 375 *Lydia Lorraine* ; 376 *Adeline Ann* ; 377 *Chas. Rice*, b Aug. 14, 1820, in Stillwater ; 378 *Julia Ann*.

### 177. MERRIMAN.

MERRIMAN COOK, son of Elam and Abigail Hall Cook, m Sally, daughter of Moses and Mary Bradley, Aug. 8, 1781. She died April 11, 1812. He married Betsey Hubbard, May 2, 1815; she died May 7, 1837. He left Cheshire, his native place, in 1809, and settled at Burton, Ohio, where he died Aug. 25, 1858. Betsey, his wife, died May 7, 1857. He was a tanner and currier by trade, shoemaker, &c., &c.

Children: 379 *John*, b Dec. 27, 1782. in Cheshire, Conn.; 380 *Hiram*, b March 21, 1781, in Cheshire, Conn.; 381 *Soalma*, b Feb. 24, 1792, m Adolphus Carlton; 382 *Eleazer*, b Aug. 30, 1799, in Cheshire, Conn.

### 178. SAMUEL.

SAMUEL COOK, son of Elam and Abigail Cook, married Sue, daughter of Aaron and Mary Cook; he died Oct. 10, 1800, ae. 37; she died Dec. 24, 1843.

Children: 383 *Clara*, b May 12, 1784, m Bellina Plum of Cheshire, she died Oct. 28, 1848; 384 *Samuel*, b 1786; 385 *Samanda*, b Nov. 6, 1788, m Silas Curtis, Dec., 1806.

### 180. EPHRAIM.

EPHRAIM COOK, son of Elam and Abigail Cook, married Sukey, daughter of Stephen and Susan Ives of North Haven, Oct. 16, 1799; he removed to Burton, Ohio, in 1814, and died there Jan. 29, 1854; she died Dec. 29, 1843.

Children: 286 *Stephen I. C.*, b April 6, 1800; 387 *Marietta*, b March 4, 1802, m John Eldridge; 388 *Harriet*, b Sept. 27, 1804, m Oliver Mastick; 389 *Sally*, b June 4, 1807; 390 *Julia Ann*, b June 27, 1809, died Sept. 12, 1809; 391 *Horace*, b Sept. 11, 1811; 392 *Esther E.*, b Oct. 12 1813, m Asa Carl; 393 *Samuel*, b Dec. 1, 1815, d June 25, 1816; 394 *Lavinia*, b Aug. 11, 1819, d June 24, 1850.

### 181. ELAM.

ELAM COOK, son of Elam and Abigail Cook, married Rebecca Bradley, Oct. 20, 1799. She died Nov 9, 1829, ae. 51 years. He died March 17, 1830, ae. 51 years.

Children 395 *Marius*, b July 19, 1800, d Aug. 2, 1804 ; 396 *Ethelbert*, b Oct. 30, 1801 ; 397 *Mariah*, b May 28, 1804, m Allen Lounsbury : 398 *Abigail*, b Aug. 29, 1806, m Perez Sanford of Prospect : 399 *Rebecca*, b March 7, 1809, m Orrin Brooks, Meriden : 400 *Emeline*, b Sept. 17, 1811, m Charles R. Miles, Cheshire : 401 *Elam*, b Aug. 15, 1815.

### 182. JOSEPH.

JOSEPH H. COOK, son of Elam and Abigail Cook, married Lucinda Hitchcock of Cheshire, in 1794. They went to Sharon, Conn., and from thence to Litchfield, Ohio.

Children : 402 *Matilda*, m Rev. Gad Smith ; 403 *Lucius*, m Cornelia Sturges.

### 187. SAMUEL.

SAMUEL COOK, son of Thaddeus and Sarah Cook, married Mary, daughter of Constant Kirtland of Wallingford. He was a thrifty farmer in the western part of the town. He died Sept. 27, 1824, ae. 66. His widow died March 10, 1839, ae. 82 years

Children : 404 *Russel*, b Sept. 8, 1778, m —— Hall of Cheshire : 405 *Eunice*, b Aug. 24, 1780, m Elias Ford Esq., late of Naugatuck ; 406 *Billious*, b Sept. 29, 1782, m Sarah Munson of Wallingford : 407 *Harriet*, b May 17, 1785, m Ira Yale Esq., of Wallingford : 408 *Turhand K.*, b 1787, m Catharine Van Bryan of Catskill ; 409 *Samuel*, b Feb. 28, 1788, m Martha Culver of Wallingford ; 410 *Thaddeus*, b April 3, 1791, m 1st. Julia Cook, 2d. Sylvia Hall, 3d. Thankful Hall. 4th, Martha Hall ; 411 *George*, b April 17, 1794, m Lavinia Culver of Wallingford ; 412 *Frinda*, b Nov. 1, 1797, m Emily Atwater of Wallingford : 413 *John*, b Dec. 2, 1799, m Mary Munson of Northford.

### 196. PEREZ

PEREZ Cook, son of Samuel and Jerusha Cook, married Nancy E. Ely of Saybrook. He died July 23, 1820, ae. 57 years. She married Calvin Ely, and died in New Haven.

Children : 414 *Samuel D. E. S.*, d Jan. 20, 1820 ; 415 *Virgilius G.*, d in New Haven, Ct. ; 416 *Louisa E. S.*, m

Augustus Barnes at New Haven; 417 *Nancy Ely*, m Dr. Miller, she died in 1850.

### 202. CORNELIUS.

CORNELIUS BROOKS COOK, son of Aaron and Mary ( Brooks) Cook, married Louisa Hotchkiss of Cheshire. He died Sept. 1, 1827, ae. 64 years. She died Aug. 4, 1832, ae. 67 years.

Children: 418 *Rufus*, b 1790 ; 419 *Charlotte*, m 1st, Elam Dickerman, 2nd, Mr. Platt ; 420, *Brooks*, b 1798 ; 421 *Polly*, m Asa Bradley of Hamden.

### 204. AARON.

AARON COOK, son of Aaron and Mary B. Cook, married Betsey Preston of Wallingford. He died July 16, 1817, ae. 44 years. She died March 26, 1820, ae. 52 years.

Children: 422 *Amasa*, b 1791, d unmarried Dec. 18, 1831 ; 423 *Hannah ;* 424 *Aaron ;* 425 *Laura*, m Marshall Ives of Cheshire ; 426 *Alfred;* 427 infant, b 1806, d April 23, 1806 ; 428 *Betsey*, b 1808, d April 6, 1808 ; 429 *Sedgwick*, d in Windham, N. Y., leaving a family ; 430 *Stephen*, d in Cheshire ; 431 *Samuel*, b Dec., 1816, d Jan. 29, 1816 ; 432 infant, d March 14, 1834.

### 205. STEPHEN.

STEPHEN COOK, son of Aaron and Mary Brooks Cook, married Eunice, daughter of John Bradley, of Wallingford. He died Sept. 4, 1800, ae. 29. She died Oct. 18, 1800, ae. 27 years.

Children: 433 *Sarah*, b 1793, d unmarried ; 434 *Julia*, b 1794, m Thaddeus Cook of Wallingford ; 435 *Mary*, m 1st, Merrit Tuttle, 2d, Wm. Todd, Jr. ; 436 *Stephen*, b June 11, 1800, d in Mass., buried in North Haven.

### 207. SAMUEL.

SAMUEL COOK, son of Stephen and Anna ( Culver ) Cook, m —— Smith, and after her death he married Abigail Mallory of East Haven. She died Nov. 4, 1851, aged 91. He died May 12, 1823, ae. 71 years.

Child by 1st marriage : 437 *Rachel*. By 2d marriage : 438 *Lovely*, b May 18, 1782, m Amos Bird, Dec. 13, 1797 ; 439 *Electa*, b Jan. 11, 1785, m Canfield Downs, Oct., 1822 ; 440 *Hubbard*, b Aug. 20, 1787, in Wallingford ; 441 *Roxanna*, b May 10, 1788, m Newton Hecock, 1814 ; 442 *Stephen*, b 1790, d ae. 3 yrs. ; 443 *Perlina*, b May, 1795, d 1813 ; 444 *Harriet*, b Dec. 25, 1797, m Samuel Washburn ; 445 *Ruth*, b 1802, d May 16, 1826 ; 446 *Charry*, b 1804, d 1808.

### 208. STEPHEN.

STEPHEN COOK, son of Capt. Stephen and Anna Cook, m Sylvia Meigs. April 20, 1777. She was born in New Haven, May 27, 1760, and died at Adams' Basin, N. Y., Sept. 7, 1849, ae. 90. He died at Chateaugay, N. Y., Aug. 28, 1829, ae. 75 years.

Children : 447 *Chauncey*, b March 9, 1778, resides in Ottawa, Illinois ; 448 *Solomon*, b April 1, 1780, resides in Grand Rapids ; 449 *Betsey*, b Sept. 10, 1782, d August 2, 1800 ; 450 *Rebecca*, b August 2, 1785, d August 7, 1825 ; 451 *Sylvia*, b Feb. 3, 1788, m J. Morton of Erie, Penn. ; 452 *Sally*, b June 5, 1790, m S. M. Moon of ———, N. Y. ; 453 *Patty*, b Feb. 5, 1793, resides near Rochester, N. Y., a widow ; 454 *Stephen*, b March 15, 1796, res. at Oberlin, Ohio ; 455 *Anna*, b Feb. 1, 1799, res. at Plattsburg, N. Y. ; 456 *Betsey*, b July 13, 1802, m C. D. Graves, Rochester, N. Y. ; 457 *Lyman*, b Mar. 20, 1804, res. at Rochester, N. Y. ; 458 *Nelson*, b Sept. 24, 1806, res. at Half Day, Illinois.

### 210. ELIHU.

ELIHU COOK, son of Stephen and Anna Cook, married Lois Thorp, and removed to New Haven, Vt., afterwards to Illinois. One son only returned to me.

Child : 458 1-2 *Sherlock*.

### 212. LYMAN.

Dr. LYMAN COOK, son of Stephen and Thankful Cook, m Sarah Lyon, and went to Westchester Co., N. Y. He was aid to Gen. Thomas with rank of Colonel in 1807, and also

V v

sheriff of the county of Westchester six years. He died at Painesville, Ohio.

Child : 459 *Caroline*, b Sept. 6, 1797, m Stephen Matthews of Painesville, Ohio, Aug. 11, 1824.

### 213. JARED.

MAJ. JARED COOK, son of Stephen and Thankful Cook, married Lucy Munson, Feb. 28, 1819. He died Aug. 14, 1828, ae. 53 years. She was burned to death in 1869.

Children : 460 *George Lambert*, b Nov. 21, 1819, d Jan. 2, 1820; 461 *Jared Philos*, b Feb. 1, 1822.

### 214. LEMUEL.

LEMUEL COOK, son of Stephen and Anna Tyler Cook, married Mrs. Hannah Sears, formerly Bunnel, in 1813. He married, 2nd, Sinai Bunnel, in 1825. He died Sept. 3, 1841, æ. 62, at Northford.

Child: 462 *Augustine*, b 1814, m S. B. Hoadley of New Haven.

### 215. MALACHI.

MALACHI COOK Esq., son of Stephen and Anna Cook, married Sarah Taintor, Dec. 25, 1802 ; he died May 27, 1858, æ. 77 yrs. She died Nov. 9, 1852, æ. 69 yrs. He was a side judge of New Haven County Court for several years.

Children: 463 *Emily Cecilia*, b April 21, 1803, m Thomas R. Lindsley ; 464 *Homer L. M.*, b April 3, 1805 ; 465 *Virgil*, b June 22, 1808 ; 466 *Ossian*, b Nov. 19, 1810 ; 467 *Hermine C.*, b June 4, 1813, m Gilbert Buck ; 468 *Grace T.*, b Sept. 16, 1815 ; 469 *Henrietta A.*, b Sept. 3, 1817, m George Butler ; 470 *Ellen*, b Oct. 21, 1819, m Alexander Brainard ; 471 *Sarah Delia*, b Jan. 19, 1823; 472 *Harriet E.*, b Oct. 23, 1827, m Bennet Atwood.

### 224. TITUS.

TITUS COOK, son of Titus and Sarah Cook, m Lucy Leete of Guilford, Conn. ; he died in Wallingford.

Children : 473 *Julia*, m George Bull of Wallingford ; 474 *Lucretia*, m —— Weber of Wallingford ; 475 *Jared R. ;*

476 *Leverett*, resides in Meriden, m —— Hotchkiss of Cheshire ; 477 *Andrew* ; 478 *Louisa*, m Henry Lane.

## 226. ATWATER.

ATWATER COOK, son of Abel and Mary Atwater Cook, m Mary Bartholomew. He went to Sheffield, Mass. ; from thence to Salisbury, Herkimer Co., N. Y., where he died, June 29, 1839, æ 80 yrs. She died July 2, 1844, ae. 86 yrs.

Children : 479 *Roxilana*, b Sept. 25, 1777, d Sept. 15, 1852 ; 480 *Rosanna*, b April 14, 1782 ; 481 *Mary*, b April 3. 1784, d Jan. 13, 1853 ; 482 *Thaddeus R.*, b July 23, 1786 ; 483 *Julia*, b July 23, 1788 ; 484 *Friend*, b Jan. 27, 1792 ; 485 *Atwater H. W.*, b Dec. 17, 1795, d Feb. 4, 1853 ; 486 *Betsey*, b April 19, 1798 ; 487 *Abel*, b Sept. 27, 1801, d ae. 21 yrs ; 488 *Delia*, b Sept. 4, 1806.

## 227. PORTER.

PORTER COOK, son of Abel and Mary Cook, married Sally Jarvis, in 1785 ; he died Dec. 26, 1848, ae. 89. She died Oct. 31, 1841, ae. 81 yrs.

Children : 489 *Alfred*, b Feb 5, 1786 ; 490 *Merrick*, b May 18, 1788 ; 491 *Randall*, b July 19, 1790 ; 492 *Philo*, b Sept. 30, 1792 ; 493 *Sally*, b Feb. 22, 1795, d in Ohio ; 494 *Franklin*, b April 1, 1797, d in Wallingford.

## 229. ABEL.

ABEL COOK, son of Abel and Mary Cook, married Mamre Bliss ; she died Dec. 10, 1790. He died May 23, 1828, æ. 63 years. His 2d wife, Viney Cook, died Dec. 28, 1848, ae. 83 years, all buried in Northford cemetery.

Children by 1st marriage : 495 *Bliss*, b April 25, 1787, d April 28, 1823, ae. 36. By 2d marriage : 496 *Leverett*, b Jan. 3, 1794 ; 497 *Cornelia*, b Feb. 21, 1797, m Wm. Everts, of Northford ; 498 *Marietta*, b Sept. 8, 1799, m Timothy Bartholomew ; 499 *Emily*, b July 23, 1802, m Chas. M. Fowler ; 500 *Philander*, b Oct. 13, 1804 ; 501 *Jennette*, b May 5, 1807, d Nov. 12, 1832.

## 233. CHESTER.

CHESTER COOK, son of Abel and Mary Cook, married 1st,

Thankful Hall, of Wallingford ; 2d, Polly Norton, widow of
Jesse Street.    Mr. Cook was a farmer and shoemaker.
Children by 1st marriage:    502 *Caroline*, b Sept. 5, 1801,
m Orrin Andrews, of Wallingford ; 503 *Marilla*, b Nov. 17,
1803, m Sherlock Avery, of Wallingford ; 504 *Hiram*, b April
27, 1805, m —— Marks.

### 231. DAVID.

CAPT. DAVID M. COOK, son of Abel and Mary Cook, married
Elizabeth Day Hall ; she died Dec., 1855.    He died 1857, ae.
91 years.    He was frequently a member of the Legislature of
the State, and selectman of the town.    He was a farmer and
shoemaker.
Children :    505 *Betsey*, b May, 1797, m Philo Hall, she d
1858 ; 506 *Eliakim*, b Nov. 8, 1801, d in childhood ; 507
*Elijah*, b Nov. 28, 1804, d in childhood ; 508 *Maria*, b June
23, 1805, m Willis Todd, and d in Northford.

### 234. OLIVER.

OLIVER DUDLEY COOK, son of Aaron and Lucretia Dudley
Cook, graduated for the ministry at Yale College, in 1793.
He married Sophia Pratt, and settled in Hartford. Conn.,
where he became an extensive bookseller and binder, accu-
mulated a very large estate, and died April 24, 1833, ae. 67
years.    His wife died March 20. 1833, ae 58 years.
Children :    509 *Edward P.*, b 1800, d Sept. 18, 1846 ; 510
*Oliver D.*, d Oct 24, 1831 : 511 a dau., m Wm. Hammersley.

### 236. KILBORN.

KILBORN COOK, son of Aaron and Lucretia Dudley Cook,
m Emma Williams ; she was born March 8, 1771, and died in
Illinois, in 1835.    He died suddenly at North Guilford, June
9, 1832.
Children :    512 *Eunice*, b Sept. 29, 1796, m Abram Coan, she
d May 28. 1859 ; 513 *Margaretta*, b Dec. 30, 1798, d June 3,
1834 ; 514 *Aaron Dudley*, resides in Illinois : 515 *Bertha*, m
Nath'l Bartlett ; 516 *Lucretia Ann*, m Erastus Benton ; 517
*Increase W.*, b Feb., 1807, d 1847 ; 518 *Caroline Jenette*, m
Erastus Benton.

### 240. APOLLOS.

APOLLOS COOK, son of Aaron and Lucretia D. Cook, married Ruth, daughter of Capt. Caleb Atwater, of Wallingford, Nov. 22, 1813, and settled at Catskill, N. Y. He died July 6, 1832, æ, 46 years.

Children : 519 *Mary A.*, b Dec. 5, 1814, m George Griffing, May 20, 1845 ; 520 *James*, b July 4, 1817, d Jan. 6, 1842 ; 521 *Frederick*, b March 19, 1819 ; 522 *Caroline E.*, b April 5, 1821, m Rev. Frank Olmsted ; 523 *John A.*, b Oct. 23, 1823 ; 524 *Emily H.*, b Feb. 25, 1826 ; 525 *Edward H.*, b June 24, 1828, d May 28, 1835 ; 526 *Francis H.*, b March 16, 1831

### 241. THOMAS.

THOMAS B. COOK, son of Aaron and Lucretia (Dudley) Cook, m Catherine, dau. of Capt. Caleb Atwater, and went to Catskill, N. Y., where he died.

Children : 527 *Frances H.*; 528 *Mary A.*; 529 *Ruth A.*, 530 *John C*; 531 *Franklin H.*, 532 *Atwater.*

### 247. JOSEPH.

JOSEPH COOK, son of Moses and Jemima Upson, married Anna Bronson, Aug. 1, 1792. She was born Dec. 25, 1770, and died Nov. 25, 1855. He died Nov. 26, 1855, æ. 87 yrs., just 10 hours before his wife died

Children : 533 *Edward B.*, b March 18, 1793 ; 534 *Samuel*, b Dec. 12, 1794 ; 535 *Susan J.*, b Oct 25, 1797, m Mark Leavenworth, Dec. 16, 1821 ; 536 *Sarah L.*, b Oct. 29, 1799, m Salome Austin of Southington ; 537 *Nancy*, b Nov. 16, 1801, m Wm. Scoville of Middletown, 1828 ; 538 *Nathan*, b Jan., 1804 ; 539 *George*, b April 8, 1806, d July 19, 1815 ; 540 *George William*, b Feb. 28, 1811.

### 249. DANIEL.

DANIEL COOK, son of Moses and Jemima Cook, married Sally Sperry, of Waterbury, Nov. 25, 1799. He died Dec. 20, 1857, æ. 85 years. She died Nov. 13, 1861, æ. 83 years.

Children : 541 *Marcus*, b Sept. 12, 1800, d Feb 9, 1831 ;

542 *Sarah P.*, b Aug. 1, 1804, m Thomas B. Segur, in 1826 ;
543 *Moses Stiles*, b 1812, resides in Waterbury, Conn.

### 259. ELUTHEROS.

ELUTHEROS COOK, son of Asaph and Sarah Parker Cook,
married Martha Caswell, of Salem, Washington Co., N. Y.
He was a lawyer in Washington Co., N. Y., before his removal to Sandusky, Ohio. He was frequently a member of
the Ohio Legislature, and was a member of Congress from
1831 to 1833. He died at Sandusky, Ohio, Dec. 27, 1864.
Children: 544 *Sarah E.*, b Jan. 16, 1816, m Wm More-
head : 545 *Pitt*, b July 23, 1819 ; 546 *Jay*, b Aug. 10, 1821,
banker in Philadelphia ; 547 *Henry D.*, b Nov. 25, 1825 ;
548 *Elutheros*, b Dec. 20, 1828, d Oct., 1850, æ. 22 ; 549
*Catherine E.*, b Sept. 15, 1831, d Oct., 1834, æ. 3.

### 262. ERASTUS.

ERASTUS COOK, son of Asaph and Sarah P. Cook, married
Fanny Anderson, Nov. 10, 1826. He went to Sandusky City,
Ohio, and was postmaster there from 1836–41. He died
in 1849.

Children: 550 *James W.*, b 1830; 551 *George A.*, b 1840 ;
552 *Emma E.*, b 1843 ; they all resided in Sandusky.

### 270. HORACE.

HORACE COOK, son of Charles and Elizabeth Cook, married Roxanna Thomas, Dec. 20, 1824, and located himself
at Sackett's Harbor, Jefferson Co., N. Y.

Children: 553 *Horace Nelson*, b Oct. 26, 1825, d Sept. 17,
1848, æ. 23 ; 554 *John Spafford*, b June 15, 1828.

### 271. CHARLES.

CHARLES COOK, son of Charles and Elizabeth Cook, married Harriet Cunningham, and resided at Roberts Corners,
N. Y.

Children : 555 *Elizabeth :* 556 *Charles :* 557 *Curtis ;*
558 *Harriet.*

### 272. ELISHA.

ELISHA COOK, son of Charles and Elizabeth Cook, removed from Sickett's Harbor to Huron Co., Ohio., where he died in 1852, æ. 51 years.

Children: 559 *Elizabeth*, b 1835; 560 *Charles*, b 1838, d Feb, 1853; 561 *Elisha*, b 1840.

### 280. AMOS

AMOS COOK, son of Amos and Rhoda Cook, married Sabrina Mix.

Children: 562 *Amos:* 563 *Rhoda.* 564 *Orrin.*

### 283. LYMAN.

LYMAN COOK, son of Amos and Rhoda Cook, married, and left Wallingford in early life.

Children: 565 *Lyman W.:* 566 *Sidney H.*

### 285. JOEL.

Capt. JOEL COOK, son of Col. Isaac and Martha Cook of Wallingford, m Rebecca Hart, Jan. 1, 1784. He entered the army of the Revolution with his father in 1776, and served through the war. In 1812 he was a distinguished officer under Gen. Harrison, in many hard fought battles with the Indians. He died at (Deer Park) Babylon, L. I., Dec. 18, 1851, ae. 92 years.

Children: 567 *Lucy*, b April 5, 1785, m James Calstead, July 22. 1804; 568 *Minerva*, b June 18, 1789; 569 *Leander*, b March 10, 1792, d at Cincinnati, Ohio; 570 *Patty*, b Nov. 27. 1794; 571 *Rebecca*, b April 5, 1798; 572 *Phebe*, b Jan 5, 1801, 573 *Jennette*, b July 8, 1804; 574 *Joel Wilcox*, b April 28, 1808, res. in Babylon, L. I.

### 286. LEMUEL.

LEMUEL COOK, son of Col. Isaac and Martha Cook, m Betsey Bates in 1784. He removed to Lewiston, Niagara Co., N. Y., in 1793. She died Sept., 1821.

Children: 575 *Lathrop*, b Nov. 23, 1785, in Wallingford; 576 *Bates*, b Dec. 23, 1787; 577 *Laura*, died in infancy in Wallingford; 578 *Laura*, b May 13, 1792, in Wallingford; 579 *Betsey*, b June 30, 1794; 580 *Amelia*, b Sept. 5, 1796; 581 *Isaac C.*, b 1803; 582 *Amanda M.*, b Nov. 6, 1805.

## 287. JAMES.

JAMES COOK, son of Col. Isaac and Martha Cook, married Chloe Royce, May 4, 1786 He was a seaman, and is supposed to have been lost or died at sea previous to 1813.

Children, all born in Wallingford: 583 *Miles;* 584 *Melissa;* 585 *Angelina;* 586 *Lucinda;* 587 *Chloe;* 588 *Eliza.*

## 289. ISAAC.

ISAAC COOK Esq., son of Isaac and Martha Cook, married Margaretta Scott, in 1792. He emigrated to Chillicothe, Ohio, in 1791, and was made an associate judge of the court of Common Pleas. He died Jan. 22, 1844.

Children: 589 *Eliza.* b Oct. 21, 1793, d Aug. 3, 1799; 590 *Martha,* b June 23, 1794, d June 24, 1796; 591 *Isaac T,* b March 6, 1797; 592 *Lucy,* b Feb. 11, 1799, d March 28, 1800; 593 *Marietta,* b March 9, 1801, m James Webb, M. D.; 594 *Matthew Scott,* b April 9, 1803; 595 *Elizabeth,* b March 27, 1805, m John Nelson; 596 *William,* b April 18, 1807; 597 *John Joseph,* b May 28, 1809; 598 *Lucy Hall,* b May 25, 1811; 599 *Phebe,* b Aug. 8, 1813, m Wm. McKell, May 26, 1836; 600 *Margaretta Scott,* b April 9, 1817, m Moses Boggs, Aug. 3, 1841.

## 294. AUGUSTUS.

CAPT. AUGUSTUS COOK, son of Caleb and Abigail Cook, m Sybel Beach, of Goshen. Sept. 2, 1790; she died Sept. 28, 1792, æ. 22 years. He married Sarah Dutton, June 30, 1793; she died April 28, 1854, ae. 80 years. He died at Middletown, Conn., where he had resided many years. April 18, 1866, ae. 79 years. He was a manufacturer of shoes.

Children: 601 *Luther Dutton,* b June 21, 1794; 602 *Sybil B.,* b June 23, 1797, m Wm. R. Catting, and d Oct. 25, 1825; 603 *Margaretta,* b Jan. 12, 1800, m Wm. S. Camp, Esq., of Middletown; 604 *Sarah,* b May 22, 1811, m Samuel Stearns, Esq., of Middletown; 605 *Catharine,* b May 22, 1813, d Sept. 23, 1813; 606 *Catharine,* b Dec. 30, 1814, m Peter Lanman, she d Jan. 4, 1834.

### 300. CALEB.

CALEB COOK, Esq., son of Caleb and Abigail Cook, m Amelia, daughter of Jared and Rhoda Lewis, Oct. 16, 1808. He left Wallingford and settled at Richland, Oswego Co., N. Y. He died at Sandusky, Ohio, on his return from a visit to his children at the West, in July, 1852, and was buried in the Oakland cemetery. She died at Pulaski, Oswego Co., N. Y., June 8, 1840.

Children : 607 *Louisa C.*, b July 10, 1809, m Rev. Henry Maltby ; 608 *Lewis*, b March 15, 1811 ; 609 *Henry C.*, b Sept. 11, 1813, d at Sidney, Ohio ; 610 *Frederick*, b June 11, 1815 ; 611 *Juliet*, b June 28, 1817, m C. Preston, she d in 1852 ; 612 *Edward H.*, d ae. 4 yrs. ; 613 *Margaretta*, b May 25, 1819, d Oct. 23, 1820 ; 614 *Augustus*, b Nov. 3, 1823, d Nov 2, 1848 ; 615 *William C.*, b July 27, 1825, resides in Richland, N. Y. ; 616 *Henrietta*, b 1828, d in Wallingford ; 617 *Henry Atwater*, b March 1, 1832, d in infancy.

### 302. CHAUNCEY.

CHAUNCEY COOK, son of Ambrose and Esther Peck Cook, married Eunice Dutton of Wallingford. He kept a tavern in Wallingford and in New Haven for a long time, and died in the latter place Jan. 22, 1827. ae. 60 years. His widow died at the residence of her son Charles C., in Ohio.

Children : 618 *Laura*, b Oct. 25, 1791, m Orrin Winchell, of New Haven ; 619 *Charles C.*, b Jan. 22, 1799, is a physician in Ohio ; 620 *Chauncey*, b Nov. 30, 1811, d July 6, 1812.

### 303. SAMUEL.

SAMUEL COOK, son of Ambrose and Esther Cook, m Martha, daughter of Benjamin Cook, Aug. 1, 1792. He died Aug. 30, 1826, aged 57. He was a shoemaker.

Children : 621 *John Milton*, b Feb. 1, 1795 ; 622 *Martha A.*, b Oct. 25, 1805, m Elihu Hall, Wallingford ; 623 *Lucy A.*, b Oct. 25, 1805.

### 306. CHARLES.

CHARLES COOK, son of Ambrose and Esther P. Cook, m

Sylvia, daughter of Elihu and Lucretia Yale ; she died at Wallingford, Feb. 1, 1825. He died at Cuyahoga Falls, Ohio, June, 1845, aged 70 years.

Children : 624 *Otis*, b April 8, 1797, m —— Butler, of Rocky Hill ; 625 *Sinai*, b Sept. 17, 1798, m John Miller White, of Middlefield, Conn. ; 626 *Peter*, b July 16, 1800; 627, *Thomas*, b Feb. 1, 1802, d in 1862, æ. 60 ; 628 *Charles*, b Aug. 13, 1804, res. in Hartford, Conn. ; 629 *Orrin*, b May 8, 1808, had no family, d at Cuyahoga Falls, Ohio ; 630 *Henry*, b Feb. 12, 1810, d 1865–6 ; 631 *Isaac*, b Aug. 17, 1813, d at St. Jago, Cuba, W. I.

### 315. MUNSON.

CAPT. MUNSON COOK, son of Benjamin and Esther Rice Cook, married Thankful Austin, Sept. 4, 1796. They went to Middletown, Ct. ; afterwards they came to Cheshire, Ct., where she died, Dec. 24, 1853. He died Aug. 18, 1862, æ. 86.

Children : 632 *Samantha*, b Sept. 4, 1797, d May 31, 1819 ; 633 *Charles B.*, b Sept. 27, 1799, d Jan. 31, 1850 ; 634 *Betsey*, b July 4, 1801, d Oct. 3, 1820 ; 635 *Caroline*, b June 8, 1803, d March 9, 1826 ; 636 *Hobart*, b Aug. 7, 1805, d Oct. 21, 1807 ; 637 *Hobart M.*, b July 9, 1807 ; 638 *Emeline*, b May 8, 1809, d March 1, 1826 ; 639 *Nathan R.*, b Aug. 10, 1811 ; 640 *Eliza Ann*, b May 1, 1813, m James R. Hall ; 641 *Ozias A.*, b Dec. 18, 1814 ; 642 *Oliver W.*, b March 21, 1817 ; 643 *Philander*, b July 3, 1819 ; 644 *Joel*, b Oct. 15, 1820 ; 645 *Henry H.*, b April 17, 1823, d July 18, 1825.

### 316. DANIEL.

DANIEL COOK, son of Benjamin and Esther Cook, married 1st, Mary Thorp, June 13, 1799. After her decease he married Catherine Smith, daughter of Stanton Smith, April 22, 1822. He moved to the State of New York and died there in 1860.

Children by 1st marriage : 646 *Phebe*, b Aug. 14, 1801 ; 647 *Alma R.*, b June 23, 1805 ; 648 *Maria*, b May 15, 1807 ; 649 *Elizur*, b Oct. 9, 1810 ; 650 *Alexander*, b March 11,

1813. By 2d marriage: 651 *Hiram*, b Feb. 20, 1823. By 3d marriage *John*, is a sailor.

### 319. JOSEPH.

JOSEPH COOK, son of Merriman and Mary Cook, married Mary A. Talman, Nov. 30, 1774, and went to Saratoga Springs, N. Y., where he was living a few years since, at the age of 94 years. His wife died April 4, 1860, æ. 86 years.

Children: 652 *Ransom*, b Nov. 8, 1794, in Wallingford; 653 *Marcus*, b Nov. 25, 1796, in Norwich, Ct. ; 654 *Andrew*, b Jan. 18, 1799, in Norwich, Ct. ; 655 *Mary A.*, b Nov. 23, 1800, in Norwich, Ct. ; 656 *Harvey*, b April 15, 1803, at Half Moon, Saratoga Co., N Y. ; 657 *Joseph*, b Nov. 1, 1805. d July 1, 1808; 658 *Nelson*, b Oct. 8, 1808. d in Saratoga Co., N. Y. ; 659 *Truman*, b Oct. 25, 1810; 660 *Eli*, b July 15, 1814, d. at Milton, N. Y., April 20, 1816 ; 661 *Julia E.*, b Aug. 14. 1817, res. at Milton, N. Y.

### 323. ELIHU.

ELIHU COOK, son of Merriman and Mary Cook. married Sarah Cooley, of Wallingford, in 1798. He died in 1855, æ. 79 years. She died several years since. He was a hatter at Ballston, Saratoga Co., N. Y.

Children: 662 *Eliza*, m Mr. Davis ; 663 *Harriet*: 664 *Merriman*, supposed to be now living at Syracuse, N. Y.

### 325 1-2. SAMUEL.

SAMUEL COOK, son of Merriman and Mary Cook, married Mary, dau. of Charles Culver, of Wallingford. She died in 1838. He married Sally Galpin, and resides at Northumberland, Saratoga Co., N. Y.

Children : 665 *Amanda*, m James Van Byring, d 1854 : 666 *Lydia*, m Reuben Wait ; 667 *Patty*. 668 *James ;* 669 *Charles*, d æ. 24 yrs. ; 670 *Samuel*, b March 27. 1819 : 671 *Alfred*. b 1824. By 2d wife : 672 *Elizabeth*, m R—— B——, in 1830 ; 673 *George*.

### 326. LYMAN.

LYMAN COOK, son of Merriman and Mary Cook, married Amy Hulin, and settled at Malta, Saratoga Co., N. Y.

Children: 674 *Alena*, b Jan. 31, 1809, m 1st, Joseph Gor-
man, Aug. 17, 1826, 2d, Samuel Hall ; 675 *Mary E.*, b April
22, 1811, m Oliver Lockwood, July 3, 1832 ; 676 *Charles H.*,
b July 20, 1813 ; 677 *Delia A* , b Nov. 26, 1815, m Henry
Warring, Jan. 9, 1839 ; 678 *Edmond*, b May 3, 1818, d Aug
3, 1818 ; 679 *Lyman W.*, b June 4, 1820; 680 *Betsey M* , b
May 12, 1822, d Nov. 26, 1826 ; 681 *Edwin D.*, b July 25,
1824 ; 682 *Henry M.*, b Feb. 18, 1827, d Dec. 26, 1827 ; 683
*John C.*, b Feb. 21, 1829, d Feb. 10, 1831 ; 684 *Sarah*, b
July 11, 1833.

### 329. SHERLOCK.

SHERLOCK COOK, son of Merriman and Mary Cook, married Milly Thurston about 1812. They removed to Western,
N. Y., and he is supposed to have died there in 1850. Only
four of his children are supposed to be living—present residence unknown.

### 332. SAMUEL.

SAMUEL COOK, son of Philip and Thankful T. Cook, married Fanny Fuller of Sandisfield, Mass., Feb. 20, 1803. They
went to Nassau, N. Y., and from thence to Ballston Spa,
where he died May 15, 1815. His 2nd wife, Harriet Cook of
Goshen, Ct., died April 15, 1828.

Children: 685 *James M.*, b Nov. 19, 1807. By 2d marriage : 686 *Samuel H.*, b July 18, 1823.

### 334. ERASTUS.

ERASTUS COOK, son of Philip and Thankful T. Cook,
married Jerusha Hewins of Richmond, Mass., in 1800. He
died at Ashtabula, Ohio, 1850.

Children: 686 *Althea*, b March 18, 1801 ; 686 1-2 *Maria T.*,
b April 19, 1802 ; 687 *Amanda*, d young ; 688 *Silas;* 689 *Joseph.*

### 338. AMASA.

AMASA COOK, son of Daniel and Eliza Cook, married 1st,
Polly Churchill. 2nd, Sally Rowe. He was accidentally
killed by a cart, while entering his barn with a load of hay,
in 1817.

Child: 690 *Philip*, b in Goshen, Ct.

### 339 PHINEAS.

PHINEAS COOK, son of Daniel and Eliza Cook, married Irene Churchill, and removed to Michigan in 1836 or 1837

Children. 691 *Betsey;* 692 *Daniel,* m Mary Kirby ; 693 *Eliza,* m Salmon Hall ; 694 *Darius,* m Jane Adams ; 695 *Mary Ann;* 696 *Plumas;* 697 *Harriet.*

### 340. GEORGE.

GEORGE COOK, son of Moses and Lydia Cook, married Roxy Grant, of Norfolk. She died Oct. 24, 1841, æ. 47 yrs. He died in 1864.

Children : 698 *Caroline M.,* b June 10, 1818 ; 699 *Ralph F.,* b May 10, 1821, has resided in New London, and Goshen, Conn.

### 343. FREDERICK.

FREDERICK COOK, son of Moses and Roxy Cook, married Louisa McKinley of Georgia, in April, 1827, and settled at Lexington, Ga., where he died April 4, 1843.

Child : 700 *Maria Elizabeth,* b Feb. 28, 1828, m Alexander Allen.

### 344. MOSES.

MOSES COOK, son of Moses and Roxy Cook, married Emily M. Beecher of Goshen. He is an inn-keeper near the center of Goshen.

Children : 701 *Harriet E.,* b Oct. 17, 1832 ; 702 *Emily,* b May 7. 1834 , 703 *Frederick A.,* b Jan. 27, 1838, 1st Lieut. 2nd Conn. Artillery ; 704 *Moses,* b March 26. 1842, d 1863. Sergt. of 2nd Comp. Artillery ; 705 *William K.,* b July 4, 1852 ; 706 *George B.,* b May 17, 1855, 1st Lieut. Comp. D, 4th Reg. Conn. volunteers.

### 345. ELIAS.

ELIAS COOK, son of Benjamin and Charity E. Cook of Guildhall, Vt., married Maria Brookins, May 26, 1825. He had been a teacher in various parts of the country ; is at this time a resident of Ware, Hocking Co., Ohio.

Children : 707 *Caroline E.,* b March 12, 1826, m Peter

Smith, May 2, 1832 ; 708 *Martha A.*, b May 10, 1827 ; 709 *Helen S.*, b May 28, 1829, m Wm. Comstock, June 16, 1849 ; 710 *Raphael G.*, b Jan. 17, 1832, d Sept., 1833 ; 711 *Raphael E.*, b June 7, 1833, U. S. Army, 1862 ; 712 *Cyrus B.*, b Dec. 1, 1834 ; 713 *Harriet E.*, b Sept. 6, 1836, m James Parden, March, 1857 ; 714 *Albert F.*, b Sept. 5, 1840 ; 715 *Emma L.*, b Dec., 1842.

### 347. BENJAMIN.

BENJAMIN COOK, son of Benjamin and Charity L. Cook, m Betsey ———; residence, Petersham, Mass.

Children ; 716 *Harriet S.*, b April 23, 1830, has been twice married ; 717 *Sandford B.*, b May 6, 1832 ; 718 *George O.*, b Oct. 14, 1834 ; 719 *Charles Elliot*, b Sept. 6, 1836 ; 720 *Mary Elizabeth*, b April 30, 1839, m Nathan Knowlton.

### 349. IRA.

IRA COOK, son of Benjamin and Charity E. Cook, married Lucy Clapp, Oct, 3, 1837, and settled at Athol Depot, Mass., as a boot and shoemaker. He married for 2d wife, Sarah Kimball, May 10, 1853. His first wife died March 12, 1852.

Children: 721 *Eliza Jane*, b Sept. 13, 1838, m Samuel Searls, May 7, 1857 ; 722 *Vernon Stiles*, b April 2, 1841, in U. S. Army, 1862 ; 723 *Lucy Ellen*, b Dec. 30, 1845, d in 1852. By 2nd marriage : 724 *Sarah Ellen*, b Oct. 18, 1855.

### 379. JOHN.

JOHN COOK, son of Merriman and Sally Cook of Cheshire, Ct., married Meroa, daughter of Josiah and Thankful Smith of Cheshire, March, 1804. He went to Ohio and settled at Burton in 1806, where he died March 21, 1848.

Children: 725 *Nabby*, b Aug. 16, 1805. d Oct. 23, 1806 ; 726 *Harriet E.*, b Aug. 20, 1807, m His Excellency Seabury Todd, Esq., of Ohio ; 727 *Josiah S.*, b May 10, 1810 : 728, *Sally R.*, b Feb. 25, 1815, m Geo. Boughton.

### 380. HIRAM.

HIRAM COOK, son of Merriman and Sally Cook, of Cheshire, married Lucinda, dau. of Ichabod and Lydia Hitch-

cock of Cheshire. They removed to Ohio in 1815, and
settled in Burton, Ohio.

Children: 729 *Sally A.*, b July 10, 1807, m Raymond Gaylord ; 730 *Lydia*, b Aug. 3, 1816, m Sherman Goodwin, M. D.;
731 *Eliza A.*, b Sept. 8, 1818, m Peter Hitchcock, Esq. ; 732
*Sarilla*, b Dec. 20, 1827, m Richard Dayton, she d in 1833.

### 382. ELZAR.

ELZAR COOK, son of Merriman and Sally Cook, married
Maria Beard of Huntington, Conn. He went to Ohio in
1807, at the age of eight years.

Child : 733 *Elizabeth*, b March 24, 1830.

### 384. SAMUEL.

SAMUEL COOK, son of Samuel and Sue Cook of Cheshire,
m Esther Curtis. Feb. 17, 1817. He was deputy sheriff for a
number of years at Cheshire, where he died Feb. 19, 1859, a:.
68 years.

Children: 734 *Samuel*, died young ; 735 *Robert H.*, b Dec.
18, 1823.

### 386. STEPHEN.

STEPHEN J. C., son of Ephraim and Sukey Cook, married
Lucinda Dudley of North Guilford, Conn., Jan. 1, 1828.

Children: 736 *Abigail*, b Dec. 23, 1829, d March 18,
1833 ; 737 *Samuel D.*, b April 14, 1832 · 738 *Abigail*, b
Aug. 18, 1836, d Sept. 12. 18,. ; 739 *Celestina*, b March 7,
1440 ; 740 *Ephraim F.*, b Feb. 21, 1843.

### 391. HORACE.

HORACE COOK, son of Ephraim and Sukey Cook. married
Lydia E. Hickox, Dec. 15, 1842, res. in Burton, Ohio.

Children: 741 *Melissa N.*, b July 24, 1845 ; 742 *Sarah*, b
Aug. 8, 1849 ; 743 *Eliza N.*, b Jan. 8, 1852.

### 396. ETHELBERT.

ETHELBERT COOK, son of Elam and Rebecca B. Cook of
Cheshire, Conn., married Philander Sanford of Prospect ; he
died March 7, 1853 ; she died Nov. 8, 1854.

Child : 744 *Lauren E.*, b April 17, 1833. m Carrie Perkins,
Nov. 12, 1860.

#### 401. ELAM.

ELAM COOK, son of Elam and Rebecca Cook of Cheshire, Ct., m Lois, daughter of Jesse and Eliza Humiston of said town.

Children: 745 *Eliza A.*, b Feb. 6, 1842 ; 746 *Theodore A.*, b March 17, 1845 ; 747 *Amelia R* , b Feb. 8, 1856.

#### 404. RUSSEL.

RUSSEL COOK, son of Samuel and Mary K. Cook ¯of Wallingford, married Miss Hall of Cheshire, where he resided for some time. From Cheshire he went, it is supposed, to Ohio, where it is supposed by his friends that he died.

#### 406. BILLIOUS.

BILLIOUS COOK, son of Samuel and Mary R. Cook, married Sarah Munson, daughter of Elizabeth. He died July 25, 1828, ae. 45 years. She died May 4, 1855, ae. 70 years.

Children : 748 *Chauncey M.*, b Oct. 10, 1805 ; 749 *Mary K.*, b Jan. 1, 1807, m Edwin L. Hall ; 750 *Russel*, b Oct. 21, 1809 ; 751 *Sarah*, b April 30, 1811, m Horace Tuttle of Hamden, Ct. ; 752 *Turhand K.*, b July 11, 1817 ; 753 *Jane R.*, b March 6, 1819, m Ambrose Todd of Fair Haven, Ct. ; 754 *Emily*, b 1824, died in infancy.

#### 408. TURHAND.

TURHAND K. COOK, son of Samuel and Mary K. Cook, married Catharine Van Bergen of Catskill, N. Y., and resided there until his decease. He was a merchant, inn-keeper and clerk of the county of Greene, N. Y. He died December 3d, 1851, aged 64 years. He married Catharine A. Allen, for his 3d wife, in January, 1848.

Children : 755 *Ann Eliza*, b Nov. 26, 1827, was at Cincinnati in 1856 ; 756 *Mary Kirtland*, b August 3, 1829, married Charles J. Russ in 1847 ; 757 *Wm. Van Buren*, b March, 1831, d Sept 24, 1849 ; 758 *John Washburton*, b Dec. 7, 1839.

#### 409. SAMUEL.

SAMUEL COOK, son of Samuel and Mary K. Cook, married Martha Culver, daughter of Benjamin. He was three years high sheriff of New Haven county, postmaster and town clerk of Wallingford. He died Dec. 18, 1843, æ. 55 years, at Cheshire. His remains were interred in Wallingford. His widow died at the house of her son Samuel A. Cook, in Waterbury, July 6, 1861, æ. 67 years.

Children: 759 *Delos Ford*, d. in Wallingford of consumption; 760 *Henry A.*, m. Delia Cook, dau. of Benj. F., 761 *Harriet*, m. Wm. Frisbie of Branford, she d. Dec. 26, 1860; 762 *Kirtland*, b. 1822, m. ——— Tuttle, d. at Cheshire 763 *Samuel A.*, m. Lucinda Hitchcock; 764 *William*. r. s. at Pond Hill, Wallingford.

### 410. THADDEUS.

Col. THADDEUS COOK, son of Samuel and Mary K. Cook, married 1st, Julia Cook, daughter of Stephen, of Cheshire; 2d, Sylvia Hall, dau. of Andrew and Diana Hall; 3d, Thankful, and 4th, Martha Hall. The two last were daughters of Josiah Hall, of Wallingford.

Child by first marriage: 765 *Julia*, m. 1st, Horace Tuttle, 2d, Wm. Francis. Child by 2d marriage: 766 *Catherine*, m. David Hall of Wallingford. Children by 4th marriage: 767 *Caroline*, m. Rev. Benjamin Paddock, of Detroit, Michigan. 768 *Sarah*, m. O. Ives Martin, of Wallingford; 769 *Emma*, m. Edwin F. Cook, son of Leander; 770 *Francelie*, b. Oct. 12, 1825, d. Feb. 25, 1836.

### 411. GEORGE.

GEORGE COOK, son of Samuel and Mary Kirtland Cook, married Lavinia, daughter of Benjamin Culver. He died at Wallingford, Feb. 18, 1844. She died Nov., 1860.

Children: 771 *Mary K.*, b. May 24, 1821; 772 *Eliza*, b. Feb. 20, 1823, m. Frederic Bartholomew, d. July 24, 1862, æ. 41 yrs.; 773 *Lavinia*, m. Samuel Parmelee; 774 *Martha*; 775 infant, died at Cheshire; 776 *Fanny*, m. Emery Morse, March 1, 1855.

### 412. FRIEND.

Dr. FRIEND COOK, son of Samuel and Mary K. Cook, graduated at Union College, studied medicine with Dr. N. Smith

W w

of New Haven, commenced practice at Windsor, Conn.
He married Emily, dau. of Dea. Joshua Atwater, of Wallingford. Afterwards he practiced his profession there until he
removed to Atwater, Ohio, where she died. He married
Sarah Folger Reynolds for his second wife. He died of a
cancer in the stomach, after a long and distressing illness,
Feb. 8, 1857.

Children: 777 *Helen A.*, b Nov. 12, 1825, d Feb. 1, 1827, in
Wallingford ; 778 *Joshua A.*, b Sept. 29, 1829, d Nov. 1,
1844, in Ohio; 779 *Frances A.*, b Nov, 25, 1833, d July 20,
1834, in Wallingford ; 780 *Emma G.*, b Nov. 29, 1836 ; 781
*Frances I.*, b May 18, 1840 ; 782 *William Shelton*, b July 13,
1862, d Dec. 31, 1848, in Ohio. Child by 2d marriage, 783
*Henry M.*, b March, 1848.

### 413. JOHN.

JOHN COOK, son of Samuel and Mary K. Cook, married
Mary Munson, June 25. 1823. He died Jan. 1, 1858, æ. 57
years.

Children: 784 *Samuel M.*, m —— Bartholomew ; 785
*Mary K.*, m Tilton E. Doolittle Esq. : 786 *Ellen*, m Charles
Jones of Wallingford ; 787 *George*, d Nov. 17, 1869.

### 418. RUFUS.

RUFUS Cook, son of Cornelius B. and Mary B. Cook,
married Betsey Curtis. He died Aug. 12, 1826, æ. 36 years,
at Cheshire, Conn.

Children: 788 *Cornelius B.*, b Dec. 15, 1810 ; 789 *Rufus*,
b July 5, 1812 : 790 *Maroa*, m Russel B. Ives. She died at
Cheshire, Conn.

### 420. BROOKS.

BROOKS COOK, son of Cornelius B. and Mary Cook, m
Sarah, dau. of Jonah Hotchkiss, of Cheshire. He died
Sept. 23, 1824, æ 26. She died Sept. 11, 1843, æ. 45 years.

Children: 791 *Mary*, d in Cheshire ; 792 *Louisa*, m George
Pardee : 793 *Amelia*, m Leverett Goodyear, of Hamden,
Conn.

### 427. AARON.

AARON COOK, son of Aaron and Betsey Cook, married Emily, dau. of Seth Hitchcock. He died in Cheshire.

Children: 794 *Elizabeth*, m Asahel Talmadge, of Cheshire , 795 *Julius*; 796 *Mary*, 797 *Melissa*, m Robert Lyman ; 798 *Julia M.*, m Wm. F. Thompkins.

### 426. ALFRED.

ALFRED COOK, son of Aaron and Mary Cook of Cheshire. He went to Windham, Greene Co., N. Y., where he married his wife. He has children, and is now ( 1869 ) in Cheshire, Conn.

### 436. STEPHEN.

STEPHEN COOK, son of Stephen and Emma Cook, married Julia E. Smith, of North Haven ; he died Oct. 21, 1840, ae. 40 yrs. His widow m Willis Smith, Esq., of Meriden.

Children: 799 *Julia E.*, b Sept. 27, 1831, m Daniel Wright; 800 *Sarah E.*, b Aug. 10, 1827, m Edward Cowell 801 *Leander D.*, b Jan. 22, 1825, d Oct. 17, 1854, ae. 29 ; 802 *Stephen C.*, b March 28, 1834, m — - - Baldwin of New Haven ; 803 *Eunice C.*, b Aug. 21, 1836, m John Riker ; 804 *Edson L.*, b April 5, 1840.

### 440. HUBBARD.

HUBBARD COOK, son of Samuel, m Abigail Dorman, Oct. 15, 1811. She died Jan. 2, 1853, and he married Ardelia Hinman, Sept. 15, 1853.

Children. 805 *Carlisle D.*, resides in Milwaukie , Wisconsin ; 806 *Jennett*, b April 30, 1813, m Job C. Phelps, Jan. 1, 1839 ; 807 *Caroline M.*, b Sept. 25, 1818, m Harrison O. Smith, Oct 1, 1842 ; 808 *Emily A.*, b Feb. 28, 1821 ; 809 *Delia*, b Dec. 16, 1824, d Aug 4, 1842, 810 *Margaret*, b April 20, 1826 ; 811 *R A* b Nov. 3, 1828, m Claxton Harrington, Oct. 16, 1850 ; 812 *Fanny D.*, b Aug. 17, 1832.

### 447. CHAUNCEY.

REV. CHAUNCEY COOK, son of Stephen and Sylvia M. Cook of Wallingford, married Mary Carpenter, Jan. 8, 1812 ; she died Dec. 15, 1814, at Adams, N. Y., ae. 23. He afterwards married Almira Cassitt, May 11, 1850 ; she died Dec. 21, 1842. Child by 1st marriage: 813 *Eliza*, b Oct. 21, 1812, m Chas. Campbell, she d June 2, 1847. By 2d marriage : 814 *Burton C.*, b May 11, 1819, m Elizabeth Hunt ; 815 *Mary*, b July 7, 1824 ; 816 *Sarah*, m West Morse, Dec. 2, 1847.

### 454. STEPHEN.

REV. STEPHEN COOK, son of Stephen and Sylvia M. Cook, married Janet Wyse, Feb. 10, 1819, resides at Oberlin, Ohio.

Children: 817 *William W.*, b April 2, 1820 ; 818 *James N.*, b Sept. 7, 1821 ; 819 *John F.*, b May 21, 1823 ; 820 *Julia A.*, b Jan. 21, 1826.

### 458. NELSON.

REV. NELSON COOK, son of Stephen and Sylvia M. Cook, married Mercy Eliza Heath, Jan. 1, 1831 ; she died Aug. 9, 1854. He married 2d, Elizabeth Arbella Leeds, Aug. 27, 1843 ; residence, Half Day, Lake Co., Illinois.

Children: 821 *Susan F.*, b. Jan. 16, 1845, d May 15, 1847 ; 822 *Gurdon L.*, b March 5, 1846, d Aug. 27, 1848 : 823 *Otis N.*, b Oct. 6, 1848, d same day ; 824 *Lyman M.*, b Jan. 23, 1850 ; 825 *Love Ann*, b May 27, 1852 ; 826 *Burton H.*, b Aug. 1, 1854.

### HENRY.

HENRY COOK, a brother of Samuel, came into Wallingford about 1674, and I suppose he married his wife Mary there, but at what date does not appear. Of his history little can be learned, except that he was a farmer, and was frequently elected to offices of trust and responsibility by his townsmen. That he was a brother of the first Samuel there is no doubt, as it is clearly shown by the records of Wallingford. He died in 1705, æ. 51 years. His widow Mary died Oct. 31, 1718.

Children : 1 *Mary*, b 1679, m Nathaniel Rexford, July 7, 1708 ; 2 *Jane*, b 1681, m Jehiel Preston, July 7, 1708 ; 3 *Henry*, b 1683 ; 4 *John*, b 1684 ; 5 *Hannah*, b 1687, m Timothy Beach, Nov. 26, 1713 ; 6 *Isaac*, b 1693 ; 7 *Elizabeth*,

b 1694, m Adam Mott, Aug. 28, 1717 ; 8 *Jonathan*, b 1698 ;
9 *David*, b 1701, settled in Wallingford where he died · 10
*Jediah*, b 17·3.

### 3 HENRY.

HENRY COOK, son of Henry and Mary Cook, married 1 t,
Experience ——— . She died Oct. 8, 1709. He married 2d,
Mary (Wheadon) Frost, dau of John and Mary Frost, of
Branford, in 1710. From Branford he went to Waterbury in
1728, and was there admitted an inhabitant His residence
was near the line of Litchfield.

Children : 11 *Sarah*, b May 5. 1720 . 12 *Ebenezer*, b March
5, 1721 : 13 *Henry*, b Aug. 17, 1723 : 14 *Thankfu*, b June,
1725, bp. in Cheshire, June 20, 1725 : 15 *Jonathan*, admitted
a freeman from Northbury, in 1748.

### 4. JOHN.

JOHN COOK, son of Mary and Henry Cook, married Abigail,
dau. of Daniel Johnson of Wallingford, Dec. 12, 1710. He
died Aug. 15, 1761, ae. 77 years. She died Aug. 15, 1761, ae.
81 years.

Children : 16 *Dinah*, b 1714 : 17 *Sarah*, b Jan. 7, 1717 ;
18 *Mary*, b Sept. 26, 1719 ; 19 *Tryphenia*, b 1722 ; 20 *Benjamin* b April 22, 1725, m Hannah Thorp, resided in the
eastern part of Wallingford, on the old Durham road ; 21
*John*, b Oct. 23, 1727.

### 6. ISAAC.

ISAAC COOK, son of Henry and Mary of Wallingford,
married Hannah ——— and removed to Branford, where he
died.

Children : 22 *Isaac Jr.*, b July 19, 1716, d at Branford,
1700 : 23 *Demetrius*, b April 23, 1718, d at Branford ;
24 *Ezra*, b May 9, 1722 , 25 *Anna*, b June 24, 1724 : 26
*Whittal*, b Jan. 28, 1727 ; 27 *Jerusha*, b Nov. 19, 1736

### 8. JONATHAN

JONATHAN COOK, son of Henry and Mary Cook, of Wallingford, married Ruth, daughter of William Luddington of

North Haven, June 15, 1735. They settled at Northbury
(then a Parish from Waterbury), now Plymouth.

Children: 28 *Jonathan*, b March 29, 1736; 29 *Jesse*, b
Feb. 1, 1739, d 1784; 30 *Titus*, b May 2, 1741; 31 *Sarah*, b
Oct. 31. 1744; 32 *Abel*, b May 18, 1747.

### 9. DAVID.

Capt. DAVID COOK, son of Henry and Mary Cook, of Wallingford. He married 1st, Rebecca Wilson; after her decease
he married Mary Lamson, of Boston. He was a very extensive ship owner, and was largely engaged in commerce, sailing
from the port of New Haven one ship and three brigs. In
religion he was a zealous friend of the church of England.
He generously paid one-quarter of the cost of building the
old church which was erected in the old Mix Lane, just opposite the residence of the late Isaac Peck. He also presented
the church an organ; this same organ was a few years since
sold to the Episcopal church in North Haven, and in 1869
they sold it to Wm. P. Gardner, an organ builder in New Haven. This organ was more than one hundred years old, and
perhaps the oldest in the state.

Children: 33 *David*, b 1723, res. in Woodbridge and New
Haven; 34 *Rachel*, b March 19, 1724, m Samuel Munson, he
d 1748; 35 *Leah*, b 1726, m Phineas Peck, she d in Wallingford; 36 *Phineas*, b April 3, 1729, settled in Middletown or
Durham; 37 *Wilson*, b April 21, 1730, left Wallingford during
the Revolutionary war and settled in Middletown; 38 *Jesse*,
b July 8, 1732; 39 *Rebecca*, b April 7, 1734, m Rev. Ichabod
Camp and went to Nova Scotia; 40 *Jedediah*, b April 4. 1735,
res. in New Haven; 41 *Benjamin*, b April 3, 1739: 42 *Nathaniel*, b May 31, 1740; 43 *Ephraim*, b 1744, res., in Wallingford.

### 10. JEDEDIAH.

JEDEDIAH COOK, son of Henry and Mary Cook, of Wallingford, married Sarah, daughter of Arthur Rexford, Aug. 10,
1727. He was a mariner, and resided in New Haven. His
dwelling house was on the south-west corner of State and

Chapel sts., New Haven. I have ascertained the name of one child only.

Child: 44 *Mary*, b Oct. 7, 1728, in New Haven.

## 12. EBENEZER

EBENEZER Cook, son of Henry and Experience Cook, of Waterbury, Conn., married Phebe, daughter of Moses Blakeslee, May 10, 1744.

Children: 45 *Huldah*, b April 26. 1744; 46 *Joel*, b Aug. 5, 1746; 47 *Justus*, b May 25, 1748, grad. at Yale College, 48 *Jonah*, b Aug. 11, 1750; 49 *Eric*, b Oct. 22, 1752; 50 *Ressell*, b May 1, 1755, grad. at Yale College, 51 *Noe*, b April 17. 1758; 52 *Arba*, b April 4, 1760; 53 *Lucinda*, b Sept. 20, 1764; 54 *Uri*; 55 *Ebenezer*, a Cong. clergyman at Montville, Conn.

## 13 HENRY.

HENRY Cook, son of Henry and Experience Cook, married Hannah, dau. of Nathan Benham, Nov. 7, 1745, and settled at Northbury, now Plymouth, Conn.

Children: 56 *Thankful*, b June 12, 1747; 57 *Mary*, b March 30, 1748, d June 11, 1760; 58 *Sarah*, b March 5, 1750, d June 15, 1760; 59 *Zuba*, b Dec. 24, 1751, d June 17, 1760; 60 *Lemuel*, b Dec. 7, 1754, d June 24, 1760; 61 *Selah*, b Dec. 10, 1756, he was a soldier in the Revolutionary war; 62 *Trueworthy*, b Sept. 29, 1759, settled with his brother Selah, in Onondaga Co., N. Y. in 1792.

## 15. JONATHAN.

JONATHAN Cook, son of Henry and Experience Cook, married Hannah, dau. of Nathan Benham, Nov. 7, 1745, and settled at Northbury, Plymouth, in 1748. No account of this family has been received.

## 22. ISAAC.

ISAAC Cook, son of Isaac and Hannah Cook, of Branford, married Mary Hubbard, of Guilford, Nov. 14, 1739. He died March 22, 1760, æ 44 years.

Children. 63 *Levi*, b Oct. 1, 1740, d 1744; 64 *Isaac*, b March 14, 1747, d Nov. 24, 1748; 65 *Rebecca*, b Nov. 12, 1751.

### 23. DEMETRIUS.

DEMETRIUS COOK, son of Isaac and Hannah Cook, married Elizabeth Rogers, of Branford,. Conn., April 26, 1739. They both died at Stony Creek, Branford, and were buried in a small grave-yard at a place called Damascus.

Children: 66 *Demetrius*, b Jan 6, 1740; 67 *Elizabeth*, b April 23, 1753; 68 *Elihu*, b Oct. 11, 1755; 69 *Jerusha*, b Jan. 19, 1760.

### 24. UZZEL.

UZZEL COOK, son of Isaac and Hannah Cook, married Zeruah Barns, of East Hampton, L. I., May 20, 1745, and settled in Branford, where they died.

Children: 70 *Desire*, b Dec. 29, 1745; 71 *Lydia*, b March 6, 1750; 72 *Abraham*, b June 1, 1754; 73 *Isaac*, b Oct. 9, 1757; 74 *Uzzel*, b July 21, 1761; 75 *Patience*, b May 13, 1764.

### 26. WAITSTILL.

WAITSTILL COOK, son of Isaac and Hannah Cook, married Elizabeth ——.

Children: 76 *Jane*, b April 10, 1751; 77 *Hannah*, b March 11, 1753; 78 *Jacob*, b July 15, 1755; 79 *Ebenezer H.*, b Sept. 6, 1759; 80 *William*, b May 9, 1762; 81 *Elizabeth*, b March 13, 1764; 82 *John*, b May 14, 1768; 83 *Huldah*, b May 14, 1768; 84 *Benjamin*, b April 6, 1771.

### 43. EPHRAIM.

EPHRAIM COOK was a son of Capt. David and Mary Cook. He was a magistrate for a long term of years, and was regarded as a sound, able and discriminating judge by all who had occasion to employ his services or come before him. He died Feb. 12, 1826, æ. 82 yrs. Mrs. Phebe, his wife, died Nov. 26, 1816, æ. 73 yrs. She was a daughter of John Tyler of Wallingford, and a sister of the Rev. John Tyler, late of Norwich, and an Episcopal clergyman.

Children: 85 *Phineas*, b Oct. 6, 1765, d Nov. 9, 1765; 86 *Elizabeth*, b April 24, 1766; 87 *Ephraim*, b March 1, 1768, m Sarah Lewis, dau. of Samuel; 88 *Darius*, b Aug. 8,

1760, d Dec. 28, 1791 ; 89 *Lyman*, b Nov. 17, 1770, d April 9, 1773 ; 90 *Mary*, b Oct. 24 1772, m Charles Rogers, d Nov. 9, 1840 ; 91 *Sylvia*, b Dec. 8, 1774, m Charles Clock of Catskill, N. Y. ; 92 *Phineas Lyman*, b June 22, 1776, d in the West Indies, May 8, 1801 ; 93 *Lucius*, b Oct. 15, 1777 ; 94 *Benjamin Tyler*, b May 30, 1778 m Diana Hull , 95 *Electa*, b April 9, 1780, d May 1, 1780 · 96 *George*, b Oct. 16, 1783 ; 97 *Nathaniel*, b April 17. 1786, m Caroline Ward, of Middletown, Conn.

## 87. EPHRAIM.

EPHRAIM COOK Jr., son of Ephraim and Phebe Cook, married Sarah, daughter of Samuel Lewis. She died Dec. 10, 1849. He died at Williamsburgh, L. I., Feb., 1868, ae. 90 yrs.

Children : 98 *Dr. Purcell*, d in N. Y., Dec. 24, 1860. no family ; 99 *Darius*, d at Catskill, N. Y., ae. 24 yrs ; 100 *Lyman*, a wealthy retired merchant in N. Y. city ; 101 *Mary*, unm in N Y. city ; 102 *Sarah Ann*, d in 1854. at Williamsburgh, L. I. ; 103 *Dr. Chauncey*, resides in Williamsburgh, N. Y. ; 194 *Delia* d at Catskill, N. Y., ae. 24 yrs.

## 93. LUCIUS.

LUCIUS COOK, son of Ephraim and Phebe Cook married 1st, Ruth Churchill ; after her death he married Mrs Phebe Ward, of Middletown and settled there. He died in 1845, ae. 79 yrs.

Child by 1st marriage : 105 *Lucius*, resides at Yellow Banks, Illinois Children by 2d marriage : 106 *Hiram*, 107 *Benjamin*, d a young man ; 108 *Lucina*, m Mr. Coe, of Middlefield, Conn

## 94. BENJAMIN.

BENJAMIN TYLER COOK, son of Ephraim and Phebe Cook, married Diana, daughter of John and Lois Hull. Mr. Cook died Jan. 30, 1851, a. 73 years. He was a large man weighing nearly 300 pounds

Children: 109 *William*, b March 3, 1803, m Julia Foster of Meriden, Ct.; 110 *Edward*, b Feb. 3, 1805; 111 *George*, b 1807, d in Chicago, Illinois; 112 *John Tyler*, b July 12, 1810, d May 29, 1811, in Wallingford; 113 *John Tyler;* 114 *Emeline*, m Lorenzo Williams, of Rocky Hill; 115 *Augustus;* 116 *Joel;* 117 *Delia*, m Henry A. Cook, of Wallingford; 118 *Phebe*, b 1817, d Feb. 24, 1817, æ. 2 weeks; 119 *David*, b 1823, d Jan. 25, 1826, æ. 2 yrs., 9 mos.; 120 *Julia*, b 1829, d May 6, 1829.

### 96. GEORGE.

GEORGE COOK, son of Ephraim and Phebe Cook, married Betsey Pierce of Catskill, N. Y., where he resided for some time, after which he removed to Newburg, N. Y., where he died Aug. 12, 1819, æ. 36 years.

Children: 121 *Sylvester*, was drowned in Hudson river; 122 *Alexander;* 123 *George Henry*, d at Burlington, N. J.; 124 *Maria*, m John Tyler Cook; 125 *Catherine*, m Lewis Germain, of N. J.

### 97. NATHANIEL.

NATHANIEL COOK, son of Ephraim and Phebe Cook, married Caroline Ward, of Middletown, Conn., after which he came to reside on the old homestead of his father, where he remained for several years, teaching school in the winter, and working the farm in the summer. He sold the old homestead, and removed his family to Earlville, Illinois, where he died April 24, 1855, æ. 69 years.

Children: 126 *Nelson*, b March 15, 1815; 127 *Emily*, b Sept. 5, 1817, m Elias Newton, Dec. 24, 1825; 128 *Phebe Tyler*, b Feb. 7, 1819, m Nehemiah Rice Ives, 1839, and Warren Baker, in 1852; 129 *Sylvester*, b Feb. 7, 1821; 130 *Caroline*, b Nov. 14, 1823, m Hiram Taft, Dec. 1, 1845; 131 *Lyman*, b Nov. 12, 1828; 132 *Ann M.*, b Jan. 12, 1831, m Jas. Ballard, of Earlville, July 4, 1850; 133 *David R.*, b Nov. 9, 1836.

## COWLES, OR COLES FAMILY.[1]

### JOSEPH.

JOSEPH COLES married Abigail Royce, July 13, 1699. She died May 24, 1714. He afterwards married Mary Wipels, May 19, 1717, and for his third wife, he married widow Ann Yale, Aug. 7, 1715. She died Feb. 27, 1715. This appears to be one of the first families of the name in Wallingford.

Children: 1 *Louis*, b April 25, 1700; 2 *Samuel*, b Dec. 10, 1701, d Feb. 18, 1704; 3 *Abigail*, b Jan. 17, 1702–3 4 *Samuel*, b Feb. 2, 1705, d Feb. 15, 1705; 5 *Hannah*, b April 11, 1706; 6 *Eunice*, b April 28, 1708, m Moses Curtis, Nov. 9, 1726; 7 *Joseph*, b March 1, 1710; 8 *Samuel*, b March 14, 1712; 9 *Hannah Waulch*, adopted daughter, d Aug. 18, 1721; 10 *Benjamin*, b Feb. 23, 1715, by Ann, 3d wife.

### WILLIAM.

WILLIAM COLES married Sarah Conger, July 27, 1688. He married 2d, Experience Gaylord, Dec. 22, 1721. This William was also among the early settlers, and doubtless a brother of the above Joseph.

Children: 11 *Samuel*, b May 7, 1688; 12 *John*, b May 18, 1691, m Mary ———; 13 *Sarah*, b Oct. 14, 1693; 14 *William*, b Feb. 15, 1696; 15 *James*, b March 7, 1707; 16 *Thomas*, b Sept. 10, 1719. By 2d marriage: 17 *Phineas*, b Jan 20, 1724; 18 *Phebe*, b 1726; 19 *Thomas*, b Sept. 10, 1722; 20 *Experience*, b March 16, 1728; 21 *David*, b Oct. 29, 1730.

### 7. JOSEPH

JOSEPH COLES married Eunice ———.

Child by Mindwell, 1st wife: 22 *Ebenezer*, b Feb. 20, 1718. By Eunice, 2d wife: 23 *Timothy*, b April 18, 1737, lived in Meriden, had a son Joel.

---

1 For collateral branches, see Andrews' Hist. of New Britain, 230, 231, 272; Doolittle's Hist Bolchertown, Mass., 270; Judd and Boltwood's Hist. and Gen. of Hadley, Mass., 471–3; Morse's Memorial of Morses, 160; Savage's Gen. Dict., I. 466.

## 11. SAMUEL.

SAMUEL COLES married 1st, Mercy Scranton, Aug. 5, 1725; 2d. Martha Brooks, Sept. 25, 1734; 3d, Susannah Cook, Dec. 1, 1735.

Children by 1st marriage: 24 *Moses*, b June 16, 1726; 25 *Mercy*, b Aug. 10, 1729. By 2d marriage: 26 *Samuel*, b July 30, 1735.

## 12. JOHN.

JOHN COLES married Mary ——, Nov. 20, 1717. He died 1761.

Children: 27 *Mary*, b Nov. 20, 1717; 28 *Comfort*, b Sept. 12, 1718; 29 *Dinah*, b March 12, 1720; 30 *Mary*, b Sept. 15, 1721; 31 *Lydia*, b Oct. 1, 1723; 32 *Timothy*, b Oct. 17, 1726, res. in Meriden; 33 *John*, b Feb. 1, 1727; 34 *Prudence*, b March 26, 1729; 35 *Thankful*, b Feb. 6, 1731; 36 *Sarah*, b March 21, 1733.

## 22. EBENEZER.

EBENEZER COLES.

Children: 37 *Elisha*, merchant and manufacturer; 38 *Ebenezer*, marble-cutter and stone-mason.

## CULVER.[1]

### JOSHUA.

JOSHUA CULVER, with Elizabeth Ford, his wife, to whom he was married Dec. 23, 1676, were among the first planters in Wallingford. He was a son of Edward Culver, Sen., of Dedham, Mass., New London, Groton and New Haven, Conn., and had three brothers in the vicinity of New London, who were heads of families at the time of his settling in Wallingford. He died April 23, 1713, ae. 70 yrs.

Children: 1 *Elizabeth*, d May 2, 1676, at New Haven, Conn.; 2 *Ann*, d Sept. 8. 1677, at New Haven, Conn.; 3–4

---

1 For collateral branches, see Caulkins' Hist. of New London, 309, 310; Howell's Hist. of Southampton, J. I., 217, 218; Savage's Gen. Dict., 1. 482, 483.

*Joshua* and *Samuel* ( twins ), 6 Sept. 21, 1684, 5 *Abigail*, b
Dec. 26, 1686 ; 6 *Sarah*, b Jan. 23, 1688 ; 7 *Ephraim*, b Sept
7, 1692.

### 3. JOSHUA.

SERGT. JOSHUA and Catharine Culver, m April 23, 1713.
He died June 14, 1730, æ. 46 yrs.

Children : 8 *Benjamin*, b Sept. 3, 1716; 9 *Stephen*, b Jan
24, 1718, d July 6, 1721 ; 10 *Samuel*, b May 10 1720; 11
*Stephen*, b May 19, 1722 ; 12 *Joshua*, b May 20, 1729 ; 13
*Daniel*, b Sept. 1, 1723; 14 *Titus*, b April 7, 1725 , 15
*Joshua*, b April 15, 1727, d July 16, 1729

### 4. SAMUEL.

SAMUEL CULVER married 1st, Sarah, 2 d, Ruth Sedgwick.
Jan. 3, 1728.

Children: 16 *Elizabeth*, b Feb. 12, 1715 ; 17 *Sarah*, b
Dec. 23, 1716 ; 18 *Abigail*, b Dec. 17, 1718 ; 19 *Esther*, b
March 17, 1721, d May 5, 1741 ; 20 *Caleb*, b Feb. 18, 1723,
m Lois ———, 21 *Anna*, b Oct. 3, 1732, d Nov. 21, 1733 ;
22 *Enoch*, b Jan. 30, 1725 . 23 *Ebenezer*, b Dec. 9, 1726.
By 2d marriage : 24 *Samuel*, b Sept. 25, 1728.

### 8. BENJAMIN.

BENJAMIN CULVER m Lydia ———.

Children : 24 *Joshua*, b Nov. 1, 1741, d ; 25 *Joshua*, b
April 4, 1743.

### 9. STEPHEN

STEPHEN CULVER m Eunice ———.

Children: 26 *Jesse*, b April 4, 1748 ; 27 *Esther*, b June 24,
1750 28 *Eunice*, b March 19, 1753 , 29 *Dan*, b May 12,
1756 : 30 *Jesse*, b April 4, 1758.

### 13. DANIEL.

DANIEL CULVER married Patience ———

Child : 31 *Samuel*, b Nov 24, 1747.

### 20. CALEB.

CALEB CULVER married Lois ———.

Children : 32 *Ruth*, b Jan 10, 1746 , 33 *Ruth*, b Nov. 25,

1751 ; 34 *Josiah*, b Sept. 7, 1748 ; 35 *Samuel*, b July 5, 1750.

## 22. ENOCH.

ENOCH CULVER married Lois ——.

Children: 36 *Esther*, b July 24, 1751 ; 37 *Lois*, b June 4, 1756.

## CURTIS.[1]

### WILLIAM.

WILLIAM CURTIS embarked in the ship Lion, June 22, 1632, and landed Dec. 16, 1632, at Scituate, Mass. He brought with him four children, Thomas, Mary, John, and Philip. He removed with his family to Roxbury, Mass., whence they removed to Stratford, Conn. By the records of Stratford, it appears that the father of these must have died before the removal of the family thither, and that previous to that event, a son William had been born to him, as the first of the name that appears on those records are John, William, and their mother, widow Elizabeth Curtis. It is stated that at the date of their removal to Stratford, John was about 28 years of age, and William about 18. Thomas died in Mass., "7th month, 1650;" widow Elizabeth died in 1658. Will proved. Nov. 4, 1658.

John married 1st, Elizabeth ———, who died in 1682 ; 2d, Margaret ———, who died in 1714. He died Dec. 6, 1707, æ. 96 years.

Children: 1 *John*, b 1642 ;. 2 *Israel*, b 1644 ; 3 *Elizabeth*,

---

1 For collateral branches, see Bradbury's Hist. Kennebunkport, Me., 235, 236; Brown's Gen. W. Simsbury. Conn.. Settlers, 31–4; Cothren's Hist. Woodbury, Conn., 531–9 ; Deane's Hist. Scituate, Mass., 251–4 ; Dod's Hist. E. Haven, Conn., 115 ; Draper's Hist. Spencer, Mass., 183 ; Paton's Hist. Thomaston, Me., 197 ; Ellis's Hist. Roxbury, Mass., 94 ; Hinman.'s Conn. Settlers, 776–88 ; Kingman's N. Bridgewater, Mass., 476; Mitchell's Hist. Bridgewater, Mass., 144 ; N. E. Hist. and Gen. Reg., XVI. 137 ; Savage's Gen. Dict., I. 484–6 ; Winsor's Hist. Duxbury, Mass., 249; Andrews' Hist. New Britain, Conn., 247 ; Barry's Hist. Hanover, Mass., 272–88.

b 1647, 4 *Thomas*, b 1648; 5 *Joseph*, b 1650; 6 *Benjamin*, b 1652; 7 *Hannah*, b 1654.

#### 4. THOMAS.

THOMAS CURTIS married Mary ———, June 9, 1674. He was born in Stratford, but removed to Wallingford.

Children: 8 *Mary*, b Oct. 13, 1675; 9 *Nathaniel*, b May 14, 1677, m Sarah Hall; 10 *Samuel*, b Feb. 3, 1678, m Elizabeth Frederick, Jan. 4, 1705°; 11 *Elizabeth*, b Sept. 11, 1680, m Nathaniel Hall; 12 *Hannah*, b Dec. 3, 1682, d Oct. 12, 1703 · 13 *Thomas*, b Aug. 16, 1685, m Mary ——— — , 14 *Sarah*, b Oct. 1, 1687, m James Parker in 1705; 15 *Abigail*, b Nov. 3, 1689, m Joseph Hall, 1709; 16 *Joseph*, b Aug. 10, 1691, d Jan. 11, 1713; 17 *Jemima*, b Jan. 15, 1694, m Nathaniel Beach; 18 *Rebecca*, b Aug. 21, 1697, m Lambert Johnson; 19 *John*, b Sept. 18 1699, m Jemima Abernathy, 1723.

#### 9. NATHANIEL.

NATHANIEL CURTIS, m 1st, Sarah Hall, April 6, 1697. She died Dec 13, 1700 He married 2nd, Sarah How, July 9, 1702.

Children: 20 *Benjamin*, b April 27, 1703, m Jemima Munson, 1727; 21 *Hannah*, b Feb. 19, 1705; 22 *Moses*, b Aug. 4, 1706; 23 *Nathan*, b May 19, 1709, m Esther Merriam, 24 *Jacob*, b Aug. 23 1710, m Abigail ——— ; 25 *Sarah*, b Mar. 30 1712; 26 *Abigail*, b April 9, 1713 · 27 *Lydia*, b March 20, 1714; 28 *Comfort*, b Oct. 30, 1716; 29 *Nathaniel*, b July 1 1718, m Lois · ———.

#### 10. SAMUEL.

SAMUEL CURTIS, married to Elizabeth Curtis, by Justice Hall, Jan. 3, 174 5.

Children: 30 *Titus*, b Jan. 28, 1733, d Jan., 1733; 31 *May*, b Nov. 8, 1736; 32 *Comfort*, b June 25, 1744; 33 *Enos*, b Jan. 27, 1746; 34 *Lois*, b March 1, 1752.

#### 16. JOSEPH.

JOSEPH CURTIS, son of Thomas and Mary Curtis, married Rebecca ———.

Children: 35 *Sybil*, b April 12, 1750; 36 *Jeptha*, b March 21, 1752.

### 19. JOHN.

JOHN CURTIS, m Jemima Abernathy, 1723. Children: 37 *John*, b Feb. 3, 1735; 38 *Giles*, b Jan. 4, 1737; 39 *Jemima*, b March 18, 1739; 40 *Elizabeth*, b April 11, 1741; 41 *Sarah*, b June 28, 1744.

### 20. BENJAMIN.

BENJAMIN CURTIS, son of Nathaniel and Sarah Curtis, married Miriam ——. Curr Children: 42 *Esther*, b Oct. 2, 1728; 43 *Abel*, b Dec. 22, 1729; 44 *Susannah*, b Nov. 9, 1732; 45 *Lois*, b Sept. 30, 1733; 46 *Benjamin*, b Oct. 27, 1735; 47 *Mariam*, b Aug. 30, 1737; 48 *Sarah*, b May 29, 1739; 49 *Aaron*, b Nov. 8, 1744.

### 23. NATHAN.

NATHAN and Esther Curtis. Children: 50 *Moses*, b May 8, 1741; 51 *Amos*, b March 24, 1743; 52 *Esther*, b March 7, 1745.

### 24. JACOB.

JACOB and Abigail Curtis. Child: 53 *Jacob*, b Oct. 1, 1738.

### 29. NATHANIEL.

NATHANIEL CURTIS married Lois ——. Children: 54 *Eunice*, b April 12, 1750; 55 *Nathaniel*, b June 13, 1756; 56 *Jacob*, b Sept. 14, 1758.

### 33. ENOS.

ENOS CURTIS, son of Samuel and Elizabeth Curtis, married Mary Yale, May 28, 1733. Children: 57 *Titus*, b Jan. 28, 1733, d Jan., 1733; 58 *Mary*, b Nov. 8, 1736; 59 *Comfort*, b June 25, 1744; 60 *Enos*, b June 27, 1746; 61 *Lois*, b March 1, 1752.

### RICHARD.

RICHARD CURTIS, who was among the first planters in Wallingford, was the father of Isaac Curtis, who married

Sarah Ford, of Branford, Aug. 13, 1682, and died July 15, 1712. Richard Curtis died in Wallingford, Sept. 17, 1631, æ. 70 years. Estate, £50

Children: 62 *Isaac*, b Nov. 6. 1683 ; 63 *Sarah*, b June 11, 1685 ; 64 *Joseph*, b July 18, 1689, m Ann Stevens Jan. 11, 1713 ; 65 *Ebenezer*, b Oct. 6, 1691, d July 20, 1717 ; 66 *Isaac*, b March 8, 1693-4, m Abigail Tuttle ; 67 *Elizabeth*, b Aug. 10. 1701 ; 68 *Benjamin*, b March 2, 1702-3 ; 69 *Moses*, b Aug. 9, 1706 ; 70 *Phebe*, d Aug. 5. 1718 , 71 *Joshua*, d July 20, 1719.

### 62. ISAAC.

ISAAC CURTIS married Abigail Tuttle ; she died, and he married Mary Tuttle, Oct. 1, 1720.

Children by 1st marriage : 72 *David*, b Aug. 7, 1707 , 73 *Phebe*, b April 4, 1718 ; 74 *Joshua*, b April 26, 1710 ; 75 *Ebenezer*, b Jan. 17, 1720.

### 64. JOSEPH.

JOSEPH CURTIS, m Ann Stephens, Jan. 11, 1713

Children : 76 *Philip*, b July 20, 1727 ; 77 *Joseph*, b Sept. 31, 1719 ; 78 *Johanna*, b June 1, 1723 ; 79 *Peter*, m Christiana Parker, Nov. 22, 1732

### 68. BENJAMIN.

BENJAMIN CURTIS married Joanna Munson, of New Haven. Children : 80 *Asa*, b May 11, 1731 ; 81 *Elizabeth*, b Dec 24, 1732 ; 82 *Asa*, b Feb. 13, 1740.

### 79. PETER.

PETER CURTIS, son of Joseph and Ann Curtis, married Christiana ———.

Children : 83 *Almer* b Aug. 8, 1738 ; 84 *Achsah*, b Oct. 5, 1739 ; 85 *Mary*, b June 6, 1741 ; 86 *Silas*, b Jan. 21, 1744 ; 87 *Eunice*, b April 2, 1746 ; 88 *Jesse*, b April 2, 1748 ; 89 *Daniel*, b Feb. 21, 1750 ; 90 *Amos*, b April 4, 1752.

### TITUS.

TITUS CURTIS, married Mary ———.

Children : 91 *Gideon*, m ——— Merriman ; 92 *Thomas* ; 93 *Rachel* ; 94 *Margaretta* ; 95 *Mary* ; 96 *Phebe*.

## DAVIDSON.

### WILLIAM.

WILLIAM DAVIDSON was the first of the name in Wallingford, where he married Elizabeth, daughter of Zachariah How,
Oct. 6, 1741. After the decease of Mr. How, he became the
owner, probably through his wife, of the farm of Mr.
How, which is the same that is now owned and occupied by the heirs
of the late Samuel Davidson and Zachariah Davidson, west
of the Falls plain, near South Meriden or Hanover.

Children: 1 *Anna*, b Dec. 21, 1742; 2 *Elizabeth*, b Dec.
23, 1744; 3 *William*, b June 6, 1747; 4 *Andrew*, b Aug. 19,
1749; 5 *John*, b Sept. 10, 1751; 6 *James*, b Oct. 6, 1753.

---

## DOOLITTLE.[1]

### ABRAHAM.

ABRAHAM DOOLITTLE, the emigrant, was the progenitor of
all who bear the name of Doolittle in this country. Himself
and his brother John were in Massachusetts very early.
John died childless at Salem, Mass. Abraham was in New
Haven before 1642, and the owner of a house. In 1644, he
took the freeman's oath, and was made the chief executive
officer (or sheriff) of the county. He was chosen by the
people of New Haven as one of the Committee to superintend the affairs of the new settlement, then (1669) just commenced at the village. The name of the village was changed
to that of Wallingford, and was incorporated May 12, 1670,
by an act of the general court, then sitting at Hartford. He
was one of the first who settled in the place, and was there before its incorporation, some two or three years. He was a
member of the vigilance committee in the time of "King
Philip's war." His dwelling was fortified during this time by

---

1 For collateral branches, see Andrews' Hist. New Britain, Conn.,
324; Doolittle's Hist. Belchertown, Mass., 273-7; N. E. Hist. and Gen.
Reg., VI. 293; Savage's Gen. Dict., II. 59.

a packet fort against any attack which might be made by the Indians. He was several times chosen a deputy from New Haven, and afterwards from Wallingford, to the general court. He was several times elected townsman, or select man, and appears to have been a very valuable and highly respected citizen. He died Aug. 11, 1690, æ. 70 years. He left an estate of £342. His 1st wife dying, he married Abigail Moss, July 2, 1663. She died Nov. 5, 1710, æ. 69 yrs.

Children by 1st marriage: 1 *Abraham*, b Feb. 12, 1649, d Nov. 10, 1732 æ. 83 years; 2 *Elizabeth*, b April 12, 1652; 3 *Mary*, b Feb. 22, 1653; 4 *John*, b June 14, 1655, m Mary Peck, Feb. 3, 1682. By 2d m: 5 *Samuel*, b July 7, 1665; 6, *Joseph*, b Feb. 12, 1666; 7 *Abigail*, b Feb. 25, 1668-9; 8 *Ebenezer*, b July 6, 1672, d Dec. 6, 1711; 9 *Mary*, b March 4, 1673, m Solomon Goff, Jan., 1713; 10 *Danj'l*, b Dec. 20, 1675; 11 *Theophilus*, b July 28, 1678.

### I. ABRAHAM.

ABRAHAM DOOLITTLE, Jr., married 1st, Mary, daughter of Wm. Hoult, of New Haven, Nov. 9, 1680. He died Dec. 15, 173-, æ. 83 years. He married for his 2d wife, Ruth Lothrop, of New London, Feb. 12, 1680. She died without issue. His 3d wife was Elizabeth Thorp, to whom he was married by Rev. Mr. Street, June 5, 1695. She died in 1736, æ. 60 years.

Children by 1st marriage: 12 *John*, b Aug. 13, 1681, m Mary Frederick, Feb. 28, 1735; 13 *Abraham*, b March 27, 1684, m Mary Lewis, Aug. 10, 1710; 14 *Sarah*, b Feb. 5, 1686; 15 *Susannah*, b April 15, 1688, m —— Armstrong. By 3d marriage: 16 *Thorp*, b Feb. 15, 1696; 17 *Samuel*, b March 14, 1698; 18 *Joseph*, b March 15, 1700, m Rachel Cole, Dec. 15, 1726; 19 *Thomas*, b May 17, 1705, m Sarah Abernathy; 20 *Lydia*, b June 26, 1710, m John Joyce.

### 4. JOHN.

JOHN DOOLITTLE, son of Abraham and Abigail Doolittle, married Mary Peck, Feb. 13, 1682. He married 2d, Grace Blakeslee, Jan. 29, 1717.

Children: 21 *Esther*, b Jan. 24, 1683; 22 *Samuel*, b Feb. 4, 1685; 23 *Sarah*, b Feb. 15, 1686; 24 *Susannah*, b April 5, 1688; 25 *Benjamin*, b July 10, 1695, grad. at Yale, 1716; 26 *Susannah*, b Feb. 24, 1706; 27 *Eunice*, b May 30, 1707; 28 *John*, b Feb. 6, 1712.

### 5. SAMUEL.

SAMUEL DOOLITTLE, son of Abraham and Abigail Doolittle, married 1st, Mary ——, 2d, Eunice ——, and settled at Middletown, Conn.

Children: 30 *Jonathan*, b Aug. 21, 1689; 31 *Samuel*, b Aug. 3, 1691, m Jane Wheeler, Aug. 1, 1714; 32 *Mary*, b Nov. 24, 1693; 33 *Abraham*, b Sept. 21, 1695; 34 *Abigail*, b 1697; 35 *Martha*, b April 6, 1698; 36 *Hannah*, b Oct. 29, 1700; 37 *Thankful*, b June 3, 1702; 38 *Joseph*, b June 20, 1704, m Mary Hitchcock, May 24, 1729; 39 *Nathaniel*, b Jan. 15, 1706, d of small pox; 40 *Esther*, b July 16, 1709; 41 *Abel*, b May 15, 1724; 42 *Benjamin*, b Jan. 17, 1730.

### 6. JOSEPH.

CAPT. JOSEPH DOOLITTLE, son of Abraham and Abigail Doolittle, married Sarah, daughter of Samuel and Sarah Brown; she was born Aug. 8, 1672, and married by Thomas Yale, Esq., April 24, 1690. He died May 15, 1733, æ. 66 years. His 2d wife was Elizabeth Hoult, whom he married Oct. 5, 1720; she died June 3, 1768, æ. 73 years.

Children: 43 *Isaac*, b Aug. 13, 1721; 44 *Enos*, b March 2, 1727, m Mary ——, he d in 1756. By 2d marriage: 45 *Dinah*, b April 24, 1729; 46 *Elizabeth*, b Jan. 3, 1731, d April 13, 1731; 47 *Ichabod*, b Aug. 21, 1732; 48 *Sarah*, b Dec. 27, 1735.

### 8. EBENEZER.

EBENEZER DOOLITTLE, son of Abraham and Abigail Doolittle, married Hannah, ——— daughter of Samuel and Hannah Hall, April 6, 1697. She was born March 11, 1673, and died July 27, 1758. He died Dec. 6, 1711; settled in Cheshire.

Children: 49 *Hannah*, b 1699; 50 *Ebenezer*, b April 15,

1700, m Lydia Warner, June 11, 1728 ; 51 *Moses*, b 1702, d April 10, 1781, m Ruth Richardson ; 52 *Sarah*, b 1704 ; 53 *Caleb*, b Feb. 3, 1706, d 1781 : 54 *Joshua*, b March 2, 1708, 55 *Zadock*, b March 17, 1711.

## 10. DANIEL.

DANIEL DOOLITTLE, son of Abraham and Abigail Doolittle, married to Hannah Cornwall of Middletown, Conn., by Mr Hamlin. After the birth of their first child they removed to Middletown, and after a residence of a few years in that place they returned to Wallingford, where he died, in 1755, æ. 80 yrs. She died Jan. 16, 1736.

Children : 56 *Hannah*, b Jan. 27, 1699. m Joseph Doolittle, Sep'. 10, 1722 ; 57 *Elizabeth*, b Oct. 15, 1700 ; 59 *Matthew*, b April 16, 1703 ; 60 *Dinah*, b Oct. 4, 17—, d Sept. 14, 1719 ; 61 *Daniel*, b Feb. 3, 1707, d Sept., 1791, v. 84 yrs. ; 62 *Joseph*, b July 3, 1709 ; 63 *Stephen*, b Sept. 14, 1710 ; 64 *Abigail*, b May 6, 1712 : 65 *Ezra*, b July 24, 1718, d Oct. 24, 1744, at Cheshire, Conn.

## 11. THEOPHILUS.

THEOPHILUS DOOLITTLE, son of Abraham and Abigail Doolittle, married to Thankful, dau. of David Hall, by Mr. Street, Jan. 5, 1698. She died June 2, 1715. He died March 26, 1740, æ. 62 yrs. He married Elizabeth Howe for his 2d wife.

Children : 67 *Thankful*, b May 2, 1700, m Timothy Page ; 68 *Sarah*, b June 1, 1703, m Isaac Tuttle, she d 1713 ; 69 *Henry*, b 1704, d 1733, æ. 29 yrs. ; 70 *Theophilus*, b June 20, 1709, m Sarah Dorch'r ( or Dorchester ), Nov. 15, 1738 : 71 *Solomon*, b Aug. 13, 1713, m Eunice Hall, Feb. 24, 17— ; 72 *Benjamin*, b Sept. 28, 1723.

## 12. JOHN.

JOHN DOOLITTLE, son of Abraham Jr. and Mercy Doolittle, married Mary Frederick, of New Haven, Feb. 28, 1705 : he married 2d, Mary Lewis. He died 1745.

Children : 73 *Benjamin*, b July 10, 17 5 , 74 *Susannah*, b Feb. 24, 1707 ; 75 *Eunice*, b May 30, 1709 , 76 *John*, b Feb.

6, 1712, m Hannah —— ; 77 *Phœbe*, b Nov. 26, 1713, m Josiah
Mix; 78 *Frederick T.*, b Oct. 20, 1715, d Sept. 2, 1746; 79
*Obed*, b Oct. 2, 1717, d Nov. 4, 1746, ae. 29 yrs.; 80 *Nathan*,
b July 22, 1720, d Aug. 20, 1728; 81 *Mary*, b Oct. 26, 1723,
d Dec. 21, 1724; 82 *Keziah*, b Jan. 31, 1728, d Sept. 22,
1746; 83 *Patience*, b June 17, 1732.

### 13. ABRAHAM.

ABRAHAM DOOLITTLE, son of Abraham Jr. and Mercy
Doolittle, married Mary Lewis, Aug. 10, 1710.   He died May
10, 1733.

Children: 84, 85 *Ezekiah*, *Josiah*, b May 25, 1711; 86
*Dinah*, d Sept. 14, 1719; 87 *Zebulon*, b March 1, 1712, d March
1, 1714; 88 *Ambrose*, b Nov. 23, 1719, m Martha Munson;
89 *Nathan*, b July 22, 1720; 89 1-2 *Mary*, b Dec. 15, 1727;
90 *Abraham*, b Aug. 29, 1728; 81 *Deliverance*, b Nov. 9, 1730.

### 17. SAMUEL.

SAMUEL DOOLITTLE, son of Abraham and Elizabeth
(Thorp) Doolittle, married Jane Wheeler, Aug. 1, 1714.

Children: 92 *Sarah*, b Sept. 24, 1714; 93 *Joseph*, b May 4,
1715; 94 *Samuel*, b Feb. 28, 1725, m Eunice —— ; 95 *Mehitable*, b Sept. 23, 1726; 96 *Benjamin*, b Jan. 17, 1730.

### 18. JOSEPH.

JOSEPH DOOLITTLE, son of Abraham and Elizabeth Doolittle, married 1st, Rachel Cowles, March 14, 1728.   He married 2nd, Martha Hitchcock, Feb. 5, 1735.

Children: 97 *Dinah*, b April 24, 1729; 98 *Ichabod*, b Aug.
31, 1731; 99 *Sarah*, b Dec. 27, 1735; 100 *Joseph*, b Jan.
25, 1738.

### 19. THOMAS.

THOMAS DOOLITTLE, son of Abraham and Elizabeth
Doolittle, married Sarah Abernathy, May 27, 1730.   He resided in Waterbury in 1764, was a Tory in the Revolution, and
joined the English.   He went to Nova Scotia with his brother
James.   He married his second wife, Hannah Fenn, March
5, 1732.

Children by 1st marriage 101 *Thomas*, b 1729, died in Cheshire, Nov. 19, 1760; 102 *Anna*, b Dec. 20, 1730; 103 *Samuel*, b Dec. 29, 1731, d Jan. 11, 1732; 104 *Jemima*, b Dec. 31, 1732; 105 *Esther*, b Aug. 30, 1734. By 2d marriage: 106 *James*, b Feb. 7, 1734; 107 *Hannah*, b Oct. 12, 1735; 108 *Catherine*, b Jan. 10, 1738; 109 *Thomas*, b Jan. 22, 1742.

## 22. SAMUEL.

SAMUEL DOOLITTLE, son of John and Mary Doolittle, married Mehitable ———, and settled in Northfield, Mass., where he died in 1736.

Children: 110 *Mary*, b June 16, 1712; 111 *Ephraim*, 112 *Moses*; 113 *Mindwell*, b June 15, 1715.

## 25. BENJAMIN.

REV. BENJAMIN DOOLITTLE, son of John and Mary Doolittle, grad. at Yale in 1716, married Lydia Todd, Oct. 14, 1717, and settled in the ministry at Northfield, Mass., in 1718. He died suddenly Jan. 9, 1748, æ. 53 years, having been settled in the ministry about 30 years. His widow died June 16, 1790, æ. 92 years.

Children: 114 *Ohrs*, b Oct. 28, 1718; 115 *Lydia*, b Aug. 24, 1720; 116 *Charles*, b July 31, 1722; 117 *Eunice*, b July 31, 1734; 118 *Susannah*, b June 13, 1726; 119 *Lucius*, b May 16, 1728; 120 *Chloe*, b May 4, 1730; 121 *Lucy*, b Feb. 27, 1731; 122 *Thankful*, b Jan. 20, 1733; 123 *Amzi*, b Nov. 15, 1737; 124 *Lucy*, b July 15, 1741.

## 28. JOHN.

JOHN DOOLITTLE, son of John and Mary, married Hannah ———. He died in Wallingford in 1746 7, æ. 35.

Children: 125 *Philemon*, b Feb. 25, 1740, m Lydia Hall, Jan. 5, 1757; 126 *Eunice*, b Jan. 31, 1741; 127 *Mary*, 128 *Hannah*, b May 12, 1744; 129 *Titus*, b June 12, 1745, m Mary, dau. of Dr. Lewis, Nov. 20, 1764.

## 31. SAMUEL.

SAMUEL DOOLITTLE, son of Samuel and Mary Doolittle, married Elizabeth ———.

Children: 130 *Elizabeth*, b Jan. 2, 1755; 131 *Ephraim*, b Sept. 30, 1756; 132 *George*, b Jan. 14, 1759.

### 33. ABRAHAM.

ABRAHAM DOOLITTLE, son of Samuel and Mary Doolittle, married Damaris ——.

Child: 133 *Abraham*, b Nov., 1754.

### 38. JOSEPH.

JOSEPH DOOLITTLE, son of Samuel and Mary Doolittle, married Mary Hitchcock, May 24, 1729. She died, and he married Mary Strickland, at Middletown, Conn., May 24, 1739. Children: 134 *Mary*, d young; 135 *Elizabeth*, d young; 136 *Joseph*, d in Middletown, Aug. 6, 1771; 137 *Seth*, b Jan. 4, 1745, m Hannah Dow, Feb. 4, 1768; 138 *Abisha*, d in Cheshire about 1837, no family; 139 *Mary;* 140 *Elizabeth;* 141 *Joseph;* 142 *Jared,* d July 13, 1769; 143 *Joel*, b July 7, 1769.

### 42. BENJAMIN.

BENJAMIN DOOLITTLE, son of Samuel and Mary Doolittle, married Elizabeth ——.

Children: 144 *Benjamin*, b July 15, 1753; 145 *Sarah*, b Feb. 21, 1756.

### 43. ISAAC.

ISAAC DOOLITTLE, son of Capt. Joseph and Sarah Doolittle, was a brass founder in New Haven, where he died, Feb. 13, 1800, ae. 99. He married Phebe Cook. He was the ancestor of Gov. English on the maternal side.

Child: *Jesse*, b Feb. 25, 1777.

### 44. ENOS.

ENOS DOOLITTLE, son of Capt. Joseph and Sarah Doolittle, married Mary ——. He died Oct. 27, 1756, ae. 22 years.

Children: 147 *Keziah*, b June 27, 1748; 148 *Katharine*, b Aug. 17, 1749; 149 *John*, b Dec. 31, 1754, d July 8, 1756; 150 *Patience*, b May 4, 1756.

### 50. EBENEZER.

EBENEZER DOOLITTLE, son of Ebenezer and Hannah, married Lydia Warner. June 11, 1728, and settled in Cheshire. He died May 20, 1774, ae. 74 years.

Children: 151 *Ruth*, b Aug. 20, 1735 ; 152 *Ebenezer*, b Oct. 12, 1736 ; 153 *Jesse*, b Aug. 12, 1738 ; 154 *Zopher*, b Aug. 7, 1740.

### 51. MOSES.

MOSES DOOLITTLE, son of Ebenezer and Hannah, married 1st, Ruth Hills ; 2d, Lydia Richardson, March 23, 1720, died April 10, 1781, ae. 79 years, at Cheshire.

Children: 155 *Thomas*, b Feb. 8, 1730, d April 13, 1731 ; 156 *Hannah*, b Nov. 9, 1731 ; 157 *Eunice*, b Oct. 27, 1733 ; 158 *Damaris*, b May 28, 1735.

### 53. CALEB.

CALEB DOOLITTLE, son of Ebenezer and Hannah, married Tamar Thompson, April 24, 1734. They settled in the south-west part of Cheshire, on land now owned and occupied by Julius Brooks, Esq., and others. He died March 11, 1781, a. 75 years.

Children: 159 *Joseph*, b April 30, 1734. was a farmer in Cheshire, near where the present Joseph Doolittle lives ; 160 *Caleb*, b Jan. 5, 1735, settled in Westwoods, Hamden. left sons and daughters ; 161 *Tamar*, b Aug. 12, 1736 ; 162 *Benjamin*, b March 5, 1738, settled in Cheshire one-half mile west of the village ; 163 *Lois*, b April 8, 1746 ; 164 *Amos*, was a farmer in the south-west part of Cheshire ; 165 *Ephraim*, b June 15, 1754.

### 54. JOSHUA.

JOSHUA DOOLITTLE, son of Ebenezer and Hannah, married Martha Hitchcock, Feb. 5, 1735, died Nov. 15, 1770, ae. 71 years. Having no children, he gave all his property to Joshua Doolittle Waterman, son of the Rev. Simeon Waterman, of Plymouth, Conn.

### 55. ZADOCK.

ZADOCK DOOLITTLE, son of Ebenezer and Hannah, married Rhoda ———.

Children: 166 *Hannah*, b July 22, 1740 ; 167 *Lidia*, b

March 3, 1742 ; 168 *Rhoda*, b June 28, 1744 ; 169 *Eunice*, b Sept. 5, 1746 ; 170 *Zachariah*, b May 13, 1749 ; 171 *Sarah*, b Sept. 24, 1751.

### 61. DANIEL.

DANIEL DOOLITTLE, son of Daniel and Hannah, married Elizabeth Dayton and settled in North Haven, two miles north of the center, on the Wallingford road.  He died Sept., 1791, ae. 84.

Children: 172 *Giles*, b Nov. 6, 1734 ; 173 *Michael*, b April 12, 1738 ; 174 *Oliver*, b Oct. 14, 1742, m —— Cook; 175 *Elizabeth*, b Jan. 8, 1745 ; 176 *John*, b Jan. 15, 1747 ; 177 *Johnson*, d in Wallingford ; 178 *Ezra*. b Jan. 3, 1752, d in Cheshire.

### 62. JOSEPH.

JOSEPH DOOLITTLE, son of Daniel and Hannah, married Mary ——.

Children: 179 *Joseph*, b Jan. 15. 1757 , 180 *Walter*, b March 27, 1759 ; 181 *Joel*, b Jan. 7, 1761.

### 63. STEPHEN.

STEPHEN DOOLITTLE, son of Daniel and Hannah, married Anna ——, May 11, 1737.  He died Nov. 8, 1772, ae. 64. She died Nov. 27, 1797, ae. 92 years.

Children: 182 *Anna*, b April 27, 1738 ; 183 *Abigail*, b Jan. 21, 1741 ; 184 *Ruth*, b Oct. 29, 1742 ; 185 *Stephen*, b Jan. 15, 1745, d Nov. 30, 1745.

### 65. EZRA.

EZRA DOOLITTLE, son of Daniel and Hannah, married Hannah ——.  He died Oct. 24, 1844, in Cheshire.

Children: 186 *Hannah*, d in 1747 ; 187 *Hannah*, b May 21, 1748.

### 70. THEOPHILUS.

THEOPHILUS DOOLITTLE, son of Theophilus and Thankful, married Sarah Dorcher, Nov. 15, 1738.

Children: 188 *Susannah*, b Aug. 2, 1739 ; 189, 190 *Solomon* and *Theophilus*, b Jan. 8, 1741, d Jan. 25, 1741 ; 191

*Theophilus*, b Feb. 5, 1742 ; 192 *Solomon*, b March 24. 1744 ; 193 *Josiah*, b July 11, 1748, married Damaris ——; 194 *Sarah*, b April 10, 1750 ; 195 *Elizabeth*, b June 1, 1751 . 196 *Stephen*, b July 12, 1752 ; 197 *Isaac*, b Aug. 27, 1754.

## 71. SOLOMON.

SOLOMON DOOLITTLE, son of Theopilus and Thankfui, married, 1st, Eunice Hall ; 2nd, Jerusha Tyler, Feb. 13, 1734

Children : 198 *Daniel*, b Oct. 4, 1706 ; 199 *Theophilus*, b March 10, 1769 ; 200 *Sarah*, b Feb. 5, 1752 ; 201 *Lucy*, b July 18. 1778 ; 202 *Ford*, b Sept. 16, 1781.

## 84. EZEKIAH.

* EZEKIAH DOOLITTLE, son of Abraham and Mary Doolittle, m Hepzibah ——.

Children : 203 *Barnabas*, b Jan. 8, 1736 ; 204 *Mehitable*, b Feb. 28, 1738 ; 205 *Hepzibah*, b Aug. 14, 1741 ; 206 *Hezekiah*, b May 4, 1742 ; 207 *Anthony*, b Jan. 31, 1744 ; 208 *Mary*, b Feb 25, 1750.

## 85. JOSIAH.

JOSIAH DOOLITTLE, son of Abraham and Mary Doolittle, married Damaris ——.

Children : 209 *Josiah*, b July 17, 1769, d July 30, 1769 ; 210 *Stephen*, b March 24. 1771.

## 87. ZEBULON.

ZEBULON, son of Abraham and Mary Doolittle, married Mary ——.

Children : 211 *Mary*, b Jan. 1, 1741 ; 212 *Sarah*, b April 7, 1745 ; 213 *John*, b May 24, 1748.

## 88. AMBROSE.

AMBROSE DOOLITTLE, son of Abraham and Mary, married Martha Munson, daughter of William and Rebecca Munson, of Cheshire. He died in Cheshire, Sept. 25, 1781, æ. 74 years.

Children : 214 *Ambrose*, b Dec. 12, 1751 ; 215 *Amos*, b May 8, 1754 ; 216 *Martha*, b Aug. 30, 1756 ; 217 *Eunice*, b June 21, 1758 ; 218 *Abner*, b July 27, 1760 ; 219 *Lois*; 220 *Thankful*; 221, 222 *Samuel* and *Silas*, b March 28, 1763, both d same day; 223 *Reuben*, b May 1, 1766; 224 *Lowly*, b June 9, 1769; 225 *Mary Ann*, b Feb. 23, 1771; 226 *Eliakim*, b Aug. 29, 1772.

## 94. SAMUEL.

SAMUEL DOOLITTLE, son of Samuel and Jane, married Eunice ——.

Child: 227 *Samuel*, b April 11, 1749.

## 125. PHILEMON.

PHILEMON DOOLITTLE, son of John and Hannah, married Lydia Hall, Jan. 5, 1757. Supposed to have died in western New York.

Children: 229 *Phebe*, b May 25, 1759, in Wallingford; 230 *Keziah*, b April 20, 1760, in Wallingford; 231 *Lydia*, b Oct. 22, 1761; 232 *John F.*, b Feb. 11, 1767; 233 *Rice*, b Aug. 27, 1769; 234 *Jared;* 235 *Jesse;* 236 *Patience;* 237 *Hannah.*

## 129. TITUS.

TITUS DOOLITTLE, son of John and Hannah, married Mary Lewis, daughter of Dr. Lewis of Wallingford, Nov. 20, 1764. He died at Westfield, Mass., Nov. 23, 1818, ae. 73 years.

Children; 239 *John*, b Jan., 1765, d in early life unm.; 240 *Elizabeth*, b 1767, m Abraham Bradley of Russell, Mass., she d April 28, 1831; 241 *Titus*, was a farmer at Westfield, Mass., m Mary Tracy in 1794, and had ten children, mostly deceased; 242 *Mary*, b 1769, m Noble Fowler of Southwick, Mass., she d March 11, 1747; 243 *Joel*, b 1774, grad. at Yale College, 1799, was a lawyer; 244 *Amasa*, b 1776, m Mary Hitchcock of Cheshire; 245 *Martha*, m Solomon Gillette of Colchester, Conn.; 246 *Mark*, a lawyer in Belchertown ,Mass., grad. at Yale College in 1804, m 1st, Betsey A. Smith, and 2d, Sarah T. Reuberteau, he d in 1818, Nov. 23, leaving no sons.

## 152. EBENEZER.

EBENEZER DOOLITTLE, son of Ebenezer and Lydia Warner Doolittle, owned and occupied the farm late the property of Landa Bristol, of Cheshire.

Children: 247 *Elkanah*, d in Brooklyn, N. Y.; 248 *Amaryllis*, m Landa Bristol, of Cheshire.

### 160. CALEB.

CALEB DOOLITTLE, son of Caleb and Tamar, married in West Woods, Hamden.

Children: 249 *Caleb;* 250 *Jesse;* 251 *Tamar,* m ———— Wooden.

### 162. BENJAMIN.

BENJAMIN DOOLITTLE, son of Caleb and Tamar.

Child: 252 *Joseph I.,* d in Prospect.

### 164. AMOS.

AMOS DOOLITTLE, son of Caleb and Tamar, married and settled in the southwestern part of Cheshire, on the farm now belonging to the heirs of his grandson, Amos Doolittle, late of Cheshire, deceased. He died March 23, 1808, ae. 75 yrs. His wife. Mrs. Abigail ————, died July 28, 1827, ae. 88 yrs.

Children: 253 *Olive,* b March 30, 1761 ; 254 *Amos,* b 1767. d May 21, 1816, ae. 49 yrs. : Lois his wife d March 27, 1828, ae. 57 yrs. ; probably Alexander and others.

### 165. EPHRAIM.

EPHRAIM DOOLITTLE, son of Caleb and Tamar, married Christiana Thorp, and settled on the farm now owned by Julius Brook, Esq., in the southwest district of Cheshire. He also owned the mills since known as Gaylord's mills. His widow married Thaddeus Rich, late of Cheshire, deceased.

Children: 255 *Julia;* 256 *Rispah,* b 1800, d ae. 50 yrs.

### 178. EZRA.

EZRA DOOLITTLE, son of Daniel and Elizabeth, married Sarah Hall, and settled on the farm now owned by h's son Levi, in the north part of Cheshire. He died suddenly on the first Monday in April, 1829.

Children: 257 *Ezra,* b May 8, 1776, settled in Barkham stead, and died there: 258 *Leonard;* 259 *Levi,* m ———— Tuttle, of Cheshire ; 260 *Sarah,* m Benjamin Dowd Doo little; 261 *Betsey;* 262 *Eunice.*

### 192. SOLOMON.

SOLOMON DOOLITTLE, son of Theophilus and Sarah, married Eunice Hall, Feb. 24, 1768.

Children: 263 *Theophilus*, b March 19, 1769, m Abiah Atwater; 264 *Sarah*, b Feb. 5, 1772; 265 *Lucy*, b July 18, 1778; 266 *Joel*, b Sept. 16, 1781.

### 214. AMBROSE.

AMBROSE DOOLITTLE, son of Ambrose and Martha, married Miss ——— Dowd of Middletown, Conn. He died in Cheshire, Conn.

Child: 267 *Benjamin Dowd*, b 1775, d May 13, 1845, æ. 70 yrs. He m Sarah Doolittle, she d July 30, 1826, æ. 44 yrs.

### 215. AMOS.

AMOS DOOLITTLE, son of Ambrose and Martha, married Abigail Ives of Cheshire, Conn., dau. of Joel Ives. He was a distinguished engraver and artist. His dwelling occupied a portion of the lot on the northwest corner of College and Elm Streets, New Haven, Conn.

Child: 267 *Mary Ann*.

### 218. ABNER.

ABNER DOOLITTLE, son of Ambrose and Martha, married. He resided in the old homestead in Cheshire, Conn., until his death; he had several daughters.

### 221. SAMUEL.

SAMUEL DOOLITTLE, son of Ambrose and Martha, married. He was insane, and died in Cheshire, Conn.

Children: 268 *Calvin*, m Matilda Wincher, he d in Cheshire, Conn.; 269 *Alfred*, m ——— Brown, and d in Cheshire, Conn.; 270 *Aaron*, married, has a large family in Cheshire, Conn.

### 222. SILAS.

SILAS DOOLITTLE, son of Ambrose and Martha. He went to Vermont, became insane and died the same hour and minute that his brother died at Cheshire.

### 231. AMASA.

AMASA DOOLITTLE, son of Titus and Mary, married Mary, daughter of Amasa Hitchcock, of Cheshire. He died in 1825, ae. 49 years.

Children: 232 *Amasa Lewis*, resides in Cheshire, on the old Lewis farm; 233 *Mary*, m Reuben Palmer, of Springfield, Mass.

### 247. ELKANAH.

ELKANAH DOOLITTLE, son of Ebenezer and ———, married 1st, —— Cook, of Cheshire. She died and he married his 2d wife in Brooklyn, N. Y., where he resided until his death. He was a graduate of Yale College.

Children: 234 *Milton*, d at Cheshire, Conn.; 235 *Edward*, d at Cheshire; 236 *Warren*; 237 *Wm. A.*, d in Brooklyn, New York.

### 254. AMOS.

AMOS DOOLITTLE, son of Amos and Abigail, married Lois ———. He died May 21, 1816, ae. 49 yrs. She died March 27, 1828, ae. 57 yrs.

Child: 238 *Amos*, b 1797, d at Cheshire about 1867, ae. 70.

### 241. TITUS.

TITUS DOOLITTLE, son of Titus and Mary Doolittle, married Mary, daughter of Rev. Stephen Tracey, of Norwich, Mass., in 1794, and had children, most of whom have died; no sons are living. His wife died in 1843. He was living at Painesville, Ohio, in 1852.

### 243. JOEL.

JOEL DOOLITTLE, son of Titus and Mary Doolittle, married Sarah P. Fitch, of Pawlet. He graduated at Yale in 1799, and was tutor in Middlebury college, Vermont He studied law and settled at Middlebury in the practice of his profession, after having filled with honor many offices in the gift of the people, as Judge of the Supreme Court, etc He died March 9, 1841, ae. 67 yrs. He left four sons and two daughters. The three sons are in Ohio.

Children: 279 *John;* 280 *Titus;* 281 *Charles Hubbard;* 282 *Joel;* 283 *Sarah;* 284 *Elizabeth.*

#### 244. AMASA.

AMASA DOOLITTLE, son of Titus and Mary Lewis Doolittle, married Mary, daughter of Amasa Hitchcock of Cheshire. He died in 1825, ae. 49 years.

Children: 285 *Amasa Lewis,* now living in Cheshire; 286 *Mary,* resides in Springfield, Mass. She married Reuben Palmer.

#### 246. MARK.

MARK DOOLITTLE, son of Titus and Mary Doolittle, graduated at Yale college, 1804; studied law and settled at Belchertown, Mass. He married for his first wife Betesy Matilda Smith, daughter of Daniel Smith Esq., of West Haven, Vt. She died Nov. 14, 1814, ae. 28. He married his 2nd wife, Sarah T. Reuberteau, of Newburyport.

Children: 287 *Lucy Maria,* m Dr. Horatio Thompson, of Belchertown, Mass., 1834; 288 *Betsey Matilda,* b May, 1814, m John Strong, a graduate of Yale in 1857, residence in Addison, N. Y. By second marriage, 289 *Sarah Lorena,* d July 29, 1849, ae. 18; 290 *Wm. C.,* d in childhood.

#### 108. ENSIGN.

ENSIGN JOSEPH DOOLITTLE, son of Joseph and Rachel, married Martha Hitchcock, and was a farmer on the west side of the river in Wallingford.

Children: 291 *Joseph;* 292 *Walter;* 293 *Joel;* 294 *Reuben.*

#### 291. JOSEPH.

JOSEPH DOOLITTLE, son of Joseph and Martha.

Children: 295 *Jared,* was a merchant in New Haven; *Nathaniel,* was the owner of the mills at Quinnipiac; 29 *Patty,* m Oliver Deming, of New Haven.

#### 293. JOEL.

JOEL DOOLITTLE, son of Joseph and Martha.

Children: 298 *Joel,* b 1790, is living at North Haven; 299

*Lucy*, no further information about her appears on the records.

REUBEN DOOLITTLE was a farmer in the south-westerly part of the town of Wallingford.

Children: 300 *Rufus ;* 301 *Almon ;* 302 *Rhoda*, m Augustus Hall Esq., of Wallingford.

## DUDLEY.

### JOHN.

JOHN and Lois Dudley, came into Wallingford about the year 1750, and settled on the west side of the river, a short distance below the present residence of Street Jones, Esq., who is the present owner of the old Dudley house. Of their history very little is now known.

### JEDEDIAH.

JEDEDIAH DUDLEY, their son, was born in Wallingford, Jan. 1, 1759, married ———, and occupied the house of his father until his decease.

Children: 1 *John*, d in Branford, buried in Wallingford, 1869 ; 2 *Caleb*, d in Wallingford ; 3 *Elias*, m Laura Preston, and died in Cheshire ; 4 *Jedediah*, d unm., and was insane several years ; 5 *Isaac*, d ; 6 a daughter.

## DUTTON.[1]

### JOSEPH.

JOSEPH DUTTON, the ancestor of the family of that name in Wallingford, was of Machimoodus, or East Haddam. He purchased land in Wallingford in 1718 and 1719, which he gave to his sons, whose names are as follows :

1 *Benjamin*, b 1696, m Mary ——— ; 2 *David*, m Lydia Cook ; 3 *Thomas*, m Abigail Merriman.

---

1 For collateral branches, see Hill's Hist. Mason, N. H., 201 ; Savage's Gen. Dict., II. 84, 85.

### 1. BENJAMIN.

BENJAMIN DUTTON, married Mary ——, had children born in Wallingford. He died in Cheshire Parish, Jan. 27, 1791, æ. 95 yrs. She died Oct. 27, 1785, æ. 80 yrs. Children: 4 *Joseph*, b Jan. 5, 1720 ; 5 *Benjamin*, b March 10, 1723 ; 6 *Susannah*, b June 17, 1725 ; 7 *John*, b Jan. 23, 1730 ; 8 *Sarah*, b Dec. 6, 1735 ; 9 *Charles*, b 1736, d Sept. 19, 1829, æ. 93 yrs. ; 10 *Elizabeth*, b July 25, 1737 ; 11 *Eunice*, b April 5, 1739 ; 12 *Daniel*, b Nov. 30, 1740.

### 2. DAVID.

DAVID DUTTON married Lydia, daughter of Samuel and Hope Cook, Sept. 14, 1722. She died Oct. 12, 1735, ae. 40. He married Sarah Doolittle, Feb. 21, 1739.

Children by 1st marriage: 13 *Mary*, b July 16, 1723, m Gideon Royce, Oct. 4, 1743 ; 14 *Charles*, b Oct. 30, 1727, m Eunice Jones, 1761, he d Oct. 9, 1789 ; 15 *Jesse*, b Dec. 24, 1729, d Feb. 4, 1745, at Cape Breton, in the old French war ; 16 *Ambrose*, b March 30, 1732 ; 17 *Joel*, b March 20, 1734 ; 18 *Lydia*, b Oct. 27, 1738, d Sept. 27, 1739. By 2d marriage : 19 *David*, b June 23, 1741 ; 20 *Amos*, b Oct. 13, 1745, d Oct. 3, 1788, æ. 61 : 21 *Jonathan*, b Jan. 25, 1743-4.

### 3. THOMAS.

THOMAS DUTTON married Abigail Merriman, May 6, 1729. Children: 22 *John*, b Feb., 1730 ; 23 *Abigail*, b Jan. 8, 1732 ; 24 *Thomas*, b Jan. 31,. 1735 ; 25 *Samuel*, b Jan. 24, 1737 ; 26 *Lois*, b Aug. 8, 1738 ; 27 *Matthew*, b Nov. 11, 1740 ; 28 *John*, b April 3, 1743 ; 29, 30 *Amasa*, and *Asahel*, b July 30, 1745 ; 31 *Nathaniel*, b June 18, 1747 ; 32 *Phebe*, b Oct. 11, 1749 ; 33 *Asahel*, b Feb. 2, 1753.

### 4. JOSEPH.

JOSEPH DUTTON, son of Benjamin and Mary, of Wallingford, married Elizabeth ——. She died Jan. 25, 1700, æ. 72. He died in Southington, Ct., Oct. 26, 1788, æ. 68 years, and was buried at Plantsville, Southington, by the side of his wife.

Child : 34 *Mindwell*, b May 18, 1746, m in Wallingford.

##### 5. BENJAMIN.

BENJAMIN DUTTON, son of Benjamin and Mary, m Abigail Jones, March 16, 1747.

Children: 35 *Eunice*, b April 5, 1749 : 36 *Abigail*, b Nov. 21, 1750

##### 14. CHARLES.

CHARLES DUTTON, son of Daniel and Lydia Dutton, married Eunice Jones, 1761. He died Oct. 9, 1781.

Children : 37 *Jesse*, settled in the State of Maine ; 38 *Amos*, b June 3, 1767, d March 21, 1845. a. 73 years ; 39 *Charles*, d in Ohio where he resided.

## FENN.[1]

##### EDWARD.

EDWARD FENN married Mary Thorp, Nov. 15, 1688. He died Feb. 2, 1728, ae. 84 yrs. She died July 24, 1725, and he married Abigail Williams, Jan. 26, 1726. He belonged in Wallingford.

Children : 1 *Mary*, b Sept. 27, 1689 ; 2 *Hannah*, b Feb. 4, 1698, d Feb. 14, 1698 ; 3 *Theophilus*, b Jan. 31, 1689 ; 4 *Elizabeth*, b April 29, 1692 ; 5 *Sarah*, b Nov. 24, 1694 : 6 *Theophilus*, b Jan. 28, 1698, m Martha —— ; 7 *John*, b March 23, 1702, m Sarah —— ; 8 *Hannah*, b Dec. 13, 1704 ; 9 *Thomas*, b Sept. 13, 1707, m Lydia —— ; 10 *Naomi*, b May 10, 1712, m Samuel Frost, March 21, 1723.

##### 6. THEOPHILUS.

THEOPHILUS FENN, m Martha Doolittle, May 24, 1722.

Children : 10 *Elizabeth*, b Oct. 25, 1723 ; 11 *Edward*, b Sept. 2, 1732 ; 12 *Martha*, b Sept. 23, 1725 ; 13 *Bethiah*, b Feb. 18, 1728 ; 14 *Benjamin*, b Aug. 3, 1730 ; 15 *Phebe*, b Feb. 12, 1735 ; 16 *Theophilus*, b Feb. 20, 1737, d Nov. 8, 1737 ; 17 *Eunice*, b March 16, 1741 ; 18 *Susannah*, b Sept. 28, 1746.

[1] For collateral branches, see Savage's Gen. Dict., II. 151, 152.

## 7. JOHN.

JOHN FENN married Sarah ———.
Children: 20 *Mary*, b Dec. 4, 1730; 21 *John*, b July 15, 1732: 22 *Lois*, b Aug. 2, 1735 ; 23 *Samuel*, b Sept. 10, 1739 ; 24 *Amos*, b May 30, 1745.

## 9. THOMAS.

THOMAS FENN, married Lydia Ackley, March 22, 1731. She died Dec. 4, 1741. He married, 2d, Christina ———. Children by 1st marriage: 25 *Lydia*, b July 11, 1733 ; 26 *Thomas*, b Dec. 1, 1735 ; 27 *Samuel*, b Dec. 27, 1737 ; 28 *Hannah*, b March 24, 1740. By 2d marriage : 29 *Esther*, b Oct. 20, 1743 ; 30 *Theophilus*, b June 29, 1744.

## FOOT.[1]

### ROBERT.

ROBERT FOOT was first of Wethersfield, afterwards of that part of New Haven now known as Wallingford, and in 1678 and thereafter, until his death at Branford, was married to Sarah *Foot*, 1659. After his decease. his widow married Aaron Blatchley of Branford, in 1686. Mr. Foot was a son of Nathaniel Foot, the settler. He died suddenly in 1681, æ. 52. John Foot, the sixth child of Robert and Sarah, was born at Branford, July 24, 1670. He married Mary ———, and had seven children. He died in 1713, ae. 43.

### JOHN.

JOHN FOOT, fourth child of John and Mary Foot, was born in 1700, and settled in North Branford. He married 1st, Elizabeth Frisbee, Dec. 25, 1733 ; she died Feb. 3, 1737, æ. 22. He married 2d, Abigail Frisbee, Aug. 16, 1738. He died Jan. 26, 1777, æ. 77. His widow Abigail died May, 1779, æ. 67.

---

[1] For collateral branches, see Brown's Gen. W. Simsbury, Conn., 53-56 ; Caulkins' Hist. New London, Conn., 308; Goodwin's Foote Family Gen. ; Judd and Boltwood's Hist. and Gen. of Hadley, Mass., 494 ; Matthews' Hist. Cornwall, Vt., 285 ; Nash's Gen. of Nash Family, 42 ; N. E. Hist. and Gen. Reg., IX. 272 ; Savage's Gen. Dict., II. 179-82.

Children by 1st marriage: 1 *Jonathan*, b Jan. 23, 1737, d
in North Branford, 1801. By 2d marriage: 2 *John*, b April 5,
1742, in North Branford, m Abigail, dau. of Rev. Samuel
Hall, of (Cheshire) Wallingford, granddaughter of Gov.
Jonathan Law, who d Nov. 19, 1788, ae. 39, m Eunice, dau. of
John Hall, Esq., Apr. 28, 1761, was grad. at Yale
College in 1765, studied Divinity, and succeeded Rev. Mr.
Hall as pastor of the Congregational Church in Cheshire, d
Aug. 31, 1813, ae. 71, his wife Eunice d Jan. 31, 1817 : 3
*Abigail Sarah Hall*, b Jan. 2, 1769, d Jan. 20, 1775 ; 4 *Mary
Ann*, b Sept. 21, 1770, d Sept. 25, 1775 ; 5 *Lucinda*, b May
19, 1772, m Dr. Thomas T. Cornwall, and was mother to
Hon. Edward A. Cornwall, of Cheshire ; 6 *John Alfred*, b
Jan. 2, 1774, d Aug. 25, 1794, ae. 20 ; 7 *Abigail M. A.*, b
Sept. 16, 1776, d Aug. 9. 1778, ae. 22 ; 8 *Wm. Lambert*, b
Oct. 10, 1778, was a physician in Cheshire ; 9 *Samuel Augus-
tus*, b Nov. 8, 1780, mem of Congress, Senator in Congress,
and Gov. of Conn. ; 10 *Roderick*, b Dec. 15, 1782, d May 16,
1791, ae. 8 ; 11 *Matilda*, b May 6, 1785, d Oct. 9, 1787.

## 8. WILLIAM.

DR. WM. LAMBERT FOOT, son of Rev. John, was a prominent man in his native town, was town clerk and judge of the
Probate court, and practiced his profession, until a short
time before his death. He married Mary, dau. of Capt. Dan
Scoville of Saybrook, March, 1801. Both died in Cheshire.

Children : 12 *William L.*, M. D., b Nov. 21, 1802, m Mary
Butler of Branford in 1827 ; 13 *Mary A.*, b May 23, 1806 ;
14 *Abigail H.*, b April 28, 1808, m Edward Doolittle, he died
March 4, 1837, ae. 29 ; 15 *Scoville D.*, b April 10, 1810, m
Martha Whiting, of Milford, Conn., June, 1836, she was born
1807 ; 16 *Eliza S.*, b June 29, 1812 , 17 *John L.*, b Sept. 14,
1817, merchant in Cheshire.

## 9. SAMUEL.

His Excellency SAMUEL A. FOOT, son of Rev. John and
Abigail, married Eudocia Hull, daughter of General Andrew
and Elizabeth Mary Ann Hull, of Cheshire. He died Sept

16, 1846, in his 66th year. She died at the residence of her
son John A. Foot Esq., Cleveland, Ohio, Jan. 12, 1849, ae. 66
years. Her remains were brought to Cheshire for interment.

Children: 18 *John Alfred*, b Nov. 22, 1803, attorney at
Cleveland, Ohio; 19 *Andrew Hull*, b Sept. 12, 1806, Rear
Admiral U. S. N., now deceased; 20 *Roderick A.*, b Oct. 1,
1808, d Feb. 24, 1810; 21 *Augustus Edwin*, b Dec. 31, 1810,
cashier at Cleveland, Ohio; 22 *Wm. Henry*, b Feb. 1, 1817,
d March 6, 1827; 23 *Edward Dorr*, b Feb. 3, 1820, d Feb.
9, 1831.

### BENJAMIN.

BENJAMIN FOOT, of Wallingford, son of Daniel and Mary
Foot, of Branford, who was the son of Daniel and Sarah Foot,
of Northford, who was the son of Joseph and Abigail Foot,
of Northford, who was the son of Robert and Sarah Foot, of
New Haven, Wallingford and Branford, who was the son of
Nathaniel the settler, was born at Northford, Conn., Aug. 1,
1778, and was the youngest but one of thirteen children. He
married, 1st, Sally P., daughter of Joel Hall, April 24, 1803;
she died, July 24, 1804, æ. 25 years; 2d, Betsey, daughter
of Andrew Hall, June 2, 1805, she died Sept. 20, 1831, æ.
44 years; 3d, Mrs. Harriet, widow of Willis Humaston, and
daughter of Newbury Button, of North Haven, May 3, 1832.
He died in Wallingford, Nov., 1869, æ. 91 years.

Children by 1st marriage: 24 *Sally H.*, b Feb., 1804, d
May 13, 1804. Children by 2d marriage: 25 *Andrew H.*, b
Nov. 15, 1806, m Frances, dau. of Simon Hoadley of New
Haven: 26 *Henry A.*, b July 14, 1809, d Oct. 2, 1818; 27
*James*, b Aug. 15, 1811, m Emeline Slead of Wallingford,
Oct. 8, 1834; 28 *Sally H.*, b Jan. 16, 1815, m Charles B. Hall
of Wallingford, Oct. 1, 1835; 29 *Benjamin*, b Oct. 18, 1817, m
Sarah, dau. of Hiel Hall of Wallingford, Nov. 19, 1840; 30
*Henry Clay*, b June 19, 1820, m Catherine W., dau. of Hiel
Hall, Aug. 17, 1842, she resided in Philadelphia, d in 1868.

# GAYLORD.[1]

## WILLIAM.

DEA. WILLIAM GAYLORD, a leading man of Windsor, Conn., was the father of Walter Gaylord, whose son Joseph was born May 13, 1649, and married July 14, 1670, Sarah, daughter of John Stanley of Farmington. Conn. It is not exactly clear as to whether he went from Windsor to Farmington, or Waterbury first ; but it is certain that he was at Mattatuck (Waterbury), in the spring of 1678, having been previously accepted as an inhabitant, Jan. 17, 1677. He had a three acre lot on the corner of East and North Main sts., which then bounded north on John Stanley. He sold his house and lot Feb. 2, 1703, reserving a quarter of an acre on which his son Joseph had built a house, after which he resided at a place called Breakneck, built a house there, and had twenty acres of land which he sold Feb. 26, 1705 or 1706. As no traces of him are found in Waterbury after this date, it is quite probable that he went to Durham in 1706, where several of his family had previously gone, and we find him there in the early part of 1706. He died in Durham previous to 1713 His children were,

1 *Sarah*, b July 11, 1671, m Thomas Judd. Jr. ; 2 *Joseph*, b April 22, 1673 or 1674, m Feb. 28, 1699, to Mary, dau. of Joseph Hickox, deceased, of Woodbury, she was born May 25, 1678.

## 2. JOSEPH.

JOSEPH GAYLORD went to Durham about the year 1705 or 1706. He built a house at Buckshill in 1703 r 1704, which he sold to Richard Welton.

Children: 3 *Elizabeth* ; 4 *Joseph*, d in infancy ; 5 *Thankful*, all b in Waterbury.

---

1 For collateral branches, see Judd and Boltwood's Hist of Hadley, Mass., 497, 498 ; Savage's Gen. Dict., II. 238, 239, Stiles' Hist. Windsor, Conn., 623-7.

## JOHN.

JOHN GAYLORD, born April 12, 1677, resided at Buckshill, adjoining his brother Joseph, on a place he bought of John Warner. He went to Durham, and subsequently to Wallingford, where he died in 1753, in what is now Cheshire. Mrs. Elizabeth Gaylord his wife, died in Cheshire, Dec. 19, 1751, æ. 73 yrs. He left an estate of £1995 in Wallingford, and of £560 in Farmington, Conn.

Children : 6 *Samuel;* 7 *Edward;* 8 *Timothy;* 9 *Nathan;* 10 *Joseph ;* 11 *John*, m Thankful ———— ; and five daughters, one of whom, 12 *Sarah*, d April 14, 1735.

## WILLIAM.

WILLIAM GAYLORD had a £40 propriety set out to him in Waterbury, in 1701, which he forfeited, and removed to Woodbury, where he joined the church, Jan. 13, 1706. Subsequently he went to New Milford, where he died about 1753. His will was proved Nov. 23, 1753, in which his wife Mercy and six children were named. Joanna, his first wife, joined the church in Woodbury, Dec. 7, 1712. His son Nathan, of New Milford, married Hannah, daughter of John Bronson, who was a son of Isaac Bronson.

Children : 13 *Benjamin*, resided in Durham and Wallingford, was in Wallingford in 1722 ; 14 *Elizabeth*, b Nov. 21, 1680, m Joseph Hickox, son of Samuel ; 15 *Mary*, m Stephen Welton, she d July 18, 1719 ; 16 *Joanna*, m Robert Royce of Wallingford, in 1716, or before ; 17 *Ruth*, m Stephen Hickox, and settled in Durham.

### 13. BENJAMIN.

BENJAMIN GAYLORD, m 1st, Jerusha Frisbie of Branford, Conn., Jan. 28, 1729. She died May 11, 1734. He married 2d, Mary Ashley, Feb. 14, 1738.

Children : 18 *Levi*, b Jan. 10, 1730 ; 19 *Jerusha*, b July 1, 1731 ; 20 *Enos*, b Jan. 27. 1733, d Jan., 1734.

### 6. SAMUEL.

SAMUEL GAYLORD, son of John and Elizabeth, married Thankful Munson, Aug. 19, 1729.

Children: 21 *Agnes*, b June 5, 1730; 22 *Justus*, b Mar. 12, 1732; 23 *Annie*, b April 24, 1734; 24 *Mamre*, b March 3, 1736.

### 7. EDWARD.

EDWARD GAYLORD, son of John and Elizabeth, m Mehitable Brooks, Aug. 16, 1733, at Cheshire, Conn.

Children: 55 *Jesse*, b Feb. 23, 1734, d; 26 *Jesse*, b Sept. 10, 1735.

### 8. TIMOTHY.

TIMOTHY GAYLORD, son of John and Elizabeth, m Prudence Royce, April 25, 1733.

Children: 27 *Prudence*, b Jan. 31, 1734; 28 *Timothy*, b May 3, 1735, d; 29 *Timothy*, b Aug. 1, 1736; 30 *Royce*, b July 17, 1737; 31 *Reuben*, b June 17, 1742.

### 9. NATHAN.

NATHAN GAYLORD, b 1724, d at Cheshire, Conn., July 2, 1802, ae. 78.

Children: 33 *John*, d in Wallingford; 34 *Nathan*, d in Cheshire; 35 *Elias*, d in Cheshire, m —— Hitchcock.

### 10. JOSEPH.

JOSEPH GAYLORD, son of John and Elizabeth, married Elizabeth Rich, Nov. 9, 1738.

Child: 32 *Charles*, b Sept 22, 1739, in Wallingford or Cheshire.

### 33. JOHN.

JOHN GAYLORD resided on Parker's farms in Wallingford, in the house now owned by Silas Y. Andrews.

Child: 36 *John*, m —— Tuttle, had a son David T. and a daughter.

### 34. NATHAN.

NATHAN died in Cheshire, and was the owner of the old mills in the south part of the town.

Children: 37 *Titus*, d in Cheshire; 38 *Hannah*, m Ebenezer Atwater; 39 *Jerusha*, m Rufus Plum; 40 *Nathan*, m ——

Bradley ; 41 *Eveline*, m Billious Brooks ; 42 *Enos*, is living-in Prospect, m Celia Moss.

### 35. ELIAS.

ELIAS GAYLORD, married 1st, —— Hitchcock. She died and he married 2d, a widow Thorp.

Children: 43 *Horace*, m —— Bradley ; 44 *Elias*, m Amanda Bristol ; 45 *Hannah*, m George Bristol.

——————

## HALL.[1]

### JOHN.

JOHN HALL senior, (the emigrant), appears first, at Boston, and afterwards at New Haven. He evidently was not an original settler at New Haven, as his name does not appear in any list which I have been able to discover until after 1650. From whence he came is uncertain. The name (Hall) is a difficult one to trace, on account of the great number of original settlers of that name, 28 having come to America previous to 1660, of whom seven bore the name of John.

That John Hall of Boston, New Haven and Wallingford

——————

1 For collateral branches, see Adams' Haven Genealogy, 2d part, 27, 28 ; Bouton's Hist. Concord, N. H., 707, 708 ; Brooke's Hist. Medford, Mass., 517-27; Clarke's Hist. Norton, Mass., 82, 83 ; Draper's Hist. Spencer, Mass., 211, 212; Eaton's Annals of Warren, Me., 396, 397 ; Eaton's Hist. Thomaston, Me., 247-50 ; Freeman's Hist. Cape Cod, Mass., II. 137, 202, 209, 214, 507, 589, 707-9, 717; Goodwin's Gen. of Foote family, 107, 108 ; Hill's Hist. Mason, N. H., 203 ; Hinman's Conn. Settlers, 1st ed., 170-8; Hudson's Hist. Lexington, Mass., 83 ; Jackson's Hist. Newton, Mass., 295-7 ; Kellogg's Memorials of Elder John White, 33 ; Kingman's Hist. North Bridgewater, Mass., 529, 530; Lewis and Newhall's Hist. Lynn, Mass., 120; Littell's Passaic Valley Gen., 160-4; Matthews' Hist. Cornwall, Vt., 286 ; Mitchell's Hist. Bridgewater, Mass., 169, 170 ; N. E. Hist. and Gen. Reg., VI. 259, 260; XIII. 15, 16 ; XV. 59, 381, 382 ; New Hampshire Hist. Soc. Coll., VII. 381, 382 ; Savage's Gen. Dict., II. 332-9; Sewell's Hist. Woburn, Mass., 616; Stiles' Hist. Windsor, Ct., 651 ; Thurston's Hist. Winthrop, Me., 186 ; Ward's Hist. Shrewsbury, Mass., 304, 305 ; Whitmore's Gen. of Hall family; Winsor's Hist. Duxbury, Mass., 263, 264.

was an emigrant, appears quite evident, from his having sons
old enough to be married in 1666. He moved to Wallingford
after the settlement had commenced, which accounts for the
non appearance of his name on the first Plantation covenant,
in 1669-70. His sons John, Thomas and Samuel, were signers to that instrument. His name appears on the covenant
of 1672, and it is quite certain that he had then been some
time in the place. In 1675, himself and his son John were
chosen selectmen of Wallingford.

John Hall senior, was freed from training in 1665, being
then in his 60th year, and was most certainly in New Haven
as early as 1639, and at Wallingford about the year 1670,
with the early settlers there. He died early in the year 1676,
ae. 71 years. The maiden name of his wife was Jane
Woolen.

Children: 1 *John*, baptized Aug. 9, 1646, d Sept. 2, 1721 ;
2 *Richard*, b July 11, 1645, m Hannah ———— ; 3 *Samuel*, b
May 21, 1646, d March 5, 1725 ; 4 *Sarah*, baptized Aug 9,
1646, at New Haven ; 5 *Thomas*, b March 25, 1649 ; 6 *Jona
than*, b April 5, 1651 ; 7 *David*, b March 18, 1652, d July 17,
1727, ae. 75 yrs.

## 1. RICHARD.

RICHARD HALL, son of John and Jane Hall, married
Hannah ————. He died in 1726, in New Haven.

Children : 8 *Samuel*, b Aug. 2, 1700, m Hannah Brown ;
9 *Hannah*, b Jan. 31, 1702 ; 10 *John*, b Jan. 17, 1714, m
Abiah Macomber ; 11 *Jonathan*, grad. at Yale in 1737 ; 12
*Mary*, b March 19, 1712, d young and before her father.

## 2. SAMUEL.

SAMUEL HALL, son of John and Jane Hall, went to Wall
ingford with the first planters in 1670. He married Hannah
Walker, May, 1668, and died March 5, 1725, ae. 77 years.
She died Dec. 20, 1728.

Children : 13 *John*, b Dec. 23, 1670, m Mary Lyman ; 14
*Hannah*, b March 11, 1673, m Ebenezer Doolittle ; 15 *Sarah*,
b June 20, 1677, d March 18, 1712 ; 16 *Samuel*, b Dec. 10,

1680, d June 15, 1770, ae. 90 yrs: 17 *Theophilus*, b Feb. 5,
1686 ; 18 *Elizabeth*, b March 6, 1690, m John Moss. ____

### 4. THOMAS.

THOMAS HALL, son of John and Jane Hall, married Grace
——, June 5, 1673, she died May 1, 1731 ; he died Sept. 17,
1731, æ. 62 years, 5 mos. and 17 days.

Children : 19 *Abigail*, b Jan. 7, 1674, m John Tyler ; 20
*Thomas*, b July 17, 1676, m Abigail, dau. of John Atwater ;
21 *Mary*, b Nov. 22, 1677 ; 22 *Jonathan*, b July 25, 1679, m
Dinah Andrews, May 12, 1703 ; 23 *Joseph*, b July 8, 1681, m
Bertha Terrel, Nov. 13, 1706 ; 24 *Esther*, b Feb. 23, 1682, m
Benoni Atkins ; 25 *Benjamin*, b April 19. 1684, m Mary Ives ;
26 *Peter*, b Dec. 28, 1686, m Rebecca Bartholomew ; 27 *Daniel*, b Jan. 27, 1689 ; 28 *Rebecca*, b Jan. 6, 1691, m Daniel
Holt, who was b Oct. 6, 1689 ; 29 *Israel*, b Oct. 8, 1696, m
Abigail Palmer.

### 5. JOHN.

JOHN HALL, son of John and Jane Hall, married Mary,
daughter of Edward Parker, at New Haven, Dec. 6, 1666.
They settled in Wallingford with the first planters, in 1670.
He died Sept. 2, 1721, æ. 86 yrs.  She died Sept. 22, 1725.

Children : 30 *Elizabeth*, b Aug. 11, 1670, in New Haven ;
31 *Daniel*, b July 26, 1672, m Thankful Lyman, March 15,
1693 ; 32 *Mary*, b June 23, 1675 ; 33 *Nathaniel*, b Feb. 8, 1677,
m Elizabeth Curtis ; 34 *John*, b March 14, 1681. m Elizabeth
Royce ; 35 *Lydia*, b Jan. 21, 1683 ; 36 *Samuel*, b Dec. 24,
1686, d Nov. 1, 1689 ; 37 *Esther*, b Aug. 30, 1693 ; 38 *Caleb*,
b Sept. 14, 1697.

### 7. DAVID.

DAVID HALL, son of John and Jane Hall, married Mary
Rutherford, of New Haven, Nov. 11, 1670 ; 2d, Sarah Rockwell, Dec. 24, 1676.  She died Nov. 3, 1732 ; he died July 7,
1727, ae. 76 yrs.

Children : 39 *Daniel*, b Aug. 9, 1672, d Jan. 13, 1673 ; 40
*Rutherford*, b April 20, 1675.  By 2d marriage : 41 *John*, b
May 9, 1678, m Thankful Doolittle ; 42 *Thankful*, b Dec. 29,

1679; 43 *Sarah*, b Dec. 28, 1681, m Nathaniel Curtis ; 44
*Ruth*, b Nov. 10, 1685 ; 45 *Jerusha*, b Oct. 28, 1687, m John
Mattoon, Oct. 20, 1706 ; 46 *Mabel*, b Aug. 15, 1691 ; 47
*David*, b Dec. 1, 1693, m Martha Doolittle, April 20, 1721.

### 13. JOHN.

JOHN HALL, son of Samuel and Hannah, married Mary
Lyman ; she died Oct. 16, 1740 ; he died April 29 1730, ae.
60 yrs.    Rev. Mr. Whittelsey preached his funeral sermon.

Children : 48 *John*, b Sept. 13, 1679 ; 49 *Esther*, b Aug.
30, 1694 ; 50 *Samuel*, b Oct. 4, 1695 ; 51 *Caleb*, b Sept. 14,
1697, graduated at Yale ; 52 *Eunice*, b March 7, 1700 ; 53
*Benjamin*, b Aug. 28, 1702 ; 54 *Benjamin*, b Dec. 17, 1704 ;
55 *Sarah*, b April 15, 1706 ; 56 *Eliakim*, b Aug. 9, 1711 ; 56
*Elihu*, b Feb. 17, 1714, graduated at Yale, was King's Attor
ney in 1770, d in London ; 58 *Nancy*.

### 16. SAMUEL.

SAMUEL HALL, son of Samuel and Hannah Hall, married
Sue, daughter of Nathaniel and Esther Royce ; 2d, Bridget
——— ; he died June 15, 1770, ae. 90 yrs.

Children : 59 *Theophilus*, b April 1, 1707 ; 60 *Samuel*, b
June 8, 1709 ; 61 *Hannah*, b July 15, 1711 ; 62 *Sarah*, b Dec.
6, 1713 ; 63 *Mehitable*, b April 1710 ; 64 *Esther*, b Nov.
7, 1719.

### 20. THOMAS.

THOMAS HALL, son of Thomas and Grace Hall, married
Abigail Atwater, April 26, 1710 ; he died Aug. 27, 1741.

Children : 65 *Thomas*, b March 10, 1712, m Lydia Curtis,
April 24, 1734 ; 66 *Phineas*, b April 12, 1715 ; 67 *Elijah*, b
April 12, 1719, d Jan. 12, 1737 ; 68 *Joshua*, b May 23, 1722.

### 22. JONATHAN.

JONATHAN HALL, son of Thomas and Grace Hall, married
Dinah Andrews, May 12, 1703 ; he was born July 25, 1679,
d Jan. 15, 1760, ae. 80 years and 17 days ; she was born
1684, and died at the age of 79 yrs., 2 mos. and 29 days.

Children: 69 *David*, b Oct. 16, 1705, m Sept. 23, 1731, to Alice ——; 70 *Jonathan*, b Jan. 13, 1708, m Dec. 15, 1739, to Sarah, dau. of John Cook; 71 *Joseph*, b May 31, 1710, m April 19, 1736, to Hannah Scoville; 72 *Anna*, b Jan. 18, 1713; 73 *Isaac*, b July 11, 1714, m Nov. 5, 1739, d March 7, 1781, m Mary Moss; 74 *Phebe*, b Feb. 12, 1717, d May 14, 1735; 75 *Ezekiel*, b May 13, 1719, m Anna Andrews, Oct. 29. 1763; 76 *Thankful*, b Sept. 20, 1722; 77 *Benjamin*, b Oct. 20, 1725; 78 *Temperance*, b April 16, 1727.

### 23. JOSEPH.

JOSEPH HALL, son of Thomas and Grace Hall, married Bertha Terrel, Nov. 13, 1706; she died Dec. 28, 1753; he died Nov. 3, 1748.

Children: 79 *Temperance*, b July 15, 1714, d Dec. 7, 1716; 80 *Joseph*, b Sept. 23, 1718, d Sept. 6, 1737; 81 *Ephraim*, b April 25, 1723, m 1st, Eunice ——, she d May 9, 1763, he m 2d, Chloe Moss, Oct. 13, 1763.

### 25. BENJAMIN.

BENJAMIN HALL, son of Thomas and Grace Hall, married Mary Ives, Dec. 27, 1752.

Children: 82 *Benjamin*, b Sept. 25, 1753, d Oct. 8, 1755; 83 *Eliab*, b Feb. 17, 1755, d in camp during the Revolution, at N. Y.; 84 *Benjamin*, b Nov. 3, 1756.

### 26. PETER.

PETER HALL, son of Thomas and Grace Hall, married Rebecca Bartholomew, Oct. 19, 1732; he died Sept. 25, 1798, æ. 90 yrs. She died Oct. 31, 1798, æ. 87 yrs.

Children: 85 *Susannah*, b Feb. 26, 1733; 86 *Hiel*, b May 6, 1735; 87 *Abigail*, b May 15, 1737: 88 *Rebecca*, b July 3, 1740; 89 *Eunice*, b Nov. 8, 1742; 90 *Josiah*, b July 3, 1743; 91 *Peter*, b June 7, 1748, d as shown by date on stone, —; 92 *Andrew*, b Sept. 16, 1750, d Oct. 14, 1776; 93 *Anna*, b March 30, 1753: 94 *Keziah*, b June 16, 1755; 95 *Lois*, b Sept. 25, 1757.

## 27. DANIEL.

DANIEL HALL, son of Thomas and Grace Hall, married Martha Doolittle, April 20, 1721.

Children: 96 *Abraham*, b Jan. 27, 1722, m Sarah Doolittle ; 97 *John*, b Jan. 29, 1724, d in Meriden, May 13, 1795, æ 72 ; 98 *Hannah*, b Sept. 11, 1725, m Benjamin Tyler, of Branford ; 99 *Daniel*, b June 1, 1727 ; 100 *Martha*, b June 14, 1729 ; 101 *Samuel*, b May 5, 1731 ; 102 *Mary*, b Sept. 7, 1733 ; 103 *Abigail*, b April 27, 1739.

## 29. ISRAEL.

ISRAEL HALL, son of Thomas and Grace Hall, m Abigail Powell, April 11, 1721.

Children: 104, 105 *Sarah*, and *Israel*, b March 14, 1722 ; 106 *Enos*, b March 30, 1726 ; 107 *Israel*, b Oct. 22, 1728 ; 108 *Abigail*, b Mar. 22, 1731, d Aug. 5, 1743 ; 109 *Jotham*, b Feb. 6, 1737 ; 110 *Abigail*, b July 5, 1744 ; 111 *Mary*, b June 23, 1749 ; 112 *Eunice*, b Feb. 6, 1751.

## 31. DANIEL.

DANIEL HALL, son of John and Mary Hall, married Thankful Lyman, March 15, 1693.

Children : 113 *Daniel*, b Jan. 4, 1693, d ; 114 *Daniel*, b Feb. 19, 1695, d 1727 ; 115 *Samuel*, b Nov. 5, 1697 ; 116 *Silence*, b Oct. 6, 1699 ; 117 *Preserved*, b Jan. 15, 1700, was an imbecile, his brother Abraham had the care of him : 118 *Sarah*, b June 21, 1703 ; 119 *Benjamin*, b Dec. 17, 1704 ; 150 *Jacob*, b 1705 ; 121 *David*, b Oct. 16, 1706 ; 122 *Abraham*, b Feb. 5, 1709, d Sept. 16, 1761, æ. 53.

## 33. NATHANIEL.

NATHANIEL HALL, son of John and Mary Hall, married Elizabeth Curtis, May, 1699 ; he died Aug. 16, 1757. She died Sept. 30, 1735, and he married Lydia Johnson, Sept 15, 1736.

Children : 123 *Amos*, b Jan. 24, 1700, m Ruth Royce ; 124 *Margaretta*, b Dec. 21, 1701, d Oct. 30, 1707 ; 125 *Caleb*, b Jan. 3, 1703, d May 11, 1766, ac. 62 yrs. ; 126 *Moses*, b June

6, 1706, d Feb. 15, 1765, ae. 59 yrs. ; 127 *Mary*, b Oct. 30, 1707 ; 128 *Nathaniel*, b April 17, 1711, d Dec. 18, 1727 ; 129 *James*, b April 23, 1713 ; 130 *Elizabeth*, b Sept. 22, 1715 ; 131 *Desire*, b June 19, 1719, 132 *Harmon*, b Oct. 17, 1720.

## 34. JOHN.

DEA. JOHN HALL, son of John and Mary Hall, married Elizabeth Rice, June 28, 1707.    He died April 27, 1766, ae. 86.    She died Sept. 2, 1755, æ. 66 years.

Children : 133, 134 *Isaac* and *Peter*, b July 22, 1709, the latter m Rebecca ———, he d Sept. 25. 1798 ; 135 *John*, b Dec. 28, 1712 ; 136 *Abel;* 137 *Asahel*, b Jan. 19, 1717 ; 138 *Royce*, b Dec. 26, 1718, grad. at Yale, 1737, d May 29, 1752 ; 139 *Abigail*, b March 7, 1723 ; 140 *Elizabeth*, b July 9, 1725 ; 141 *Benjamin*, b April 4, 1728, m Phebe Hall, d Dec. 11, 1806 ; 142 *Elisha*, b Sept. 15, 1730 ; 143 *Sarah*, b Aug. 25, 1732.

## 47. DANIEL.

DANIEL HALL, son of Daniel and Sarah Hall, was born Dec. 1, 1693, married Martha Doolittle, April 20, 1721.

Children : 144 *Abraham*, b Jan. 27, 1722, m Sarah Doolittle ; 145 *John*, b Jan. 29, 1724, settled in Meriden ; 146 *Hannah*, b Sept. 11, 1725, m Benajah Tyler ; 147 *Daniel*, b June 1, 1727, settled in Meriden ; 148 *Martha*, b June 14, 1729 ; 149 *Samuel*, b May 5, 1731 ; 150 *Mary*, b Sept. 7, 1733 ; 151 *Abigail*, b April 27, 1739.

## 48. JOHN.

JOHN HALL, son of John and Mary Lyman Hall, married Mary Street, March 5, 1716.    She died Oct. 12, 1778, aged 81 years.    He died June 18, 1773, ae. 80 years.

Children : 152 *Hannah*, b Jan. 29, 1717 ; 153 *John*, d April 25, 1737 ; 154 *Eunice*, m Dr. Dickinson of Middletown, Conn. ; 155 *Lyman*, Gov., b April 12, 1724, signed the Declaration of Independence ; 156 *Street*, b Nov. 12, 1721, d in Wallingford ; 157 *Susannah*, b April 9, 1726, m —— Whittelsey ; 158 *Giles*, b Feb. 18, 1733, d March 11, 1789, ae. 56 ; 159 *Rhoda*, b April 14, 1734, d Aug. 23, 1751, ae. 17 ; 160 *Mary*, m —— Foote.

### 50. SAMUEL.

Rev. Samuel Hall, son of John and Mary Lyman Hall, grad. at Yale in 1716, married Anna Law, Jan. 25, 1727, and was settled as a minister over the Congregational church at Cheshire in 1724. He died Feb. 26, 1776. She was born in Milford, Aug. 1, 1702, died Aug. 23, 1775.

Children: 161 *Samuel*, b July 23, 1727, d Aug. 23, 1727 ; 162 *Jonathan*, b July 11, 1728, d July 12, 1728 ; 163 *Benoni*, b Nov. 4, 1729, d Nov. 19, 1729 ; 164 *Lucy*, b Sept. 11, 1730, m Chas. Whittelsey, 165 *Samuel*, b Jan. 11, 1732, d May 10, 1732 ; 166 *Ann*, b May 10, 1733 ; 167 *Samuel*, b May 31, 1735, grad. at Yale ; 168 *Mary*, b Nov. 5, 1736 ; 169 *Brenton*, b April 2, 1738, d Nov. 25, 1820, ae. 82 ; 170 *Elisha*, b March 10, 1740, grad. at Yale in 1764 ; 171 *Sarah*, b Aug. 8, 1742 ; 172 *Jonathan*, b July 19, 1745, settled in Cheshire, kept a tavern ; 173 *Abigail*, b Dec. 7, 1748, m Rev. John Foote of Cheshire.

### 51. CALEB.

Caleb Hall, son of John and Mary Lyman Hall, married Damaris Atwater, May 15, 1721 ; he died July 27, 1749 ; she died July 29, 1762, æ. 64 years.

Children: 174 *Damaris*, b Nov. 25, 1722, d Feb. 22, 1740 ; 175 *Stephen*, b Nov. 7, 1724, m Ruth Miles in 1762, d July 27, 1749 ; 176 *Ruth*, b April 26, 1729 ; 177 *Caleb*, b Aug. 29, 1731, grad. at Yale in 1752 ; 178 *Jeremiah*, b Sept. 1, 1733, d Sept. 4, 1740 ; 179 *Lydia*, b Aug. 26, 1730 ; 180 *Timothy*, m Abigail Miles.

### 54. BENJAMIN.

Benjamin Hall, son of John and Mary Lyman Hall, married Abigail, daughter of Rev. Nathaniel Chauncey, of Durham, Feb. 20, 1727, and settled in Cheshire on the place now known as the Law farm.

Children: 181 *Benjamin*, b Nov. 22, 1727, d Dec. 3, 1727 ; 182 *Charles Chauncey*, b Dec. 12, 1728, d Dec. 20, 1776, æ. 48 ; 183 *Sarah*, b July 20, 1730, m Thaddeus Cook ; 184 *Dorothy*, b Feb. 29, 1732, d May 13, 1737 ; 185 *Dorothy*, m

Z z

Charles, son of John Peck; 186 *Abigail*, b Oct. 11, 1733, d
April 15, 1737; 187 *Benjamin*, b Sept. 27, 1736, grad. at Yale
in 1754, d 1786, æ. 50; 188 *Abigail*, b May 1, 1737, m Moses
Moss; 189 *Eunice*, b March 4, 1742, m Rev. Mr. Waterman.

### 56. ELIAKIM.

ELIAKIM HALL, son of John and Mary Lyman Hall, married Ruth Dickerman Oct. 17, 1734; she died Dec. 18, 1752,
and he married Elizabeth ———— : she died Aug. 9, 1803;
he died April 19, 1794, æ. 80 years.

Children : 190 *Isaac*, b Nov. 4, 1735; 191 *Mary*, b Nov.
6, 1737; 192 *Eliakim*, b Feb. 13, 1740; 193 *Hezekiah*, b
July 13, 1743; 194 *Ruth*, b May 1, 1750.

### 57. ELIHU.

COL. ELIHU HALL, son of John and Mary Lyman Hall,
married Lois Whittelsey, Jan. 2, 1734, was King's Attorney
in 1750; went to England and died in London in 1784, æ.
70; his widow died Sept. 29, 1780, ae. 66 yrs; he was a
grad. of Yale College.

Children: 195 *Lois*, b May 11, 1735; 196 *Hezekiah*, b
May 4. 1737 ; 197 *Sarah*, b July 24, 1729 ; 198 *John*, b Jan.
18, 1739, m Mary Jones ; 199 *Damaris*, b Oct. 6, 1741 ; 200
*Elihu*, b Aug. 13, 1744 ; 201 *Elihu*, b March 15, 1745, m
Sarah ———— ; 202 *Eunice*, b March 2, 1749; 203 *Lucy*, b Nov.
14, 1781 ; 204 *Eunice*, b Aug. 11, 1754.

### 59. THEOPHILUS.

REV. THEOPHILUS HALL, son of Samuel and Love Hall,
married Hannah Avery, May 21, 1734, graduated at Yale in
1727, was ordained Oct. 29, 1729, and was the first settled
minister of the Congregational church in Meriden ; he died
March 25, 1769, ae. 60 yrs., in the thirty-eighth year of his
ministry.

Children: 205 *Hannah*, b March 11. 1735 ; 206 *Theophilus*,
b Aug. 5, 1736, d May 9, 1739 ; 207 *Avery*, b Dec. 2, 1737,
he was a clergyman ; 208 *Samuel*, b July 16, 1739 ; 209,
210 *Theophilus* and *Lucy*, b Aug. 26, 1741, the former married

Elizabeth Couch, d May 17, 1804, ae. 63 yrs ; 211 *Elisha*, b 1742, d Jan. 2. 1757, ae. 9 yrs ; 212 *Mary*, b June 24, 1743 : 213 *Elisha*, b March 3, 1745, m Ann Hopkins, Feb. 25, 1767 ; 214 *Mehitable*, b 1751, d Sept. 11, 1767.

## 60. SAMUEL.

SAMUEL HALL, son of Samuel and Love Hall, was born June 8, 1709. He married Sarah Hull, Dec. 7, 1732 ; he died Dec. 24, 1771.

Children : *Samuel*, b July 11, 1732, d in infancy : 215 *Hezekiah*, b Dec. 27, 1733 ; 216 *Louisa*, b June 30, 1736 ; 217 *Sarah*, b Dec. 5, 1737 ; 218 *Esther*, b Jan. 21, 1740 : 219 *Love*, b April 30, 1742 ; 220 *Elizabeth*, b Jan 23, 1745 ; 221 *Samuel*, b Feb. 28, 1750, d Feb. 27, 1821 ; 222 *Damaris*, b Jan. 23, 1754.

## 65. THOMAS.

THOMAS HALL, son of Thomas and Abigail Hall, married Lydia Curtis. She died Sept. 24, 1777. He was born March 12, 1712.

Children : 223 *Ambrose*, b Feb. 3, 1735 ; 224 *Titus*, b June 28, 1737, d May 1. 1773 : 225 *Abigail*, b Aug. 27, 1741 ; 226 *Thomas*, b Dec. 28, 1743 : 227 *Amasa*, b Feb. 9, 1746 ; 228 *Lydia*, b Sept. 6, 1749 : 229 *Rhoda*, b June 6, 1753.

## 66. PHINEAS.

PHINEAS HALL, son of Thomas and Abigail Hall, married Anna ———.

Children : 230 *Abigail;* 231 *Thankful:* 232 *Phineas:* 233 *Levi:* 234 *Eunice:* 235 *Barnabas;* 236 *Annis*.

## 68. JOSHUA.

JOSHUA HALL, son of Thomas and Abigail Hall, married Hannah ———.

Children : 237 *Susannah*, b Nov. 16, 1742 ; 238 *Medad*, b July 26, 1743 : 239 *Abigail*, b April 5, 1745 ; 240, 241 *Giles*, and *Abigail*, b Feb. 24, 1747 ; 242 *Samuel*, b Jan. 29, 1749 ; 243 *Joshua*, b Sept. 9, 1767.

## 69. DAVID.

DAVID HALL, son of Jonathan and Dinah Andrews Hall, married Alice Hale, Sept. 23, 1730 ; he died about 1755. Children: 244 *Alice*, b Sept. 8, 1731 ; 245 *David*, b Nov. 2, 1732, d March 21, 1795, æ. 63 ; 246 *Benijah*, b Feb. 12, 1734, left no family ; 247 *Asaph*, b June 11, 1735 ; 248 *Bates*, b Dec. 5, 1736 ; 249 *Phebe*, b June 24, 1739 ; 250 *Lois*, b Feb. 2, 1741, d Nov. 11, 1760; 251 *Elkanah*, b Oct. 20, 1742, d Nov. 30, 1763 ; 252 *Lucy*, b July 24, 1744. .

## 70. JONATHAN.

JONATHAN HALL, son of Jonathan and Dinah Hall, married Sarah Cook, Dec. 15, 1739; she died Aug. 12, 1740; he married 2d, Abigail ——, and she died Nov. 19, 1779; he married 3d, Jerusha Gaylord.

Child : 253 *Sarah*, b Aug. 12, 1740, d Aug. 13, 1740.

## 71. JOSEPH.

JOSEPH HALL, son of Jonathan and Dinah Hall, married 1st, Abigail Judd ; she died July 31, 1751, æ. 39 ; he married 2d, Rebecca Plum, Nov. 7, 1753 ; she died Feb. 24, 1769, æ. 47 yrs.

Children : 254 *Phebe*, b March 26. 1738 ; 255, *Phebe*, 256, *Abigail*, b March 30, 1740 ; 257 *Esther*, b July 21, 1742 ; 258 *Esther*, b March 19, 1743 ; 259 *Joseph*, b July 9, 1746 ; 260 *David*, b June 20, 1758 ; 261 *Phebe*, b Sept. 15, 1761.

## 73. ISAAC.

DR. ISAAC HALL, son of Jonathan and Dinah Hall, was the first physician of Meriden. He married Mary Morse, Nov. 5, 1739; died March 7, 1781, æ. 66 years. She died Oct. 9, 1791, æ. 74 years.

Children: 262 *Mary*, b Oct. 6. 1742. m John Ives, grandfather of Rev. Dr. Levi Silliman Ives ; 263 *Isaac*, b May 7, 1745. m Lois Buckley ; 264 *Joel*, b April 3, 1747, d Oct. 22, 1748 ; 265 *Esther*, b March 18, 1751 : 266 *Elizabeth*, b June 11, 1752 ; 267 *Jonathan*, b Dec 11, 1757. m Martha Collins, he died June 6, 1832.

## 75. EZEKIEL.

EZEKIEL HALL, son of Jonathan and Dinah Hall, married Annah Andrews, Oct. 20, 1743.

Children: 268 *Ezekiel*, b Oct. 24, 1744; 269 *Titus*, b Oct. 19, 1746, d Sept. 4, 1748; 270 *Eben*, b May 25, 1749; 271 *Benijah*, b 1762, m Ruth ———.

## 77. BENJAMIN.

BENJAMIN HALL, son of Jonathan and Dinah Hall, married Mary Ives, Dec. 27, 1752.

Children: 272 *Benjamin*, b Sept. 25, 1753; 273 *Eliab*, b Feb. 17, 1755; 274 *Benjamin*, b Nov. 3, 1756.

## 81. EPHRAIM.

EPHRAIM HALL, son of Joseph and Bertha Hall, married Eunice ———. She died May 9, 1763, and he married Chloe Moss, Oct. 13, 1763.

Children: 275 *Temperance*, b Aug. 10, 1764. By 2nd marriage: 276 *Joseph*, b March 17, 1776; 277 *Ephraim*, b Oct. 5, 1768; 278 *Chloe*, b Nov. 13, 1770; 279 *Comfort*, b Feb. 25, 1773, settled on a farm in Middletown, Westfield society, where he died; 280 *Reuben*, b 1775; 281 *David Moss*, b Oct. 24, 1777; 282 *Content*, b March 15, 1780; 283 *Bethiah*, b March 27, 1782.

## 86. HIEL.

HIEL HALL, son of Peter and Rebecca Hall, married Catharine ———; she died June 4, 1788, ae. 42 yrs; he died Sept. 7, 1707, ae. 73 yrs.

Children: 284 *Josiah*, b 1774, d Dec. 15, 1821, ae. 47; 285 *Catharine*, b Jan. 2, 1776; 286 *Andrew*, b 1777, d June 25, 1812, ae. 35; 287 *Chauncey*, b Sept. 8, 1778, m Marilla Hall; 288 *Peter*, b May 31, 1780, m Delight Kirtland; 289 *Hiel*, b Feb. 7, 1782, m Sarah Kirtland; 290 *Ria*, b May 2, 1784; 291 *Justus*, d Feb. 14, 1777.

## 91. PETER.

PETER HALL, son of Peter and Rebecca Hall, married

762     HISTORY OF WALLINGFORD.

Lydia Brown of Cheshire, March 17, 1774. She died May 2, 1805, æ. 52. He died Sept. 25, 1732, æ. 86 yrs.

Children: 292 *Jesse;* 293 *Wooster;* 294 *Roxy*, b 1779, d Sept. 26, 1756; 295 *Marcus;* 296 *Major Atwater*, b July 18, 1785, d March 28, 1848; 297 *Philo*, m Thankful Morse; 298 *Albert;* 299 *Peter Ufford*, d in Southington, in 1836; 300 *Sally;* 301 *Betsey.*

### 92. ANDREW.

ANDREW HALL, son of Peter and Rebecca Hall, married Sept. 16, 1750, Thankful ———. She died Oct. 14, 1776.

Children: 302 *John Todd;* 303 *Merritt;* 304 *Charry;* 305 *Anna*, b Feb. 3, 1773; 306 *Thankful*, b Aug. 4, 1776.

### 96. ABRAHAM.

ABRAHAM HALL, son of Daniel and Abigail Hall, married Sarah Doolittle, May 5, 1741; he died Sept. 16, 1761, æ. 53 yrs. She died March 14, 1781, æ. 77 yrs.

Children: 307 *Eldad*, b Feb. 4, 1742; 308 *Medad*, b July 26, 1745; 309 *Bildad*, b Sept. 3, 1747; 310 *Isaac*, b July 26, 1749; 311 *Isaac*, b Aug. 11, 1753.

### 107. ISRAEL.

ISRAEL HALL, son of Israel and Abigail Powell Hall, married Eunice Rice, Feb. 26, 1778.

Children: 312 *Elisha*, b Dec. 26, 1778; 313 *Eunice*, b Jan. 6, 1787.

### 109. JOTHAM.

JOTHAM HALL, son of Israel and Abigail Powell Hall, married Elizabeth ———.

Children: *Sarah*, b May 11, 1758; 314 *Jotham*, b March 1, 1761; 315 *Elizabeth*, b Aug. 27, 1763; 316 *George*, b April 27, 1768; 317 *Mary*, b Sept. 23, 1770; 318 *Joseph*, b July 23, 1773; 319 *Chloe*, b July 11. 1775.

### 120. JACOB.

JACOB HALL, son of Daniel and Thankful Hall, married Elizabeth Royce, Dec. 21, 1726.

Children: 320 *Phebe*, b Dec. 26, 1727; 321 *Mindwell*, b

May 21, 1730; 322 *Jacob*, b July 20, 1731; 323 *Giles*, b June 7. 1732; 324 *Lydia*, b April 20, 1736; 325 *Daniel*, b July 21, 1738; 326 *Daniel*, b Nov. 17, 1740, d Oct. 24, 1789; 327 *Thankful*, b July 29, 1744; 328 *Lois*, b Nov. 5. 1746.

### 121. DAVID.

DAVID HALL, son of Daniel and Thankful Hall, married Alice ——: he was born Feb. 19, 1695.

Children: 329 *David*, b Nov. 2, 1732, d March 2, 1795, a. 63, m Thankful ——: 330 *Benajah*, b Feb. 12, 1734; 331 *Asaph*, b June 15, 1735; 332 *Kate*, b Dec. 5, 1736; 333 *Phebe*, b June 24, 1737; 334 *Lucy*, b July 25, 1747, æ. 51.

### 123. AMOS.

AMOS HALL, son of Nathaniel and Elizabeth Hall, was born Jan. 24, 1700; he married Ruth Royce, June 8, 1720. She died Feb. 2, 1775, ae. 75. He died Nov. 30, 1752, ae. 52 years.

Children: 335 *Reuben*, b Dec. 20, 1721, m Mary ——; 336 *Amos*, b Sept. 9, 1722, d Dec. 24, 1782, ae. 31 yrs.; 337 *Eunice*, b Aug. 21, 1724, m Abner Avered; 338 *Lois*, b Oct. 26, 1727, m Caleb Culver; 339 *Moses*, b Aug. 25, 1735, m Elizabeth How, Dec. 21, 1726. she d and he m Elizabeth Johnson, March 20, 1754.

### 125. CALEB.

CALEB HALL, son of Nathaniel and Elizabeth Hall, was born Jan. 3, 1703, m Esther Umberfield, May 11, 1726; he died May 11, 1766, ae. 62 yrs.

Children: 340 *Margaret*, b March 28, 1727, d Nov. 14, 1749; 341 *Esther*, b April 24, 1729, m Ichabod Lewis; 342 *Nathaniel*, b April 8, 1732; 343 *Caleb*, b Sept. 12, 1734; 344 *Moses*, b May 13, 1736; 345 *Lydia*, b July 9, 1738; 346 *Desire*, b June 20, 1740, m Moses Holt; 347 *Sarah*, b April 10, 1742, m Noah Todd; 348 *Margaret*, b Aug. 31, 1744; 349 *Titus*, b Aug. 16, 1746; 350 *Rhoda*, b June 15, 1748, d Oct. 10, 17—; 351 *Jonah*, b Feb. 23, 1749-50; 352 *Rhoda*, b July 4, 1753; 353 *Lucretia*, b Feb. 16, 1757.

### 126. MOSES.

MOSES HALL, son of Nathaniel and Elizabeth Hall, was born June 6, 1706, married Elizabeth Howe, Dec. 21, 1726. He married 2d, Phebe ———. He died Feb. 15, 1765, ae. 59. His will gave his property to Caleb and Heman his brothers, and to Amos, Moses and Miles, his cousins. No children.

### 129. JAMES.

JAMES HALL, son of Nathaniel and Elizabeth Curtis Hall, was born Aug. 23, 1713, married Hannah Cook, Sept. 15, 1735. Children: 354 *Miles*, b Oct. 17, 1736; 355 *Bethia*, b April 13, 1740; 356 *Phebe*, b Nov. 16, 1741; 357 *James*, b July 22, 1743; 358 *Olive*, b May 20, 1745.

### 133. ISAAC.

ISAAC HALL, son of John and Elizabeth Hall, was born July 23, 1709, married Mary Moss Nov. 5, 1739. She died Oct. 9, 1721, ae. 75. He died March 7, 1781.
Children: 359 *Mary*, b Oct. 5, 1742; 360 *Isaac*, b March 7, 1745; 361 *Joel*, b April 3, 1747, d Oct. 22, 1748; 362 *Esther*, b March 18, 1751; 363 *Elizabeth*, b June 11, 1752; 364 *Jonathan*, b Nov. 8, 1755, d 1756, ae. ten mos.; 365 *Jonathan*, b Dec. 11, 1757.

### 135. JOHN.

JOHN HALL, son of John and Elizabeth Hall, born Dec. 28, 1712, married Abigail Russel; June 11, 1739, died May 13, 1795.
Children: 366 *Elias*, b March 10, 1740; 367 *Jared*, b July 19, 1741; 368 *Abigail*, b Oct. 16, 1743; 369 *John*, b Dec. 6, 1744; 370 *Elizabeth*, b Sept. 28, 1745; 371 *William*, b June 15, 1747; 372 *Mary*, b Jan. 23, 1749; 373 *Eunice*, b July 6, 1751; 374 *Anna C.*, b Aug. 15, 1755; 375 *Benjamin*, b July 2, 1757, m Lydia ———.

### 136. ABEL.

ABEL HALL, son of John and Elizabeth Hall, married Ruth Johnson, May 12, 1743.

Children : 376 *Elizabeth*, b Feb. 12, 1743-4 ; 377 *Abel*, b Oct. 12, 1745 ; 378 *Ruth*, b Oct. 19, 1748 ; 379 *Rica*, b May 28, 1750 ; 380 *John*, b Dec. 23, 1751, m Hannah Atwater ; 381 *Lucy*, b Oct. 3, 1753 ; 382 *Esther*, b July 10, 1754 ; 383 *Hezekiah*, b April 20, 1757, m Susannah —— ; 384 *Simon*, b Oct. 6, 1759 ; 385 *Daniel Johnson*, b July 4, 1761 ; 386 *Mary*, b July 17, 1764.

### 137. ASAHEL.

ASAHEL HALL, son of John and Elizabeth Hall, born June 10, 1717, m Sarah Goldsmith, July 29, 17—. She died Feb. 25, 1784. He died Nov. 11, 1795.

Children : 387 *Catharine*, b Aug. 6, 1739 ; 388 *Joel*, b May 21, 1741 ; 389 *Sarah*, b March 5, 1743 ; 390 *Asahel*, b March 15, 1745, d April 20, 1745 ; 391 *Jerusha*, b Aug. 31, 1746, d March 10, 1752 ; 392 *Sarah*, b June 9, 1748, d Dec. 25, 1747 ; 393 *Asahel*, b July 16, 1750, d March 4, 1752 ; 394 *Mehitable*, b March 13, 1753 ; 395 *Aaron*. b July 28, 1755, d Oct. 6, 1756 ; 396 *Charles*, b Nov. 12, 1757 ; 397 *Asahel*, b Jan. 14, 1759, m Ruth Johnson, Sept. 21, 1786 ; 398 *Aaron*, b Nov. 4, 1760 ; 399 *Sarah*, d Feb. 5, 1749.

### 141. BENJAMIN.

BENJAMIN HALL, son of John and Elizabeth Hall, born April 4, 1728. died Dec. 11, 1806, ae 79 ; he married Phebe Hall, she died Dec. 12, 1779.

Children : 400 *Susannah*, b Jan. 15, 1759 ; 401 *Bela*, b Sept. 16, 1764 ; 402 *Statira*, b March 20, 1766 ; 403 *Benjamin*, b June 30, 1767 ; 404 *Samuel*, b April 19, 1771.

### 142. ELISHA.

SERGT. ELISHA HALL, son of John and Elizabeth Royce Hall, born Sept 15, 1730, married Thankful Atwater, June 14, 1755. He died Jan. 19, 1800, ae. 70 yrs. She died Jan. 28, 1792, æ. 59 yrs.

Children : 405 *Phebe*, b Feb. 10, 1756, m —— Parmelee, of Durham ; 406 *Sarah*, b April 5, 1758, m John Fields, of Cheshire ; 407 *Joseph*, b July 25, 1759, m Mercy Cornwall,

May 31, 1799; 408 *Lydia*, b July 17, 1761, m ——— Curtis, and went to Durham ; 409 *Sally*, b Dec 8, 1763 ; 410 *Elizabeth*, b Oct. 3, 1765, m Benjamin Hall ; 411 *Hannah*, b Jan. 26, 1769 ; 412 *John*, b July 13, 1770, m Grace D. Hall ; 413 *Eunice*, b Aug. 1, 1772, m Miles, son of Nicholas Peck.

### 144. ABRAHAM.

ABRAHAM HALL, son of Daniel and Martha Hall, was born June 27, 1722, married Mary Prindle, June 23, 1746. She died May 12, 1747. For his second wife he married Hannah ———. He died 1757.

Children by 1st marriage : 414 *Mary*, b May 10, 1747. By 2d marriage : 415 *Rufus*, b July 25, 1751 ; 416 *Sarah ;* 417 *Josiah ;* 418 *Abraham.*

### 145. JOHN.

JOHN HALL, son of Daniel and Martha Hall, born Jan. 29, 1724, settled in Meriden, married Elizabeth Prindle, May 4, 1749 ; he died May 13, 1795, ae. 72 yrs. She died Oct 21, 1802, ae. 71 yrs.

Children : 419 *Prindle*, b June 30, 1750, d Dec. 6, 1821 ; 420 *John*, b May 8, 1752, d 1764 ; 421 *Mary*, b Sept. 10, 1754, d March 1, 1825 : 422 *Elizabeth*, b April 20, 1757, died March 30, 1847 ; 423 *Sarah*, b May 11, 1759, d 1760; 424 *David*, b Sept. 16, 1761, d Aug. 3, 1843 ; 425 *Sarah*, b Feb. 13. 1764, d 1777 ; 426 *Abigail*, b Feb. 24, 1766, d Oct. 28, 1828 ; 427 *John*, b Jan. 9, 1768, d April 21, 1851 : 428 *Joseph*, b Oct. 28, 1770, d March 13, 1831, m Hannah —— ; 429 *Jedutham*, April 25, 1773, d July 9, 1851 ; 430 *Isaac*, b May 28, 1776, d Jan. 1, 1838.

### 149. SAMUEL.

SAMUEL HALL, son of Daniel and Martha Hall, was born May 5. 1731, married Mamre Ives, Aug. 28, 1755.

Children : 431 *Jesse*, b Jan. 24, 1757 ; 432 *Sarah*, b Jan. 24, 1758 ; 433 *Samuel*, b July 4, 1760.

### 155. LYMAN.

LYMAN HALL, son of John and Mary Street Hall, was

graduated at Yale college in 1747, Representative in Congress from the state of Georgia, signer of the Declaration of Independence in 1776. He died in 1791, he left no children, was Governor of the state of Georgia in 1790.

### 156. STREET.

Col. STREET HALL, son of John and Mary Street Hall, was born Nov. 12, 1721. He died 1809 ; he married Hannah Fowler, June 30, 1748.

Children · 434 *Hannah*, b July 3, 1751 ;. 435 *Anna*, b Feb. 28, 1753, d Dec. 24, 1755 ; 436 *Thaddeus*, b Feb. 28, 1757 ; 437 *Rebeca*, b Feb. 15, 1758 ; 438 *Street T.*, b Feb. 26, 1762 ; 439 *Mary A.*, b June 9, 1764 : 440 ———.

### 158. GILES.

GILES HALL, son of John and Mary Street Hall, was born Feb. 18, 1733, married 1st, Martha Robinson, Nov., 1759, m 2d, Thankful Merriman, of Wallingford. He died March 17, 1789, æ. 41 yrs. Mrs. Thankful died July 14, 1796, æ. 47 years.

Children: 441 *Lucy*, b April 11, 1771 ; 442 *David M.*, b 1773, d April 21, 1792 ; 443 *Martha R.*, b Aug. 22, 1777 ; 444 *Mary Street*, b March 17, 1780 ; 445 *John*, b July 27, 1782 ; 446 *Hannah*, b 1783 : 447 *Elizabeth*, b May 2, 1785 ; 447 *Giles*, b June 7, 1788 ; 449 *Lois*, b Feb. 82, 1789 ; 450 *John*, b April 20, 1793, d Feb. 26, 1835, ae. 53 yrs.

### 169. BRENTON.

BRENTON HALL, son of Rev. Samuel and Ann Hall, was born April 2, 1738, married Lament Collins, Feb. 18, 1762, and settled in the eastern part of Meriden, where he died Nov. 25, 1820, ae. 82 yrs. His 2d wife Abigail ———, died May 5, 1837, ae. 88 yrs.

Children: 451 *Wm Brenton*, b May 31, 1764 ; 452 *Collins*, b Jan. 8, 1766 ; 453 *Samuel*, b June 10, 1768 ; 454 *Lamert*, b July 14, 1776 ; 455 *Joab*.

### 170. ELISHA.

ELISHA HALL, son of Rev. Samuel and Ann Hall of

Cheshire, Conn., graduated at Yale College in 1774. He married for his 2d wife, Oct. 22, 1795, Lois, widow of Jesse Street, and daughter of Col. Thaddeus Cook. She was mother of Col. Thaddeus Street, late of Cheshire.

### 172. JONATHAN.

JONATHAN HALL, son of Rev. Samuel and Ann Hall, married Mary ———. He was a farmer and inn-keeper in Cheshire, for many years.

Children: 456 *Millicent;* 457 *Lucy;* 458 *George;* 459 *Salmon;* 460 *Leverett;* 461 *Sylvester.*

### 177. CALEB.

CALEB HALL, son of Caleb and Damaris Hall. He graduated at Yale College in 1752, studied medicine and became a physician. He married Prudence Holt. She died Nov. 30, 1807, æ. 67 yrs. He died Sept. 21, 1783, æ. 67 yrs.

Children: 462 *Caleb Johnson,* b Sept. 22, 1763; 463 *Augustus,* b Aug. 16, 1765; 464 *Abigail,* b Jan. 29, 1767, m 1st, Lemuel Carrington, 2d, Nehemiah Rice; 465 *Eunice,* b Aug. 24, 1770; 466 *Benjamin,* b July 26, 1772; 467 *Horatio Gates,* b Jan. 17, 1778, d at Wallingford; 468, 469 *George* and *Damaris,* b Feb. 10, 1782.

### 180. TIMOTHY.

TIMOTHY HALL, son of Caleb and Damaris Hall, married Abigail Miles, and settled on Cheshire street; he was a farmer. She died Nov. 22, 1748. He married Athildred Parker, June 10, 1748-9.

Children: 470 *Jeremiah,* b April 20, 1750; 471 *Aaron,* b June 27, 1751; 472 *Timothy,* b Oct. 13, 1752; 473 *Amasa,* b Dec. 7, 1754; 473 1-2 *Abigail,* b Dec. 5, 1756; 474 *Archibald,* b May 23, 1758; 475 *Zenas,* b June 8, d Nov. 6, 1759; 476 *Zenas,* b Oct. 7, 1759; 477 *Josiah,* b Nov. 6, 1761; 478 *Aaron.*

### 182. CHARLES.

CHARLES CHAUNCEY HALL, son of Benjamin and Abigail Hall, married Lydia Holt, Dec. 5, 1751, and died at Cheshire.

Children: 479 *Abigail*, b July 8, 1753 ; 480 *Benjamin Holt*, b Oct. 6, 1754, died at Cheshire, a farmer ; 481 *Lydia*, b May 26, 1755 ; 482 *Charles C.*, b March 9, 1762, died at Cheshire, a farmer ; 483 *Rachel*, b July 4, 1764 ; 484 *Charlotte*, b Jun. 20, 1769 ; 485 *Lyman*, b Jan. 4, 1761, died at Cheshire, a farmer.

### 187. BENJAMIN.

BENJAMIN HALL, son of Benjamin and Abigail Hall, born at Cheshire, Sept. 27, 1736, grad. at Yale in 1754, married Mary Ives, Dec. 27, 1752. He built the house late the property of Wm. Law, Esq., and more recently of Sheldon Spencer, Esq.

Children. 486 *Eliab*, b Feb. 17, 1755 ; 487 *Benjamin*, d Oct. 8, 1755 ; 488 *Benjamin*, b Nov. 3, 1756.

### 190. ISAAC.

ISAAC HALL, son of Eliakim and Ruth Hall, was born Nov. 4, 1737, married Esther Mosely, Dec. 1, 1764, died Feb. 7, 1796 æ. 61. His widow Esther, died March 22, 1827, æ. 86 yrs.

Children : 489, 490 *Abner* and *Elizabeth*, b April 28, 1764, d in infancy ; 491 *Esther*, b Dec. 15, 1765 ; 492 *Mary*, b Nov. 24, 1767 ; 493, 494 *Elizabeth*, and *Eliakim*, b Jan. 21, 1770 ; 495 *Dickerman*, b 1774, d Sept. 18, 1838, æ. 64 yrs. ; 496 *Isaac*, b July 19, 1776, went to Wallingford, Vt. ; 497 *Abigail*, b Nov. 22, 1778 ; 498 *Day*, b Aug. 20, 1781 ; 499 *Lyman*, b March 31, 1784.

### 192. ELIAKIM.

ELIAKIM HALL, Esq., son of Eliakim and Ruth Hall, was born Feb. 13, 1740, married Eunice Morse, May 29, 1769. She died July 18, 1789 ; he married 2d, Sarah ——. she died Sept. 27, 1806, æ. 56 yrs. He died Sept. 6, 1806, æ. 67 yrs

Children : 500 *Eunice*, b Feb. 19, 1770 ; 501 *Pamelia* b Dec. 13, 1771 ; 502 *Sarah*, b June 19, 1773 ; 503 *John Morse*, b May 25, 1775, d Dec. 11, 1837, æ. 62 yrs. ; 504 *Phebe*, b Dec. 8, 1777 ; 505 *Sophia*, b Dec. 1, 1782 ; 506 *Eleta*, b Oct. 27, 1785 ; 507 *Elizabeth*, b Jan. 29, 1788.

### 193. HEZEKIAH.

HEZEKIAH HALL, son of Eliakim and Ruth Hall, was born July 13, 1743, married Elizabeth Merriman, Oct. 30, 1769 ; he died Sept. 7, 1815, ae. 73 yrs. She died Nov. 21, 1801, ae. 50 yrs.

Children : 508 *Ruth*, b Feb. 8, 1771, m Nehemiah Rice ; 509 *Elizabeth*, b March 14, 1772, m David M. Cook ; 510 *Thankful*, b May 25, 1775, m Chester Cook ; 511 *Hope*, b Sept. 26, 1780, m Samuel Francis ; 512 *Lucy*, b Oct. 9, 1782, m Jacob Francis ; 513 *Ophelia*, b March 1, 1785 ; 514 *Nathan*, b Nov. 6, 1788, d Aug. 18, 1741, ae. 53 yrs ; 515 *Laura*, b 1792.

### 198. JOHN.

JOHN HALL, son of Elihu and Lois Hall, married Mary Jones, Oct. 19, 1772.

Child : 516 *Nicholas Street*, b March 27, 1773.

### 201. ELIHU.

ELIHU HALL, son of Elihu and Lois Hall, was born Mar. 15, 1795, m Sarah ———. This person commenced life with a large fortune, his possessions being much larger than those of most young men. For many years he owned large tracts of land in Wallingford, and the whole township of Guild- hall, in the State of Vermont, besides slaves, horses, cattle, etc. His entire want of economy and tact in the management of his business cost him in a few years his whole estate, and he died a subject of the town's charge. His wife died some years before him.

Children : 517 *John*, b May 20, 1774, left Wallingford ; 518 *Frederick*, b Jan. 8, 1777 ; 519 *Lois*, b June 18, 1779 ; 520 *Louisa*, m a Mr. Armour, and died in New Haven, May 1, 1850.

### 207. AVERY.

AVERY HALL, son of Rev. Theophilus and Hannah Hall of Meriden, was b Dec. 2, 1737. He settled in the ministry at Rochester, New Hampshire.

## 208 SAMUEL.

SAMUEL HALL, son of Rev. Theophilus and Hannah Hall of Meriden, married Eunice Lee, Feb. 10, 1757.

Children: 521 *Samuel*, b May 27, 1759 ; 522 *Eunice*, b April 16, 1765 ; 523 *Caleb*, b Nov. 9, 1768 ; 524 *Eunice*, b June 22, 1770.

## 209 THEOPHILUS.

THEOPHILUS HALL, son of Rev. Theophilus and Hannah Hall, m Elizabeth Couch, March 10, 1768. He died May 17, 1804, æ. 63. She died March 11, 1824, æ. 74. in Meriden.

Children: 525 *Mehitable*, b March 23. 1769, died Sept. 30, 1776 ; 526 *Clarissa*, b April 3, 1771 ; 527 *Theophilus*, b April 20, 1773, d Sept. 26, 1815, æ. 62 yrs. ; 528 *Mehitable*, b Aug. 4, 1777 ; 529 *Avery*, b May 25, 1779 ; 530, 531 *Hannah* and *Elizabeth*, b Jan. 20, 1782.

## 213. ELISHA.

ELISHA HALL, son of Rev. Theophilus and Hannah Hall, married Ann Hopkins, June 25, 1767. He died March 13, 1759.

Children: 532 *Luther Elisha*, b Sept. 3, 1770 ; 533 *Ann Lane*, b Dec. 20, 1772 ; 534 *Sylvester*, b May 13, 1778.

## 221. SAMUEL.

DEA. SAMUEL HALL, son of Samuel and Sarah Hall, b Feb. 28, 1750, m Elizabeth Parsons, May 10, 1774. He died Feb 27, 1821, ae. 71. She died Sept. 27, 1823, ae. 71 yrs.

Children: 535 *Samuel*, b Dec. 2, 1776 ; 536 *Hezekiah*, b June 11, 1778 ; 537 *George*, b Aug. 13, 1780 ; 538 *Marilla*, b Dec. 28, 1782, married Chauncey Hall ; 539 *Richard*, b Jan. 26, 1785 ; 540 *Jared*, b Aug. 24, 1792, d April 24, 1861

## 224. TITUS.

TITUS HALL, son of Thomas and Lydia Hall, was one of the first separates in Wallingford ; he married Elizabeth Mack, Aug. 23, 1762, and died in 1773, æ. 36.

Children. 541 *Thomas ;* 542 *Elizabeth*, b Feb. 25, 1765 ; 543 *Titus*, b July 30, 1767 ; 544 *Elias*, b Aug. 24, 1769 ; 545 *Lydia*, b April 17, 1771.

### 227. AMASA.

AMASA HALL, son of Thomas and Lydia Hall, married Dinah Ives, Dec. 15, 1775.

Children : 546, 547 *Major* and *Phebe*, b Feb. 17, 1775 ; 548 *Hannah*, b Feb. 17, 1777.

### 232. PHINEAS.

PHINEAS HALL, son of Phineas and Annah Hall, born April 12, 1715, married Agnes Yale, Nov. 18, 1774, a widow. Children ; 549 *Mary*, b July 28, 1775 ; 550 *Abigail;* 551 *Thankful;* 552 *Phineas;* 553 *Levi;* 554 *Eunice;* 555 *Barnabas;* 556 *Annis.*

### 240. GILES.

GILES HALL, son of Joshua and Hannah Hall, was born Feb. 24, 1747, married Lois Ives.

Children : 557 *Abel,* b Dec. 10, 1778, d at Atwater, Ohio ; 558 *Sarah,* b Aug. 20, 1780 ; 559 *Giles,* d April 21, 1791 ; 560 *Joshua;* 561 *Lois,* m Andrew Andrews ; 562 *Lucy;* 563 *Hannah;* 564 *John.*

### 243. JOSHUA.

JOSHUA HALL, son of Joshua and Hannah Hall.

Children : 565 *Susannah,* b Nov. 16, 1742 ; 566 *Abigail,* b April 25, 1745 ; 567 *Giles,* b Feb. 24, 1747 ; 568 *Samuel,* b Jan. 29, 1749.

### 245. DAVID.

DAVID HALL, son of David and Alice Hall.  He died 1795, æ. 63 years.

Child : 569 *Elkanah,* b Nov. 30, 1767.

### 247. ASAPH.

ASAPH HALL, son of David and Alice Hall.

Children : 570 *Benajah,* b 1762 ; 571 *Asa;* 572 daughter, m —— Hopson.

### 267. JONATHAN.

DR. JONATHAN HALL, son of Isaac and Mary Hall, residence Meriden, Ct., married Martha Collins, May 14. 1777. He died June 6, 1832, ae. 54.  She died May, 1841, ae. 83, in the state of New York. He settled at New Hartford, N. Y., in 1787.

Children : 573 *Isaac*, b Feb. 22, 1778 ; 574 *Keturah*, b Nov. 17, 1780 ; 575 *Sylvia*, b Sept. 18, 1782 ; 576 *Jonathan*, b Aug. 14, 1784 ; 577 *Eli*, b May 14, 1786 ; 578 *Ira*, b July 10, 1788 ; 579 *Mary Moss*, b April 12, 1790 ; 580 *Agnes Collins*, b Aug. 6, 1793 ; 581 *Amos Hull*, b Feb. 13, 1796 ; 582 *Jede-dith Sanger*, b Nov. 2, 1797 ; 583 *Sarah T.*, b May 6, 1799.

### 269. TITUS.

TITUS HALL, son of Ezekiel and Anna Hall, was born Oct. 19, 1746, married Olive Barnes, Nov. 26, 1767.

Children : 584 *Abigail*, b Sept. 21, 1768 ; 585 *Caleb*, b Jan. 11, 1771 ; 586 *Lucy*, b Dec. 14, 1775 ; 587 *Caleb*, b Aug. 27, 1781 ; 588 *Ransley*, b Feb. 7, 1784.

### 271. BENAJAH.

BENAJAH HALL, son of Ezekiel and Annah Hall, was born 1762, married Ruth Francis, Aug. 19, 1784.

Children : 589 *Orrin*, b June 5, 1785 ; 590 *Esther*, b June 13, 1787 ; 591 *Ruth*, b Aug. 25, 1789 ; 592 *Nancy*, b Nov. 9, 1792 ; 593 *Martha*, b July 13, 1795 ; 594 *Philo*, b May 13, 1798 ; 595 *Jacob*, b April 5, 1801 ; 596 *Joseph*, b Oct. 17, 1803 ; 597 *Joel*, b Nov. 3 1806 ; 598 *Lovineas*, b July 21, 1810.

### 274. BENJAMIN.

BENJAMIN HALL, son of Benjamin and Mary Hall, married Phebe ———, April 28, 1757, settled at Plymouth.

Children : 599 *Benjamin* ; 600 *Mary*, b Jan. 29, 1758 , 601 *Andreas*, b Aug. 15, 1759 ; 602 *Mary*, b Aug. 6, 1761 ; 603 *Phebe*, b Aug. 20, 1763, m ——— Hart ; 604 *Linus*, b Sept. 25, 1765 ; 605, 606 *David*, *Jonathon*, b Nov. 17, 1761 ; 607 *Erastus*, b Feb. 12, 1770 ; 608 *Admah*, b May 8, 1772 ; 609 *Salmon*, b 1774 ; 610 *Elijah*, b Dec. 11, 1776, settled in North Killingworth ; 611 *Grace Denison*, b May 5, 1776 ; 612 *Asaph*, b Oct. 1, 1781.

### 280. REUBEN.

REUBEN HALL, son of Ephraim and Chloe Hall, b Feb., 1735, m Sally Miller, May 25, 1797.

A A A

Children: 613 *Alma*, b March 23, 1798; 614 *Horace*, b April 17, 1800; 615 *Milla*, b Jan. 8, 1802 ; 616 *Eli*, M. D., b Nov. 5, 1803 ; 617 *William*, b Feb. 21, 1806 ; 618 *Reighly*, b April 1, 1808.

### 281. DAVID.

DAVID MOSS HALL, son of Ephraim and Chloe Hall, married Mindwell ———. He left Wallingford.

Child: 619 *Orrilla*, b Nov. 5, 1800.

### 284. JOSIAH.

DEA. JOSIAH HALL, son of Hiel and Catherine Hall, married Martha Hall, daughter of Giles Hall, April 2, 1793.

Children: 620 *Thankful*, b May 23, 1796, m Thaddeus Cook; 621 *Catherine*, b May 18, 1798 ; 622 *Eliza*, b May 15, 1800, died; 623 *Eliza*, b July 25, 1801 ; 624 *Edward* L., b May 13, 1804, m Mary K. Cook, dau. of Billious Cook; 625 *George Chauncey*, b April 19, 1706 ; 626 *Martha R.*, b Oct. 19, 1808, m Thaddeus Cook ; 627 *Josiah*, b June 15, 1812 ; 628 *Ogden*, b Sept. 13, 1815 ; 629 *David M.*, b May 27, 1818, m Catherine Cook ; 630 *James*, b April 11, 1821.

### 286. ANDREW.

DR. ANDREW HALL, son of Hiel and Catherine Hall, married Lydia, daughter of Ambrose Cook, Sept. 11, 1803.

Children: 631 *Alexander W.*, b May 28, 1805; 632 *Sarah R.*, b Oct. 14, 1806, m Medad W. Munson, Esq. ; 633 *Andrew C.*, b June 7, 1810, d in Phila., interred in Wall. ; 635 *Franklin D.*, b Sept. 20, 1811.

### 287. CHAUNCEY.

CHAUNCEY HALL, son of Hiel and Catherine Hall, married Marilla, daughter of Samuel and Catherine Hall, Feb. 6, 1803.

Children: 635 *Henry C.*, b Jan. 19, 1804 ; 636 *Samuel R.*, b Nov. 11, 1805; 637 *Elihu*, b June 2, 1807, m Martha, dau. of Samuel Cook; 638 *Lucretia*, b Dec. 1, 1809 ; 639 *Louisa*, b Jan, 29, 1812 ; 640 *Lucy A.*, b April 18, 1814, m Ira Yale, Jr.; 641 *Sidney*, b July 12, 1816; 642 *Elizabeth;* 643 *Marietta;* 644 *Celia*.

### 288. PETER.

PETER HALL, son of Hiel and Catherine Hall, married Delight Kirtland, Sept. 8, 1808.

Child : 645 *Charles*, m Miss Foote.

### 290 RICE.

DR. RICE HALL, son of Hiel and Catherine Hall, married Esther Hall, Nov. 19, 1806.

Children: 646 *Hiel Beverly*, b Feb. 18, 1811 ; 647 *John M.*; 648 *Marilla*, b May 25, 1813 ; 649 *Ophelia*, b June 2, 1818 , 650 *Henrietta E.*, b Aug. 8, 1815 ; 651 *Elizur Rice*, b June 25, 1821 ; 652 *Philander*.

### 293. WOOSTER.

WOOSTER HALL, son of Peter and Lydia Hall, married Chloe Cooley, July 27, 1806.

Children : 653 *Samuel B.*, b Sept. 20, 1808 ; 654 *Lydia*, b Nov. 16, 1810 ; 655 *Lydia*: 656 *Asahel*, b May 3, 1812 ; 657 *Dinah*, b Oct. 7, 1814 ; 658 *Lois*, b Feb. 14, 1817.

### 326. DANIEL.

DANIEL HALL, son of Jacob and Elizabeth Hall, married Sarah Atwater, Oct. 7, 1761.

Children : 659 *Mary*, b June 24, 1762 ; 660 *Elizabeth*, b June 21, 1764 ; 661 *Lemuel*, b March 20, 1766 ; 662 *Aaron*, b May 2, 1768 ; 663, 664 *Ira*, and *Asa*, b Aug. 18, 1770 ; 665 *Joshua*, b Aug 5, 1772 ; 666 *Abigail*, b Dec. 16. 1776 ; 667 *Lemuel*, b May 2, 1779, d in New Haven. Conn. ; 668 *Sally*, b June 8, 1781 ; 669 *Patty*, b Sept. 3, 1783 ; 670 *Alma*, b Nov. 15, 1785 ; 671 *Phebe*, b Aug. 21, 1787.

### 329 DAVID.

DAVID HALL, son of David and Thankful (Morse) Hall, was born Nov. 2, 1732, died March 25, 1825. She died Sept. 24, 1826, ae. 61.

Children : 672 *Abner*, b Sept. 10, 1793, d in Wallingford ; 673 *Alethea*, b Oct. 11, 1795, m Wooster Martin ; 674 *Charlotte*, b July 24. 1791. m ——— Lindley ; 675 *Stephen*, went west, supposed to Ohio.

### 335. REUBEN.

REUBEN HALL, son of Amos and Ruth Hall, married Mary ———. He was born Dec. 20, 1721.

Children: 676 *Mary*, b Oct. 17, 1742; 677 *Elizabeth*, b Feb. 12, 1743; 678 *Abel*, b Oct. 12, 1745.

### AMOS.

AMOS HALL,·SON of Asaph and Ruth Hall, died Dec. 24, 1782, ae. 31 years.

Children: 679 *Reuben;* 680 *Moses;* 681 *Eunice;* 682 *Louis.*

### 336. MOSES.

MOSES HALL, son of Amos and Ruth Hall.

Children: 683 *Moses*, b Dec. 26, 1754; 684 *Enos*, b March 8, 1756.

### 342. NATHANIEL.

NATHANIEL HALL, son of Caleb and Esther Hall, born April 8, 1732, married Lydia ———. She died Jan. 15. 1760. Child : 685 *Lurena*, b Feb. 21, 1759.

### 343. CALEB.

CALEB HALL, son of Caleb and Esther Hall, b Sept. 12, 1734. Child : 686 *Susannah*, b Feb. 8, 1759.

### 349. TITUS.

TITUS HALL, son of Caleb and Esther Hall, was born Aug. 16, 1746, married Olive Barnes, Nov. 26, 1767.

Children: 687 *Abigail*, b Sept. 21. 1768; 688 *Caleb*, b Jan. 21, 1771, d Nov. 12, 1824; 689 *Lucy*, b Dec. 14, 1775 ; 690 *Caleb*, b Aug. 29, 1781 ; 691 *Ransley*, b Feb. 7, 1784.

### 354. MILES.

MILES HALL, son of James and Hannah C. Hall, born Oct. 17, 1736, married Abigail Tyler, Sept. 30, 1764.

Children: 692 *Abigail*, b Dec. 3, 1767 ; 693 *James*, b Oct. 14, 1769 ; 694 *William Tyler*, b Jan. 15, 1772.

### 357. JAMES.

JAMES HALL, son of James and Hannah C. Hall, born July 22. 1743.

Child: 695 *Phebe*, b Nov. 16, 1741.

### 360. ISAAC.

ISAAC HALL, son of Isaac and Mary Moss Hall, was born March 7, 1745, married Phebe Ives, Sept. 6, 1764.

Children: 696 *Mary*, b July 21, 1766; 697 *John*, b July 3, 1768; 698 *Phebe*, b Jan. 31, 1770; 699 *Elizabeth*, b Sept. 23, 1771; 700 *Isaac*, b May 19, 1775: 701 *Jonathan*, b Sept. 15, 1776; 702 *Clarissa*, b Aug. 12, 1779; 703 *Abijah*, b 1781; 704 *Sally*, b 1784.

### 365. JONATHAN.

JONATHAN HALL, son of Isaac and Mary Hall, was born Dec. 11, 1757, married Martha Collins, May 14, 1777.

Children: 705 *Isaac*, b Feb. 22, 1778 706 *Katurah*, b Nov. 17, 1780.

### 366. ELIAS.

ELIAS HALL, son of John and Abigail Hall, was born Mar. 10, 1740, married 1st, Mary Humiston, Dec 15, 1763. She died Aug. 14, 1774, and he married 2d, Rubama ——.

Children by 1st marriage: 707 *Martha*, b Sept. 26, 1764; 708 *Mary*, b May 26, 1766; 709 *Ruth*, b Feb. 28, 1768; 710 *Eliakim*, b May 31, 1778; 711 *Benjamin*, b Feb. 20, 1770. By 2d marriage: 712 *Rubama*, b Jan. 16, 1776.

### 367. JARED.

JARED HALL, son of John and Abigail Hall, born July 19, 1741, married Lucy Hall, July 5, 1770.

Children: 713 *Lemuel*, b Aug. 16, 1771; 714 *Amos*, b May 21, 1773: 715 *Rufus*, b Jan. 9, 1775

### 369. JOHN.

JOHN HALL, son of John and Abigail Hall, born Dec. 6, 1743, married Lucy ——.

Child: 716 *Millicent*, b Sept. 3, 1768.

### 371. WILLIAM.

WILLIAM HALL, son of John and Abigail Hall, married Rebecca ——. He was born June 15, 1747.

Children: 717 *Benj. Russel*, b Aug. 1, 1775; 718 *Abigail*, b Sept. 20, 1777; 719 *Ambrose*, b Dec. 7, 1779.

### 375. BENJAMIN.

BENJAMIN HALL, son of John and Abigail Hall, married Lydia ———— ; he was born July 2, 1757, died March 12, 1770. Children : 721 *Lyman*, b March 20, 1798 ; 722 *Mary*, b June 12, 1799 ; 723 *Emeline*, b April 14, 1800 ; 724 *Orrin*, b March 22, 1803.

### 377. ABEL.

ABEL HALL, son of Abel and Ruth Hall, born Oct. 12, 1745, married Ruth Morse, Jan. 3, 1771. Child : 725 *Esther*.

### 383. HEZEKIAH.

HEZEKIAH HALL, son of Abel and Ruth Hall, born April 20, 1757, married Susannah ————. Children : 726 *Charity*, b Oct. 3, 1784 ; 727 *Isaac*, b Aug. 21, 1786.

### 388. JOEL.

JOEL HALL, son of Asahel and Sarah Goldsmith Hall, born May 21, 1741 ; he was a large and thrifty farmer, married Hannah Parmalee, Oct. 30, 1765. Children : 728 *Andrew*, b March 4, 1767, m Diana Cook, Jan. 11, 1778, he d 1796 ; 729 *Augustus*, b May 3, 1769, m Pamelia Hall, April 12, 1786 ; 730 *Joel*, b July 26, 1771 ; 731 *Luther*, b Aug. 16, 1776, m Sarah ————, 2d, wid. Bassett ; 732 *Sarah P.*, b June 3, 1779 ; 733 *Asahel W.*, b May 12, 1781 ; 734 *James*, b Oct. 12, 1783.

### 396. CHARLES.

CHARLES HALL, son of Asahel and Sarah Goldsmith Hall, b Nov. 12, 1757, married Sarah ————. Children : 735 *Jerusha*, b Oct. 23, 1772 ; 736 *Daniel Root*, b Aug. 30, 1779 ; 737 *Rice*, b Jan. 26, 1782 ; 738 *Sylvester*, b Aug. 29, 1784 ; 739 *Thomas G.*, b Aug. 17, 1787 ; 740 *Sarah*, b Nov. 25, 1789 ; 741 *Susan*, b Dec. 2, 1791 ; 742 *Charles ;* 743 *Sarah.*

### 397. ASAHEL

ASAHEL HALL, son of Asahel and Sarah Goldsmith Hall,

born Jan. 14, 1750, married Ruth Johnson, Sept. 21, 1786.

Children: 744 *Catherine*, b April 17, 1787 ; 745 *Asahel*, b April 8, 1789 ; 746 *John D.*, b June 22, 1790 ; 747 *Sarah*, b April 5, 1792.

## 398. AARON.

AARON HALL, son of Asahel and Sarah Hall, was born Nov. 4, 1760, married Elizabeth Cook, May 24, 1781 ; she died and he married 2d, Sarah, widow of Charles Hall, Dec. 11, 1820 ; 3d, Anna Brooks, June 18, 1827. He died Sept. 30, 1839, ae. 79 yrs.

Children: 748 *Benjamin Atwater*, b April 6, 1782 ; 749 *Elizabeth*, b Oct. 23, 1783 ; 750 *Electa*, b Sept. 9, 1785 ; 751 *Aaron C.*, b Nov. 11, 1787, went to Catskill, N. Y. ; 752 *Mary*, b Jan. 20, 1790 ; 753 *Asahel*, b April 6, 1792 ; 754 *Salmon*, b Aug. 12, 1793 ; 755 *Anna*, b Jan. 6, 1796 ; 756 *Caroline*, b Dec. 21, 1798 ; 757 *B Kirtland*, b July 4, 1805.

## 407. JOSEPH.

JOSEPH HALL, son of Elisha and Thankful Hall, married Mercy Cornwall, May 31, 1790.

Child : 758 *Sarah G.*, m Israel Harrison, Oct. 21, 1841.

## 412. JOHN.

JOHN HALL, 3d son of Elisha and Thankful Hall, married Grace Denison Hall, April 3, 1800 She died Jan. 21, 1840, ae. 69.

Children : 759 *Jeremiah Atwater*, b 1806 ; 760 *John*, b Oct. 8, 1808 ; 761 *Thankful A.*, b Sept. 6, 1801. m ———— Hopson : 762 *Lovely*, b April 21, 1804, m ———— Johnson ; 763 *Phebe*, b Dec 18, 1810 ; 764 *Denison D.*, b Dec. 9, 1815 ; 765 *Grace D.*, b July 18, 1813, m George Simpson ; 766 *Elisha*, b March 15, 1818 ; 767 *Jennett*, b May 31, 1820 ; 768 *Patty*.

## 415. RUFUS.

RUFUS HALL, son of Abraham and Hannah Hall, b July 25, 1751, married Experience Foster, Nov. 14, 1772.

Children: 769 *Hannah*, b Nov. 20, 1776 ; 770 *Abraham*, b May 5, 1778 ; 771 *Anne*, b Aug. 13, 1779.

#### 419. PRINDLE.

PRINDLE HALL, son of John and Elizabeth Prindle Hall, b June 19, 1750, married Anna Mix, Dec. 5, 1771.

Children : 772 *Ebenezer*, b March 26, 1773 ; 773 *Annah*. b March 9, 1774 ; 774 *Anna*, b Oct. 7, 1776 ; 775 *Lydia*, b Sept. 13, 1778 ; 776 *Sarah*, b April 25, 1780.

#### 438. STREET.

STREET T. HALL, son of Col. Street and Hannah Hall, born Feb. 26, 1762.

Children: 777 *Sherlock*, b Nov. 3, 1792 ; 778, 779 *Elisha* and *Rebecca Ann*, b Feb. 17, 1795 ; 780 *Alfred*, b July 17, 1797 ; 781 *Ransom*, b April 28, 1803 ; 782 *Carlos*, b July 4, 1806 ; 783 *Wm. Street*, b March 6, 1809 ; 784 *Mary Ann*, b July 8, 1841.

#### 448. GILES.

GILES HALL, son of Giles and Martha Hall, married Susan Hall, and occupies the old home of his father.

Children: 785 *Elizabeth*, b Oct. 21, 1815, m Elijah Rice.; 786 *Wm. Cook*, b April 12, 1818, m Julia A. Johnson, Sept. 12, 1843 ; 787 *Emily*, b Aug. 16, 1820 ; 788 *Henry Lyman*, b Nov. 25, 1824, a school teacher and farmer.

#### 450. JOHN.

JOHN HALL, son of Giles and Martha Hall, married 1st, Abigail ———. She died, and he married Dency Strong.

Children by 1st marriage : 789 *Stanley*, b March 20, 1805 ; 790 *Apollos*, b July 12, 1807 ; 791 *Henry Franklin*, b June 28, 1807. By second marriage : 792 *Dency;* 793 *Dwight*, b Aug. 19, 1814, hotel-keeper in the village ; 794 *Elizur*, b Jan. 25, 1817, d Sept. 26, 1857 ; 795 *Adeline*. b June 2, 1820, d Aug. 5, 1834 ; 796 *Wolcott*, b Oct. 30, 1824.

#### 452. COLLINS.

COLLINS HALL, son of Brenton and Lament Hall, was born Jan. 8, 1766, m Rebecca ———, March 17, 1795. She was born Jan. 10, 1764.

Children: 797 *Abigail*, b Nov. 25, 1796 : 798 *Alma*, b Oct 5, 1799 : 799 *Elisha*, b May 1, 1803 ; 800 *Erastus*, b Jan. 2, 1805 ; 801 *Augustus*, b Oct. 30, 1806.

### 467. HORATIO.

HORATIO G. HALL, son of Caleb and Prudence Hall, married Polly, daughter of Benjamin Byington. She was born Aug. 25, 1777.

Children: 802 *Augustus*, b July 14, 1799, m Rhoda Doolittle; 803 *Lyman*, b May 7, 1801, m ——— Button, d at Yalesville, Conn.; 804 *Horace*, b May 25, 1804, m 1st ———, 2d, ——— Bull ; 805 *Mary*, b March 16, 1807, m Leverett Allen ; 806 *Josiah H.*: 807 *Abigail*.

### 482. CHARLES.

CHARLES C. HALL, son of Charles Chauncey and Lydia H. Hall, was born March 9, 1762.

Children: 808 *Charles C.* ; 809 *Eliza*, m Jesse L. Nichols of Wolcott ; 810 *Lyman*, d in New Haven ; 811 *Augustus*, res. in Branford ; 812 *George*, res. in Cheshire ; 813 *James R.*, res. in Cheshire, m ——— Cook.

### 485. LYMAN.

LYMAN HALL, son of Charles C. and Lydia Hall, was born Jan. 4, 1761.

Children: 814 *William*, m Mary Horton ; 815 *Charles C.*

### 494. ELIAKIM.

COL. ELIAKIM HALL, married Clarissa Cook, March 13, 1794 ; he kept an inn in the Muddy River district.

Children : 816 *Sukey*, b Jan. 15, 1797 ; 817 *Ogden*, b 1802, d Feb. 23, 1803, æ. 6 mos. , 818 *Jane Ann*, b Aug. 5, 1806 ; 819 *Margaret*, b Jan. 5, 1810.

### 495. DICKERMAN.

DICKERMAN HALL, son of Isaac and Esther Mosely Hall, married 1st, Lucy Hough, March 13, 1796, and 2d, Miss ——— Bishop, in 1803. He died Sept. 18, 1838.

Children: 820 *Rebecca*, b Feb. 23, 1797 ; 821 *Hannah*, b

March 22, 1799, m 1st, John Hull, 2d, ——— Andrews ; 822
*Lucy*, b July 2, 1801 ; 823 *Henrietta*, b June 28, 1804 ; 824
*William Mosely*, b Feb. 11, 1806 ; 825 *Mary Ann*, b Oct. 31,
1807 ; 826 *Cornelia*, b Feb. 17, 1811 ; 827 *Frances A.*, b Oct.
9, 1813 ; 828 *Harriet*.

### 503. JOHN MORSE.

JOHN MORSE HALL, son of Eliakim and Eunice Morse
Hall, was born May 25, 1775, married Lizzie Meigs, April
14, 1800; he died Dec. 11, 1837, æ. 62 yrs.    His wife died
Dec. 13, 1843, æ. 63 yrs.

Children : 829 *Lizzie*, b Nov. 17, 1801 ; 830 *Mary*, b Dec.
6, 1802 ; 831 *John Meigs*, d July 3, 1851, in Wallingford, m
Miss ——— Gilbert, a sister of Rev. E. R. Gilbert,; 832 *Ellen
A.*; 833 a daughter ; 834 *Eliza M.;* 835 *Helen;* 836 *Mary*.

### 514. NATHAN.

NATHAN HALL, son of Hezekiah and Elizabeth Merriman
Hall, married Polly Andrews, daughter of Nathaniel ; he
died, æ. 53.

Children : 837 *Ruth*, b March 16, 1815, m Sherman Austin ; 838 *Hezekiah*, b June 4, 1817, m ——— Coe of Meriden ;
839 *Lucretia D.*, b March 18, 1821 ; 840 *Viney*, b Dec. 23,
1822.

### 529. AVERY.

AVERY HALL, son of Theophilus and Elizabeth Hall,
was born Nov. 9, 1768.

Children : 841 *Selden*, b Sept. 21, 1801 ; 842 *Alfred*, b
May 18, 1803.

### 537. GEORGE.

GEORGE HALL, son of Samuel and Elizabeth P. Hall, born
Aug. 13, 1780, married Lucinda ———.

Children : 843 *Mary A.*, b Nov. 11, 1843 ; 844 *Julia E. H.*,
b Sept. 14, 1815 ; 845 *George*, b July 28, 1818 ; 846 *Lament
P.*, b Oct. 7, 1820 ; 847 *Nancy*, b Oct. 3, 1822 ; 848 *Julia*, b
Dec. 23, 1834.

### 539. RICHARD.

RICHARD HALL, son of Samuel and Elizabeth P. Hall, b Jan. 26, 1785, married Nancy, daughter of Ambrose Cook.

Children. 849 *Philander*, b July 25, 1806; 850 *Susan*, b Sept. 16, 1808, m —— Phinney; 851 *Jerusha*, b Nov. 9, 1809, m Wm. Elton; 852 *Eliza*, m Wm. Lewis.

### 560. JOSHUA.

JOSHUA HALL, son of Giles and Lois Hall, married Sophronia Gates, March 21, 1804.

Children: 853 *Wm. Chauncey*, b May 5, 1805; 854 *Roderick*, b Dec. 21, 1806; 855 *James M.*, b March 3, 1809; 856 *Delight*, b Jan. 24, 1811; 857 *Delilah*, b March 29, 1813; 858 *Henrietta*, b June 24, 1815; 859 *Lois*, b Feb. 3, 1818; 860 *Jennette*, b Dec. 18, 1821; 861 *Alexander*, b Aug. 24, 1824, m —— Potter of Northford.

### 569. ELKANAH.

ELKANAH HALL, son of David and Alice Hall, was born in 1761, died March 23, 1738, æ. 71 years, married Sarah ——.

Children: 862 *Harry*, b July 28, 1797; 863 *Eliakim*, b Nov. 19, 1799; 864 *Isaac N.*, b Feb. 14, 1802; 865 *Alexander*, b Jan., 1805.

### 578. IRA.

IRA HALL, son of Dr. Jonathan and Martha Collins Hall, married 1st, Kate Rose and 2d, Marcia Rounds. He died Jan. 10, 1860, in New York, ae. 71 yrs., 5 mos.

Children: 866 *Nathan Kelsey*, b March 28, 1810; 867 *Ira F.*, b Aug. 3, 1811; 868 *Ira*, b Aug. 4, 1814; 869 *Catherine*, b Dec. 3, 1816; 870 *Mary*, b Sept. 17, 1819, 871 *Eli Q.*, b June 21, 1822; 872 *Sylvester R.*, b July 3, 1826; 873 *Sarah*, b March 1, 1829; 874 *Marie*, b Sept. 29, 1831; 875 *Jane*, b April 4, 1836.

### 594. PHILO.

PHILO HALL, son of Benajah and Ruth Hall, was born May 13, 1798, married Thankful Morse.

Children: 876 *Lavinia*, b March 13, 1823; 877 *Bennet*, b

May 10, 1824; 878 *Philo Fayette*, b Sept. 15, 1825 ; 879 *Emery Osgood*, b Sept. 1, 1827 ; 880 *Almira C.*, b Feb. 18, 1828 ; 881 *Truman Gerrard*, b Jan. 24, 1832 ; 882 *Harriet Newell*, b Feb. 18, 1833.

### 601. ANDREWS.

ANDREWS HALL, son of Benjamin and Phebe Hall, born Aug. 15, 1759, married Sylvia Blakeslee, Dec. 3, 1800.

Children: 883 *William A.*, b June 8, 1803 ; 884 *Sylvia*, b April 18, 1805 ; 885 *Abigail*, b June 14, 1807 ; 886 *Mary*, b April 24, 1810, m ——— McKenzie.

### 608. ADNAH.

ADNAH HALL, son of Benjamin and Phebe Hall, married Elizabeth ———, she died 1860; he died June 17, 1838, æ. 66 yrs.

Children : 887 *Valucia*, b March 29, 1811 ; 888 *Wilfred*, b July 25, 1815 ; 889 *Temperance*, b May 24, 1817 ; 890 *Harvey S.*, b April 9, 1819 ; 891 *Ezekiel*, b Jan. 23, 1822.

### 612. ASAPH.

ASAPH HALL, son of Benjamin and Phebe Hall, born Oct. 1, 1781, married Thankful ———; he died Feb. 12, 1839, æ. 58 years.

Children: 899 *Merab*, b June 24, 1812, m George Peck, of Cheshire, Conn.; 900 *Benjamin H.*, b Aug. 2, 1815 ; 901 *Asa*, b July 6, 1821.

### 663. IRA.

IRA HALL, son of Daniel and Sarah Hall, married Abigail ———.

Children: 902 *Elizur*, b June 28, 1798 ; 903 *Cornelia*, b Nov. 20, 1800 ; 904 *Edward*, b Sept. 30, 1802 ; 905 *Abigail*, b June 27, 1807 ; 906 *Elizabeth*, b Oct. 2, 1816.

### 667. LEMUEL.

LEMUEL HALL, son of Daniel and Sarah Hall, was a merchant in New Haven. He built and was the owner of the store now owned by Austin & Gilbert, on the corner of Elm and Church-sts.

Children: 907 *Henry*, d in New Haven ; 908 *Grace;* and several other children.

### 672. ALMER.

DEA. ALMER HALL, son of Daniel and Thankful Hall, married 2d, widow of Merrick Cook ; he was a merchant and deacon of the Baptist church for several years.

Child : 909 *Almer L.*, m —— Hall.

### 728. ANDREW.

ANDREW HALL, son of Joel and Hannah Hall, was born Jan. 11, 1757, married Diana Cook.

Children : 910 *Betsey*, b Feb. 3, 1788 ; 911 *Russell*, b Oct. 18, 1789, m Polly Kirtland ; 912 *Liverius*, b Aug. 13, 1790 ; 913 *Clarissa C.*, b Nov. 28, 1793, m Almer Hall, Esq. ; 914 *Susan*, b March 18, 1795 ; 915 *Sylvia*, b March 13, 1797, m Thaddeus Cook ; 916 *Sinai*, b June 25, 1799, m Frederick Lewis ; 917 *Wm. Cook*, b Jan. 11, 1802.

### AUGUSTUS.

AUGUSTUS HALL, son of Joel and Hannah Hall, married Pamelia Hall, Feb. 10, 1794 ; he died in Wallingford.

Children : 918 *Eunice*, b March 3, 1796 ; 919 *Joel*, b July 6, 1799.

### 731. LUTHER.

LUTHER HALL, son of Joel and Hannah Hall, married Sarah ——.

Children : 920 *Emily*, b Sept. 6, 1800 ; 921 *Julia A.*, b Oct. 6, 1801 ; 922 *William*, b Jan. 10, 1804 ; 923 *Sally E.*, b May 17, 1806 ; 924 *Abraham R.*, b Sept. 25, 1808 , 925 *Betsey P.*, b May 8, 1815.

### 866. NATHAN.

NATHAN KELSEY HALL, son of Ira and Catharine Hall, of Skaneateles, N. Y., married Emily Payne. She was born Aug 5, 1811, married Nov. 16, 1832. He is a lawyer at Buffalo, N. Y.

Children : 926 *Nathan K.* Jr., b Oct. 13, 1833, d at Buffalo, Oct. 22, 1835 ; 927, *Frederick Aug.*, b Jan. 10, 1836, d at Andover, N. Y., Jan. 7, 1852 ; 928 *Emily A.*, b Oct. 9, 1838, m George Gorham of Canandagua, N. Y. ; 929 *Frank*, b Jan. 7, 1845, d at Washington, D. C., May 23, 1848 ; 930 *Grace*, b May 16, 1850.

#### 701. JONATHAN.

JONATHAN HALL, son of Isaac and Mary Morse Hall, married 1st, Elizabeth, daughter of John G. Hoadley, 2d, Sally, daughter of William Jencks. He died Feb. 22, 1741, ae. 64 years, 5 mos., 29 days. Residence of this family was at Leyden, Lewis Co., N. Y.

Children: 931 *Jehiel*, b Nov. 16, 1803, m Louisa Wilson, Aug. 10, 1826; 932 *Daniel*, b July 30, 1805, m Mary D. Sperry, Oct. 23, 1834 ; 933 *Mary*, b June 23, 1812, m Silas Cary, Feb. 6, 1812 ; 934 *Abigail*, b Dec. 22, 1813, m Rev. David A. Barney, March 5, 1834 ; 935 *Jonathan*, b Aug. 22, 1815, m Ann Henry, Nov. 9, 1840 ; 936 *Sally*, b April 28, 1817, m Robert Harvey, Sept. 9, 1839 ; 937 *Isaac*, Capt., b Nov. 6, 1818, m Amanda Thayer, May 1, 1845 ; 938 *Julia*, b April 5, 1820; 939 *William Jencks*, b Dec. 22, 1821, m Emeline Stone ; 940 *Phebe Ives*, b Feb. 18, 1824, m Amos Chamberlain, Nov. 3, 1844; 941 *Eunice*, b Feb. 18, 1827, m Franklin A. Thomas, April 26, 1866 ; 942 *Newton*, Maj., b Sept. 16, 1829, m Elmira Brainard, April 26, 1866 ; 943 *Maria K.*, b July 4, 1831, m Charles G. Dewey, Nov. 16, 1854.

#### 911. RUSSEL.

COL. RUSSEL and Polly Hall.

Children : 944 *Caroline Diana*, b Sept. 3, 1815 ; 945 *Eliza Ann*, b Sept. 13, 1817 ; 946 *George Kirtland*, b July 7, 1819 ; 947 *Mary Augusta*, b May 11, 1822 ; 948 *Sarah Potter*, b July 26, 1824.

#### 428. JOSEPH.

JOSEPH HALL, son of John and Elizabeth Prindle Hall, married Hannah ——.

Children : 949 *Sherman*, b April 26, 1806 ; 950 *John*, b June 5, 1808, d July 9, 1836 ; 951 *Emery*, b Sept. 29, 1809, d Dec. 6, 1869 ; 952 *Lucy*, b May 27, 1811, d Feb 18, 1813 ;

953 *Julius*, b June 7, 1813, m Laura F. Parker, May 1, 1852, 6 children ; 954 *Maria*, b August 30, 1815, d May 5, 1846, ae. 30 years.

## HARRIMAN.

### SAMUEL.

SAMUEL HARRIMAN was in New Haven at an early date, where he had a considerable family. Among his children was John, who graduated at Harvard College in 1663. He went to Wallingford with the first planters in 1670, and was the acting minister among the people of the village for two years, though not an ordained minister. Mrs. Elizabeth Harriman, his mother, died in Wallingford, Sept. 23, 1684. His wife died Jan. 10, 1680. His house lot was that on which the houses of the late Mr. Almer Hall and Liverius Carrington now stand.

Children : 1 *John*, b Jan. 25, 1660, d Nov. 21, 1683, ae. 17 years ; 2 *Samuel*; 3 *Anna*, b July 6, 1678 ; 4 *Mary*, b Nov. 7, 1680 ; 5 *Leonard*, b June 5, 1683 ; 6 *Richard*, b Aug. 9, 1685.

## HART.[1]

### HAWKINS.

HAWKINS HART of Farmington came to Wallingford at the age of 24 years, and married Sarah Royce, who was nineteen years of age. Their marriage was consummated Sept. 17, 1701. She died Jan. 31, 1733. He died May 24, 1735. They resided after their marriage a short time in Farmington, but returned to Wallingford Oct. 4, 1705, where they resided for the remainder of their lives.

---

1 For collateral branches, see Andrews' Hist. New Britain, Conn., 149–51, 163–4, 170–8, 183–91 ; Davis' Gen. Hart Family, Lewis and Newhall's Hist. Lynn, Mass., 227 ; Littell's Passaic Valley Gen., 179 ; Savage's Gen. Dict., II. 367–8 ; Sibley's Hist. Union, Me 459.

Children : 1 *Nathaniel*, b June 19, 1702, in Farmington, Ct. ; 2 *Ruth*, b Aug. 13, 1704, in Farmington, Ct. ; 3 *Hawkins*, b Sept. 16, 1706, d in Wallingford, Sept. 22, 1706 ; 4 *Hawkins*, b March 1, 1708, m 1st, Mary Street, Jan. 30, 1734, 2nd, Abigail Hall, Feb. 12, 1761 ; 5 *Sarah*, b March 21, 1710 ; 6 *Esther*, b Aug. 12, 1712 ; 7 *Thomas*, b Sept. 29, 1714 ; 8 *Mary*, b June 21, 1719 ; 9 *Benjamin*, b Jan. 28, 1722. Mr. Hart married for his 2nd wife, Mary, daughter of Rev. Joseph and Mary Elliot of Guilford, 1734. She was born 1688, and had 10 *Samuel*, born July 13, 1735, who was a lieutenant in the American army, and was wounded in the battle at Saratoga during the Revolutionary war. He died at Durham, Ct., Jan. 12, 1805.

### 1. NATHANIEL

NATHANIEL HART m Martha Lee, Dec. 21, 1727. He died Oct. 2, 1750, ae. 48 years.

Children : 11 *Nathaniel*, b Sept. 5, 1729, m Alice Hall, Jan. 23, 1753, he went to Goshen where he d ae. 80 years, had Nathaniel, b Nov. 8, 1754 ; 12 *Timothy*, b May 24, 1731 ; 13 *Martha*, b June 21, 1733 ; 14 *Ebenezer*, b March 26, 1739 ; 15 *Josiah*, b Feb. 22, 1742 ; 16 *Phebe*, b April 22, 1746, m 1st, Stephen Yale, 2nd, Eliasaph Preston, Feb. 17, 1764.

### 4. HAWKINS.

LIEUT. HAWKINS HART, married to Susannah Merriman by Rev. Theophilus Hall, Nov. 20, 1730. After her decease he married Mary Street, Jan. 30, 1734. She died, and he married Abigail Hall, Feb. 12, 1761. He died April 17, 1756.

Children : 17 *Samuel ;* 18 *Sarah*, b 1750, d Nov. 27, 1765 ; 19 *Susannah*, b 1747, d Oct. 26, 1757 ; 20 *Benjamin*, b 1751, d Oct. 7, 1836, m Jerusha Rich, Feb. 25, 1776, she d Aug. 26, 1832.

### 20. BENJAMIN.

BENJAMIN HART, son of Lieut. Hawkins Hart, married Jerusha Rich.

Children : 21 *Esther*, b Nov. 8, 1776, m Marvel Andrews

for his 4th wife, 22 *Lucy*, b Dec. 20, 1779; 23 *Susannah*, b Jan. 15. 1782; 24 *Webb*, b Feb. 21, 1786; 25 *Jerusha*, b Sept. 11. 1788, m Abel D. Clark; 26 *Samuel, J.*, b Nov. 22, 1792.

### 26. SAMUEL.

SAMUEL IVES HART, son of Benjamin and Jerusha Rich Hart, married Abigail D. Hall, Sept. 20, 1814; he is now living in the east part of Meriden.

Children: 27 *Daniel H.*, b June 19, 1815, m Harriet G. Miller; 28 *Edmund*, b Aug. 12, 1817; 29 *Edmund*, b Feb. 16, 1818; 30 *Jerusha*, b Aug. 22, 1822, m Horace Pratt of Meriden; 31 *Elizabeth*, b Aug. 22, 1822, m Edward B. Miller of Meriden.

## HOW.[1]

Four persons of this name were early at New Haven, viz.: Jeremiah Sen., Ephraim, Zachariah Sen., and Nathaniel. These persons all but Ephraim, went to Wallingford, in 1670. and he followed them in 1672, as appears by the records, having been at New Haven then, about 20 years. John How, one of the sons, returned to New Haven about the year 1700.

### JEREMIAH.

Children: 1 *Jeremiah*, b July 8, 1650; 2, 3 *John* and *Ebenezer*, b June 26, 1656; all born in New Haven. John married Abigail ——.

### EPHRAIM.

EPHRAIM How is supposed to have removed from Wallingford, as no mention of marriages or deaths are found on the Wallingford records.

Children born in New Haven: 4 *Ephraim*, b April 3, 1653

---

[1] For collateral branches, see Bond's Hist. Watertown, Mass., 303-4; Kidder's Hist. New Ipswich, N. H., 391; Morse's Memorial of Morses, Appendix No. 67 3-4; N. E. Hist. and Gen. Reg XVI. 314; Worcester Mag. and Hist. Jour., II. 130-1.

B B B

5 *Sarah*, b June 25, 1654 ; 6 *Nancy*, b Nov. 17, 1656; 7 *Samuel*, b 1658 ; 8 *Daniel*, b Jan. 4, 1663 ; 9 *Isaac*, b Aug. 26, 1666 ; 10 *Abigail*, b April 23, 1668 ; 11 *Esther*, b Nov. 28, 1671 ; 12 *Mary*, b Dec. 8, 1674.

### NATHANIEL.

NATHANIEL and Elizabeth How were with the first planters in Wallingford ; she died Dec. 29, 1713, æ. 70 yrs. He married 2d, Sarah Curtis, August 9, 1714 ; he died at Wallingford, Feb. 12, 1722.

Children : 13 *Elijah*, b Sept. 9, 1673, m Mary Bellamy, Jan. 25, 1703 ; 14 *Lydia*, b Nov. 6, 1675 ; 15 *Daniel*, b Mar. 8, 1677, m 1st, Margery ——, 2d, Sarah —— ; 16 *Abigail*, b Aug. 7, 1680.

### ZACHARIAH.

ZACHARIAH How died at Wallingford, Sept. 22, 1740 ; he died June, 1703.

Children born in New Haven : 17 *John*, b Jan. 16, 1666, m Abigail —— ; 18 *Zachariah*, b May 30, 1669, m Elizabeth Hemingway, he d May 12, 1712 ; 19 *Nathaniel*, b Jan. 2, 1672, m Mary Tracey, Oct. 15, 1711 ; 20 *Matthew*, b Jan. 2, 1672, m Elizabeth Winston, Dec. 31, 1717, both born in Wallingford ; 21 *Sarah*, b Oct. 30, 1675, d Feb. 2, 1713, æ. 36 yrs. ; *Mary*, b Dec. 14, 1677.

### I. JEREMIAH.

JEREMIAH How married Elizabeth ——, Oct. 29, 1674. He died at Wallingford, Sept. 22, 1740, æ. 90 yrs. ; Elizabeth, his wife died Oct. 4, 1704. He married a widow, Mary Cook, April 9, 1705.

Children by 1st marriage, born at Wallingford : 22 *Jeremiah*, b Sept. 15, 1675; *Jerusha*, b Sept. 13, 1677 ; *Ephraim*, b Feb. 20, 1681 ; 25 *Martha*, b Aug. 2, 1684 ; 26 *Maria*, b Sept. 20, 1687 ; 27 *Ebenezer*, b March 3, 1690 : 28 *Joshua*, b Dec. 2, 1702. Children by 2d marriage : 29 *Sarah*, b April 16, 1709 ; 30 *Dinah*, b Feb. 28, 1716 ; 31 *Ichabod*, b Sept. 11. 1717 ; 32 *Joshua*, b April 1, 1720.

## 22. JEREMIAH.

JEREMIAH How married Judith Cook, April 20, 1704 ; she died March 20, 1708. He was living June 28, 1745.

Children : 33 *Judith*, b Oct. 22, 1703, m Elihu Yale ; 34 *Jeremiah*, b Feb. 17, 1705, m Elizabeth Gaylord.

## 34 JEREMIAH

JEREMIAH How of Wallingford married Elizabeth Gaylord, March 11, 1730. He was designated as Jeremiah How 3d : he emigrated to Goshen in the summer of 1747.

Children born in Wallingford : 35 *Judith*, b Dec. 19, 1730 ; 36 *John*, b Oct. 1, 1732 ; 37 *Jeremiah*, b Dec. 24, 1734, d 1736 ; 38 *Jeremiah*, b Nov. 17, 1736, m Martha North ; 39 *Elizabeth*, b Sept. 18, 1738, m Daniel Norton : 40 *Benjamin*, b Oct. 26, 1739, d ; 41 *Benjamin*, b Jan. 22, 1740 ; 42 *Joel*, d Jan. 28, 1745 ; 43 *Esther*, b March 5, 1744, m Daniel Merrills ; 44 *Joseph*, b Nov. 9, 1746, m Prudence Norton ; 45 *Ruth*, b Oct. 4, 1748, m Royce Orvis, she was b in Goshen.

## 36. JOHN.

JOHN How married Mary Wadams, daughter of Noah Wadams of Goshen. She died, and he married Lydia Norton, April 15, 1766.

Children born in Goshen : 46 *Mary*, b Sept. 10, 1757, m Wait Hinman ; 47 *Experience*, b Dec. 29, 1759, m Nathan Norton ; 48 *Anna*, b April 10, 1762, m Israel Everett and went to Vermont ; 49 *Deliverance*, b June 25, 1764. By second marriage : 50 *John*, b April 22, 1767, m Esther Walter of Cornwall, Conn. ; 51 *Ichabod*, b June 5, 1769, m C. Moss Norton of Cornwall, Conn ; 52 *Isaac*, b 1771, d æ. 8 yrs : 53 *Luman*, b Aug. 6, 1774, m Esther Meacham ; 54 *Daniel* 55 *Seth*, m Achsah Washburn of Penn. ; 56 *Lydia*, committed suicide at the age of 14 yrs.

The above John How remained in Goshen, Conn., till Dec. 30, 1766, when he sold to Wistal Willoughby, and removed to Canaan, Conn.

### 41. JOSEPH.

JOSEPH How married Prudence Norton, Oct. 24, 1768, daughter and youngest child of Joseph, who was from Durham, Conn. ; he died at Goshen, April 17, 1807, æ. 61 yrs. She died Jan. 15, 1825.

Children: 57 *Prudence,* b Oct. 15, 1769, m Amasa Robinson of Litchfield, Conn. ; 58 *Melzar,* b Oct. 19, 1772, m ———— Willoughby ; 59 *Philo,* m Roxy Tuttle ; 60 *Clara,* m Allen Dean.

## HITCHCOCK.[1]

### JOHN.

JOHN and Abigail Hitchcock were the first of the name who came into the town of Wallingford, which was about 1675.

Children: 1 *Mary,* b Dec. 10, 1676 ; 2 *Nathaniel,* b April 18, 1679, d May 12, 1710, ae. 31 ; 3 *Margery,* b Sept. 9, 1681 ; 4 *Elizabeth,* b April 8, 1684 ; 5 *John,* b Oct. 18, 1685, m Marlow Munson, Nov. 21, 1712 ; 6 *Matthias,* b May 26, 1688, m Thankful Andrews ; 7 *Hannah,* b Jan. 9, 1690 ; 8 *Damaris,* b June 11, 1693 ; 9 *Benjamin,* b March 24, 1696, m Elizabeth Ives.

### 2. NATHANIEL.

NATHANIEL HITCHCOCK m Sarah Lewis Jennings, April 3, 1704. He died May 12, 1714.[D]

Children: 10 *Sarah,* b March 13, 1705 ; 11 *Elizabeth,* b Jan. 26, 1707 ; 12 *Hannah,* b June 11, 1709.

### 5. JOHN.

JOHN HITCHCOCK, m Marlow Munson, Nov. 21, 1712. She died July 1, 1739.

Children: 13 *Peter,* b Oct. 14, 1713 ; 14 *Martha,* b April 1,

---

1 For collateral branches, see Dodd's Hist. E. Haven, Conn., 126, 127 ; Kellogg's Memorials of Elder John White. 121 ; Savage's Gen. Dict., II. 428, 429; Wilbraham, Mass., Centennial Celebration, 1863, 298, 299.

1715 ; 15 *John*, b May 11, 1717 ; 16 *Eliakim*, b Sept. 7, 1710, d April 5, 1723 ; 17 *Jotham*, b Feb. 4, 1722, m Mary —— ; 18 *Dan*, b March 14, 1724, m Esther ——— ; 19 *Eliakim*, b June 13, 1726 ; 20 *Titus*, b Jan. 31, 1729, m Hannah Munson July 30, 1759 ; 21 *Catherine*, b July 10, 1731.

## 6. MATTHIAS.

MATTHIAS HITCHCOCK m Thankful Andrews, Dec. 27, 1710. Children: 22 *Oliver*, b Nov. 14, 1716 ; 23 *Jason*, b Aug. 10, 1718 ; 24 *William*, b Oct. 16, 1720 ; 25 *Matthias*, b June 19, 1711, d April 7, 1726 ; 26 *Nathaniel*, b Oct. 15, 1712 ; 27 *Valentine*, b Feb. 14, 1715 ; 28 *Nathaniel*, b May 7, 1733 ; 29 *Thankful*, b March 29, 1725 ; 30 *Matthias*, b Feb. 11, 1727, m Sarah —— ; 31 *Ebenezer*, b Sept. 14, 1728 ; 32 *Tabitha*, b Feb. 26, 1730 ; 33 *Enos*, b April 27, 1735 ; 34 *Hannah*, b April 27, 1735.

## 9. BENJAMIN.

CAPT. BENJAMIN HITCHCOCK was married to Elizabeth Ives by Capt. Yale, Oct. 1, 1718. He died Feb. 12, 1767. She died Aug. 8, 1762.

Children : 35 *Bela*, b Oct. 27, 1719 ; 36 *Hannah*, b Sept. 12, 1721 ; 37 *Benjamin*, b Feb. 23, 1724 ; 38 *Joseph*, b July 12, 1737 ; 39 *Abigail*, b May 10, 1728 ; 40 *David*, b June 29, 1742 ; 41 *Samuel*, b April 1, 1730 ; 42 *Damaris*, b Sept. 3, 1745 ; 43 *Nathaniel*, b June 20, 1732 ; 44 *Nathaniel*, b Sept. 20, 1739 ; 45 *Damaris*, b Nov. 25, 1756.

## 15. JOHN.

JOHN and Elizabeth Chatterton Hitchcock, married Nov. 29, 1739.

Children : 46 *Amos*, b Dec. 28, 1740 ; 47, 48 *Elizabeth* and *Elisha*, b Oct. 24, 1743 ; 49 *David*, b Sept. 27, 1742.

## 17. JOTHAM.

JOTHAM and Mary Hitchcock.

Children : 50 *Sarah*, b Sept. 11, 1747 ; 51 *Lyman*, b March 15, 1749 ; 52 *Mary*, b Dec. 4, 1750 ; 53 *Marlow*, b Dec. 26, 1752 ; 54 *Jotham*, b Nov. 6, 1754.

### 13. PETER.

PETER HITCHCOCK married Hannah Smith, June 18, 1737. Children: 55 *Reuben*, b May 11, 1738; 56 *Amasa*, b Oct. 3, 1739; 57 *Valentine*, b April 18, 1741; 58 *Peter*, b May 17, 1743, d May 16, 1744; 59 *Peter*, b Feb. 6, 1743; 60 *David*, b Nov. 10, 1754.

### 18. DAN.

DAN HITCHCOCK married Esther Miles, of Cheshire, Aug. 17, 1743.

Children: 61 *Asahel*, b Dec. 24, 1743; 62 *Martha*, b April 10, 1748; 63 *Susannah ;* 64 *Eunice*, b Nov. 28, 1754; 65 *Seth ;* 66 *Lydia ;* 67 *Benajah :* 68 *Eliakim*, b Aug. 8, 1746; 69 *Esther*, b May 23, 1750; 70 *Dan*, b Oct. 19, 1752; 71 *Sarah*, b Sept. 6, 1757; 72 *Miriam :* 73 *George*.

### 19. ELIAKIM.

ELIAKIM HITCHCOCK married Esther ——; he died June 19, 1788, æ. 62 yrs.

Children: 74 *Abigail*, b Dec. 6, 1756; 75 *Rufus*, b April 1, 1760, was a Judge of Probate, Town Clerk, etc. ; 76 *Jared*, b July 30, 1758.

### 20. TITUS.

TITUS HITCHCOCK married Hannah Munson, July 30, 1759. Child: 77 *Obedience*, b Oct. 8, 1761.

### 22. OLIVER.

OLIVER HITCHCOCK married Thankful Parker, Oct. 19, 1744.

Children: 78 *Mary*, b July 8, 1745; 79 *Thankful*, b May 13, 1747; 80 *Rebecca*, b Jan. 18, 1749; 81 *Hannah*, b Oct. 11, 1750, d Nov. 5, 1752; 82 *Oliver*, b Feb. 24, 1755; 83 *Sarah*, b March 19, 1757; 84 *Damaris*, b Nov. 6, 1758; 85 *Dinah*, b Nov. 23, 1760.

### 23. JASON.

JASON HITCHCOCK, married Lydia Cook, Sept. 20, 1743; she died Dec. 30, 1753.

Children: 86 *William*, b June 26, 1744; 87 *Thomas*, b

Dec. 20, 1746; 88 *Lemuel*, b Dec. 20, 1749 , 89 *Jason*, b July 12, 1752; 90 *Jason*, b Oct. 10, 1755 ; 91 *Ichabod*, b Dec. 18, 1756; 92 *Thankful*, b March 20, 1761.

### 30. MATTHIAS.

MATTHIAS HITCHCOCK married Sarah ———.

Children: 93 *Oliver;* 94 *Jason;* 95 *Thankful;* 96 *Matthias;* 97 *Ebenezer;* 98 *Tabitha.* 99 *Nathaniel;* 100 *Hannah.*

### 35 BELA.

BELA HITCHCOCK married Sarah Atwater, Dec. 25, 1744 , she died Oct. 23. 1746; he married Hannah Cook, and she died June 28. 1805, æ. 83 ; he died Oct. 12, 1796, æ. 77 yrs., in Cheshire.

Child by 1st marriage : 101 *Isaac*, b Jan. 23, 1746, d Jan. 28. 1746. Children by 2nd marriage : 102 *Isaac*, b Oct. 26, 1748, d May 27, 1749 ; 103 *Bela*, b Sept. 21, 1750 ; 104 *Hannah*, b Dec. 31, 1752 ; 105 *Asa*, b Feb. 11, 1755 ; 106 *Sarah*, b Aug. 1, 1757 ; 107 *Aaron*, b Dec. 6, 1759.

### 37. BENJAMIN.

BENJAMIN HITCHCOCK married Rhoda Cook, Feb. 27, 1745. Children: 108 *Thaddeus*, b Dec. 13, 1745 ; 109 *Hannah*, b March 9, 1748 ; 110, 111 *Benjamin* and *Rhoda*, b Nov 24, 1752 ; 112 *Lucy*, b March 24, 1755 ; 113 *Damaris*, b Dec. 5, 1756 ; 114 *Thaddeus*, b Dec. 10, 1760.

### 56. AMASA.

Children : 115 *Amos;* 116 *Silas;* 117 *James;* 118 *David;* several daughters.

### 57. VALENTINE.

Children : 119 Hon. *Peter;* 120 Rev. *Roger;* 121 *Polly.*

### 60. DAVID.

Children ; 122 *Marcus;* 123 *David;* 124 *Gaius.*

### 63. ELIAKIM.

ELIAKIM HITCHCOCK, son of Dan and Esther Hitchcock, married Betty Hill, July 23. 1734, she died Nov. 21, 1754.

Child : 125 *Betty Hill*, b March 2, 1754.

### 61. ASAHEL.

ASAHEL HITCHCOCK lived in the village of Cheshire. Child : 126 *Miles*, went to New York, where he died.

### 70. DAN.

DAN HITCHCOCK was a blacksmith, and resided, when living, in a house then standing a little east of the late residence of Titus and Almon Preston.

Children : 127 *Samuel;* 128 *Clarissa*, m —— Perkins ; 129 *Chauncey;* 130 *Esther;* 131 *Lyman;* 132 *Rebecca*, m A. Perkins ; 133 *Dan;* 134 *Annah*, m John Reed ; 135 *Matilda;* 136 *Betsey*, m Amos Bristol.

### 73. RUFUS.

RUFUS HITCHCOCK was twice married ; he died in 1832, was a Judge of Probate, Town Clerk, etc.

Children : 137 *Wm. Rufus*, m Mary Hall, d in Waterbury ; 138 *Lucretia*, m Rev. P. G. Clark.

### 91. ICHABOD.

ICHABOD HITCHCOCK, son of Jason and —— Hitchcock, died in Cheshire.

Children : 139 *Pliny*, m —— Bradley ; 140 *Sarilla*, m Geo. Stevens ; 141 *Jason;* 142 *Hannah*, m T. L. Gaylord ; 143 *Lucinda*, m Richard Beach. By 2d marriage : 144 *Abigail*, m and went to Kentucky.

### 65. SETH.

SETH HITCHCOCK, son of Dan and Esther Miles Hitchcock, died in Cheshire.

Children ; 145 *Alfred;* 146 *Emily*, m Aaron Cook, late of Cheshire.

### HOLT.[1]

William Holt died in Wallingford, Sept. 1, 1683, aged 83; consequently was born in 1600, in the old country. He was buried in the cemetery at Wallingford, where his tomb-stone

---

1 For collateral branches, see Abbot's Hist. Andover, Mass., 22;

still remains to mark his grave. Benjamin Holt also died in
Wallingford, Aug. 2, 1693, aged 32 years.

#### JOSEPH.

JOSEPH HOLT was an early settler in Wallingford, though
not an original subscriber. He was married to Elizabeth
French or Tench, by Major Nash, Nov. 20, 1684. He died
Dec. 10, 1697, ae. 42 years.

Children: 1 *Joseph*, b Sept. 10, 1685, m Abigail Curtis,
June 8, 1709 ; 2 *Daniel*, b Oct. 6, 1687, m Rebecca ——— ;
3 *Benjamin*, b Sept. 3, 1690, m Abigail Curtis ; 4 *Mary*, b
Jan. 20, 1691 ; 5 *Elizabeth*, b March 23, 1696 ; 6 *John*.

#### 1. JOSEPH.

JOSEPH HOLT married Abigail Curtis, June 8, 1709. She
died Jan. 12, 1730.

Children : 7 *Tamar*, b Oct. 31, 1711 ; 8 *Susannah*, b Feb.
12, 1716 ; 9 *Mary*, b Feb. 9, 1714 ; 10 *Samuel*, b May 14,
1718 ; 11 *Lucy*, b Dec. 12, 1722 ; 12 *Lydia*, b April 24, 1725 ;
13 *Abigail*, b July 20, 1727 ; 14 *Prudence*, b Dec. 29, 1728 ;
15 *Mehitable*, b Dec. 26, 1729 ; 16 *Mabel*, d Dec. 28, 1727.

#### 2. DANIEL.

DANIEL and Rebecca Holt.

Children : 17 *Phebe*, b Dec. 24, 1716 ; 18 *Hannah*, b April
28, 1719 ; 19 *Mary*, b May 21, 1718 ; 20 *Thomas*, b Jan. 22,
1721 ; 21 *Eunice*, b Nov. 26, 1724 ; 22 *Uriah*, b Jan. 22,
1721 ; 23 *Joseph*, b Feb. 25, 1726 ; 24 *Levis*, b Oct. 30, 1726 ;
25, 26 *Rebecca* and *Abigail*, b May 11, 1738 ; 27 *Daniel*, b
May 27, 1729.

#### 3. BENJAMIN.

BENJAMIN and Abigail Holt.

Children : 28 *Elizabeth*, b Dec. 25, 1729 ; 29 *Prudence*, d
May 23, 1737 ; 30 *Lydia*, b August 15, 1732 ; 31 *Benjamin*, b

Caulkins' Hist. New London, Ct., 314, 315 ; Dodd's Hist. East Haven,
Ct., 127, 128 ; Durrie's Gen. of Holt Family ; Savage's Gen. Dict., II.
454, 455.

June 14, 1734, d May 2, 1735 ; 32 *Benjamin*, b August 22, 1737.

## HOTCHKISS.[1]

### SAMUEL.

SAMUEL HOTCHKISS came from Essex, England, and is supposed to have been a brother of John Hotchkiss, who settled at Guilford, Conn. This name is spelled in some instances, Hodghe, Hodgkins, and Hotchkins. He was at New Haven as early as 1641. In Aug., 1642, he married Elizabeth Cleverly ; he died Dec. 28, 1663.

Children : 1 *John*, b 1643, m Elizabeth Peck, Dec. 4, 1672, and remained in New Haven ; 2 *Samuel*, b 1645, m Sarah Talmadge in 1678, settled at East Haven, Conn. ; 3 *James*, b 1647 ; 4 *Joshua*, b Sept. 16, 1651, m two or three wives, resided in New Haven ; 5 *Thomas*, b 1654, m Sarah Wilmot ; 6 *David*, b 1657, m Esther Sperry.

### 1. JOHN.

JOHN HOTCHKISS married Elizabeth Peck, daughter of Henry Peck of New Haven, Dec. 4, 1672. They had John, born 1673 ; he married Mary Chatterton in 1694, and settled on the west side of Wallingford, now Cheshire.

Child : 7 *John*, b 1694, m Miriam Wood, March 10, 1717, he d in Cheshire, April 30, 1732, she d Jan 10, 1765, æ. 65 yrs.

### 7. JOHN.

Children : 8 *Robbins*, b May 12, 1709 ; 9 *Mary*, b Feb. 20, 1712, d Aug., 1718 ; 10 *Henry*, b April 1, 1715 ; 11 *Benjamin*, b May 10, 1718 ; 12 *Jason*, b May 12, 1719, m Abigail ———, she d Feb. 22, 1773, ae. 40 yrs. ; 13 *Sarah*, b July 13, 1721 ; 14 *Dorothy*, b Dec. 28, 1723 ; 15 *Hannah*, b July 30, 1726 ; 16 *Naomi*, b Feb. 23, 1731 ; 17 *John*, b Sept. 16, 1733.

1 For collateral branches, see Andrews' Hist. New Britain, Conn., 155, 156, 171, 172, 224. 295 ; Bronson's Hist. Waterbury, Conn., 505-8 ; Cothren's Hist. Woodbury, Conn.. 579, 580 ; Dodd's Hist. East Haven, Conn,, 512-19.

### 12. JASON.

JASON HOTCHKISS married Abigail ———, he died in Cheshire, May 19, 1776, ae. 58 years. She died Feb. 22, 1773, ae. 49 yrs.

Children: 18 . *Abigail*, b July 12, 1746 ; 19 *David*, b March 8, 1752 ; 20 *Jonathan*, b May 7, 1754 ; 21 *Abigail*, b Sept 19, 1756; 22 *Sarah*, b May 1, 1758, m William Law Esq. of Cheshire, and was the mother of Samuel Law Esq. of Meredith, N Y., and of William and Jonathan Law of Cheshire, and John of Whitehall, N. Y., all deceased.

### 2. SAMUEL.

SAMUEL HOTCHKISS married Sarah Talmadge in 1678.

Children, born in East Haven : 23 *Mary* , 24 *Sarah* , 25 *Samuel*; 26 *James*, b 1747, m Tamar ———; 27 *Abigail*, 28 *Eben*; 29 *Enos*.

### 4. JOSHUA.

ENS. JOSHUA HOTCHKISS was twice or more times married. The name of his last wife was Mary Hotchkiss. She died Nov. 15, 1787, ae. 88 yrs. He died 17██ ae. ██ yrs. ; he resided in New Haven, and was a leading man there.

Children: 30 *Mary*, b April 30, 1679 ; 31 *Stephen*, b Aug. 12, 1681, settled in Wallingford, parish of Cheshire ; 32 *Martha*, b Dec. 14, 1680, m Thomas Brooks of New Haven, in 1702, and settled in Cheshire (then Wallingford); 33 *Priscilla*, b 1688 ; 34 *Abraham*, settled in Bethany, Conn., d 1702 ; 35 *Desire*, d 1702 ; 36 *Isaac*, b June, 1701. Among the children were Abraham, Isaac and Jacob, all residents of Bethany, as was their father. 37 *Jacob*, b Feb. 7, 1704, remained on the old homestead in New Haven for some time, and subsequently removed to Hamden, one of his sons went to Derby, Conn. ; 38 *John*, b Feb. 27, 1733 ; 39 *Elizabeth*, b March 23, 1735 ; 40 *Mary*, b Aug. 11, 1737, d ; 41 *Mary*, b June 17, 1738.

### 5. THOMAS.

THOMAS HOTCHKISS married Sarah Wilmot, Nov. 28, 1697. He died in 1711. Children: 42 *Samuel*; 43 *Anna*; 44 *Sarah*

## 6. DAVID.

DAVID HOTCHKISS married 1st, Esther Sperry, June 20, 1683. He married 2nd, Eunice ——. He died in 1712.

Children : 45 *Eliza ;* 46 *Daniel,* m Mamre —— ; 47 *Oba-* *diah,* m Eunice Beach, Jan., 1716, they had Lewis, b Jan. 16, 1717 ; 48 *Thankful,* b Feb. 15, 1753 ; 49 *Eunice,* b Jan. 8; 1755 ; 50 *Rebecca ;* 51 *Isaac,* b March 4, 1757 ; 52 *Hannah,* b June 5, 1761 ; 53 *Rebecca.*

## 10. HENRY.

CAPT. HENRY HOTCHKISS married Sarah ——, and settled at Wallingford, in the parish of Cheshire, where he was married Nov. 23, 1736. He died June 9, 1799, ae. 84. She died Nov. 19, 1751, ae. 34 years.

Children : 54 *Henry,* b Sept. 2, 1737 ; 55 *Joseph,* b Dec. 18, 1738 ; 56 *Henry,* b 1723, d Sept. 29, 1742 ; 57 *Jonah,* d July 26, 1741 ; 58 *Sarah,* b Feb. 5, 1742 ; 59 *Mary,* b Feb. 1, 1745 ; 60 *Jonah,* b Oct. 28, 1748.

## 31. STEPHEN.

DEA. STEPHEN HOTCHKISS, b 1681, son of Joshua, m Elizabeth, daughter of John Sperry of New Haven, Dec. 12, 1704. He purchased land in Cheshire in 1706, and settled upon it in 1707. He died March 5, 1755, ae. 74 years. He was deacon of the church at Cheshire for 31 years.

Children : 61 *Joshua,* b Aug. 26, 1705 ; *Elizabeth,* b 1706, d 1788 ; 62 *Mary,* b July 1, 1708, m Nathan Burns M. D.; 63 *Hannah,* b Jan. 10, 1710, m Stephen Atwater ; 64 *Esther,* b Feb. 8, 1712 ; 65 *Elizabeth,* b Aug. 15, 1715 ; 66 *Gideon,* b Dec. 5, 1715, first Dea. of the Congregational Church in Salem ; 67 *Stephen,* b Dec. 1, 1717 ; 68 *Silas,* b Nov. 20, 1719, m widow Alcott ; 69, 70 *Hannah* and *Stephen,* b Feb. 23, 1722 ; 71 *Bashua,* b Sept. 7, 1726 ; 72 *Benjamin,* b Feb. 1, 1728, m Elizabeth Roberts ; 73 *Noah,* b Nov. 24, 1731, d Jan. 13, 1760.

## 26. JAMES.

JAMES HOTCHKISS, son of Samuel and Sarah, married Tamar ——.

Children: 74 *Asa*, b Nov. 24, 1731 ; 75 *Robert*, b June 17, 1733 ; 76 *Eunice*, b March 28, 1734 ; 77 *Tamar*, b Aug. 24, 1736 ; 78 *Reuben*, b Feb. 5, 1743 ; 79 *Lydia*, b Aug. 11, 1745.

### JOSIAH.

JOSIAH HOTCHKISS married Abigail ————. He died of small pox in May, 1732, at Cheshire ; she died of the same disease near the same time.

Children : 80 *Josiah*, b Oct. 13, 1716 ; 81 *Josiah*, b April 3, 1720 ; 82 *Elizabeth*, b Jan. 25, 1723 ; 83 *Ludwick*, b Jan. 15, 1720 ; 84 *Tyrrel*, b 1718 ; 85 *Lent*, b June 2, 1726.

### 66. GIDEON.

DEA. GIDEON HOTCHKISS, m Anna Brockett, Jan. 18, 1737. She died, and afterwards he married Mabel, daughter of Isaac Stiles, of Southbury. He located on a farm in the southeasterly part of Waterbury in 1736, and was chosen a Deacon of the Congregational Church at Salem now (Naugatuck), at its organization. He was one of the principal men who founded the Congregational Church at Prospect (then Columbia), and was a leading man there. He served in the French and Revolutionary wars, and died full of years, Sept. 3, 1807, æ. 91 years, leaving 105 grandchildren, 155 great grandchildren, and four of the fifth generation.

Children : 86 *Isaac*, b 1738 ; 87 *David*, b 1743 ; 88 *Gideon*, b Dec., 1744 ; 89 *Huldah*, b June 27, 1747, m Josiah Paine ; 90 *Anna*, b Oct. 22, 1749, m Reuben Williams ; 91 *Amos*, b Nov. 24, 1751 ; 92 *Submit*, b June 2, 1753, m David Paine ; 93 *Titus*, . b June 26, 1755, m Rachel Guernsey ; 94 *Eben*, b Dec. 13, 1757, m Mary, dau. of Gideon Sanford, Feb. 15, 1781 ; 95 *Asahel*, born Feb. 16, 1760 ; 96 *Benoni*, born ———— : 97 *Mabel*, born May 23, 1764, m Chauncey Judd, May 5, 1797 ; 98 *Phebe*, b Aug. 3, 1765, m Reuben Williams ; he died in 1780 ; 99 *Stiles*, b Jan. 1, 1768, m Polly Horton, and had five children ; 100 *Olive*, b Nov. 21, 1769, m William Jones ; 101 *Millicent*, b May 2, 1771, m David Sanford ; 102 *Amzi*, b July 3, 1774, resided in Meriden.[1]

1 See Bronson's Hist. of Waterbury, 505–8, for descendants of above.

## HOUGH.[1]

### SAMUEL.

SAMUEL HOUGH married Susannah, daughter of Simeon Wrotham, of Farmington, Conn. His father, William Hough, was a son of Edward Hough, of Westchester, Cheshire Co., England. Samuel was born in New London, Conn., and was by trade a mill-wright. He came to Wallingford to assist in the construction of the first mill in the township. Mrs. Hough died in Wallingford, Sept. 5, 1684. He married 2d, Mary, daughter of James Bates, of Haddam, Aug. 18, 1685 ; he died March 14, 1714.

Children : 1 *William*, b Aug. 22, 1680, m Mehitable ———— ; 2 *Samuel*, b Feb. 15, 1681, d Nov. 30, 1702, ae. 21 yrs. ; 3 *Susannah*, b Nov. 27, 1683, m ———— Andrews, of Farmington, Conn. By 2d marriage : 4 *James*, b Dec. 15, 1688, m Sarah Newhall, July 29, 1718 ; 5 *Hannah*, b Nov. 8, 1691.

### 1. WILLIAM.

WILLIAM HOUGH, son of Samuel and Susannah Hough, married Mehitable ———— ; she died Feb. 5, 1726. He married 2d, Elizabeth ———— ; she died June 3, 1740.

Children : 6 *Mary*, b Sept. 10, 1710 ; 7 *Samuel*, b July 5, 1712, d Oct. 8, 1713 ; 8, 9 *William*, and *Mehitable*, b Aug. 14, 1714 ; 10 *Deborah*, b Dec. 17, 1716 ; 11 *Anna*, b Dec. 28, 1718 ; 12 *Abiah*, b May 15, 1721. By 2d marriage : 13 *Nathaniel*, b Dec. 28, 1727 ; 14 *Simeon*, b Jan. 11, 1734.

### 4. JAMES.

JAMES HOUGH, son of Samuel and Susannah, married Sarah Newhall, July 19, 1718.

Children : 15 *Ephraim*, b April 9, 1719 ; 16 *Daniel*, b March 6, 1721, d July 25, 1768, ae. 49 yrs ; 17 *Ebenezer*, b Jan. 22, 1726, m Lydia ————, d July 20, 1737, she d July

---

1 For collateral branches, see Andrews' Hist. of New Britain, Conn., 352 ; Babson's Hist. Gloucester, Mass., 105 ; Caulkins' Hist. New London, Conn., 302, 303 ; Caulkins' Hist. Norwich, Conn., Ed. 1867, 233 ; Savage's Gen. Dict., II. 468-9 ; Wadsworth's Hyde Gen., II. 1100-11, 1152-9.

19, 1757, 18 *David*, b Feb. 8, 1728, d Oct. 18, 1729 ; 19 *Sarah*, b Oct. 18, 1730, d Nov. 10. 1741 : 20 *David*, b Jan. 28, 1733, d June 27, 1752, ae. 19 yrs. ; 21 *James*, b March 24, 1735, m Lucy ——, she d Oct. 5, 1775, æ. 51 ; 22 *Barnabas*, b Sept. 5, 1736 : 23 *Mary*, b Nov. 25, 1739.

## 8. WILLIAM.

WILLIAM HOUGH, son of William and Mehitable Hough, married Mary Hall, Dec. 20, 1752.

Children : 24 *Susannah*, b May 24, 1754, d Nov. 24 1756 ; 25 *Mary*, b June 22, 1756.

## 15. EPHRAIM.

EPHRAIM HOUGH, son of James and Sarah Newell Hough, married Hannah ——.

Children : 26 *Abigail*, b Nov. 29, 1740, d Aug. 16. 1743 : 27 *Sarah*, b Jan. 26, 1742 : 28 *Abigail*, b Aug. 10, 1743, d Aug. 16, 1743 ; 29 *Abigail*, b Feb. 21, 1744 ; 30 *Ephraim*, b Jan. 6, 1746 ; 31 *Andrew*, b Dec. 27, 1747 ; 32 *Andrew*, b Dec. 17, 1749 ; 33 *Hannah*, b Jan. 17, 1751 ; 34 *Thankful*, b May 29, 1753, d Aug. 18. 1780 ; 35 *Ambrose*, b Sept. 2, 1754 ; 36 *Lois*, b June 3, 1756.

## 16. DANIEL.

DANIEL HOUGH, son of James and Sarah (Newell), married 1st, Mindwell . ——. She died March 21, 1741-2. He married for 2d wife, Violet Benton, Nov. 29, 1743. He settled in Meriden where he died.

Children : 37 *Mindwell*, b May 5, 1745 : 38 *Ensign*, M. D., b Sept. 1, 1746 ; 39 *Elijah*, b Jan. 23, 1747 : 40 *Samuel*, b March 12, 1750-1 ; 41 *Eunice*, b March 30, 1755 ; 42 *Dolly*, b Jan. 30, 1756 ; 43 *Caleb*, b Feb. 13, 1757 ; 44 *Hannah*, b Feb. 4, 1762.

## 17. EBENEZER.

EBENEZER HOUGH, son of James and Sarah, married Lydia ——. She died July 20, 1757.

Children : 45 *Buel*, b June, 1743 ; 46 *Lydia*, b Aug 28, 1749, d July 19, 1759 : 47 *Lucy*, b April 23, 1756.

## SAMUEL.

SAMUEL HOUGH married Hannah ——. Supposed son of Samuel and Hannah was in W., about 1700.

Children: 48 *Samuel*, b July 12, 1712, m Mehitable ——; 40 *Phineas*, b April 11, 1714, d Sept. 1, 1797, ae. 83 years.

## ENSIGN.

DR. ENSIGN HOUGH, son of Daniel and Violet Hough, of Meriden, died in 1813. He kept a hotel and practiced his profession as a physician.

Children: 50 *Dr. Isaac I.*, b 1781, d in Meriden, unmarried, Feb. 26, 1825 ; 51 *Ensign*, d in Meriden ; he had other children.

## 49. PHINEAS.

PHINEAS HOUGH, son of Samuel and Hannah Hough, married Hannah ——.

Children: 52 *Rachel*, b May 27, 1740 ; 53 *James*, b July 31, 1743 ; 54 *Phineas*, b Sept 16, 1745 ; 55 *Mary*, b Aug. 14, 1747 ; 56 *Rachel*, b April 22, 1750 ; 57 *Anna*, b April 18, 1752.

## JOSEPH.

JOSEPH HOUGH married Catherine, daughter of Capt. Theophilus and Sarah Street Yale, June 27, 1745. He was born 1717, and died Jan. 5, 1809, ae. 92 years. Catherine, his wife, died Oct. 5, 1767, ae. 46 years.

Children: 58 *Joseph*, b Sept. 12, 1745 ; 59 *Mary*, b July 15, 1746 ; 60 *Lois*, b June 24, 1747, d Nov. 12, 1748 ; 61 *Lent*, b April 4, 1751 ; 62 *Lois*, b Dec. 5, 1752 ; 63 *David*, b Nov. 2, 1754 ; 64 *Joel*, b Jan. 27, 1757, d Sept. 9, 1843, in Hamden, Ct. ; 65 *James*, d Dec. 3, 1762 ; 66 *James*, d in Wallingford ; 67 *Catherine*, m Edmund Smith ; 68 *Sarah*, m —— Rice, and settled at Homer, N. Y.

## 58. JOSEPH.

CAPT. JOSEPH HOUGH, son of Joseph and Catherine Yale Hough, settled on the farm of his father at Clapboard Hill. He built the house now occupied by his grandson Joseph Hough. He died Sept. 11, 1811.

Children : 69 *Chauncey*, m Lura, daughter of James Rice, of Wallingford, and had Mary, Elizabeth, Joseph and Chauncey : 70 *Betsey*, m Salmon Carter of W. and had Salmon, Betsey and William ; 71 *Horace*, went to New Haven, Ohio, and died there, leaving several sons.

### 61. LENT.

LENT HOUGH, son of Joseph and Catherine Vale Hough, married 1st, Rebecca Tuttle. She died Aug. 22, 1798, ae. 44. He married Mary Andrews, who was Mary Pierrepont of North Haven before her 1st marriage. She died June 27, 1832, ae. 75. He died Oct. 8, 1837, ae. 87 yrs.

Children by 1st marriage : 72 *Lucy :* 73 *Hannah ,* 74 *Serrajah*, b March 26, 1780, m Elizabeth S. Avery in 1801. By 2d marriage : 75 *Almira*, b Nov. 6, 1797, m Eveline Dutton, Nov. 6, 1821, d in Canada, May 15, 1841, æ. 42 yrs.

### 64. JOEL.

JOEL HOUGH, son of Joseph and Catherine Hough, settled in Hamden, Mt. Carmel society, where he died ; he was a shoemaker and farmer.

Children : 76 *Ira*, settled in Wolcott, Conn., and d there ; 77 *Joseph*, settled in Cheshire, Conn., m —— Moss, dau. of Bowers Moss, of that place ; 78 *Eze.*——, went to western New York ; 79 *Amos*, m Nancy, dau. of Nehemiah Rice, of Wallingford, d at Hamden in 1869 ; 80 *Joel*, went to the state of N. Y.

### 66. JAMES.

JAMES HOUGH, son of Joseph and Catherine Vale Hough, married and settled in the North Farms district, Wallingford, where he died. He was a farmer.

Children : 81 *James*, m Mary, dau. of Nehemiah Rice, they had Elijah, and daughters ; 82, daughters ; 83 *Joel*, m, is now on the farm of his father in Wallingford.

### 74. SERRAJAH.

SERRAJAH HOUGH, only son of Lent and Rebecca Hough, m Elizabeth S., daughter of Abner Avery, of Wallingford, Feb.

18, 1801. She was born Sept. 27, 1782. Mr. Hough died at Meriden, Aug. 3, 1853, æ. 73 years.

Children : 84 *Lyman Worcester*, b March 7, 1802, d Aug. 1834, in Meriden ; 85 *Lent Serrajah*, b Jan. 20, 1804, m Hannah Smith, of Wallingford, July 12, 1831, settled in Wolcott, Conn. ; 86 *Nancy Avery*, b Feb. 1, 1806, d March 11, 1823, ae. 17 years ; 87 *Rebecca Tuttle*, b Jan. 3, 1808, m Rev. Sam'l. F. Curtis, she died March 25, 1842 ; 88 *Alonzo Bennett*, b Mar. 25, 1810, resided in Vineland, N. J. ; 89 *George Sherman*, b Oct. 7, 1812, now at Pittsburg, Pa., 1867 ; 90 *John Meers*, b Oct. 12, 1815, resides in Tyrrell Co., N. C. ; 91 *Wm. Augustus*, b Aug. 14, 1818, d at Ravenna, Ohio, Dec. 25, 1837 ; 92 *Julius Ogden*, b July 21, 1822, d at Wallingford Jan. 1, 1823, ae. 6 months.

## HULL.[1]

This name was early in Connecticut, and came from Derbyshire, England. George Hull was at Windsor, Conn., in 1636, and was a surveyor at Wethersfield the same year, and a member of the General Court 1637–8–9. He married Elizabeth Loomis in 1641.

Richard and Andrew Hull were both at New Haven in 1639, and had families.

### JOHN.

DR. JOHN HULLS, as he wrote his name, was at Stratford in 1661, when he was admitted a planter. It is not quite certain whether he came from England, or was a son of Richard Hull of New Haven. Dr. John was at Derby in 1668, and at Wallingford in 1687. He died Dec. 6, 1711, at the latter place. He was probably somewhat advanced in life when he came to Wallingford. He married Mary Jones, Oct. 19, 1672, probably his second wife ; she dying, he married

---

1 For collateral branches, see Am. Antiq. Soc. Coll., III. 269 ; Andrews' Hist. New Britain, Conn., 367 ; Cothren's Hist. Woodbury, Conn., 577–9 ; Rhode Island Hist. Soc. Coll., III. 292, 293 ; Savage's Gen. Dict., II. 492–5 ; Stiles' Hist. Windsor, Conn., 672, 673.

Rebecca Turner, Sept. 23, 1699. He exchanged his house and land at Stratford, with Benjamin Lewis, for his house and land at Wallingford, in 1687. The town of Wallingford set out to Dr. Hull a tract of land which they supposed contained 700 acres, lying between the north side of Broad Swamp and the Quinnipiac river, the east and west boundaries not being so clearly defined. This grant was more than a mile square, and was known as Dr. Hull's large farm.

Children : 1 *John*, b March 14, 1661, m Mary ——— ; 2 *Samuel*, b Feb. 4, 1663 ; 3 *Mary*, b Oct. 31, 1666 ; 4 *Joseph*, b 1668, m Mary Nichols of Derby : 5 *Benjamin*, M. D., b Oct. 7, 1672. m Elizabeth Andrews, Dec 14. 1695 ; 6 *Ebenezer*, b 1673, m Lydia Mix, Mar. 4, 1706, he died in 1709 : 7 *Richard*, b 1674 ; 8 *Jeremiah*, M. D., b 1679, at Derby, m Hannah Cook, of Wallingford . 9 *Archer*.

### 1. JOHN.

JOHN HULL, son of Dr. John Hull, was born in Stratford, March 14, 1661–2, married Mary ——, and settled in Derby.

Children : 10 *Deborah*, b 1691, at Derby ; 11 *John*, b 1693 ; 12 *Daniel*, m May 2, 1732 ; 13 *Miles*, b 1700, m Mary Tuttle, Dec. 4 1729 : 14 *Ebenezer*, m Hannah Bates, Sept. 1, 1734 15 *Mary;* 16 *Martha ;* 17 *Priscilla*, b 1702.

### 4. JOSEPH.

CAPT. JOSEPH HULL, of Derby, was a son of Dr. John Hull of Wallingford. He married Mary Nichols of Derby, where they lived and died. The name of his second wife was Hannah ———, whom he left a widow.

Children : 18 *Samuel*, b 1692, had a family in Derby : 19 *Joseph*, b 1694. left 3 children, Sarah, b 1720, Joseph, b 1737, Elizabeth, b 1738 : 20 *Caleb*, b Feb 4, 1695, settled in Cheshire by request of his grandfather ; 21 *Abijah*, b 1697 ; 22 *Abner*, b 1698 ; 23 *Sarah*, m ——— Beach of Stamford ; 24 *Mary*, m ——— Russel of Derby, Conn.

### 5. BENJAMIN.

DOCT. BENJAMIN HULL, son of Dr. John Hull, came to Wallingford with his father in 1687, married Elizabeth Andrews, Dec. 14, 1693. She died April 27, 1732. He died March 30, 1741.

Children: 25 *Andrew*, b Aug. 17, 1694, d Dec. 10, 1717; 26 *Mary*, b Aug. 31, 1696, m Ebenezer Bronson; 27 *Elizabeth*, b April 8, 1698, m Nathaniel Merriman, Nov. 12, 1725; 28 *Damaris*, b Feb. 4, 1700, m Elnathan Street; 29 *John*, M. D., b Oct. 6, 1702, m Mary Andrews; 30 *Abigail*, b Feb. 14, 1704, m Ens. Merriman; 31 Capt. *Samuel*, b Sept. 1, 1706, m Sarah Hall, Feb. 21, 1733; 32 *Sarah*, b March 30, 1710, m Samuel Hall, Dec. 27, 1733; 33 *Benjamin*, M. D., b July 6, 1712, m Hannah Parmalee, Dec. 17, 1735.

### 6. EBENEZER.

EBENEZER HULL, son of Dr. John Hull, married Lydia Mix, May 7, 1706; he died Nov. 9, 1709, æ. 36 years. His widow Lydia administered on the estate.

Child: 34 *Hannah*, b March 23, 1708.

### 8. JEREMIAH.

DR. JEREMIAH HULL, son of Dr. Benjamin Hull of Wallingford, married Hannah, daughter of Samuel and Hope Cook, May 24, 1711, at Wallingford; she died Dec. 11, 1741; he died May 14, 1736, in Wallingford.

Children: 35 *John*, b Nov. 13, 1712, m Mary Andrews, Oct. 26, 1735; 36 *Moses*, b Dec. 26, 1714, d June 3, 1736, æ. 22 yrs.: 37 *Tabitha*, b March 3, 1717; 38 *Hannah*, b March 18, 1720; 39 *Anna*; 40 *Jeremiah*, b Jan. 5, 1729, m Mary Merriman in 1753; 41 *Joseph*, b March 24, 1733, m Hannah Corbitt in 1754; 42 *Patience*, b Oct. 20, 1735; 43 *Keturah*.

### 11. JOHN.

JOHN HULL, son of John and Mary Jacobs Hull, of Derby, was born Jan. 1, 1695.

Children: 44 *John*, b Oct. 22, 1703; 45 *Tamar*, b Nov. 27, 1705; 46 *Mary*, b Feb. 17, 1708; 47 *Ebenezer*, b Oct. 18, 1715; 48 *Susannah*, b Sept. 29, 1726.

### 12. DANIEL.

DANIEL HULL, son of John of Derby, who was son of

Dr. John Hulls of Wallingford, married Elizabeth Lane of Derby, in 1731 or 1732.

Children: 49 *Daniel*, b 1734; 50 *Samuel*, b 1735; 51 *Elizabeth*, b 1738; 52 *Ebenezer*, b 1741; 53 *John*, b 1744.

### 13 MILES.

MILES HULL, son of John of Derby, who was son of Dr John Hulls of Wallingford, married Mary Tuttle of Wallingford, and settled in that place.

Children: 54 *Martha*, b Nov. 29, 1730, d in infancy; 55 *Martha*, b Nov. 23, 1732; 56 *Esther*, b Sept. 15, 1733; 57 *Elizabeth*, b 1735; 58 *Elijah*, b March 10, 1736, d May 10, 1736; 59 *Eunice*, b March 29, 1738; 60 *Mary*, b July 15, 1740; 61 *Miles*, b March 24, 1743 m Eunice Hulls, Dec. 4, 1761; 62 *Abigail*, b June 11, 1745, m Elam Cook, Jan. 8. 1761; 63 *Abijah*, b June 10, 1747.

### 14. EBENEZER.

EBENEZER HULL, son of John and Mary Hull of Derby, married Hannah Bates, Sept. 1, 1731; he died in Wallingford in 1774.

Children: 64 *Joseph*, b Sept., 1731, d March 13, 1732; 65 *Daniel*, b Feb. 29, 1732; 66 *Lydia*, b April 14, 1734, m Nicholas Andrews of Wallingford; 67 *Eunice*, b 1736, m Miles Hull of Cheshire; 68 *Esther*, b 1737; 69 *Anna*, b Oct. 13, 1738, m Elijah Gaylord of Wallingford; 70 *Mary*, m ———— Tuttle of Wallingford; 71 *Joseph*, b 1740; 72 *Rena*, 73 *Joseph*, b March 1, 1742; 74 *Sarah*, m Benjamin Sperry of Wallingford; 75 *Ebenezer*, b 1750, m Patience ————; 76 *Esther*, b March 27, 1756, survived her father.

### 18. SAMUEL.

SAMUEL HULL, son of Capt. Joseph Hull of Derby, who was a son of Dr. John Hull of Wallingford.

Children. 77 Infant, b 1725; 78 *Hannah*, b 1726; 79 *Eunice*, b 1727.

### 19. JOSEPH.

JOSEPH HULL, son of Capt. Joseph Hull of Derby, who

was son of Dr. John Hull of Wallingford, was twice married:
1st, to Bertha ——, 2d, to Sarah ——; he died June 12,
1778, æ. 85 yrs.   Mrs. Sarah died at the age of 92 yrs.
Child by 1st marriage : 80 *Temperance*, b 1714.   By 2d
marriage: 81 *Sarah*, b 1726, m Rev. Dr. Mansfield of
Derby, Conn. ; 82 *Joseph*, b 1727, m Elizabeth Masters, she
d Feb. 11, 1825, æ. 94 yrs. ; 83 *Elizabeth*, b 1728, d in 1738,
ae. 10 yrs.

### 20. CALEB.

CALEB HULL, son of Capt. Joseph and Mary Hull, and
grandson of Dr. John Hull, of Wallingford, married Mercy
Benham, of Wallingford, May 1, 1724; he was then 28
years old.   The chimney-place of his residence in 1751 is
now visible, at Broad swamp, so called, near the north-
eastern part of Cheshire, east nearly a mile from the
Jared Bishop place, late the residence of Capt. Munson Cook,
and now of his son Joel Cook.   She died April 19, 1766.
He died Sept., 1788.   In 1710, he, Caleb, then fourteen years
old, received from his grandfather, Dr. John Hull, 100 acres
of land, deeded to Joseph from Caleb, conditioned that Caleb
should come and live with him till 21 years old, or until
his decease.   Dr. Hull died Dec. 6, 1711.   Doubtless Caleb
went.   The 100 acres is on record.

Children : 84 *Sarah*, b April 25, 1725, m Reuben Atwater
of Cheshire ; 85 *Andrew*, b Aug. 23, 1726, d Sept. 21, 1774,
ae. 49 yrs., m Lowly Cook ; 86 *Mary*, b Apr. 27, 1728, m
Jonathan Hitchcock, Oct. 3, 1745 ; 87 *Samuel*, b Mar. 22,
1730, m Eunice Cook in 1753 ; 88 *Joseph*, b Aug. 29, 1732 ;
89 *Abijah*, b Oct. 11, 1733, d Dec. 14, 1733 ; 90 *Joseph*, b June
10, 1734, d Dec. 4, 1735 ; 91 *Caleb*, b May 21, 1735, d Aug. 8,
1735 ; 92 *Submit*, b Dec. 12, 1736, d Feb. 13, 1737 ; 93
*Patience*, b Oct. 15, 1740, d Sept., 1764, ac. 25 ; 94 *Joseph*, b
April 18, 1741 ; 95 *Caleb*, b Dec. 16, 1742, d June 4, 1767, ae.
25. m Mary Street.

### 21. ABIJAH.

ABIJAH HULL, son of Capt. Joseph and Mary Hull, and

grandson of Dr. John and Mary Hull of Wallingford, m Abigail Harger, of Derby, Nov. 20, 1727.

Children : 96 *Esther*, b 1728 ; 97, daughter.

### 29. JOHN.

DR. JOHN HULL, son of Dr. Benjamin and Elizabeth Hull. married Sarah Ives, June 21, 1727. She died Nov. 29, 1760. He married for his 2d wife, Damaris Frost, Oct. 20, 1761. He died May 22, 1762-3.

Children · 98 *Zephaniah*, b Aug. 15, 1728, m Hannah Doolittle, March 28, 1749 ; 99 *John*. d May 27, 1739 ; 100 *Elizabeth*, b Feb. 14, 1733, m Ephraim Cook. Jan. 1, 1752, in Cheshire ; 101 *Sarah*, b 1737, d Jan. 23, 1740 ; 102 *John*, b Apr. 17, 1739 ; 103 *Desire*, b June 6, 1740 ; 104 *Sarah*, b Sept. 17. 1741 : 105 *John*, b Feb. 15, 1744 ; 106 *Amos*, b May 27, 1745, m 1st, Martha Hitchcock, 1764, 2d, —— Norton.

### 31. SAMUEL.

CAPT. SAMUEL HULL, son of Dr. Benjamin and Elizabeth Hull, married Sarah Hall, Feb. 21, 1733. and settled in Cheshire, where he died Jan. 17. 1789, ae. 82 years. She died June 11, 1763, ae. 50 years. He was born in 1707.

Children : 107 *Sarah*, b Jan. 26, 1734, d May 3, 1734 ; 108 *Samuel*, b April 6, 1735, d May 22, 1735 ; 109 *Samuel*, b Aug. 12, 1737, m Sarah Humiston, Jan. 22, 1761, she died Sept. 4, 1775, ae. 31 ; 110, 111 *Sarah* and *Love*, b Aug. 27, 1738, the latter m Thomas Atwater, Dec. 8, 1757 ; 112 *Jesse*, b Jan. 27, 1745, m Ruth Preston, he settled on a farm at Broad Swamp, Cheshire ; 113 *Benjamin*, b about 1775, m Mary Andrews ; 114 *Levi*, d Oct. 30, 1751. The last two were by 2d marriage.

### 33. BENJAMIN.

DR. BENJAMIN HULL, son of Dr. Benjamin, son of Dr. John Hull, of Wallingford, married Hannah Parmalee, Dec. 17, 1735.

Children : 115 *Patience*, b 1736 ; 116 *Phebe*, b May 2, 1737 ; 117 *Hannah*, b May 3, 1739 ; 118 *Dr. Benjamin*, b Oct. 20, 1741, m Esther ——, in 1763 ; 119, 120 *Eliakim*, and

*Charles*, b May 1, 1744, the latter settled in Wallingford, m
Sarah Atwater, he died May 4, 1819 ; 121 *Sybil*, b Aug. 15,
1746, d June 2, 1758; 122 *Joel*, b Aug. 6, 1749, settled in
Yalesville, m Sarah ———, she d Aug. 23, 1816 ; 123 *Beda*,
b April 11, 1753; 124 *Lois*, b Jan. 1, 1757 ; 125 *Asahel*, b
Aug. 4, 1759, settled in Wallingford ; 126 *Ephraim*. b 1767.

### 35. JOHN.

DR. JOHN HULL, son of Dr. Jeremiah and Hannah Cook
Hull, married Mary Andrews, Oct. 26, 1735 ; he died Aug.
15, 1755 ; m 2d, Damaris Frost, Oct. 20, 1761.

Children : 127 *Sarah*, b Jan. 12, 1736 ; 128 *Molly*, b March
12, 1738, m Thomas Shephard, May 5, 1732 ; 129 *Sarah*, b
Sept. 17, 1741, m Col. Asa, father of Hoadly Brothers, late
of East Haven ; 130 *Moses*, m Mary Ives, April 28, 1757 ;
131 *John*, b March 7, 1741-2, m Lois Beadles, March, 1759 ;
132 *Nathaniel*. b March 17, 1743, m Mehitable Beadles, April
13, 1763 ; 133 *Aaron*, b July 17, 1745 ; 134 *Abigail*, b Dec.
1, 1747 ; 135 *Hannah*, b July 6, 1750.

### 40. JEREMIAH.

JEREMIAH HULL, son of Dr. Jeremiah and Hannah
Cook Hull, and grandson of Dr. John Hull, married Mary
Merriman, Jan. 18, 1753.    She died Aug. 22, 1774, ae. 41
years.    He died Aug. 24, 1790, ae. 60.    He was twice
married.

Children : 136 *Caleb*, b Dec. 1, 1753, m —— Tyler ; 137
*Jeremiah*, m 1st, Sarah ———, 2nd, Phebe Hart ; 138, *Sam-
uel*, m Lois Peck of Wallingford ; 139 *Ann*, m Jacob Rice.
By 2nd marriage : 140 *Benjamin ;* 141 *Levi*, m and settled
near his brother Jeremiah in Wallingford ; 142 *Hannah*, m
—— Heath in Wallingford ; 143 *Eunice*, m —— Pratt of
Essex, Ct.

### 41. JOSEPH.

JOSEPH HULL, son of Dr. Jeremiah and Hannah Cook
Hull, married Hannah Corbitt in 1754.    I have been unable
to ascertain when they died.    They may have removed from
Wallingford in early life.

Correction

_ _ _ _ _ _ _ _ _ _ _ _ _ _ _ _ _ _ _ _ _ _ _ _

Children of Andrew Hull of Wallingford.

The name "Mary" should be Mercy.

Proof

The Will of Andrew Hull recorded

at Wallingford reads:

To my daughters- Damaras, Lowly,

Hannah, Sarah, Ursula, Mercy, Esther, and

Lovica.

Mercy's name is repeated twice in

said will.

New York, April 25, 1911.

~221 Eastern Parkway,

Brooklyn, N. Y.

A decendant of Mercy.

Children. 144 *Mary*, b Sept. 20, 1755, 145 *Caldwell*, b Jan. 2, 1759.

## 61. MILES.

CAPT. MILES HULL, son of Miles and Mary Hull, married Eunice, daughter of Ebenezer and Hannah Hull of Wallingford, Dec. 4, 1761. He died at Cheshire. When living he owned the farms of the late Jared Bishop, and Capt. Munson Cook.

Children: 146 *Amzi*, went to Canada; 147 *Luther;* 148 *Miles;* 149 *Polly*, m Levi Douglas of Meriden; 150 Daughter, m —— Sizer, of Meriden.

## 75. EBENEZER.

EBENEZER HULL, son of Ebenezer and Hannah Bates Hull, m Patience ——. He was a farmer at what is now Yalesville, where he died June 10, 1807, ae. 57 years. She died a few years later.

Children: 151 *Joseph*, m Rebecca, daughter of Josiah Mix; 152 *Ira*, d unmarried in 1812, at Broadswamp, Cheshire; 153 *Sarah*, m Amos Austin of Meriden: 154 *Amy*, m Lyman Hitchcock, son of Dan ——.

## 85. ANDREW.

ANDREW HULL, son of Caleb, son of Capt. Joseph, son of Dr. John Hull of Wallingford, married Lowly Cook, daughter of Capt. Samuel and Hannah Cook of Wallingford, Oct. 17, 1730. He died Sept. 21, 1774, ae. 49. He owned the large farm which Elias Gaylord's heirs and George Bristol now own, near Cheshire street, bounded north by the river. Mrs Lowly Hull died about 1785.

Children: 155 *Damaris*, b Sept. 29, 1749; 156 *Lowly*, b July 16, 1753; 157 *Hannah*, b Dec. 16, 1754; 158 *Damaris* b Sept. 18, 1755; 159 *Andrew*, b Oct. 6, 1758, m Elizabeth Mary Ana Atwater; 160 *Sarah;* 161 *Ursula*, b Nov. 10, 1760; 162 *Mary·* 163 *Esther*, 164 *Susan;* 165 *Josiah*, m Dr. Hall, went to Vermont.

✻ See Correction

## 87. SAMUEL.

SAMUEL HULL. son of Caleb, son of Capt. Joseph, the son of Dr. John Hulls of Wallingford, married Eunice Cook, daughter of Capt. Samuel and Hannah Cook of Wallingford. Dec. 26, 1753. He died April 27, 1791, ae. 62. She died May 9, 1803, ae. 68 years.

Children: 166 Infant son, b Jan. 1, 1755 ; 167 *Jedediah*, b ; Feb. 26, 1756 ; 168 Infant son, b Feb 2, 1758, d same day ; 169 *Samuel*, b May 27, 1759, d Feb. 20, 1840, ae. 80 years ; 170 *Zephaniah*, b May 1, 1761, settled in Wallingford, Vt., and d Feb. 20, 1840 ; 171 *Epaphras*, b April 9, 1763; d April 13, 1827, in Wallingford, Vt. ; 172 *Eunice*, b April 16, 1765, d Dec. 18, 1820, m Sheriff Whipple, Cazenovia, N. Y. ; 173 *Lois*, b Feb. 1, 1769, d Oct. 20, 1777 ; 174 *Caleb*, b Nov. 9, 1768, d Aug. 9, 1816, at Wallingford, Vt. ; 175 *Elizabeth*, b Oct. 28, 1770, d Oct. 13, 1777 ; 176 *Josephus*, b Aug. 24, 1772, d March 18, 1813, at Wallingford, Vt. ; 177 *Hannah*, b Oct. 11, 1775, m A. Meacham, Wallingford, Vt., d 1850.

## 95. CALEB.

CALEB HULL, son of Caleb, son of Capt. Joseph, son of Dr. John Hulls, of Wallingford, married Mary Street ; he died June 4, 1767, æ. 25.

Children: 178 *Ambrose;* 179 *Abraham;* 180 *Mary*, m —— Hudson, he was drowned.

## 98. ZEPHANIAH.

DR. ZEPHANIAH HULL, son of Dr. John, son of Dr. Benjamin and Elizabeth Hull, married Hannah Cook, March 28, 1749, and settled in Bethlem, Conn., probably through the inducement of Rev. Dr. Bellamy, with whom a close intimacy and warm friendship existed until death separated them. He died Nov. 10, 1760. She died the same day, both suddenly.

Children: 181 *Lydia*, b Dec. 22, 1749, d Feb. 21, 1750 ; 182 *Titus*, *M. D.*, b March 25, 1751, he went to Danbury in 1805, then to State of N. Y. ; 183 *Lydia*, b July 23, 1753, m Ja. Judson, March 21, 1769, by whom she had four children, marri d 2d, Amasa Clark, of Cheshire ; 184 *Andrew*, b Dec 8, 1754, settled at Cheshire ; 185 *Hannah*, b Jan. 28, 1757, d Nov. 16, 1760 ; 186 *Sarah*, b May 17, 1759, d Nov. 16, 1760.

### 105. JOHN.

JOHN HULL, son of Dr. John and Sarah Ives Hull, married Hannah Hitchcock, Dec. 13, 1764.

Child : 187 *John*, b Oct. 8, 1765.

### 106. AMOS.

DR. AMOS HULL, son of Dr. John and Sarah Hull, married Martha Hitchcock, March 2, 1764.

Child : 188 Dr. *Amos G.*, m Lydia Cook, dau. of Aaron of Wallingford, for his last wife.

### 109. SAMUEL.

SAMUEL HULL, son of Capt. Samuel and Sarah Hull of Cheshire, married Sarah Humiston, Jan. 22, 1761. She died Sept. 4, 1775, ae. 31 years. He married Hannah —— for 2d wife, and she died April 4, 1811, ae. 62 years.

Child : 189 *Samuel*, b 1777, m Alma, dau. of Jesse and Lois Humiston, of Cheshire, he was a saddler and harness-maker of Cheshire, he died May 5, 1831, ae. 54, leaving one daughter, Alma, wife of Wm. Kelsey, Esq..

### 112. JESSE.

JESSE HULL, son of Capt. Samuel and Sarah Hull, was six years in the war of the Revolution, married Ruth Preston, and settled in Cheshire, where they died

Children : 190 *Samuel*, b 1769, d in Cheshire, ae. 90 , 191 *Thelus*, went to Ohio, and has descendants there , 192 eight daughters, most of whom went to western New York.

### 113. BENJAMIN.

BENJAMIN HULL, son of Capt. Samuel and Hannah Hull, married Mary ———— ; he was a large landholder in Broad Swamp, Cheshire. He died May 3, 1835, ae. 63 years. She died Nov. 3, 1838, ae. 63 years.

Children : 193 *Rice Andrew*, went to Canada ; 194 *Lucy*, m

Samuel U. Beach, of Cheshire ; 195 *Chauncey*, b 1794, d Aug. 2, 1830, æ. 36 yrs. ; 196 *Darius*, m Martha ———— ; 197 *Amasa*, b 1806, d in Cheshire ; 198 *Benjamin*, b 1806, d April 6, 1812, æ. 6 yrs. ; 199 *Abiathar*, b 1814, d Oct. 10, 1839, æ. 25 yrs. ; 200 *Samuel Lee*, b 1818, d Jan. 8, 1838, æ. 20 yrs.

#### 118. BENJAMIN.

DR. BENJAMIN HULL, son of Dr. Benjamin and Hannah Hull, married Esther ————, 1763.

Child : 201 *Benjamin*, b Dec. 11, 1763.

#### 120. CHARLES.

CHARLES HULL, son of Dr. Benjamin and Hannah Hull, married Sarah Atwater, and when living, owned what is now known as the Ruggles farm at Yalesville in Wallingford ; he died May 4, 1819, æ. 75. His widow married Aaron Hall of Wallingford.

Children : 202 *Lucinda*, b 1760, d April 11, 1833, æ. 73 yrs., m Thomas Ruggles ; 203 *Lucia*, b 1778, d Sept. 8, 1848, æ. 70 yrs, m Barney McCarthy.

#### 122. JOEL.

JOEL HULL, son of Dr. Benjamin and Hannah Hull, m Sarah ——. She died Aug 23, 1816, ae. 59, in Wallingford. He sold his farm, which is the one now owned by the heirs of Ransom Jeralds at Yalesville, and removed to Ohio, where he died.

Child : 204 *Anson*, an only son, d in Ohio.

#### 130. MOSES.

MOSES HULL, son of Dr. John and Mary Hull, married Mary Ives, April 28, 1757. He lived, and I suppose, built the house where Thomas Berry lived in his old age, and where he died. The grandson of Mr. Berry now ( 1870 ) occupies the old house.

#### 131. JOHN.

JOHN HULL, son of Dr. John and Mary Hull, married 1st, Lois Beadles, March 20, 1759. She died Sept. 6, 1802, ae.

59 yrs. He married Phebe —— for his second wife. She died Sept. 3, 1834, ae. 93. He died Oct. 6, 1828, ae. 88 yrs. He was a large and enterprising farmer, and owned and occupied the house and land now belonging to Mr. Durand, near Yalesville.

Children: 205 *Nathaniel*, b Sept. 7, 1759, d in infancy; 206 *Mary*, b Aug. 30, 1762, m —— Beach; 207 *Sarah*, m Samuel Wolcott; 208 *Sally*, m Reuben Ives; 209 *Fanne*, m Ephraim A. Humiston; 210 *Melinda*, m Samuel J. Simpson; 211 *Diana*, m Benjamin T. Cook.

### 132. NATHANIEL.

NATHANIEL HULL, son of Dr. John and Mary Hull, married Mehitable Beadles, April 13, 1760.

Children: 212 Daughter, m Jonsey Curtis; 213 *Hull's*, b 1760, m Mehitable Mix, sister of John Mix, he d May 8, 1830, ae. 70; 214 *Mary;* 215 *George.*

### 133. AARON.

AARON HULL, son of Dr. John and Mary Hull, settled in Meriden, was a farmer and a peddler of tin ware.

Children: 216 *Joel*, m Hannah Hall, of Wallingford, daughter of Dickerman Hall; 217 *Cornelius.*

### 137. JEREMIAH.

JEREMIAH HULL, son of Jeremiah and Mary Hull, m 1st, Sarah ————, 2d, Phebe, daughter of Nathaniel Hart of Wallingford. He was a noted peddler and farmer. Mrs. Sarah died at the age of 27 years. Mrs. Phebe died Nov 9, 1855, ae. 84. He died Oct. 10, 1843, ae. 81 yrs.

Children by 1st marriage: 218 *Alma*, m Ira Morse of Wallingford; 219 *Julia*, m Ira Andrews of Wallingford. By 2d marriage: 220 *Philo*, m Betsey Cook of Wallingford; 221 *Hiram*, m Caroline Ives of Wallingford; 222 *Mary*, res. Wallingford, old homestead; 223 *Lucy*, m Senator Blakeslee, of Wallingford; 224 **Orrin**, m Ann Dowd; 225 *Jeremiah*, m Sophronia Dudley.

### 138. SAMUEL.

SAMUEL HULL, son of Jeremiah and Mary Hull, married Lois Peck, and settled on the old homestead of his father; he was an enterprising farmer in the north part of Wallingford.

Children: 226 *William*, m Alma, dau. of Reuben Hall; 227 *Sylvester*, m Delilah, dau. of Benijah Morse; 228 *Lois*, m Miles, son of Ichabod Ives.

### 151. JOSEPH.

JOSEPH HULL, son of Ebenezer and Patience Hull, married Rebecca, daughter of Josiah Mix; he died of a wound in his knee joint, produced by an axe in his own hands while pruning apple trees for the late Chester Cook, March, 1818.

Children: 229 *James Mix;* 230 *Maria*, m Jonathan Ives, of Meriden; 231 *Nancy;* 232 *Rebecca*.

### 152. IRA.

IRA HULL, son of Ebenezer and Patience Hull, died unmarried at Cheshire in 1812, and by his will gave his real estate to his sister Amy, she paying the legacies named therein.

### 159. ANDREW.

GEN. ANDREW HULL, son of Andrew and Lowly Hull, of Cheshire, married Elizabeth Mary Ann, daughter of Reuben Atwater, of Cheshire. He was a highly respectable gentleman, merchant and farmer; he died in Cheshire.

Children: 233 *Eudocia*, m Gov. Samuel A. Foot, of Cheshire; 234 infant son, d in infancy; 235 *Merab*, m Henry Whittelsey, of Cheshire; 236 *Elizabeth*, m Rev. Dr. A. Todd, of Stamford; 237 *Mary A.*, m Wm. R. Hitchcock, of Cheshire; 238 *Sarah*, m Rev. Mr. Cloud; 239 *Adeline*, m Rev. Mr. Mason.

### 169. SAMUEL.

SAMUEL HULL, son of Samuel and Eunice Hull, married Abigail Doolittle; she was born May 26, 1766. He was a farmer in the northern part of Cheshire, where he died, Oct. 27, 1828, ae. 70 yrs. Mrs. Abigail died Oct. 10, 1835, ae. 69.

Children: 240 *Stella*, b March 27, 1786, m Jonathan Law, Esq., she d Dec. 13, 1841, ae. 56 yrs. ; 241 *Jedediah*, b 1788, was insane ; 242 *Ann*, b 1793, d Aug. 27, 1818, ae. 25 yrs. ; 243 *Abigail Ann*, b Jan. 13, 1794 ; 244 *Linda*, b Feb. 6, 1796, m David Brooks of Cheshire, she d ae. 69 yrs. ; 245 *Eunice*, b Nov. 12, 1798, m Birdsey Booth, late of Cuyahoga Falls, Ohio ; 246 *Charlotte L.*, b Sept. 9, 1800, m John Olmstead, late of Hartford, Conn. ; 247 *Samuel Cook*, b Aug. 4, 1802, d Aug. 26, 1804 ; 248 *Samuel*, b Feb. 4, 1805, d at Morris, Grundy Co., Illinois ; 249 *Julius*, b July 1, 1807, m Lucy Ives, and went to Ohio ; 250 *Andrew Franklin*, b Jan 13, 1811, m Adeline Munson, he d Jan. 1, 1845, ae. 34 yrs.

## 182. TITUS.

DR. TITUS HULL, son of Dr. Zephaniah and Hannah Hull, studied medicine with Dr. Seth Bird, of Litchfield, and settled in Bethlem ; went in 1805 to Danbury. Ct. In the autumn of 1807, he went to the state of New York. He married Lucy Parmelee, daughter of Jonathan of Chatham, by whom he had two children, both of whom died in infancy. Mrs. Lucy died in Nov., 1776. In 1778 he married Olive Parmelee, widow of Abram of Goshen, her mother being a descendant of the Strong family of Northampton, Mass. He died Sept. 3, 1852.

Children : 251 *Lawrence*. M. D., b June 6, 1779, m Dorcas Ambler of Bethlem, in 1803, and had 6 sons and 3 daus. ; 252 *Althea*, b Aug. 18, 1780, has six sons and a daughter ; 253 *Charles*, b Jan. 4, 1782, was a physician, and practiced in Oneida Co., N Y., and d in 1833, leaving a son and 3 daus., all married ; 254 *Betsey M.*, b Sept. 17, 1783 ; 255 *Elias*, b April 3, 1786, has 2 chil. and lived in Alabama ; 256 *Lucy*, b Aug. 23, 1788, m Ezra Starr, Oct. 17, 1807 ; 257 *Olive E.*, b May 13, 1790, m Col. Elijah Morse of Eaton ; 258 *Andrew C.*, b Oct. 28. 1792, m Betsey Morse, in 1818, at Eaton ; 259 *Laverett*, b Dec. 3, 1796, m Julia Scoville of Salisbury, Ct., in 1829 ; 260 *Rufus Lewis*, died in childhood.

### 184. ANDREW.

ANDREW HULL, son of Dr. Zephaniah and Hannah Hull, after the decease of his father, went to live with his great-grandfather on his mother's side, at Cheshire, from whom he received an estate on which he continued to reside until his death. He married Naomi ———. She died Oct. 28, 1824, æ. 70 yrs. He died March 31, 1824, æ. 70 yrs., much lamented.

Child: 261 *Naomi II.*, m Mr. Wm. Brown, of New Haven, who was lost at sea. She was the mother of Wm. A. Brown, of Cheshire, and also of Mrs. Alfred Doolittle.

### 187. JOHN.

JOHN HULL, son of Dr. John and Sarah Hull, married Hannah Hitchcock, Dec. 13, 1764. I find no further account of them.

Child : 262 *John*, b Oct. 8, 1765.

### 188. AMOS.

DR. AMOS GOULD HULL, son of Dr. Amos Hull, who married a daughter of Dr. Norton of Cheshire, and was the inventor of the celebrated Hull truss, married Lydia Cook, daughter of Aaron and Elizabeth Cook of Wallingford.

Child by Lydia, 2d or 3d wife: 263 *Aaron Cook*, was a physician at Brooklyn, N. Y., is deceased.

### 190. SAMUEL.

SAMUEL HULL, son of Jesse and Ruth Preston Hull, married ——— Manwaring, of Essex, and settled at the old home of his father, where he died Dec. 8, 1857, ae. 90 years. He was a farmer, and during his long life maintained the character of an honest man.

Children: 264 *Caleb E.*, resides near Wallingford line, Cheshire ; 265 *Josiah M.*, resides in Cheshire, a farmer ; 266 *Samuel T.*, resides in Cheshire, a farmer ; 267 *Richard S.*, grad. at Yale College, is a lawyer in New Haven.

### 195. CHAUNCEY.

CHAUNCEY HULL, son of Benjamin and Mary Hull, married Hannah, daughter of Jonah Hotchkiss, of Cheshire ; he died Aug. 2, 1830, leaving several children, most of whose names are to me unknown.

Child: 268 *Chauncey*, d Jan. 1, 1821, æ. 4 yrs.

196. DARIUS.

DARIUS HULL, son of Benjamin and Mary Hull, married Martha ———— She died March 16, 1858, æ 53 yrs. He has a considerable family of children, names unknown to me. He still lives at Cheshire.

## HUMISTON.

### HENRY.

HENRY HUMISTON was at New Haven as early as 1650; he married Joanna Walker, Aug. 28, 1651. He died Jan. 16, 1663.

Children: 1 *Samuel*, b Aug. 7, 1650; 2 *Nathaniel*, b Jan. 13, 1654; 3 *Thomas*, b Oct. 19, 1656; 4 *Abigail*, b May 17, 1661.

Two of the name were at Wallingford about the commencement of the last century, viz., James and John, both from New Haven. John Humiston married Hannah Royce, of Wallingford, June 28, 1711, but it does not appear that he settled in Wallingfo—. James Humiston married Sarah Atwater, Jan. 7, 1719, and remained in Wallingford. He died Aug. 17, 1747.

Children: 5 *Daniel*, b Nov. 16, 1721, m Lydia ————; 6 *Stephen*, b Nov. 9, 1723; 7 *Noah*, b March 1, 1729, d Sept. 3, 1729; 8 *James*, b Oct. 28, 1734, m Abiah Ives, Feb. 4, 1755–6, 2d Hannah ————; 9 *Noah*, d June 13, 1745.

### 5. DANIEL.

DANIEL HUMISTON, son of James and Sarah Humiston, married Lydia ————, and settled in Cheshire, where he died July 27, 1767, ae. 46 yrs. She died Jan. 1, 1809, ae. 83 yrs.

Children: 10 *Sarah.*, b Dec. 14, 1744; 11 *Hannah*, b March 2, 1745; 12 *Stephen*, b July 17, 1751; 13 *Lydia*, b

D D D

March 17, 1754; 14 *Patience*, b Nov. 28, 1756; 15 *Daniel*, b April 10, 1759; 16 *Daniel*, b 1760, d Nov. 7, 1783; 17 *John*, b June 30, 1761 ; 18 *Jesse*, b March 12, 1764, m Lois, dau. of Amos Doolittle, of Cheshire.

### 8. JAMES.

JAMES HUMISTON, son of James and Sarah Humiston, married Abiah or Abigail ———, and settled on a farm at Gitteau's Corner, now known as the Humiston farm. He died in Wallingford, Feb. 18, 1812, ae. 77 yrs. She died Dec. 19, 1761.

Children : 19 *James*, owner of Humiston's Mills, Wallingford ; 20 *Linus*, went to Ohio.

### 18. JESSE.

JESSE HUMISTON, son of Daniel and Lydia Humiston of Wallingford, marrièd Lois, daughter of Amos Doolittle of Cheshire, and settled on a farm about a mile west of the railroad depot, in Cheshire. His decease occurred March 12, 1832, at the age of 68 ; Mrs Lois Humiston died Feb. 8, 1847, ae. 87 years.

Children : 21 *Daniel*, m Juliana Ives, daughter of Jared ; 22 *Jesse A.*, m Lois Preston, dau. of Reuben ; 23 *Alma*, m Samuel Hull of Cheshire ; 24 *John*, m Rhoda Nichols, of Wolcott, Conn.

### 19. JAMES.

JAMES HUMISTON was the proprietor of the mills about a mile west of the village of Wallingford, and was extensively engaged in wool-carding and cloth-dressing, as well as milling.

Children : 25 *Chauncey;* 26 *Nancy*, m Almon Preston ; 27 *Betsey*, m Harmon Morse ; 28 *Maria*, m Samuel Allen ; *Lyman*, m Jennie Johnson ; *Charles*, m Lucy Bronson.

### 20. LINUS.

LINUS HUMISTON went to Ohio many years ago, with his family. When in Wallingford, he resided on the old Humiston place, Gitteau's Corner.

Children : 29 *Miles;* 30 *Samuel;* 31 *Philo;* 32 *Mary;* 33 *Hannah.*

### 21. DANIEL.

DANIEL HUMISTON, son of Jesse and Lois Humiston, married Juliana, daughter of Jared Ives, of Cheshire. He died in 1866.

Children: 34 *Chauncey A.*; 35 *John D.*, m Emily Barns, of Cheshire; 36 *Julia Ann*, b 1822.

### 22. JESSE.

JESSE A. HUMISTON, son of Jesse and Lois Humiston, married Lois Preston.

Children: 37 *Lauren A.*, m Hannah Moss; 38 *Lois*, m Elam Cook.

### 24. JOHN.

JOHN HUMISTON, son of Jesse and Lois Humiston, married Rhoda Nichols, daughter of the late Samuel Nichols, of Wolcott. He died in Cheshire.

Children: 39 *Jesse*, removed to the state of New York 40 *John Latimer*, res. in Cheshire.

### EPHRAIM.

EPHRAIM A. HUMISTON came from North Haven, and married a daughter of John Hull, and settled on the old Henry and Russel farm, and died there.

Children: 41 *Sherlock*; 42 *Hiram*; 43 *Diana*; 44 *Willis*, has become wealthy, and res. in Troy, N. Y.

### IVES.[1]

### JOHN.

JOHN IVES was the first of the name that settled at Wallingford. He was a farmer in Meriden. I have been unable to determine his previous residence or place of nativity.

Children: 1 *John*, b Nov. 16, 1669, d 1738 æ. 69 yrs; 2 *Hannah*, m Joseph Benham, Aug. 17, 1682; 3 *Joseph*, b Oct. 14, 1674, m Esther Benedict, May 11, 1697; 4 *Gideon*, m Mary Royce, Feb 20, 1700; 5 *Nathaniel*, b May 31, 1677, m

---

[1] See Savage's Gen. Dict., II. 525.

Mary Cook, April 5, 1699 ; 6 *Ebenezer*, m Elizabeth ——; 7 *Samuel*, b June 5, 1696 ; 8 *Benjamin*, b Nov. 22, 1699.

### 1. JOHN.

JOHN Ives, son of John and Mary Ives, married Mary Gillette, Dec. 6, 1693. He died in Meriden, 1738, ae. 69 yrs. Children: 9 *John*, b Sept. 28, 1694, m Hannah Royce, he d Aug. 4, 1745 ; 10 *Samuel*, b Jan. 5, 1696, m Phebe Royce, Jan. 28, 1720 ; 11 *Benjamin*, b Nov. 22, 1699, m 1st, Rebecca Merriman, 2d, Hannah Moss ; 12 *Abijah*, b March 14, 1700, m Abigail Mix, May, 1730 · 13 *Mary*, b March 10, 1702 ; 14 ∨ *Lazarus*, b Feb. 5, 1703, m Mabel Jerome, Jan. 5, 1730 ; 15 *Daniel*, b Feb. 19, 1706, m Abig  ——; 16 *Hannah*, b Feb. 10, 1708 ; 17 *Abraham*, b Sept. 2, 1709, m Elizabeth Stanley, he d Aug. 4, 1735 ; 18 *Bezaleel*, b July 4, 1712, d Oct. 28, 1714 ; 19 *Bezaleel*, b 1726, m Hannah Merriman.

### 3. JOSEPH.

DEA. JOSEPH IVES, son of John, married Esther Benedict, May 11, 1697, in the south-west part of Wallingford. He married Mamre Munson for his second wife, June 13, 1733 ; he died March 18, 1755, ae. 81 yrs.

Children : 20 *Thomas*, b May 30, 1698 ; 21 *Elizabeth*, b Feb. 6, 1700 ; 22 *Hannah*, b Oct. 13, 1701 ; 23 *Abigail*, b Aug. 27, 1704 ; 24 *Esther*, b Jan. 17, 1706 ; 25 *Joseph*, b Dec. 10, 1709, m Maria —— · 26 *Phineas*, b April 8, 1711 ; 27 *Nathaniel*, b Jan. 15, 1714 ; 28 *Ephraim*, b Jan. 4, 1717 ; 29 *Dinah*, b April 4, 1721.

### 4. GIDEON.

GIDEON IVES, son of John, m Mary Royce, Feb. 20, 1706 ; he was at Wallingford before 1700. She died Oct. 15, 1742, ae. 56 yrs.

Children : 30 *Sarah*, b Sept. 8, 1708 ; 31 *Jotham*, b Sept. 20, 1710, d Sept. 2, 1753 ; 32 ...... , b Aug. 24, 1712 ; 33 *Rhoda*, b Dec. 12, 1714 ; 34 *Martha*, b A... 12 1716 ; 35 *Amasa*, b Nov. 15, 1718 ; 36 *Gideon*, b Sept. 24, 1720 ; 37 *Joel*, b Jan. 13, 1723 ; 38 *Mary*, b Dec. 16, 1724 ; 39 *Susannah*, b May 26, 1727 ; 40 *Esther*, b Oct. 14, 1729.

### 5. NATHANIEL.

NATHANIEL IVES, son of John, married Mary Cook, April 5, 1690, and settled in the south west part of the town ; he died Nov. 6, 1711.

Children : 41 *Caleb*, b Feb. 3, 1700, d Nov. 6, 1710 : 42 *Caleb*; 43 *Stephen*, b March 24, 1704, m Sarah Hart, O t. 25, 1730 ; 44 *Thankful*, b Aug. 4, 1708 ; 45 *Abel*, b May 6, 1711, m Sarah Reed, March 25, 1736.

### 9. JOHN.

JOHN IVES, son of John and Mary Ives, married Hannah Royce, Dec. 18, 1719. He died Aug. 4, 1795. She died Nov. 5, 1770, ae. 70 yrs., at Meriden ; was daughter of Samuel and Hannah Royce.

Children : 46 *Eunice*, b April 20, 1721, d Sept. 11, 1727 ; 47 *Anna*, b April 20, 1725 ; 48 *Eunice*, b Sept. 11, 1727, d Sept. 13, 1727 ; 49.*John*, b July 4, 1729 ; 50 *Titus*, b Feb. 17, 1732 ; 51 *Levi*, b Jan. 19, 1733 ; 52, 53 *Joseph* and *John*, b April 2, 1735 : 54 *Levi*, b July 30, 1736, d Dec. 20, 1739 ; 55 *Jesse*, b April 2, 1738 ; 56 *Joseph*, b June, 1745 ; 57 *Jesse*.

### 10. SAMUEL.

SAMUEL IVES, son of John and Mary Ives, married Phebe Royce, Jan. 28, 1720. He died Aug. 29, 1734.

Children : 58 *Mehitable*, b March 29, 1724 ; 59 *Bezaleel*, b Dec. 14, 1726 ; 60 *Samuel*, b Jan. 28, 1733.

### 11. BENJAMIN.

BENJAMIN, son of John and Hannah Royce, married 1st, Hannah Moss, May 6, 1728.

Children : 61 *Rebecca*, b March 29, 1723, d Dec. 9, 1724 ; 62 *Rebecca*, b Nov. 18, 1725 ; 63 *Benjamin*, b April 15, 1727, d June 19, 1727 : 65 *Benjamin*, b Jan. 26, 1729 ; 66 *Hannah*, b Dec. 18, 1732 ; 67 *Lois*, b March 10, 1734 ; 68 *David*, b July 9, 1736, d Feb 20 1737 : 69 *Ruth*, b Jan 31, 1738 ; 70 *Dorcas*, b Jan. 15, 1740 ; 71 *Levi*, b July 23. 1743 : 72 *Thankful*, b Jan. 1, 1746 . 73 *Levi*, b Sept. 18, 1748.

12. ABIJAH.

ABIJAH IVES, son of John and Hannah Ives, married
⎰ ————. She died May 6, 1753. He died July 17, 1762.
Children : 74 *Moses*, b March 6, 1731 ; 75 *Mary*, b Sept.
22, 1732 ; 76 *Abijah*, b March 24, 1734, d Aug. 16, 1741 ; 77
*Aaron*, b May 26, 1736, d Nov. 24, 1742 ; 78 *Abigail*, b Feb.
14, 1738 ; 79 *Phebe*, b March 23, 1740 ; 80 *Martha*, b May
17, 1742 ; 81 *Prudence*, b June 19, 1744 ; 82 *Aaron*, b April 6,
1746 ; 83 *Anna*, b Feb. 21, 1749, d June 25, 1751.

14. LAZARUS.

LAZARUS IVES, son of John and Mary, married Mabel
Jerome, Jan. 5, 1731.   His 2d wife was Isabella ————.
Children by 1st marriage : 84 *Timothy*, b Oct. 16, 1731 ;
85 *Mary*, b Sept. 10, 1733 ; 86 *Lazarus*, b Nov. 2, 1734.
By 2d marriage : 87 *Ambrose*, b May 22, 1736 ; 88 *Isabella*,
b April 19, 1738 ; 89 *Joshua*, b March 16, 1740 ; 90 *Amasa*,
bap. March 13, 1743 ; 91 *John*, bap. May 17, 1747 ; 92
*Phebe*, bap. Nov. 26, 1752.

15. DANIEL.

DANIEL IVES, son of John and Mary Ives, married Abigail
Parker, Oct. 28, 1738.
Children : 93 *Abigail*, b July 30, 1736 ; 94 *Lydia*, b June
11, 1738 ; 95 *Martha*, b Feb. 29, 1740 ; 96 *Olive*, b Nov. 29,
1741 : 97 *Daniel*, b Jan. 31, 1743 ; 98 *Samuel*, b March 9,
1745 ; 99 *John*, b Feb. 19, 1747 ; 100 *Levi*, b March 29, 1750.

17. ABRAHAM.

ABRAHAM IVES, son of John and Mary Gillette Ives, married Elizabeth Stanley.   She died Aug. 4, 1735, and he
married Barbara Johnson, May 11, 1736.
Children : 101 *Elizabeth*, b July 22, 1735 ; 102 *Sarah*, b
Dec. 23, 1736 ; 103 *Reuben*, b Dec. 11, 1738 ; 104 *Barbara*,
b Oct. 9, 1739 ; 105 *Abraham*, b June 8, 1743 ; 106 *Abraham*,
b March 8, 1746 ; 107 *Barbara*, b Oct. 5, 1747 ; 108 *Ambrose*,
b June 30, 1748, m Lucy ————; 109 *Sarah*, b Oct. 8, 1749.

### 19. BEZALEEL.

CAPT. BEZALEEL IVES, son of John and Mary Gillette Ives, married Hannah Merriman, Feb. 14, 1753. He died Nov. 24, 1798, ae. 72 yrs. She died March 21, 1815, ae. 84 yrs.

Child: 110 *Capt. Samuel*, b Jan. 5, 1752, m Lucretia, dau. of John Ives, d in Meriden, Oct. 18, 1803.

### 20. THOMAS.

THOMAS IVES, son of Dea. Joseph and Esther Ives, married Abigail How, Sept. 2, 1702 ; he married 2d, Rebecca Hotchkiss, Nov. 15, 1720.

Children: 111 *Isaac*, b Nov. 8, 1721 ; 112 *Andrew*, b July 2, 1724; 113 *Lent*, b May 17, 1726, d July 11, 1726 ; 114 *Enos*, b May 14, 1727.

### 25. JOSEPH.

JOSEPH IVES, son of Dea. Joseph and Esther Ives, married Maria ———.

Children: 115 *Mary*, b March 26, 1734; 116 *Lent*, b Sept. 12, 1735 ; 117 *Joseph*, b Jan. 17, 1737.

### 26. PHINEAS.

PHINEAS IVES, son of Dea. Joseph and Esther Ives, married Margery Munson, Jan. 26, 1738.

Child: 118 *Phineas*, b Oct. 31, 1746.

### 27. NATHANIEL.

NATHANIEL IVES, son of Dea. Joseph and Esther Ives, married Zeruah ———. ?

Children: 119 *Mary*, b Sept. 6, 1746 ; 120 *Abigail*, b Oct. 17, 1748 ; 121 *Joseph*, b June 15, 1749 ; 122 *Nathaniel*, b April 23, 1741 ; 123 *Zeruah*, b Dec. 15, 17.. ; 124 *Samuel*, b May 1, 1756.

### 28. EPHRAIM.

EPHRAIM IVES, son of Dea. Joseph and Esther Ives, married Elizabeth Atwater, March 12, 1741.

Children. 125 *Sarah*, b Nov. 19, 1741 ; 126 *Ephraim*, b Jan. 7, 1744 ; 127 *Phineas*, b June 12, 1746 ; 128 *Elnathan*, b Dec. 21, 1748 ; 129 *Elizabeth*, b Nov. 6, 1751 ; 130 *Eunice*, b Feb. 19, 1755.

### 42. CALEB.

CALEB IVES, son of Nathaniel and Mary Ives, married 1st, Mary ———, 2d, Sarah ———, 3d, Elizabeth Plant, Feb. 27, 1733. He died April 13, 1752.

Children: 131 *Nathaniel*, b Jan. 12, 1722 ; 132 *Sarah*, b Aug. 6, 1725, d Feb. 15, 1735. By 3d marriage: 133 *Charles*, b Sept. 5, 1734 ; 134 *Eunice*, b Sept. 13, 1736 ; 135 *Elizabeth*, b Dec. 25, 1738 ; 136 *Olive*, b May 10, 1742 ; 137 *Caleb*, b May 19, 1745 ; 138 *Caleb*, b Feb. 9, 1748 ; 139 *Amos*, b May 1, 1750.

### 43. STEPHEN.

STEPHEN IVES, son of Nathaniel and Mary Ives, married Sarah Hart, Oct. 25, 1730.

Children: 140 *Sarah*, b May 29, 1733 ; 141 *Mary*, b April 16, 1735 ; 142 *Lois*, b Jan. 9, 1737.

### 45. ABEL.

ABEL IVES, son of Nathaniel and Mary Ives, married Sarah Read. March 25, 1736. She died Jan. 1, 1787, æ. 85 years. He died Jan. 31, 1781, æ. 80 years.

Children: 143 *Elizabeth*, b Aug. 30, 1730 ; 144 *Abel*, b Dec. 9, 1736 ; 145 *Anna*, b Dec. 20. 1739 ; 146 *Anna*, b Aug. 1st, 1740 ; 147 *Sarah*, b June 24, 1743 ; 148 *Elizabeth*, b Aug. 30, 1746 ; 149 *Esther*, b June 4, 1751 ; 150 *Lois*, b Mar. 27, 1754.

### 53. JOHN.

JOHN IVES, son of John and Hannah, married Sarah ———.
Child : 151 *Sarah*, b Jan. 12, 1737–

### 56. JOSEPH.

JOSEPH IVES, son of John and Hannah, married Mary ——.
Child : 152 *Anna*. b Dec. 7, 1750.

### 36. GIDEON.

GIDEON, son of Gideon and Mary Royce Ives, married and settled in Wallingford in a house still in existence, and standing a little north and in the rear of the residence of the late Benajah Morse. *d.* *d.* 1, 2 1777

Children: 153 *Amos*, bap. Jan. 5, 1752 ; 154 *Enos*, bap. Dec. 2, 1753 ; 155 *Gideon*, bap May 15, 1757 ; 156 *Jerusha*, bap. Oct. 12, 1755. Moses *bap.* 168 *n . . rd* *k* 7i 3

ELNATHAN.

Children: 157 *Elnathan*, bap. March 21, 1731, m Ann Yale, March 9, 1758 ; 158 *Abigail*, bap. Feb. 11, 1732 ; 159 *Jerusha*, bap. Feb. 28, 1735 ; 160 *Josiah*, bap. March 18, 1738 ; 161 *Reuben*, bap. March 13, 1744 ; 162 *Huldah*, bap. Jan. 17, 1748.

### 31. JOTHAM.

JOTHAM IVES, son of Gideon and Mary Royce Ives, married Abigail Burroughs, Feb. 28, 1736. He died Sept. 2, 1753, ae. 43.

Child : 163 *Zachariah*, b Jan. 31, 1737, settled near the Honey Pot brook in Cheshire. March 9, 1815, ae. 78, nd with his wife Lois was buried in the Episcopal churchyard, Cheshire. Children of Zachariah : 164 Rev. *Reuben*, b in 1761, gradu t Yale in 1785, ordained by Bishop Seabury in 1786, Rector of St. P ter's Church, Cheshire, about thirty ears 1 Oct. 14, 18 , 5 yrs.; 165 *Chauncy*, b in 1762, 1 Nov. 17, 1778, in h. ar ; 166 *Lucy*, m Seth De Wolf ; 67 *d*, a farmer, d in Cheshire ; 168 *Amos H.*, m Lois Cook, d in Cheshire ; 169 *Jesse*, settled on a farm in Meriden.

### 40. JOHN.

JOHN, son o John and Hannah Royce Ives, b July 4, 1729, m 1st, Mary, d. f Dr. Isaac Hall. She d Feb., 1788. d 2nd, Sarah whe d Nov. 24, 1804. He d I b., 1816.

Children : 170 *Lu m* Capt. Samuel Ives ; 171 *John*, m Martha M 1/2 *Isaac* m 1st, Benedict, m 2d, W ry : 173 *Levi*, m Fanny Silliman, June 18, 178 Bishop Ives ; 174 *Sarah*, m Lu ughter 1; 175 *J l* m Hart ; 176 *David*, b ug. 1779, married 1st, Sarah, daughter of

Nathaniel Yale, Oct 28, 1800, m 2d, Rosetta Yale, Oct. 26, 1815; 177 *Titus*, m Ximena Yale; 178 *Eli*, d unmarried; 179 *Anna*, m Noah Foster; 180 *Folly*, m John Hooker; 181 *Meriel*, m —— Clark, and moved to Canada.

### 177. OTHNIEL.

OTHNIEL, son of John and Mary Hall Ives, lived in the east part of Meriden in the house now occupied by Othniel jr.

Children: 182, *Eliza*, b Jan. 17, 1804, m Edwin R. Yale, March 14, 1824, she died March 9, 1846; 183 *Elias*, b Jan. 7, 1806, m Cornelius Pomeroy, Aug. 22, 1827; 184 *Eli*, b Jan. 7, 1809, m Gelina Ann Pomeroy; 185 *Othniel*, b Nov. 26, 1812, m 1st, Julia Cook, 2d, Mary Howard; 186 *Isaac I.*, b. Jan. 21, 1817, m Eloise White of Danbury, 1847, d Oct. 14, 1850; 187 *Sarah Rosetta*, b Nov. 23, 1818, m Harvey Miller; 188 *Juliette*, b May 13, 1822, m Eli Butler, Nov. 10, 1842, d March 1, 1855; 189 *John*, b Dec. 26, 1825, m 1st, Alina Birdsey, Oct. 12, 1847, 2d Wealthy Merwin; 190 *Frederick W.*, b Jan. 27, 1828, m Frances Jones; 191 *Russell Jennings*, b July 17, 1830, m 1st, Flora Ann White, Sept. 15, 1853, 2d, Eliza, daughter of Deacon John Yale.

---

## JOHNSON.[1]

Fitz James came from Normandy with William the Conqueror about the 11th century, and settled in the north of England. It was customary before the Conquest to change a name by adding *son*, as we find *Grimkelson*, *Gamelson*, &c.,

---

1 For collateral branches, see Abbot's Hist. Andover, Mass., 35, 36; Barry's Hist. Framingham, Mass., 303, 304; Bond's Hist. Watertown, Mass., 539-42; Brown's Gen. W. Simsbury Settlers, 88, 89; Chase's Hist. Haverhill, Mass., 276, 634-37; Cope's Record of Cope family of Penn. 52, 115, 116; Cothren's Hist. Woodbury, Ct., 600-2; Deane's Hist. Scituate, Mass., 296, 297; Eaton's Hist. Thomaston, Me., 284, 285; Ellis's Hist. Roxbury, Mass., 122; Fox's Hist. Dunstable, Mass., 246; Gage's Hist. Rowley, Mass., 446; Heraldic Journal, III. (867,) 43-5, 182, 183; Hudson's Hist. Lexington, Mass., 111, 112; Hudson's Hist. Marlborough, Mass., 403-6; Kellogg's Memorial of John White, 37; Leland's Gen. of

in the time of Edward the Confessor, if not earlier. The
Norman *Fitz*, a corruption of *fils*, was used the same way, and
among the conquered Saxons was sometimes adopted in-
stead. Thus, Fitz Harding became *Hardingson;* Fitz Clark,
*Clarkson;* Fitz James, *Jameson;* and Fitz John, *Johnson.*[1]
The Fitz James mentioned above, changed his name to *Johnson*, and had a numerous family. One branch of it went to
Scotland, where the name became quite numerous. Some
of these added a *t* to the name, and thereby made it read
*Johnston*.[2] In the reign of Queen Elizabeth one branch
went to Ireland, and became quite numerous. Sir William
Johnston was of this branch of the family. In later ages the
family were settled in Kingston-on-Hull. At the time of Dr.
Johnson's visit, as agent from Connecticut, to England, he
found the family almost extinct, there being but one, a maiden
lady of thirty years, left in the place. On visiting the churchyard, he found a large number of tomb-stones and monuments
with the name of Johnson inscribed upon them. Three
brothers had gone from Kingston to North America, one of
whom, a clergyman, settled near Boston, and was killed by
the Indians. He left a considerable family, from whom have
descended most of the name in Massachusetts and Rhode
Island. One settled in the western part of Connecticut.
Most of his descendants went to New Jersey, and were

Leland Family, 249, 250; Littell's Passaic Valley Gen., 192–5; Mitchell's
Hist. Bridgewater, Mass., 204–6; Morse's Gen. Reg. Sherborn and Holl-
iston, Mass., 155, 156; N. E. Hist. and Gen. Reg., VIII. 232, 358–62;
Pierce's Hist. Gorham, Me., 180; Poor's Hist. and Gen. Researches, 107;
Savage's Gen. Dict., II. 540–59; Sewall's Hist. Woburn, Mass., 73–6,
165–8, 617, 61ˣ; Ward's Hist. Shrewsbury., Mass., 334–6; Washburn's
Hist. Leicester, Mass., 379, 380.

1 The use of the prefix Fitz, has, with propriety, been revived in modern times. The eldest son of Harris, Earl of Malmsbury, is, by title of
courtesy, Viscount FitzHarris.

2 Most of the persons bearing the name of Johnston in Scotland,
derive the name from the village of Johnston in Renfrewshire. The family
are descended from Hugo de Johnstone, in the time of Alexander II.

numerous.   Robert, the 3d brother, settled in New Haven, Conn., and was one of its first founders.

Children : 1 *John;* 2 *Robert;* 3 *Thomas;* 4 *William*, and possibly others.   ·

Edward Johnson originated from Kent, in England, in a parish within which county, called in his will Heron Hill, i. e. Herne Hill, or Herne, and at a place in that parish called Waterham.   ͺHe probably came to this country in the fleet with Winthrop, in 1630.   He died April 23, 1672.   He left five sons : Edward, George, William, Matthew and John, and two daughters, Susan and Martha.   They have many descendants in Massachusetts.

#### 4. WILLIAM.

WILLIAM JOHNSON, son of Robert, the emigrant, appeared early in New Haven.   He was one of the original subscribers to the compact for the settlement of Wallingford, in 1670, and had assigned him a lot. bounded as follows : " 20 rods wide north and south, 19 rods and 4 ft. east and west, and bounded east by yͤ street, and north by Jeremiah How, and west by Nathan Andrews.''   This piece of land he sold, with consent of his wife Sarah ——, to Isaac Curtis, in 1694.   Mr. Johnson does not appear to have ever had a residence in Wallingford, but was simply a subscriber for the benefit of his heirs who might settle in the place.

#### JACOB.

JACOB JOHNSON, son of William, married Abigail Hitchcock, Dec. 14, 1693.   He built his house on the north side of the road that leads past the residence of the late Col. Thaddeus Cook, and nearly opposite the barn built within the last few years by Chauncey M. Cook.   He was a tailor by trade ; he died July 26. t 19, æ. 80 yrs.   Mrs. Abigail ᵗ ᵗ 9, 726.   He married 2d, Parkis Lindley, 1726.

Children : 5 *Reuben*, b Aug. 27, 1694, m Mary ——; 6 *Isaac*, b Feb. 25, 1696-7, m Sarah Osborne, he d April 23, 1779, ae. 84 ; 7 *Enos*, b 1698, d Jan. 31, 1786, ae. 88 ; 8 *Abigail*, b 1699 ; 9 *Israel;* 10 *Abner*, b Aug. 2, 1702. m

Charity Dayton, Dec 14, 1726; 11 *Caleb*, b 1733-4, d Oct. 15, 1777, ae. 73 yrs., m Rachel Brockett, Jan. 26, 1731, was a merchant in Wallingford ; 12 *Daniel*, b 1709, d Oct. 14, 1780, ae. 72 yrs. ; 13 *Sarah*, b 1710, m Matthew Bellamy, Mar h 31, 1721 ; 14 *Jacob*, b April, 1713, grad. of Yale, was Cong. min., settled at Groton, Conn. ; 15 *Lydia*, d June 3, 1729.

### 5. REUBEN.

REUBEN JOHNSON married Mary Dayton, March 11, 1718, and settled on the place now owned by Almon Doolittle, and built a house there.

Children : 16 *Justus*, b April 6, 1720, d May 12, 1720 ; 17 *Justus*, b March 26, 1721 ; 18 *Ephraim ;* 19 *Rebecca*, b Jul, 14, 1723 ; 20 *Zaccheus ;* and probably others. Ephraim occupied the old house where his father lived ; he took it down and built the one now owned by Mr. Rufus Doolittle. Zaccheus lived in the house that stood opposite the Caleb Dudley house.

### 6. ISAAC.

DEA. ISAAC JOHNSON married Sarah Osborne, March 26, 1723. She died Nov. 16, 1766, ae. 65. He built and occupied the Caleb Dudley house, and lived there ; he died April 29, 1779. ae. 84 yrs.

Children : 21 *Isaac ;* 22 *Abigail*, b Feb. 11, 1722 ; 23 *Joseph*. b Jan. 21, 1725 ; 24 *Sarah*, b Feb. 10, 1729 ; 25 *Isaac*, b June 23, 1731. m Elizabeth —— ; 26 *Esther*, b Nov. 31, 1735 ; 27 *Lois*, b Feb. 15, 1738 ; 28 *Rachel*, b March 6, 1740.

### 7. ENOS.

ENOS JOHNSON lived in the house of his father Jacob.
Child : 29 *Enos*.

### 9. ISRAEL.

ISRAEL JOHNSON married Sarah Miles, Jan. 26, 1732. His house was built by Caleb Johnson, and stood on the lot just east of the present residence of Turhand Cook. He also lived on the place now owned by the heirs of the late Liverius Carrington, in the village. He was a smith of some kind, and a worker of brass, &c., &c. He died 1747, leaving an Estate of £2226 12s.

Children: 30 *Eunice*, b Jan. 13, 1734; 31 *Prudence*, b Jan. 11, 1738; 32 *Caleb*, b Sept. 17, 1739; 33 *Anna*, b Apr. 12, 1736; 34 *Miles*, b Oct. 31, 1741; 35 *Rebecca*, b Aug 4, 1744; 36 *Warren*, b Apr. 17, 1747; 37 *Silas*, b Jan. 21, 1749; 38 *Jacob*, b July 21, 1742.

### 10. ABNER.

CAPT. ABNER JOHNSON married Charity Dayton, Dec. 14, 1726, and lived on the place where afterward his son Hezekiah lived. He died Dec. 28, 1757.

Children: 39 *Dayton*, b Feb. 8, 1728, m Hannah ———; 40 *Hezekiah*, b March 12, 1732; 41 *Abner*, b Aug. 26, 1738, graduated at Yale College and settled in Waterbury; 42 *Anna*, b Apr. 18, 1736; 43 *Charles*, b May 19, 1736; 44 *Jacob*, b July 21, 1742; 45 *Lydia*, m E. Fitch Esq.; 46 *Charity*, b May 19, 1736.

### 15. DANIEL.

DANIEL JOHNSON married Joanna Preston, Dec. 24, 1734, and first occupied a house that stood a little east of where his father Jacob lived. He afterwards removed to the Sam'l Parker place. He died Oct. 14, 1780, ae. 72. She died Jan. 18, 1781.

Children: 47 *Charles*, b Nov. 13, 1735, d at sea, brought to New Haven and buried; 48 *Solomon*, b May 4, 1740, built the John B. Johnson house; 49 *Dan*, b Mar. 24, 1746; 50 *Israel*, b July 8, 1748, settled in Meriden near Hanging Hills; 51 *Justin*, b Mar. 4, 1752; 52 *Mindwell*, b May 19, 1738, m ——— Merrow; 53 *Joanna*, b Apr. 4, 1743, m ——— Lee; 54 *Abigail*, b Dec. 23, 1753; 55 *Joshua*, b July 26, 1757, m ——— Brockett; 56 *Rebecca*, b March 29, 1759, d March 31, 1759; 57 *Rebecca*.

### JOHN.

JOHN JOHNSON, the son of John, the son of Robert, married 1st, Mary Chatterton of New Haven, came to Wallingford before 1710; the date of this marriage is Dec. 12, 1710. She died within that year, and he married Sarah Hitchcock, July 12, 1711. His house occupied the same piece of ground as that now occupied by the dwelling-house of Russell Cook, and formerly known as the Pond house or place. He died July 24, 1748, ae. 64 years. Born 1687.

Children: 58 *Esther*, b May 4, 1712, m Merriman Munson; 59 *Barbara*, b Feb. 5, 1714, m Abraham Ives: 60 *Damaris*, b June 31, 1716; 61 *Daniel*, b Dec. 14, 1717, m Ruth —— , he d in 1761; 62 *Phebe*, b April 28, 1720. m Dydimus Parker; 63 *Jennings*, b Jan. 7, 1722, m Sarah ——, 1745, owned the Pond place; 64 *Ruth*, b Oct. 10, 1723; 65 *Amos*, b March 4, 1726, d during the Revolutionary war near White Plains, N. Y.; 66 *Patience*, b July 28, 1728.

#### 18. EPHRAIM.

EPHRAIM JOHNSON, son of Reuben and Mary Dayton, married Hannah ——.

Children: 67 *Content*, b July 14, 1755; 68 *Luther*, b June 25, 1759.

#### 20. ZACCHEUS.

ZACCHEUS JOHNSON, son of Reuben and Mary Dayton, married Phebe ——.

Children: 69 *Justus*, b Dec. 6. 1756; 70 *Sybil*, b Jan. 27, 1769.

#### 39. DAYTON.

DAYTON JOHNSON, son of Abner and Charity Dayton Johnson, married Hannah ——— She died Jan. 6, 1723, ae. 46 yrs. He died Feb. 19, 1798, ae. 70 yrs.

Children: 71 *Mamre*, b Aug. 15, 1752; 72 *Eliakim*, b Dec. 31, 1753; 73 *Hannah*, b April 28, 1756.

#### 40. HEZEKIAH.

HEZEKIAH JOHNSON, son of Abner and Charity Dayton Johnson, married Ruth ———.

Children: 74 *Caleb*, b July 11, 1759; 75 *George*, b March 11, 1760; 76 *Charles*, b Nov. 21, 1761.

#### 48. SOLOMON.

SOLOMON JOHNSON, son of Daniel and Joanna Preston Johnson, married Mary, daughter of John Barker. She died Sept. 7, 1825. He died April 4, 1779, ae. 59

Child: 77 *John Barker*, married —— Munson, he d in Wallingford.

### 49. DAN.

DAN JOHNSON, son of Daniel and Joanna P. Johnson, married 1st, Rebecca Hitchcock. She died July 25, 1813, ae. 65. His 2d wife, Lucy Dudley, died Jan. 22, 1825, ac. 69. He died Sept. 2, 1830, ae. 85.

Children : 78 *Cephas*, m —— Frost ; 79 *Dan*, b on the old Humiston place, m —— Dudley; 80 *Willard;* 81 *Augustus*, m —— Frost ; 82 *Ransom;* 83 *Laura*, m Amos Curtis of Meriden.

### 50. ISRAEL.

ISRAEL JOHNSON, son of Daniel and Joanna Preston Johnson, settled near the Hanging Hills in the parish of Meriden. Some of the family are still on that farm.

Children: 84 *Andrew;* 85 *Peter;* 86 *William*, still living on the farm, a bachelor ; 87 *Huldah*.

### 63. JENNINGS.

JENNINGS JOHNSON, son of John and Sarah H. Johnson, married Sarah Johnson. He cut the stone cider mill trough that was afterwards Samuel Cook's.

Children: 88 *Sarah*, b June 4, 1749 ; 89 *Damaris*, b June 26, 1753 ; 90 *Stephen*, b March 18, 1754 ; 91 *Esther*, b March 27, 1756 ; 92 *Rachel*, b Oct. 29, 1759.

### 65. AMOS.

AMOS JOHNSON, son of John and Sarah H. Johnson, married Abigail ———.

Children: 93 *Lucy*, b Sept. 11, 1747 ; 94 *Esther*, b Nov. 16, 1749 ; 95 *Sybil*, b Sept. 16, 1751.

----

# JONES.

## THEOPHILUS.

THEOPHILUS and Hannah Jones are the first recorded of that name in Wallingford; he married Hannah Mix, Dec.

26, 1711. She died Nov. 26, 1754. He married 2d, Sarah
Moss, Sept. 22, 1755.

Children : 1 *Nathaniel,* b March 30, 1717, m Sarah Merri
man ; 2 *Theophilus,* b Nov. 1, 1723, m Anna Street ; 3 *Caleb,*
b Nov. 4, 1712, m Mary How, Oct. 6, 1741 ; 4 *Lydia,* b Nov.
9, 1714, m Joseph Moss, Feb. 4, 1735 ; 5 *Hannah,* b Oct. 4,
1720, m Jehiel Merriman, Aug. 5, 1740 ; 6 *Abigail,* b Dec. 28,
1726, m Benjamin Dutton, March 16, 1747 · 7 *Daniel,* b Oct.
28, 1731, d May 1, 1737 : 8 *Nicholas,* b Dec. 17, 1729, m 1st,
Mary ———, 2d, Eunice ———.

## 1. NATHANIEL.

NATHANIEL JONES, son of Theophilus and Hannah, mar
ried Sarah Merriman, June 8, 1743, in Wallingford.

Children · 9 *Abigail,* b Sept. 26, 1744 ; 10 *Daniel,* b Oct.
17, 1748 ; 11 *Sarah,* b Aug. 16, 1750 ; 12 *Eunice,* b Jan. 27,
1752 : 13 *Benjamin,* b Feb. 5, 1757 ; 14 *Amos,* b Aug. 3,
1758 ; 15 *Reuben,* b Oct. 11, 1759, m Sarah ———, he d Oct.
6, 1840 ; 16 *Hannah,* b Feb. 25, 1761.

## 2. THEOPHILUS.

THEOPHILUS JONES, son of Theophilus and Hannah, mar
ried Anna Street, May 24, 1757 · she died Aug. 10, 1811, ae.
76 yrs. He died Oct. 8, 1815, ae. 91 yrs.

Children : 17 *Sarah,* b March 30, 1758, m Elisha Whittelsey ; 18 *Nicholas,* b Nov. 25, 1760, d Aug. 25, 1848, ae. 88 ;
19 *Anna,* b 1772, d Oct. 1, 1776.

## 3. CALEB.

CALEB JONES, son of Theophilus and Hannah, married
Mary How, dau. of Zachariah.

Children : 20 *Anna,* b August 19, 1742 ; 21 *Zachariah H.,*
b Sept. 3, 1744 ; 22 *Hannah,* b Jan. 8, 1746 : 23 *Caleb,* b
Sept. 3, 1748 , 24 *Samuel,* b May 15, 1754.

## 8. NICHOLAS.

NICHOLAS JONES, son of Theophilus and Hannah, married
1st, Mary ———, 2d, Eunice ———. He died April 24, 1760.

Children by 1st marriage : 25 *Charles,* b May 19, 1752 ,

E E F

26 *Patience*, b March 27, 1754. By 2d marriage: 27 *Mary*, b April 30, 1756, d May 6, 1760; 28 *Eunice*, b Feb. 26, 1758, d March 31, 1758; 29 *Mary*, b Feb. 26, 1760.

## 15. REUBEN.

REUBEN, son of Nathaniel and Sarah Jones, married Sarah ——. He lived about a mile east of Wallingford village, where his descendants are still living, 1869. He died Oct. 6, 1843, æ. 84 years. Mrs. Sarah his wife d March 12, 1833, æ. 72 years.

## 18. NICHOLAS.

NICHOLAS JONES, son of Theophilus and Anna Jones, married Elizabeth ——, and remained on the old farm of his fathers, on the west side of the river, where his son Street Jones Esq. now resides. He was a very enterprising and prosperous farmer, and died Aug. 25. 1848, ae 88 yrs., and his wife died Feb. 8, 1845, ae. 81 yrs.

Children: 30 *Betsey*, m Rufus Bradley, Cheshire; 31 *Anna*, b 1785, d Nov. 19, 1861, ae. 76, m Jared Doolittle of North Haven; 32 *Street*, m 1st, —— Eastman, 2d —— Parsons; 33 *Sarah*, m Dea. Ezra Dickerman of Hamden.

## SAMUEL.

SAMUEL JONES was, with his wife Sarah, born in Wallingford. previous to 1721; she died Nov. 9, 1760. He was possibly a brother of Theophilus Jones. He married Esther Pratt, April 12, 1762.

Children: 34 *Mary*, b Dec. 5, 1721; 35 *William*, b May 31, 1722; 36 *Diadate*, b March 15, 1724; 37 *Hester*, b March 9, 1727, m Dennis Covert, March 10, 1758; 38 *Eaton*, b Aug. 26, 1730; 39 *John*, b May 25, 1747; 40 *Daniel*, b March 18, 1745–6.

## KIRTLAND.[1]

The name of Kirtland is of Scotch descent; and among the first 36 settlers of Saybrook in 1635, was John Kirtland.

---

[1] For collateral branches, see Chapman's Gen. of Chapman family, 71

who came from Silver-street, London. He had a son John, who was the father of Daniel, who was the father of the noted missionary, Rev. Samuel Kirkland, who was born in 1701, graduated at Yale in 1720, under the name of Kirtland.

### JOHN.

JOHN KIRTLAND was married to his first wife in Saybrook, March 3, 1703 ; 2d, Lydia Baldwin.

Children : 1 *Hester*, b March 10, 1704 ; 2 *John*, b July 5, 1708, d March, 1787 ; 3 *Temperance*, b Nov. 10, 1710. By 2d marriage : 4 *Elisha*, b July 21, 1718 ; 5 *Elisha*, b Aug. 17, 1719, killed at Fort Edward, March 16, 1756 ; 6 *Lydia*, b Oct. 29, 1721, d June 30, 1770, at Horton, Nova Scotia ; 7 *Parnel*, b Jan. 29, 1724 ; 8 *Constant*, b Jan. 24, 1726, d young ; 9 *Constant*, b Dec. 24, 1727, d at Wallingford ; 10 *Ezra*, b Oct. 11, 1730, d at Saybrook, Aug., 1801 ; 11 *Elizabeth*, b Oct. 13, 1732 ; 12 *Dorothy*, b Sept. 21, 1735.

### 8. CONSTANT.

CONSTANT KIRTLAND, son of John and Lury Kirtland, of Saybrook, married Rachel, daughter of Isaac and ——— Brockett, of Wallingford, April 19, 1753. She was born May 23, 1732, died at Northford, Feb. 17, 1812.

Children : 13 *Isaac*, b March 9, 1754, d Sept. 30, 1807, in Wallingford ; 14 *Turhand*, b Nov. 16, 1755, d Aug. 16, 1854, at Poland, Ohio ; 15 *Mary*, b Dec. 23, 1757, m Samuel Cook, d March 3, 1839 ; 16 *John*, b Dec. 20, 1759, d at Granville, N. Y., May 19, 1843 ; 17 *Billious*, b June 9, 1762, d Oct. 25, 1805, at Wallingford ; 18 *Rachel*, b July 9, 1764, m Col. Edward Barker, d June 13, 1823, at Wallingford ; 19 *Jared*, b Aug. 8, 1766, d April 16, 1831, at Poland, Ohio ; 20 *George*, b July 2, 1769, d April 10, 1793, at Wallingford ; 21 *Lydia*, b Feb. 27, 1772, m Jonathan Fowler, of Guilford, d Aug. 16, 1850, at Poland, Ohio ; 22 *Sarah*, b March 19, 1778, m Capt.

72, 96, 133; Lewis and Newhall's Hist. Lynn, Mass., 154 ; N. E. Hist. and Gen. Reg., XIV. 241-5; Savage's Gen. Dict., III. 31, 32.

Wm. Douglass, and had John, Sarah, Benjamin and William, d Sept. 28, 1842, at Northford.

### 13. ISAAC.

ISAAC KIRTLAND, son of Constant and Rachel Kirtland, married Sarah Ives.

Children : 23 *Delight*, m Peter Hall, of Wallingford ; 24 *Sarah*, m Jehiel Hall, of Wallingford ; 25 *Constant*, m Caroline Carrington, he died in N. Y. ; 26 *Clarissa*.

### 14. TURHAND.

TURHAND KIRTLAND, son of Constant and Rachel Kirtland, married Mary, daughter of Moses Beach, of Wallingford ; she died Nov. 24, 1792. Married 2d, Polly, daughter of Dr. Jared Potter, Jan. 19, 1793 ; she was born in New Haven, Feb. 10, 1772, and died at Poland, Ohio, March 21, 1850.

Children : 27 *Jared Potter*, M. D., b Nov. 10, 1793, m Caroline, dau. of Joshua Atwater, May, 1814 ; 28 *Henry Turhand*, b Nov. 16, 1795, m 1st, Thalia Fitch ; 29 *Mary Beach*, b Sept. 12, 1798, m Richard Hall, d in Poland, Ohio ; 30 *Nancy*, b Jan. 1, 1801, m Elkanah Morse ; 31 *Billious*, b Aug. 29, 1807, m Ruthan A. Frame, resides in Poland, Ohio ; 32 *George*, m Helen, dau. of Randall Cook, of Wallingford.

### 16. JOHN.

JOHN KIRTLAND, son of Constant and Rachel Kirtland, married 1st, Lucy A. Burbank, April 10, 1788 ; she was born Jan. 10, 1771, d Aug. 17, 1728. Married 2d, widow Mary Tyler Benham, dau. of Moses Tyler, and widow of Silas Benham, formerly of Meriden. June 7, 1829. She died April 4, 1836, æ. 57 years.

Children : 33 *Henrietta*, b Jan. 23, 1789, m Wm. Sweetland, of Plattsburg, Nov. 19, 1811 ; 34 *Wm. Henry*, b Jan. 11, 1791, d April 6, 1821 ; 35 *Lucy Fitch*, b April 3, 1793, m Peter J. H. Myers, of Whitehall, Jan. 29, 1815 ; 36 *George Washington*, b April 11, 1795, m Frances Davis, Oct. 6, 1828, he is a lawyer ; 37 *Ann Burbank*, b April 5, 1797, d May 11,

1797. 38 *Ann Burbank*, b April 27, 1798, m Wm. Haile, April 15, 1822, d Nov. 26, 1859 ; 39 *Eliza Cornelia*, b Sept. 17, 1800, m John B. Shaw, Oct. 13, 1825, d July 22, 1842 ; 40 *Lydia Maria*, b March 25, 1802, m S Myers, Oct. 23, 1827, d Nov 9, 1864 ; 41 *Rach'l Brockett*, b Feb. 11, 1804, m Thos. A. Tomlison, May 16, 1833 ; 42 *John*, b Oct. 13, 1805, m Catherine Campbell, Sept. 13, 1836 ; 43 *Isaac Billhous*, b Oct. 14, 1807, m Lucy Sperry, Dec. 8, 1835 ; 44 *Edward*, b July 23, 1810, m Maria Foot, Jan. 24, 1837 : 45 *Jared Turhand*, b Nov. 3, 1816, m Ann T. Palmer, Sept. 6, 1849, d May 19, 1861.

### 17. BILLIOUS.

DR. BILLIOUS KIRTLAND, son of Constant and Rachel Kirtland, married Sarah, daughter of Dr. Jared Potter.

Children : 46 *Eliza*, m Liverius Carrington ; 47 *Polly*, m Col. Russell Hall ; 48 *George*, d 1869 ; 49 *Sarah*, m Liverius Carrington.

### 19. JARED.

JARED KIRTLAND, son of Constant and Rachel Kirtland, married 1st, Lois, daughter of Elisha and Lucretia Stanley Yale, of Wallingford. He removed to Poland, Ohio, in 1802, where he died, April 16, 1831. She died Oct. 3, 1814, ae 38 yrs., at Cookstown, Penn. He left a widow. 2d wife.

Children by 1st marriage : 50 *Lucretia*, b Nov. 2, 1796. m Dr. —— Manning ; 51 *Rachel*, b Dec. 9, 1798, m Col. Caleb Wicks ; 52 *Eliza*, b Aug. 2, 1803, m Philo Cook, of Walling ford ; 53 *Sarah*, b Oct. 8, 1805, m Geo. G. Hills ; 54 *Lois Yale*, b Sept. 21, 1813, m Eli Mygatt, M. D., of Poland, Ohio.

## LEWIS.[1]

### BENJAMIN.

BENJAMIN LEWIS was the first of the name in Wallingford. He came from Stratford in 1670, and had assigned him lot ———, which he sold to Dr. John Hull, who had come

1 For collateral branches, see Alden's Coll. of Am. Epitaphs, v. 68-70 ;

from Derby to settle in the place as a physician. Mr Lewis soon after left Wallingford, and returned to his old home in Stratford.

Children: *Mary*, b Nov. 1, 1671, d in Wallingford; *John*, b Sept. 20, 1672 ; *Mary*, b Nov. 9, 1674 ; *Edmund*, b 1679, m Hannah Beach, May 21, 1702. He d in 1757, æ. 78 yrs.

### EBENEZER.

EBENEZER LEWIS, blacksmith, married Elizabeth Merriman, Dec. 2, 1685, and settled in the eastern part of the town in 1684. He was a son of William Lewis, of Farmington. He died in 1709.

Children : 1 *Hezekiah*, b Oct. 12, 1686, d 1711, m Abigail ———; 2 *Caleb*, b Oct. 15, 1691, m Sarah Cook, Nov. 25, 1713 ; 3 *Selckey*, b Oct. 25, 1693 ; 4 *Elizabeth*, b Oct. 15, 1695 ; 5 *Barnabas*, b Nov. 4, 1697, m Elizabeth ———; 6 *Hannah*, b Oct. 10, 1699, m Samuel Cook Esq.; 7 Dr. *Benjamin*, b Sept. 21, 1701, m Esther Matthews, Nov. 3, 1724 ; 8 *Malachi*, b Oct. 4, 1703, settled in Middletown ; 9 *Agape*, b Jan. 10, 1705.

### 2. CALEB.

CALEB LEWIS, son of Ebenezer and Elizabeth, married Sarah, dau. of Samuel and Hope Cook, Nov. 28, 1713.

Children : 10 *Ichabod*, b April 13, 1714, d March 1, 1718 ; 11 *Caleb*, b Feb. 28, 1717, m Eunice Welton, Jan. 10, 1736 ; 12 *Ichabod*, b 1716, m Sarah ———, 1777 ; 13 *Ebenezer*, b

Andrews' Hist. New Britain, Ct., 160, 161, 167, 277, 306, 307, 332, 354 ; Bradbury's Hist. Kennebunkport, Me., 257 ; Bronson's Hist. Waterbury, Ct., 518, 519 : Caulkins' Hist. New London. Ct., 295, 296 ; Deane's Hist. Scituate, Mass., 303, 304; Fields' Hist. Haddam, Ct., 46; Freeman's Hist. Cape Cod, Mass., I. 614, II. 285, 404, 465, 471, 480, 481, 507, 661, 676; Howe's Hist. Col. Virginia, 181–3 : Hudson's Hist. Lexington, Mass., 281 ; Judd & Boltwood's Hist. Hadley, Mass., 530, 531 ; Lewis & Newhall's Hist. Lynn, Mass., 180–2 ; Meade's Old Churches and Families of Virginia, II. 231–3, 325, 326 ; N. E. Hist. and Gen., Reg., XVII. 162–6 ; Pierce's Hist. Gorham, Me., 181–3 ; Savage's Gen. Dict, III. 84–90 ; Sheppard's Account of Lewis Family ; Smith's Hist. Delaware Co., Penn., 478–80 ; Virginia Hist. Reg., V. 24, 25.

April 14, 1715, m Sarah Avered, June 12, 1735 ; 14 *Hezakiah*, b Oct. 14, 1720, m Abigail Chamberlain, April 25, 1744.

### 5. BARNABAS.

BARNABAS LEWIS, son of Ebenezer and Elizabeth, married Elizabeth ———— ; he died Oct. 1, 1729.

Children : 15 *Lucy*, b March 23, 1724 ; 16 *Lois*, b May 26, 1728.

### 7. BENJAMIN.

DR. BENJAMIN LEWIS, son of Ebenezer and Elizabeth, married Esther Matthews, Nov. 3, 1724.

Children : 17 *Bela*, b Sept. 28, 1724 , 18 *Bela*, b Jan. 10, 1725 ; 19 *Elizabeth*, b March 6, 1727, m Cornelius Johnson, Dec. 9, 1746 ; 20 *Benjamin*, b Jan. 11, 1728, m Mary Malthie, April 3, 1773 ; 21 *Barnabas*, b Aug. 17, 1733, m Rachel Curtis, Feb. 24, 1762 ; 22 *Jesse*, b Jan. 29, 1734 ; 23 *Caleb*, b May 22, 1736, m Lucy Holt, March 13, 1748-9 ; 24 *Samuel*, b March 8, 1741 ; 25 *Esther*, b Oct. 23, 1738, m Nathaniel Douglass, Feb. 1, 1759 ; 26 *Mary*, b Oct. 10, 1743 ; 27 *Mary*, b June 11, 1747 ; 28 *Levi*, b Oct. 19, 1750 ; 29 *Levi*, b Oct. 19, 1751 ; 30 *Lucy*, b March 23, 1754, m Zebulon Frisbie.

### 11. CALEB.

CALEB LEWIS, son of Caleb and Sarah, married Eunice Welton, Jan. 10, 1736.

Children : 31 *Jacob*, b Sept. 7, 1736 ; 32 *Eunice*, b April 6, 1738 ; 33 *Amy*, b Jan. 31, 1715 ; 34 *Caleb*, b April 15, 1752.

### 12. ICHABOD.

ICHABOD LEWIS, son of Caleb and Sarah, married 1st, Sarah ————, 2d, Esther ———— ; she was burned to death in 1812.

Children : 35 *Samuel*, b Oct. 9, 1748, m Esther ————, he d Feb. 8, 1824, ae. 76 ; 36 *Elihu*, b June 10, 1752, settled in Albany, N. Y. ; 37 *Esther*, b July 11, 1756, m John Mansfield ; 38 *Jared*, b May 10, 1761, m Rhoda Munson.

### 13. EBENEZER.

EBENEZER LEWIS, son of Caleb and Sarah Cook Lewis, married Sarah Avered, June 12, 1735.
Children: 39 *Hannah*, b Oct. 9, 1736 ; 40 *Malachi*.

### 14. HEZEKIAH.

HEZEKIAH, son of Caleb and Sarah Cook Lewis, m Abigail Chamberlain, April 28, 1744.
Children: 41 *John*, b May 22, 1745 ; 42 *Ebenezer*, b Oct. 14, 1746 ; 43, 44 *Mary* and *Hezekiah*, b April 27, 1755 ; 45 *Benjamin*, b Nov. 18, 1757 ; 46 *Abel*, b Dec. 25, 1760.

### 18. BELA.

BELA LEWIS, son of Benjamin and Esther Lewis, married Abigail ——.
Child : 47 *Joseph*, b May 6, 1743–4.

### 21. BARNABAS.

BARNABAS LEWIS, son of Dr. Benjamin and Esther Lewis, married Rachel Curtis, Feb. 24, 1762.
Children: 48 *Rachel*, b March 20, 1768 ; 49 *Levi*, b March 5, 1775 ; 50 *Merriam*, b Feb. 14, 1777.

### 35. SAMUEL.

SAMUEL LEWIS, son of Ichabod and Sarah Lewis, died Feb. 8, 1824, ae. 76 yrs. He married Esther ——.
Children: 51 *Sarah*, b Sept. 8, 1773 ; 52 *Esther*, b July 15, 1776, m Ephraim Cook, of Wall. ; 53 *Elihu*, b March 12, 1777.

### 38. JARED.

JARED LEWIS, son of Ichabod and Sarah Lewis, married Rhoda Munson. He died in Wallingford.
Children: 54 *Isaac*, m Esther Beaumont, kept a hotel and store in Meriden ; 55 *Frederick*, m Sinai Hall, of Wallingford.

### JACOB.

JACOB LEWIS married Mary Martin, June 22, 1773.
Children: 56 *Jacob*, b March 10, 1776 ; 57 *Ezekiel*, b July 6, 1777.

ISAAC.

DR. ISAAC LEWIS married Keziah ———. He lived on the west side of the river.

Children: 58 *Charles*, b May 8, 1772 ; 59 *Isaac*, died May 9, 1772, ae. 25 yrs. ; 60 *Keziah*, d May 29, 1772, ae. 10 yrs.

Joseph Lewis of Windsor and Simsbury, had sons, Joseph and John, who had a numerous posterity, who settled in Waterbury.

Joshua Lewis, a Baptist Clergyman, came from Wales about 1780, and settled in Connecticut. His son Joshua, likewise a Baptist Clergyman, resided in Conn. and R. I., where he had a son Joshua, who removed to Saratoga, N. Y., and married a Miss Grinelle, and had a son John, who moved to the neighborhood of Auburn, N. Y., where he married Delecta Barbour, and became a farmer. They had five children, one of whom is Dr. Dio Lewis, of Lexington, Mass., born in 1825.

The name of Lewis is derived from the Welsh *Lluaws*, signifying a multitude. The name of Lewes is derived from the same source, as is also the ancient town of Lewes in Sussex, England.

## MARTIN.[1]

The Martins of Plymouth, Devonshire, were originally from Kent. Capt. John Martin, of this family, went round the world with Drake, in 1577.

The name of Martin was adopted as a surname at a very early date ; and few names have had a greater number to bear them. The earliest record containing it which I have found, is the "roll of Battle Abbey," on which appears the name of Le Sire de S. Martin. Battle Abbey was dedicated to St

---

1 For collateral branches, see Babson's Hist. Gloucester, Mass., 115; Cothren's Hist. Woodbury, Conn., 620–31 ; Eaton's Hist. Thomaston, Me., 324; Hough's Hist. Lewis Co., N. Y., 172–4; Littell's Passaic Valley Gen., 278 ; Savage's Gen. Dict., III. 161–4.

Martin, and the date of its roll is 1066.    The name was not
only numerous on the other side of the water, but has been
the same in this country from its first settlement.    There was
a William Martin at London, England, who assisted the Puritans in preparing for their voyage to Plymouth Rock ; but it
does not appear that he came with them.    John Martyn, afterwards Capt. John Martyn or Martin of Plymouth, and son of
—— Martin of Bridgetown, near Totness, who had male issue
living at that place in 1620, sailed round the globe with Sir
Francis Drake, leaving Plymouth Nov. 15, 1577, and returning
to the same port Sept. 26, 1580.

Christopher Martin with his wife and son Christopher, and
one whose name is not given, came over in the Mayflower in
1620; but they all died during the first winter.    Others of the
name however, came in almost every ship that brought over a
company, for some years.    They settled in various parts of
Massachusetts, Connecticut, Virginia and other colonies.
Anthony died at Middletown, Conn., 1693 ; William of Stratford at Woodbury, Conn.    It is proposed in this to trace only
the Wallingford families.    As early as 1684, John and
Elizabeth Martin made their appearance in Wallingford, and
were married by Mr. Moss, Jan. 15, 1684 ; how long they
continued in the place does not now appear.    In 1735, Robert Martin and his wife Abigail appear to have been in Wallingford.

Children : 1 *James*, b March 3, 1735, m Agnes Crawford,
March 8, 1718 ; 2 *Lydia*, b Oct. 27, 1740 ; 3 *Elizabeth*, b
Sept. 23, 1742 ; 4 *Samuel*, b May 1, 1744 ; 5 *Abigail*, b Dec.
9, 1745 ; 6 *Isaac*, b April 25, 1748 ; 7 *Mary*, b Aug. 30, 1750 ;
8 *John*, b Sept. 27, 1754.

### WOOSTER.

WOOSTER MARTIN came into Wallingford early in the
present century, and settled on the North Farms as a wagon-
maker, and by industry and perseverance accumulated a
very handsome estate.    He was twice married ; 1st, to Althea

Hall, 2d. Delilah Morse, widow of the late Sylvester Hull.
He died in Wallingford, May 4, 1862, ae. 72.

Children by 1st marriage : 9 *Othniel Ives*, m ——, daughter of Augustus Hall, 2d, —— Cook, daughter of Colonel
T. Cook ; 10 ——-——; 11 *Henry*, m —— Hall, daughter of
Joel Hall.   By 2d marriage, 12 ————.

### I. JAMES.

JAMES MARTIN, son of Robert and Abigail, m Agnes
Crawford, March 8, 1758.

Children  13 *Mary*, b Dec. 28, 1758, in Wallingford ;  14
*James*, b Nov. 10, 1761, in Wallingford.

## MANSFIELD.

CAPT. JOHN MANSFIELD married Esther Lewis, and owned
and occupied the house and lot now owned and occupied by
Mr. Harrison, and formerly by John Hiddleson, Esq.  Mr.
Mansfield was in the service of his country during the Revolution, and received for that service a pension from the
government.   He died highly respected.

Children : 1 *Ira*, he settled at Atwater, Ohio ; 2 *Sybil*, 1.
John Hiddleson of Georgetown, S. C. ; both 1 in Wallingford.

## MATTOON.[1]

Philip, son of Philip and Mary Mattoon, was doubtless
the first of the name in Wallingford.  He settled in the
northeast part of the town.

### JOHN.

JOHN MATTOON, son of Philip and Mary, who also settled
in Wallingford, was born in 1682, and married Jerusha Hall,
Oct. 20, 1706.  He died Feb. 10, 1754 ; she died Sept. 28,
1760, ae. 71 yrs.

Children : 1 *Eleazer*, b Dec. 13, 1727, no knowledge of

1 For collateral branches, see Judd & Loltman's Hist. and Gen. Hadley,
Mass., 535, 536 ; Savage's Gen. Dict., III. 177, 178.

him or family; 2 *Gershom*, b Aug. 18, 1730; 3 *Ebenezer*, b
April 4, 1735, m Martha ——, she d Nov. 10, 1802, he d May
27, 1814; 4 *David*; 5 *Isaac*; 6 *Nathaniel*; 7 *Sarah*; 8
*Mary*, m —— Brooks; 9 *John*, d Jan. 6, 1808, ae. 51.

### 4. DAVID.

DAVID MATTOON m Phebe Curtis, Oct., 5, 1742.
Children: 10 *Charles*, b Dec 12, 1744; 11 *Phebe*, b Jan.
15, 1748; 12 *Eunice*, b March 19, 1751.

### 6. NATHANIEL.

NATHANIEL MATTOON married Mary Curtis, Feb. 17, 1745.
Children: 13 *Joel*, b Jan. 24, 1749; 14 *Seth*, b March 21,
1753.

---

# MERRIMAN.

This name is often spelled on the old records Merriam and
Merriman, both names referring to the same person.  Joseph
Merriam took the freeman's oath in Lexington, Mass., March
14, 1638.  He died Jan. 1, 1641, and some of his descendants assumed the name of, or were recorded as Merriman.

### NATHANIEL.

CAPT. NATHANIEL MERRIMAN was one of the original settlers in Wallingford in 1670.  Lots Nos. 1 and 2 were set him
on the north, west and east corners of the south cross street,
also No. 2 adjoining the west lot.  These corner lots are now
owned by Peter Whittelsey, Esq., and Rev. Edgar J. Doolittle.
These extra lots were set to him in consideration of some out
land which the committee had given out to other parties to
his damage.  Capt. Merriman built his house on the lot
where Mr. Whittelsey's house now stands, but a short distance
to the west of it.  A large elm tree stands nearly in front
of the old site.  He died Feb. 13, 1693, ae. 80 years.

Children: 1 *John*, d Sept. 26, 1651; 2 *Hannah*, b May 16,
1651; 3 *Abigail*, b April 18, 1654; 4 *Mamre*, b July 12, 1657,
m Samuel Munson; 5 *John*, b Feb. 28, 1659, m 1st, Hannah

Lines, 2d. Mary Doolittle , 6 *Samuel*, b Sept 29, 1662. m 1st, Anna — —, 2d, Elizabeth Peck ; 7 *Caleb*, b May, 1665, m Mary Preston ; 8 *Moses*, b 1667 ; 9 *Elizabeth*, b Sept. 14. 1669, m Ebenezer Lewis, Dec. 2, 1685.

## 5. JOHN.

JOHN MERRIMAN married 1st, Hannah Lines of New Haven, March 28, 1682. He married 2d, Mary Doolittle, and after her decease married Elizabeth Peck, March 20, 1690.

Children: 10 *Esther*, b Jan. 24, 1683 ; 11 *Abigail*, b Feb 1, 1685 ; 12 *George*, b July 14, 1688, m Susanna Abernathy By 3d marriage : 13 *John*, b Oct 16, 1691 ; 14 *Israel*, b June 23, 1693, m Comfort Benham, June 23. 1715 ; 15 *Sarah*, b Feb. 17, 1702 16, 17 *Elizabeth* and *Susanna*, b July 20, 1703 ; 18 *Mercy*, b March 15, 1705 ; 19 *Caleb*, b April 25, 1707, m Ruth ——.

## 6. SAMUEL.

SAMUEL MERRIMAN married 1st, Anna ——, 2d, Elizabeth Peck.

Children. 20 *Nathaniel*, b May 22, 1687 ; 21 *Nathaniel*, b March 16, 1690 ; 22 *Theophilus*, b April 28, 1692, m Mary —— May 6, 1714 , 23 *Samuel*, b Dec. 19, 1694, m Sarah ——.

## 7. CALEB.

CALEB MERRIMAN married Mary Pinton (or atron) ——. He died July 9, 1703. Estate £439

Children : 24 *Moses*, b Oct. 31. 1691 ; 25 *Elizabeth*, b May 4, 1691 ; 26 *Eliasaph*, b May 21, 1695, m Abigail Hall, Dec 10, 1719 ; 27 *Phebe*, b June 17. 1697 ; 28 *Hannah*, b Sept. 10, 648 ; 29 *Phebe*, b Sept. 16, 1699, m Waitstill Munson, Dec 10, 1719 , 30 *Lydia*, b Dec. 3. 1701 ; 31 *Lydia*, b Nov. 12, 1702.

## 8. MOSES.

MOSES MERRIMAN m Martha ——.

Children : 32 *John*, b Oct. 28. 1713 ; 33 *Esther*, b Nov. 11, 1716, d April 3d, 1734 ; 34 *Phebe*, b March 27. 1720 ; 35

*Benjamin,* b Jan. 21, 1722 ; 36 *Martha,* b Dec. 30, 1723 ; 37 *Mary,* b Feb. 26, 1726 ; 38 *Lent,* b May 25, 1731.

### 12. GEORGE.

GEORGE MERRIMAN married 1st, Susannah Abernathy, June 28, 1713 ; 2d, Ruth ——.
Children : 39 *Nathan,* b Nov. 30, 1713 ; 40 *Nathan,* b July 16, 1717 : 41 *Lois,* b Nov. 10, 1720; 42 *Susannah,* b Sept. 13, 1723 ; 43 *Daniel,* b Feb. 22, 1727 ; 44 *Molly,* b July 6, 1730 ; 45 *Sarah,* b May 25, 1733.

### 14. ISRAEL.

ISRAEL MERRIMAN m Comfort Benham, June 23, 1715.
Children : 46 *Joseph,* b Aug. 20, 1716 ; 47 *Comfort,* b Oct. 3, 1720 ; 48 *Jelin,* b Feb 16, 1724; 49 *Israel,* b Nov. 30, 1732 ; 50 *Elizabeth,* b March 11, 1734.

### 19. CALEB.

CALEB MERRIMAN married Ruth ——, Aug. 31, 1732. She died before him.   He died of small pox, June 2, 1770.
Children : 51 *Sarah,* b May 25, 1733 ; 52 *George,* b 1736, d Sept. 24, 1787 ; 53 *Elizabeth,* b Nov. 24, 1739 ; 54 *Ruth,* b Nov. 1, 1741 ; 55 *Anna,* d July 4, 1751 ; 56 *Jerusha,* d July 5, 1751 ; 57 *Abigail,* d Oct. 3, 1761 ; 58 *Caleb,* b Feb. 26, 1751, d Oct. 9, 1751.

### 21. NATHANIEL.

NATHANIEL MERRIMAN married Mehitable ——.
Children : 59 *Samuel,* b May 3, 1712 ; 60 *David,* b Feb. 11, 1715 ; 61 *Thankful,* b May 31, 1717 ; 62 *Nathaniel,* b May 31, 1720, m Prudence Austin, Dec. 19, 1743.

### 22. THEOPHILUS.

THEOPHILUS MERRIMAN married Mary ——.
Children : 63 *Anna,* b Sept. 1, 1715 ; 64 *Theophilus,* b Aug. 20, 1717.

### 23. SAMUEL.

SAMUEL MERRIMAN married Sarah Wilcher.
Children : 65 *Samuel,* b Aug. 24, 1728 ; 66 *Samuel,* b Oct. 14, 1734 ; 67 *Catherine,* b Dec. 28, 1736 ; 68 *Nicholas,* b Feb.

17. 1737 ; 69 *Anna*, b March 10, 1737 ; 70 *Samuel*, b Feb. 28, 1739 ; 71 *Sarah*, b Jan. 28, 1742 ; 72 *Stephen*, b March 25, 1743 ; 73 *Miles*, b June 11, 1744 ; 74 *Hannah*, b Dec. 1, 1750 ; 75 *Eunice*, b Aug. 21, 1753.

### 26. ELIASAPH.

ELIASAPH MERRIMAN married Abigail Hall ; she with her daughter Abigail were killed by lightning, Aug. 4, 1758 He died Aug. 14, 1758, ten days after.

Children : 76 *Eunice*, b Oct. 7, 1720, d : 77 *Eunice*, b Jan. 12, 1722, d : 78 *Eunice* b Nov. 24, 1722 ; 79 *Sarah*, b Nov. 18, 1723 ; 80 *Titus*, b Aug 28, 1727 ; 81 *Caleb*, b Sept. 3, 1729 ; 82 *Amasa*, b about 1730 ; 83 *Elizabeth*, b July 27, 1732 ; 84 *Esther*, b Dec. 2, 1734 ; 85 *Abigail*, killed by lightning, Aug. 4, 1758 ; 86 *Elizabeth*.

### 38. LENT.

LENT MERRIMAN married Catherine ———.

Children : 87 *Luce*, b Feb. 14, 1755 ; 88 *Joel*, b Sept. 11, 1756 ; 89 *Mamre*, b June 30, 1758 ; 90 *Katherine*, b May 23, 1760 ; 91 *Moses*, b Oct. 30, 1761.

### 46. JOSEPH.

JOSEPH MERRIMAN married Deborah ———.

Children : 92 *Joseph*, b Dec. 20, 1732 ; 93 *Susannah*, b Sept. 9, 1745.

### AMASA.

AMASA and Sarah Merriman, of Wallingford.

Children. 94 *Charles*, b Aug. 20, 1762. He enlisted into the army of the Revolution as a drummer, in 1776, became drum major, and served through the war. He married Anna Punderson, of New Haven, May 16, 1784, and settled in Watertown, where he commenced the business of tailor, which he was compelled to relinquish in consequence of ill health. After having "ridden post" from New Haven to Suffield, Conn., four years, and made a voyage to the West Indies, he commenced the mercantile business in Watertown, in which he continued until 1829. He died Aug. 26, 1829, leaving ten children

## MILES.[1]

John Miles was in New England in 1630, and was made free in 1732.

### THOMAS.

MAJ. THOMAS MILES of New Haven, married Abigail Mix, daughter of Thomas Mix. Sept. 7, 1709. His father, Richard Miles, died in New Haven in 166?. and his mother, Mrs. Katherine Miles, died in Wallingford, Jan. 27, 1683, æ. 95 yrs. Anna, the wife of Rev. Mr. Samuel Street, was their daughter. The tomb-stone of Mrs. Catherine Miles is still in the cemetery at Wallingford. Maj. Thomas Miles died Oct. 5, 1741.

Children: 1 *John*, b Jan. 14. 1711, m Sarah ——; 2 *James*, b Dec. 18, 1713, m Phebe Thompson, Jan. 10, 1733; 3 *Elizabeth*, b Sept. 18, 1718, m Daniel Clark, she d April 17, 1755; 4 *Mary*, b Nov. 19, 1719, m Josiah Stanley, March 14, 1739; 5 *Martha*, b Nov. 5, 1723; 6 *Eunice*, b Dec. 6, 1726, m Stephen Culver, Feb. 12, 1745-6; 7 *Abigail*, b April 2, 1727.

### 1. JOHN.

JOHN and Sarah Miles. He died Nov. 18, 1760. She died Nov. 25, 1760.

Children: 8 *Samuel*, b Dec. 18, 1714; 9 *Sarah*, b Aug. 28, 1717; 10 *John*, b Oct. 4, 1723; 11 *Esther*, b Aug. 26, 1726; 12 *Mehitable*, May 2, 1741, she died May 2, 1757.

### 2. JAMES.

CAPT. JAMES and Phebe Miles of Wallingford. He was Town Clerk of his native place for a great number of years. She died Oct. 23, 1756.

Children: 13 *Thomas*, b Oct. 14, 1733; 14, 15 *Samuel*, and *Anna*, b Mar. 24, 1735; 16 *Joseph*, b March 7, 1737; 17

1 For collateral branches, see Allen's Hist. Worcester, Mass. Association, 165, 166; Hill's Hist. Mason, N. H., 205; Miles' Gen. of Miles Family; Savage's Gen. Dict., III. 206–8; Smith's Hist. Delaware Co., Penn., 485; Ward's Hist. Shrewsbury, Mass., 368–70; Westminster, Mass. Centennial Celebration, 30.

*John*, b Nov. 24, 1739; 18 *Catherine*, b Nov. 23, 1741;
19 *James*, b Feb. 19, 1743-4; 20 *Abigail*, b Nov. 9, 1746; 21
*Sarah*, b May 20, 1749; 22 *George*, b April 22, 1752.

### 8. SAMUEL.

SAMUEL MILES m Phebe Tuttle, Nov. 29, 1736, and re
sided in Wallingford

Children: 21 *Joseph*, b March 7, 1737; 22 *Amos*, b Feb.
6, 1738; 23 *Ruth*, b May 24, 1739, m Stephen Hall, April 21,
1762; 24 *Mabel*, b Oct. 1, 1741, m John McCleave; 25
*Martha*, b June 28, 1743; 26 *Joel*, b Nov. 18, 1749; 27
*Isaac*, b Aug, 25, 1752; 28 *Samuel*, b Aug. 12, 1757

### 10. JOHN.

JOHN MILES m Martha Curtis, Nov. 14, 1743, and resided
in Wallingford.

Children: 29 *John*, b Aug. 31, 1745; 30 *Simeon*, b April 4,
1746; 31 *Sarah*, b Sept. 30, 1749.

### DANIEL.

DANIEL MILES married Anna ———, of Wallingford.
He died Dec. 12, 1756.

Children: 32 *Samuel*, b Oct. 9, 1746; 33 *Charles*, b Feb.
8, 1748; 34 *Susannah*, b Sept. 6, 1750; 35 *Mary*, b Oct. 19,
1753; 36 *Anna*, b April 4, 1756.

### 22. GEORGE.

GEORGE MILES son of Capt. James Miles, came to Wall
ingford some thirty-five or forty years since, and remained
there, until his decease, a single man, greatly advanced in
life. He died Feb. 13, 1838, ae. 86 years. He was the last
of the male members of the Miles family in Wallingford.

## MIX.[1]

### JOHN.

JOHN MIX was the first of the name who was in Walling
ford. He had assigned to him in 1670 lot No. 12, the same

---

1 For collateral branches, see Savage's Gen Dict, III. 222, 223.

F F F

on which now (1870) stand the houses of Joel Peck, deceased, and the heirs of the late Hon. Edgar Atwater. He was the eldest son of Thomas Mix Sen., of New Haven. Daniel, his brother, also settled in Wallingford, married Ruth 〜〜〜〜, May 2, 1678.

Children: 1 *Thomas*, b March 25, 1678-9, m Deborah Royce, March 2, 1705 ; 2 *Lydia*, b July 31, 1682, m Ebenezer Hall ; 3 *Daniel*, b June 1, 1685, m Lydia Erwin, May 24, 1732.

### 1. THOMAS.

THOMAS MIX, son of Daniel and Ruth, married Deborah Royce, daughter of Samuel and Hannah Royce ; she died Dec. 15, 1738.

Children: 4 *Abigail*, b Jan. 29. 1706 ; 5 *Josiah*, b Nov. 20. 1707 ; 6 *Thomas*, b Nov. 27, 1709 ; 7 *Daniel*, b April 27, 1712 ; 8 *Deborah*, b March 17, 1744 ; 9, 10 *Hannah* and *Sarah*, b Jan. 30. 1716 ; 11 *Stephen*, b May 8, 1718, m Rebecca —— ; 12 *Enos*, b May 29, 1720 ; 13 *Sarah*, b April 1, 1723, m Christopher Robinson, April 14, 1757 ; 14 *Martha*, b July 18, 1725 ; 15 *Timothy*, b Dec. 28. 1727 ; 16 *Enos*, b May 29, 1730, d Dec. 20, 1737.

### 3. DANIEL.

DANIEL MIX married Lydia Erwin, May 28, 1712. He was a son of Daniel and Ruth Mix.

Children: 17 *Benjamin*, b Aug. 13. 1713 ; 18 *Lydia*, b Sept. 21, 1716 ; 19 *Ruth*, b Oct. 5, 1718 ; 20 *Benjamin*, b Dec. 11, 1720 ; 21 *Isaac*, b June 7, 1723, d ; 22 *Isaac*, b Nov. 5, 1727 ; 23 *Daniel*, b Nov. 31, 1730 ; 24 *Jeremiah*, b Nov. 12, 1737.

### 5. JOSIAH.

JOSIAH MIX, son of Thomas and Deborah Mix, married 1st. Sybil Holt; she d Aug. 5, 1731. He married 2d, Abigail Porter, Dec. 20, 1742.

Children: 25 *Jesse*, b Oct. 22, 1731, m Deborah Parker; 26 *Eldad*, b Oct. 4, 1733 ; 27 *Titus*, b Dec. 4, 1735, d ; 28 *Sybil*, b April 5, 1738. By 2d marriage: 29 *Titus*, b Dec. 4, 1745.

## 6. THOMAS.

THOMAS MIX, son of Thomas and Deborah Mix, married Ruth ——.

Children: 30 *Samuel*, b Feb. 3, 1740 , 31 *Thomas*, b Aug. 12, 1745 : 32 *Enos*, b Feb. 2, 1747 : 33 *John*, b Aug. 23, 1750, d in Wallingford : 34 *Amos*, b Dec. 2, 1753.

## 11. STEPHEN.

STEPHEN MIX married Rebecca ——.

Children: 35 *Rebecca*, b May 13, 1747 : 36 *Stephen*, b Nov. 2, 1748 ; 37 *Sarah*, b Dec. 31, 1749.

## 25. JESSE.

JESSE MIX married Deborah Parker, Nov. 22, 1753.

Children: 38 *Ruth*, b Sept. 15, 1754 : 39 *Josiah*, b Aug. 22, 1755. m 1st, Mindwell Royce, 2d, Keziah Royce.

## THEOPHILUS.

THEOPHILUS and Damaris Mix were married Jan. 17, 1729. He died in Meriden July 3, 1750, ae. 53 years.

Children: 40 *Moses*, b Jan. 3, 1730, died 1 ch 14, 1750 ; 41 *Mary*, b April 3, 1731 ; 42 *Sarah*, b Aug. 26, 1732 ; 43 *Mary*, b Aug. 4, 1734, d ; 44 *Mary*, b Aug., 1735. d Sept. 3, 1735 : 45 *Eber*.

## 39. JOSIAH.

JOSIAH MIX was twice married, 1st to Mindwell Royce, Aug. 17, 1777. She died in 1802. He married he·sister Keziah Royce, Jan. 2, 1803. He formerly owned and occu pied the house, late the residence of Harley Morse, at Yalesville. In 1816, he, with his family, removed to Ohio and settled at Atwater. He died at Rootstown, Ohio, in his 91st year. His wife Keziah died at Atwater, Ohio, ae. 82 yrs.

Children: 46 *James*, b June 7, 1778, m Miss Curtis : 47 *Josiah*, b Sept. 15, 1779, m Sarah Mattoon, d Feb. 4, 1867 : 48 *Sarah*, b June 7, 1782, m Joseph Rice, d in 1818 ; 49 *Mindwell*, b June 1, 1784 ; 50 *Rebecca*, b May 1, 1787, m 1st, Joseph Hull, 2d, Joseph Parker, d in Wallingford ; 51 *Stephen*, b Feb. 14, 1790, m Polly Owens, d Jan. 10, 1832 · 52

*Amanda*, b April 13, 1792, m Earl Hawkins, Oct. 24, 1823; 53 *Julia*, d June 10, 1801 ; 54 *Phebe*, b Feb. 7, 1799, m James Webber, March 1, 1827, is living in Atwater, Ohio. By 2d marriage : 55 *Julia*, b Feb. 4, 1804, m Chauncey Andrews ; 56 *Emeline*, b March 14, 1805, m John B. Whittelsey, Oct. 15, 1827, d Sept. 19, 1863 ; 57 *Samuel*, b Feb. 23, 1807, m Jàne Case, is living at Rootstown, Ohio ; 58 *Lucy*, b Feb. 8, 1809, m Dr. L. W. Trask.

### JOHN.

JOHN MIX married Elizabeth ———, and settled on the North Farms in Wallingford, as a blacksmith. He raised a large family of sons who learned their trades of him. He died Oct. 3, 1821, ae. 75 years. Mrs. Elizabeth died Sept. 7, 1845, ae. 81 years.

Children : 59 *John*, b 1784, m Olive Ives ; 60 *Titus*, b 1787, d Aug. 31, 1833, ae. 46 ; 61 *Eli*, b 1802, d Dec. 16, 1848, ae. 46 ; 62 *Elias*, d in Prospect ; 63 *William*, died at Cheshire, was a miller at Hough's Mills ; 64 *Thomas*, m a daughter of Abel Sanford.

### 59. JOHN.

JOHN MIX married Olive Ives of Wallingford. He was a blacksmith at Yalesville or Tyler's Mills, for several years. He died April 5, 1849, ae. 65 years.

Children : 65 *Joel ;* 66 *John*, m ——— Barnes, residence Cheshire ; 67 *Butler*, d unmarried at Prospect ; 68 *Garry I.*, is a manufacturer at Yalesville, Conn. ; 69 *William*, resides in New Haven ; 70 *Erwin*, resides in Cheshire ; 71 *Olive :* 72 *Sylvia*, m William Haywood, and resides at Brooklyn, N. Y.

### 60. TITUS.

TITUS MIX, son of John and Elizabeth, was a blacksmith in the southeastern part of Meriden, and was at one time celebrated as a plough-maker.

Child : 73 *Titus Mix*, lives in Cheshire.

### DANIEL.

DANIEL and Ruth Mix were in Wallingford as early as 1667. The name of his 2d wife was Deborah ———.

Children by 1st marriage : 74 *Thomas*, b March 25, 1678 ; 75 *Lydia*, b July 22, 1682 ; 76 *Daniel*, b July 1, 1684. m Lydia ——, May 28, 1712. By 2d marriage, 77 *Daniel*, b April 2, 1702 ; 78 *Abigail*, b Jan. 20, 1706 ; 79 *Josiah*, b Nov. 20, 1707 ; 80 *Thomas*, b Nov. 27, 1709.

### 76. DANIEL.

DANIEL MIX m Lydia ——.

Children : 81 *Deborah*, b March 17, 1714 ; 82 *Hannah*, b Jan. 20, 1716 ; 83 *Enos*, b March 29, 1720, d Dec. 20, 1737 ; 84 *Sarah*, b April 21, 1723 ; 85 *Isaac*, b Nov. 5, 1724 ; 86 *Martha*, b July 18, 1725 ; 87 *Joanna*, b March 13, 1726 , 88 *Timothy*, b Dec. 28, 1727 ; 89 *Daniel*, b March 31, 1730.

### THEOPHILUS.

THEOPHILUS MIX married Damaris ——.

Children : 90 *Moses*, b Jan. 3, 1730 ; 91 *Mary*, b Aug. 4 1733 ; 92 *Eben*, b Sept. 3, 1735.

## MOSS [1]

### JOHN.

JOHN MOSS, the ancestor of all who bear the name in these parts, was in New Haven as early as 1615, and perhaps before that date. He was a prominent man there, frequently representing the people in the General Court. As early as 1667, we find him in what is now Wallingford, perambulating the country in that region for the purpose of settling a village there. In 1670, at the age of 67 years, we find him exerting himself before the General Court at Hartford, to procure an act of incorporation, changing the name of the village to that of Wallingford, which was carried into effect the 12th day of May, 1670. At this time he was a member of the General Court from New Haven. Afterwards he was frequently a member of said Court, as a representative from Wallingford. He was a very active member of the company,

[1] For collateral branches, see Savage's Gen. Dict., III. 246, 247.

and a leader among the settlers, who were constantly filling up the place.

He was at first located on a lot at the south end of the village, a short distance below the present residence of Constant Webb, and adjoining his friends, John Brockett and Samuel Brown, to whom was assigned the lot on which the Beach house now stands. Failing to settle on it within the time limited, his title was forfeited, and the committee to whom such matters were referred, gave it to John Moss Jr., and the same remained in the possession of his heirs and descendants, until the death of the late Ebenezer Morse.

John Moss sen. died in 1707, at the advanced age of 103 years.

His sons, 1 *Mercy*, and 2 *John*, were among the early settlers of Wallingford.

### MERCY.

MERCY MOSS, son of John the emigrant, married and settled in New Haven; was for a time in Wallingford.

Child: 3 *John*, b Jan. 7, 1677.

### 2. JOHN.

JOHN MOSS Jr., son of John the emigrant, m Martha Lathrop, 1677. She died Sept. 21, 1719, and he died March 31, 1717. He settled on the Moses Y. Beach lot, and built a house upon it, in which I suppose he died.

Children: 4 *Mary*, b Jan. 7, 1677; 5 *Esther*, b Jan. 5, 1678; 6 Dea. *Samuel*, b Nov. 18, 1680, m Susannah Hall, Dec. 15, 1703; 7 *John*, b Nov. 10, 1682, m Elizabeth Hall, Feb. 25, 1708; 8 *Martha*, b Dec. 22, 1684; 9 *Solomon*, b July 9, 1690, m Ruth Peck, Jan. 28, 1714; 10 *Isaac*, b July 6, 1692, m Hannah Royce, May 2, 1717; 11 *Mary*, b July 23, 1694, m Solomon Munson, June 28, 1714; 12 *Israel*, b Dec. 31, 1696, m Lydia ———; 13 *Benjamin*, b Feb. 10, 1702, m Abigail ———.

### 6. SAMUEL.

DEA. SAMUEL MOSS, son of John and Martha Lathrop Moss, married Susannah Hall, Dec 15, 1703. He died July

29, 1765, æ. 85 yrs., she died March 4, 1766, æ. 83 yrs. Children: 14 *Theophilus*, b Oct. 24, 1704; 11 Ruth Bunny · 15 *Martha*, b June 7, 1706; 16 *Susannah*, b Dec. 5, 1708; 17 *Samuel*, b April 4, 1711, m Hannah ———; 18 *Esther*, b July 30, 1713; 19 *Isaac*, b Dec. 5, 1715, m Hannah ———, 2d, Keziah Bowers; 20 *Sarah*, b Feb. 10, 1718; 21 *Isaiah*, b Oct. 16, 1720; 22 *Bethiah*, b March 2, 1723.

### 7. JOHN

JOHN Moss, son of John and Martha Moss, married Elizabeth ____. She died Jan. 27, 1754, he died May 14, 1755.

Children: 23 *Hannah*, b Nov. 11, 1709; 24 *Elizabeth*, b Oct. 6, 1710; 25 *Samuel*, b April 4, 1711, m Mary ———; 26 *Joseph*, b Feb. 9, 1714, m Lydia Jones, Feb. 4, 1735; 27 *Mary*, b April 22, 1716; 28 *John*, b Nov. 14, 1720; 29 *Levi*, b Sept. 30, 1722; 30 *Eunice*, b Feb. 6, 1728. 31 *Thankful*, b April 26, 1729.

### 9. SOLOMON.

SOLOMON Moss, son of John and Martha Moss married Ruth Peck. She died March 29, 1728. He married Sarah ————.

Children by 1st marriage: 32 *Martha*, b June 7, 1706; 33 *Susannah*, b Dec. 5, 1708; 34 *Daniel*, b May 15, 1716; 35 *David*, b Oct. 28, 1717, m Mary Watts, Oct. 3, 1737; 36 *Abigail*, b March 7, 1718; 37 *Solomon*, b Oct. 31, 1719, m Sarah ————; 38 *Ruth*, b Aug. 5, 1721; 39 *Martha*, b Sept. 30, 1723; 40 *Abigail*, b July 9, 1729. Children by 2d marriage: 41 *Lois*, b Jan. 7, 1730; 42 *Jonathan*, b Feb. 8, 1731; 43 *Sarah*, b Nov. 28, 1734.

### 10. ISAAC.

ISAAC Moss, son of John and Martha Moss, married Hannah Royce, May 2, 1717.

Children: 44 *Heman*, b July 21, 1718, d May 9, 1721; 45 *Hannah*, b March 7, 1722; 46 *Orzel;* 47 *Jesse*, b March 10, 1729; 48 *Elihu*, b May 25, 1731; 49 *Mehitable*, b May 9, 1735.

### 12. ISRAEL.

ISRAEL MOSS, son of John and Martha, married Lydia ——.
Children : 50 *Nathaniel*, b Dec. 19, 1722 ; 51 *Isaiah*, b Apr.
10, 1725 ; *Lydia*, b March, 1727 ; 53 *Isaiah*, b Dec. 15, 1731 ;
54 *Keziah*, b Dec. 9, 1734, d Jan. 20, 1737 ; 55 *Asahel*, b
Feb. 22, 1737 : 56 *Keziah*, b July 27, 1739.

### 13. BENJAMIN.

BENJAMIN Moss, son of John and Martha, married Abi-
gail ——.
Children : 57 *Abigail*, b Dec. 28, 1728 ; 58 *Benjamin*, b
Nov. 27, 1729 ; 59 *Barnabas*, b Dec. 27, 1733 : 60 *Timothy*, b
March 17, 1736 ; 61 *Abigail*, b Sept. 30, 1740 ; 62 *Joseph*, b
Dec. 17, 1742 ; 63 *Martha*, b Jan. 27, 1744-5 ; 64 *Eunice*, b
Aug. 12, 1747.

### 17. SAMUEL.

SAMUEL Moss, son of Samuel and Susannah Moss, married 1st, Mary Judd, May 28, 1734 ; she died, and he married
2d, Hannah ——, Jan. 28, 1748.
Children : 65 *Susannah*, b Oct. 20, 1735, d Feb. 1, 1747 :
66 *Samuel*, b March 31, 1739 ; 67 *Joshua*, b Jan. 18, 1742 ;
68 *Sarah*, b April 30, 1745 ; 69 *Thomas*, b Jan. 21, 1747 ; 70
*Thomas*, b July 27, 1751 ; 71 *Mary*, b April 9, 1753 ; 72
*Martha*, b May 10, 1755 ; 73 *Bethia*, b May 21, 1757.

### 19. ISAAC.

ISAAC Moss, son of Samuel and Susannah, married Hannah
——. She died March 31, 1731, ae. 40. He married 2d,
Keziah Bowers, Oct. 4, 1736.
Children : 74 *Ebenezer*, b June 15, 1723 ; 75 *Heman*, b Jan.
2, 1727 ; 76 Capt. *Jesse*, b Dec. 16, 1729, d at Cheshire,
March 20, 1793, ae. 64 years ; 77 *Mehitable*, d May 9, 1735 ;
78 *Isaac*, b Nov. 5, 1734. By 2d marriage : 79 *Keziah*, b March
18, 1746.

### 26. JOSEPH.

JOSEPH Moss, son of John and Elizabeth, married Lydia
Jones, Feb. 4, 1735. He died at Cheshire, July 10, 1775, ae.
62 yrs.

Children: 80 *Rhoda*, b Jan. 9, 1736 ; 81 *Moses*, b March 18, 1738 ; 82 *Flavia*, b Aug. 18, 1740 ; 83 *Eunice*, b May 5, 1742 ; 84 *Hannah*, b April 9. 1745 , 85 *Joseph*, b March 21, 1747 ; 86 *Elizabeth*, b May 31, 1750 ; 87 *Isaac*, b March 29, 1754 ; 88 *Sarah*, b March 22, 1757 ; 89 *Amos*, b Oct. 2, 1760.

## 28. JOHN.

JOHN Moss, son of John and Elizabeth, married Lydia —— She died and he married for second wife, Sarah ——. Children by 1st marriage: 90 *Amasa*, b April 22, 1746 ; 91 *John*, b Sept. 3, 1747 ; 92 *Joel*, d Jan. 12, 1726 ; 93 *Eunice*, b Oct. 30, 1750 ; 94 *John*, b April 7, 1753. By 2d marriage : 95 *Sarah ;* 96 *Phebe*, b May 6, 1760.

## 29. LEVI.

LEVI Moss, son of John and Elizabeth, married Martha —— . . . . ( Children : 97 *Amos*, b Nov. 17, 1744 ; 98 *Levi*, b Nov. 16, 1746 ; 99 *Elizabeth*, b Dec. 3, 1748 ; 100 *Eunice*, b Oct. 30, 1750 ; 101 *John*, b Feb. 14, 1751 ; 102 *Martha*, b Aug. 18, 1753 ; 103 *Martha*, b Nov. 28, 1755 ; 104 *Stephen*, b Feb. 6, 1758 ; 105 *Hannah*, b July 24, 1760.

## 35. DANIEL.

DANIEL Moss, son of Solomon and Ruth, married Mindwell ——. Children : 106 *Chloe*, b Dec. 6, 1739 ; 107 *Simeon*, b Oct. 16, 1740 ; 108 *David*, b Sept. 30, 1742.

## 47. JESSE.

JESSE Moss, son of Isaac and Hannah Moss, married Mary ——. Children : 109 *Hannah* b June 16, 1754 ; 110 *Joel*, b Dec. 17, 1755, d Nov. 22, 1756 ; 111 *Jesse*, b Sept. 10, 1757 ; 112 *Reuben*, b June 11, 1759 ; 113 *Job*, b April 25, 1761 ; 114 *Job*, b April 25, 1762.

## 50. NATHANIEL.

NATHANIEL Moss, son of Israel and Lydia Moss, married Mary ———.

Children: 115 *Stephen*, b Oct. 6, 1752 ; 116 *Nathaniel*, b
April 15, 1754 ; 117 *Keziah*, b May 13, 1756 : 118 *Mary*, b
July 19, 1758 ; 119 *Lydia*, b Aug. 26, 1760.

## 53. ISAIAH.

ISAIAH MOSS, son of Israel and Lydia Moss, married
Phebe Doolittle, April 11, 1738 ; she died May 10, 1758.
Children : 120 *Phebe*, b June 3, 1739 ; 121 *Hezekiah*, b Jan.
20, 1741, d July 10, 1742 ; 122 *Mehitable*, b Nov. 15, 1743 ;
123 *Hezekiah*, b Nov. 3, 1746 ; 124 *Phebe*, b Aug. 18, 1752 ;
125 *Linus*, b March 2, 1761.

---

## MUNSON.[1]

### SAMUEL.

SAMUEL MUNSON, the first of the name in Wallingford,
married Martha Bradley of New Haven, Oct. 26, 1665.   She
died Jan. 9, 1707.  He married for his 2d wife, Mary Merriman, March 10, 1708.   He was a shoemaker and tanner of
leather, and owned the lot on which now stands the house of
Ahner I. Hall, Esq.  He died in Wallingford, Nov. 24, 1741.
ae. 74 years.

Children by 1st marriage : 1 *Martha*, b May 6, 1667, in New
Haven ; 2 *Samuel*, b Feb. 28, 1669 ; 3 *Thomas*, b March 12,
1670, in New Haven, d in Cheshire, Sept. 28, 1746, ae. 76 ; 4
*John*, b Jan. 28, 1672 ; 5 *Theophilus*, b Sept. 1, 1675 ; 6 *Joseph*,
b Nov. 1, 1677 ; 7 *Stephen*, b Dec. 5, 1679 ; 8 *Caleb*, b Nov. 19,
1682, m Elizabeth ——— ; 9 *Joshua*, b Feb. 7, 1684, d Dec.
9, 1711 ; 10 *Israel*, b March 6, 1686 ; 11 *Solomon*, b Feb. 18,
1689, m Mary Cooley ; 12 *Samuel*, b Aug. 25, 1691, m
Rachel Cook ; 13 *Marlo*, b Feb. 15, 1693 ; 14 *William*, b
Oct. 13, 1695, m Rebecca ———, in 1750 ; 15 *Waitstill*, b
Dec. 12, 1697 ; 16 *Eunice*, b Sept. 13, 1700 ; 17 *Obedience*, b
Oct. 13, 1792 ; 18 *Katherine*, b June 3, 1704. m John Mitchell,
Oct. 12, 1702.  By 2d marriage : 19 *Tamar*, b Dec. 5, 1709.

---

1 Machias Centennial Celebration, 171 ; Savage's Gen. Dict., III. 257 ;
Temple's Eccles. Hist. Whately, Mass., 36.

##### 5. THEOPHILUS.

THEOPHILUS MUNSON, son of Samuel and Martha, married to Mary Moss, by Mr. Hall, June 28, 1714.
Child: 20, *Eliasaph*, b Nov. 17, 1719.

##### 6. JOSEPH.

JOSEPH MUNSON, son of Samuel and Martha Munson, married Margery Hitchcock, March 10, 1699.
Children: 21 *Abel*, b Jan. 10, 1701, m Sarah Peck; 22 *Abigail*, b April 3, 1704, m Ichabod Merriman, Oct. 17, 1725, 23 *Joseph*, b Dec. 21, 1705; 24 *Desire*, b Feb. 7, 1707; 25 *Thankful*, b Jan. 8, 1708; 26 *Ephraim*, b Nov. 15, 1714; 27 *Margery*, b Oct. 10, 1717; 28 *Jemima*, b March 27, 1720; 29 *Auger*, b April 7, 1725, d Dec. 17, 1726.

##### 8. CALEB.

CALEB MUNSON, son of Samuel and Martha Munson, married Elizabeth Brewer, March 26, 1706.
Children: 30 *Keziah*, b Jan. 13, 1706; 31 *Caleb*, b Aug. 19, 1709, m Abigail Brockett, April 23, 1735; 32 *Elizabeth*, b March 31, 1717; 33 *Merriam*, b April 12, 1720.

##### 9. JOSHUA.

JOSHUA MUNSON, son of Samuel and Martha Munson, married Katharine, daughter of Rev. Samuel Street, Dec. 20, 1710. He died Dec. 9, 1711.
Children: 34 *Joshua*, b Aug. 2, 1710; 35 *Mary*, b March 2, 1712.

##### 11. SOLOMON.

SOLOMON MUNSON, son of Samuel and Martha Munson, married Mary Moss, June 28, 1714; m Sarah Peck, June 14, 1753.
Children: 36 *Martha*, b Sept. 14, 1715; 37 *Samuel*, b Sept. 15, 1717; 38 *Elizabeth*, b Nov. 17, 1719. By 2d marriage: 39 *Jonathan*, b June 30, 1756; 40 *Eunice*, b Nov. 19, 1754; 41 *Sarah*, b Dec. 11, 1760.

##### 12. SAMUEL.

SAMUEL MUNSON, son of Samuel and Martha, married

2. Mary Merriman, March 10, 1708.  She died Nov. 28, 1755. He died Nov. 23, 1741.

Children : 42 *Samuel*, b Feb. 5, 1709 ; 43 *Merriman*, b Nov. 30, 1710 ; 44 *Mamre*, b Dec. 16, 1712 ; 45 *Lent*, b Mar. 6, 1714.

#### 14. WILLIAM.

WILLIAM MUNSON, son of Samuel and Martha, married Rebecca ——, in 1750.

Children : 46 *Martha*, b April 2, 1729, m Ambrose Doolittle ; 47 *William*, b July 5, 1731 ; 48 *Eunice*, b Aug. 15, 1733 ; 49 *Peter*, b Nov. 22, 1735, d at Cheshire in 1833, ae. 98 yrs. ; 50 *Hannah*, b Sept 6, 1737 ; 51 *George*, b Oct. 7. 1739 ; 52 *Samuel :* 53 *Amasa*, b Jan. 27, 1741.

#### 15. WAITSTILL.

WAITSTILL MUNSON, son of Daniel and Martha, married Phebe Merriman, Dec. 10, 1719.

Children : 54 *Reuben*, b May 9, 1721 ; 55 *Hannah*, b Feb. 20, 1723 : 56 *Samuel*, b Dec. 7, 1724 ; 57 *Phebe*, b Jan. 14, 1726 ; 58 *Solomon*, b March 19, 1728, m Sarah Peck, June 14, 1753 : 59 *Waitstill*, b Nov. 24, 1729 ; 60 *Mamre*, b Jan. 20. 1734, m Timothy Carrington, Sept. 26, 1751 ; 61 *Martha*, b June 11. 1738.

#### 21. ABEL.

ABEL MUNSON, son of Joseph and Margery, married Sarah Peck, Nov. 7, 1728.

Children : 62 *Mary*, b May 2. 1732. m Joseph Doolittle, March 11, 1756 : 63 *Titus*, b July 5, 1734 ; 64 *Lud*, b May 5, 1736 ; 65 *Levi*, b Aug. 29, 1738 ; 66 *Sarah*, b Sept. 6, 1740 ; 67 *Nathaniel*, b Oct. 20, 1742 ; 68 *Abigail*, b Sept. 2, 1744 ; 69 *Margery*, b Nov. 3, 1746 ; 70 *Lydia*, b Oct., 1748 ; 71 *Abel*, b Jan 3. 1749 : 72 *Joseph*, b Nov. 16, 1751.

#### 30. CALEB.

CALEB MUNSON, son of Caleb and Elizabeth Munson, married Abigail Brockett, April 3, 1735.  He died July 25, 1747.

Children: 73 *Mabel*, b June 2, 1730; 74 *Abner*, b March 2, 1736; 75 *Harmon*, b Oct. 28, 1738; 76 *Caleb*, b March 13, 1741; 77 *Cornelius*, b April 16, 1742; 78 *Benjamin*, b Aug. 23, 1744.

### 33. JOSHUA.

JOSHUA MUNSON, son of Joshua and Katherine Munson, married Anna ———.

Children: 79 *Joshua*, b Feb. 4, 1750; 80 *Elizabeth*, b Feb. 29, 1752; 81 *Joshua*, b Aug. 2, 1754; 82 *Lucy*, b Feb. 3, 1757; 83 *Anna*, b June 28, 1760.

### 42. MERRIMAN.

DEA. MERRIMAN MUNSON, son of Samuel and Mary Munson, married 1st, Esther ———. She died April 6. 1757; he m 2d, Thankful Peck, June 23, 1758.

Children: 84 *Sarah*, b Dec. 16, 1734; 85 *Esther*, b March 25, 1740; 86 *Samuel*, b Dec. 8, 1741; 87 *Mamre*, b Aug. 12, 1745, d Sept. 17, 1745. By 2d marriage: 88 *Sarah*, b Oct. 7, 1758.

### 44. LENT.

LENT MUNSON, son of Samuel and Mary Munson, married Mary ———.

Children: 89 *Mamre*, b Dec. 9, 1749, d Aug. 31, 1751; 90 *John*, b Aug. 25, 1754; 91 *Luce*, b Feb. 14, 1755; 92 *Mary*, b Sept. 29, 1756.

### 46. WILLIAM.

WILLIAM MUNSON, son of William and Rebecca, married Phebe ———.

Children: 93 *Mehad*, b Aug. 31, 1731; 94 *Martha*, b Jan. 16, 1740.

### 48. PETER.

PETER MUNSON, son of William and Rebecca, married and settled in Cheshire, where he died ae. 92 years.

Children: 95 *Waitstill*, d in New York a Methodist minister, left numerous descendants; 96 *Reuben*, d in N. York; 97 *Levi*, d in Cheshire, Conn.

### 53. REUBEN.

REUBEN MUNSON, son of Waitstill and Phebe, married Mary Chittenden, Dec. 21, 1741.

Children: 98 *Stephen*, b Sept. 23, 1742 ; 99 *Moses*, b Sept. 24, 1744 ; 100 *Reuben*, b Dec. 22, 1746.

### 57. SOLOMON.

SOLOMON MUNSON, son of Waitstill and Phebe, married Sarah ——.

Children: 101 *Eunice*, b Nov. 19, 1754 ; 102 *Jonathan*, b June 3, 1756.

### 58. WAITSTILL.

WAITSTILL MUNSON, son of Waitstill and Phebe, married ——.

Children: 103 *Martha*, b June 11, 1738 ; 104 *Zerah*, was a shoemaker ; 105 *Hunn*.

### 6?. TITUS.

TITUS MUNSON, son of Abel and Sarah, married Lydia Lindsley, Sept. 22, 1759.

Child: 106 *Irene*, b March 9, 1758.

### 92. REUBEN.

REUBEN MUNSON, son of Peter and Rebecca Munson, married and settled in the city of New York, and became a wealthy manufacturer of combs. He had a large family of children, among whom were William and others whose names I have not learned.

### 96. LEVI.

LEVI MUNSON, son of Peter and ——, married Tenny Brooks of Cheshire, and settled on the old homestead of his father, about a mile and a half north of the village of Cheshire, where he died.

Children : 107 *Levi ;* 108 *Abbey*, m Rier Bristol of Cheshire ; 109 —— ; 110 *Benjamin F.*, m 1st, Abigail Atkins, 2d, Anna Cook ; 111 *Truman*, m W. Hitchcock.

## 98. MOSES.

MOSES MUNSON, son of Reuben and Mary, married Phebe ———.

Children : 112 *John*, b Aug. 2, 1740 ; 113 *Thomas F.*, b April 5, 1742 ; 114 *Margoretta*, b April 14, 1744 ; 115 *Caleb*, b May 22, 1746 ; 116 *Hannah*, b May 17, 1748 ; 117 *Moses*, b Aug. 13, 1750.

### EBENEZER.

EBENEZER and Abigail Munson.

Children : 118 *Thomas*, b Oct. 24, 1741 ; 119 *Lydia*, b Jan. 30, 1745 ; 120 *Elizabeth*, b Jan. 13, 1746 ; 121 *Patience*, b Aug. 31, 1749 ; 122 *Jesse*, b July 5, 1751 ; 123 *John*, b Dec. 3, 1752.

### OBADIAH.

OBADIAH MUNSON married 1st, Rachel Tyler, Feb. 28, 1753, 2d, Mary Williams, Oct. 15, 1755.

Children : 124 *Barnabas*, b Sept. 24, 1754 ; 125 *Wilmot*, b July 23, 1755 ; 126 *Lydia*, b Aug. 11, 1756 ; 127 *Hannah*, b Jan. 12, 1757 ; 128 *Stephen*, b Sept. 10, 1759 ; 129 *Daniel*, b March 23, 1761.

## 129. DAVID.

DAVID and Sarah Munson.

Children : 130 *David*, b Jan. 23, 1741 ; 131 *Amos*, b Oct. 13, 1745.

### WALTER.

WALTER MUNSON married Phebe ———.

Child : 132 *Martha*, d Jan. 26, 1740.

### ELIASAPH.

ELIASAPH MUNSON married Rebecca ———, and settled on a farm on the west side of the river in Wallingford. He died Jan. 1, 1826, ae. 75. Mrs. Rebecca died Aug. 9, 1849, ae. 90 years.

Children : 132 *Chauncey*; 133 *Rachel*, m John B. Johnson; 134 *Sarah*, m Billious Cook.

## NOYES.[1]

### JAMES.

REV. JAMES NOYES came from England in 1634, and is the ancestor of the Noyes family in Connecticut. He was born in 1608, in Choulderton, Wiltshire, England. His father was a minister of that place, and was a very learned man. He came to this country because he could not comply with the ceremonies of the Church of England. He was married to Miss Sarah Brown of Southampton, not long before he came to this country, which was in 1634. He was first called to preach in Mystic, and continued there nearly a year. Afterward he settled in Newbury, Mass., and was pastor of the church in that place for more than twenty years. He died Oct. 22, 1656, in the 48th year of his age. He had six sons and two daughters, all of whom lived to be married, and had children. Three of his sons graduated at Harvard College, and settled in the ministry.

James was pastor of a church in Stonington, Conn. Moses settled in Lyme, Conn., and died 1729, in his 86th year, after having resided with his people 60 years. Nicholas, brother of Rev. James, settled in Salem, Mass.

### JAMES.

REV. JAMES NOYES of Stonington, married Dorothy Stanton, Sept. 11, 1674. He was one of the founders and first trustees of Yale College ; was pastor of the church in Stonington 50 years. He died Dec. 30, 1719-20, æ. 80 yrs.

Children : 1 *James*, born in England, his sons were John, b 1619, d in Roxbury, Mass., 1682, and Robert, who settled

---

1 For collateral branches, see Coffin's Hist. Newbury, Mass., 312 ; Hobart's Hist. Abingdon, Mass., 423–6 ; Journals of Smith and Dean of Portland, Me., 158 ; Kingman's Hist. North Bridgewater, Mass., 582–4 ; Noyes' Gen. of Noyes Family ; Poor's Hist. and Gen. Researches, 119, 120, 136–40, 168, 169 ; Savage's Gen. Dict., III. 296–299 ; Ward's Hist. Shrewsbury, Mass., 388–90 ; Wyman's Hunt Family Gen., 119, 120 ; also p. 291 of this history.

in Roxbury, m Sarah Lynde ; 2 *Thomas*. 3 *John* ; 4 *Joseph*, m Abigail Pierrepont ; 5 *Moses* . 6 *Dolly*.

### 3. JOHN.

JOHN NOYES, son of Rev. James of Stonington, married Mary Fish, at Stonington, Nov. 16, 1758.

Children : 8 *Rebecca*, b Nov. 22, 1759, d at Stonington, May 14, 1760 ; 9 *Joseph*, b Feb. 14, 1761, m —— Burr ; 10 *John*, b Aug. 27, 1762, m —— Skidmore ; 11 *James*, b Aug. 14, 1764, m Anna Holbrook ; 12 *Mary*, b June 21, 1766 d Aug., 1770 ; 13 *Anna*.

Mary, the wid. of John Noyes, m ried 2d, Gen. Gold S. Silliman of Fairfield, Conn., in 1775, and had two children* by her second marriage : Gold S. Silliman. Esq., lawyer, of Brooklyn, N. Y., and the late Prof. Benjamin Silliman of Yale College.

### 4. JOSEPH.

REV. JOSEPH NOYES, son of Rev. James of Stonington, was born in 1688, graduated in Yale College in 1709. After receiving his first degree, being then about 22 years of age, he became tutor in Yale College, and served four years in that office. He was ordained and installed over the church in New Haven, July, 1716. He married Nov. 6, 1716, Miss Abigail Pierrepont, dau. of his predecessor, Rev. James Pierrepont. None of their children lived to be married except one son and two daughters, viz.: John, Abigail, who married Thomas Darling, Esq., of New Haven, and Sarah, who married Col. Chester, of Wethersfield, Conn. He died June 16, 1761, æ. 73 yrs.

### 7. JOHN.

REV. JOHN NOYES, son of Rev. Joseph, graduated at Yale College in 1756, and was licensed to preach, May 31, 1757. He died Nov. 5, 1767, æ. 32 yrs.

### 10. JOHN.

REV. JOHN NOYES, son of Rev. John Noyes, was born Aug. 27, 1760, graduated at Yale College, Sept., 1779, and was licensed to preach, in Oct., 1783, by the Western Asso-

G G G

ciation of Fairfield Co., Conn. He was ordained and installed at Northfield parish, town of Weston, Fairfield Co., Conn., May 30, 1786. He married Eunice Sherwood, March 8, 1786.

Children : 14 *Samuel Sherwood,* b May 20, 1787 ; 15 *Mary,* b Nov. 3, 1788; 16 *John,* b May 11, 1788 ; 17 *William,* b May 23, 1792 ; 18 *Ebenezer,* b March 27, 1794 ; 19 *Benjamin,* b Feb. 5, 1796, d April 21, 1815 ; 20 *Charles,* b June 23, 1798, d July 9, 1821 ; 21 *Eunice,* b Aug. 21, 1800, d Feb. 13, 1804 ; 22 *Burr,* b Aug. 31, 1803, d July 3, 1830.

Mrs. Eunice, wife of Rev. John Noyes, died March 25, 1824, æ. 64 yrs. Rev. John Noyes married 2d, Fanny Swann of Stonington, Conn., Oct. 16, 1827 ; she was born July 9, 1776. He died in Northfield, May 15, 1846, æ. nearly 84 yrs. He had written the discourse for the 60th anniversary of his ministry, and it was to have been delivered by him two weeks from the Sabbath on which he was interred.

### 14. SAMUEL.

SAMUEL SHERWOOD, son of Rev. John Noyes, born May 20, 1787, married Esther Chapman, who was born June 5, 1790, on Nov. 3, 1812.

Children: 23 *Samuel,* b March 12. 1815 ; 24 *Benjamin,* b Nov. 10, 1816 ; 25 *William,* b Dec. 10, 1818 ; 26 *Julia Chapman,* b July 25, 1820 ; 27 *Charles,* b Aug. 7, 1822, d March 12, 1857 ; 28 *Josiah Chapman,* b Jan. 22, 1824, d May 22, 1849 ; 29 *John,* b April 11, 1826, d Oct. 22, 1853 ; 30 *Elizabeth,* b May 14, 1828 ; 31 *James Burr,* b Sept. 17, 1830, d. Dec. 4. 1851.

Dr. Samuel S. Noyes studied medicine and was licensed to practice in 1810. He settled in New Canaan, Fairfield Co., in 1811.

### 22. BURR.

REV. BURR NOYES, son of Rev. John Noyes, graduated at Yale College, Sept., 1824. He settled at Chester, Saybrook, Conn., was very successful in his profession, and won the confidence and esteem of the people. He died July 2, 1830.

## 9. JOSEPH.

JOSEPH NOYES ESQ., son of Rev. John Noyes, was born Feb. 14, 1761, died in 1817, ae. 56 yrs. He was married to Amelia Burr, Dec. 11, 1783. She was born Dec. 7, 1764, and died May 7, 1802 ; he married Lucy Norton, May 24, 1804 ; she died July 12, 1850, ae. 79 yrs.

Children : 32 *Joseph Fish*, b Oct. 9, 1784 ; 33 *John Noyes*, b Aug. 7, 1786 ; 34 *James*, b Oct. 21, 1788 ; 35 *Samuel*, b Sept. 15, 1791 ; 36 *Rebecca*, b March 3, 1794. By 2d marriage : 37 *Benjamin Silliman*, b May 5, 1805 ; 38 *Joseph Chester*, b Aug. 5, 1808 ; 39 *Thomas Norton*, b Oct. 3, 1799 ; 40 *Harriet Norton*, b Oct. 5, 1796 ; 41 *Mary Ann*, b Sept. 7, 1813.

## 11. JAMES.

REV. JAMES NOYES, son of Rev. John Noyes, was born Aug. 4. 1764, and died in Wallingford, Feb. 18, 1844, in the 80th year of his age, being the oldest minister in the county of New Haven. He married Anna Holbrook, of Derby, Conn., Jan. 22, 1769. She died Jan. 1, 1838, ae. 69 yrs.

Children : 42 *Catharine*, b Feb. 1, 1789, d March 19, 1811 ; 43 *Anna*, b Feb. 1, 1790 ; 44 *James*, b May 23, 1792, d Oct. 26, 1794 ; 45 *Mary*, b May 13, 1794, d April 23, 1844 ; 46 *Sally*, b Feb. 11, 1796, d Jan. 12, 1834 ; 47 *James*, b Jan. 27, 1798, d 1869. in East Haddam ; 48 *Cornelia*, b March 23, 1800, d Jan. 16, 1835 ; 49 *Esther*, b March 21, 1802, d Oct. 16, 1839 ; 50 *Abigail*, b May 13, 1804, d April 24, 1844 ; 51 *Eunice*, b March 12, 1806, d Oct 3, 1824 ; 52 *Joseph Fish*, b July 3, 1808 ; 53 *John*, b July 15, 1810, d Oct. 11, 1810 ; 54 *Catharine*, b May 27, 1812, d Jan. 27, 1833 ; 55 *Harriet*, b Aug. 11, 1814.

# PARKER.[1]

Parker has always been a common name in New England. We find Abraham, Amariah, Edmund, George, Jacob, James,

---

1 For collateral branches, see Abbott's Hist. Andover, Mass., 20 ; Bar-

Joseph, Matthew, Nicholas, Robert. Thomas, two or more
Williams, and as many Johns, appearing in nearly as many of
the different settlements in Massachusetts and Connecticut,
at an early day. Abraham Parker was the first of the family
in this country. It is supposed that he came from Wiltshire,
England. He first settled in Woburn, Mass., where he married Rose Whitlock, Nov. 18, 1644.

### I. WILLIAM.

WILLIAM PARKER was early in Hartford and Saybrook, and
had three children: 2 *William;* 3 *Ralph*, died in 1690; 4
*John*, who removed to New Haven; he had 5 *John*, b Oct.
8, 1648, m Nov. 8, 1670, Hannah, dau. of Wm. Bassett; 6
*Mary*, b April 27, 1649, m John Hall, 1666; 7 *Hope*, b May
26, 1650, m Samuel Cook, May 2, 1677; 8 *Lydia*, b May 26,
1652-3, m John Thomas, Jan. 12, 1671; 9 *Joseph*, m Hannah
Gilbert, 1673.

### 5. JOHN.

JOHN PARKER and HANNAH his wife were among the early
planters in Wallingford, and settled at Parker's farms, about
two miles west of the village, which first gave the name to
that locality. He was an active business man, and did much
in advancing the interests of the settlement. He died in
1711. Hannah his wife died June 7, 1726.

ry's Hist. Framingham, Mass., 349–51; Bouton's Hist. Concord, N. H.,
682; Bridgman's Granary Burial Ground, 136-44; Butler's Hist., Groton,
Mass., 421, 476,494; Caulkins' Hist. of New London, Conn., 306; Deane's
Hist. Scituate, Mass., 320; Freeman's Hist. Cape Cod, Mass., II. 438, 466,
472, 642; Hill's Hist. Mason, N. H., 205; Howell's Hist. Southampton,
L. I., 260; Hudson's Hist. Lexington, Mass., 169-76; Jackson's Hist.
Newton, Mass., 375-81; Kidder's Hist. New Ipswich, N. H., 417-19;
Littell's Passaic Valley Gen., 311; Morse's Gen. Reg. of Sherborn and
Holliston, Mass., 185; Morse's Memorial of Morses, Appendix, No. 54;
N. E. Hist. & Gen. Reg., IV. 139, VI. 375, 376, XVI. 41, 91-4; Poor's Hist.
& Gen. Researches, 113-15, 124-8; Savage's Gen. Dict., III. 349-58;
Sewall's Hist. Woburn, Mass., 628; Shattuck's Memorial, 375-7; Smith's
Hist. Delaware Co., Penn., 490; Stoddard's Gen. of Stoddard Family, ed.
1865, 14, 38, 39, 63-8; Temple's Eccles. Hist. Whately, Mass., 29; Ward's
Hist. Shrewsbury, Mass., 400-4.

Children : 10 *Hannah*, b Aug. 20, 1671, m Wm. Andrews, Jan. 12, 1692 ; 11 *Elizabeth*, m Josiah Royce, March 24, 1693 ; 12 *John*, b March 26, 1675, m Mary Kibbe of Springfield, Nov. 1, 1699 ; 13 *Rachel*, b June 16, 1680, m Thomas Kelzea of New Haven, 1700 : 14 *Joseph*, m Sarah Curtis, June 7, 1705 ; 15 *Eliphalet*, m Hannah Beach, Aug. 5, 1708 ; 16 *Samuel*, m Sarah Goodsell of Middletown, July 16, 1713 ; 17 *Edward*, b 1692, m Jerusha ——, he d Oct. 21, 1776, she d Dec. 27, 1745 ; 18 *Mary*, m Joseph Clark, Nov. 27, 1707 ; 19 *Abigail*, b March 3, 1710, m Joseph Bradley Dec. 8, 1765.

### 12. JOHN.

JOHN, son of John and Hannah Parker, married 1st, Mary Kibbe, 2d Sarah ——.

Children by 1st marriage : 20 *Rachel*, b Jan. 6, 1701–2 ; 21 *John*, b Oct., 1703, m Deborah, dau. of Thomas Matthews, Oct. 17, 1727 ; 22 *Aaron*, b July 8, 1704, d Jan. 12, 1727 ; 23 *Mary*, b Feb. 8, 1706 ; 24 *Elisha*, b Oct. 25, 1708, m Susanna Tuttle, Feb. 28, 1728 ; 25 *Abigail*, b March 3, 1710, m Robert Martin, July 15, 1734 ; 26 *Elizabeth*, b June 3, 1716 ; 27 *Lois*, b July 20, 1718, m Thomas, son of Timothy Beach, Nov. 5, 1740 ; 28 *Isaac*, b 1720, m Hannah, dau. of Timothy Beach, Aug. 11, 1742 ; 29 ——, d April 27, 1773, m Lois Royce. By 2d marriage : 30 *Sarah*, b July 22, 1739.

### 14. JOSEPH.

JOSEPH son of John and Hannah Parker, married Sarah Curtis.

Children : 31 *Joseph*, b Aug. 6, 1706, d July 25, 1712 : 32 *Joseph*, b July 25, 1707 : 33 *Andrew*, m Susanna Blakeslee ; 34 *Thomas*, b June 7, 1709, m Abigail Dutton and settled in Waterbury, Conn., in 1756 ; 35 *Hannah*, b Aug. 30, 1700 ; 36 *Ebenezer*, b March 5, 1713, m Lydia Barnes, April 1, 1735 ; 37 *Joseph*, b April 3, 1716, m 1st, Lucy Parmalee, Feb. 23, 1742, 2d, Mary Andrews, March 30, 1758 : 38 *Ralph*, b Jan. 9, 1718, went to Vermont ; 39 *Waitstill*, b July 24, 1721, m Jemima, dau. of Joseph Munson, Oct. 27, 1742 ; 40 *Sarah*, b

Oct. 18, 1725, m Asaph, son of Samuel Cook, Jan. 15, 1744-5.

### 15. ELIPHALET.

ELIPHALET, son of John and Hannah Parker, married Hannah Beach ; he died in 1757, ae. 76 yrs.

Children: 41 *Eliada*, b April 2, 1710, d March 24, 1712 ; 42 *Eliada*, b April 22, 1712, m Sarah Curtis Dec. 21, 1732 ; 43 *Chestina*, b April 18, 1714, m Peter Curtis Nov. 22, 1732 ; 44 *Aaron*, b Feb. 17, 1716, m Sarah Martin, March 11, 1756 ; 45 *Gamaliel*, b June 6, 1718, d Dec. 3, 1799, he m Elizabeth ———— : 46 *Didymus*, b Jan. 14, 1721, m Phebe, daughter of John Johnson, Dec. 22, 1742 ; 47 *Eliphalet*, b Jan. 19, 1721, m Thankful Hitchcock, May 21, 1745 ; 48 *Joanna*, b July 8, 1723, m Amos Bristol of Cheshire, June, 1740 ; 49 *Bethuel*, b April 2, 1727, m Tabitha, daughter of Matthias Hitchcock, July 19, 1749, he d March 13, 1778 ; 50 *Benjamin*, b Feb. 12, 1729, m Mary Atwater and removed to Simsbury, Conn. ; 51 *Thankful*, m Oliver Hitchcock.

### 16. SAMUEL.

SAMUEL, son of John and Hannah Parker, m 1st, Lydia ———— ; 2d. Sarah Goodsell, July 16, 1713 ; 3d, Mary Chamberlain, Jan. 9. 1744.

Children by 1st marriage : 52 *Thomas*, b June 7, 1709 ; 53 *Sarah*, b May 17, 1714 ; 54 *Abiah*, b Aug. 2, 1716, m Daniel, son of John Ives, Oct. 28, 1735 ; 55 *Joseph*, b Aug. 2, 1716, m Lucy Parmalee, Feb. 23, 1742-3. By 2d marriage : 56 *Abraham*, b March 24, 1720, m Damaris, daughter of William Abernathy, Sept, 9, 1747, d July 26, 1775 ; 57 *Jacob*, b April 24, 1722, m Elizabeth, daughter of John Beecher, April 26, 1749, d Sept. 24, 1767 ; 58 *Titus*, b Feb. 23, 1728. By 3d marriage : 59 *Thankful*, b Oct. 8, 1745 ; 60 *Martha*, b Sept. 10, 1749 ; 61 *Lent*, b July 8, 1752.

### 17. EDWARD.

EDWARD, son of John and Hannah Parker, married Jerusha ————. They settled in Cheshire parish, on what is now called Cheshire street, where she died Dec. 27, 1745.

He married 2d, Rebecca Ives, Dec. 1, 1748; she died May 23, 1762, ae. 65. He married 3d, Ruth Merriman Merwin, Sept. 30, 1762.

Children: 62 *Ralph*, b Jan. 9, 1718, m Martha, daughter of Gideon Ives, Dec. 25, 1740; 63 *Athildred*, b July 1, 1719, m Timothy Hall, Jan. 10, 1748; 63 1-2 *Edward*, b March 11, 1721, m Sarah Burroughs, Aug. 21, 1744; 64 *Joel*, b Feb. 24, 1723, m Susannah Hotchkiss, Dec. 25, 1746; 65 *Ephraim*, b Aug. 23, 1725, m Bathsheba Parsons, Nov. 11, 1747; 66 *Amos*, b Nov. 26, 1726, d Aug. 20, 1748; 67 *William*, b 1728, d May 2, 1752; 68 *Eldad*, b Sept. 14, 1731, m Thankful, daughter of Matthew Bellamy, April 24, 1755, d July 6, 1779; 69 *Joseph Merriam*, b Feb. 2, 1734, d March 21, 1734; 70 *Joseph*, b Oct. 9, 1735, m Mary Andrews, May 30, 1758.

### 21. JOHN.

JOHN, son of John and Mary Parker, married Deborah Matthews. He died March 28, 1740.

Children: 71 *Abiah*, d Aug. 14, 1728; 72 *John*, b Dec. 25, 1730, m Eunice Beach, June 16, 1752, and had John, b Dec. 8, 1755; 73 *Deborah*, b May 4, 1834, m Jesse, son of Josiah Mix, Nov. 26, 1753; 74 *Jesse*, b March 16, 1736, m Dorothy Spenser, Feb. 16, 1758; 75 *Reuben*, b March 12, 1738, m Hannah Chapman of Waterbury Dec. 10, 1764; 76 *Gideon*, b July 5, 1740, m Elizabeth ——, b Nov. 11, 1743; 77 *Isaiah*, b June 14, 1746, m Susanna or Damaris Yale, Feb. 14, 1771.

### 24. ELISHA.

ELISHA PARKER, son of John and Mary, married Susanna Tuttle. 7

Children: 78 *Ruth*, b Feb. 28, 1728; 79 *Aaron*, b April 9, 1730, m Sarah, dau. of Robert Martin, March 11, 1756; 80 *Elisha*, b July 25, 1735, m Esther Spencer, Aug. 10, 1750; 81 *John*, b Sept. 17, 1739; 82 *Dan*; 83 *Damaris*, b July 16, 1743, m Enos Parker, Dec. 2, 1761; 84 *Susanna*, b Dec. 7, 1745.

### 28. ISAAC.

ISAAC PARKER, son of John and Mary, m. Hannah Beach.

Children : 85 *Keziah*, b Feb. 12, 1743 ; 86 *Lois*, b April 30,
1746 ; 87 *Ruth*, b July 11, 1750, m Gershom Mattoon, Dec. 5,
1776 ; 88 *Isaac*, b Sept. 4, 1754, m Annie Parker, March 19,
1778 ; 89 *Mary*, b Aug. 14, 1755, m Amos Austin, Aug. 17,
1777 ; 90 *Timothy*, b Aug. 14, 1757 ; 91 *John*, b Feb. 21,
1762 ; 92 *Phineas*, b July 14, 1765.

### 34. THOMAS.

THOMAS PARKER, son of Joseph and Sarah Curtis Parker,
married Abigail Dutton, Aug. 30, 1748, and settled in Waterbury.   He died in 1788.

Children : 93 *Thomas*, b April 3, 1749 ; 94 *Amasa*, b Feb.
28, 1751, graduate of Yale, m Thankful Andrews, Aug. 28,
1771 ; 95 *Peter*, b March 11, 1753, removed to the State of
N. Y. ; 96 *Abigail*, b Aug. 28, 1755 ; 97 *Abner*, removed to
the State of N. Y. ; 98 *Joseph*, was a physician in Litchfield
Co. ; 99 *Daniel*, m Miriam Curtis, Nov. 18, 1762.

### 36. EBENEZER.

EBENEZER PARKER, son of Joseph and Sarah Curtis Parker,
married Lydia Barnes.

Children : 100 *Desire*, b June 7, 1735, m Aaron Bellamy,
Dec. 20, 1753 ; 101 *Ebenezer*, b July 6, 1737, m Anna ——,
d Dec. 11, 1762 ; 102 *Caleb*, b March 30, 1739 ; 103 *Joshua*,
b April 17, 1741, m Mary, dau. of Oliver Hitchcock, Oct. 30,
1765 ; 104 *Jared*, b Nov. 16, 1743 ; 105 *Lydia*, b March 8,
1745, m Abel Parker, April 23, 1762 ; 106 *Stephen*, b Oct. 27,
1747 ; 107 *Eliakim*, b July 10, 1751, m Phebe Carrington,
Feb. 20, 1775, and had Eliakim, b March 13, 1777, m 2d,
wid. Lois Ives, Nov. 11, 1777, and had three children ; 108
*Caleb*, b Nov. 2, 1759, m Dolly Peck, Nov. 3, 1783.

### 39. WAITSTILL.

WAITSTILL PARKER, son of Joseph and Sarah Curtis
Parker, married 1st, Jemima Munson. 2d, Jemima Beach.

Children : 109 *Margery*, b March 20, 1743-4, d Oct. 1,
1744 ; 110 *Justus*, b Jan. 1, 1747-8 ; 111 *Margery*, b Feb. 25,
1749, m Eliada Parker, Jr.   By 2d marriage : 112 *Jemima*, b

June 2, 1753; 113 *Rhoda*, b March 25, 1755. By 3d marriage: 114 *Charles*, b Aug. 21, 1760, m Charity Dibble, Oct. 21, 1784; 115 *Eunice*, b Aug. 9, 1762; 116 *Justus*, b May 23, 1764; 117 *Martha*, b April 17, 1766; 118 *Abigail*, b June 10, 1768; 119 *Sarah*, b April 2, 1771.

### 33. ANDREW.

ANDREW, son of Joseph and Sarah Curtis Yale Parker, married Susannah Blakeslee.

Children: 120 *Ambrose*, b March 6, 1738, m Comfort Parker, March 22, 1758; 121 *Grace*, b Dec. 10, 1739, d Dec. 11, 1739; 122 *Patience*, b Dec. 10, 1739, d Dec. 13, 1739; 123 *Zeruiah*, b Nov. 28, 1741, m David Miller, Jan. 3, 1765; 124 *Oliver*, b Nov. 20, 1743, m Lucy Parker, Dec. 3, 1764, and had Thaddeus, b Jan. 26, 1766; 125 *Ezra*, b Dec. 2, 1745; 126 *Susannah*, b Dec. 2, 1747; 127 *Rachel*, b Dec 28, 1749; 128 *Sybil*, b Feb. 9, 1753; 129 *Jason*, b Aug. 17, 1764.

### 42. ELIADA.

ELIADA, son of Eliphalet and Hannah Beach Parker, married Sarah Curtis.

Children: 130 *Martha* b July 8, 1734; 131 *Lettis*, b Sept. 18, 1736; 132 *Comfort*, b Sept. 16, 1738, m Ambrose Parker, March 22, 1758; 133 *Eliada*, b Nov. 24, 1740, d March 23, 1742; 134 *Sarah*, b Jan. 23, 1743-4; 135 *Hannah*, b Sept. 23, 1746; 136 *Patience*, b Aug. 18, 1748, m Joseph Parker, June 29, 1769; 137 *Eliada*, m Margery Parker, May 10, 1770, d Sept. 12, 1776; 138 *Phebe*, b Oct. 31, 1752; 139 *Levi*, b June 8, 1757, m Lydia Bradley, July 22, 1779.

### 45. GAMALIEL.

GAMALIEL, son of Eliphalet and Hannah Beach Parker, married Elizabeth ——.

Children: 140 *Joel*, b Jan. 4, 1741, m Lydia Parker, Aug. 23, 1762; 141 *Elizabeth*, b Jan. 7, 1742-3; 142 *Eunice*, b Jan. 6, 1744-5; 143 *Gamaliel*, b Dec. 9, 1745, d Oct. 29, 1765; 144 *Amos*, b Jan. 20, 1748-9; 145 *Miriam*, b Jan. 28, 1753; 146 *Gamaliel*, b Oct. 22, 1755, d Nov. 8, 1755; 147 *Garretiel*, b

Nov. 2, 1756, m Martha Parker, May 2, 1782 ; 148 *Anna*, b
Feb. 8, 1759 ; 149 *Amos*, b Dec. 11, 1761, m Mary Curtis,
Dec. 5, 1785.

### 46. DIDYMUS.

LIEUT. DIDYMUS, son of Eliphalet and Hannah Beach
Parker, married Phebe Johnson.

Children : 150 *Enos*, b March 12, 1744, m Damaris Parker, Dec. 2, 1761 ; 151 *Ichabod*, b Jan. 2, 1748–9, married
Susannah Cook, Dec. 3, 1766.

### 47. ELIPHALET.

ELIPHALET, son of Eliphalet and Hannah Beach Parker,
married Thankful Hitchcock.

Children : 152 *Valentine*, b March 5, 1745–6, d Dec. 14,
1760 ; 153 *Matthias*, b Sept. 24, 1747 ; 154 *Eliphalet*, b Jan.
22, 1754 ; 155 *Thankful*, b April 3, 1756, d Nov. 28, 1763 ;
156 *Michael*, b Oct. 15, 1758.

### 49. BETHUEL.

BETHUEL, son of Eliphalet and Hannah Beach Parker,
married Tabitha Hitchcock.

Children : 157 *Jerusha*, b April 6, 1750, m William Smith,
July 10, 1777 ; 158 *David*, b March 9, 1752, d Sept. 6, 1753 ;
159 *Olive*, b March 9, 1754, m Joseph Distance, Feb. 27,
1777 ; 160 *David*, b March 18, 1756, d Oct. 9, 1776 ; 161
*Martha*, b Dec. 12, 1757, m Gamaliel Parker, May 2, 1782 ;
162 *Joanna*, b June 18, 1760 ; 163 *Tabitha*, b Nov. 16, 1762 ;
164 *Bethuel*, b Feb. 21, 1765 ; 165 *Simon*, b April 15, 1767, d
Sept. 13, 1773 ; 166 *Thankful*, b June 15, 1769 ; 167 *Asa*, b
Dec. 4, 1771 ; 168 *Mary*, b Sept. 29, 1776, d Dec. 15, 1777.

### 55. JOSEPH.

JOSEPH, son of Samuel and Lydia Parker, married Lucy
Parmalee.

Children : 169 *Esther*, b Jan. 11, 1742–3, d Feb. 8, 1744–5 ;
170 *Joseph*, b Nov. 5, 1746, m Patience Parker, June 29,
1769 ; 171 *Lucy*, b March 13, 1748–9 ; 172 *Esther*, b March
27, 1754 ; 173 *Charles*, b Feb. 26, 1756.

### 56. ABRAHAM.

ABRAHAM, son of Samuel and Sarah Goodsell Parker, m Damaris Abernathy.

Children: 174 *Sarah*, b July 16. 1748 ; 175 *Abraham*, b July 20, 1753, d May 1. 1754 ; 176 *Benjamin*, b May 27, 1755, m Lucinda Curtis, and had two daus., June 25, 1778 ; 177 *Abraham*, b Aug. 23, 1757 ; 178 *William*, b Dec. 19, 1759 : 179 *Mehitable*, b June 30, 1762.

### 57. JACOB.

JACOB, son of Samuel and Sarah Goodsell Parker, married Elizabeth Beecher.

Children: 180 *Samuel*, b Jan. 10, 1749. and had Jared. b April 22, 1777. 181 *Solitary*, b Jan. 7, 1752, d Aug. 31, 1754 : 182 *Elizabeth*, b May 18, 1754; 183 *Jacob*, b Jan. 13, 1756. d Sept. 17, 1756 ; 184 *Jacob*, b July 1, 1757 ; 185 *Rebeca*, b Feb. 27, 1759 ; 186 *James*, b March 3, 1760 ; 187 *Solomon*, b April 12, 1762 ; 188 *Adah*, b Feb. 23, 1765 : 189 *Abiah*, b March 8, 1767.

### 62. RALPH.

RALPH, son of Edward and Jerusha Parker, m Martha Ives.

Children: 190 *Jerusha*, b Nov. 1, 1741, m Robert Roys, May 27, 1762 ; 191 *Ralph*, b Feb. 8, 1743-4 ; 192 *Medad*, b March 29, 1746 ; 193 *Martha*, b April 18, 1749.

### 63 1-2. EDWARD.

EDWARD, son of Edward and Jerusha Parker, married Sarah Burroughs.

Children: 194 *Sarah*, b in Cheshire, Aug. 28, 1745 ; 195 *Elizabeth*, b June 7. 1748. m Enos Clark, of Southington ; 196 *William*, b June 18, 1752. m Desire Bunnel, Feb. 25, 1770 : 197 *Abigail*, b July 7, 1755, m Dr. Benjamin Yale, Dec. 17, 1777 : 198 *Edward*, b April 21. 1760, m Rebecca Hendrick, removed to Cazenovia, N. Y.

### 64. JOEL.

JOEL, son of Edward and Jerusha Parker, married Susanna Hotchkiss.

Children b in Cheshire: 199 *Alhildred*, b Sept. 17, 1747, m Asa Bronson, Feb. 5, 1772 ; 200 *Amos*, b Oct. 22; 1749, m Hannah Hough ; 201 *Susanna*, b March 8, 1752, m Allen Bronson; 202 *Joel*, b Jan. 17, 1754: 203 *Stephen*, b Aug. 5, 1759, m 1st, Sally, dau. of Joseph Twiss, May 27, 1787, m 2d, widow Rebecca Stone, dau. of Joshua Ray, b Jan. 6, 1805, d July 1, 1846.

### 68. ELDAD.

ELDAD, son of Edward and Jerusha Parker, m Thankful Bellamy.

Children b in Cheshire: 204 *Phebe*, b July 23, 1756 ; 205 *Thankful*, b Oct. 6, 1757 ; 206 *Anne*, b Jan. 1, 1760, m Wm. Starke, Chenango Co., N. Y. ; 207 *Thankful*, b March 8, 1762, 208 *Eldad*, b Sept. 27, 1763 ; 209 *Levi*, b Sept. 28, 1765 ; 210 *Levi*, b March 19, 1767, m Phebe Scovill ; 211 *Oliver*, b March 19, 1771 ; *Thankful*, b May 12, 1769 ; *Rebecca*, b March 16, 1773, m Abisha Cowles.

### 70. JOSEPH.

JOSEPH, son of Edward and Jerusha Parker, married Mary Andrews.

Children, born in Cheshire : 212 *Beckey*, b March 29, 1760 ; 213 *Joseph Merriam*, b Oct. 10, 1762 ; 214 *Eldad;* 215 *Zephaniah*, b Feb. 26, 1769 ; 216 *Mary*, b Jan. 24, 1767.

### 74. JESSE.

JESSE, son of John and Deborah Matthews Parker, married Dorothy Spencer.

Children: 217 *Jesse*, b May 30, 1759 ; 218 *Lucy*, b Sept. 17, 1761 ; 219 *Jared*, b Jan. 31, 1764 ; 220 *Jotham*, b Feb. 2, 1767 ; 221 *Dorothy*, b Aug. 5, 1770.

### 79. AARON.

AARON, son of Elisha and Susanna Tuttle Parker, married Sarah Martin.

Children: 222 *Mamre*, b Feb. 14, 1757 ; 223 *Robert*, b Feb. 12, 1759 ; 224 *Susanna*, b Feb. 20, 1762 ; 225 *Abigail*, b April 1, 1764 ; 226 *Sally*, b March 20, 1766 ; 227 *Lyman*, b

April 17, 1768; 228 *Eunice*, b Jan. 11, 1771; 229 *Ruth* b Feb. 1, 1774; 230 *Lyman*, b Feb. 30, 1776.

## 80. ELISHA.

ELISHA, son of Elisha and Susannah Tuttle Parker, married Esther Spencer.

Children: 231 *Elisha*, b April 28, 1761; 232 *Katherine*, b March 30, 1763; 233 *Chloe*, b Dec. 28, 1765; 234 *Arabel*, b April 2, 1768; 235 *Poly*, b March 20, 1773; 236 *Shubel*, b Aug. 28, 1775; 237 *Polly*, b Sept. 13, 1778

## 101. EBENEZER.

EBENEZER, son of Ebenezer and Lydia Barnes Parker, married Anne ——

Children: 238 *Ebenezer*, b June 4, 1762; 239 *Jabez*, b July 18, 1763; 240 *Jemima Doolittle*, b Nov. 16, 1764; 241 *Thomas*, b May 1, 1767; 242 *Ebenezer*, b May 7, 1771.

## 103. JOSHUA.

JOSHUA, son of Ebenezer and Lydia Barnes Parker, married Mary Hitchcock.

Children: 243 *Stephen*, b April 1, 1766; 244 *Lydia*, b May 23, 1769; 245 *Hannah*, b April 21, 1773; 246 *Chestina*, b June 20, 1777; 247 *Eber*, b March 28, 1779; 248 *Jared*, b March 22, 1781; 249, 250 *Mary* and *Miriam*, b Nov. 1, 1782

## 114. CHARLES.

CHARLES, son of Waitstill and Jemima Beach Parker, married Charity Dibble.

Children: 251 *Charles Pierce*, b Dec. 1, 1785, d Feb. 25 1788; 252 *Pierce*, b March 20, 1788; 253 *Ruth*, b Feb. 1, 1790, m Sydney Smith. Dec 16, 1807; 254 *Nancy*, b Dec. 13, 1791; 255 *Charles*, b Jan. 27, 1797.

## 120. AMBROSE.

AMBROSE, son of Andrew and Susanna Blakeslee Parker, married Comfort Parker.

Children: 256 *Ambrose*, b Jun. 15, 1759; 257 *Giles*, b Sept 15, 1760; 258 *Lydia* b May 26, 1763; 259 *Comfort*, b May 23, 1766.

### 137. ELIADA.

ELIADA PARKER, son of Eliada and Sarah Curtis Parker, married Margery Parker.

Children: 260 *Munson*, b Feb. 18, 1771; 261 *Chester*, b Oct. 20, 1773; 262 *Linus*, d Feb. 9, 1776.

### 108. CALEB.

CALEB PARKER, son of Ebenezer and Lydia Barnes Parker, married Dolly Peck.

Children: 263 *Augustus*, b Sept. 10, 1784; 264 *Caleb*, b Jan. 30, 1787; 265 *Paulina*, b Dec. 30, 1789; 266 *Nancy*, b July 5, 1792; 267 *Juliana*, b Nov. 21, 1794.

### 139. LEVI.

LEVI PARKER, son of Eliada and Sarah Curtis Parker, married Lydia Bradley.

Children: 268 *Sybil*, b April 28, 1780, m Amos Peck, Sept. 22, 1799; 269 *Polly*, b Sept. 25, 1782; 270 *Eliada*, b May 31, 1784, m Elizabeth Oswald, Feb. 15, 1807; 271 *Ammi Bradley*, b July 11, 1787; 272 *Lyman*, b April 3, 1790, m Malinda Harrison, March 24, 1818; 273 *Alfred*, b Oct. 19, 1792, m Fanny ——; 274 *Belinda*, b Sept. 18, 1795; *Philo* and *Orrin*, b April 18, 1798, d April 18, 1800.

### 44. DANIEL.

DANIEL, son of Arnon and Sarah Martin, married Miriam, daughter of Benjamin Curtis, Nov. 18, 1762.

Children: 275 *Ruth*, b Feb. 3, 1764; 276 *Denison*, b Sept. 28, 1766; 277 *Leman*, b Dec. 21, 1768; 278 *Lucinda*, b July 24, 1771; 279 *Ruth*, b Dec. 10, 1774; 280 *Daniel*, b May 24, 1775; 281 *Ruth*, b Dec. 27, 1777; 282 *Betsey*, b July 16, 1780.

### 147. GAMALIEL.

GAMALIEL, son of Gamaliel and Elizabeth Parker, married Martha Parker.

Children: 283 *Joel*, b April 17, 1783; 284 *Chester*, b Aug. 19, 1784; 285 *Martha Hall*, b Aug. 20, 1786; 286 *Gamaliel*, b Sept. 13, 1788; 287 *Luroxa*, b Nov. 18, 1790; 288 *Zera*, b

July 13, 1792 ; 289 *Laura*, b Sept. 4, 1796 ; 290 *Fannie*, b Dec. 28, 1798.

### 150. ENOS.

ENOS, son of Didymus and Phebe Johnson Parker, married Damaris Parker.

Children : 291 *Dorcas*, b Dec. 17, 1761 ; 292 *Dan*, b March 18, 1764.

### 164. BETHUEL.

BETHUEL, son of Bethuel and Tabitha Hitchcock Parker, married Eunice ——.

Children : 293 *Bethuel Virgil*, b Oct. 1, 1796, m 1st, Polly Beach, Sept. 7, 1825, 2d. Lowly Thomas, March 30, 1835 ; 294 *Jason*, b Feb. 14, 1798 ; 295 *Rhoda*, b Sept. 29, 1800.

### 167. ASA.

ASA, son of Bethuel and Tabitha Hitchcock Parker, married Keziah ——.

Children : 296 *Laura*, b Feb. 13, 1796 ; 297 *Liverius*, b March 25, 1798 ; 298 *James*, b May 16, 1800 ; 299 *Lemuel*, b April 11, 1804 ; 300 *Asa*, b May 14, 1806.

### 170. JOSEPH.

JOSEPH, son of Joseph and Lucy Parmalee Parker, married Patience Parker.

Children : 301 *Jehiel*, b Sept. 26, 1770 ; 302 *Lena*, b Feb. 23, 1773 ; 303 *Lucy*, b Nov. 20, 1775 ; 304 *Sarah*, 305 *Amy*, b Oct. 16, 1780.

### 196. WILLIAM.

WILLIAM, son of Edward and Sarah Burroughs Parker, married Desire Bunnel.

Children : 306 *Sarah*, b Nov. 7, 1770, m Chas. F. Hill ; 307 *William*, m wid. Rebecca Hull ; 308 *Nancy*, m Divan Lusk ; 309 *Anson* ; 310 *Abigail*, m Elnathan Beach ; 311 *Fanny*, m 1st, Simeon Perkins, 2d, Simeon Hersey ; 312 *Marcus*, m Mehitable Mathews.

### 198. EDWARD.

EDWARD, son of Edward and Sarah Burroughs Parker, married Rebecca Hendrick of Cazenovia, N. Y.

Children: 313 *Chauncey*, b Oct. 9, 1786, m Lydia Atwater ; 314 *Elizabeth*, b Jan. 25, 1788, d June 7, 1794 ; 315 *Oren*, b March 9, 1790, d Aug. 4, 1790 ; 316 *Oren*, b July 11, 1791, d 1812 ; 317 *Edward*, b Sept. 2, 1793, d June 8, 1794 ; 318 *Edward*, b March 15, 1795, m Philomela Hitchcock, rem. to Elyria, Ohio ; 319 *Don Carlos*, b April 27, 1797, m Julia Strake ; 320 *Louisa*, b June 18, 1799 ; 321 *Wm. Hendrick*, b Aug. 9, 1801 ; 322 *Abigail:* 323 *Harriet A.*, m Eliakim Hall.

### 203. STEPHEN.

STEPHEN, son. of Joel and Susanna Hotchkiss Parker, m 1st, Sally Twiss, 2d, wid. Rebecca Stone.

Children by 1st marriage : 324 *Clarissa*, b June 10, 1788, d May 27, 1789 ; 325 *Zeri*, b Aug. 1, 1790 ; 326 *Stephen*, b July 17, 1792, d Jan. 15, 1794 ; 327 *Stephen*, b Nov. 3, 1794, d May, 1826 ; 328 *Sarah*, b March 11, 1797 ; 329 *Clarissa*, b March 10, 1800 ; 330 *Joel*, b March 11, 1801 ; 331 *Isabella*, b Nov. 25, 1803. By 2d marriage : 332 *John*, b Aug. 30, 1805, m 1st, March, 1832, Emily Ward, she d June 1, 1867, and he m 2d, Jan. 22, 1868, Grace A. Belden ; 333 *Betsey*, b May 1, 1807 ; 334 *Charles*, b Jan. 2, 1809, m Abi, daughter of Thomas Eddy, Oct. 6, 1831 ; 335 *Edmund*, b Feb. 9, 1811, m Jennette Bradley of Branford, Conn., and had seven children, four of whom are living, he d April 19, 1866.

## PARMALEE.

### LEANDER.

LEANDER PARMALEE came into Wallingford a carpenter and joiner, and continued to prosecute that business until elected sheriff of the county of New Haven, which office he successively held for twelve years, to the great satisfaction of his constituents, and all who came in contact with him as an officer. He married —— Blakeslee, daughter of the late Joseph Blakeslee of Wallingford. They both died in Wallingford.

Children : 1 *Samuel B.*. m Lavinia, dau. of George Cook ; 2 ——, m Lorenzo Lewis, Esq.; 3 *Leander;* 4 dau.

## PRESTON.[1]

The name of Preston is of great antiquity in North Britain, and was assumed by the family from their territorial possessions in Mid Lothian, in the time of Malcolm, King of the Scots. The first of this family upon record is Leolphus De Preston, living in the time of William the Lion, about 1040, whose grandson, Sir Wm. De Preston, was one of the Scotch nobles summoned to Berwick by Edward the First, in competition for the Crown of Scotland between Bruce and Baliol, it having been submitted to Edward for decision. After the death of King Alexander III., 1291, Sir William was succeeded by his son Sir Nicol De Preston, one of the Scottish barons who swore fealty to King Edward I. He died in the beginning of the reign of David II. of Scotland, son of Robert Bruce, and was succeeded by his son, Sir Lawrence De Preston, who was succeeded by Richard De Preston, who was seated at Preston Richard in Westmoreland, in time of Henry II. Sir Richard De Preston, the fifth in descent from the above Richard, of Preston Richard, represented the county of Westmoreland in Parliament, in seventeen Edward III. His son, Sir Richard De Preston, had likewise the honor of being Knight of the shire for Westmoreland in the same reign (twenty seven Edward III.), and in the same year (1368) obtained a license to impark five hundred acres. His successor, Sir John De Preston of Preston Richard and Preston Patrick, was a member of Parliament for Westmoreland, in the thirty sixth, thirty ninth and forty sixth years of Edward III.

Children: 1 *Richard*, who left a family of daughters only; 2 *John*, who was a Judge of the Court of Common Pleas, in the reign of Henry IV. and VI., and retired from the bench

1 For collateral branches, see Abbot's Hist. Andover, Mass., 30; Adams' Hist. of G—n., 2d part, 32; Brown' Gen. of Brown Family; Cothren's Hist. of Woodbury, Conn.; Hudson's Hist. Lexington, Mass., 18, 138; Kidder's Hist. New Ipswich, N. H., 421-3; N. E. Hist. and Gen. Reg., XIV. 26; Savage's Gen. Dict., III. 482.

in consequence of his great age, in 1427. He left John, a clergyman ; Richard, his heir ; and a daughter.

In 1593 there was a William Robert Preston, who was a relative of Sir Edward Coke.

### WILLIAM.

WILLIAM PRESTON, son of John, son of George of Valley Field, England, was created Baronet of Nova Scotia in 1637. He came to America in the ship Truelove in 1635, at the age of 44 years, from Yorkshire, England, with his wife Mary, ae. 34 years. They had on their arrival in Massachusetts, four children, as follows :

Children: 1 *Elijah*, b 1624. ae. 11 yrs.; 2 *Sarah*, b 1627, ae. 8 yrs.; 3 *Mary*, b 1629, ae. 6 yrs.; 4 *John*, b 1632, ae. 3 yrs. Children born in New Haven, Conn.: 5 *Jehiel*, b 1640, removed to Stratford where he had land let to him, Sept. 21, 1668; 6 *Hackaliah*, b 1643. settled at Woodbury, Conn., in 1681 ; 7 *Eliasaph*, b 1643, lived at Stratford and Wallingford ; 8 *Joseph*, b Jan. 24, 1647.

### 7. ELIASAPH.

DEA. ELIASAPH PRESTON married 1st, Mary Wilcoxen, widow of Thomas Kimberly, of Stratford, July 9, 1673. She died April 16, 1674. He m 2d, Elizabeth, dau. of John Beach, of Stratford. He went to Wallingford in 1674. He was their first Town Clerk and schoolmaster, and was an energetic and very valuable member of the colony, both for the church of which he was deacon, and the township at large. He died in 1705, ae. 70 years.

Children by 1st marriage : 9 *Mary*, b April 25, 1674, m Caleb Merriman, July 9, 1690. By 2d marriage : 10 *Elizabeth*, b Jan. 29, 1676 ; 11 *Hannah*, b July 12, 1678, m Wm. Andrews, May 12, 1692 ; 12 *Eliasaph*, b Jan. 26, 1679, m Deborah Merriman, Jan. 2, 1717 ; 13 *Joseph*, b March 10, 1681, m Jane Cook, July 7, 1708 ; 14 *Esther*, b Feb 28, 1683; 15 *Lydia*, b May 5, 1686 ; 16 *Jehiel*, b Aug. 25, 1688, d Nov. 24, 1689.

### 12. ELIASAPH.

ELIASAPH PRESTON married Rebecca Wilcoxen; she died Sept. 2, 1716. He married 2d, Deborah Merriman, Jan. 2, 1717. He married 3d, Hannah Mott, Nov. 26, 1726

Children by 1st marriage: 17 *Ephraim*, b Sept 8, 1703, 19 Patience ———; 18 *Elizabeth*, b Aug. 8, 1711, d 1715; 19 *Joanna*, b March 18, 1714 By 2d marriage: 20 *John*, b Sept. 11, 1719, m Thankful Sedgwick, Oct. 21, 1741, 21 *Rebecca*, b Sept. 25, 1721; 22 *Elizabeth*, b Dec. 28, 1727, m Abner Bunnel, Feb. 19 1745 By 3d marriage: 23 *Isaac*, b Oct. 1 1729; 24 *Moses*, b and d April 8, 1733; 25 *Moses*, b Oct 30, 1734; 26 *Lois*, b Feb. 3, 1737 8.

### 13. JOSEPH

JOSEPH PRESTON married Jane Cook. July 7, 1708. He married Sarah How, Jan. 30, 1734.

Children by 1st marriage: 27 *Eliasaph*, b May 9, 1700; 28 *Eliasaph*, b May 1, 1710; 29 *Joseph*, b April 7, 1711; 30 *Jonathan*, b Jan., 1713, m Sarah Williams July 28, 1736, 31 *Samuel*, b Aug. 27, 1715; 32 *John*, b June 22, 1715; 33 *Ebenezer*, b Sept. 17, 1725. By 2d marriage: 34 *Dinah*, b Nov. 10, 1734; 35 *Samuel*, b Sept. 30, 1737.

### 17. EPHRAIM.

LIEUT. EPHRAIM PRESTON married Rebecca ———, 2d, Patience ———. She died May 4, 1753; he died April 8, 1772, æ. 69 yrs.

Children by 1st marriage: 36 *Mary*, b Jan. 8, 1731; 37 *Phebe*, b March 6, 1732; 38 *Ephraim*, b Aug. 6, 1734, m Eunice Doolittle, March 25, 1754. Children by 2d marriage: 39 *Reuben*, b May 27, 1736; 40 *Phebe*, b Oct. 3, 1737; 41 *Patience*, b March 30, 1738, d April 18, 1738; 42 *Lent*, b March 5, 1739; 43 *Eliasaph*, b Nov. 28, 1740, m Phebe Hart, Feb. 27, 1764, d April 11, 1717, æ. 37; 44 *Titus*, b Jan. 29, 1743; 45 *Benjamin*, b Dec. 27, 1745; 46 *Elizabeth*, b Dec 7, 1750.

### 20. JEHIEL.

SERGT. JEHIEL PRESTON m Thankful Sedgwick, Oct. 21, 1741. He died Nov. 22, 1758.

Children: 47 *Sarah*, b Aug. 23, 1742 ; 48 *Esther*, b April 1, 1744; 49 *Samuel*, b April 24, 1746 ; 50 *Caleb*, b April 24, 1746 ; 51 *Rebecca*, b Sept. 11, 1750; 52 *Thankful*, b Dec. 10, 1752 ; 53 *Ruth*, b Jan. 28, 1757.

### 28. ELIASAPH.

ELIASAPH PRESTON married Hannah ———.

Children : 54 *Isaac*, b Oct. 1, 1727; 55 *Moses*, b April 8, 1733 ; 56 *Lois*, b Feb. 3, 1737–8.

### 29. JOSEPH.

JOSEPH PRESTON married Sarah ———.

Children : 57 *Dinah*, b Nov. 19, 1734 ; 58 *Samuel*, b Sept. 30, 1737.

### 38. EPHRAIM.

EPHRAIM PRESTON married 1st, Eunice Doolittle, March 25, 1754 : 2d, Esther ———. He died April 8, 1772, ae. 69.

Children : 59, 60 *Joel* and *Ebenezer*, twins, d Dec. 11, 1763.

### 39. REUBEN.

REUBEN PRESTON married Elizabeth ———.

Children : 61 *Charles*, d May, 1753 ; 62 *Mary*, b Jan., 1757.

### 43. ELIASAPH.

ELIASAPH PRESTON married Phebe Hart, Feb. 17, 1764. He died April 12, 1777, ae. 37 years. She m 2d, Stephen Ives.

Children : 63 *Titus*, d in Wallingford ; 62 *Reuben*, d in Cheshire ; 65 *Elizabeth*, d in Prospect.


### REYNOLDS.[1]

#### HEZEKIAH.

HEZEKIAH REYNOLDS was born in Watertown, Conn., July 4, 1756. From there he went to Roxbury, Conn., and from

---

1 For collateral branches, see Caulkins' Hist. Norwich, Conn.; ed. 1867,

thence to North Branford. He married Martha Davenport Wolcott, a daughter of Doct. Jeremiah Wolcott. She was born at Branford, Aug. 18, 1762, and died Aug. 19, 1839, ae. 77 years, at Wallingford. He died June 30, 1833, ae. 77 years. He came to Wallingford about the close of the last century, and resided for sometime in the west part of the town in what was the old Beadles house at Popple Hill. From this place he removed into the village, bought the house nearly the residence of Rev. Samuel Andrews, who was an Episcopal Clergyman before the Revolution.

Children : *Hezekiah*, b Dec., 1773, in Roxbury, Conn. ; 2 *Wolcott*, b June 18, 1779 ; 3 *James*, b April 12, 1783, d Mar. 31, 1807, ae. 47 ; 4 *John D.*, b Apr. 27, 1785 ; 5 *Luanna*, b Apr. 23, 1784, m Nehemiah Carrington of New Haven, Dec. 23, 1825 ; 6 *Martha*, b Feb. 13, 1794, m Col. Thaddeus Street of Cheshire, 1823 ; 7 *Sarah*, b Jan. 12, 1796, m Alexander Harrison, 1819 ; 8 *Thomas G.*, b March 16, 1798, d Sept. 26, 1826, ae. 28 ; 9 *William A.*, b April 1, 1800, m Jane Lynde, of New Haven ; 10 *Beverly*, b Nov. 15, 1806, d Nov. 5, 1807.

### I. HEZEKIAH.

HEZEKIAH REYNOLDS, son of Hezekiah and Martha Wolcott Reynolds, married Anna Wilson, at Savannah, Georgia, in 1806.

Child : 12 *Martha Ann*, b 1807, m Henry Belden, Esq., of Hartford, Conn., in 1828.

### 2. WOLCOTT.

CAPT. WOLCOTT REYNOLDS, son of Hezekiah and Martha W Reynolds, married Serephina Beaumont, in 1804 He died Sept. 28, 1842, ae. 44 years.

Child : 13 *Serephina*, b Jan. 16, 1805, d ae. 28 years.

### 3. JOHN.

HON. JOHN DAVENPORT REYNOLDS, son of Hezekiah and

107, 108; Chapman's Gen. of Chapman Family, 110 ; Kingman's Hist. N. Bridgewater, Mass., 62 r-55; Mitchell's Hist Bridgwater, Mass., 282, 283 ; Rogers' Hist. & Gen. Researches, 110 , Savage's Gen. Dict., III. 525, 526.

Martha D. Reynolds, married Lydia, daughter of John Scarritt, in 1822. He was a man eminently fitted by nature to fill
almost any place of a public character in the gift of the people. He was often a Representative in the Legislature of the
State from Wallingford, and a Senator from the sixth Senatorial district, and Judge of the Probate Court for the district
of Wallingford, for a number of years. The duties of those,
and all other public offices, he discharged with marked ability.
He died Oct. 18, 1853, ae. 68 years. Mrs. Lydia, his wife,
died July 28, 1862, ae. 65 years.

Children: 14 *Martha*, b March 27, 1826: 15 *John D.*, b
April 20, 1828: 16 *Serephina*, b March 15, 1833, m S. N.
Edmonds. Oct. 4, 1852.

### 10. WILLIAM.

WILLIAM A. REYNOLDS, ESQ., son of Hezekiah and Martha
W. Reynolds, was born in Wallingford, married Jane Lynde,
of New Haven, was a merchant and for several years a member of the firm of Harrison & Reynolds, in State-st., and for
the last thirty years has been a respectable broker in New
Haven.

Children: two daughters and two sons, living in 1870.

### ROYCE.[1]

Among the first planters in Wallingford was 1 *Isaac*, and
2d *Nehemiah* Royce, who made their appearance in the place
in 1671; 3 *Nathaniel*, 4 *Samuel*, 5 *Joseph*, and 6 *Robert* Royce,
were also there soon after, all of whom had families, and are
believed to be sons of Robert Royce who was at Stratford in
1644.

### I. ISAAC.

ISAAC and Elizabeth Royce were in Wallingford early in
1671. He died in the autumn of 1682, leaving an estate of

---

[1] For collateral branches, see Andrews' Hist. New Britain, Conn., 190;
Caulkins' Hist. New London, Conn., 293–4; Caulkins' Hist. Norwich,
Conn., ed. 1867, 199; Savage's Gen. Dict., III. 569–70.

£101. His widow married Ebenezer Clark for her second
husband in 1696.

Children: 7 *Isaac*, b Oct. 28. 1673, d Dec. 8, 1673, 8
*Robert*, b Sept. 4, 1674; 9 *Sarah*, b March 10, 1677; 10
*Martha*, b June 1. 1679.

## 2. NEHEMIAH.

NEHEMIAH ROYCE (shoemaker) was in Wallingford with
his wife Hannah, among the first settlers. She died June 19,
1677, and he married Esther ——, who died Sept. 12, 1706.
He died Nov. 7. 1706, ae. 72 years. He was the original
owner of the James Rice place at the head of Main-st., in
Wallingford.

Children: 11 *Mary*, b Aug. 12, 1673, d Aug. 12, 1675 ; 12
*Mercy*, b Feb. 4, 1675, d Feb. 24, 1675 ; 14 *Esther*, b Oct.
15, 1678; 15 *Lydia*, b May 28, 1680, m Daniel Messenger ;
16 *Nehemiah*, b May 18, 1682-3, m Keziah Hall, Feb. 9, 1700 ;
17 *Margery*, d Sept. 12, 1683.

## 3. NATHANIEL.

NATHANIEL ROYCE married Esther ——, Oct. 27, 1673.
She died June 19, 1677. He was married to Sarah Lathrop
by Mr. Moss, April 21, 1681. She died Nov. 11, 1706. He
then married Hannah Farnham. Aug. 24, 1707. She died
Feb. 6, 1708, and he married Abigail Hoyt, Aug. 25, 1708.
She died and he married Phebe Clark, Dec. 27, 1720. He
died Feb. 8. 1736 ; was by trade, a carpenter and joiner and
blacksmith in 1687.

Children by 1st marriage : 18 *John*, b April 11, 1675 ; 19
*Benjamin*, b May 6, 1677. m Rebecca Wilcoxen, d Oct. 20,
1703. By 2d marriage : 20 *Sarah*, b April 3, 1683 ; 21 *Hester*,
b Sept. 10, 1685, d Oct. 14, 1703, ae. 18 yrs. ; 22 *Lois*, b July
29. 1687, m Samuel Hall ; 23 *Elizabeth*, b Dec. 28, 1689. By
3th marriage : 24 *Daniel*, b Sept. 29, 1726 ; 25 *Lois*. b March
27. 1728 ; 26 *Robert*, b Nov. 19, 1729 ; 27 *Elisha*, b Oct. 27,
1731 ; 28 *Nathaniel*, b July 1, 1733.

SAMUEL ROYCE married 1st, Sarah Baldwin, June 5, 1690,[1]
2d, Hannah Benedict, Dec. 12, 1695. He died in Meriden,
May 14, 1757, ae. 85 years. Mrs. Hannah died in Meriden,
Jan. 12, 1761, ae. 90 yrs.

Children by 1st marriage: 29 *Abigail*, b Nov. 24, 1677, m
Joseph Cole ; 30 *Prudence*, b July 26, 1680; 31 *Deborah*, b
Sept. 8, 1683, m Thomas Mix ; 32 *Isaac*, b March 10, 1688 ;
33 *Ebenezer*, b Sept. 25, 1691 ; 34 *Nathaniel*, b Oct. 21, 1692 ;
35 *John*, b April 25, 1693 ; 36 *Mary*, b Feb. 17, 1695 ; 37
*Jacob*, b April 11, 1697, m Thankful Beach, dau. of Moses ;
By 2d marriage : 38 *Hannah*, b Feb. 19, 1697-8, m John Ives ;
39 *Ezekiel*, b Feb. 10, 1699, m Anna Merwin, Apr. 26, 1723 ; 40
*Samuel*, b Oct. 5, 1702, settled in Cheshire, in Martha Moss,
1728 ; 41 *Abel*, b Jan. 10, 1700; 42 *Benjamin*, b May 23,
1705, m Mindwell Royce, April 11, 1729, was clerk of the
mines, d Jan. 30, 1758 ; 43 *Mehitable*, b July 30, 1709 ; 44
*Ebenezer*, b Aug. 21, 1713, d Oct. 18, 1752, in Meriden,
aged 39.

## 5. JOSEPH.

JOSEPH ROYCE, married to Mary Porter, by the Hon. J.
Wadsworth, Oct. 1, 1684. He died March 19, 1704, or 1707,
æ. 44 yrs.

Children : 45 *Mary*, b Jan. 12, 1686 ; 46 *Joseph*, b May 1,
1689, d June 27, 1689 ; 47 *Joseph*, b May 2, 1690. m Anna
Andrews, March, 1710 ; 48 *Thomas*, b Aug. 13, 1692, m Mary
—— ; 49 *Nathaniel*, b Oct. 21, 1693 ; 50 *James*, b July 31,
1695, d Dec. 22, 1695 ; 51 *Hannah*, b Nov. 6, 1696, d ; 52
*Sarah*, b Feb. 24, 1699. d Dec. 6, 1711 ; 53 *Hannah*, b March
18, 1701 : 54 *Reuben*, b Dec. 18, 1703, d Sept. 10, 1790, æ.
77 yrs.

## 8. ROBERT.

ROBERT ROYCE married 1st, Mary ——, June 2, 1692 ; 2d,
Abigail Benedict, March 14, 1709. He died in 1759, ae.
94 yrs.

Children : 55 *Nathaniel*, b Oct. 23, 1694, m Phebe Clark, Dec. 20, 1720 ; 56 *Dinah*, b Feb. 24, 1696 ; 57 *Josiah*, b July 10, 1698 ; 58 *Ruth*, b Sept., 1701 ; 59 *Sarah*, b April 4, 1703, d Aug. 5. 1723 ; 60 *Timothy*, b June 2. 1705. m Mindwell Wassles, May 16, 1727 ; 61 *Mary*, b July, 1707 ; 62 *Elizabeth*, b Aug., 1709 ; 63 *Gideon*, b May 4. 1711, m Rebecca —— ; 64 *Prudence*, b April 11, 1714 ; 65 *Moses*, b Sept. 24. 1716, m Thankful *Austin* ; 66 *Martha*, m Edmund Scott, March 16, 1730 ; 67 *Lydia*, b Nov. 20, 1719.

### 19. BENJAMIN.

BENJAMIN ROYCE, son of Nehemiah and Hannah, married Rebecca Wilcoxen of Stratford, Conn. : he d Oct. 20, 1701.

Child : 68 *Mindwell*, b Oct. 12. 1703, m Benjamin Royce, April 11, 1729.

### 16. NEHEMIAH.

NEHEMIAH ROYCE, son of Nehemiah and Hannah, married Keziah Hall. His farm was at the head of Falls Plain.

Children : 69 Capt. *James*, b June 30, 1711, d Jan. 20, 1796, ae. 85 yrs. ; 70 *Hannah*, b Nov.. 1713, d Dec. 14, 1713 ; 71 *Phineas*, b June 16, 1715 ; 72 *Ephraim*, b Feb. 9, 1717 ; 73 *Hannah*, b May 15, 1720, m Eunice —— ; 74 *Keziah*, b March 16, 1726.

### 32. ISAAC.

ISAAC ROYCE, son of Samuel and Sarah, m Hannah - - – Children : 75 *Richard*, b March 16, 1759 ; 76 *Hannah*, b May 20, 1761.

### 33. ELENTZER.

ELENEZER ROYCE, son of Samuel and Sarah, married Abigail Roct, March 4, 1741. He died in Meriden, Oct. 18, 1752. ae. 39 years.

Children : 77 *Hannah*, b Jan. 5. 1743 ; 78 *Huldah*, b Jan. 16, 1745 ; 79 *Oliver*, b March 1, 1747, d at Meriden Dec. 6, 1755, ae. 7 years ; 80 *Samuel*, b Oct. 25, 1751.

### 34. NATHANIEL.

NATHANIEL ROYCE, son of Samuel and Sarah, married Phebe Clark Dec. 27. 1720.

Children: 81 *John*, b Feb. 14, 1723 ; 82 *Dinah*, b Nov. 6,
1724 ; 83 *David*, b Sept. 29, 1726 ; 84 *Lois*, b March 27,
1728 ; 85 *Robert*, b Nov. 16, 1729 ; 86 *Nathaniel*, b July 1,
1733 ; 87 *Phebe*, b May 15, 1735 ; 88 *John*, b March 22,
1737 ; 89 *Josiah*, b March 2, 1738 ; 90 *Elisha*, b Oct. 27,
1739 ; 91 *Clark*, b Oct. 4, 1740.

### 37. JACOB.

JACOB ROYCE, son of Samuel and Sarah Royce, was
married to Thankful Beach by Capt. Hall, Sept. 28, 1724.
He died Nov. 13, 1727.

Children : 92 *Amos*, b Nov. 1, 1725, m Sarah —— ; 93
*Experience*, b Dec. 1, 1727.

### 39. EZEKIEL.

EZEKIEL, son of Samuel and Hannah Royce, married
1st, Anna Merwin, April 25, 1723. She died Dec. 20, 1725;
He married 2d, Abigail Alling, Nov. 30, 1726.    He died in
Meriden, Sept. 4, 1765, ae. 66 years.

Children by 1st marriage : 94 *Samuel*, b Jan. 29, 1724 ; 95
*Barnabas*, b Dec. 12, 1725.    By 2d marriage : 96 *Anna*, b
July 3, 1727 ; 97 *Rachel*, b Oct. 4, 1728 ; 98 *Ezra*, b June 7,
1730, m Anna —— ; 99 *Lucy*, b March 4, 1732 ; 100 *Deborah*,
b Aug. 17, 1734 ; 101 *Ezekiel*, b July 23, 1736 ; 102 *Ezekiel*, b
Oct. 15, 1739, m Lydia ——, d Sept., 1808, ae. 69 years ; 103
*Abigail*, b July 14, 1751.

### 40. SAMUEL.

SAMUEL ROYCE, son of Samuel and Hannah, married
Martha Moss, Dec. 25, 1728.

Children : 104 *Samuel*, b May 9, 1732, m Sarah —— ;
105 *Nathaniel*, b May 20, 1734, m Sybil —— ; 106 *Sarah*,
b Nov. 27, 1737 ; 107 *Ebenezer*, b April 13, 1740 ; 108 *Levi*,
b Oct. 29, 1744 ; 109 *Reuben*, b June 22, 1750.

### 41. ABEL.

ABEL ROYCE, son of Samuel and Hannah Royce, was
married to Joanna Beach, Oct. 23, 1723, by Thomas Yale.

Children : 110, *Rhoda*, b Dec. 13, 1725 ; 111 *Hester*, b

Dec. 21, 1727 ; 112, 113 *Abel* and *Joanna*, b March 30, 1730; 114 *Benedict*, b Feb. 19, 1735 ; 115 *Mehitable*, b April 1, 1737 ; 116 *Hezekiah*, b Dec. 16, 1739 ; 117 *Huldah*, b Nov. 6, 1742.

### 42. BENJAMIN.

BENJAMIN ROYCE, son of Samuel and Hannah Royce, married Mindwell ⸺, April 11, 1729.

Children : 118 *Benjamin*, b April 1, 1730, m Phebe ⸺, she d June 13, 1776, ae. 46, he d in Meriden, Feb., 1777 ; 119 *Solomon*, b Jan. 31, 1741.

### 44. EBENEZER.

EBENEZER ROYCE, son of Samuel and Hannah Royce, married Abigail Root, March 4, 1741.

Children : 120 *Hannah*, b Jan. 5, 1743 ; 121 *Huldah*, b Jan. 16, 1745 ; 122 *Olive*, b March 1, 1747 ; 123 *Samuel*, b Oct. 28, 1751.

### 48. THOMAS.

THOMAS ROYCE, son of Joseph and Mary Royce, married Mary Holt, Dec. 23, 1714, residence in Meriden He married Anna Child, July 21, 1730.

Children : 124 *Sarah*, b June 23, 1716 ; 125 *Joseph*, b July 16, 1719, m Eunice ⸺ ; 126 *Mary*, b Feb. 12, 1723 ; 127 *Benjamin*, b June 26, 1724, m Anna Chamberlain, May 29, 1750 ; 128 *Thomas*, b June 29, 1727 ; 129 *Enos* ; 130 *Anna*, b Sept. 15, 1731 ; 131 *Samuel*, b Nov. 20, 1733 ; 132 *Phebe*, b Dec. 30, 1742.

### 54. REUBEN.

REUBEN ROYCE, son of Joseph and Mary Royce, married Keziah Moss, Nov. 18, 1736. She died Oct. 3, 1770, ae. 53. He died Sept. 10, 1790, ae. 77 years.

Children : 133 *Anna*, b Aug. 5, 1737 ; 134 *Rachel*, b Nov. 26, 1753.

### 57. JOSIAH.

JOSIAH ROYCE, son of Robert and Abigail, married Elizabeth Parker, March 24, 1693. Married 2d, Abigail Clark, May 1, 1722.

Children: 135 *Ebenezer*, b Jan. 22, 1713.  By 2d marriage: 136 *Sarah*, b June 5, 1723; 137 *Justus*, b 1725; 138 *Thankful*, b 1727; 139 *Charles*, b 1731; 140 *Stephen*, b 1733; 141 *Caleb*, b 1734.

### 60. TIMOTHY.

TIMOTHY ROYCE, son of Robert and Abigail, married Mindwell Wassles, May 16, 1727.

Children: 142 *Hannah*, b Dec. 29, 1727; 143 *Lydia*, b Feb. 11, 1730; 144 *Timothy*, b June 25, 1732, m Abigail ——; 145 *Ruth*, b Aug. 31, 1735.

### 63. GIDEON.

GIDEON ROYCE, son of Robert and Abigail, m 1st, Mary ——, 2d, Rebecca ——.

Children: 146 *Mary*, b May 10, 1743; 147 *Titus*, b Feb. 4, 1745; 148 *Wait*, b July 11. 1748; 149 *Gideon*, b Dec. 26, 1751; 150 *Mary*, b Oct. 30, 1753; 151 *Justice*, b Dec. 8, 1756, m Lois Perkins, of Meriden; 152 *Rebecca*, b April 16, 1758; 153 *Jonathan*, b March 18, 1760.

### 65. MOSES.

MOSES ROYCE, son of Robert and Abigail, married Thankful Austin, Jan. 6, 1740.

Children: 154 *Thankful*, b July 5, 1747; 155 *Amasa*, b March 21, 1751, d Dec. 12, 1797, ae. 47 yrs.; 156 *Abner*, b Jan. 4, 1753; 157 *Joel*, b Feb. 16, 1754; 158 *Amos*, b March 19, 1757.

### 69. JAMES.

CAPT. JAMES ROYCE, son of Nehemiah and Keziah, married Miriam ——.  She died Aug. 20, 1757, ae. 37 years. He died Jan. 20, 1796, ae. 85 years.

Children: 159 *Elizabeth*, b Jan. 6, 1744; 160 *Keziah*, b July 27, 1746, m Janet Tyler, of Wallingford; 161 *James*, b Dec. 18, 1748, m Mary Tyler; 162 *Joel*, b Jan. 10, 1751, d July 27, 1756, ae. 6 yrs.

### 72. EPHRAIM.

EPHRAIM ROYCE, son of Nehemiah and Keziah, married Eunice ——.

Children: 163 *Mindwell*, b Aug. 12, 1740 ; 164 *Keziah*, b May 12, 1742 ; 165 *Margery*, b March 17, 1742 ; 166 *Ephraim*, b June 30, 1744 ; 167 *Stephen*, b Sept. 2, 1752 ; 168 *Mary*, b Dec. 31, 1754.

### 85. ROBERT.

ROBERT ROYCE, son of Nathaniel and Phebe, married Hannah ~~Hart~~ Nov. 5, 1752.

Children: 169 *Bennet*, b Nov. 11, 1752 ; 170 *Hannah*, b Jan. 27, 1755 ; 171 *Chauncey*, b April 20, 1757 ; 172 *David*, b Feb. 24, 1760.

### 86. NATHANIEL.

NATHANIEL ROYCE, son of Nathaniel and Phebe, married Sybil ———.

Children : 173 *Martha*, b Jan. 3, 1756 ; 174 *Sibil*, b April 11, 1760.

### 88. JOHN.

JOHN ROYCE, son of Nathaniel and Phebe, married Hannah ———.

Children : 175 *Mary*, b May 8, 1751 ; 176 *Hannah*, b Jan. 18, 1753, d ; 177 *Matthew*, b Oct. 13, 1759 ; 178 *Hannah*, b June 2, 1761.

### 92. AMOS.

AMOS ROYCE, son of Jacob and Thankful, m Sarah ———.

Children : 179 *Sarah*, b Sept. 3, 1754 ; 180 *Jacob*, b Dec. 9, 1756, m —— Hull ; 181 *John*, b Nov. 15, 1758 ; 182 *Hannah*, b May 22, 1761.

### 94. SAMUEL.

SAMUEL, son of Ezekiel and Anna Royce, married Deborah ———.

Children : 183 *Stephen*, b Oct. 21, 1756 ; 184 *Hannah*, b April 28, 1758 ; 185 *Ebenezer*, b March 24, 1760.

### 98. EZRA.

EZRA, son of Ezekiel and Anna Royce, married Anna Royce, Nov. 25, 1746 ; res. in Meriden before 1793.

Children : 186 *Jesse*, b Oct. 3, 1746 ; *Rachel*, b Oct. 20, 1747 , 187 *Joseph*, b April 14, 1756 ; *Mehitable*, b April 3,

1750 ; 188 *Sarah*, b Nov. 9, 1751 ; *Seth*, b June 6, 1752 ; 189 *Esther*, b Aug. 2, 1754 ; *Asa*, b Sept. 1, 1754 ; 190 *Deborah*, b Sept. 6, 1757 ; *Lucy*, b Oct. 26, 1757 ; 191 *Thomas*, b Sept. 26, 1749 ; 192 *Ezra*, b Oct. 30, 1759, res. in Meriden.

### 102. EZEKIEL.

EZEKIEL, son of Ezekiel and Anna Royce, married Lydia ——. She died Oct. 28, 1813, ae. 73 yrs. He died Sept. 3, 1808, ae. 69, in Meriden.

Child : 193 *Oliver*, b July 26, 1760, d in Meriden, April 28, 1794, ae. 34 yrs.

### 104. SAMUEL.

SAMUEL, son of Samuel and Martha Royce, married Sarah ——.

Children : 194 *Mindwell*, b Nov. 8, 1756, m Josiah Mix in 1777 ; 195 *Phebe*, b Nov. 10, 1758 ; 196 *Lucy*, b May 1, 1761 ; 197 *Keziah*, b March 25, 1768, m Josiah Mix, he d in Ohio, May 13, 1845, ae. 91.

### 116. HEZEKIAH.

HEZEKIAH, son of Abel and Joanna Royce, died in Meriden at a very advanced age.

Children : 198 *Benajah*, d near South Meriden ; 199 *Porter*, d in Wallingford.

### 123. SAMUEL.

SAMUEL, son of Ebenezer and Abigail Royce, married Deborah ——.

Children : 200 *Stephen*, b Oct. 21, 1756 ; 201 *Hannah*, b April 28, 1758 ; 202 *Ebenezer*, b March 24, 1760.

### 125. JOSEPH.

JOSEPH, son of Thomas and Mary Royce, married Eunice ——.

Child : 203 Capt. *Joseph*, b 1748, d Sept. 10, 1790, ae. 77.

### 144. TIMOTHY.

TIMOTHY, son of Gideon and Rebecca Royce, married Abigail ——.

Children : 204 *Mindwell*, b April 27, 1754 ; 205 *Timothy*, b

May 12 1751, 20. *Elijah*, b July 26. 1756   207 *Charl...* b
Sep'' 7. 1757. 2 8 *Jemima*, b Sept. 27. 175i   200 *Kath rin.*
b Oct 4. 1760.

## 151. JESTER.

JESTER ROYCE, son of Gideon and Rebecca Royce, mar
ried Lois Perkins of Meriden.  She died in Wallingford and
was buried there.

Children: 210 *Roswell*, d in Wallingford ; 211 *Jotham.*
went west: 212 *Ann*, m Moses Taylor ; 213 *Mary*, d in
Meriden ; 214 *Titus*, resides in Wallingford now. 1870

## EVAN.

EVAN ROYCE married Rachel Parker. May 20, 1724.  He
does not appear to be of the same family of any of the preceding, yet it is quite possible that he was.

Children: 215 *John*, b May 25. 1725 ; 216 *Anna*, b June
23. 1724 ; 217 *Evan*, b June 18, 1729 ; 218 *Charles*,  b March
28. 1731 ; 219 *Mary*, b Feb. 5, 1733 ; 220 *James*, b Jan. 1.
1735 ; 221 *Lois*, b Nov. 4. 1740 ; 222 *Rachel*, b June 30. 1743 ;
223 *Hannah*, b March 25, 1759 : 224 *James*, b Feb. 1, 1757.

## 161. JAMES.

JAS. ROYCE, son of Capt. Jas. and Miriam Royce, when li\-
ing, owned and occupied the house and lot at the head of Main
Street, in the village of Wallingford.  The old house and lot
had been owned by the family from 1670 down to 1808.  Mr.
James Royce died Feb. 17, 1827, ae. 79 years  His wife died
Aug 6, 1834, ae. 83 years.  The maiden name of his wife
was Mary, daughter of William Tyler, and sister of Samuel
and Fred Tyler, late of Wallingford.

Children: 225 *Nehemiah*, b 1774, m 1st, Ruth Hall, 2d,
Abigail, daughter of Caleb Hall, Esq., he d April 8 1851.
ae. 57 years. 226 *Ambrose*, b 1777, d Aug. 21, 181\-. ae. 33
years ; 227 *Miriam*, m Isaac Peck of Wallingford  228
*Samuel*, d in western N. Y., a Baptist minister ; 226 *Lucy*,
m Chauncey Hough of Wallingford ; 230 *Fred*, b 1786, m
Lucretia Vale, d Dec. 21, 1828 ; 231 *James*, resides in west

ern N. Y. ; 232 *Mary*, b 1782, d Aug., 1859, ae. 77 ; 233 *Henrietta*, b 1791, d of measles, Feb. 18, 1818, ae. 27 years ; 234 *Sylvester*, b 1793, d April 1, 1820, ae. 27 years.

### 218. CHARLES.

CHARLES, son of Evan and Rachel Royce, married Lois ——.

Child ; 235 *Thaddeus*, b Nov. 3, 1757, res. near Gitteau's corner.

## STANLEY.[1]

The ancestor of the Wallingford Stanleys was John Stanley, who died on his passage over from England, leaving a son John, and a daughter Ruth, both of whom were married (the same day), Dec. 5, 1645. John the son was nephew of Timothy Stanley, of Cambridge and Hartford.

John Stanley, the grandfather of the Wallingford branch, was born in 1625, came to New England in 1634, settled early in Windsor and Farmington, joined the church in Farmington July 12, 1753, was a deputy from Farmington, four sessions to the General Court, was a Captain in King Philip's War, and a leading man in Farmington. He married Sarah, daughter of Thomas Scott, Dec. 5 1645. He married 2d, Sarah, daughter of John Fletcher, of Milford, June 26, 1661. He died Dec. 19, 1706, and his 2d wife and widow died May 15, 1713.

Children : 1 *John*, b in Hartford, Nov. 3, 1647 ; 2 *Thomas*, b in Farmington, Nov. 1, 1649, m in 1690, Anne, daughter of Rev. Jeremiah Peck, she d May 23. 1718 ; 3 *Sarah*, b Feb., 1651-2, m Joseph Gaylord ; 4 *Timothy*, b March 17, 1653-4, m Mary, dau. of John Strong, in 1676, and d childless ; 5

---

[1] For collateral branches, see Andrews' Hist. New Britain, Conn. ; Dagget's Hist. Attleborough, Mass., 94, 95 ; Judd and Boltwood's Hist. Hadley, Mass., 582 ; Leonard's Hist. Dublin, N. H., 396-7 ; Morse's Memorial of Morses, App. No. 55 ; Savage's Gen. Dict., IV. 163-6; Thurston's Hist. Winthrop, Me., 196-7.

*Elizabeth*, b April 1, 1657, d , 6 *Abigail*, b July 25, 1669, m John Hooker, Nov. 1687 ; 7 *Elizabeth*, b Nov. 28, 1672, m John Wadsworth, she d Oct. 5, 1713 ; 8 *Isaac*, b Sept. 22, 1660, was an imbecile.

### 1. JOHN.

JOHN STANLEY appears to have been a prominent man in Waterbury. He was the first recorder of the town and pro prietors. He was appointed first by the committee, and afterward, Dec. 26, 1682, by the town, which offi e he filled until his removal to Farmington. He was a good penm n and well qualified for the office, as the records fully demon strat-. He married Esther, daughter of Thomas Newell of Farmington, and d May 16, 1729 : she d in 1740.

Childr n: 9 *Esther*, b Dec. 2, 1672, in Farmington, d 1676, ae. 4 years ; 10 *John*, b April 9. 1675, in Farmington, m Dec 14, 1714, d Sept. 8, 1748 , 11 *Samuel*, b 1677, m Eliza beth, daughter of Abraham Bro son of Lyme, July 15, 1702 12 *Nathaniel*, b 1679, m Sarah Smith and settled in Goshen, d 1770 ; 13 *Thomas*, b May 25 1684 in Farmington ; 14 *Sarah*, b July 4, 1686 ; 15 *Timothy*, b June 6, 1689, m Martha Smith of Farmington, settled in Goshen after 1735.

### 11. SAMUEL.

SAMUEL STANLEY married Elizabeth, daughter of Abraham Bronson of Lyme. He died in 1737 ; he was a mill wright and carpenter, and lived in Wallingford Farmington and Durham

Child n: 16 *Samuel*, b in Waterbury ; 17 *Abraham*, b April 13, 1705, m Prudence, dau. of Isaac Pinn y, of Wind sor, Conn. ; 18 *John* ; 19 *Esther* ; 20 *Ebenezer* ; 21 *Anna*, b March 8, 1713, all b in Wallingford ; 22 *Elizabeth*, b 1715 ; 23 *Asa*, b 1717 ; 24 *Ruth* ; 25 *Josiah*, all b in Farmington.

### 17. ABRAHAM.

ABRAHAM STANLEY married Prudence Pinney of Windsor. He ettled on a farm a little west of Yalesville He died Feb. 17, 1788, ae 85 yr

I I I

Children: 26 *Abraham*, b Dec. 7, 1731; 27 *Prudence*, b
May 13, 1734, m Laban Andrews, April 5, 1758; 28 *Oliver*,
b Oct. 10, 1743, grad. at Yale, 1768, was a lawyer; 29 *Lucretia*,
b Aug. 7, 1748, m Elihu Yale.

### 18. JOHN.

JOHN STANLEY married Hannah Ives, May, 29, 1735. She
died in Wallingford, July 13, 1750.

Children: 30 *Hannah*, b June 6, 1736, d June 28, 1750, ae.
14 yrs.; 31 *John*, b Dec. 26, 1737; 32 *Mary*, b June 11,
1740; 33 *Thomas*, b July 1, 1743; 34 *Sarah*, b July 2, 1745.

### 25. JOSIAH.

JOSIAH STANLEY married Mary Miles, of Wallingford,
March 14, 1739. He died Oct. 31, 1756.

Children, 35 *Abigail*, b June 9, 1742; 36 *Mary*, b Aug. 9,
1744; 37 *Benjamin*, b June 3, 1748.

### 28. OLIVER.

OLIVER STANLEY ESQ. married ——. He was graduated
at Yale College in 1768, and became a lawyer of considerable
note in his native village. He owned the house and lot
where Mrs. Edgar Atwater now lives ( 1869 ), and died there.

Children: 38 *George Washington*, graduated at Yale; 39
*Sarah*, m Medad Baker.

### 38. GEORGE.

GEORGE WASHINGTON STANLEY ESQ. married ——. He
practiced his profession as a lawyer in his native place for
several years, with great success; and was Town Clerk and
Judge of the Probate Court. In 18— he went to Middletown, where he was made Attorney for the State. He remained
there several years, and subsequently went to Cleveland, Ohio,
where he soon became distinguished as a learned, discreet
and faithful counselor. He died at an advanced age, leaving
one son to perpetuate his name. and who is reported to be a
successful business man at Cleveland.

## SCARRITT.

James Scarritt was from Branford, Conn. In 1758 he was in the old French war with Miles Yale, Col. Isaac Cook, Samuel Parsons, and old Samuel Barnes. These men used to meet often and relate their experiences in that war, to the great gratification of any who might be present. Mr. Scarritt was a weaver and schoolmaster. He taught school before the Revolution, and until within the memory of the writer. He was the honored father of John Scarritt, who was also a schoolmaster, and also the highly respected Town Clerk of New Haven, for many consecutive years. He died in New Haven.

Children: 1 *Amanda*, m W. Lyon, she d in 1869 ; 2 *Lydia*. m John D. Reynolds ; 3 *Marcus*, 4 *Louisa*; 5 *James*. m ——— Johnson, and removed to Waterbury.

## STREET.[1]

### NICHOLAS.

REV. NICHOLAS STREET came from England and settled at Farmington, Mass. In 1649 he went to New Haven where he died April 22, 1674.

Children : *Samuel*, b 1735, grad. at Harvard, 1664 ; *Susannah* ; *Sarah* ; *Abiah* ; *Hannah*.

### I. SAMUEL.

REV. SAMUEL STREET married Anna, daughter of ~~Samuel~~ Richard Miles, Nov. 3, 1664. He was one of the original subscribers to the settlement of Wallingford in 1670, and was the first settled clergyman in the place. Four years after the settlement commenced, he was called to settle there, and continued in the work of ministry there until his decease, Jan 17, 1717, a period of nearly 45 years. Mrs. Anna Street died July 19, 1730

Children 1 *Anna*, b 1665, in New Haven : 2 *Samuel*, b

1 For collateral branches, see Dodd's Hist. East Haven, Conn., 153 ; Savage's Gen. Dict., IV 222-3.

1667, in New Haven ; 3 *Mary*, b 1670, m John Hall of Wallingford ; 4 *Susanna*, b June 15, 1675, in Wallingford ; 5 *Nicholas*, b July 14. 1677, settled in Groton, Conn. ; 6 *Katharine*, b Nov. 19, 1679 ; 7 *Sarah*, b Jan. 15, 1681, m Theophilus Yale.

### 2. SAMUEL.

SAMUEL STREET JR. married Madeline Daniels, Nov. 1, 1684. She died and he married Hannah Glover, July 14, 1690. She died July 3, 1715, and he married for his third wife, Elizabeth ——, Dec. 20, 1716.

Children by 1st marriage : 8 *Samuel*, b Nov. 3, 1685 ; 9 *James*, b Dec. 28, 1686, m Rebecca Scoville, Sept. 6, 1731 ; 10 *Anna*, b Aug. 26, 1688. By 2d marriage : 11 *Eleanor*, b Dec. 3, 1690 ; 12 *Nathaniel*, b Jan. 19, 1692 ; 13 *Elnathan*, b Sept. 2, 1695, m Damaris Hull. Feb. 6, 1722 ; 14 *Mehitable*, b Feb. 15. 1699 ; 15 *John*, b Oct. 25, 1703, m Hannah Hall, June 9, 1734 ; 16 *Samuel*, b May 10, 1707, d Oct. 15, 1752.

### 5. NICHOLAS.

NICHOLAS STREET married Jerusha Morgan, April 22, 1707. Children : 17 *James*. b Feb. 10, 1708 ; 18 *Elizabeth*, b Apr. 24, 1709.

### 9. JAMES.

JAMES STREET m Rebecca Scoville. Children : 19 *Samuel*, b Sept. 6, 1731 ; 20 *James*. b Sept. 14, 1733.

### 13. ELNATHAN.

ELNATHAN STREET married Damaris Hall. Feb. 6, 1722.

Children : 21 *Benjamin*, b May 18, 1723 ; 22 *Samuel*, b Jan. 10, 1725, d Jan. 18, 1725 ; 23 *Samuel*, b Dec. 8, 1728 ; 24 *Nicholas*, b Feb. 21, 1730, graduated at Yale, 1751, ordained Oct. 8, 1755, d at East Haven, Oct. 3, 1706 ; 25 *Elnathan*, b Feb. 20, 1732 ; 26 *Anna*, b Feb. 16, 1736 ; 27 *Mary*, b June 28, 1738 ; 28 *Jesse*, b April 24, 1741, m Lois Cook.

### 15. JOHN.

JOHN STREET married Hannah Hall, June 5, 1734.

Children : 29 *Thaddeus*, b March 15. 1735, d March 16, 1735 ; 30 *Hannah*, b June 7, 1736 ; 31 *Sarah* b July 8 1738 ; 32 *Mary* b May 4, 1740 ; 33 *Elisha*, b Dec. 17, 1742.

### 16. SAMUEL.

SAMUEL STREET married 1st, Keziah Munson, Nov. 12, 1734 ; 2d, Sarah ———. She died Oct. 1, 1795, ae. 68 years ; he died in Wallingford, 1792, ae. 85 years.

Child by 1st marriage: 34 *Glover*, b May 1, 1735. Children by 2d marriage: 35 *Titus*, b June 4, 1750, m ——— Atwater, of Cheshire ; 36 *Caleb*, b Oct. 23 1753

## THOMPSON.[1]

There are few names more common among the early set tlers of New England than that of Thompson, most of whom came from London and Hertfordshire, and were probably related to each other. Of these, the principal individuals connected with the New England settlements were David Thompson, who emigrated to Portsmouth, N. H., in 1622, where he established fisheries, and in 1623, removed to an island in Boston Harbor, which still bears his name ; James Thompson, who was one of the first settlers of Woburn, Mass., in 1634 : Major Robert Thompson, who resided in Boston in 1639, and was a man of wealth and respectability ; Maurice Thompson, a merchant of London, Governor of the East India Co., who established fisheries at Cape Ann, in 1639 ; Rev. William Thompson, who came to York, Maine, in 1637, and Anthony Thompson, of New Haven, Conn.

1 For collateral branches, see Andrews' Hist. New Britain, Conn., 162 232 ; Barry's Hist. Hanover, Mass., 400, 410 ; Bradbury's Hist. Kennebunkport, Me., 297-80 ; Cothren's Hist. Woodbury, Conn., 727-37 ; Dodd's Hist. East Haven, Conn., 154-6 ; Eaton's Hist. Thomaston, Me., 427-9 ; Hooker's Memorials of James and Augustus Thompson ; Journals of Smith and Dean of Portland, Me., 68 ; Kingman's Hist N. Bridgewater, 414, 315 ; N. E. Hist. and Gen. Reg., IV. 18 , XVII. 112-16, 318-20 , Savage's Gen. Dict., IV. 283-90 ; Sewall's Hist. Woburn, Mass., 30, 40°, 643-5 ; Stiles's Hist Windsor, Ct, 815 ; Thompson's Gen. of Thompson Family ; Thompson's Hist. Long Island, N. Y., 11. 425-31

## JOSEPH.

JOSEPH THOMPSON and his wife Elizabeth were in Wallingford among the first planters, though not an original subscriber.   He was collector of taxes in 1681.

Children: 1 *Joseph*, m Hannah Clark, Feb. 1, 1700; 2 *John*, b Feb. 1, 1685, m Sarah Culver, June 23, 1710; 3 *Hannah*, b April 16, 1687.

### 1. JOSEPH.

JOSEPH THOMPSON, son of Joseph and Elizabeth Thompson, married Hannah Clark.   He died ae. 67 years.

Children: 4 *Elizabeth*, b Oct. 23, 1710; 5 *Samuel*. b Nov. 10, 1713; 6 *Tamar*, b Sept. 18, 1715; 7 *Phebe*, b April 12, 1720; 8 *Hannah*, b Sept. 10. 1725; 9 *Keziah*, b Jan. 15, 1728.

### 2. JOHN.

JOHN THOMPSON, son of Joseph and Elizabeth Thompson, married Sarah Culver, June 23. 1710.

Children: 10 *Abel*, b and d Jan. 14, 1715; 11 *Abel*, b 1717, d 1798; 12 *Anna*, b Jan. 28, 1719, m Benjamin Sedgwick; 13 *Mabel*, b Nov. 11, 1721; 14 *Sarah*, b Oct. 5, 1724, m John Moss: 15 *John*, b Jan. 26, 1726.

### 5. SAMUEL.

SAMUEL THOMPSON, son of Joseph and Hannah Thompson, married Rachel ———.

Children: 16 *John*, b Feb. 24, 1747; 17 *Samuel*, b June 11, 1751; 18 *Phebe*, b Feb. 20, 1753; 19 *Rachel*, b April 20, 1755; 20 *Samuel*, b Oct. 5, 1757.

### 11. ABEL.

ABEL THOMPSON, son of John and Sarah Culver Thompson, married ———.   He was the father of Abel, who was the father of Capt. Caleb Thompson, late of Wallingford, deceased.

Children: 21 *Edward*, d in Wallingford; 22 *Stiles H.*, d 1863; 23 *Lodema*, m E. S. Ives, Esq.; 24 daughter.

### JOSEPH.

Joseph and Abigail Thompson had the following family in Wallingford.

Children: 25 *Elihu*, b Oct. 9. 1745; 26 *J. W.*, b July 22, 1757

### THORP.[1]

#### SAMUEL.

Sergt. Samuel Thorp was an early settler in the eastern part of Wallingford, near Muddy river. His house stood on the east side of said river, on an old highway which is closed, and which ran south from the east side of the late Col. Russel Hall's barn. Lot No. 14 on the east side of the main street, in the village, was assigned him for a house lot. He died at the age of 84, Feb. 2, 1728. Mary Thorp, his wife, died March 1, 1718.

Children: 1 *Elizabeth*, b Feb. 15, 1668; 2 *Samuel*, b Mar. 8, 1670; 3 *Hannah*, b Sept. 9, 1678; 4 *Abigail*, b Jan. 31, 1681, m John Boulcott, Oct. 18, 1708; 5 *John*, b July 6, 1686 6 *Samuel*, b Apr. 11, 1687; 7 *Hannah*.

#### 6. SAMUEL.

Samuel Thorp married 1st, Hannah ——— 2d, Elizabeth How. He died March 14, 1704. She died Oct. 19, 1756.

Children by 1st marriage: 8 *Samuel*, b Mar. 24, 1707; 9 *Joseph*, b Dec. 8, 1708; 10 *Elizabeth*, b Oct. 3, 1710; 11 *David*, b Jan. 4, 1711; 12 *Hannah*, b Nov. 18, 1712; 13 *Samuel*, b Apr. 10, 1715; 14 *Julia*, b Oct. 31, 1714; 15 *Abigail*, b Nov. 1, 1716; 16 *Thomas*. 17 *Benjamin*, b Sept. 3, 1715 18 *John*, b Aug. 2, 1718; 19 *Oliver*, b Mar. 14, 1711. By 2d marriage: 20 *Hannah*, b Feb. 11, 1722; 21 *Mabel*, b Jan. 12 1724, 22 *Mary*, d Oct. 19, 1767; 23 *Abner*, b Oct. 14, 1725; 24 *Lucy*, b Oct. 14, 1727; 25 *Phebe*, b Apr. 1, 1728; 26

---

1 For collateral branches, see Savage's Gen. Dic., V. 2.

*Elnathan*, b Aug. 13, 1729 ; 27 *Sarah*, b Dec. 10, 1734 ; 28 *Tamar*, b Sept. 18, 1735.

### 9. JOSEPH.

JOSEPH THORP, married Abigail ———. He died Sept. 13, 1755.
Children: 29 *Sarah*, b July 7, 1741 ; 30 *Jared*, b Oct. 27, 1744 ; 31 *Joseph*, b May 1, 1750 ; 32 *Titus*, b Mar. 1, 1751 ; 33 *Abigail*, b Apr. 22, 1753.

### 11. DANIEL.

DANIEL THORP married Elizabeth ———. She died Oct. 16, 1751.

Child : 34 *Mary*, d Oct. 16, 1751.

### 13. SAMUEL.

SAMUEL THORP, son of Samuel and Hannah.
Children : 35 *Thomas ;* 36 *Lois*, b Feb. 26, 1736 ; 37 *Sarah*, b Apr. 16, 1737 ; 38 *Lydia*, b Oct. 9, 1741 ; 39 *Lynes*, b Oct. 12, 1743.

## TUTTLE.[1]

### WILLIAM.

WILLIAM TUTTLE, his wife and three children, and a brother John came from Devonshire, England, in the ship Planter, as passengers, and were registered April, 1635. John was born in 1596, and settled at Ipswich, Mass. ; he left numerous descendants. William's age was put at twenty-six years, his wife 'Elizabeth's at 23 yrs., John, their eldest child, at 3 1-2 yrs., Ann, 2 1-2 yrs., and Thomas at three months. Mrs. Elizabeth united with the church in Boston, July 24, 1636, and brought to be baptized a son, Jonathan, July 2, 1637, and another, David, April 7, 1639. Soon after, the family re-

---

1 For collateral branches, see Cothren's Hist. Woodbury, Conn., 723-7 ; Dodd's Hist. East Haven, Conn., 156-8 ; Hall's Hist. Rec. Norwalk, Ct., 203-241, 267-269, 281-290, 297 ; Hudson's Hist. Lexington, Mass., 248, 249 ; N. E. Hist. and Gen. Reg., VIII. 132-42 ; Otis's Gen. Otis Family; Savage's Gen. Dict., IV. 350-2 ; Wyman's Hunt Family Hist., 529.

moved to New Haven, there he became a man of consequence, and was much employed in public affairs. He
resided in that part of the town now called North Haven,
and was there in 1659, on land that belonged to the estate of
Gov. Eaton. He died in 1673, at the age of 64 years. Mrs.
Elizabeth died Dec. 30, 1684, at 81 years. He was a subscriber to the compact for the settlement of East Haven. Estate, £440.

Children: 1 *John*, b 1631, in England, m Catharine Lane,
2 *Anna*, b 1633, in England; 3 *Thomas*, b 1635, m Hannah
Powell, May 21, 1670. 4 *Jonathan*, b July 2, 1637, in Boston,
m Rebecca, dau. of Francis Bell; 5 *David*, b April 7, 1639,
in Boston, d in 1693; 6 *Joseph*, b Nov. 22, 1640, in New
Haven, m Hannah Munson; 7 *Sarah*, b April 1642, m John
Hanson, Nov. 11, 1663; 8 *Elizabeth*, b Nov., 1645, m
Timothy Edwards of Windsor, 1667. 9 *Simon*, b March 28,
1647, settled at Wallingford in 1670. 10 *Benjamin* b Oct. 29,
1648; 11 *Mercy*, b April 27, 1650, m Samuel Brown of New
Haven, 12 *Nathaniel*, b Feb. 20, 1652, m Sarah, dau. of
Ephraim How, and settled at Woodbury, Conn., where he d
Aug. 20, 1721. Cothren, in Hist. of Woodbury, gives his
descendants.

### 1. JOHN.

JOHN TUTTLE, eldest son of William and Elizabeth Tuttle,
was born in England in 1628, came to America with his
parents in 1635, in the ship Planter, married Catherine Lane,
Nov. 8, 1653, and died in 1683. Estate, £79.

Children: 13 *Hannah*, b Nov. 3, 1655, m Samuel Clark
Nov. 7, 1672; 14 *John*, b Spt. 16 1657; 15 *Samuel*, b Jan.
9, 1659, m Sarah Newman, b 1658, 16 *Sarah*, b Jan. 22,
1661-2, m john Humiston, Sept 10, 1685; 17 *David*, b
April 12, 1664, d 1700, at Milford, ic. 36 years. 18 *Mary*, b
April 13, 1664 m John Ball, June 6, 1716; 19 *Elizabeth*, b
Nov. 26, 1666; 20 *David*, b Nov. 14, 1668.

### 3. THOMAS.

THOMAS TUTTLE, 2d son of William and Elizabeth Tuttle,

was born in England in 1634-5, and was brought to America by his parents in the ship Planter. He married Hannah Powell, May 21, 1661.

Children : 21 *Hannah*, b Feb. 24, 1661, m Samuel Clark, Nov. 7, 1672 ; 22 *Abigail*, b Jan. 17, 1663 ; 23 *Mary*, b June 14, 1665, d Aug. 12, 1683 ; 24 *Thomas Jr.*, b Oct. 27, 1667, m Mary Sanford, June 28, 1692, he d Jan. 30, 1703 ; 25 *John*, b Dec. 5, 1669 ; 26 *Esther*, b April 9, 1672, m Samuel Russell, Feb. 25, 1694 ; 27 *Caleb*, b Aug. 29, 1674, m Mary Hotchkiss, March 1, 1699 ; 28 *Joshua*, b Dec. 19, 1676, m Mary Mix, Feb 25, 1710 ; 29 *Martha*, b May 23, 1679, d Jan. 25, 1699, ae. 20.

### 4. JONATHAN.

JONATHAN, son of William and Elizabeth Tuttle, was born in Boston, and came to New Haven when a child with his parents. He married Rebecca Bell of Norwalk. Conn., and settled on a farm in what is now North Haven, and on which some of his descendants continue to reside to this day ( 1870 ). He died in 1700. Estate, £100. His wife Rebecca died May 2, 1676.

Children : 30 *Rebecca*, b Sept. 10, 1664 ; 31 *Mary*, b Feb. 7, 1666, m Ebenezer Frost, Oct. 4, 1704 ; 32 *David*, b Nov. 14, 1668 ; 33 *Jonathan*, b April 6, 1669 ; 34 *Simon*, b March 11, 1671 ; 35 *William*, b May 25, 1673 ; 36 *Nathaniel*, b Feb. 25, 1676.

### 5. DANIEL.

DANIEL, son of William and Elizabeth Tuttle, was a proprietor in 1685. For some cause which does not now appear, he was in 1687 put under the charge of his brother Thomas, and died in 1692, ae. 55 years, without children. He had lot 16, east side of Main-st. in Wallingford, 1670. Estate, £29.

### 6. JOSEPH.

JOSEPH, son of William and Elizabeth Tuttle, married Hannah, daughter of Thomas Munson, May 2 1667. He died in Sept., 1690. She afterwards married Nathan Bradley in 1694, and died in 1695. Estate, £269 This family was of East Haven, Conn.

Children: 37 *Joseph*, b March 18, 1668, m Elizabeth San ford, Dec. 10. 1691-2 ; 38 *Samuel*, b July 15, 1670, m Sarah Hart, Dec. 11, 1695 ; 39 *Stephen*, b May 20, 1673. m Ruth ——, settled at Woodbridge, N. J.; 40 *Jeanna*, b Feb. 25, 1675, m Stephen Panbonna ; 41 *Timothy*, b Sept. 30. 1678, d Nov. 21, 1678 ; 42 *Susannah*, b Feb. 20, 1679 ; 43 *Elizabeth*, b July 12, 1683 ; 44 *Hannah*, b May 14, 1685, d in infancy ; 45 *Hannah*, b Feb. 26, 1686.

## 8. ELIZABETH.

ELIZABETH TUTTLE, daughter of William and Elizabeth Tuttle, married Richard Edwards of Windsor, Conn. She was the maternal ancestor of the late Gov. Henry W. Edwards, of New Haven.

Children: 46 *Mary*, b 1668 ; 47 *Timothy*, b May 14, 1669, m Esther Stoddard ; 48 *Abigail*, b 1671 ; 49 *Elizabeth*. b 1675, 50 *Ann*, b 1678 : 51 *Mabel*, b 1685 ; 52 *Cynthia* ——

## 9. SIMON.

SIMON TUTTLE, son of William and Elizabeth Tuttle, married Miss Abigail, daughter of John Beach, and was among the first subscribers to the compact for the settlement of New Haven village ( now Wallingford ), in 1669-70, and settled there near his father Beach's land, perhaps on a portion of it. His house lot was No. 13, east side Main st., with 8 acres of out land. He died April 16, 1719. ae. 72 years. Mrs Abigail died Aug., 1722.

Children: 53 *Daniel*, b Nov. 11, 1680, m Ruth How, Oct. 18 1711 ; 54 *Dea. Timothy*, b 1681, m 1st. Thankful Doolittle, Nov. 2, 1706, she d Nov 23, 1728, 2d, Mary Bewford, Sarah Humiston, June 28, 1749, he died April 15, 1756, ae. 75 ; 55 *Thankful*; 56 *Rebecca*, b April 30, 1698 ; 57 *Jonathan*, b Sept. 18, 1701 : 58 *Isaiah*, b July 10, 1704, m Susannah Doolittle, June 4. 1727 ; 59 *Elizabeth*, b Nov. 8, 1705 ; 60 *Deborah*, b Jan. 1, 1709 , 61 *David*, b April 25, 1713.

### 11. MERCY.

MERCY TUTTLE, daughter of William and Elizabeth Tuttle, married Samuel Brown, who was among the original subscribers to the compact for the settlement of the village of Wallingford, and had assigned to him the lot on which now stands the residence of the late Moses Y. Beach, Esq. ; but as he did not settle on it within the time prescribed, he lost his title, and it was assigned to John Moss.   Dea. Philo Brown, of the firm of Brown, Elton & Co., of Waterbury, is a direct descendant of her.    See " Bronson's Waterbury."

Children : 62 *Abigail,* b March 11, 1669, d young ; 63 *Sarah,* b Aug. 8, 1672 ; 64 *Rachel,* b Aug. 14, 1677 ; 65 *Francis,* b Oct. 7, 1679 ; 66 *Gideon,* b July 12, 1685 ; 67 *Samuel,* b Oct. 29, 1699.

### 12. NATHANIEL.

NATHANIEL TUTTLE son of William and Elizabeth Tuttle, married Sarah How, Aug. 10, 1682.   He settled in Woodbury, Conn., about 1680, where he raised a considerable family.   He died Aug. 20, 1721, leaving a widow, Sarah. His descendants are somewhat numerous in Woodbury and vicinity, to this day.

Children : 68 *Mary,* bap. May, 1683, d before 1721 ; 69 *Ephraim,* bap. July 20, 1683, m Dinah Wheeler, Feb. 13, 1706 ; 70 *Temperance,* bap. Nov. 24, 1674, d Nov., 1749 ; 71 *Hezekiah,* m Martha Huthwith, April 11, 1711, d in 1753 ; 72 *Isaac.* b Feb. 3, 1698, m 1st. Prudence Wheeler, Jan. 10, 1729, she d 1730, m 2d, Mary Warner, she died Oct. 28, 1746 ; 73 *Anna,* d July 22, 1753.

### 35. WILLIAM.

WILLIAM, son of Jonathan and Rebecca Tuttle, m ————.

Children : 74 *Aaron.* b Nov. 25, 1698, m Mary Munson, Feb. 6, 1723–4 ; 75 *Mary.* b Aug., 1702 ; 76 *Susannah,* b Nov. 10, 1708 ; 77 *Lydia,* b Feb. 22, 1710–11 , 78 *Jemima,* b Feb. 13, 1712 ; 79 *Hannah,* b Nov. 10, 1715 ; 80 *Dan,* b Aug. 1, 1718, d young ; 81 *Dan,* b Aug. 30, 1722, m Abigail Frederick, Jan. 26, 1743, at Wallingford.

### 37. NATHANIEL.

NATHANIEL, 2d son of Jonathan and Rebecca Tuttle, married and settled in New Haven.

Children : 82 *Jonathan*, b 1701 ; 83 *Silence*, b 1703 ; 84 *Mary*, b May 8, 1704 ; 85 *Nathaniel*, b M., 29, 1714 m Mary Tod l, Jan. 16. 1737–8.

### 53. DANIEL.

CAPT. DANIEL TUTTLE. son of Simon and Abigail Tuttle, settled on lot 16, east side of the main street in Wallingford village, married Ruth How. Oct. 18, 1711 ; he died in 1740.

Children : 86 *Daniel*, b 1714, d Aug. 12, 1767, ae. 53 ; 87 *John*, b Aug. 7, 1717, m Hannah Hull, Aug 31, 1742 , 88 *Abiah*; 89 *Phebe*, b Jan 8, 1719, d ; 90 *Lydia*, b April 15, 1722, m Benj. Culver of Wallingford ; 91 *Eunice*, b April 9, 1725, d April 12, 1726 ; 92 *Eunice*, b July 12, 1726, m Gideon Ives, Jr , Oct. 19, 1745 ; 93 *Ambrose*, b Sept. 25, 1728, m Esther Ives, May 31, 1748 ; 94 *Enos*, b Jan. 3, 1732, m Sarah Francis, April 21, 1757 ; 95 *Mary*, b Oct. 11, 1733, m Joseph Francis, Aug. 31 1750 ; 96 *Phebe*, b Jan. 8 1734, m Samuel Miles ; 97 *Lois*, b March 9, 1737, m Abel Ives, June 19, 1760 ; 98 *Martha*, b Feb. 25, 1720, d Jan. 1, 1742.

### 54. TIMOTHY.

DEA. TIMOTHY TUTTLE, son of Simon and Abigail Tuttle, married Thankful Doolittle, Nov. 2, 1706. She died Nov. 23, 1728. He married 2d Mary Rowe of New Haven, June 9 1729 ; she died Jan. 22, 1747–8. He married 3d, Sarah Humiston, June 28, 1749. He died at Cheshire, April 15, 1756, æ. 76 yrs.

Children : 99 *Rachel*, b April 10, 1706, m Nathan Tyler ; 100 *Ebenezer*, b May 18, 1708, d Dec 3. 1736, ae 28 yrs. ; 101 *Ephraim*, b April 10, 1710, m Hannah Pride, Jan. 10. 1734 ; 102 *Mary*, b Oct 3, 1712, m Miles Hull of Derby, Dec. 4. 1729 ; 103 *Gershom*, b Aug. 11, 1714, settled in Bristol, Conn., d ae. 74 yrs. ; 104 *Timothy*, b Dec. 4. 1716, m Hannah Wadhams of Goshen, Conn. ; 105 *Abigail*, b April 11, 1719 m John Gaylord of Cheshire ; 106 *Simon*, b June 12,

1721, settled in Bristol, Conn.; 107 *Moses*, b Dec. 18, 1723, settled in Cheshire; 108 *Thankful*, b Nov. 15, 1726, d Dec. 9, 1747; 109 *Mehitable*, b Nov. 15, 1730, m Andrew Clark; 110 *Ichabod*, b July 2, 1732, d Jan. 9, 1747–8.

### 57. JONATHAN.

JONATHAN, son of Simon and Abigail Tuttle, married Rebecca Gilbert, Dec. 8, 1724.

Child: 111 *Simon*, b Nov. 16, 1725.

### 58. ISAIAH.

ISAIAH, son of Simon and Abigail Tuttle, married Susanna Doolittle, June 4, 1727.

Children: 112 *Jonathan*, b May 19, 1728, settled in Wallingford; 113 *Theophilus*, b March 4. 1729, settled in Wallingford, d Nov. 17, 1787, ae. 58; 114 *Isaiah*, b Feb. 6, 1732, d in childhood; 115 *David*, b Jan. 21, 1733, d in 1765; 116 *Elizabeth*, b June 17, 1736; 117 *Sarah*, b July 13, 1738; 118 *Isaiah*, b Nov. 29, 1742, d young; 119 *Solomon*, b Aug. 19, 1746.

### 71. HEZEKIAH.

HEZEKIAH, son of Nathaniel and Sarah Tuttle, had a son who settled in North Haven, and has numerous descendants, some of whom reside in New Haven, Conn. ( 1870 ).

### 86. DANIEL.

DANIEL TUTTLE, son of Daniel and Ruth Tuttle, married Phebe ———.

Children: 120 *Zopher*, b July 19, 1743; 121 *Prudence*, b Jan. 24, 1745; 122 *Dan*, b Nov. 27, 1746; 123 *Ichabod*, b Feb. 14, 1748; 124 *Benoni*, b Sept. 30, 1749; 125 *Jabez*, b July 20, 1751; 126 *Ichabod*, b Nov. 28, 1757, d Oct. 31, 1834, ae. 77 years; 127 *Beri*, b Apr. 29, 1761, drowned May 11, 1809, ae. 47 years.

### 87. JEHIEL.

JEHIEL TUTTLE, son of Daniel and Ruth Tuttle, married Hannah Hull, Aug. 30, 1742.

Children: 128 *Daniel*, b Jan. 9, 1743–4; 129 *John*, b Apr. 30,

1746, 130 *Charles*, b Dec. 24, 1747, 131 *Jeremiah*, b Nov 25, 1750; 132 *Charles*, b Jan. 26, 1753, settled at Windham, Greene Co., New York; 133 *Joel*, b July 25, 1756.

### 93. AMBROSE.

AMBROSE TUTTLE, son of Daniel and Ruth Tuttle, married Esther Ives, May 31, 1748. He died in 1757.

Children: 134 *Samuel*, b Dec. 22, 1748, d May 9, 1755; 135 *Ambrose*, b Oct. 11, 1752; 136 *Martha*, b Oct. 9, 1750, 137 *Benjamin*, b Sept. 5, 1754; 138 *Samuel*, b Dec. 22, 1757.

### 94. ENOS.

ENOS TUTTLE, son of Daniel and Ruth Tuttle, married Sarah Francis, April 21, 1757. Probably left Wallingford when a young man.

Child: 139 *Sarah*, b Feb. 19, 1758.

### 101. EPHRAIM.

EPHRAIM TUTTLE, son of Dea. Timothy and Thankful Tuttle, married 1st, Esther Hotchkiss, June 11, 1731. She died May, 1732, of small pox. He m 2d, Hannah Paine, Jan 16, 1734. She died May 22, 1756, ae. 42. He m 3d, Thankful Preston, Dec. 16, 1761. He died in Cheshire, Feb 2, 1775, ae. 64 yrs.

Children: 140 *Edmund*, M. D., b Nov. 26, 1733-4, d May 5, 1763, ae. 30 yrs.; 141 *Esther*, b Feb. 10, 1736; 142 *Ebenezer*, b Oct. 15, 1737, m Eunice ——; 143 *Ephraim*, b March 20, 1739, m 1st, Mary Hall, Aug. 2, 1754, 2d, Elizabeth Atwater; 144 *Noah*, b June 30, 1741, d July 23, 1742, 145 *Timothy*, b July 1, 1743, d young; 146 *Noah*, b Dec. 18, 1744, d June 30, 1828, at Camden, N. Y., ae. 84 yrs. 147 *Timothy*, b May 17, 1745, went to Ohio; 148 *Hannah*, b Jan. 4, 1746-7; 149 *Lucius*, b Dec. 4, 1749, d June 27, 1846 ae. 97 yrs.; 150 *Thankful*, b March 13, 1752. By 2d marriage. 151 *Ruth*, b Jan. 3, 1761-2; 152 *Edmund*, b Dec. 30, 1764, m Sarah L. Royce, Dec. 6, 1784, he d Jan. 1, 1846, ae. 90.

### 103. GERSHOM.

GERSHOM TUTTLE, son of Dea. Timothy and Thankful

Tuttle, married and settled in Goshen, Conn.   He died Oct. 23, 1760.

Children:  153 *Noah*, b March 26, 1742, m Ruth Beach; 154 *Mary*, b Dec. 1, 1743 ; 155 *Ichabod*, b June 23, 1744, was killed at Wyoming. by the Indians ; 156 *Amos*, b Feb. 9, 1745; 157 *Elisha*, b Nov. 24, 1746, m Elizabeth Matthews, Feb. 20, 1772 ; 158 *Deliverance*, b Oct. 14, 1753, d Oct. 8, 1760 ; 159 *Timothy*, b Jan. 13, 1755 ; 160 *David*, b Dec. 26, 1756, d Oct. 10, 1760 ; 161 *Hannah*, b May 10, 1758 ; 162 *Thankful*, b May 30, 1759, m Philip Cook ; 163 *Lois*, b May 21, 1760.

### 104. TIMOTHY.

TIMOTHY, son of Dea. Timothy and Thankful Tuttle, married Hannah Wadams Jan. 27, 1743, and settled at Goshen, Conn.

Children :  164 *Mary*, b Dec. 1, 1743, m —— Sedgwick of Cornwall Hollow ; 165 *Amos*, b Feb. 4, 1745 ; 166 *Elisha*, b Nov. 24, 1746, d in Goshen, July 28, 1825 ; 167 *Ichabod*, b June 23, 1748, m Elizabeth Matthews, Feb. 20, 1772, killed by Indians at Wyoming, Pa. ; 168 *Noah*, b March 26, 1752, m Ruth Beach, was hotel keeper several years in Canada ; 169 *Deliverance*, b Oct. 14. 1753, d Oct. 8, 1760 ; 170 *Timothy*, b June 10, 1755, m Abigail —— ; 171 *David*, b Dec. 26, 1756, d Oct., 1760 ; 172 *Hannah*, b Aug. 10, 1758 ; 173 *Thankful*, b May 30, 1759, m Phillip Cook of Goshen, Conn. ; 174 *Lois*, b May 21, 1760.

### 107. MOSES.

MOSES, son of Dea. Timothy and Thankful Tuttle, married Sybil Thomas, June 2, 1746.   He died in Cheshire, Jan. 17, 1809, ae. 86 yrs.   She died July 16, 1804, ae. 80 yrs.   Both are buried in the Episcopal yard, Cheshire.

Children :  175 *Ichabod*, b Feb 14, 1748. m Sarah Hitchcock ; 176 *Sybil*, b April 15, 1749, m Amos Hitchcock, May 31, 1764, settled in Canada and died there ; 177 *Sarah*, b Aug. 19, 1750, m Isaac Moss ; 178 *Rebecca*, b Feb. 21, 1752, m Reuben Merriman ; 179 *Moses*, b Oct. 24, 1753, settled in Prospect ; 180 *Anna*, b Oct. 24. 1753 ; 181 *Freelove*, b April

8, 1752, m John Benham. 182 *Thaddeus*, b Aug. 18, 1777 m
Cornelia Atwate 183 *Samuel*, b April 16, 1759. m M rel
Hull, settled in Vermont; 184 *Lydia* b July 9, 1761. m
Abner Doolittle of Cheshire.

## 112. JONATHAN.

JONATHAN TUTTLE, son of Josiah Tuttle of North Haven,
married Hannah Barns, Feb. 6, 1754, and settled in the south
west corner of Wallingford, near the foot of the Blue Hills
The locality has ever since borne the name of Tuttle's farm
He died May 27, 1795. ae. 65 years. Hannah his relict di-I
Nov. 6, 1831, ae. 97 years.

Children: 185 *Rebecca*, b Dec. 21, 1754. m Lent Hough, of
Wallingford; 186 *Isaiah*, b May 5. 1757 m Sarah Yale, thei
children were Samuel, Jonathan, Harvey. Romanth i, ar d Rev
Anson, all went to Ohio; 187 *Hannah*, b Jan. 2, 1760. m
Bethiel Todd; 188 *Sarah*, b Dec. 18, 1762. m Reuben Jones,
of Wallingford. 189 *David Justus*, b Jan 27, 1765, m Polly
Tuttle. April 29, 1790, she d Jan. 9, 1813. ae 48; 190,
*Samuel*, b 1771, m Abigail Cook, Oct. 25, 1792; 191 *Polly*,
m Samuel Johnson, of Wallingford.

## 127. BERI.

BERI TUTTLE, son of Daniel and Phele Tuttle, of Wallingford, was drowned while at work on the bridge at Hamis
ton Mills, May 11, 1807, ae. 47 years. He married Charity
Johnson. She died Jan. 31, 1814. ae. 52 years.

Children: 192 *Nancy*; 193 *Laura*, b 1788, m Asa Tuttle
and l in Chshire; 194 *Clarissa*; 195 *Merrit*, b 1795. m
Mary, dau. of Stephen Cook; 196 *Franklin*, b 180- I Nov
18, 1811, ae. 11 yrs. 197 *Ira* Esq., b June 30, 1805, m Mary
dru. of John B. Johnson Esq., d Jan. 10, 1870, ae. 64.

## 132. CHARLES.

CHARLES TUTTLE, son of Jehiel of Wallingford, settled at
Windham, Greene Co., N. Y.

Children: 198 *Marire*; 199 *Anna*; 200 *Charles*, 201
*Daniel Bliss*, b July, 1797, m Abigail Clark Stimpson; 202
*Sallie*; 203 *Ephraim*, d 1866.

k k k

### 201. DANIEL.

DANIEL BLISS. son of Charles and —— Tuttle, married Abigail Clark Stimpson.

Children : 204 *Lemuel S.*, b at Windham, Greene Co., N. Y. ; 205 *Sarah B.;* 206 *Daniel ;* 207 Rev. *David Sylvester*, b Jan. 26, 1837, m Harriet M. Foote, he was consecrated a Bishop of the Protestant Episcopal Church of Idaho, Montana and Utah, May 1, 186-, his children were George M., b Sept. 23, 1866, and Herbert Edward, b June 14, 1869.

### 142. EBENEZER.

EBENEZER TUTTLE, son of Ephraim and Hannah Tuttle, married Eunice ——.

Children : 208 *Mary*, b March 12, 1761 ; 209 *Phebe*, b Aug. 15, 1763 ; 210 *Ebenezer*, b July 28, 1765 : 211 *Joseph*, b Aug. 9, 1767.

### 143. EPHRAIM.

EPHRAIM TUTTLE, son of Ephraim and Hannah Tuttle, married 1st, Mary Hull, Aug. 20, 1764. She died in 1768. He married 2d, Elizabeth Atwater. She died in 1808. He died in Cheshire, Conn., 1811, ae. 72 years.

Child by 1st marriage : 212 *Uri*, b Oct. 31, 1765, m 1st, Peggy Morrison, she d Oct. 17, 1813, ae. 46 yrs, he m 2d, —— Stowe. By 2d marriage : 213 *Ephraim*, b Feb. 28, 1776, m Lois, dau. of Capt. David Hitchcock ; 214 *Lucy*, m Gideon Walker, settled in Southington, Conn. : 215 *Mary*, b in 1769, m S. Ufford Beach, she d Feb. 1, 1854 ; 216 *Elizabeth*, m Nath'l Royce, of Southington, Conn. ; 217 *Hannah*, m Eliasaph Preston, of Prospect, Conn. ; 218 *Abigail*, m John Peck, of Homer, N. Y. : 219 *Stephen*, m Catharine Smith, and went to Burton, Ohio.

### 149. LUCIUS.

CAPT. LUCIUS TUTTLE, son of Ephraim and Hannah Tuttle, married Hannah, daughter of Andrew and Lowly Hull, of Cheshire. He was a prominent man in Cheshire for many years, and during the Revolution was under General Washington's command at Boston and Long Island. and himself had grown out of a compromise of her temper and of the latter which resulted in the surrender of General Burgoyne, in his army in 1777. He died at the house of his son Lucius, in Wolcott at the age of 97 years.

Children: 220 *Justus Hull*, b. Aug. 25, 1775; 221 *Levius*, b. Aug. 7, 1776, settled in Wolcott Conn., had a family there; 222 *Rosa Ann*, b. April 8, 1778, m. Samuel Benham, of Cheshire; 223 *Marcus*, b. March 25, 1780; 224 *Lucy*, b. Dec. 20, 1781, d. Sept. 19, 1853, ae. 32; 225 *William B.*, b. Feb. 11, 1784, d. Jan. 6, 1821, ae. 33 yrs.; 226 *Hannah*, b. March 24, 1782, d. unm. June 9, 1849, ae. 50; 227 *Edward*, b. July 5, 1736, d. ae. 67 yrs. in Cheshire; 228 *Esther*, b. Dec. 30, 1790, m. Levi Doolittle, and died in Cheshire.

## 152. EPHRAIM.

EPHRAIM TUTTLE, son of Ephraim and Thankful Tuttle, married Sarah S. Royce, Dec. 6, 1784. He died at Cheshire, Jan. 1, 1846, ae. 82 years. She died Dec. 6, 1856, ae. 89 yrs.

Children: 229 *Sybel Stella*, m. John Hull, April, 1826; 230 *Lucy*, d. Nov. 18, 1813, ae. 17 yrs.; 231 *Edward*, d. Jul. 11, 1793, in infancy; 232 *Lois S.*, m. James Merriman, of Southington; 233 *Nancy*, d. Jan. 4, 1827, ae. 24 yrs.; 234 *Laura Ann*, d. Sept. 20, 1821, ae. 23 yrs.; 235 *Myra*, m. Jesse Brooks, of Cheshire; 236 *Ruth*, m. John Peck, and died in Cheshire, Conn.

## 175. ICHABOD.

ICHABOD TUTTLE, son of Moses and Sybel Thomas Tuttle, married Sarah Hitchcock, daughter of Dan and Esther Hitchcock, of Cheshire, and was for many years owner of the farm now known as the Doolittle farm, situated about a mile and a quarter east of Cheshire village. She died Oct. 30, 1834, ae. 77 years.

Children: 237 *Dan*, m. Hannah Holdreden, settled at Great Bend in Penn.; 238 *Sail*, m. Roderon Smith; 239 *Cora*, m. Titus Smith; 240 *Jerusha*, m. Jared Linn, and died in Penn.; 241 *Susannah*, m. Green Spring of Cheshire; 242 *Abner*, d. unmarried at Cheshire; 243 *Mary*, m. Ethural Bristol, of

Cheshire ; 244 *Ichabod*, d at Vergennes, Vermont, by his wife Elizabeth, he had Calvin, Luther and Ichabod ; 245 *Benajah*, d in Vergennes, Vt. ; 246 *Lavinia*, m Gaius Hitchcock of Cheshire, in 1791, he d May 27, 1862, ae. 71 years ; 247 *Zephaniah*, m Betsey Hotchkiss, he d in S. C. ; 248 *Sarah Julia*, m 1st, Capt. Wm. Harwood, 2d, Harry Davidson ; 249 *Maria*, m 1st, Cyrus Bradley, 2d, Sheldon Lewis, of Bristol.

### 179. MOSES.

MOSES TUTTLE, son of Moses, and Sybil Tuttle, married Damaris ———, and settled in Prospect, Conn., where he died Jan. 17, 1835, ae. 82 years. He was the honored father of Mrs. Joel Merriman, of Cheshire, and of Mrs. Benjamin Dutton Beecher, of Cheshire and Prospect, and others whose ' names I have been unable to ascertain. She died July 25, 1835, ae. 77 years.

Child: *Wooster*, m Mercy ———, d in Prospect, Feb. 26, 1843, ae. 65 yrs.

### 189. DAVID.

DAVID JUSTUS, son of Jonathan and Hannah Tuttle of Wallingford, died Jan. 9, 1813, ae. 48. Mrs. Polly Tuttle, his widow, died Sept. 22, 1836, ae. 67 years.

Children : 250 *Rebecca Hough*, b March 7, 1801, m Augustus Hitchcock ; 251 *Betsey*, b Nov. 1, 1790, m John Gaylord of Wallingford ; 252 *Sally*, b June 29, 1792, d Sept. 21, 1810 ; 253 *Harry*, b Oct. 20, 1796, m Mary Bronson of Wolcott ; 254 *Julius*, b Dec. 2, 1798, m Sylvia, dau. of Ambrose Tuttle of Hamden ; 255 *Jesse*, b Sept. 22, 1794, res. in Wallingford ; 256 *Merwin*, m Eliza Hemingway, and died at East Haven, Conn ; 257 *Caroline*, m Allen Tuttle of Hamden, res. North Haven ; 258 *Eliza*.

### 190. SAMUEL.

SAMUEL, son of Jonathan and Hannah Tuttle, married 1st, Abigail Cook. She died July 6, 1808, ae 36. He then married Lucy ———, who died Dec, 2, 1823, ae. 56 yrs. He died Feb. 3, 1824, ae. 53 yrs. He was a man of note in Wallingford.

Children : 259 *Lucy*, b Sept. 20, 1793 , 260 *Anna*, b Nov. 5, 1795 ; 261 *Orren*, b Jan. 18, 1801, deceased while a young man ; 262 Rev. *Bri*, Baptist minister in Ohio.

### 195. MERRIT.

MERRIT TUTTLE, son of Ben and Charity Tuttle, married Mary, daughter of Stephen Cook, of Cheshire. He died June 20, 1844, ae. 49 years. She married Wm. Todd for her 2d husband, and died Oct. 2, 1864.

Children : 263 *Sarah*, 264 *Caroline*; 265 *Marietta*; 266 *Benajah*, killed by falling into a cider mill, Nov. 12, 1813, ae 11 yrs. ; 267 *Julia*; 268 *Ira A.*, m Maria, dau. of Hiram Bristol ; 269 *Selden*, m 1st, Ellen Doolittle, April 11, 184 , 2d, Sarah L. Chatfield, Dec. 24, 1862 ; 270 *Henry Clay*, b June, 1832, m Cornelia Blakeslee, April 14, 1804 ; 271 *Merrit*; 272 *Louisa*.

### 212. URI.

URI TUTTLE, son of Ephraim and Mary Tuttle, married 1st, Peggy Morrison, she died : he married 2d, Catharine Stow He died in New Haven.

Children : 273 *Henry Hopkins*, b May 18, 1794 ; 274 *Wm. Imes*, b Jan. 22, 1796, resides in Auburn, N. Y. ; 275 *Elizabeth Mary*, b Nov. 20, 1797, m Wm Hall ; 276 *Harriet*, b April 12, 1801, m —— Smith : 277 *Jane C.*, b Sept. 17, 1803, d Aug 17, 1805. By 2d marriage : 278 *Charles*, b Oct. 3, 1815, d Oct. 23, 1854 ; 279 *Jane*, b Jan. 5, 1818, d Jan. 9, 1818 ; 280 *Chester Allen*, b Oct. 20, 1819, d Sept. 10, 1820 ; 281 *Frances*, b Jan 28, 1821, m Henry How ; 282 *Frederick*, b 1822, d ae. 14 yrs. ; 283 *George E.*, b Oct. 28, 1823, m Maria Antoinette, dau. of Rev. W. Brown, of New York city, a graduate of Yale College in 1818 ; 284 *Chester Uri*, b June 9, 1825.

### 213. EPHRAIM.

EPHRAIM TUTTLE, on of Ephraim and Elizabeth Tuttle, married Lois, daughter of Capt. David Hitchcock, of Cheshire, June 15, 1806. She was born Sept. 2, 1781, and died Feb. 11, 1843, ae. 62 years. He died July 4, 1860, ae 84 years.

Children: 285 *Marus*, b March 6, 1807, m Fannie Tyon
of Colchester, Conn. ; 286 *Ephraim*, b Jan. 20, 1809, m
Elizabeth Ives, of Middletown, Conn. ; 287 *Abner*, b Jan. 27,
1811, m Hannah Beecher, of Bristol. Conn. ; 288 *Henry*, b
Sept. 8, 1812, m Abigail Ames, of Ohio ; 289 *Edmund*, b
Sept. 6, 1814, m Betsey Hubbard, of Wallingford ; 290 *Peter
Green*, b Sept. 7, 1816, m Mary A. Roberts ; 291 *Lucy Ann*,
b July 24, 1818, m Henry Lane, she d Jan. 14, 1855 ; 292
*David*, b May 6, 1820, d ae. 6 weeks ; 293 *Joseph*, b March
26, 1822 ; 294 *James*, b March 26, 1822, d ae. 3 weeks ; 295
*James*, b Feb. 14, 1822, m 1st, Levia Root, of Southington.
Conn., 2d, Calista Darrow, of Bristol, Conn.

### 264 STEPHEN.

CAPT. STEPHEN TUTTLE, son of Ephraim and Elizabeth
Tuttle, married Catharine Smith, of Cheshire, Conn. He
went to Burton, Geauga Co., Ohio, and died there about
1866-7.

Children: 296 *Augustus F.*, res. in New Haven ; 297
*Mary*, m Silas Gaylord, of Cheshire, and settled in Ohio ;
298 *Elizabeth*.

### 227. GAIUS.

GAIUS TUTTLE, son of Capt. Lucius and Hannah Tuttle,
married Bella Gaylord, of Wallingford. He was a farmer
and resided about a mile and a quarter from the village of
Cheshire, eastward, on the road to Meriden. He died in
Cheshire, ae. 67 years.

Children: 299 *Phebe N.*, b Jan. 24, 1811, m Stephen
Beecher, Aug. 8, 1844 ; 300 *Samuel Anson*, b Aug. 18, 1814,
m 1st, Eunice Pierrepont, May 1, 1844, she d Sept. 17, 1850,
ae. 29, he m 2d. Emily R. Royce, dau. of Dea. Silas Royce
of Meriden, May 11, 1854.

### JOTHAM.

JOTHAM TUTTLE, a descendant of Jonathan and Rebecca
Tuttle, son of Nathaniel and Mary Tuttle, married Keziah
Munson, and settled at Tuttle's farm, in Wallingford, where
he died, ae. 66 years. His 2d wife was Elizabeth Perkins.

Children by 1st marriage. 301 *Eli*, m Asenath Perkin,
and settled in Hamden; 302 *Asa*, m Laura Tuttle, and set
tled in Cheshire, where he d, she d in 1870; 303 *Mary*; 304
*Ethel*. By 2d marriage. 305 *Hannah*, went west many
years ago.

## TYLER.

Roger, John and William Tyler, supposed brothers, were
the first of the name in Wallingford.   Roger Tyler married
Sarah Humiston, Jan. 10, 1698.   John Tyler married Phebe
Beach.   William and Mary Tyler were the first of the name
in Wallingford.

### JOHN.

JOHN TYLER, married to Abigail Hall, by Rev. Samuel
Street, Jan. 14, 1694.   She died Nov. 20, 1741.

Children: 1 *Esther*, b Sept. 20, 1695, m Moses Beach of
Wallingford; 2 *John*, b Jan. 29, 1697; 3 *Abigail*, b Jan.
29, 1697, m Saul Andrews, of Wallingford; 4 *Nathan*, b Apr.
17, 1701, m Rachel ———, she died in Cheshire, Nov. 2,
1749, ae. 44 years; 5 *Lois*, b Nov. 7, 1705; 6 *Thomas* b Nov.
26, 1708, m Lydia ———; 7 *John*, b Jan 14, 1710, m Phebe
Beach, April 7, 1731; 8 *Isaac*, b Jan. 17, 1713, m Susannah
Miles, Nov. 27, 1732, 9 *Joseph*, b March 21, 1716, m Mehitable ———; 10 *Experience*; 11 *Hannah*, m Macock Ward.

### WILLIAM.

WILLIAM TYLER married Mary ———.   She died in
Wallingford, March 11, 1754.   H, in company with Mr.
Samuel Stanley, purchased the mills at Yalesville in 1703.
He bought the interest of Mr. Stanley in 1704.   From thi

For the lateral branches see Bradbury's Hist. Kennebunkport, 16, 581;
Bridgman's King's Chapel Burial Ground, 280-91; Daggett Hist.
Attleborough, Mass., 65; Eaton's Hist. Thomston, Me., 44; Field's
Hist. Haddam, Conn., 46; Heraldic Journal, III. (1867) 184; Holden's
Gen. Cipron Family, part I. 101; Hudson's Hist. Lexington Mass., 281;
Savage's Gen. Dict., IV. 354

date, they remained in the family until after the decease of the late Mr. Samuel Tyler, in 1822, when they were set out to his daughter Merab, whose guardian, the late Nehemiah Rice, sold them to Charles Yale Esq.

Children : 11 1-2 *Mary*, b Sept. 7. 1695, m Francis Sedgwick, Feb. 5, 1734; 12 *Sarah*, b Nov. 25, 1697 ; 13 *Phebe*, b Oct. 5, 1700; 14 *Samuel*, b Aug. 11, 1702, m Jerusha Sedgwick Feb. 15, 1734; 15 *Martha*, b Oct. 4, 1706, m Jacob Francis, Jan. 20, 1763 ; 16 *Mehitable*, b Nov. 14, 1707 ; 17 *Abiah*, b Nov. 10, 1708; 18 *Ephraim*, b April 18, 1713, m Elizabeth De Wolf, Feb. 13, 1734; 19 *Mehitable*, b Nov. 17, 1718, m Stephen Merwin, April 12, 1743 ; 20 *Asa*, b July 30, 1722.

### NATHAN.

NATHAN TYLER m Rachel ————. She died at Cheshire, Nov. 25, 1749, ae. 44 years.

Children : 21 *Lois*, b May 12, 1731 ; 22 *Thankful*, b April 18. 1733 ; 23 *Rachel*, b Nov. 24, 1736 ; 24 *Tirzah*, b March 6, 1738 ; 25 *Barnabas*, b Aug. 30, 1739, d Sept. 20, 1749 ; 26 *Heber*, b and d Sept. 30, 1749.

### 6. THOMAS.

THOMAS and Lydia Tyler were of Wallingford.

Children : 27 *Elizabeth*, b Nov. 18, 1736 ; 28 *Reuben*, b Sept. 19, 1738 ; 29 *Rispie*, b Dec. 8, 1740 ; 30 *Joseph*, b Feb. 19, 1743, d Feb. 25, 1752 ; 31 *Experience*, b Aug. 18. 1745 ; 32 *Obedience*, b Nov. 24. 1747.

### 7. JOHN.

JOHN TYLER married Phebe Beach, April 7, 1731. After her decease he married Mary Doolittle, Nov. 9, 1741.

Children : 33 *Benjamin*, b Jan, 14, 1732, d Feb. 25, 1732 ; 34 *Benjamin*, b Feb. 23. 1733 ; 35 *Lydia*, b June 28. 1735 ; 36 *Patience*. b March 6, 1739. By 2d marriage : 37 *John*, b Aug. 15, 1742 ; 38 *Phebe*, b Nov. 10, 1743.

### 8. ISAAC.

ISAAC TYLER married Susannah Miles ; she died Jan. 25,

1760. He died April 12, 1801, at 89 years, at Cheshire

Children: 39 *Abraham*, b June 9, 1735 ; 40 *Enos*, m Obedience Smith ; 41 *Abraham*, b 1738 ; 42 *Miles* C. ; 43 *Levi*, b March 23, 1740 ; 44 *Amos* ; 45 *Jacob*, b March 20, 1742 ; 3 , 46 *Susannah*, b April 8, 1745 ; 47 *Hannah*, b July 20, 1747 ; 48 *Sarah*, b March 2, 1749, m Jesse, son of Stephen Welton, of Waterbury ; 49 *Nathaniel*, b Oct. 9, 1753 ; 50 *Lunice*.

## 9. JOSEPH.

JOSEPH TYLER married Mehitable ———. She died Aug. 28, 1757. He died Oct., 1741, leaving an estate of £518.

Child : 51 *Sybil*, b Dec. 31, 1740, m Benjamin Cook, Aug. 28, 1757.

## 14. SAMUEL.

SAMUEL TYLER married Jerusha, daughter of Samuel and Ruth Sedgwick, of Hartford.

Children : 52 *Lathrop*, b June 22, 1734, he built the original mill known as Humiston Mill ; 53 *Samuel*, b Dec. 14, 1735, m Damaris Atwater, April 21, 1763 ; 54 *Daniel*, b March 17, 1738, he built the mill in the south-east part of the town ; 55 *Moses*, b March 15, 1740, d Jan. 15, 1743 ; 56 *Jerusha*, b July 23, 1743, d May 3, 1744 ; 57 *Jared*, b Nov. 5, 1744, m Keziah Rice, she died 1817, æ. 73 yrs. ; 58 *Moses*, b Feb. 12, 1746, d Nov. 22, 1776, in Wallingford ; 59 *Jason*, b May 23, 1749 ; 60 *Mary*, b 1751, m James Rice, he d in Wallingford ; 61 *Jerusha*, b Jan. 4, 1754.

## 40 ENOS.

ENOS TYLER married Obedience Smith, who died July 28, 1771, ae 38 years. He then married Lydia ———, and she died Oct. 27, 1744, ae. 36 years.

Children : 62 *Reuben*, b May 30, 1759 ; 63 *Enos* 64 *Nathaniel*, b Jan. 22, 1761 ; 65 *Bede* ; 66 *Sarah* ; 67 *Mary* ; 68 *Lydia*.

## 53. SAMUEL.

SAMUEL, son of Samuel and Jerusha Sedgwick Tyler married Damaris, daughter of Phineas and Mary Atwater, April

21, 1763. He was the last male in the Tyler line that owned the mills at Yalesville, and was himself constantly employed about the mills during a long life. Bennet Jeralds Esq. has recently erected a new house on the site of the old one. The new Episcopal church at Yalesville occupies the ground on which formerly stood the large barn of Mr. Tyler. . He died March 13. 1823, ae. 88 yrs. She died April 24, 1810, aged 72 yrs.

Children: 69 *Merab*, b 1763 ; 70 *Selina*, m Sherlock Andrews of Wallingford ; 71 son, d young ; 72 *Julia*, m Dr. James Gilbert of New Haven ; 73 *Lavinia*, b March 14, 1781, m Harry Whittelsey of Catskill, N. Y.

### 54. DANIEL.

DANIEL, son of Samuel and Jerusha Tyler. He built the mills at the south-east part of the township, which are still in the possession of his descendants. He was killed by an insane person named Coles, for the crime ( as the insane man claimed ), of being a tory of the Revolution.

Children : 74 *Royal D. ;* 75 *Samuel*, d at the south.

### 57. JARED.

JARED, son of Samuel and Jerusha Tyler, married Keziah Royce, July 15, 1772. He died March 17. 1816. She died Feb. 8, 1819, ae. 73. He owned and occupied a large farm at what is now Yalesville. Miles Clark is the present owner of the house in which Mr. Tyler lived.

Children : 76 *Jared Royce*, b Sept. 2, 1776, m Rhoda ——, went to Vermont, where he died ; 77 *Kezia*, b April 18, 1784, m Ethelbert Benham of Cheshire, she d July 19, 1830 ; 78 *Ford*, b about 1774, m 1st, Esther Hough, in 1798, 2d, P. Blakeslee, he d in 1831, in Lockport. N. Y., had Jared, James, Jane and Amanda, all deceased ; 79 *Elizabeth*, b 1794, m Ebenezer Allen and went to Ohio, where she d at the age of 74 ; 80 *Amanda*, b April 2, 1780, m Capt. Wm. Davidson of Milford, was lost at sea ; 81 twins, b 1796, d early.

### 58. MOSES.

MOSES, son of Samuel and Jerusha Tyler, married Lois ---- She died Aug., 1800, æ. 51 yrs. He died Nov. 22 1770, æ. 31 yrs. He was the owner of a large house which was occupied as a hotel, and stood on the ground now occupied by Mr McKenzie's house at Yalesville. The old tavern was burned some sixty or seventy years since, with all its contents.

Children: 82 *Noble*, b 1802, d Mar. 22, 1844, æ. 42. 83 *Lois*, m Capt. John Nott of Wethersfield, both died in Wallingford; 84 *Mary*, m 1st, Silas Benham of Meriden, and had Jared Nelson Tyler Benham, an only son, she m for her 2d husband John Kirtland Esq.

### 78. JOEL.

JOEL TYLER, son of Jared and Keziah Tyler, was born about 1774, married Esther Hough about 1798; after her death he married Polly Blakeslee. He died in Lockport, N. Y., in Feb. or March, 1831.

### 76. JARED.

JARED ROYCE TYLER, son of Jared and Keziah Tyler, was born Sept. 2, 1776. He died Nov. 14, 1844, æ. 68 yrs., in Lockport, N. Y., leaving a widow, Rhoda, but had no children born to them.

### 80. AMANDA.

AMANDA TYLER, daughter of Jared and Keziah Tyler was born April 2, 1780, married Capt. William Davidson, of Milford, in the year ----. He with his vessel and crew were lost while returning from the West Indies. The last heard from him was that he left the island with his vessel heavy laden with salt, just before a severe gale. She married 1st, Abijah Carrington, in Milford, in the year ----, and died Milford, in the year ----.

### 77. KEZIAH.

KEZIAH TYLER, daughter of Jared and Keziah Tyler, was born April 18, 1784, married Ethelbert Benham, of Cheshire Conn., Oct., 1800, died July 19, 1830, in Cheshire, Conn.

### 79. ELIZABETH.

ELIZABETH TYLER, daughter of Jared and Keziah Tyler, was born in 1794, married Ebenezer Allen, of Bristol, at the age of 25, and died ae. 74 yrs. and 11 months. She died in Geneva, Ohio.

## WHITTELSEY.[1]

### JOHN.

JOHN WHITTELSEY is believed to be the first person of the name who emigrated to the United States, and the ancestor of all the Whittelseys who have lived here. He came from England about 1650, and became a tanner and shoemaker at Saybrook, Conn. The town of Saybrook, by authority of the General Court, gave to Mr. Whittelsey and Wm. Dudley the right to establish a ferry over the Connecticut river, near which he lived, in 1663. This still belongs to his descendants. He died April 15, 1704; his wife died Sept. 29. 1714. Their descendants were:

(a) *John*, settled in Saybrook; (b) *Stephen*, attorney at Saybrook; (c) *Joseph*, settled at Saybrook; (d) *Eliphalet*, settled at Wethersfield, married Mary Pratt, Dec. 1, 1702; (e) *Ebenezer*, settled at Saybrook; (f) *Jabez*, settled at Bethlem, deacon; (g) *Samuel*, settled at Wallingford, minister; (h) *Elizabeth;* (i) *Ruth.*

### SAMUEL.

REV. SAMUEL WHITTELSEY was the youngest son and child of John and Ruth Dudley Whittelsey of Saybrook, and was born there in 1686, was graduated at Yale college in 1705, married Sarah, daughter of Rev. Nathan Chauncey, son of Rev. Charles Chauncey, President of Harvard College. He

---

1 For collateral branches, see Andrews' Hist. New Britain, Conn., 235, 317, 355, 376; Cothren's Hist. Woodbury, Conn., 756-65; N. E. Hist. and Gen. Reg., xx. 321; Scranton's Gen. of Scranton Family, 43; Savage's Gen. Dict., IV. 537; Whittelsey's Memorial of Whittelsey Family.

was ordained at Wallingford as colleague to Rev. Mr Street,
April 10, 1710, after having preached one year on probation.
He died April 15, 1752, having nearly completed the 42d year
of his ministry.[1] His widow died Oct. 23, 1767, ae. 84 y.

Children: 1 *Samuel*, b July 10, 1713, m Susanna Newton
of Milford, Sept 21, 1743; 2 *Lois*, b Nov. 28, 1714, m Co
Elihu Hall, Jan. 2, 1734; 3 *Chauncey*, b Oct. 8, 1717, m
1st Elizabeth Whiting, Oct. 17, 1751, 2d, Martha Newton,
Aug. 13, 1753; 4 *Sarah*, b Jan. 19, 1720, d Aug 23, 1725
5 *Elisha*, b Oct 10, 1721, m Susanna Hall of New Haven,
April 8, 1754; 6 *Charles*, b Jan. 16, 1723, m Lucy Hall of
Cheshire, June 13, 1751; 7 *Sarah*, b Oct. 20, 1726, d Nov 2,
1746; 8 *Katherine*, b Dec. 26, 1728, m Rev. Jam s Dana,
May 8, 1759; he was born May 10, 1735, and d Aug. 28
1793, at New Haven; she d Aug. 18, 1812.

### 1. SAMUEL.

SAMUEL WHITTELSEY grad. at Yale College in 172 . He
was a tutor in that college from 1732 to 1738. Master of Arts
from Yale and Harvard colleges; settled in the ministry at
Milford, where his virtues, piety, and good deeds shone with
peculiar brightness and beauty. His life was unceasingly
devoted to faithful labor in sacred things, and the advance
ment of religion among his people in Milford, who with com
mendable zeal honor his memory. His wife, to whom he was
married Sept. 21, 1743, died May 10, 1803, ae. 87. He died
Oct. 22, 1769.

Children: 9 *Samuel*, b Aug. 3, 1745, m Mary Hubbard,
was a physician in Milford, d Oct. 22, 1776; 10 *Susanna*, b
Jan. 26, 1747, m Dr. Edward Carrington of Milford, d Jan 1,
1801; 11 *Sarah*, b Oct. 31, 1749, m John Chandler, who grad.
at Yale, 1764, and was sheriff of New Haven Co., she d July 1,
1803; 12 *Reed Newton*, b Feb. 24, 1754, m Ann Woodruff of
South Farms, April 20, 1775.

### 3 CHAUNCEY.

CHAUNCEY WHITTELSEY was graduated at Yale College,

1 See p 115, ante.

1738, ordained March 1, 1758, over the 1st church in New Haven; preached election sermon, May 14, 1778. President Stiles says of him, "He was an excellent classical scholar, well acquainted with the three learned languages Latin, Greek and Hebrew, also with Geography, Mathematics, Natural Philosophy and Astronomy, with Moral Philosophy and History. and with the general Cyclopædia of an academic life; and amassed by laborious reading, a great treasure of wisdom. In Literature, he was in his day, oracular at College, for he taught with facility and success in every branch of knowledge." One of his most distinguished pupils said of him at his funeral, "I shall never forget the pathetic and earnest recommendations of early piety which he gave to us in the course of his tutorship."

It was this man of whom David Brainard said, " He had no more grace than this chair." Peabody, in his life of Brainard ( p. 274 ) said in reference to this language, that it was "a phrase which that individual justified by his subsequent proceedings." Dr. Bacon in his historical discourses ( pp. 248, 249 ) refutes this charge, and shows the spirit which dictated the utterance of such language. He was licensed to preach, Sept. 30; 1740. "In 1745 he resigned his office in college, and for reasons which do not appear, relinquished the design of entering the ministry, and settled in New Haven as a merchant. He continued in business ten years ; during this time he was an active member of the first Church and Society. He was brought forward by his fellow citizens into public life. He represented this town in the General Assembly of the colony, and in a variety of public trusts. he discharged himself with fidelity and growing influence. He was subsequently settled as colleague with Mr. Noyes."[1] When settled in the ministry he applied himself to theological studies and the duties of the pastoral office with an ardor, zeal and assiduity equaled by few. His

[1] See Bacon's Historical Discourses, pp. 243, 266.

affability and dignity of manner, philanthropy and integrity, joined to an accurate knowledge of men and the affairs of life, commanded esteem and veneration.[1] He married 1st. Elizabeth, daughter of Col. Whiting, and ed, Martha Newton, a sister of his brother Samuel's wife

Children  13 *Chauncey*, b Oct. 27, 1746, m Lucy Wetmore, Feb. 12 1770 ; 14 *Samuel Joseph*, b July 13, 1749, d Aug. 3, 1751 ; 15 *Elisha*, b Oct. 14, 1751, d Oct. 23, 1751 ; 16 *Newton*, b June 1, 1754, grad. at Yale, 1773, m Beulah Fuller ; 17 *Martha*, b Sept. 1, 1756, m Capt. Wm. Van Duerson, he d May 3, 1763 ; 18 *Elizabeth*, b July 1, 1758, d Aug. 1, 1758 ; 19 *Elizabeth*, b May 2, 1760, d July, 1760 ; 20 *John Bryan*, b June 15, 1763, d Aug. 27, 1763 ; 21 *Samuel*, b Feb. 10, 1763, grad. at Yale college in 1779, m Sarah Van Duerson, Dec 10, 1788 ; 22 *Charles*, b Oct. 18, 1764, m Anna Cutler Oct 9, 1792 ; 23 *Susannah*, b Feb. 25, 1766, m Judge Dyer White 24 *Bryan*, b Aug. 6, 1768, d at New Haven, Jan 9, 1835 ; 25 *John*, b Sept. 8, 1770, grad. at Yale college in 1791, m Ann Kerwood ; 26 *Elizabeth*, b Sept. 18, 1773.

## 5. ELISHA.

ELISHA WHITTLESEY married Susanna Hall of New Haven, April 8, 1754. He was an attorney at Wallingford, and died at that place Feb. 25, 1808, ae. 87 yrs. She d Oct 19, 1798.

Children : 27 *Elisha*, b Jan. 1, 1755, m Sarah Jones ; 28 *Susanna*, b Sept. 2, 1756, m Caleb Street ; 29 *Sarah* b Mar 15, 1759, d June 23, 1764, m Wallingford ; 30 *Mary*, b April 9 1751, m Dr. Wm. Cook ; 31 *Elizabeth*, b April 4, 1763, m Dr. Liberty Kimberly, in 1788  she d in Derby, 1807 ; 32 *Charles*, b Nov. 12, 1764, d May 26, 1768  33 *Sarah* b Dec 6, 1766, d Nov. 8 1774 ; 34 *Charles*, b Sept. 20, 1768, d Jun. 9, 1769

## 12. ROGER.

ROGER NEWTON WHITTLESEY married Ann Woodruff, April 20, 1775 ; sh. was born April 5, 1756, and died March

1 See Dana's sermon on the Close of the 18th Century, Note F p. 10.

7, 1825, at Litchfield. South Farms.  He was a farmer, and died March 15, 1835 ; he was for many years a Justice of the Peace for Litchfield County.

Children : 35 *Samuel*, b Dec. 18, 1775, was a minister in New York. m Abigail Goodrich ; 36 *Newton*, b Oct. 31, 1777, m Esther Robbins of Claremont, N. H. ; 37 an infant son, b Dec. 29, 1779, d Jan. 7, 1780 ; 38 *Chauncey*, b Dec. 13, 1781, m Mary Bacon of Roxbury, Conn., Dec. 11, 1811 ; 39 *Susanna*, b Feb. 12, 1784, m Capt. Stephen Cogswell of New Preston, Conn. ; 40 *Jabez*, b Feb. 8, 1786, m Nancy Parker of Terryville, Conn. ; 41 *William*, b July 28, 1788, m Abigail Mills of Boston, Mass. ; 42 *Henry*, b May 18, 1790, m Abby Ray of New York ; 43 *Frederick*. b Jan. 25, 1792, m Hannah Ray of South Farms ; 44 *Charles*, b Aug. 23, 1793, m Elizabeth Fuller of Avon, Conn. ; 45 *Anna*, b May 28, 1795, m Dea. Chester Stone of Franklin, N. H. ; 46 *Lucy*, b Oct. 10, 1797, m Stephen Cogswell Jr. of New Preston ; 47 *George Washington*, b Aug. 10, 1799, m 1st, Cornelia Keeler, 2d, Elizabeth G. Boardman, res., New Milford.

### 13. CHAUNCEY.

CHAUNCEY WHITTELSEY married Lucy Wetmore of Middletown, Conn., Feb. 12, 1770 ; he graduated at Yale College in 1764, and was licensed to preach, but gave it up on account of his health, after two years ; he was elected deacon, Sept. 17, 1778, and served twenty-three years; was Alderman and Collector of the Port at Middletown ; his wife was an only daughter of Seth Wetmore, and her mother was a sister of Pres. Edwards.

Children : 48 *Lucy*, b Oct. 4. 1773, m Capt. Joe. Alsop, of Middletown, Conn., Nov. 5, 1797 ; 49 *Hannah*, b May 10, 1775 ; 50 *Betsey*, b May 24, 1780, m Capt. Joseph Williams. May 25, 1817 : 51 *Chauncey*, b Jan. 18, 1783, m Seth Lathrop Tracy, April 14, 1818, an attorney.

### 16. NEWTON.

NEWTON WHITTELSEY, married Beulah Fuller, of Middle-

town, Conn. He graduated at Yale, in 1773. Was a mer
chant. He died Dec. 4, 1785, æ. 64 years.

Child: 52 *Martha*, b Nov. 6, 1785, m Julius Dunning, Nov
25, 1808, settled in Shelby Center, N. Y.

SAMUEL WHITTLESEY, married Sarah Van Duerson, of Vincennes, Ind., Dec. 16, 1788. She was born May 3, 1763,
and died Apr. 1811, æ. 65 yrs., at Vincennes, Ind. He grad.
at Yale, in 1779. He was an attorney. He died March 7,
1838, æ. 71 years.

Children: 53 *Catharine Van Duerson*, b Sept 9. 1790, res
Clark, Ind.; 54 *Wm. Chauncey*, M. D., b Dec. 26, 1792, m
Ann Elizabeth Rapine Nov. 20, 1822; 55 *Samuel Gilbert*, b
in 1794, d; 56 *Samuel Gilbert*, b Dec., 1796, d June, 1810;
57 *Isaac Newton*, b July 19, 1798, m A. Elizabeth Van Buren,
April 12, 1831; 58 *Eliza Roberts* b April 16, 1800, m Dr.
James K. Oliver, Dec. 6, 1825; 59 *Chas. Ecker*, M. D., b
March 24, 1802, d Sept. 4, 1824.

CHARLES WHITTLESEY, married Ann Cutler, Oct. 9, 1792.
She was born in New Haven, July 12, 1773, and died Feb. 8,
1853. He was a merchant at New Haven, and died March
12, 1828, æ. 64 years.

Children: 60 *Mary Cutler*, b Aug. 12, 1793, d in New
Haven, Dec. 5, 1853; 61 *Chauncey*, b Aug. 5, 1795, d Aug.
21, 1795; 62 *Susannah*, b Dec. 5, 1796, m 1st, Rev. Samuel
B. Ingersoll, 2d, Wm. L. Fustice, of Boston; 63 *Charles
Hayward*, b Dec. 12, 1798, m Jane B. Willard, went, settled in
New Haven, d, 1799, b Sept 26, 1801, was a master
d March 12, 1826; 65 *John Cutler*, b Nov. 1, 1803, m Eliza
Weller, June 7, 1829, she was b in 1807; 66 *Henry Newton*,
b Feb. 9, 1825, m Elizabeth A. Wilson, of New Haven, Nov
30, 1837; 67 *Martha Ann*, b Oct 13, 1811, m Rev George
Oviatt, Oct. 17, 1839, d April 2, 1841.

## 24. BRYAN.

BRYAN WHITTELSEY was lame from his birth. He died at New Haven, Jan. 9, 1835.

## 25. JOHN.

JOHN married Ann Kerwood, June 1. 1799. He grad. at Yale, 1791, was U. S. Inspector in N. Y. city. He died May 12, 1849, at New Haven.

Children: 68 *Elizabeth K.*, b May 12, 1800, d ae. 3 years; 69 *Edward*, b May 2, 1801, a merchant, d in New York, July 9, 1842; 70 *John Newton*, b Feb. 11, 1803, d in New Orleans, La., July 9, 1803; 71 *Mary Elizabeth*, b June 29, 1805, d in New Haven; 72 *Charles*, b Nov. 3, 1807, m Maria Tuthill, Nov. 3, 1837. she was b Dec. 28, 1816; 73 *John Russel*, b Oct. 10, 1809, m Martha Butler, Jan. 12, 1835, she was b March 29, 1809; 74 *Wm. Kerwood*, b Aug. 27, 1812, d at Tipton, Iowa, Sept. 15, 1849; 75 *Martha Newton*, b April 17, 1815, m Moses H. Baldwin April 23, 1839, Pittsfield, Mass.; 76 *Jane Ann*, b Feb. 2, 1818, d Sept. 20, 1825.

## 27. ELISHA.

ELISHA WHITTELSEY married Sarah Jones of Wallingford, Sept, 8, 1777. She was born March 30, 1758, and died Sept. 15, 1836. He was a merchant and town clerk of his native town for many years. He died greatly lamented, Sept. 16, 1822, ae. 67 years.

Children: 77 *John Hall*, b June 4, 1778, m 1st, Sally Chittenden, Dec. 14, 1798, 2d, wid. Clara Bostwick, Aug. 4, 1824; 78 *Nancy*, b March 15, 1780, m 1st, Wolcott Reynolds, 2d, John Hunt of New Haven; 79 *Henry*, b Feb. 2, 1782, m 1st, Lavinia Tyler of Wallingford, May 2, 1811, 2d, Merab Hall of Cheshire, May 12, 1828: 80 *Eunice*, b Sept. 26, 1784, d July 31, 1819, in Wallingford; 81 *Jared Potter*, b March 8, 1777, m Lydia G. Acker, Oct. 22, 1814, d Jan. 25, 1869; 82 *Lucy*, b Feb. 16, 1789, m Drake Andrews of Wallingford; 83 *Sarah*, b May 29, 1792, d Nov. 11, 1792; 84 *Peter*, b Feb. 8, 1794, m Betsey Hunt, April 16, 1823.

### 35  SAMUEL.

SAMUEL married Abigail Goodrich.  He graduated at Yale in 1803, licensed to preach in June, 1804, ordained at New Preston, Dec. 30, 1807, settled nine years, during which time 142 were added to the church, April 30, 1817, took charge of the Deaf and Dumb Asylum at Hartford, became Principal of the Ontario Female Seminary, April, 1826 afterwards removed to the Seminary at Utica became publisher of the Mother's Magazine, 1833, removed to New York city in 1833.[1]

Children: 85 *Samuel Goodrich*, b Nov. 8, 1809, m Anna Cook Mills ; 86 a son, b March 26, 1811, d March 28, 1811 ; 87 *Charles Chauncey*, b Sept. 2, 1812, d April 29, 1818 ; 88 *Elizabeth*, b Sept. 29, 1815, d Jan. 26, 1848 ; 89 *Henry Martyn*, b Aug. 12, 1821 lawyer in N. Y. city ; 90 *Charles Augustus*, b Oct. 20, 1823, a seaman ; 91 *Emily Chauncey*, b Jan. 17, 1825, m Rev. Lucius Curtis, of Woodbury.

## WILCOX.

The family of Wilcox is of Saxon origin, and was seated at Bury St. Edmonds, in the county of Suffolk. England, before the Norman Conquest.  Sir John Dugdale, in his visitation of the county of Suffolk, mentions fifteen generations of this family previous to 1600.  In the reign of King Edward III., Sir John Wilcox was entrusted with several important commands against the French, and had command of the cross bowmen from Norfolk, Suffolk and Essex.  Jno. Wm. Wilcox, of Bury Priory in Suffolk, an eminent Queen's counsel, is the representative of this ancient family.  Sir George Lawrence Willcocks, of Broadend, County Tyrone, Ireland, is the eldest son of the late George Willcocks Esq. of Coal Island, County Tyrone, by Isabella, daughter of the Rev. Charles Caulfield.  He was born in 1820, educated at Dungannon, and is a magistrate for County Tyrone.  This family is a

[1]  See Cothren's Hist. of Woodbury, Conn., p. 270.

branch of the family of Willcockses of Tottenham High Cross, Middlesex, but has been settled in Ireland for about two centuries. They have been, and some branches are still members of the Society of Friends. On the old records the name is spelled both Wilcox and Wilcocks. It is derived from *William*.[1]

William Wilcox, who was chosen Lieut. Governor in the early times of the Massachusetts Colony, was the first of the name who is recorded on the list of the early officers. He was an officer of the artillery company, and died at Cambridge, November, 1653. He is there stated to have come to this country from the county of Suffolk. Nine of his descendants graduated at the New England colleges up to the year 1823.

## JOHN.

JOHN WILCOX of Hartford was an original proprietor in 1639. He had a son John who accompanied him from England. This son John was born in England, and married 1st, Sarah, eldest daughter of Wm. Wadsworth, Sept. 17, 1646 ; 2d, Catherine, daughter of Thomas Stoughton, Jan. 18, 1650 ; 3d Mary ——, who died 1671 ; 4th, Esther, daughter of Wm. Cornwall.

Child by 1st marriage : 1 *Sarah*, b Oct. 3, 1648. By 2d marriage : 2 *John*, b Oct. 29, 1650 ; 3 *Thomas*; 4 *Mary*, b Nov. 13, 1654 ; 5 *Israel*, b June 19, 1656 ; 6 *Samuel*, b Nov. 9, 1658. By 3d marriage : 7 *Ephraim*, b July 9, 1672 ; 8 *Esther*, b Dec. 9, 1673 ; 9 *Mary*, b March 24, 1676. John Wilcox died May 24, 1676.

## 5. ISRAEL.

ISRAEL WILCOX was in Middletown in 1675; he mar-

---

[1] This name has become the parent of a greater number of sirnames than any other baptismal appellation ; among which may be mentioned Wilcox, Wilkes, Wilkins, Wilmot, Willis, Wilson and Williams. Gillet, and Gillot are also from the same source. In France this Christian name has produced Guillot, Guillemin, Guillemette, Villemain, etc. See *Mem. Soc. Ant. Normandie*, XIII.

died Sarah, daughter of John Savage, March 28, 1678 ; he died Dec. 20, 1689. She died Feb. 8, 1724.

Children : 11 *Israel*, b Jan. 16, 1680 ; 11 *John*, b July 5, 1682 ; 12 *Samuel*, b Sept. 26, 1685 ; 13 *Thomas*, b July 5, 1687 . 14 *Sarah*, b Nov. 30 1689.

## 6. SAMUEL.

SAMUEL WILCOX of Middletown, born Nov. 9, 1658, married Abigail, daughter of Francis Whitmore, May 9, 1683 ; he died March 16, 1714.

Children : 15 *Samuel*, b Feb. 20, 1684 ; 16, 17 *Francis* and *Abigail*, b July 5, 1687, Abigail d in 1688, and her mother a fortnight after.

## 7. EPHRAIM.

EPHRAIM WILCOX removed to Middletown, and married, Aug. 23, 1698.

Children : 18 *Esther*, b Jan. 4, 1707 ; 19 *Ephraim*, b June 4, 1709 ; 20 *John*, b Aug. 8, —— .

## 20. JOHN.

JOHN WILCOX born Aug. 8, 17—, married Hannah ——, lived in Middletown.

Children : 21 *John*, b Jan. 15, 1740, d April 25, 1823 ; 22 *Samuel*, b May 8, 1742, d Sept. 4, 1807 . 23 *Hezekiah*, b Mar. 4, 1744, d Sept. 11, 1776 ; 24 *Joseph*, b March 29, 1746, d Jan. 31, 1832 ; 25 *Hannah*, b Jan. 28. 1748, d Feb. 19, 1826 . 26 *Gibbs*, b Jan. 2, 1750 ; 27 *Simeon*, b Feb. 25, 17—, d Oct. 13, 1827 ; 28 *Submit*, b Dec. 5, 1754, d Aug. 16, 1803 ; 29 *Comfort*, b Feb. 17, 175—, m Patty Doolittle, Aug. 10, 1780 ; 30 *Sarah*, b Feb. 7, 1750, m Abel North, Feb. 11, 1788, 11 had five children

## 21. JOHN.

JOHN WILCOX, son of John and Hannah, married Eunice Norton, Oct. 16, 1766.

Children : 31 *Seth*, b July 31, 1767, m Mitty Bacon, Mar. 21, 1736 , 32 *Jotutham*, b Nov. 18, 1768, m Sally Fisk, May, 1793 ; 33 *John*, b Sept. 15, 1771, m Sibel Gibbs, 1795 ; 34

*Eunice*, b July 4, 1774 ; 35 *Jedediah*, b June 1, 1778, d Oct. 10, 1789.

### 22. SAMUEL.

SAMUEL WILCOX, son of John and Hannah, married 1st, Ruth Roberts, 1784, and 2d, Ruth Wood, 1796. Child: 36 *Ruth*, b Aug. 12, 1798. After his death his widow married Thomas Scofel, Feb. 17, 1779.

### 23. HEZEKIAH.

HEZEKIAH WILCOX, son of John and Hannah, married Rachel Boardman, Nov. 9, 1775. Child: 37 *Hezekiah*, b Oct. 11, 1776, d Jan. 18, 1792.

### 24. JOSEPH.

JOSEPH WILCOX, son of John and Hannah, married Miriam, daughter of Josiah and Sybil Bacon, Nov. 30, 1785. She was born Feb. 7, 1762, d March 19, 1825.

Children : 38 *Sarah*, b Oct. 29, 1786, d Nov. 4, 1847 ; 39 *Jedediah*, b Feb. 7, 1788, d 1856 ; 40 *Submit*, b Nov. 11, 1789 ; 41 *Joseph*, b Oct. 21, 1791, d Jan., 1858 ; 42 *Hezekiah*, b March 28, 1793 ; 43 *Elisha B.*, b June 20, 1795 ; 44 *Lavinia*, b Jan. 31, 1797, d Sept. 24, 1843 ; 45 *Maria* ( or *Miriam*), b March 19, 1801, d March 1847.

### 26. GILES.

GILES, son of John and Hannah Wilcox, married Rachel Dove, Nov. 9, 1775.

Children : 46 *Olive*, b Nov. 1, 1776, m Amos Churchill, April 21, 1796 ; 47 *Giles*, b Aug. 28, 1779 ; 48 *Sylvester*, b Feb. 14, 1782 ; 49 *Samuel*, b Oct. 20, 1786 ; 50 *Sarah*, b Nov. 30, 1788.

### 42. HEZEKIAH.

HEZEKIAH, son of Joseph and Miriam Wilcox, married Rama Roberts, Nov. 7, 1816. She was born Dec. 23, 1792, and died Jan. 10, 1869.

Children born in Westfield : 51 *Joseph Alston*, b Oct. 15, 1817, m Lucy Ann Bacon : 52 *Ann*, b Sept. 7, 1821, d March 7, 1826 : 53 *Phœbe Miranda*, b Dec. 4, 1822, m Hollister Ris-

ley, 54 *Irene* b July 29, 1825, m Wm Hall of Meriden;
55 *Hezekiah*, b Dec. 23, 1827, d Nov. 16, 1853; 56 *Horace*, b
May 30, 1830. m Sarah Dunham.

### 43. ELISHA.

ELISHA B., son of Joseph and Miriam Wilcox, married
Hepsibah ——, Jan. 26, 1818.

Children, born in Westfield: 57 *Irene Sophia*, b June 3,
1819, m Edwin Savage, Nov., 1837; 58 *Lucy Maria*, b June
15, 1820, m George Miller, Aug. 5, 1845; 59 *Hannah Jane*,
b April 13, 1822; 60 *Horace Cornwall*, b Jan 26, 1824; 61
*Julia*, b Jan. 7, 1826, m Newell H Bowers, Sept. 2, 1846;
62 *Jedediah*, b March 4, 1827; 63 *Dennis Cornwall*, b Dec.
14, 1831; 64 *Edson*, b March 14 1831, d Oct. 1, 1851; 65
*Hezekiah*, b Oct. 12, 1832; 66 *Edmund North*, b Aug. 7,
1830; 67 *Mary Ellen*, b Oct., 1838; 68 *Elisha Watson*, b July
27, 1840.

Israel and Jedediah Wilcox were the first of the name in
Westfield, Conn.; both came from Middletown, Upper
houses.

The arms of the Wilcoxes of England are, per fesse, *or*
and *az.* a fesse, gules, over all a lion rampant, counterchanged.

Crest: a demi lion rampant, *az.* The lion rampant indi-
cates that he to whom the arms were granted, had gained a
victory whilst in command of the army.

------

# YALE.

### THOMAS.

THOMAS YALE married Mary, daughter of Capt. Nathaniel
Turner, of New Haven in 1645. Capt. Turner was of Lynn
Mass. in 1630; he moved to New Haven in 1638. He was
Captain of Mr. Lamberton's Phantom ship, which sailed from
New Haven on a voyage to the old country, and was lost
with all on board, Jan., 1666.

Mr. Yale came to America in 1637, with his father-in-law
Gov. Eaton, his mother, brother David and sister Ann, who

became the wife of Gov. Hopkins. He was a merchant at
New Haven ; his house stood on the ground now owned and
occupied by Yale College, in that city.

Gov. Theophilus Eaton. his step-father. having deceased,
Mrs. Eaton and her son Thomas Yale, went to England,
with Elihu, afterwards Gov. Yale, the distinguished donor of
Yale College, accompanied by David Yale his brother, and
Hannah Eaton, a daughter of the Governor. Returning to
New Haven the following year he purchased land in North
Haven near the present location of the bridge (Mansfield
bridge). of Gov. Eaton's estate, and settled on it in 1660.
He was evidently a man of energy and business tact, and was
frequently called to fill many important offices, by the citizens of New Haven. He died March 27. 1683, ae. 67
years. His wife, Mary Turner, died Oct. 15, 1704.

Children : 1 *John*, b 1646, settled in North Haven ; 2
*Thomas*, b 1647, settled in Wallingford in 1670 ; 3 *Elihu*, b
April 5, 1648, donor of the College at New Haven : 4 *Mary*,
b Oct. 26, 1650 m Capt. Joseph Ives ; 5 *Nathaniel*, b Jan. 3,
1652 ; 6 *Martha*, b May 6, 1655, d Jan. 15. 1670 : 7 *Abigail*,
b May 5, 1660 ; 8 *Hannah*, b July 6, 1662, m Enos Talmage ;
9 *Elizabeth*, b Jan. 29, 1667, m Joseph Pardee, of East Haven.

### 2. THOMAS.

CAPT. THOMAS YALE, son of Thomas and Mary Yale, of
New Haven, was born in that place in 1647. married Rebecca,
daughter of William Gibbards. Esq., Dec. 11, 1667. She
died, ———. He married 2d, Sarah, daughter of John Nash.
She died May 27, 1716. He married 3d, Mary Beach. of
Wallingford, July 31, 1716. He was one of the first and most
active settlers in the village of Wallingford in 1670, to which
place he removed that year. In 1710 he with the Rev. Samuel Street were the only surviving signers of the Plantation
Covenant of Wallingford. He was a Justice of the Peace
and Captain of the Train band, Surveyor of land and generally moderator of the business meetings of the town. &c.

He died Jan. 26, 1736, ae. 89 years. Mrs Reb-cc Yale was born Feb. 26, 1650.

Children: 10 *Hannah*, b July 27, 1669 : 11 *Rebeca* b Oct. 2, 1671 : 12 *Elizabeth*, b July 15, 1673 : 13 *Theophilus*, b Nov. 13, 1675 ; 14 *Thomas*, b March 20, 1678 ; 15 *Nathaniel*, b July 12, 1681 ; 16 *Mary*, b Aug. 27, 1684 . 17 *John*, b Dec. 8, 1687.

## NOTE TO BENHAM FAMILY [1]

UEL BENHAM was born December 26, 1730, died April 2-, 1832, at Cheshire. Lois his wife was born Oct. 16, 1747, died Dec. 26, 1827, at Cheshire.

Children: *Sarah*, b Oct. 11, 1769 ; *Uri*, b Oct. 23, 1771, d Oct. 23, 18_6 ; *Lois*, b Sept. 25, 1773, d Nov. 27, 1774 , *Mary Lois*, b Oct. 27, 1775 : *Uel*, b March 25, 1778, d Oct. 18, 1836 ; *Ethelbert*, b July 14, 1780, d Jan. 26, 1840 , *Amanda*, b Jan. 1, 1783 : *Joseph*, b Jan. 26, 1785, d Oct 29, 1853 : *Martha*, b March 2, 1788, d March 7 1836.

[This work has increased to such an extent that it has been found advisable to omit the Yale genealogy [2] for which material had been gathered. Mr. Elihu Yale, of New Haven, a few years ago published a genealogy of the family, to which the reader is referred].

1 See pp. 655-656, ante.

2 See p. 546, ante.

# APPENDIX.

## A.

SUCCESSION OF TOWN CLERKS IN WALLINGFORD,

FROM 1670.

NEW HAVEN COMMITTEE, to April 28, 1673, 3 years. NA-
THANIEL MERRIMAN, from April 28, 1673, to Dec. 15, 1682,
9 years. ELIASAPH PRESTON, from Dec. 15, 1682, to April
26, 1687, 5 years. JOSEPH HOULT, from April 26, 1687, to
April 28. 1696, 9 years. JOSEPH ROYCE, from April 28, 1696,
to Dec. 28, 1697. 1 year, 8 mos. THOMAS HALL. from Dec.
28, 1697, to Dec. 25, 1711, 14 years. SAMUEL MUNSON, from
Dec. 25, 1711, to Dec. 23, 1740, 29 years. THOMAS MILES,
from Dec. 23, 1740, to Oct. 20, 1741, 10 mos. JAMES MILES,
from Oct. 20, 1741, to Feb. 6, 1766, 25 years. CALEB HALL,
from Feb. 6, 1766, to Dec. 20, 1774, 8 years. CALEB COOK,
from Dec. 20, 1774, to Dec. 19, 1775, 1 year. CALEB HALL,
from Dec. 19, 1775, to Dec. 16, 1783, 8 years. ELISHA
WHITTELSEY, from Dec. 16, 1783, to Nov. 11, 1800, 17 years.
GEO. W. STANLEY, from Nov. 11, 1800, to Nov. 8, 1803, 3
years. HUNN MUNSON, from Nov. 8, 1803, to Oct. 6, 1834,
31 years. FRIEND COOK, from Oct. 6, 1834, to Oct. 5. 1835,
1 year. JAMES CARRINGTON, from Oct. 5, 1835, to Aug. 15,
1836, 10 mos. JAMES W. CARRINGTON, from Aug. 15, 1836,
to Oct 3, 1836, 2 mos. SAMUEL COOK, from Oct. 3, 1836,
to Oct. 5, 1840, 4 years. DELOS FORD COOK, from Oct. 5,
1840, to Oct. 22, 1840, less than one month. HENRY A.
COOK, from Oct. 22, 1840, to Oct. 4, 1841, 1 year. LORENZO
LEWIS, from Oct 4, 1841, to Oct. 6, 1856, 5 years. E. S.

IVES, from Oct. 6, 1856, to Sept. 29, 1860, 4 years    LORENZO
LEWIS, from Oct. 8, 1860, to Oct. 7, 1861, 1 year    F. S.
IVES, from Oct. 7, 1861, to April 1, 1863, 2 years    J. B.
POMEROY, assistant T. C., from April 1, 1863, to Sept. 7,
1863, 4 mos.    ARGALUS HALL, from Sept. 7, 1863, to Sept.
27, 1864. 1 year.    E. S. IVES, from Sept. 27, 1864 to Jan.,
1868 3 years.    GEORGE W. BARTHOLOMEW, from Jan., 1868,
to April 15, 1868. 3 mos    EDWARD F. COOK, from April 15,
1868, to Sept. 6, 1869, 1 year, 5 mos.    FRANKLIN FLAGG,
elected April 6, 1860.

## B.

### PHYSICIANS IN CHESHIRE.

DR. ELNATHAN BEACH was located in the center of the
village.    He built the house known as the Bronson house.
DR. GOULD NORTON owned and occupied the house since
owned by the late Pliny Hitchcock.    DR. PIERRE E. BRAN-
DON, a Frenchman, lived and died in Cheshire.    He was a
skillful physician and had an extensive practice.    DR.
THOMAS TRYON CORNWALL had a large practice.    DR. LAM-
PERT FOOTE was an excellent physician for many years.    DR.
CHARLES SHELTON was eminent in his profession    He died
in 1832, ae. 50 years.    DR. ASA J. DRIGGS is still practising
(1870) in Cheshire, where he has been for many years.    DRS.
CHAMBERLAIN and URSON recently removed to Cheshire
DR. WILLIAMS, a homoeopathic physician, is practising in
Cheshire.

## C

On page 233 in speaking of the division of the society
we said that the 1st Congregational society dound not
return the church records.    In order that we may not be
misconstrued, we annex the following note:

*"Meriden, Dec.* 31, 1847.

"The Church met after preparatory lecture. A communication was read from the Congregational society connected with this Church, stating that the new house of worship was nearly completed, and inviting the Church to occupy it for the service of the sabbath, whereupon resolved:

"That the invitation from the society to remove our place of worship be accepted, and our Pastor requested to appoint all meetings on the Sabbath in the new Church immediately after it shall have been completed.

"Resolved further, that so many of the members of the Church as choose to remain in the old house of worship, be affectionately recognized as a Church of Christ whenever duly organized, and that our Pastor be authorized to terminate their connection with this Church on their intimating to him their wishes to that effect, and that they thus reserve one-half of the Church property.

"Resolved further, that the brethren thus leaving us for the purpose of forming another Church, be allowed to take a copy of the Church records.    Meeting adjourned.

"G. W. PERKINS, Moderator."

A true copy.    B. H. Catlin, Moderator.

*Meriden, Aug.* 2. 1870.

————

## D.

### REVOLUTIONARY SOLDIERS.

In addition to those found on pp. 368–70.    Lieut. Ephraim Chamberlain.    Lieut. Dan Johnson, Benajah Rice.    Daniel Atwater was killed in a skirmish with British troops at Camp's Hill, April 28, 1777.    Asaph Cook was at the battle of Lexington.    Capt. Joel Cook served with his father Capt. Isaac, through the war.    In 1812, he was an officer under Gen. Harrison, in many hard fought battles with the Indians.    Lieut. Samuel Hart was wounded at Saratoga.    Charles Merriman

was a drummer; in 1776 he was drum major, and served
through the war. Capt. Lucian Tuttle was under Gen. Washington at Boston and Long Island, and had command of
company of his townsmen at the battle which resulted in the
surrender of Gen. Burgoyne and his army in 1777.

## E.

### OFFICERS IN THE CIVIL WAR.

It was found that the second group of officers intended
for this work could not be finished in time; it is therefore
omitted. It will probably be published in the Soldier's Memorial. CHARLES L. UPHAM was born in Townshend, Vt.,
May 24, 1839, enlisted as Orderly Sergt. in Falls Co. 1st 2d
Reg. Conn. Vols., May 14, 1861, mustered into the U. S.
Vol. service as Captain Co. K. 8th Reg. Conn Vol. Inf.,
Sept, 23, 1861, promoted to Major, same Reg., Dec. 1862, to Lieut. Col. Apr. 2 1867, to Col. 15th Reg. Apr. 1,
1865, mustered out of service at the close of the war, June
27, 1865, was in the following engagements: Bull Run,
Roanoke Island, Newbern, severely wounded, South Moun-
tain, Antietam, Fredericksburg, Com. the 16th Conn. Reg.,
Siege of Suffolk, Edenton Road, Providence Church Road,
Kinston.

WM. McLAIN PRATT was born in Meriden, December
12, 1837, enlisted and mustered in 8th Conn. Vol. Infantry,
May 14, 1862, as private, wounded and taken prisoner at
the battle of Antietam, September 17, 1862, promoted to
2d Lieutenant, November 17, 1862, 1st Lieut. and Adj.
May 29, 1863, Major, November 1, 1864, Lieut. Col.
April 25, 1863, resigned Oct. 30, 1865, and was on detached
service in North Carolina as A. D. C. to Brig. Gen. Edward
Harland Com Feb., 1864, to Feb., 1865, served with the
Regiment the rest of the time from date of enlistment to
resignation, commanded the regiment from Feb., 1865,
through the final struggle, was at the capture of Richmond
April 3, 1865.

THEODORE BYXBEE was born in New York City, Nov. 29, 1834, enlisted April 16, 1861, and was mustered in at New Haven, April 21, 1861, as captain of Co. F. 1st Reg. Conn. Vols., promoted to Major, June 1, 1861, engaged in the first battle of Bull Run, July 21, 1861, re-enlisted Sept. 3, 1862, as captain of Co. G, 27th Reg. Conn. Vols., promoted to Major, Oct. 2, 1862, mustered in U. S. service, Oct. 21, 1862, was engaged in the battle of Fredericksburg, Dec. 17, 1862.

ROGER M. FORD was born in New Marlborough, Mass. Dec. 28, 1834, enlisted April 17, 1861, for three months, as private in Co. F, 1st Reg. Conn. Vols., mustered in April 23, 1861, promoted to Corporal, July 6, 1861, at Falls Church, Va., was at the battle of Bull Run, discharged July 31. 1861, enlisted Sept. 21, 1861, for three years, in Co. K, 8th Reg. Conn. Vols., Inf., mustered in as 2d Lieut., Sept. 22, 1861, promoted to 1st Lieut. March 18, at Newbern, and to Captain of Co. G, March 7, 1863, at Newport News, Va., discharged Sept. 2, 1864, at Annapolis, Md., on account of wounds received at Petersburg, Va., June 25, 1864, enlisted at New Haven, Jan. 3, 1865, as private in the 8th Reg. Conn. Vols., Inf., promoted to 1st Sergt. Co. E, Feb. 6, 1865, at Chapin's farm, Va., mustered out Dec. 12, 1865, was in the following battles : Roanoke Island, Newbern. Fort Macon, South Mountain, Antietam, Fredericksburg, Wallthal Junction, Swift Creek, Drury's Bluff, Cold Harbor, Petersburg, and at the taking of Richmond, April 3, 1865.

JARED R. COOK was captain of Rifle Co. B, 3d Reg. Conn. Vols., and was mustered into service, May 14, 1861. May 23, the Regiment arrived at Washington, and on the 24th of June went to Virginia, where it was placed in the extreme front of the Union center. Capt. Cook was at the battle of Bull Run, and was honorably discharged Aug. 12, 1861.